CASES AND MATERIALS ON CIVIL LIBERTIES

AUSTRALIA
The Law Book Company Ltd.
Sydney : Melbourne : Brisbane

CANADA AND U.S.A.
The Carswell Company Ltd.
Agincourt, Ontario

INDIA
N. M. Tripathi Private Ltd.
Bombay
and
Eastern Law House Private Ltd.
Calcutta
M. P. P. House
Bangalore

ISRAEL
Steimatzky's Agency Ltd.
Jerusalem : Tel Aviv : Haifa

MALAYSIA : SINGAPORE : BRUNEI
Malayan Law Journal (Pte.) Ltd.
Singapore

NEW ZEALAND
Sweet & Maxwell (N.Z.) Ltd.
Auckland

PAKISTAN
Pakistan Law House
Karachi

CASES AND MATERIALS

ON

CIVIL LIBERTIES

By

PAUL O'HIGGINS, M.A., Ph.D.

of the King's Inns and of Lincoln's Inn, Barrister,
Fellow of Christ's College, University
Reader in Labour Law, Cambridge

LONDON
SWEET & MAXWELL
1980

Published in 1980 by
Sweet & Maxwell Ltd. of
11 New Fetter Lane, London
Photoset by Promenade Graphics Ltd., Cheltenham.
Printed in Great Britain by
Page Bros. (Norwich) Ltd.

British Library Cataloguing in Publication Data

O'Higgins, Paul
  Cases and materials on civil liberties.
  1. Civil rights — Great Britain
  I. Title
  342' .41'085   KD4080.A25

  ISBN 0-421-25050-X
  ISBN 0-421-25060-7 Pbk

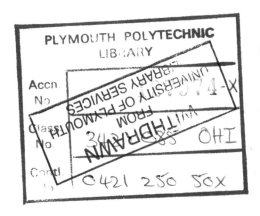
©
Paul O'Higgins
1980

PREFACE

Courses on civil liberties or on human rights are taught in an increasing number of law schools. It is the purpose of this collection to be of assistance to students and teachers involved in such courses. Many students of political science are concerned with the activities of government and law enforcement agencies in areas involving issues of individual freedom. This collection should also be of use to them. There are an increasing number of people who are concerned with the emergence of trends in our society which are potentially dangerous to the degree of individual liberty which people feel they are entitled to. This collection should be of interest to them as well.

An initial difficulty in the compilation of this material is to define the scope of what is meant by "Civil Liberties." There must inevitably be considerable variation in what is regarded as essential to this subject. Existing courses show a surprising variation of emphasis, but there is still a sufficient hard core of common ground between them for this collection to be found relevant to all of them. A further difficulty has been the sheer bulk of relevant materials, a suprisingly large proportion of which is statutory. In the past the approach of a compiler of a collection such as this might well have been to concentrate on the case law (*cf.* the space devoted in existing collections on constitutional law to case law). It is believed that such an emphasis would be wrong and misleading. The mass of relevant materials has meant inevitably in a work of limited size such as this the exclusion quite arbitrarily of a number of topics which may be regarded as highly relevant, such as the right to life itself, criminal procedure, sexual and social discrimination, etc. Exclusion of such topics is not a denial of their importance, only an acknowledgement of the impossibility of including everything which the compiler regards as important. A further choice had to be made with regard to the inclusion of comparative material. Again reasons of space have dictated the exclusion of comparative material except very occasionally, as in the Appendix.

It has been felt essential to include a selection of international materials. This is for two main reasons. The United Kingdom has now adhered formally to a growing number of international standards (for the most part treaties) which directly affect basic individual and collective rights. It is an important starting point for the discussion of these rights to determine whether or not the United Kingdom is living up to the standards she has accepted, often a matter of international legal obligation. Secondly, in many cases there exists machinery for the "enforcement" on an international plane of the rights embodied in these international standards. It is therefore important when considering the remedies open to an individual or group denied the enjoyment of the rights guaranteed to be aware that, in addition to any action, legal or political, taken within the United Kingdom, there may also be the possibility of taking some further action before an international forum.

Organisation of material

The material has been organised under a number of principal chapter headings together with cross references to material elsewhere in the collection that may be relevant. Within the chapters the material may often be further divided under sub-headings. Where it is practicable an indication is given of relevant reading under the principal sub-headings. This guidance to reading indicates first of all whether, and if so where, a number of basic works (listed in the table of abbreviations) have discussed the issues raised by the particular sub-heading. Secondly, there appears a list of other books where useful additional material may be found. Finally, reference is made to any articles in periodicals which seem to be particularly relevant. The aim of these references to other reading is not to indicate what is the best that is written on the subject but rather to indicate the books and articles in which will be found a discussion of the issues which in the past people have seen as being the important ones arising out of that particular topic.

Following an indication of suitable reading there may also be a comment pinpointing some particular aspects of the topic dealt with. At the end of any particular extract there may be further notes where considered relevant or helpful.

Finally, under some sub-headings will be found some suggested projects or questions the working out of which may be found to be helpful to illuminate some of the main issues.

Few other countries have contributed so much of value and importance to the discussion and understanding of civil liberties as has Great Britain. The compiler was very tempted to include lengthy extracts from some of the great British classics in this area. While there may be a need for an anthology of this kind, reasons of space have prevented the inclusion of such extracts here. However, reference will be found in the Select Bibliography to some of the more important British contributions in this area. No one's education as a citizen, let alone as a political scientist, political activist or lawyer is complete, unless one has absorbed as part of one's cultural heritage some of the principles to be derived from the writings of earlier libertarian thinkers.

April 1980   Paul O'Higgins
                                                                   Christ's College

ACKNOWLEDGMENTS

In an area so multi-faceted as civil liberties it is impossible to list the many students and teachers who have influenced my thinking. Amongst my teachers I should like to mention particularly a debt owed to Professor F. E. Dowrick of Durham University, formerly of Trinity College, Dublin, and amongst my students I should like to thank particularly the classes who over many years have argued their way through the postgraduate Civil Liberties course at Cambridge.

I am very grateful for the help and advice received from Peter Duffy, LL.B., co-author with A. B. McNulty of an important work on the European Convention on Human Rights and Fundamental Freedoms. I should have liked to have acted upon more of his advice but space has not permitted me to do this in this work.

I owe a special debt to my publishers, Sweet & Maxwell Ltd. and its staff, who have shown a forebearance and patience above and beyond that which it is reasonable to expect of any publisher.

For permission to quote material in this collection I am very grateful to the Advertising Standards Authority Ltd., the British Broadcasting Corporation; the B.B.C. Complaints Commission; Butterworths; the Controller of Her Majesty's Stationery Office; the Council of Europe; the Incorporated Council of Law Reporting for England and Wales; the Independent Broadcasting Authority; Industrial Relations Services Ltd. and the Press Council.

CONTENTS

TABLE OF CASES

[References in italic type denote reproduction of a report]

xi

TABLE OF STATUTES

[References in italic type denote reproduction of the text of the Act.]

TABLE OF STATUTORY INSTRUMENTS

[References in italic type denote reproduction of the text of the S.I.]

TABLE OF CONVENTIONS, TREATIES AND REPORTS

[References in italic type denote reproduction of the text of the Convention, Treaty or Report]

SELECT BIBLIOGRAPHY

This is intended to supplement the references to be found in the main text. Consequently, items listed here will not usually have been elsewhere referred to. This list is intended to provide suggestions for further reading into the subject of civil liberties. The Council of Europe has produced a very valuable *Bibliography relating to the European Convention of Human Rights* (Strasbourg, 1978).

1. SPECIALIST PERIODICALS

Censorship. London. Quarterly. Vol. 1, No. 1 (1964)—Vol. 3, No. 1 (1967). Publication suspended.

European Human Rights Reports. London. Quarterly. Vol. 1, No. 1 (1979)—in progress.

The Human Rights Review. Oxford. Quarterly. Vol. 1 (1976)—in progress.

Index on Censorship. London. Quarterly. Vol. 1, No. 1 (1972)—in progress.

Revue des Droits de l'Homme/Human Rights Journal. Paris. Quarterly. Vol. 1, No. 1 (1968)—in progress.

Rights (The Newspapers of the NCCL). London. Monthly. Vol. 1, No. 1 (September 1976)—in progress.

State Research Bulletin. Institute for the Study of Conflict, London. Monthly. No. 1 (October 1977)—in progress.

2. THE CLASSICS

Bury, J. B., *A History of Freedom of Thought* (O.U.P., 1913: reprinted many times).

Chesterfield, Lord. *The E— of C—f—d's Speech in the H—se of L—ds, against the Bill for Licensing all Dramatic Performances* (Dublin, 1749; Reprinted O'Higgins, 165–74).

Dicey, A. V. *Introduction to the Study of the Law of the Constitution* (1885) (Ed. Wade, MacMillan, 1961).

Forster, E. M. *Two Cheers for Democracy* (Penguin, 1965).

Forster, E. M. *Abinger Harvest* (Penguin, 1967).

Laski, H. J. *Liberty in the Modern State* (3rd ed., 1948 Allen & Unwin).

Lecky, W. E. H. *History of European Morals* (Longmans, 1910).

Lecky, W. E. H. *History of the Rise and Influence of the Spirit of Rationalism in Europe* (Longmans, 1910).

Lecky, W. E. H. *Democracy and Liberty* (London, 1913).

Locke, J. *Two Treatises of Government* (1690) (C.U.P., 1967).

Locke, J. *Letter on Toleration*, (1690); *A Second Letter*, (1690); *A Third Letter*, (1692) (many eds.).

Mill, J. S. *On Liberty* (1859; many later eds.; the latest is in the Penguin series).

Milton, J. *Areopagitica* (London, 1644; many subsequent eds.).

Morley, J., *On Compromise* (London, 1921; a number of reprints).

Paine, *Rights of Man* (London, 1791; innumerable eds.; the latest is by Penguin Books).

Pollard, R. S. W., *Conscience and Liberty* (London, 1940; Facsimile reprint, Garland Publishing, Inc., New York, 1977).

3.   GENERAL WORKS

Anderson, Sir N., *Liberty, Law and Justice* (Sweet & Maxwell, 1978).

Angel, Sir N., *Why Freedom Matters* (Penguin, 1940).

Archer, P., and Lord Reay, *Freedom at Stake* (Bodley Head, 1966).

"Barrister", *Justice in England* (Gollancz, 1938).

Bell, C. *On British Freedom* (Chatto & Windus, 1923).

Berlin, I., *Four Essays on Liberty* (O.U.P., 1969).

Birch, F., *This Freedom of Ours* (C.U.P., 1937).

Blackburn, R., *The Erosion of Freedom* (Times Press, Isle of Man, 1964).

Cannon, G., *Freedom* (Headley Bros., 1917).

Carstairs, G. M., *This Island Now* (Penguin, 1964).

Clark, G., *Democracy in the Dock* (Thomas Nelson, 1943).

Comfort, A., *Darwin and the Naked Lady* (Routledge & Kegan Paul, 1961).

Conservative Political Centre, *Liberty in the Modern State* (London, 1957).

Cox, B., *Civil Liberties in Britain* (Penguin, 1975).

Cranston, M., *Human Rights Today* (Allen & Unwin, 1962).

Curtis, J., *The Land of Liberty* (Seckes & Warburg, 1938).

Dworkin, R., *Taking Rights Seriously* (Duckworth, 1977).

Field, M., *Freedom Is More than a Word* (University of Chicago Press, 1945).

Finley, M. I., *Democracy Ancient and Modern* (Chatto & Windus, 1973).

Grant, L., Hewitt, P., Jackson, C., and Levenson, H. *Civil Liberty: The NCCL Guide to your Rights* (N.C.C.L., 1972).

Hailsham, Lord, *Elective Dictatorship* (London, 1976).

Haynes, E. S. P., *The Decline of Liberty in England* (Srant Richards, 1916).

Haynes, E. S. P., *The Case of Liberty* (Srant Richards, 1919).

Haynes, E. S. P., *The Enemies of Liberty* (Srant Richards, 1923).

Hobson, J. A., *Democracy and a changing Civilisation* (John Lane, The Bodley Head, 1934).

Hodann, M., *History of Modern Morals* (Heinemann, 1917).

Hogben, L. *Dangerous Thoughts* (Allen & Unwin, 1939).

Hook, S. *The Paradoxes of Freedom* (University of California Press, 1967).

Huxley, A., *Science, Liberty and Peace* (Chatto, 1947).

Jackson, T. A., *Trials of British Freedom* (Lawrence & Wishart, 1945).

Jaeger, M., *Liberty versus Equality* (Thomas Nelson, 1943).

Johnston, A. W., *Law and Liberty* (Angus & Robertson, 1910).

Kidd, R., *British Liberty in Danger* (Lawrence & Wishart, 1940).

Laski, H. J., *Reflections on the Revolution of our Time* (Allen & Unwin, 1944).

Leacock, S. *Our Heritage of Liberty* (London, 1942).

Lindsay, J. and Rickwood, E., *A Handbook of Freedom* (Lawrence & Wishart, 1939).

Lucas, E., *What is Freedom?* (O.U.P., 1963).

Lucas, J. R., *Democracy and Participation* (Penguin, 1976).

Macmurray, J., *Freedom in the Modern World* (Faber, 1935).

Marshall, G. and Moodie, G. C., *Some Problems of the Constitution* (Hutchinson, 1959).

Marshall, G., *Constitutional Theory* (O.U.P., 1973).

Morgan, C., *Liberties of the Mind* (MacMillan, 1951).

Muir, R., *Future for Democracy* (Nicholson & Watson, 1939).

Muir, R., *Civilisation and Liberty* (Jonathan Cape, 1940).

Nevinson, H. W., *The Growth of Freedom* (T. C. & E. C. Jack).

Nevinson, H. W. (ed.)., *England's Voice of Freedom* (Gollancz, 1929).

Orwell, G., *Inside the Whale and other Essays* (Penguin, 1962).

Pearl, G., *The Girl with the Swansdown Seat* (Bobs Merrill, 1958).

Purdom, C. B., *The New Order* (Dent, 1941).

Radcliffe, Lord, *The Problem of Power* (Secker & Warburg, 1958).

Rayner, R. M., *British Democracy* (Longmans Green, 1946).

Roberts, A., *Forbidden Freedom* (Linden Press, 1960).

Robinson, R., *An Atheist's Values* (Blackwell, 1964).

Scarman, Sir L., *English Law: The New Dimension* (Stevens & Sons, 1974).

Stein, P. and Shand, J., *Legal Values in Western Society* (Edinburgh U.P., 1974).

Thompson, A. A., *Big Brother in Britain Today* (Michael Joseph, 1970).

Thompson, W. H., *Civil Liberties* (Gollancz, 1938).

UNESCO., *Freedom and Culture* (London, n.d.).

Watson, G. *The Unservile State* (Allen & Unwin, 1957).

Williamson, H. R., *Who is for Liberty?* (Michael Joseph, 1939).

Wilson, G., *Case and Materials on Constitutional and Administrative Law* (2nd. ed., 1976, C.U.P.)

ABBREVIATIONS

De Smith	S. A. De Smith, *Constitutional and Administrative Law* (3rd ed., Penguin, 1977).
Dicey	A. V. Dicey, *Introduction to the Study of the Law of the Constitution* (10th ed., with an introduction by E. C. S. Wade, Macmillan, 1959).
O'Higgins	Paul O'Higgins, *Censorship in Britain* (Nelson, 1972).
Smith and Hogan	J. C. Smith and B. Hogan, *Criminal Law* (4th ed., Butterworths, 1978).
Street	Harry Street, *Freedom, the Individual and the Law* (4th ed., Penguin, 1977).
Wade and Phillips	E. C. S. Wade and Godfrey Phillips, *Constitutional and Administrative Law* (Eds. A. W. Bradley and T. St. J. Bates, 9th ed., Longmans, 1977).

Chapter 1

GENERAL CONSIDERATIONS

(a) Introductory

The degree of freedom enjoyed in the United Kingdom today is historically and geographically a departure from what is the norm of human experience. It is far from perfect but it must be seen in perspective, if it is to be preserved let alone extended and improved upon. Conventional complacency and conventional cynicism are both threats to its preservation. If it is to be understood properly, there are certain questions, outside the scope of this work, which must be considered carefully by anyone concerned with civil liberties, because the answers to them must colour very significantly attitudes to their protection and extension.

How far is it true, as Abel-Smith and Stevens say on the first page of *Lawyers and the Courts* (Heinemann, 1971) that "civil liberties, traditionally thought of in connection with the common law, in so far as they are protected, are protected primarily by political and social pressures rather than by the activities of the courts?"

How far does the recognition and enjoyment of civil liberties in any society depend upon the economic and social organisation of that society? Is freedom of economic competition essential to the enjoyment of liberty in a meaningful sense? Is social welfare legislation consistent with the enjoyment of liberty? These are the kinds of issues which absorb not only politicians but writers like F. A. Hayek, author of *The Constitution of Liberty* (Routledge, 1960) and many other books; C. B. Macpherson, *Democratic Theory* (O.U.P., 1973) and *The Life and Times of Liberal Democracy* (O.U.P., 1977), and Milton Friedman, *Capitalism and Freedom* (University of Chicago Press, 1960) and *Free to Choose* (Secker & Warburg, 1980).

Another basic question is whether the effectiveness with which civil liberties are protected should be assessed from the point of view of a conventional middleclass citizen comfortably employed with conventional politics or whether it should be assessed from the point of view of the black; the poor; the subversive; the atheist; the "lunatic fringe," etc.?

The special feature of the United Kingdom is that there is no written constitution nor even a Bill of Rights with a special legal status guaranteeing certain basic rights. From this flow many consequences. In particular, the ground upon which it is possible to challenge decisions of the law enforcement agencies do not include the ground that what has been done by them involves a violation of a constitutional right. See *Arrowsmith* v. *Jenkins*, below, p. 9.

(b) Rights and liberties

It is usual in the United Kingdom to talk of civil *liberties* rather than civil *rights*. Lacking a written constitution many matters which would be legally protected rights under other systems, such as freedom of speech or assembly, are not so protected here, and their content has to be defined in terms of what it is not unlawful to do by way of speech or assembly. Professor Glanville Williams has said, "A liberty . . . means any occasion on which an act or omission is not a breach of a duty." He continues: "A right exists where there is a positive law on the subject; a liberty where there is no law against it. A right is correlative to a duty in another, while a liberty is not." (See "The Concept of Legal Liberty" in Robert S. Summers, *Essays in Legal Philosophy* (O.U.P., 1970), pp. 121-45). This distinction has not prevented English judges from describing what is technically a liberty, *e.g.* freedom of the press, as a right and then attaching the taint of illegality to those who interfered with it (see Lord Denning in *Associated Newspapers Group Ltd.* v. *Wade* [1979] I.R.L.R. 201, see below, p. 312). This has been particularly common when the judiciary were seeking to limit the scope for industrial action on behalf of trade unions.

Entick v. Carrington (1765), 19 St. Tr. 1030

Common Pleas

In an action for trespass for breaking and entering the plaintiff's house and removing his papers the defendants, King's Messengers, pleaded as a defence the warrant of a Secretary of State who had ordered them to find the plaintiff and bring him and his books and papers before the Secretary of State. (**LORD CAMDEN**) C.J. delivered a verdict for the plaintiff.

. . . [T]he defendants having failed in the attempt made to protect themselves by the statute of the 24th of Geo. 2, are under a necessity to maintain the legality of the warrants, under which they have acted, and to shew that the secretary of state in the instance now before us, had a jurisdiction to seize the defendants' papers. If he had no such jurisdiction, the law is clear, that the officers are as much responsible for the trespass as their superior.

This, though it is not the most difficult, is the most interesting question in the cause; because if this point should be determined in favour of the jurisdiction, the secret cabinets and bureaus of every subject in this kingdom will be thrown open to the search and inspection of a messenger, whenever the secretary of state shall think fit to charge, or even to suspect, a person to be the author, printer, or publisher of a seditious libel.

The messenger, under this warrant, is commanded to seize the person described, and to bring him with his papers to be examined before the secretary of state. In consequence of this, the house must be searched; the lock and doors of every room, box, or trunk must be broken open; all the papers and books without exception, if the warrant be executed according to its tenor, must be seized and carried away; for it is observable, that nothing is left either to the discretion or to the humanity of the officer.

This power so assumed by the secretary of state is an execution upon all the party's papers, in the first instance. His house is rifled; his most valuable secrets are taken out of his possession, before the paper for which he is charged is found to be criminal by any competent jurisdiction, and before he is convicted either of writing, publishing, or being concerned in the paper.

This power, so claimed by the secretary of state, is not supported by one single citation from any law book extant. It is claimed by no other magistrate in this kingdom but himself: the great executive hand of criminal justice, the lord chief justice of the court of King's-bench, chief justice Scroggs excepted, never having assumed this authority.

The arguments, which the defendant's counsel have thought fit to urge in support of this practice, are of this kind.

That such warrants have issued frequently since the Revolution, which practice has been found by the special verdict; though I must observe, that the defendants have no right to avail themselves of that finding, because no such practice is averred in their justification.

That the case of the warrants bears a resemblance to the case of search for stolen goods.

They say too, that they have been executed without resistance upon many printers, booksellers, and authors, who have quietly submitted to the authority; that no action hath hitherto been brought to try the right; and that although they have been often read upon the returns of Habeas Corpus, yet no court of justice has ever declared them illegal.

And it is further insisted, that this power is essential to government, and the only means of quieting clamours and sedition.

These arguments, if they can be called arguments, shall be all taken notice of; because upon this question I am desirous of removing every colour or plausibility.

Before I state the question, it will be necessary to describe the power claimed by this warrant in its full extent.

If honestly exerted, it is a power to seize that man's papers, who is charged upon oath to be the author or publisher of a seditious libel; if oppressively, it acts against every man, who is so described in the warrant, though he be innocent.

It is executed against the party, before he is heard or even summoned; and the information, as well as the informers, is unknown.

It is executed by messengers with or without a constable (for it can never be pretended, that such is necessary in point of law) in the presence or the absence of the party, as the messengers shall think fit, and without a witness to testify what passes at the time of the transaction; so that when the papers are gone, as the only witnesses are the trespassers, the party injured is left without proof.

If this injury falls upon an innocent person, he is as destitute of remedy as the guilty: and the whole transaction is so guarded against discovery, that if the officer should be disposed to carry off a bank-bill, he may do it with impunity, since there is no man capable of proving either the taker or the thing taken.

It must not be here forgot, that no subject whatsoever is privileged from this search; because both Houses of Parliament have resolved, that there is no privilege in the case of a seditious libel.

Nor is there pretence to say, that the word 'papers' here mentioned ought in point of law to be restrained to the libellous papers only. The word is general, and there is nothing in the warrant to confine it; nay, I am able to affirm, that it has been upon a late occasion executed in its utmost latitutde: for in the case of Wilkes against Wood, when the messengers hesitated about taking all the manuscripts, and sent to the secretary of state for more express orders for that purpose, the answer was, "that all must be taken, manuscripts and all." Accordingly, all was taken, and Mr. Wilkes's private pocket-book filled up the mouth of the sack.

I was likewise told in the same cause by one of the most experienced messengers, that he held himself bound by his oath to pay an implicit obedience to the commands of the secretary of state; that in common cases he was contented to seize the printed impressions of the papers mentioned in the warrant; but when he received directions to search further, or to make a more general seizure, his rule was to sweep all. The practice has been correspondent to the warrant.

Such is the power, and therefore one should naturally expect that the law to warrant it should be clear in proportion as the power is exorbitant.

If it is law, it will be found in our books. If it is not to be found there, it is not law.

The great end, for which men entered into society, was to secure their property. That right is preserved sacred and incommunicable in all instances, where it has not been taken away or abridged by some public law for the good of the whole. The cases where this right of property is set aside by positive law, are various. Distresses, executions, forfeitures, taxes, &c. are all of this description; wherein every man by common consent gives up that right, for the sake of justice and the general good. By the laws of England, every invasion of private property, be it ever so minute, is a trespass. No man can set his foot upon my ground without my licence, but he is liable to an action, though the damage be nothing; which is proved by every declaration in trespass, where the defendant is called upon to answer for bruising the grass and even treading upon the soil. If he admits the fact, he is bound to shew by way of justification, that some positive law has empowered or excused him. The justification is submitted to the judges, who are to look into the books; and if such a justification can be maintained by the text of the statute law, or by the principles of common law. If no such excuse can be found or produced, the silence of the books is an authority against the defendant, and the plaintiff must have judgment.

According to this reasoning, it is now incumbent upon the defendants to shew the law, by which this seizure is warranted. If that cannot be done, it is a trespass.

Papers are the owner's goods and chattels: they are his dearest property; and are so far from enduring a seizure, that they will hardly bear an inspection; and though the eye cannot by the laws of England be guilty of a trespass, yet where private papers are removed and carried away, the secret nature of those goods will be an aggravation of the trespass, and demand more considerable damages in that respect. Where is the written law that gives any magistrate such a power? I can safely answer, there is none; and therefore it is too much for us without such authority to pronounce a practice legal, which would be subversive of all the comforts of society.

But though it cannot be maintained by any direct law, yet it bears a resemblance, as was urged, to the known case of search and seizure for stolen goods.

I answer, that the difference is apparent. In the one, I am permitted to seize my own goods, which are placed in the hands of a public officer, till the felon's conviction shall intitle me to restitution. In the other, the party's own property is seized before and without conviction, and he has no power to reclaim his goods, even after his innocence is cleared by acquittal.

The case of searching for stolen goods crept into the law by imperceptible practice. It is the only case of the kind that is to be met with. No less a person than my lord Coke (4 Inst. 176,) denied its legality; and therefore if the two cases resembled each other more than they do, we have no right, without an act of parliament, to adopt a new practice in the criminal law, which was never yet allowed from all antiquity.

Observe too the caution with which the law proceeds in this singular case.—There must be a full charge upon oath of a theft committed.—The owner must swear that the goods are lodged in such a place.—He must attend at the execution of the warrant to shew them to the officer, who must see that they answer the description.—And, lastly, the owner must abide the event at his peril: for if the goods are not found, he is a trespasser; and the officer being an innocent person, will be always a ready and convenient witness against him.* . . .

What would the parliament say, if the judges should take upon themselves to mould an unlawful power into a convenient authority, by new restrictions? That would be, not judgment, but legislation.

I come now to the practice since the Revolution, which has been strongly urged, with this emphatical addition, that an usage tolerated from the æra of liberty, and continued downwards to this time through the best ages of the constitution, must necessarily have a legal commencement. Now, though that pretence can have no place in the question made by this plea, because no such practice is there alleged; yet I will permit the defendant for the present to borrow a fact from the special verdict, for the sake of giving it an answer.

If the practice began then, it began too late to be law now. If it was more ancient, the Revolution is not to answer for it; and I could have wished, that upon this occasion the Revolution had not been considered as the only basis of our liberty . . .

With respect to the practice itself, if it goes no higher, every lawyer will tell you, it is much too modern to be evidence of the common law; and if it should be added, that these warrants ought to acquire some strength by the silence of those courts, which have heard them read so often upon returns without censure or animadversion, I am able to borrow my answer to that pretence from the Court of King's-bench, which lately declared with great unanimity in the Case of General Warrants, that as no objection was taken to them upon the returns, and the matter passed *sub silentio*, the precedents were of no weight. I most heartily concur in that opinion; and the reason is more pertinent here, because the Court had no authority in the present case to determine against the seizure of papers, which was not before them; whereas in the other they might, if they had thought fit, have declared the warrant void, and discharged the prisoner *ex officio*.

This is the first instance I have met with, where the ancient immemorable law of the land, in a public matter, was attempted to be proved by the practice of a private office. The names and rights of public magistrates, their power and forms of proceeding as they are settled by law, have been long since written, and are to be found in books and records. Private customs indeed are still to be sought from private tradition. But who ever conceived a notion, that any part of the public law could be buried in the obscure practice of a particular person?

---

*Leach's Hawkins's, *Pleas of the Crown,* Bk.2, c.13, s.17.

To search, seize, and carry away all the papers of the subject upon the first warrant: that such a right should have existed from the time whereof the memory of man runneth not to the contrary, and never yet have found a place in any book of law; is incredible. But if so strange a thing could be supposed, I do not see, how we could declare the law upon such evidence.

But still it is insisted, that there has been a general submission, and no action brought to try the right.

I answer, there has been a submission of guilt and poverty to power and the terror of punishment. But it would be strange doctrine to assert that all the people of this land are bound to acknowledge that to be universal law, which a few criminal booksellers have been afraid to dispute.

The defendants upon this occasion have stopped short at the Revolution. But I think it would be material to go further back, in order to see, how far the search and seizure of papers have been countenanced in the antecedent reigns.

First, I find no trace of such a warrant as the present before that period, except a very few that were produced the other day in the reign of king Charles 2.

But there did exist a search-warrant, which took its rise from a decree of the Star-Chamber. The decree is found at the end of the 3d volume of Rushworth's Collections. It was made in the year 1636, and recites an older decree upon the subject in the 28th of Elizabeth, by which probably the same power of search was given.

By this decree the messenger of the press was empowered to search in all places, where books were printing, in order to see if the printer had a licence; and if upon such search he found any books which he suspected to be libellous against the church or state, he was to seize them, and carry them before the proper magistrate.

It was very evident, that the Star-Chamber, how soon after the invention of printing I know not, took to itself the jurisdiction over public libels, which soon grew to be the peculiar business of that court. Not that the courts of Westminster-hall wanted the power of holding pleas in those cases; but the attorney-general for good reasons chose rather to proceed there; which is the reason, why we have no cases of libels in the King's-bench before the Restoration.

The Star-Chamber from this jurisdiction presently usurped a general superintendance over the press, an exercised a legislative power in all matters relating to the subject. They appointed licensers; they prohibited books; they inflicted penalties; and they dignified one of their officers with the name of the messenger of the press, and among other things enacted this warrant of search.

After that court was abolished, the press became free, but enjoyed its liberty not above two or three years; for the Long Parliament thought fit to restrain it again by ordinance. Whilst the press is free, I am afraid it will always be licentious, and all governments have an aversion to libels. This parliament, therefore, did by ordinance restore the Star-Chamber practice; they recalled the licences, and sent forth again the messenger. It was against the ordinance, that Milton wrote that famous pamphlet called Areopagitica. Upon the Restoration, the press was free once more, till the 13th and 14th of Charles 2, when the Licensing Act passed, which for the first time gave the secretary of state a power to issue search warrants: but these warrants were neither so oppressive, nor so inconvenient as the present. The right to enquire into the licence was the pretence of making the searches; and if during the search any suspected libels were found, they and they only could be seized.

This act expired the 32d year of that reign, or thereabouts. It was revived again in the 1st year of king James 2, and remained in force till the 5th of king William, after one of his parliaments had continued it for a year beyond its expiration.

I do very much suspect, that the present warrant took its rise from these search-warrants, that I have been describing; nothing being easier to account for than this engraftment; the difference between them being no more than this, that the apprehension of the person in the first was to follow the seizure of papers, but the seizure of papers in the latter was to follow the apprehension of the person. The same evidence would serve equally for both purposes. If it was charged for printing or publishing, that was sufficient for either of the warrants. Only this material difference must always be observed between them, that the search warrant only carried off the criminal papers, whereas this seizes all.

When the Licensing Act expired at the close of king Charles 2's reign, the twelve judges were assembled at the king's command, to discover whether the press might not be as effectually restrained by the common law, as it had been by that statute.

I cannot help observing in this place, that if the secretary of state was still invested with a power of issuing this warrant, there was no occasion for the application to the judges: for though he could not issue the general search-warrant, yet upon the least rumour of a libel he might have done more, and seized every thing. But that was not thought of, and therefore the judges met and resolved:

First, that it was criminal at common law, not only to write public seditious papers and false news; but likewise to publish any news without a licence from the king, though it was true and innocent.

Secondly, that libels were seizable. This is to be found in the State Trials; and because it is a curiosity, I will recite the passages at large . . . [Quotes from Trial of Harris for Libel, 7 st. Tr. 929.]

These are the opinions of all the twelve judges of England; a great and reverend authority.

Can the twelve judges extrajudicially make a thing law to bind the kingdom by a declaration, that such is their opinion?—I say No.—It is a matter of impeachment for any judge to affirm it. There must be an antecedent principle or authority, from whence this opinion may be fairly collected; otherwise the opinion is null, and nothing but ignorance can excuse the judge that subscribed it. Out of this doctrine sprang the famous general search-warrant, that was condemned by the House of Commons; and it was not unreasonable to suppose, that the form of it was settled by the twelve judges that subscribed the opinion.

The deduction from the opinion to the warrant is obvious. If you can seize a libel, you may search for it: if search is legal, a warrant to authorize that search is likewise legal: if any magistrate can issue such a warrant, the chief justice of the King's bench may clearly do it.

It falls here naturally in my way to ask, whether there be any authority besides this opinion of these twelve judges to say, that libels may be seized? If they may, I am afraid, that all the inconveniences of a general seizure will follow upon a right allowed to seize a part. The search in such cases will be general, and every house will fall under the power of a secretary of state to be rummaged before proper conviction.—Consider for a while how the law of libels now stands . . .

I can find no other authority to justify the seizure of a libel, than that of Scroggs and his brethren.

If the power of search is to follow the right of seizure, every body sees the consequence. He that has it or has had it in his custody; he that has published, copied, or maliciously reported it, may fairly be under a reasonable suspicion of having the thing in his custody, and consequently become the object of the search-warrant. If libels may be seized, it ought to be laid down with precision, when, where, upon what charge, against whom, by what magistrate, and in what stage of the prosecution. All these particulars must be explained and proved to be law, before this general proposition can be established.

As therefore no authority in our books can be produced to support such a doctrine, and as many Star-Chamber decrees, ordinances, and acts have been thought necessary to establish a power of search, I cannot be persuaded, that such a power can be justified by the common law.

I have now done with the argument, which has endeavoured to support this warrant by the practice since the Revolution.

It is then said, that it is necessary for the ends of government to lodge such a power with a state officer; and that it is better to prevent the publication before than to punish the offender afterwards. I answer, if the legislation be of that opinion, they will revive the Licensing Act. But if they have not done that, I conceive they are not of that opinion. And with respect to the argument of state necessity, or a distinction that has been aimed at between state offences and others, the common law does not understand that kind of reasoning, nor do our books take notice of any such distinctions.

Serjeant Ashley was committed to the Tower in the 3d of Charles 1st, by the House of Lords only for asserting in argument, that there was a 'law of state' different from the common law; and the Ship-Money judges were impeached for holding, first, that state-necessity would justify the raising money without consent of parliament; and secondly, that the king was judge of that necessity.

If the king himself has no power to declare when the law ought to be violated for reason of state, I am sure we his judges have no such prerogative.

Lastly, it is urged as an argument of utility, that such a search is a means of detecting offenders by discovering evidence. I wish some cases had been shewn, where the law forceth evidence out of the owner's custody by process. There is no process against papers in civil causes. It has been often tried, but never prevailed. Nay, where the adversary has by force or fraud got possession of your own proper evidence, there is no way to get it back but by action.

In the criminal law such a proceeding was never heard of; and yet there are some crimes, such for instance as murder, rape, robbery, and house-breaking, to say nothing of forgery and perjury, that are more atrocious than libelling. But our law has provided no paper-search in these cases to help forward the conviction.

Whether this proceedeth from the gentleness of the law towards criminals, or from a consideration that such a power would be more pernicious to the innocent than useful to the public, I will not say.

It is very certain, that the law obligeth no man to accuse himself; because the necessary means of compelling self-accusation, falling upon the innocent as well as the guilty, would be both cruel and unjust; and it should seem, that search for evidence is disallowed upon the same principle. There too the innocent would be confounded with the guilty.

Observe the wisdom as well as mercy of the law. The strongest evidence before a trial, being only *ex parte*, is but suspicion; it is not proof. Weak evidence is a ground of suspicion, though in a lower degree; and if suspicion at large should be a ground of search, especially in the case of libels, whose house would be safe?

If, however, a right of search for the sake of discovering evidence ought in any case to be allowed, this crime above all others ought to be excepted, as wanting such a discovery less than any other. It is committed in open daylight, and in the face of the world; every act of publication makes new proof; and the solicitor of the treasury, if he pleases, may be the witness himself . . .

I have now taken notice of every thing that has been urged upon the present point; and upon the whole we are all of opinion, that the warrant to seize and carry away the party's papers in the case of a seditious libel, is illegal and void.

Note: See also pp. 251, 260 and 262.

Question

"This is perhaps the central case in English constitutional law"—D. L. Keir & F. H. Lawson, *Cases in Constitutional Law* (5th. ed., O.U.P., 1967), p. 307. Do you agree? How have the principles expounded by Lord Camden been regarded in practice by later cases?

Arrowsmith v. Jenkins [1963] 2 Q.B. 561

Divisional Court.

Pat Arrowsmith held a meeting at a spot in Bootle traditionally used for the holding of meetings. It was part of the highway. In the past the police had facilitated the holding of meetings at this spot. She was convicted on a charge of wilfully obstructing the highway contrary to the Highways Act 1959, s. 121. An appeal by case stated was made.

LORD PARKER C.J. stated the facts and continued: I think that the defendant feels that she is under a grievance because—and one may put it this way—she says: "Why pick on me? There have been many meetings held in "this street from time to time. The police, as on this occasion, have attended "those meetings and assisted to make a free passage, and there is no evidence "that anybody else has ever been prosecuted. Why pick on me?" That, of course, has nothing to do with this court. The sole question here is whether the defendant has contravened section 121 (1) of the Highways Act, 1959. That section provides: "If a person, without lawful authority or excuse, in any "way wilfully obstructs the free passage along a highway he shall be guilty of "an offence and shall be liable in respect thereof to a fine not exceeding forty "shillings."

I am quite satisfied that section 121 (1) of the Act of 1959, on its true construction, is providing that if a person, without lawful authority or excuse, intentionally as opposed to accidentally, that is, by an exercise of his or her free will, does something or omits to do something which will cause an obstruction or the continuance of an obstruction, he or she is guilty of an offence. Mr. Wigoder, for the defendant, has sought to argue that if a person—and I think that this is how he puts it—acts in the genuine belief that he or she has lawful authority to do what he or she is doing then, if an obstruction results, he or she cannot be said to have wilfully obstructed the free passage along a highway.

Quite frankly, I do not fully understand that submission. It is difficult, certainly, to apply in the present case. I imagine that it can be put in this way: that there must be some mens rea in the sense that a person will only be guilty if he knowingly does a wrongful act. I am quite satisfied that that consideration cannot possibly be imported into the words "wilfully obstructs" in section 121 (1) of the Act of 1959. If anybody, by an exercise of free will, does something which causes an obstruction, then an offence is committed. There is no doubt that the defendant did that in the present case.

I am quite satisfied that quarter sessions were right, and I would dismiss this appeal.

Ashworth and Winn, JJ. agreed.

Note: This case appears to imply that one cannot challenge a police decision to prosecute selectively, where the grounds upon which the particular person is selected for prosecution, is that they were of a particular political persuasion or had been exercising some basic right to the annoyance of the police. See A. F. Wilcox, *The Decision to Prosecute* (Butterworths, 1972). In the United States, given a written constitution, there is a limited possibility to challenge a discriminatory prosecution. See *U.S.* v. *Falk*, 479 F.2d 516 (noted 72 *Michigan Law Review* 1113), and *U.S.* v. *Crowther* 456 F.2d 1074 (4th Cir. 1972).

(c) Local Legal Rules

Further Reading

O'Higgins, pp. 44–47 and Chap. 5; Wade & Phillips, pp. 358–360; I. Brownlie, *The Law Relating to Public Order,* (Butterworths, 1968), Chaps. 3 and 15.

Apart from rules applying within one of the three legal systems which make up the United Kingdom, there are also many rules of limited geographical application which affect civil liberties, in particular by regulating meetings and processions, sometimes establishing criminal liability for acts which are not generally criminal in the state as a whole, by conferring special powers of arrest, search and seizure on the police, and by establishing liability for acts which are regulated by the general law in such a manner as to allow the law enforcement agencies to opt between acting under general legislation or under local legislation which is often less stringent as regards safeguards for the individual. These rules are found principally in byelaws, in public acts of local application, and in local or private acts of parliament. They constitute an astonishing undergrowth of legal rules, still showing an astonishing variation from one community to another. Efforts are made by central government to encourage uniformity, particularly in the light of the Local Government Act 1972, section 262. This provided generally that except where a particular local Act was continued in force by ministerial order, all existing local Acts were to cease to operate in Metropolitan counties at the end of 1979 and elsewhere at the end of 1984. In consequence the re-enactment of local acts believed to be necessary by local authorities has given an opportunity for such local legislation to be subject to Parliamentary scrutiny.

Rules are made by a wide variety of bodies, public and private, which may affect the area of civil liberties. Universities, clubs, trade unions, nationalised industries, harbour boards, water boards, employers, etc. all make rules. Many of these depend for their legal authority, if any, upon statute or statutory instrument. Some derive their force from the law of contract.

No proper study has yet been undertaken of the relevance of these kinds of rules for civil liberties. Given below are some examples of rules which are fairly typical.

DISCIPLINARY RULES, CAMBRIDGE UNIVERSITY

Whereas it is the duty of the University to maintain good order and discipline within the University:

1. No member of the University shall intentionally or recklessly disrupt or impede or attempt to disrupt or impede the activities and functions of the University, or any part thereof, or of any College.

2. No member of the University shall intentionally or recklessly impede freedom of speech or lawful assembly within the Precincts of the University.

3. No member of the University shall intentionally occupy or use any property of the University or of any College except as may be expressly or by implication authorized by the University or College authorities concerned.

4. No member of the University shall intentionally or recklessly damage or deface or knowingly misappropriate any property of the University or of any College.

5. No member of the University shall intentionally or recklessly endanger the safety, health, or property of any member, officer, or employee of the University within the Precincts of the University.

6. No candidate shall make use of unfair means in any University examination or knowingly have in his possession at an examination any book, paper, or other material relevant to the examination unless specifically authorized. No member of the University shall assist a candidate to make use of such unfair means.

7. No member of the University shall forge or falsify or knowingly make improper use of any degree certificate or other document attesting to academic achievement nor shall he knowingly make false statements concerning standing or concerning results in examinations.

8. All members of the University shall comply with any instruction given by a University officer, or by any other person authorized to act on behalf of the University, in the proper discharge of his duties.

9. All members of the University shall state their names and the Colleges to which they belong when asked by a Proctor or Pro-Proctor, or other person in authority in the University or in any of the Colleges in the University.

[*Grace 1 of 19 February 1975.*]

BOOTLE CORPORATION ACT 1970

Power of police to search

97.—(1) A police constable may within the borough enter upon and search any vehicle upon or in which there shall be reason to suspect that any thing stolen or unlawfully obtained may be found, and also any person who may be reasonably suspected of having or conveying in any manner any thing stolen or unlawfully obained.

(2) The powers of this section shall not be exercised with respect to licensed pawnbrokers or their servants, apprentices or agents in a licensed pawnbroker's shop.

COUNTY OF SOUTH GLAMORGAN ACT 1976

Part V Public Order and Public Safety

Notice of street processions.

25.—(1) No procession shall pass through the streets of a district unless notice stating—
  (a) the route by which and the date and time on and at which it will so pass; and
  (b) the name of a person responsible for organising the procession and the purpose of the procession;
has been delivered at the offices of the chief executives of the county council and of the district council respectively and the chief superintendent of police of the district in which the procession is to take place at least thirty-six hours (exclusive of Sundays) before the time so stated.

(2) If any procession passes through the streets of a district in contravention of the foregoing subsection or by a route or at a time other than that stated in the notice delivered with respect thereto under that subsection any person organising or conducting the procession shall be liable on summary conviction to a fine not exceeding £50.

(3) In this section the expression "procession" means any public, protest or ceremonial procession or any circus procession or procession of wild animals:

Provided that nothing in this section shall apply to any public or ceremonial procession habitually held.

TEESSIDE CORPORATION (GENERAL POWERS) ACT 1971

Notice of street processions.

104.—(1) No procession shall pass through the streets of the borough unless written notice stating the route by which, and the date and time on and at which, it will pass has been delivered at the office of the town clerk, and at the principal police station in the borough, by midday on the day next but one before the date stated, treating as not an intervening day a Sunday, Christmas Day, Good Friday, bank holiday or day appointed for public thanksgiving or mourning.

(2) If a procession passes through the streets of the borough in contravention of the foregoing subsection, or by a route, or at a time, other than that stated in the notice delivered with respect thereto under that subsection, any person organising or conducting the procession shall be guilty of an offence.

(3) In this section "procession" means any public or ceremonial procession or any walk organised by or for the benefit of a charity, or any circus procession or procession of wild animals:

Provided that nothing in this section shall apply to a public or ceremonial procession habitually held.

OXFORDSHIRE COUNTY COUNCIL ACT 1971

Notice of street processions.

68.—(1) No procession shall pass through the streets of an urban district unless written notice stating the route by which, and the date and time on and at which, it will pass has been delivered at the office of the clerk of the local authority of that district, and at the principal police station in the district, by mid-day on the day next but one before the date stated, treating as not an intervening day a Sunday, Christmas Day, Good Friday, bank holiday or day appointed for public thanksgiving or mourning.

(2) If a procession passes through the streets of an urban district in contravention of the foregoing subsection, or by a route, or at a time, other than that stated in the notice delivered with respect thereto under that subsection, any person organising or conducting the procession shall be liable to a fine not exceeding twenty pounds.

(3) In this section "procession" means any public or ceremonial procession or any circus procession or procession of wild animals:

Provided that nothing in this section shall apply to a public or ceremonial procession habitually held.

BOURNEMOUTH CORPORATION ACT 1971

Notice of street processions.

46.—(1) No procession shall pass through the streets of the borough unless written notice stating the route by which, and the date and time on and at which, it will pass has been delivered at the office of the town clerk, and at the principal police station in the borough, by midday on the day next but three before the date stated, treating as not an intervening day a Sunday, Christmas Day, Good Friday, bank holiday or day appointed for public thanksgiving or mourning.

(2) If a procession passes through the streets of the borough in contravention of the foregoing subsection, or by a route, or at a time other than that stated in the notice delivered with respect thereto under that subsection, any person organising or conducting the procession shall be liable to a fine not exceeding twenty pounds.

(3) In this section "procession" means any public or ceremonial procession or any circus procession or procession of wild animals:

Provided that nothing in this section shall apply to a public or ceremonial procession habitually held.

TORBAY CORPORATION ACT 1971

Notice of street processions.

70.—(1) No procession shall pass through the streets of the borough unless written notice stating the route by which, and the date and time on and at which, it will pass has been delivered at the office of the town clerk, and at the principal police station in the borough, by midday on the day next but one before the date stated, treating as not an intervening day a Sunday, Christmas Day, Good Friday, bank holiday or day appointed for public thanksgiving or mourning.

(2) If a procession passes through the streets of the borough in contravention of the foregoing subsection, or by a route, or at a time, other than that stated in the notice delivered with respect thereto under that subsection, any person organising or conducting the procession shall be guilty of an offence.

(3) In this section "procession" means any public or ceremonial procession or any walk organised by or for the benefit of a charity, or any circus procession or procession of wild animals:

Provided that nothing in this section shall apply to a public or ceremonial procession habitually held.

Note: See a comment on recent bills promoted by local authorities containing provisions regarding notice of processions, by Lord Avebury speaking on a motion to set up a Select Committee of the House of Lords to consider Bills being promited by local authorities of Greater Manchester, the Isle of Wight, South Yorkshire and Tyne and Wear:

Lord AVEBURY:

My Lords, I wonder whether I might make a few remarks about this Motion which, as the Lord Chairman of Committees has said, deals with the four Bills in the second batch of those brought forward as a result of the provisions of Section 262 of the Local Government Act 1972, which provided that all local legislation then in force, with a few exceptions, was to be repealed on certain dates from 1980 to 1984. To the extent that the powers contained in those Acts were still needed, the local authorities had to bring forward fresh legislation for enactment. There was an inheritance of what the Lord Chairman of Committees called a "hotch-potch of powers". It was to tidy up that "hotch-potch" that Parliament required the new local authorities to come back and prove again the need for such powers as they wished to retain.

It was considered that some of the matters dealt with in the old local Acts would be better dealt with in public general legislation . . .

At the same time, as a result of this procedure I am afraid there will be a sacrifice of the uniformity or consistency which it is the aim of this procedure to achieve. I am sorry to say that the consistency is not even achieved as between Bills in the same batch, let alone as between the first and second batches of four Bills which your Lordships have considered . . .

It seemed to me, on reading these debates, that what is concealed by the terminology is the lack of any fixed principle in deciding whether to accept particular clauses or variants of them. That was illustrated very well in the case of the public processions clauses which we had dealt with in an Instruction that I moved on the Greater Manchester Bill but which your Lordships at that time did not see fit to accept.

If one looks at the old local Acts, one finds that the vast majority of authorities which did require notice of processions were content to make do with 24 hours' warning, in the case of 43, or 36 hours, in the case of 56. A mere seven required two days' notice; two required three days and two wanted longer than three days. If one looks at a few examples of the local authorities which had these provisions, there are inexplicable variations between them. Oxfordshire had 36 hours' notice; Cambridgeshire had no notice; Rochester had no notice; Chatham required 24 hours; the West Riding of Yorkshire, 36 hours, the East Riding, none; Derby, 24 hours and Leicester, 36. So it appears that up to 1972 very many councils did not find it necessary to have these powers at all, and the ones that did have them were, in the very large majority, content with either 24 or 36 hours. Apparently it never occurred to the Governments of the day to consider whether, in general, it was a good idea to lay a statutory obligation on the organisers of processions, which the overwhelming majority of them would have been quite happy to do voluntarily, in any case.

There is a danger, once a provision of this kind has appeared in a large number of private Acts, that that will be taken as sufficient justification for its continuance in one form or other. We find in these Bills which are now appearing that the length of the notice has been increased to three or seven days. Three days is the period which is suggested in the General Powers Bill Common Clauses; seven days is the period of notice which is required in Northern Ireland. I think that that is where the local authorities which have chosen this period got the precedent from; but, of course, the circumstances in Northern Ireland are totally different, as I think your Lordships would agree.

Of the Bills that have been considered in your Lordships' House so far, four have gone to the Commons—the West Midlands Bill, where the notice clause has been taken out on an Instruction of the House; the West Yorkshire Bill, where the promoters have stated their intention of withdrawing the notice clause; the Merseyside Bill, where the promoters have agreed to reduce the notice from seven days to three, and the Cheshire Bill which still has to have its Second Reading, but it is rumoured that the promoters will agree to three days.

In the case of the four Bills which we now have, and which have been referred to the Committee, the Tyne and Wear Bill has no notice; the Isle of Wight Bill has seven days; the Greater Manchester Bill has seven days and, in the case of the South Yorkshire Bill, I understand that the promoters will agree to withdraw the clause requiring three days, when it gets into Committee.

So that there are these tremendous variations between one Bill and another. I realise that the Select Committee, which is concerned with unopposed clauses, will be dealing only with the Isle of Wight, but it will no doubt have regard to the fact that it now looks as though no authority will have seven days' notice and, in many cases, even three will be abandoned. If the promoters of the West Midlands Bill do not seek to restore the clause which was knocked out by the Instruction, when that Bill comes up for Report in another place, then four out of these eight Bills, which are at various stages in each House, could have no notice at all, and it would be necessary to probe the necessity for it in the others even more closely than the Select Committee would have done otherwise.

If I may say so, the general approach of the Conservative Party to legislation, with which I have a certain amount of sympathy, is that we have too much legislation, and that whenever opportunities occur of striking out redundant provisions from the Statute Book, then we should act accordingly.

It is for that reason that I have ventured to make these remarks this afternoon, not only because I respectfully hope that the Select Committee might take note of them, but also with the object of saving the promoters time and money by reducing the areas of controversy.

[400 *H.L. Deb., Cols* 717-21 (14 *June* 1979).]

DURHAM COUNTY COUNCIL ACT 1968

Defacing of road surface, etc.

21.—(1) The highway authority may expunge or remove any picture, letter, sign or other mark painted or otherwise inscribed or affixed upon the surface of a highway or upon a tree, structure or works on or in a highway contrary to paragraph (*cc*) of subsection (1) of section 117 of the Act of 1959.

Note: Highways Act 1959, s.117 provides:
Penalty for damaging highway, etc.
(1) If a person, without lawful authority or excuse,— ...
(*cc*) paints or otherwise inscribes or affixes upon the surface of a highway, or upon any tree, structure or works on or in a highway, any picture, letter, sign or other mark, or ...
he shall be guilty of an offence.

CLYDE PORT AUTHORITY (HUNTERSTON ORE TERMINAL) ORDER CONFIRMATION ACT 1973

Amendments and repeals

6.—(2) For subsection (1) of section 467 (Offences relating to amenity) of the Order of 1967 there shall be substituted the following subsection:—
"(1) (*a*) A person shall not—
(i) in any street distribute any handbill for the purpose of selling or advertising any article or obtaining custom or
(ii) lay or spread out any handbill on the surface of any street.
(*b*) In this subsection 'handbill' includes a pamphlet, leaflet or other printed matter or article."

CROUCH HARBOUR ACT 1974

64.—(1) The Authority may from time to time make byelaws, as they think fit, for all or any of the following purposes:—
(*c*) for securing the good and orderly conduct and the safety of persons in charge of or using vessels or houseboats in the harbour;
(*d*) for preserving order and preventing and suppressing nuisances and offences against decency in the harbour ...

MOTHERWELL AND WISHAW BURGH EXTENSION, ETC.
ORDER CONFIRMATION ACT 1964

Separation of sexes in houses let in lodgings.

37.—(1) The Town Council as the local authority of the burgh under the Act of 1897 may make byelaws applicable to houses let in lodgings and persons occupying and using the same requiring that persons of different sexes above the age of ten years (other than husband and wife) shall not occupy the same sleeping apartment.

(2) The power of the Town Council to make byelaws under this section shall be in addition to and not in derogation of their power to make byelaws under section 72 of the Act of 1897.

GLASGOW CORPORATION CONSOLIDATION (GENERAL POWERS)
ORDER CONFIRMATION ACT 1960

Part IX Offences and Penalties

Penalties for certain offences.

152. Any person who is guilty of any of the following acts or omissions shall in respect thereof be guilty of an offence and shall be liable on summary conviction to penalties not exceeding those hereinafter respectively mentioned (that is to say):—

To a fine of twenty pounds or to imprisonment without the option of a fine for sixty days every person who—

(1) behaves in a riotous disorderly violent or indecent manner;

(2) occupies a building or part of a building and suffers any breach of the peace or riotous or disorderly conduct within the same;

(3) occupies a building or part of a building or other place of public resort for the sale or consumption of provisions or refreshments of any kind and knowingly harbours prostitutes or suffers persons of notoriously bad fame or dissolute boys or girls to assemble therein;

(4) publishes makes prints or offers for sale or distribution or sells distributes or publicly exhibits any profane indecent or obscene article book paper print photograph drawing painting or representation:

To a fine of ten pounds or to imprisonment without the option of a fine for thirty days every person who—

(5) alters or defaces the name or address or the distinctive mark or inscription on any barrel box bag plank or other article which does not belong to him without the authority of the owner;

(6) wilfully prevents obstructs or hinders any officer of the Corporation in the performance of his duty or aids or incites any other person to do so; . . .

(8) uses any words or behaviour with intent to provoke a breach of the peace or whereby a breach of the peace may be occasioned;

(9) without proper cause sets on or urges any dog or other animal to attack worry or put in fear any person or animal:

To a fine of ten pounds every person who—

(10) finds any goods or any parcel bank note money or other article of value and does not either return the same to the owner or deliver it to a constable on duty at a police office within forty-eight hours thereafter. Provided

that this paragraph shall not apply to any property found in or on any railway property or in or on any public service vehicles tramcars trolley vehicles or any subway carriage used on the subway railway of the Corporation;

(11) keeps any dog or other animal or any poultry which has been found by the magistrate to be an annoyance to the neighbourhood and has been ordered to be removed;

(12) occupies a building or part of a building or other place of public resort for the sale or consumption of provisions or refreshments of any kind and knowingly suffers to remain in his premises any constable on duty unless for the purpose of quelling any disturbance or restoring order or directly or indirectly supplies such constable with liquor:

To a fine of five pounds every person who—

(13) occupies a building or part of a building or other place of public resort for the sale or consumption of provisions or refreshments of any kind and opens his premises for business before five o'clock in the morning or keeps them open or does business therein after midnight unless specially allowed by the chief constable; . . .

Penalty for begging.

153. Any person who in any public place or from door to door begs or acts in any way for the purpose of inducing the giving of alms shall be guilty of an offence and shall be liable on summary conviction to a fine not exceeding ten pounds or to imprisonment without the option of a fine for thirty days:

Provided that nothing in this section shall make it an offence to take part in any collection licensed under or deemed to be licensed under or authorised by any enactment.

Penalty for vagrancy.

154. Any person who is found wandering abroad or lodging in any unoccupied building or in the open air or under a tent or in any cart or waggon or on any common stair or common passage shall unless he proves that he has a fixed place of residence and a lawful means of getting his livelihood be guilty of vagrancy and shall be liable on summary conviction to a fine of ten pounds or to imprisonment without the option of a fine for thirty days.

Offences by vagrants known thieves etc.

155.—(1) (a) Any person who is found in or on any building or in any enclosed space for any unlawful purpose shall be guilty of an offence.

(b) Any person who having been convicted of vagrancy or of any of the crimes specified in the next following subsection or any known thief or associate of a known thief who—

  (i) has in his possession any picklock key crowbar jack bit or other implement usually employed in house-breaking;

  (ii) is found in or on any premises or in any public place or in any vehicle with intent to commit any of the crimes specified in the next following subsection; or

  (iii) has in his possession any money or article without being able to give a satisfactory account of his possession thereof;

  shall be guilty of an offence.

(c) Any person found guilty of an offence under this subsection shall be liable on summary conviction to imprisonment for sixty days and without prejudice to the provisions of any enactment dealing with the forfeiture of implements shall be liable to forfeit any article or money forming the subject matter of the offence.

(2) The crimes referred to in the last foregoing subsection are robbery theft reset of theft house-breaking with intent to steal fraud and any other crime inferring dishonest appropriation of property and any attempt to commit any of these crimes.

(3) It shall not be necessary for the purpose of proving the commission of an offence under sub-paragraph (ii) of paragraph (b) of subsection (1) of this section to show that the accused did any particular act tending to indicate his intention and he may be convicted of such offence if from the circumstances of the case and from his known character as proved to the court it appears to the court that his intention was to commit any of the crimes specified in subsection (2) of this section.

(4) Any article or money forfeited in pursuance of this section shall if not claimed within six months by the owner thereof be vested in the Corporation and be applied for police purposes.

(5) Any constable may take into custody without warrant any person who has committed or whom he believes with reasonable cause to have committed an offence under this section or under the two immediately preceding sections of this Order.

Gaming and betting houses.

156.—(1) Any constable having good grounds for believing that any house room or place is kept or used as a gaming or betting house may—
  (a) enter such house room or place;
  (b) if needful use force for the purpose of effecting such entry;
  (c) take into custody all persons who are found therein; and
  (d) seize all tables for and instruments of gaming and all lists cards or other documents relating to betting found in such house room or place and all moneys and securities for money found therein.

(2) The owner or keeper of any house room or place kept or used as a gaming or betting house or other person having the care or management thereof and also any person who acts in any manner in conducting gaming or betting in any such house room or place shall be guilty of an offence and shall be liable on summary conviction to a fine not exceeding fifty pounds.

(3) Upon conviction of any such offender all tables for and instruments of gaming and all lists cards or other documents relating to betting found in any such house room or place shall be destroyed and all the moneys and securities for money which have been seized as aforesaid shall be paid and applied in the same way and manner as penalties under this Order are directed to be paid and applied.

(4) Any person found within a gaming or betting house without lawful excuse shall be guilty of an offence and shall be liable on summary conviction to a fine not exceeding ten pounds.

(5) Nothing in this section shall be in derogation of the provisions of the Small Lotteries and Gaming Act 1956.

Proof of gaming for money not necessary in support of prosecution.

157. It shall not be necessary in support of any prosecution under the provisions of this Order in respect of gaming in or suffering any game or gaming in any gaming or betting house or keeping or using or being concerned in the management or conduct of such house to prove that any person found playing therein at any game was playing for any money wager or stake.

Penalty for betting in streets etc.

158.—(1) If any two or more persons assemble together in any street or public place for the purpose of engaging in lotteries betting or gaming each of such persons shall be guilty of an offence and shall be liable on summary conviction to a fine not exceeding five pounds.

(2) If any person who conducts business of any kind in lotteries betting or gaming engages in any street or public place in lotteries betting or gaming or does any act for the purpose of inducing or enabling any other person to engage in any lottery betting or gaming he shall be guilty of an offence and shall be liable on summary conviction to a fine not exceeding twenty pounds.

(3) Any constable may take into custody without warrant any person who commits an offence under this section in view of such constable.

Penalty for soliciting etc.

159.—(1) Every person who in any street commits any of the following offences shall be guilty of an offence and shall be liable on summary conviction to a fine not exceeding ten pounds (that is to say)—

(a) being a common prostitute or street-walker loiters about or importunes passengers for the purpose of prostitution;

(b) habitually or persistently importunes or solicits or loiters about for the purpose of importuning or soliciting women or children for immoral purposes.

(2) For the purposes of this section "street" includes any harbour railway station station or depot of any operators of public service vehicles canal depot wharf towing-path public park common or open area or space and any other public place.

Offences in streets and other places.

160. Any person who is guilty of any of the following acts or omissions on or in any street or on the outside of any building adjoining the same or in any public place shall be guilty of an offence and shall be liable on summary conviction to penalties not exceeding those hereinafter respectively mentioned (that is to say):—

To a fine of ten pounds every person who—

(1) rides any horse or other animal or rides drives or propels any vehicle not being a vehicle to which sections 11 and 12 of the Road Traffic Act 1930 (which relate respectively to reckless or dangerous driving and careless driving) apply recklessly or in a manner which is dangerous to the public having regard to all the circumstances of the case or without due care and attention or without reasonable consideration for other persons;

(2) fails to protect by means of a sufficient iron grating or other covering any opening in the foot pavement which he is authorised to make or use or who fails to protect by means of a sufficient fence any area pit or sewer of

which he has charge or who leaves such area pit or sewer without a sufficient light during the hours of darkness;

To a fine of five pounds every person who—

(3) writes or draws any indecent or obscene word figure or representation on any wall fence or building or sings or recites any profane or obscene song or ballad or uses any profane indecent or obscene language;

(11) leaves unattended on any street or does not immediately remove therefrom any furniture goods or other articles or places or uses on any foot pavement any standing place stool bench stall or showboard;

(14) affixes or causes to be affixed to any building any sign or signboard without the consent of the proprietor and occupier;

(15) writes upon soils defaces or marks any wall fence hoarding or building with chalk or paint or in any other way;

(16) without authority affixes or causes to be affixed to any church chapel or schoolhouse or without the consent of the proprietor and occupier to any other building or to any wall fence or hoarding any bill or other notice;

(29) being the occupier of any building or part of a building causes or suffers any female to stand on the sill of any window in order to clean paint or perform any operation upon the outside of such window or upon any other building unless such window be in the sunk or basement storey;

(30) wilfully or wantonly continues by loud calls or noises whether by the voice or by horns bells or other instruments and whether for the purpose of proclaiming sales or of hawking or collecting articles or otherwise to cause annoyance or disturbance to any of the lieges after having been requested by a constable to cease;

(31) wilfully or wantonly continues to play any instrument of music or to sing opposite or near any building to the annoyance or disturbance of the owner or occupier of any part of such building after having been requested by him personally or through his servant or a constable to cease;

(32) occasions any kind of obstruction nuisance or annoyance in any street public place or doorway or obstructs or incommodes hinders or prevents free passage along or through the same or prejudices or annoys in any manner whatsoever any other person using the same;

(33) plays at any game of football cricket or other sport or game to the obstruction or annoyance of the lieges.

Prevention of assemblies causing obstruction

161.—(1) Where—

(a) any demonstration or display in any shop window;

(b) any notice placard advertisement or announcement;

(c) the playing of any musical instrument; or

(d) the use of a loudspeaker in any premises;

causes persons to assemble and obstruct the free passage in any street common stair or common passage any constable not below the rank of sergeant may require the owner or occupier of the premises in or upon which such demonstration or display is taking place or such notice placard or announcement is exhibited or such musical instrument is being played or loudspeaker is situated to—

(i) discontinue such demonstration or display;
(ii) remove or at the option of the owner or occupier screen from public view such notice placard advertisement or announcement; or
(iii) discontinue the playing of such musical instrument or the use of such loudspeaker.

(2) Any such owner or occupier who fails to comply forthwith with any such requirement shall be guilty of an offence and shall be liable on summary conviction to a fine not exceeding five pounds.

Pernicious literature etc.

162.—(1) Any magistrate may on a complaint by the procurator fiscal grant warrant to any constable not under the rank of inspector to enter into and search from time to time during any period not exceeding thirty days from the date of such warrant any house shop room building part of a building or other place in which the magistrate has reasonable ground for believing that any profane indecent or obscene article book paper print photograph drawing painting or representation is kept for sale or for lending on hire or for publication for purposes of gain. Such warrant may if the magistrate thinks fit include power to search—
(a) the occupier of any such house shop room building part of a building or other place; and
(b) any person found therein engaged or assisting the management thereof.

(2) Any such constable acting under the authority of such warrant may enter (using if necessary force for the purpose) such house shop room building part of a building or other place and may seize and carry away all profane indecent or obscene articles books papers prints photographs drawings paintings or representations as aforesaid found therein and may apprehend and convey to the police office any of the persons mentioned in the immediately preceding subsection of this section.

(3) In the event of any profane indecent or obscene articles books papers prints photographs drawings paintings or representations being found in such house shop room building part of a building or other place or on any occupier or person hereinbefore in this section mentioned such occupier or person shall on its being proved to the satisfaction of the magistrate that such occupier or person has kept such articles books papers prints photographs drawings paintings or representations for sale or for lending on hire or for publication for purposes of gain be guilty of an offence and shall be liable to a fine not exceeding twenty pounds or to imprisonment for sixty days.

(4) Upon the conviction of such occupier or person the magistrate shall order all such articles books papers prints photographs drawings paintings or representations so seized as aforesaid to be destroyed unless it shall be necessary to preserve the same for some further or other proceedings and if the magistrate is satisfied that the same or any of them are not of the character stated in the warrant or have not been kept for any of the purposes aforesaid he shall forthwith direct them to be restored to the said occupier or person.

(5) Nothing in this section shall apply to any premises in respect of which a licence under the Cinematograph Acts 1909 and 1952 is for the time being in force.

Project

Find out what local acts and byelaws apply in the community where you live. Obtain copies of them—the local town hall or local library should be able to help. See what special rules affecting police powers, meetings, processions, etc., are contained in these local rules. Find out what use is made by the local police of the powers given them by these rules. How often are prosecutions brought under these local rules; the clerk to the local justices should be able to help, and see if you can find out why prosecutions are brought under special local rules in cases where there is either a common law or statutory offence of general application covering the same factual situation.

Question

Consider the offences prescribed in Part IX of the Glasgow Corporation Consolidation (General Powers) Order Confirmation Act 1960. How far does the Act merely provide an alternative ground upon which to prosecute people for actions which are already unlawful under the general law of the land? Are there any significant differences in the elements necessary to establish liability for the offences under Part IX as compared to those necessary to establish legal liability under the general law?

CHAPTER 2

THE INTERNATIONAL LEGAL FRAMEWORK

Further Reading

P. Archer, *Human Rights* (Fabian research series no. 274, London, 1974); I. Brownlie (ed.), *Basic Documents on Human Rights* (O.U.P., 1971); R. P. Claude (ed.), *Comparative Human Rights* (John Hopkins University Press, 1976); F. E. Dowrick (ed.), *Human Rights: Problems, Perspectives and Texts* (Saxon House, 1979); C. Ezejiofor, *Protection of Human Rights under the Law* (Butterworths, 1964); Louis Henkin, *The Rights of Man Today* (Stevens, 1979); E. Kamenka and A. Erh-Soon Tay, *Human Rights* (Edward Arnold, 1978); H. Lauterpacht, *International Law and Human Rights* (Sweet & Maxwell, 1951); E. Luard (ed.), *The International Protection of Human Rights* (Thames & Hudson, 1967); R. St. J. Macdonald, D. M. Johnston and G. L. Morris, *The International Law and Policy of Human Welfare* (Alphen aan den Rijn, North Holland); B. G. Ramchara (ed.), *Human Rights: Thirty Years after the Universal Declaration* (Nijhoff, The Hague, 1976); L. B. Sohn & T. Burgenthal, *Basic Documents on the International Protection of Human Rights* (Bobbs-Merrill, 1973), and H. G. Wells, *Rights of Man* (Penguin, 1940).

See also *Accession of the Communities to the European Convention on Human Rights Commission Memorandum,* E. C. Bull. Supp. 2/79.

Since the end of the second World War there has been an enormous increase in the number of international instruments establishing standards in the area of human rights, covering not only the more traditional political and civil rights but also now economic, social and cultural rights. Taken together these instruments are sometimes referred to as "The International Bill of Rights." However not all of the rules in this "Bill" are legal rules, some embody desirable standards, but where the line is to be drawn between desirable aims and legal obligations is often unclear. It is necessary to commence any discussion of civil liberties with the "International Bill of Rights" in the United Kingdom for two reasons. First of all these standards represent a starting point from which to analyse, and indeed criticise British law and practice. These standards represent, very often, standards which the United Kingdom has undertaken to comply with or to aim at. Secondly, a breach of these standards, quite apart from any remedy available to any person who suffers thereby under English law, may also entitle the injured person, on certain conditions, to some kind of remedy before an international forum.

Treaties and other standards affecting civil liberties have been drawn up, principally, under the aegis of the following organisations (a) The United Nations Organisation; (b) the International Labour Organisation; (c) the Council of Europe, and (d) the European Communities.

A. UNITED NATIONS ORGANISATION

I. Universal Declaration of Human Rights

**Adopted and proclaimed by General Assembly,
resolution 217 A (III) of 10 December 1948**

Preamble

Whereas recognition of the inherent dignity and of the equal and inalienable rights of all members of the human family is the foundation of freedom, justice and peace in the world,

Whereas disregard and contempt for human rights have resulted in barbarous acts which have outraged the conscience of mankind, and the advent of a world in which human beings shall enjoy freedom of speech and belief and freedom from fear and want has been proclaimed as the highest aspiration of the common people,

Whereas it is essential, if man is not to be compelled to have recourse, as a last resort, to rebellion against tyranny and oppression, that human rights should be protected by the rule of law,

Whereas it is essential to promote the development of friendly relations between nations,

Whereas the peoples of the United Nations have in the Charter reaffirmed their faith in fundamental human rights, in the dignity and worth of the human person and in the equal rights of men and women and have determined to promote social progress and better standards of life in larger freedom,

Whereas Member States have pledged themselves to achieve, in co-operation with the United Nations, the promotion of universal respect for and observance of human rights and fundamental freedoms,

Whereas a common understanding of these rights and freedoms is of the greatest importance for the full realization of this pledge,

Now, therefore,

The General Assembly

Proclaims this Universal Declaration of Human Rights as a common standard of achievement for all peoples and all nations, to the end that every individual and every organ of society, keeping this Declaration constantly in mind, shall strive by teaching and education to promote respect for these rights and freedoms and by progressive measures, national and international, to secure their universal and effective recognition and observance, both among the peoples of Member States themselves and among the peoples of territories under their jurisdiction.

Article 1

All human beings are born free and equal in dignity and rights. They are endowed with reason and conscience and should act towards one another in a spirit of brotherhood.

Article 2

Everyone is entitled to all the rights and freedoms set forth in this Declaration, without distinction of any kind, such as race, colour, sex, language, religion, political or other opinion, national or social origin, property, birth or other status.

Furthermore, no distinction shall be made on the basis of the political, jurisdictional or international status of the country or territory to which a person belongs, whether it be independent trust, non-self-governing or under any other limitation of sovereignty.

ARTICLE 3

Everyone has the right to life, liberty and the security of person.

ARTICLE 4

No one shall be held in slavery or servitude; slavery and the slave trade shall be prohibited in all their forms.

ARTICLE 5

No one shall be subjected to torture or to cruel, inhuman or degrading treatment or punishment.

ARTICLE 6

Everyone has the right to recognition everywhere as a person before the law.

ARTICLE 7

All are equal before the law and are entitled without any discrimination to equal protection of the law. All are entitled to equal protection against any discrimination in violation of this Declaration and against any incitement to such discrimination.

ARTICLE 8

Everyone has the right to an effective remedy by the competent national tribunals for acts violating the fundamental rights granted him by the consitution or by law.

ARTICLE 9

No one shall be subjected to arbitrary arrest, detention or exile.

ARTICLE 10

Everyone is entitled in full equality to a fair and public hearing by an independent and impartial tribunal, in the determination of his rights and obligations and of any criminal charge against him.

ARTICLE 11

1. Everyone charged with a penal offence has the right to be presumed innocent until proved guilty according to law in a public trial at which he has had all the guarantees necessary for his defence.

2. No one shall be held guilty of any penal offence on account of any act or omission which did not constitute a penal offence, under national or international law, at the time when it was committed. Nor shall a heavier penalty be imposed than the one that was applicable at the time the penal offence was committed.

ARTICLE 12

No one shall be subjected to arbitrary interference with his privacy, family, home or correspondence, nor to attacks upon his honour and reputation. Everyone has the right to the protection of the law against such interference or attacks.

ARTICLE 13

1. Everyone has the right of freedom of movement and residence within the borders of each State.

2. Everyone has the right to leave any country, including his own, and to return to his country.

ARTICLE 14

1. Everyone has the right to seek and to enjoy in other countries asylum from persecution.

2. This right may not be invoked in the case of prosecutions genuinely arising from non-political crimes or from acts contrary to the purposes and principles of the United Nations.

ARTICLE 15

1. Everyone has the right to a nationality.

2. No one shall be arbitrarily deprived of his nationality nor denied the right to change his nationality.

ARTICLE 16

1. Men and women of full age, without any limitation due to race, nationality or religion, have the right to marry and to found a family. They are entitled to equal rights as to marriage, during marriage and at its dissolution.

2. Marriage shall be entered into only with the free and full consent of the intending spouses.

3. The family is the natural and fundamental group unit of society and is entitled to protection by society and the State.

ARTICLE 17

1. Everyone has the right to own property alone as well as in association with others.

2. No one shall be arbitrarily deprived of his property.

ARTICLE 18

Everyone has the right to freedom of thought, conscience and religion; this right includes freedom to change his religion or belief, and freedom, either alone or in community with others and in public or private, to manifest his religion or belief in teaching, practice, worship and observance.

ARTICLE 19

Everyone has the right to freedom of opinion and expression; this right includes freedom to hold opinions without interference and to seek, receive and impart information and ideas through any media and regardless of frontiers.

ARTICLE 20

1. Everyone has the right to freedom of peaceful assembly and association.

2. No one may be compelled to belong to an association.

ARTICLE 21

1. Everyone has the right to take part in the government of his country, directly or through freely chosen representatives.

2. Everyone has the right of equal access to public service in his country.

3. The will of the people shall be the basis of the authority of government; this will shall be expressed in periodic and genuine elections which shall be by universal and equal suffrage and shall be held by secret vote or by equivalent free voting procedures.

ARTICLE 22

Everyone, as a member of society, has the right to social security and is entitled to realization, through national effort and international co-operation and in accordance with the organization and resources of each State, of the economic, social and cultural rights indispensable for his dignity and the free development of his personality.

ARTICLE 23

1. Everyone has the right to work, to free choice of employment, to just and favourable conditions of work and to protection against unemployment.

2. Everyone, without any discrimination, has the right to equal pay for equal work.

3. Everyone who works has the right to just and favourable remuneration ensuring for himself and his family an existence worthy of human dignity, and supplemented, if necessary, by other means of social protection.

4. Everyone has the right to form and to join trade unions for the protection of his interests.

ARTICLE 24

Everyone has the right to rest and leisure, including reasonable limitation of working hours and periodic holidays with pay.

ARTICLE 25

1. Everyone has the right to a standard of living adequate for the health and well-being of himself and of his family, including food, clothing, housing and medical care and necessary social services, and the right to security in the event of unemployment, sickness, disability, widowhood, old age or other lack of livelihood in circumstances beyond his control.

2. Motherhood and childhood are entitled to special care and assistance. All children, whether born in or out of wedlock, shall enjoy the same social protection.

ARTICLE 26

1. Everyone has the right to education. Education shall be free, at least in the elementary and fundamental stages. Elementary education shall be compulsory. Technical and professional education shall be made generally available and higher education shall be equally accessible to all on the basis of merit.

2. Education shall be directed to the full development of the human personality and to the strengthening of respect for human rights and fundamental freedoms. It shall promote understanding, tolerance and friendship among all nations, racial or religious groups, and shall further the activities of the United Nations for the maintenance of peace.

3. Parents have a prior right to choose the kind of education that shall be given to their children.

ARTICLE 27

1. Everyone has the right freely to participate in the cultural life of the community, to enjoy the arts and to share in scientific advancement and its benefits.

2. Everyone has the right to the protection of the moral and material interests resulting from any scientific, literary or artistic production of which he is the author.

ARTICLE 28

Everyone is entitled to a social and international order in which the rights and freedoms set forth in this Declaration can be fully realized.

ARTICLE 29

1. Everyone has duties to the community in which alone the free and full development of his personality is possible.

2. In the exercise of his rights and freedoms, everyone shall be subject only to such limitations as are determined by law solely for the purpose of securing due recognition and respect for the rights and freedoms of others and of meeting the just requirements of morality, public order and the general welfare in a democratic society.

3. These rights and freedoms may in no case be exercised contrary to the purposes and principles of the United Nations.

ARTICLE 30

Nothing in this Declaration may be interpreted as implying for any State, group or person any right to engage in any activity or to perform any act aimed at the destruction of any of the rights and freedoms set forth herein.

Note: The Universal Declaration has been followed up by two U.N. Covenants, accepted by the United Kingdom which came into force in 1976, on Economic, Social and Cultural Rights and on Civil and Political Rights (for texts of these see I. Brownlie, *op. cit.*). The United Kingdom has *not* however acceded to the Optional Protocol to the Covenant on Civil and Political Rights, which gives a right to individuals to bring complaints against signatory states.

B. INTERNATIONAL LABOUR ORGANISATION

Further Reading

E. B. Haas, *Human Rights and International Action: The Case of Freedom of Association* (Stanford University Press, 1970); I.L.O., *Trade Union Rights and their Relation to Civil Liberties* (Geneva, 1969); *ibid. International Labour Standards: A Workers' Education Manual* (Geneva, 1978); C. W. Jenks, *The International Protection of Trade Union Freedom* (Stevens, 1957); *ibid. Human Rights and International Labour Standards* (Stevens, 1960); *ibid. Social Justice in the Law of Nations* (O.U.P., 1970); G. A. Johnston, *The International Labour Organisation: Its Work for Social and Economic Progress* (Europa Publications, 1970); E. A. Landy, *Effectiveness of International Supervision: Thirty Years of I.L.O. Experience* (Oceana Pubrs. and Stevens, 1966), and N. Valticos, *Droit International du Travail* (Dalloz, Paris, 1970; Supplement, 1973).

Despite the work of the I.L.O. for improvement of labour standards since 1919 there are some who deny that social rights are *properly* speaking human rights. See for example M. Cranston, *What are Human Rights?* (Allen & Unwin, 1973), Chapters 8 and 9.

G. A. Johnston has said, with special reference to the adherence of the United Kingdom to I.L.O. Conventions, "While some countries ratify Conventions before taking any steps to bring their legislation into conformity with the Conventions, the United Kingdom ratifies a Convention only when United Kingdom law and practice are considered to be in full conformity with the requirements of the Convention" ("The Influence of International Labour Standards on Legislation and Practice in the United Kingdom," 90 *International Labour Review* (1968) 465–87 at 466). Sadly this does not appear to be true either generally with regard to human rights conventions to which the United Kingdom becomes a party or even with respect to I.L.O. Conventions. One need only mention in this context the United Kingdom's adherence to the European Convention on Human Rights which in Article 8 provides for a right of privacy, which does not yet exist in British law (see pp. 302 and 339); to the fact that despite its adherence in 1951 to I.L.O. Convention No. 98 on the Right to Organise and Collective Bargaining, the United Kingdom did not provide workers with the protection against acts of anti-union discrimination by employers until the Industrial Relations Act 1971 (see Chap. 6); and to the gap which exists between the provisions of the Employment Protection Act 1975 and the relevant EEC Directive on consultations over pending redundancies 1975 (see B. A. Hepple and P. O'Higgins, *Employment Law* (3rd ed., Sweet & Maxwell, 1979), paras. 702–704).

Although there is no express guarantee of the right to strike in the I.L.O. Conventions to which the United Kingdom has adhered (see I.L.O. Conventions Nos. 87, 198 and 135) the I.L.O. Governing Body's Committee on Freedom of Association, to which complaints of violations of Conventions 87, 98 and 135 are referred, has interpreted these Conventions as to imply into them a *right* to strike (see *Freedom of Association: Digest of Decisions of the Freedom of Association Committee of the Governing Body of the I.L.O.* (2nd ed., Geneva, 1976), *passim*.

C. COUNCIL OF EUROPE

I. EUROPEAN CONVENTION ON HUMAN RIGHTS AND FUNDAMENTAL FREEDOMS
Entry into force: September 3, 1953

The United Kingdom has recognised the competence of the Commission on Human Rights to receive individual petitions (under Article 25.I) and of Court in all matters concerning the interpretation and application of the Convention (under Article 46.I).

Further Reading

R. Beddard, *Human Rights and Europe* (Sweet & Maxwell, 1973); F. Castberg, *The European Convention on Human Rights* (Allen & Unwin, 1974); N. R. Engel, *Twenty Five Years of the Human Rights Convention of the Council of Europe* (Council of Europe, 1975); J. E. S. Fawcett, *The Application of the European Convention on Human Rights* (O.U.P., 1969); F. G. Jacobs, *The European Convention on Human Rights* (O.U.P., 1975); A. B. McNulty and P. J. Duffy, *The European Convention on Human Rights* (Butterworths, 1980); A. H. Robertson *Human Rights in Europe* (Manchester University Press, 1963); *ibid.* (*ed.*), *Human Rights in National and International Law* (Manchester University Press, 1968).

The Council of Europe publishes regularly *The Yearbook of the European Convention on Human Rights*. Regular *Collections of Decisions of the European Commission of Human Rights* are published. The decisions of the European Court of Human Rights are published. The Secretariat of the European Commission of Human Rights publishes periodically *Stocktaking on the European Convention on Human Rights,* and Case Law Topics: No. 1, *Human Rights in Prison* (1971); No. 2, *Family Life* (1972); No. 3 *Bringing an Application before the European Commission of Human Rights* (1972), and No. 4, *Human Rights and Their Limitations* (1973).

The Governments signatory hereto, being Members of the Council of Europe.

Considering the Universal Declaration of Human Rights proclaimed by the General Assembly of the United Nations on 10th December 1948;

Considering that this Declaration aims at securing the universal and effective recognition and observance of the rights therein declared;

Considering that the aim of the Council of Europe is the achievement of greater unity between its Members and that one of the methods by which that aim is to be pursued is the maintenance and further realisation of human rights and fundamental freedoms;

Reaffirming their profound belief in those fundamental freedoms which are the foundation of justice and peace in the world and are best maintained on the one hand by an effective political democracy and on the other by a common understanding and observance of the human rights upon which they depend;

Being resolved, as the Governments of European countries which are likeminded and have a common heritage of political traditions, ideals, freedom and the rule of law, to take the first steps for the collective enforcement of certain of the rights stated in the Universal Declaration;

Have agreed as follows:

Article 1*

The High Contracting Parties shall secure to everyone within their jurisdiction the rights and freedoms defined in Section I of this Convention.

SECTION I

Article 2

1. Everyone's right to life shall be protected by law. No one shall be deprived of his life intentionally save in the execution of a sentence of a court following his conviction of a crime for which this penalty is provided by law.
2. Deprivation of life shall not be regarded as inflicted in contravention of this article when it results from the use of force which is no more than absolutely necessary:

   a. in defence of any person from unlawful violence;

   b. in order to effect a lawful arrest or to prevent the escape of a person lawfully detained;

   c. in action lawfully taken for the purpose of quelling a riot or insurrection.

Article 3

No one shall be subjected to torture or to inhuman or degrading treatment or punishment.

Article 4

1. No one shall be held in slavery or servitude.
2. No one shall be required to perform forced or compulsory labour.
3. For the purpose of this article the term "forced or compulsory labour" shall not include:

   a. any work required to be done in the ordinary course of detention imposed according to the provisions of Article 5 of this Convention or during conditional release from such detention;

*N.B. Text given as amended by Protocols.

b. any service of a military character or, in case of conscientious objectors in countries where they are recognised, service exacted instead of compulsory military service;

c. any service exacted in case of an emergency or calamity threatening the life or well-being of the community;

d. any work or service which forms part of normal civic obligations.

Article 5

1. Everyone has the right to liberty and security of person. No one shall be deprived of his liberty save in the following cases and in accordance with a procedure prescribed by law:

a. the lawful detention of a person after conviction by a competent court;

b. the lawful arrest or detention of a person for non-compliance with the lawful order of a court or in order to secure the fulfilment of any obligation prescribed by law;

c. the lawful arrest or detention of a person effected for the purpose of bringing him before the competent legal authority on reasonable suspicion of having committed an offence or when it is reasonably considered necessary to prevent his committing an offence or fleeing after having done so;

d. the detention of a minor by lawful order for the purpose of educational supervision or his lawful detention for the purpose of bringing him before the competent legal authority;

e. the lawful detention of persons for the prevention of the spreading of infectious diseases, of persons of unsound mind, alcoholics or drug addicts or vagrants;

f. the lawful arrest or detention of a person to prevent his effecting an unauthorised entry into the country or of a person against whom action is being taken with a view to deportation or extradition.

2. Everyone who is arrested shall be informed promptly, in a language which he understands, of the reasons for his arrest and of any charge against him.

3. Everyone arrested or detained in accordance with the provisions of paragraph 1. *c.* of this article shall be brought promptly before a judge or other officer authorised by law to exercise judicial power and shall be entitled to trial within a reasonable time or to release pending trial. Release may be conditioned by guarantees to appear for trial.

4. Everyone who is deprived of his liberty by arrest or detention shall be entitled to take proceedings by which the lawfulness of his detention shall be decided speedily by a court and his release ordered if the detention is not lawful.

5. Everyone who has been the victim of arrest or detention in contravention of the provisions of this article shall have an enforceable right to compensation.

Article 6

1. In the determination of his civil rights and obligations or of any criminal charge against him, everyone is entitled to a fair and public hearing within a reasonable time by an independent and impartial tribunal established by law. Judgment shall be pronounced publicly but the press and public may be excluded from all or part of the trial in the interests of morals, public order or national security in a democratic society, where the interests of juveniles or the

protection of the private life of the parties so require, or to the extent strictly necessary in the opinion of the court in special circumstances where publicity would prejudice the interests of justice.

2. Everyone charged with a criminal offence shall be presumed innocent until proved guilty according to law.

3. Everyone charged with a criminal offence has the following minimum rights:

    a. to be informed promptly, in a language which he understands and in detail, of the nature and cause of the accusation against him;

    b. to have adequate time and facilities for the preparation of his defence;

    c. to defend himself in person or through legal assistance of his own choosing or, if he has not sufficient means to pay for legal assistance, to be given it free when the interests of justice so require;

    d. to examine or have examined witnesses against him and to obtain the attendance and examination of witnesses on his behalf under the same conditions as witnesses against him;

    e. to have the free assistance of an interpreter if he cannot understand or speak the language used in court.

Article 7

1. No one shall be held guilty of any criminal offence on account of any act or omission which did not constitute a criminal offence under national or international law at the time when it was committed. Nor shall a heavier penalty be imposed than the one that was applicable at the time the criminal offence was committed.

2. This article shall not prejudice the trial and punishment of any person for any act or omission which, at the time when it was committed, was criminal according to the general principles of law recognised by civilised nations.

Article 8

1. Everyone has the right to respect for his private and family life, his home and his correspondence.

2. There shall be no interference by a public authority with the exercise of this right except such as is in accordance with the law and is necessary in a democratic society in the interests of national security, public safety or the economic well-being of the country, for the prevention of disorder or crime, for the protection of health or morals, or for the protection of the rights and freedoms of others.

Article 9

1. Everyone has the right to freedom of thought, conscience and religion; this right includes freedom to change his religion or belief and freedom, either alone or in community with others and in public or private, to manifest his religion or belief, in worship, teaching, practice and observance.

2. Freedom to manifest one's religion or beliefs shall be subject only to such limitations as are prescribed by law and are necessary in a democratic society in the interests of public safety, for the protection of public order, health or morals, or for the protection of the rights and freedoms of others.

Article 10

1. Everyone has the right to freedom of expression. This right shall include freedom to hold opinions and to receive and impart information and ideas

without interference by public authority and regardless of frontiers. This article shall not prevent States from requiring the licensing of broadcasting, television or cinema enterprises.

2.   The exercise of these freedoms, since it carries with it duties and responsibilities, may be subject to such formalities, conditions, restrictions or penalties as are prescribed by law and are necessary in a democratic society, in the interests of national security, territorial integrity or public safety, for the prevention of disorder or crime, for the protection of health or morals, for the protection of the reputation or rights of others, for preventing the disclosure of information received in confidence, or for maintaining the authority and impartiality of the judiciary.

Article 11

1.   Everyone has the right to freedom of peaceful assembly and to freedom of association with others, including the right to form and to join trade unions for the protection of his interests.

2.   No restrictions shall be placed on the exercise of these rights other than such as are prescribed by law and are necessary in a democratic society in the interests of national security or public safety, for the prevention of disorder or crime, for the protection of health or morals or for the protection of the rights and freedoms of others. This article shall not prevent the imposition of lawful restrictions on the exercise of these rights by members of the armed forces, of the police or of the administration of the State.

Article 12

Men and women of marriageable age have the right to marry and to found a family, according to the national laws governing the exercise of this right.

Article 13

Everyone whose rights and freedoms as set forth in this Convention are violated shall have an effective remedy before a national authority notwithstanding that the violation has been committed by persons acting in an official capacity.

Article 14

The enjoyment of the rights and freedoms set forth in this Convention shall be secured without discrimination on any ground such as sex, race, colour, language, religion, political or other opinion, national or social origin, association with a national minority, property, birth or other status.

Article 15

1.   In time of war or other public emergency threatening the life of the nation, any High Contracting Party may take measures derogating from its obligations under this Convention to the extent strictly required by the exigencies of the situation, provided that such measures are not inconsistent with its other obligations under international law.

2.   No derogation from Article 2, except in respect of deaths resulting from lawful acts of war, or from Articles 3, 4 (paragraph 1) and 7 shall be made under this provision.

3. Any High Contracting Party availing itself of this right of derogation shall keep the Secretary General of the Council of Europe fully informed of the measures which it has taken and the reasons therefor. It shall also inform the Secretary General of the Council of Europe when such measures have ceased to operate and the provisions of the Convention are again being fully executed.

Article 16

Nothing in Articles 10, 11 and 14 shall be regarded as preventing the High Contracting Parties from imposing restrictions on the political activity of aliens.

Article 17

Nothing in this Convention may be interpreted as implying for any State, group or person any right to engage in any activity or perform any act aimed at the destruction of any of the rights and freedoms set forth herein or at their limitation to a greater extent than is provided for in the Convention.

Article 18

The restrictions permitted under this Convention to the said rights and freedoms shall not be applied for any purpose other than those for which they have been prescribed.

SECTION II

Article 19

To ensure the observance of the engagements undertaken by the High Contracting Parties in the present Convention, there shall be set up:

a. A European Commission of Human Rights, hereinafter referred to as "the Commission";

b. A European Court of Human Rights, hereinafter referred to as "the Court".

SECTION III

Article 20

The Commission shall consist of a number of members equal to that of the High Contracting Parties. No two members of the Commission may be nationals of the same State.

Article 21

1. The members of the Commission shall be elected by the Committee of Ministers by an absolute majority of votes, from a list of names drawn up by the Bureau of the Consultative Assembly; each group of the Representatives of the High Contracting Parties in the Consultative Assembly shall put forward three candidates, of whom two at least shall be its nationals.

2.   As far as applicable, the same procedure shall be followed to complete the Commission in the event of other States subsequently becoming Parties to this Convention, and in filling casual vacancies.

Article 22

1.   The members of the Commission shall be elected for a period of six years. They may be re-elected. However, of the members elected at the first election, the terms of seven members shall expire at the end of three years.
2.   The members whose terms are to expire at the end of the initial period of three years shall be chosen by lot by the Secretary General of the Council of Europe immediately after the first election has been completed.
3.   In order to ensure that, as far as possible, one half of the membership of the Commission shall be renewed every three years, the Committee of Ministers may decide, before proceeding to any subsequent election, that the term or terms of office of one or more members to be elected shall be for a period other than six years but not more than nine and not less than three years.
4.   In cases where more than one term of office is involved and the Committee of Ministers applies the preceding paragraph, the allocation of the terms of office shall be effected by the drawing of lots by the Secretary General, immediately after the election.
5.   A member of the Commission elected to replace a member whose term of office has not expired shall hold office for the remainder of his predecessor's term.
6.   The members of the Commission shall hold office until replaced. After having been replaced, they shall continue to deal with such cases as they already have under consideration.

Article 23

The members of the Commission shall sit on the Commission in their individual capacity.

Article 24

Any High Contracting Party may refer to the Commission, through the Secretary General of the Council of Europe, any alleged breach of the provisions of the Convention by another High Contracting Party.

Article 25

1.   The Commission may receive petitions addressed to the Secretary General of the Council of Europe from any person, non-governmental organisation or group of individuals claiming to be the victim of a violation by one of the High Contracting Parties of the rights set forth in this Convention, provided that the High Contracting Party against which the complaint has been lodged has declared that it recognises the competence of the Commission to receive such petitions. Those of the High Contracting Parties who have made such a declaration undertake not to hinder in any way the effective exercise of this right.

2.   Such declarations may be made for a specific period.
3.   The declarations shall be deposited with the Secretary General of the
Council of Europe who shall transmit copies thereof to the High Contracting
Parties and publish them.
4.   The Commission shall only exercise the powers provided for in this article
when at least six High Contracting Parties are bound by declarations made in
accordance with the preceding paragraphs.

Article 26

The Commission may only deal with the matter after all domestic remedies
have been exhausted, according to the generally recognised rules of international law, and within a period of six months from the date on which the
final decision was taken.

Article 27

1.   The Commission shall not deal with any petition submitted under Article
25 which:
   a. is anonymous, or
   b. is substantially the same as a matter which has already been examined by
the Commission or has already been submitted to another procedure of international investigation or settlement and if it contains no relevant new
information.
2.   The Commission shall consider inadmissible any petition submitted
under Article 25 which it considers incompatible with the provisions of the
present Convention, manifestly ill-founded, or an abuse of the right of
petition.
3.   The Commission shall reject any petition referred to it which it considers
inadmissible under Article 26.

Article 28

In the event of the Commission accepting a petition referred to it:
   a. it shall, with a view to ascertaining the facts, undertake together with the
representatives of the parties an examination of the petition and, if need be,
an investigation, for the effective conduct of which the States concerned shall
furnish all necessary facilities, after an exchange of views with the
Commission;
   b. it shall place itself at the disposal of the parties concerned with a view to
securing a friendly settlement of the matter on the basis of respect for human
rights as defined in this Convention.

Article 29

After it has accepted a petition submitted under Article 25, the Commission
may nevertheless decide unanimously to reject the petition if, in the course of
its examination, it finds that the existence of one of the grounds for non-
acceptance provided for in Article 27 has been established.
   In such a case, the decision shall be communicated to the parties.

Article 30

If the Commission succeeds in effecting a friendly settlement in accordance
with Article 28, it shall draw up a report which shall be sent to the States

concerned, to the Committee of Ministers and to the Secretary General of the Council of Europe for publication. This report shall be confined to a brief statement of the facts and of the solution reached.

Article 31

1.   If a solution is not reached, the Commission shall draw up a report on the facts and state its opinion as to whether the facts found disclose a breach by the State concerned of its obligations under the Convention. The opinions of all the members of the Commission on this point may be stated in the report.
2.   The report shall be transmitted to the Committee of Ministers. It shall also be transmitted to the States concerned, who shall not be at liberty to publish it.
3.   In transmitting the report to the Committee of Ministers the Commission may make such proposals as it thinks fit.

Article 32

1.   If the question is not referred to the Court in accordance with Article 48 of this Convention within a period of three months from the date of the transmission of the report to the Committee of Ministers, the Committee of Ministers shall decide by a majority of two-thirds of the members entitled to sit on the Committee whether there has been a violation of the Convention.
2.   In the affirmative case the Committee of Ministers shall prescribe a period during which the High Contracting Party concerned must take the measures required by the decision of the Committee of Ministers.
3.   If the High Contracting Party concerned has not taken satisfactory measures within the prescribed period, the Committee of Ministers shall decide by the majority provided for in paragraph 1 above what effect shall be given to its original decision and shall publish the report.
4.   The High Contracting Parties undertake to regard as binding on them any decision which the Committee of Ministers may take in application of the preceding paragraphs.

Article 33

The Commission shall meet *in camera.*

Article 34

Subject to the provisions of Article 29, the Commission shall take its decisions by a majority of the members present and voting.

Article 35

The Commission shall meet as the circumstances require. The meetings shall be convened by the Secretary General of the Council of Europe.

Article 36

The Commission shall draw up its own rules of procedure.

Article 37

The secretariat of the Commission shall be provided by the Secretary General of the Council of Europe.

SECTION IV

Article 38

The European Court of Human Rights shall consist of a number of judges equal to that of the Members of the Council of Europe. No two judges may be nationals of the same State.

Article 39

1. The members of the Court shall be elected by the Consultative Assembly by a majority of the votes cast from a list of persons nominated by the Members of the Council of Europe; each Member shall nominate three candidates, of whom two at least shall be its nationals.
2. As far as applicable, the same procedure shall be followed to complete the Court in the event of the admission of new Members of the Council of Europe, and in filling casual vacancies.
3. The candidates shall be of high moral character and must either possess the qualifications required for appointment to high judicial office or be jurisconsults of recognised competence.

Article 40

1. The members of the Court shall be elected for a period of nine years. They may be re-elected. However, of the members elected at the first election the terms of four members shall expire at the end of three years, and the terms of four more members shall expire at the end of six years.
2. The members whose terms are to expire at the end of the initial periods of three and six years shall be chosen by lot by the Secretary General immediately after the first election has been completed.
3. In order to ensure that, as far as possible, one third of the membership of the Court shall be renewed every three years, the Consultative Assembly may decide, before proceeding to any subsequent election, that the term or terms of office of one or more members to be elected shall be for a period other than nine years but not more than twelve and not less than six years.
4. In cases where more than one term of office is involved and the Consultative Assembly applies the preceding paragraph, the allocation of the terms of office shall be effected by the drawing of lots by the Secretary General immediately after the election.
5. A member of the Court elected to replace a member whose term of office has not expired shall hold office for the remainder of his predecessor's term.
6. The members of the Court shall hold office until replaced. After having been replaced, they shall continue to deal with such cases as they already have under consideration.

Article 41

The Court shall elect its President and Vice-President for a period of three years. They may be re-elected.

Article 42

The members of the Court shall receive for each day of duty a compensation to be determined by the Committee of Ministers.

Article 43

For the consideration of each case brought before it the Court shall consist of a Chamber composed of seven judges. There shall sit as an *ex officio* member of the Chamber the judge who is a national of any State Party concerned, or, if there is none, a person of its choice who shall sit in the capacity of judge; the names of the other judges shall be chosen by lot by the President before the opening of the case.

Article 44

Only the High Contracting Parties and the Commission shall have the right to bring a case before the Court.

Article 45

The jurisdiction of the Court shall extend to all cases concerning the interpretation and application of the present Convention which the High Contracting Parties or the Commission shall refer to it in accordance with Article 48.

Article 46

1. Any of the High Contracting Parties may at any time declare that it recognises as compulsory *ipso facto* and without special agreement the jurisdiction of the Court in all matters concerning the interpretation and application of the present Convention.
2. The declarations referred to above may be made unconditionally or on condition of reciprocity on the part of several or certain other High Contracting Parties or for a specified period.
3. These declarations shall be deposited with the Secretary General of the Council of Europe who shall transmit copies thereof to the High Contracting Parties.

Article 47

The Court may only deal with a case after the Commission has acknowledged the failure of efforts for a friendly settlement and within the period of three months provided for in Article 32.

Article 48

The following may bring a case before the Court, provided that the High Contracting Party concerned, if there is only one, or the High Contracting Parties concerned, if there is more than one, are subject to the compulsory jurisdiction of the Court or, failing that, with the consent of the High Contracting Party concerned, if there is only one, or of the High Contracting Parties concerned if there is more than one:

    a. the Commission;
    b. a High Contracting Party whose national is alleged to be a victim;
    c. a High Contracting Party which referred the case to the Commission;
    d. a High Contracting Party against which the complaint has been lodged.

Article 49

In the event of dispute as to whether the Court has jurisdiction, the matter shall be settled by the decision of the Court.

Article 50

If the Court finds that a decision or a measure taken by a legal authority or any other authority of a High Contracting Party is completely or partially in conflict with the obligations arising from the present Convention, and if the internal law of the said Party allows only partial reparation to be made for the consequences of this decision or measure, the decision of the Court shall, if necessary, afford just satisfaction to the injured party.

Article 51

1. Reasons shall be given for the judgment of the Court.
2. If the judgment does not represent in whole or in part the unanimous opinion of the judges, any judge shall be entitled to deliver a separate opinion.

Article 52

The judgment of the Court shall be final.

Article 53

The High Contracting Parties undertake to abide by the decision of the Court in any case to which they are parties.

Article 54

The judgment of the Court shall be transmitted to the Committee of Ministers which shall supervise its execution.

Article 55

The Court shall draw up its own rules and shall determine its own procedure.

Article 56

1. The first election of the members of the Court shall take place after the declarations by the High Contracting Parties mentioned in Article 46 have reached a total of eight.
2. No case can be brought before the Court before this election.

SECTION V

Article 57

On receipt of a request from the Secretary General of the Council of Europe any High Contracting Party shall furnish an explanation of the manner in which its internal law ensures the effective implementation of any of the provisions of this Convention.

Article 58

The expenses of the Commission and the Court shall be borne by the Council of Europe.

Article 59

The members of the Commission and of the Court shall be entitled, during the discharge of their functions, to the privileges and immunities provided for in Article 40 of the Statute of the Council of Europe and in the agreements made thereunder.

Article 60

Nothing in this Convention shall be construed as limiting or derogating from any of the human rights and fundamental freedoms which may be ensured under the laws of any High Contracting Party or under any other agreement to which it is a Party.

Article 61

Nothing in this Convention shall prejudice the powers conferred on the Committee of Ministers by the Statute of the Council of Europe.

Article 62

The High Contracting Parties agree that, except by special agreement, they will not avail themselves of treaties, conventions or declarations in force between them for the purpose of submitting, by way of petition, a dispute arising out of the interpretation or application of this Convention to a means of settlement other than those provided for in this Convention.

Article 63

1. Any State may at the time of its ratification or at any time thereafter declare by notification addressed to the Secretary General of the Council of Europe that the present Convention shall extend to all or any of the territories for whose international relations it is responsible.
2. The Convention shall extend to the territory or territories named in the notification as from the thirtieth day after the receipt of this notification by the Secretary General of the Council of Europe.
3. The provisions of this Convention shall be applied in such territories with due regard, however, to local requirements.
4. Any State which has made a declaration in accordance with paragraph 1 of this article may at any time thereafter declare on behalf of one or more of the territories to which the declaration relates that it accepts the competence of the Commission to receive petitions from individuals, non-governmental organisations or groups of individuals in accordance with Article 25 of the present Convention.

Article 64

1. Any State may, when signing this Convention or when depositing its instrument of ratification, make a reservation in respect of any particular provision of the Convention to the extent that any law then in force in its territory is not in conformity with the provision. Reservations of a general character shall not be permitted under this article.
2. Any reservation made under this article shall contain a brief statement of the law concerned.

Article 65

1. A High Contracting Party may denounce the present Convention only after the expiry of five years from the date on which it became a Party to it and after six months' notice contained in a notification addressed to the Secretary General of the Council of Europe, who shall inform the other High Contracting Parties.

2. Such a denunciation shall not have the effect of releasing the High Contracting Party concerned from its obligations under this Convention in respect of any act which, being capable of constituting a violation of such obligations, may have been performed by it before the date at which the denunciation became effective.

3. Any High Contracting Party which shall cease to be a Member of the Council of Europe shall cease to be a Party to this Convention under the same conditions.

4. The Convention may be denounced in accordance with the provisions of the proceeding paragraphs in respect of any territory to which it has been declared to extend under the terms of Article 63.

Article 66

1. This Convention shall be open to the signature of the Members of the Council of Europe. It shall be ratified. Ratifications shall be deposited with the Secretary General of the Council of Europe.

2. The present Convention shall come into force after the deposit of ten instruments of ratification.

3. As regards any signatory ratifying subsequently, the Convention shall come into force at the date of the deposit of its instrument of ratification.

4. The Secretary General of the Council of Europe shall notify all the Members of the Council of Europe of the entry into force of the Convention, the names of the High Contracting Parties who have ratified it, and the deposit of all instruments of ratification which may be effected subsequently.

Note: For Notices of Derogation by the United Kingdom in respect of Northern Ireland see *The Protection of Human Rights in by Law in Northern Ireland,* Cmnd. 7009 (1977), pp. 103–6.

For cases before the European Court of Human Rights see pp. 149, 177, 359, 405 and 408.

Protocols to the European Convention

No. 1. Enforcement of certain Rights and Freedoms not included in Section I of the Convention.
Entry into force: May 18, 1954.

Article 1

Every natural or legal person is entitled to the peaceful enjoyment of his possessions. No one shall be deprived of his possessions except in the public interest and subject to the conditions provided for by law and by the general principles of international law.

The preceding provisions shall not, however, in any way impair the right of a State to enforce such laws as it deems necessary to control the use of property in accordance with the general interest or to secure the payment of taxes or other contributions or penalties.

Article 2

No person shall be denied the right to education. In the exercise of any functions which it assumes in relation to education and to teaching, the State shall respect the right of parents to ensure such education and teaching in conformity with their own religious and philosophical convictions.

Article 3

The High Contracting Parties undertake to hold free elections at reasonable intervals by secret ballot, under conditions which will ensure the free expression of the opinion of the people in the choice of the legislature.

Article 4

Any High Contracting Party may at the time of signature or ratification or at any time thereafter communicate to the Secretary General of the Council of Europe a declaration stating the extent to which it undertakes that the provisions of the present Protocol shall apply to such of the territories for the international relations of which it is responsible as are named therein.

Any High Contracting Party which has communicated a declaration in virtue of the preceding paragraph may from time to time communicate a further declaration modifying the terms of any former declaration or terminating the application of the provisions of this Protocol in respect of any territory.

A declaration made in accordance with this article shall be deemed to have been made in accordance with paragraph 1 of Article 63 of the Convention.

Article 5

As between the High Contracting Parties the provisions of Articles 1, 2, 3 and 4 of this Protocol shall be regarded as additional articles to the Convention and all the provisions of the Convention shall apply accordingly.

Article 6

This Protocol shall be open for signature by the Members of the Council of Europe, who are the signatories of the Convention; it shall be ratified at the same time as or after the ratification of the Convention. It shall enter into force after the deposit of ten instruments of ratification. As regards any signatory ratifying subsequently, the Protocol shall enter into force at the date of the deposit of its instrument of ratification.

The instruments of ratification shall be deposited with the Secretary General of the Council of Europe, who will notify all Members of the names of those who have ratified.

No. 2. Conferring upon the European Court of Human Rights Competence to give Advisory Opinions

Article 1

1.   The Court may, at the request of the Committee of Ministers, give advisory opinions on legal questions concerning the interpretation of the Convention and the Protocols thereto.

2.   Such opinions shall not deal with any question relating to the content or scope of the rights or freedoms defined in Section 1 of the Convention and in the Protocols thereto, or with any other question which the Commission, the Court or the Committee of Ministers might have to consider in consequence of any such proceedings as could be instituted in accordance with the Convention.

3.   Decisions of the Committee of Ministers to request an advisory opinion of the Court shall require a two-thirds majority vote of the representatives entitled to sit on the Committee.

Article 2

The Court shall decide whether a request for an advisory opinion submitted by the Committee of Ministers is within its consultative competence as defined in Article 1 of this Protocol.

Article 3

1.   For the consideration of requests for an advisory opinion, the Court shall sit in plenary session.

2.   Reasons shall be given for advisory opinions of the Court.

3.   If the advisory opinion does not represent in whole or in part the unanimous opinion of the judges, any judge shall be entitled to deliver a separate opinion.

4.   Advisory opinions of the Court shall be communicated to the Committee of Ministers.

Article 4

The powers of the Court under Article 55 of the Convention shall extend to the drawing up of such rules and the determination of such procedure as the Court may think necessary for the purposes of this Protocol.

Article 5

1.   This Protocol shall be open to signature by member States of the Council of Europe, signatories to the Convention, who may become Parties to it by:

   a. signature without reservation in respect of ratification or acceptance;
   b. signature with reservation in respect of ratification or acceptance, followed by ratification or acceptance.

Instruments of ratification or acceptance shall be deposited with the Secretary General of the Council of Europe.

2.   This Protocol shall enter into force as soon as all States Parties to the Convention shall have become Parties to the Protocol, in accordance with the provisions of paragraph 1 of this article.

3.   From the date of the entry into force of this Protocol, Articles 1 to 4 shall be considered an integral part of the Convention.

4.   The Secretary General of the Council of Europe shall notify the member States of the Council of:

   a. any signature without reservation in respect of ratification or acceptance;
   b. any signature with reservation in respect of ratification or acceptance;
   c. the deposit of any instrument of ratification or acceptance;
   d. the date of entry into force of this Protocol in accordance with paragraph 2 of this article.

No. 3. Amending Articles 29, 30, and 94 of the Convention.

Note: This has been incorporated into text of Convention as printed.

No. 4. Protecting Certain Additional Rights

Entry into force: May 2, 1968.

Article 1

No one shall be deprived of his liberty merely on the ground of inability to fulfil a contractual obligation.

Article 2

1.   Everyone lawfully within the territory of a State shall, within that territory, have the right to liberty of movement and freedom to choose his residence.
2.   Everyone shall be free to leave any country, including his own.
3.   No restrictions shall be placed on the exercise of these rights other than such as are in accordance with law and are necessary in a democratic society in the interests of national security or public safety, for the maintenance of *ordre public*, for the prevention of crime, for the protection of health or morals, or for the protection of the rights and freedoms of others.
4.   The rights set forth in paragraph 1 may also be subject, in particular areas, to restrictions imposed in accordance with law and justified by the public interest in a democratic society.

Article 3

1.   No one shall be expelled, by means either of an individual or of a collective measure, from the territory of the State of which he is a national.
2.   No one shall be deprived of the right to enter the territory of the State of which he is a national.

Article 4

Collective expulsion of aliens is prohibited.

Article 5

1.   Any High Contracting Party may, at the time of signature or ratification of this Protocol, or at any time thereafter, communicate to the Secretary General of the Council of Europe a declaration stating the extent to which it undertakes that the provisions of this Protocol shall apply to such of the territories for the international relations of which it is responsible as are named therein.
2.   Any High Contracting Party which has communicated a declaration in virtue of the preceding paragraph may, from time to time, communicate a further declaration modifying the terms of any former declaration or terminating the application of the provisions of this Protocol in respect of any territory.
3.   A declaration made in accordance with this article shall be deemed to have been made in accordance with paragraph 1 of Article 63 of the Convention.

4. The territory of any State to which this Protocol applies by virtue of ratification or acceptance by that State, and each territory to which this Protocol is applied by virtue of a declaration by that State under this article, shall be treated as separate territories for the purpose of the references in Articles 2 and 3 to the territory of a State.

Article 6

1. As between the High Contracting Parties the provisions of Articles 1 to 5 of this Protocol shall be regarded as additional articles to the Convention, and all the provisions of the Convention shall apply accordingly.

2. Nevertheless, the right of individual recourse recognised by a declaration made under Article 25 of the Convention, or the acceptance of the compulsory jurisdiction of the Court by a declaration made under Article 46 of the Convention, shall not be effective in relation to this Protocol unless the High Contracting Party concerned has made a statement recognising such right, or accepting such jurisdiction, in respect of all or any of Articles 1 to 4 of the Protocol.

Article 7

1. This Protocol shall be open for signature by the Members of the Council of Europe who are the signatories of the Convention; it shall be ratified at the same time as or after the ratification of the Convention. It shall enter into force after the deposit of five instruments of ratification. As regards any signatory ratifying subsequently, the Protocol shall enter into force at the date of the deposit of its instrument of ratification.

2. The instruments of ratification shall be deposited with the Secretary General of the Council of Europe, who will notify all Members of the names of those who have ratified.

II. EUROPEAN SOCIAL CHARTER

Entry into force: February 26, 1965.

The United Kingdom has accepted (under Article 20) to be bound by the following Articles in Part II: 1, 2 (not para. 1) 3, 4 (not para. 3) 5, 6, 7 (not paras. 1, 4 and 7), 8 (not paras. 2 and 3), 9, 10, 11, 12 (not para. 1), 13, 14, 15, 16, 17, 18 and 19. For text see I. Brownlie, *op. cit.*

M. Evans, "The European Social Charter," in *Fundamental Rights* (Bridge, J.W. *et. al.* ed. University of Virginia Press, 1973), at pp. 278–90; D. J. Harris, "The European Social Charter," (1964) 13 *International and Comparative Law Quarterly* 1076–87; *ibid. The European Social Charter* (University of Virginia Press, 1980); Sir Otto Kahn Freund, "The European Social Charter," in *European Law and the Individual* (Jacobs, F.G. ed.) (Amsterdam, 1976), pp. 181–211.

D. THE EUROPEAN COMMUNITIES

The United Kingdom became a member of the European Communities on January 1, 1973 and so is subject to the law of those Communities. See European Communities Act 1972.

Further Reading

De Smith, pp. 77–81; Wade & Phillips, Chapter 8.

W. R. Bohning, *The Migration of Workers in the United Kingdom and the European Community* (London, 1972); J. W. Bridge, "Fundamental Rights in the European Economic Community," in *Fundamental Rights* (Bridge, J.W. *et. al.* ed. 1973), pp. 291–305; T. C. Hartley, "The International Scope of the Community Provisions Concerning Free Movement of Workers," in *European Law and the Individual* (Jacobs, F.W. ed. 1976), pp. 19–38; M. Hilf, "The Protection of Fundamental Rights in the Community," in Jacobs, *op. cit.,* pp. 145–60; "The Protection of Fundamental Rights in the European Community," in *Bulletin of the European Communities,* Supplement 5/76. This contains a Report by the Commission of the Communities on the protection of fundamental rights as Community law is created and developed, and a study by R. Bernhardt, "The problems of drawing up a catalogue of fundamental rights for the European Communities"; B. Sundberg-Weitman, *Discrimination on Grounds of Nationality* (North Holland Publishing Company, 1977).

CHAPTER 3

BILLS OF RIGHTS

Further Reading

De Smith, pp. 439–443; Street, pp. 312–315; Wade & Phillips, pp. 540–543. S. A. De Smith, *The New Commonwealth and its Constitutions,* (Sweet & Maxwell, 1964), Chap. 5; I. W. Duncanson, "Balloonists, Bills of Rights and Dinosaurs" (1978) *Public Law* pp. 393–408; J. E. Fawcett, "A Bill of Rights for the United Kingdom?" (1976), 1 *Human Rights Review,* pp. 57–64; Joseph Jaconelli, "The European Convention of Human Rights—The Test of a British Bill of Rights" (1976), *Public Law* pp. 226–255; *ibid. Enacting a Bill of Rights: The Legal Problems,* (O.U.P., 1980); Lord Lloyd of Hampstead, "Do We Need a Bill of Rights?" (1976) 39 Modern Law Review pp. 121–129; F. A. Mann, "Britain's Bill of Rights," (1978), *Law Quarterly Review* pp. 512–533; A. J. M. Milne, "Should We Have a Bill of Rights," (1977) 40 Modern Law Review pp. 389–396; G. Marshall, *Constitutional Theory* (O.U.P., 1971), Chap. 6; Frank Stacey, *A New Bill of Rights for Britain* (Newton Abbot, 1973); Standing, Advisory Commission of Human Rights, *Bill of Rights:* A Discussion Paper (Belfast, 1976); P. Wallington and J. McBride, *Civil Liberties and A Bill of Rights** (Cobden Trust, 1976); M. Zander, *A Bill of Rights?* (Chichester, 1975).

Note: The discussion over whether or not the United Kingdom should have a Bill of Rights has been precipitated by a number of quite different factors. There has been the issue raised whether or not a constitutional safeguard for minority rights in Northern Ireland might have contributed to heading-off or lessening the violence that has occurred there. *(cf.* Government of Ireland Act 1920, section 5, below at p. 99). There has been the problem created by the fact that although the United Kingdom is a party to the European Convention on Human Rights and Fundamental Freedoms its law is patently not in conformity with some of its provisions. One way of resolving this might be to enact the European Convention as British law. From a quite different point of view concern has been expressed at the possibility of a government elected to power on a minority of votes making fundamental changes for which it has no mandate.

It is not of course possible to envisage the enactment of a British Bill of Rights without also discussing the legal status of such a document. Is it to

*This work has a very useful bibliography.

be an ordinary statute which may be repealed by later inconsistent legislation, but itself repealing earlier inconsistent legislation? Or is it to be
entrenched against repeal in some way? Or is it to be merely a statutory formulation of some presumptions of statutory interpretation?

Precursors

The United Kingdom has of course experienced legal instruments in the
past which shared some features in common with what are nowadays
referred to as "Bills of Rights" and like them partook of a special constitutional, although not necessarily legal status. Magna Charta 1215, the
Act of Union with Scotland 1706, the Bill of Rights 1688, the Government
of Ireland Act 1920 all have features in common with "Bills of Rights."

The Union with Scotland Act 1706

Article XVIII

Laws concerning public rights; private rights.—That the laws concerning
regulation of trade customs and such excises to which Scotland is by virtue of
this treaty to be liable be the same in Scotland from and after the union as in
England and that all other laws in use within the kingdom of Scotland do after
the union and notwithstanding thereof remain in the same force as before (except such as are contrary to or inconsistent with this treaty) but alterable by
the Parliament of Great Britain with this difference betwixt the laws concerning publick right policy and civil government and those which concern
private right that the laws which concern publick right policy and civil
government may be made the same throughout the whole United Kingdom.
But that no alteration be made in laws which concern private right except for
evident utility of the subjects within Scotland.

Note: See *MacCormick* v. *Lord Advocate* 1953 S.C. 396; J. D. B. Mitchell,
Constitutional Law (2nd ed. Edinburgh, 1968), pp.69-74, and Wade &
Phillips, 77-80.

The Bill of Rights 1688

*An Act declaring the Rights and Liberties of the Subject
and Settling the Succession of the Crowne*

Whereas the lords spirituall and temporall and comons assembled at Westminster lawfully fully and freely representing all the estates of the people of
this realme did upon the thirteenth day of February in the yeare of our Lord
one thousand six hundred eighty eight present unto their Majesties then
called and known by the names and stile of William and Mary Prince and
Princesse of Orange being present in their proper persons a certaine declaration in writeing made by the said lords and comons in the words following viz
  Whereas the late King James the Second by the assistance of diverse evill
councillors judges and ministers imployed by him did endeavour to subvert

and extirpate the Protestant religion and the lawes and liberties of this kingdome.

By assumeing and exerciseing a power of dispensing with and suspending of lawes and the execution of lawes without consent of Parlyament.

By committing and prosecuting diverse worthy prelates for humbly petitioning to be excused from concurring to the said assumed power.

By issueing and causeing to be executed a commission under the great seale for erecting a court called the court of commissioners for ecclesiasticall causes.

By levying money for and to the use of the Crowne by pretence of prerogative for other time and in other manner then the same was granted by Parlyament.

By raising and keeping a standing army within this kingdome in time of peace without consent of Parlyament and quartering soldiers contrary to law.

By causing severall good subjects being protestants to be disarmed at the same time when papists were both armed and imployed contrary to law.

By violating the freedome of election of members to serve in Parlyament.

By prosecutions in the Court of King's Bench for matters and causes cognizable onely in Parlyament and by diverse other arbitrary and illegall courses.

And whereas of late yeares partiall corrupt and unqualifyed persons have beene returned and served on juryes in tryalls and particularly diverse jurors in tryalls for high treason which were not freeholders.

And excessive baile hath beene required of persons committed in criminall cases to elude the benefitt of the lawes made for the liberty of the subjects.

And excessive fines have beene imposed.

And illegall and cruell punishments inflicted.

And severall grants and promises made of fines and forfeitures before any conviction or judgement against the persons upon whome the same were to be levyed.

All which are utterly and directly contrary to the knowne lawes and statutes and freedome of this realme.

And whereas the said late King James the Second haveing abdicated the government and the throne being thereby vacant his Highnesse the Prince of Orange (whome it hath pleased Almighty God to make the glorious instrument of delivering this kingdome from popery and arbitrary power) did (by the advice of the lords spirituall and temporall and diverse principall persons of the commons) cause letters to be written to the lords spirituall and temporall being protestants and other letters to the several countyes cityes universities boroughs and cinque ports for the choosing of such persons to represent them as were of right to be sent to Parlyament to meete and sitt at Westminster upon the two and twentyeth day of January in this yeare one thousand six hundred eighty and eight in order to such an establishment as that their religion lawes and liberties might not againe be in danger of being subverted, upon which letters elections haveing beene accordingly made.

And thereupon the said lords spirituall and temporall and commons pursuant to their respective letters and elections being now assembled in a full and free representative of this nation takeing into their most serious consideration the best meanes for attaining the ends aforesaid doe in the first place (as their auncestors in like case have usually done) for the vindicating and asserting their auntient right and liberties, declare

[1] *Suspending power.*—That the pretended power of suspending of laws or

the execution of laws by regall authority without consent of Parlyament is illegall.

Late dispensing power.—That the pretended power of dispensing with laws or the execution of laws by regall authoritie as it hath been assumed and exercised of late is illegall.

Ecclesiastical courts illegal.—That the commission for erecting the late court of commissioners for ecclesiastical causes and all other commissions and courts of like nature are illegal and pernicious.

Levying money.—That levying money for or to the use of the Crowne by pretence of prerogative without grant of Parlyament for longer time or in other manner then the same is or shall be granted is illegal.

Right to petition.—That it is the right of the subjects to petition the King and all commitments and prosecutions for such petitioning are illegal.

Standing army.—That the raising or keeping a standing army within the kingdome in time of peace unlesse it be with consent of Parlyament is against law.

Subjects' arms.—That the subjects which are protestants may have arms for their defence suitable to their conditions and as allowed by law.

Freedom of election.—That election of members of Parlyament ought to be free.

Freedom of speech.—That the freedome of speech and debates or proceedings in Parlyament ought not to be impeached or questioned in any court or place out of Parlyament.

Excessive bail.—That excessive bail ought not to be required nor excessive fines imposed nor cruel and unusual punishment inflicted.

Juries.—That jurors ought to be duly impanelled and returned.

Grants of forfeiture.—That all grants and promises of fines and forfeitures of particular persons before conviction are illegal and void.

Frequent Parliaments.—And that for redress of all grievances and for the amending, strengthening and preserving of the laws Parliament ought to be held frequently . . .

THE ACT OF SETTLEMENT 1700

An Act for the further Limitations of the Crown and better securing the Rights and Liberties of the Subject

2. The persons inheritable by this Act, holding communion with the church of Rome, incapacitated as by the former Act, to take the oath at their coronation, according to Stat. 1, W. & M. c. 6

Provided always and it is hereby enacted that all and every person and persons who shall or may take or inherit the said crown by vertue of the limitation of this present Act and is are or shall be reconciled to or shall hold communion with the see or church of Rome or shall profess the popish religion or shall marry a papist shall be subject to such incapacities as in such case or cases are by the said recited Act provided enacted and established. And that every King and Queen of this realm who shall come to and succeed in the imperiall crown of this kingdom by vertue of this Act shall have the coronation oath administered to him her or them at their respective coronations according to the Act of Parliament made in the first year of the reign of his Majesty and the said late Queen Mary intituled An Act for establishing the coronation oath and shall make subscribe and repeat the declaration in the Act first above recited mentioned or referred to in the manner and form thereby prescribed.

3. Further provisions for securing the religion, laws, and liberties of these realms

And whereas it is requisite and necessary that some further provision be made for securing our religion laws and liberties from and after the death of his Majesty and the Princess Ann of Denmark and in default of issue of the body of the said princess and of his Majesty respectively Be it enacted by the Kings most excellent Majesty by and with the advice and consent of the lords spirituall and temporall and commons in Parliament assembled and by the authority of the same

That whosoever shall hereafter come to the possession of this crown shall joyn in communion with the Church of England as by law established

That in case the crown and imperiall dignity of this realm shall hereafter come to any person not being a native of this kingdom of England this nation be not obliged to ingage in any warr for the defence of any dominions or territories which do not belong to the crown of England without the consent of Parliament . . .

That after the said limitation shall take effect as aforesaid no person born out of the kingdoms of England Scotland or Ireland or the dominions thereunto belonging (although he be . . . made a denizen (except such as are born of English parents) shall be capable to be of the privy councill or a member of either House of Parliament or to enjoy any office or place of trust either civill or military or to have any grant of lands tenements or hereditaments from the Crown to himself or to any other or others in trust for him . . .

That no pardon under the great seal of England be pleadable to an impeachment by the commons in Parliament.

Note: See Aliens Employment Act 1955, s.1; Army Act 1955, s.21 (4); Air Force Act 1955, s.21 (4) and Armed Forces Act 1966, s.36. These permit aliens to serve in the armed forces and allow command over British armed forces to be vested in foreigners.

The status of the European Convention on Human Rights and Fundamental Freedoms in United Kingdom Law.

Note: Although not incorporated by legislation in British law the Convention is not without its effects.

Standing Advisory Commission on Human Rights,

The Protection of Human Rights by Law in Northern Ireland. Cmnd. 7009, 1977

5.23. . . . . The United Kingdom is among the minority of States in which the Convention does not form part of the internal law. The United Kingdom is also in the unique position among the member countries of the Council of Europe of having no written constitution with provisions on fundamental rights and freedoms. The individual has a remedy in the United Kingdom courts for violations of the Convention only to the extent that the Convention rights and freedoms are reflected in the common law or statute law. And, as the Government's Discussion Document has indicated[1] there is no complete certainty about the effect of the Convention within our legal system at present. 5.24 Although the European Convention has not been incorporated into United Kingdom law, the House of Lords and the Court of Appeal in both England and Northern Ireland have recently recognised the Convention as a source of legal interpretation. In *Waddington v. Miah* Lord Reid, whose speech was approved unanimously by the other members of the House of Lords, stated[2] that in the light of Article 7 of the Convention it was hardly credible that any Government department would promote, or that Parliament would pass, retrospective criminal legislation, and he construed the Immigration Act 1971 accordingly. In *Broome v. Cassell & Co* Lord Kilbrandon stated[3] that a constitutional right of free speech must be recognised in United Kingdom law at least since the date when the Convention was ratified. In *Blathwayte v. Baron Cawley* Lord Wilberforce acknowledged[4] that a widely accepted treaty like the Convention might point the direction in which common law concepts of public policy, as applied by the courts, ought to move. In *R. v. Secretary of State for the Home Department, ex p. Bhajan Singh* Lord Denning MR stated[5] that:

> 'It is to be assumed that the Crown, in taking part in legislation, would do nothing which was in conflict with treaties. So the court should now construe the Immigration Act 1971 so as to be in conformity with [the] Convention . . . immigration officers and the Secretary of State in exercising their duties ought to bear in mind the principles stated in the Convention.'

In *R. v. Secretary of State for the Home Department, ex p. Phansopkar* Lord Justice Scarman stated[6] that it was the duty of public authorities in administering the law—including the Immigration Act 1971—and of the courts in interpreting and apply the law to have regard to the Convention. In *R. v. Chief Immigration Officer, Heathrow Airport, ex parte Salamat Bibi* Lord Denning referred[7] to his previous observation in the *Bhajan Singh* case that immigration officers ought to bear in mind the principles stated in the Convention, and said that he now thought that this would be asking too much of them. They could not be expected to known or apply the Convention. They should go simply by the immigration rules laid down by the Secretary of State. The Convention was drafted in a style very different from that used in our own legislation. It contained wide general statements of principle. They were apt to lead to much difficulty in application; because they gave rise to much uncertainty. Lord Justice Roskill believed that the statements of Lord Justice Scarman in the *Phansopkar* case were somewhat too wide and might call for reconsideration. He also agreed with Lord Denning that he had gone too far in the *Bhajan Singh* case. There were no grounds for imposing on immigration officers the additional burden of considering in every case the application of the Convention. Lord Justice Geoffrey Lane considered that whatever persuasive force the Convention might have in resolving ambiguities it could not have the

[1]*Legislation on Human Rights: A Discussion Document,* June 1976, para. 3.25.
[2][1974] 1 W.L.R. 683, 694 (HL).
[3][1972] A.C. 1027, 1133 (HL).
[4][1976] A.C. 397, 426 (HL).
[5][1976] Q.B. 198, 207 (CA).
[6][1976] Q.B. 606, 626 (CA).
[7][1976] 3 All ER 843, 847 (CA).

effect of overriding the plain provisions of the 1971 Act and the rules made thereunder. In *Ahmad v. Inner London Education Authority* Lord Justice Scarman (dissenting) broadly construed[1] Section 30 of the Education Act 1944 (prohibiting the disqualification of a teacher by reason of his religious opinions or of his attending or omitting to attend religious worship) so as to be in conformity with Article 9 of the European Covention. However, Lord Denning (with whose judgment Lord Justice Orr concurred) stated that the Convention was no part of English law but that the Courts did their best to see that their decisions were in conformity with it. Article 9 was in such vague terms that it could be used for all sorts of unreasonable claims and provoke all sorts of litigation. And there was nothing in the Convention to give the appellant teacher any right to manifest his religion in derogation of his contract of employment (by missing about 45 minutes of his teaching duty every Friday to attend prayers at the nearest mosque).

In *R. v. Deery* a more recent Northern Ireland (firearms) case[2] (the Lord Chief Justice of Northern Ireland) Sir Robert Lowry gave explicit recognition to the Convention as a source of legal interpretation. Citing *Salomon v. Commissioners of Customs and Excise* [1966] 3 All ER 871 at p. 875G, he stated that although effect must be given to the terms of a domestic Act when those terms are clear and unambiguous (even when they conflict with Treaty obligations), in a case in which domestic legislation is unclear or ambiguous, the terms of international treaty obligations (in this case the European Convention) are a strong guide to the meaning of the ambiguous provisions when a court has to make its choice between possible interpretations of that legislation.

5.25 In the light of these cases the present status of the European Convention in United Kingdom law is uncertain and unpredictable. For example, it is not clear:

   (i) whether the presumption of conformity with the Convention applies only to legislation enacted after our ratification of the Convention or whether it also applies to legislation existing at the date of ratification;

   (ii) whether Ministers or their civil servants have a duty to have regard to the Convention in exercising their discretionary powers;

   (iii) whether rules made by Ministers with Parliamentary approval or administrative circulars issued by the Government Departments are subject to a presumption of conformity with the Convention;

   (iv) whether the exercise of legislative or executive powers by a subordinate legislature or executive (such as the former Northern Ireland Assembly and Executive) is subject to a duty to have regard to the Convention;

   (v) whether the Convention is to be regarded as a source from which to derive common law concepts of public policy, and, if so, whether this should be done in all cases or only in cases against public authorities.

6.04. .... [W]ould it now be right to make any move at all in the direction of comprehensive legislation giving special protection to fundamental rights. We attempted to:

---

[1] The Times Law Report, 22 March 1977.
[2] See *Construction of Statutes: R. v. Deery*, Criminal Law Review (September 1977) pp. 550–551.

identify the main arguments which were relevant to this question in paragraphs 10 and 11 of the Discussion Paper which we published in March 1976. The views which have subsequently been expressed in response both to that document and to the Government's Discussion Document have naturally tended to emphasise the argument in different ways. But we believe that the general arguments were correctly identified in our Discussion Paper as follows:

'On the one hand it may be argued that:

(1) It is complacent to assume that there is no need for new legal safeguards in Northern Ireland or indeed elsewhere in the United Kingdom. The existing legislative and common law safeguards against abuse of power are less comprehensive and effective than in many advanced democratic countries. For example:

    (a) there are inadequate constitutional guarantees against the abuse of power by the government or Parliament;

    (b) there is no modern and coherent system of administrative law enabling the citizen to obtain prompt, speedy and adequate legal redress for the misuse of administrative powers by public authorities;

    (c) there are important gaps in our legal system where basic rights and freedoms (e.g. in relation to freedom of expression conscience and association, respect for privacy and family life, or the right to a fair and public hearing in the determination of civil rights or criminal charges) are not adequately guaranteed;

    (d) the need for greater protection is especially important in relation to the increased powers and responsibilities of regional and local government and private institutions whose activities affect the basic rights and freedoms of the citizen; and

    (c) the absence of a Bill of Rights enforceable by the courts against the misuse of public powers may have contributed to the present situation in Northern Ireland.

(2) A Bill of Rights would remove certain fundamental values out of the reach of temporary political majorities, governments and officials and into the realm of legal principles by the courts. This would not be undemocratic because the exercise of political power in a democracy should not be beyond criticism or restraint.

(3) A Bill of Rights would be especially important in the context of the devolution of the present powers of Central Government in maintaining a national framework of law and order, and guaranteeing the basic rights of citizens throughout United Kingdom.

(4) A Bill of Rights would encourage a more actively and socially responsive judicial role in protecting basic rights and freedoms; it would alter the method of judicial law-making, so as to enable the courts to recognise the fundamental importance of certain values and the relationship between them.

(5) The European Convention contains a minimum Bill of Rights for Council of Europe countries and is also being used as a source of guidance about common standards within the European Community in relation to human rights questions arising under the EEC Treaty. The enactment of a Bill of Rights in this country would enable the United Kingdom to be manifestly in conformity with its international obligations and would also enable the citizen to obtain redress from United Kingdom courts without needing, except in the last resort, to have recourse to the European Commission in Strasbourg.

(6) A Bill of Rights would not necessarily hamper strong, effective and democratic government because it could recognise that interference with certain rights would be justifiable if they were necessary in a democratic society, for example, in the interests of national security, public safety or the economic well-being of the country, for the prevention of disorder or crime, for the protection of health or morals, or for the protection of the rights and freedoms of others.

(7) The generality of a Bill of Rights makes it possible for the interpretation of such a document to evolve in accordance with changing social values and needs. This process of giving fresh meaning to basic human rights—and the obligations which flow from them—from generation to generation is valuable for its own sake, as a means of educating public opinion, and as a rallying point in the State for all who care deeply for the ideals of freedom.

(8) A Bill of Rights would not be a substitute for more specific statutory safeguards against specific abuses (*e.g.* anti-discrimination legislation or the Parliamentary Commissioner for Administration). It would supplement and strengthen those safeguards where they were incomplete.

(9) Although it would be difficult and perhaps divisive to envisage introducing a wholly new and comprehensive Bill of Rights except as part of a widely supported major constitutional settlement, this does not rule out more limited guarantees (*e.g.* on the lines of the European Convention); nor would such limited guarantees involve fettering the ultimate sovereignty of Parliament.

On the other hand it may be argued that:

(1) Because of the general nature of Bills of Rights and the increased powers of judicial law-making which they require, the scope and effect of such documents is uncertain and unpredictable.

(2) A Bill of Rights would create expectations which could not be satisfied in practice. It would be regarded as a panacea for all grievances whereas its real value (if any) would be only a limited one. It would be least effective when it was most needed: *i.e.* to protect fundamental rights and freedoms against powerful currents of intolerance, passion, usurpation and tyranny.

(3) A Bill of Rights might be interpreted by the courts in a manner which would hamper strong, effective or progressive government, and the role of the courts would result in important public issues being discussed and resolved in legal or constitutional terms rather than in moral or political terms. It would risk compromising the necessary independence and impartiality of the judiciary by requiring the judges to work in a more political arena.

(4) Most Bill of Rights stem from a constitutional settlement following revolution, rebellion, liberation or the peaceful attainment of independence. It would be difficult and perhaps divisive to seek to obtain a sufficient degree of political consensus about the nature and scope of a Bill of Rights in present circumstances.

(5) Human Rights are at least as well protected in the United Kingdom as in countries which have Bills of Rights since they are adequately safeguarded by traditional methods, *i.e.,* legislative measures to deal with specific problems, combined with the unwritten but effective constitutional conventions; the sense of responsibility and fair dealing in legislators and administrators; the influence of a free press and the force of public opinion; the independence of the judiciary in upholding the rule of law; and free and secret elections.

(6) The United Kingdom differs from many advanced democratic countries in lacking (a) a written constitution, (b) a system of public law, and (c) a

codified legal system. A Bill of Rights involves features of all three of these distinctive characteristics of other legal systems. It would therefore represent a
fundamental departure from the existing legal tradition.

(7) A Bill of Rights which did not (i) contain a modern definition of the
rights and freedoms relevant to the particular circumstances obtaining
whether in the United Kingdom in general or in Northern Ireland in particular, (ii) have priority over other laws, (iii) create legally enforceable rights
and (iv) apply to violations of human rights by private individuals and
organisations as well as by public authorities would not satisfy some promi-
nent supporters of such a measure. On the other hand a Bill of Rights which
did have these characteristics would be unlikely to obtain widespread public
support.

(8) A Bill of Rights would create wasteful duplication in relation to existing
statutory safeguards for human rights and would generate unnecessary
litigation.

(9) In Northern Ireland existing safeguards (e.g. Part III of the Northern
Ireland Constitution Act 1973) have not in practice tended to be relied upon
by those alleging that their human rights have been infringed. There is no
evidence that this situation would be altered by the introduction of a Bill of
Rights'.

6.05   None of the arguments which we have summarised on each side of the
question is 'right' or 'wrong'. Some of the arguments on each side are controversial, but there are important points in all of them. However, the unanimous conclusion which we have reached in answer to our first question is
that the legal protection of human rights in Northern Ireland should be increased and that one of the ways in which this should be done is by the enactment of an enforceable Bill of Rights. We believe that the most appropriate
way of doing this would be to incorporate the European Convention into the
domestic legal system of the United Kingdom. Later in this Chapter we shall
outline other measures which we also think should be taken.

6.06   We would summarise our main reasons for answering the first question
in this way by referring to:
   (a) the value of ensuring express compliance with the international
       obligations imposed by the European Convention which are designed
       to secure to everyone within the United Kingdom the rights and
       freedoms guaranteed by the Convention and to provide effective
       remedies for violations of those rights and freedoms by public
       authorities;
   (b) the value of giving explicit and positive recognition in our con-
       stitutional and legal system to respect for basic human rights and
       freedoms;
   (c) the need for effective legal safeguards against the misuse of power by
       public authorities;
   (d) the necessity in a genuinely democratic society to ensure that govern-
       ments respect the rights and freedoms of minorities;
   (e) the importance of legislating expressly for comprehensive and effective
       guarantees of human rights which are applicable to the United
       Kingdom as a whole so that the basic rights of the individual do not de-
       pend upon the particular part of the United Kingdom in which the in-
       dividual was born or lives;
   (f) the importance of having general principles or criteria to assist

legislators and administrators, as well as judges, in matters concerning human rights;

(g) the need to encourage legislators, administrators and judges to be more systematically and consciously concerned with fundamental values when they perform their public functions (as part of the necessary process of adaptation to the legislative, administrative and judicial techniques of the other member countries of the European Community and of the Council of Europe);

(h) the advantages of a more actively and socially responsive judicial role in settling constitutional disputes and in protecting basic rights and freedoms;

(i) the need to remove the uncertainties about the present status and effect of the European Convention in the law of the United Kingdom;

(j) the benefits of a Bill of Rights as a source of public education about the values of a democratic society.

Some of these reasons, although of general application, have a particular relevance to the situation in Northern Ireland today—see Chapter 2.

6.07 The present state of opinion, . . . demonstrates wide agreement, both in Northern Ireland and among political groups and independent experts in Great Britain, in favour of modelling a Bill of Rights upon the European Convention rather than attempting to introduce a Bill of Rights which stands free from the Convention. We share this view. We doubt whether a sufficient degree of consensus could be obtained (whether in Northern Ireland alone or in the United Kingdom as a whole) as to the scope and effect of a free-standing Bill of Rights, especially if, as some have argued, such a change were to be made in advance of a new constitutional settlement involving entrenched rights and legal restraints on Parliamentary sovereignty, judicially enforced.

6.08 In our view, some of the arguments against any enforceable Bill of Rights (which we have summarised in paragraph 6.04) would have more force in relation to the introduction of a new free-standing Bill of Rights which was constitutionally entrenched. However, their force would be greatly diminished if the proposal were confined to the incorporation of the European Convention into our legal system. In particular, we consider that:

(1) although incorporation would introduce some uncertainty into our legal system, it would also clarify the present uncertain status of the Convention and provide our courts with the benefit of the guidance of the case law of the Convention organs;

(2) in view of the modest nature of the process of incorporation, it would be unlikely to be widely misconstrued as a panacea for grievances; on the other hand, because more effective domestic remedies would be available, the risks of violations of human rights might be reduced;

(3) anxiety about the manner in which our courts might interpret the Convention would be allayed by the fact that the courts would be obliged to have regard to the Strasbourg case law and that appeals would lie to the Convention organs;

(4) there would be no need to obtain a political consensus about the nature and scope of a Bill of Rights modelled on the Convention; the rights and obligations are already defined in the Convention itself; incorporation would create no new rights or obligations but would only give greater effect to existing rights and obligations;

(5) the Convention contains only the minimum international standards of human rights; its incorporation would therefore be no substitute for

but rather a reinforcement of our traditional methods (*i.e.*, legislative measures to deal with specific problems, combined with the unwritten but effective constitutional conventions; the sense of responsibility and fair dealing in legislators and administrators; the influence of a free press and the force of public opinion; the independence of the judiciary in upholding the rule of law; and free and secret elections);

(6) the incorporation of the Convention would be consistent with the implications of our membership of the European Community;

(7) although incorporation of the Convention would not satisfy some supporters of a Bill of Rights the modest nature of the exercise would make it more widely acceptable (*e.g.*, because it would not create new sources of legal liability for trade unions and other non-governmental organisations nor fetter the sovereignty of Parliament);

(8) incorporation of the Convention would not affect existing statutory safeguards for human rights but would supplement them; the normal risk as to costs and the inherent powers of the courts would discourage unnecessary litigation under the Convention;

(9) there have already been many applications from individuals in Northern Ireland complaining to the European Commission of violations of the Convention; if the Convention were incorporated there would be more effective domestic remedies which would have to be exhausted before recourse to Strasbourg; given adequate legal assistance and enforcement machinery, it is therefore likely that greater use would be made of the Convention than has been the case as regards existing legal safeguards.

6.09 In view of the prominence which has been given to this matter during the public debate about the Bill of Rights issue, we should emphasise that, in our view, the incorporation of the European Convention into our law would not require a new constitutional settlement, entrenching the Convention rights and freedoms against the possibility of change by Parliament and thereby fettering the sovereignty of Parliament. We note that the other States parties to the Convention have not found it necessary to give such overriding priority to the Convention when making its provisions part of their domestic law. In our view, it would be sufficient to give the same priority to the Convention under our law as has been given to Community law . . . The fact that the Convention would remain binding in international law upon future United Kingdom Governments would no doubt in practice inhibit Parliament from exercising its sovereignty in a manner which would violate the Convention; but we do not consider that a major constitutional departure should be undertaken by seeking to deprive Parliament of the power to act in breach of international law if it were minded to do so. Nor, in our view, would it be necessary to seek to entrench the Convention against the possibility of change by Parliament in order to persuade our courts to give sufficient priority and importance to the Convention in their work. Provided that the incorporating statute were to contain sufficient guidance (similar to that contained in the European Communities Act 1972 in relation to Community law) we believe that our courts would give proper weight to the Convention and to the evolving body of case law on the international plane. The Convention, like any Bill of Rights, would be no substitute for the vital role of democratic institutions in protecting human rights. Parliament must necessarily remain at the centre of our constitutional arrangements for redressing grievances by making specific changes in the law and calling the responsible bodies to account.

However, there are clear limits to the reliance which can be placed on the operation of the democratic process in individual cases. Human rights cannot always be protected by the parliamentary process and unfortunately cases may occur of the misuse of power by central or devolved government or other public authorities.

6.10 The second question—whether any changes should be confined to Northern Ireland alone or should apply to the United Kingdom as a whole—was referred to in Part III of our Discussion Paper, where we gave the following brief summary of the arguments on each side:

'On the one hand it may be argued in favour of a measure limited to Northern Ireland that:

(1) Northern Ireland has special problems which call for special solutions, including special kinds of rights and exceptions. It would not be practicable to devise a United Kingdom measure capable of being applied to present circumstances to Northern Ireland.

(2) By well-established custom and convention both before and since Direct Rule the Westminster Parliament has not normally applied human rights legislation (on such matters as race relations, equal pay and sex discrimination) directly to Northern Ireland. A Northern Ireland Bill of Rights would therefore be in accordance with past practice.

(3) Whereas there appears to be widespread support in Northern Ireland for a Bill of Rights, support seems at present to be less widespread at this stage in the rest of the United Kingdom.

(4) To await the introduction of a United Kingdom Bill would involve unnecessary delay for Northern Ireland.

On the other hand it may be argued in favour of a United Kingdom measure that:

(1) It would be impracticable to introduce a Bill of Rights exclusively in Northern Ireland where fundamental rights and freedoms have been under the greatest strain and where it would be difficult, if not impossible, at this stage to obtain a sufficient degree of consensus about the nature and scope of the rights guaranteed and the means by which they would be enforced.

(2) The majority of political opinion in Northern Ireland appears to favour a United Kingdom measure using the European Convention as a guide for a Bill of Rights.

(3) It is extremely unusual to introduce constitutional guarantees of fundamental rights in only one part of a country's territory. It would be especially unusual to incorporate the European Convention into only part of the legal system of a contracting State.

(4) A measure for the whole of the United Kingdom would underline the common character of the rights of all its citizens; on the other hand, an exclusively Northern Ireland measure would lack the moral and legal force of wider measures applied to the United Kingdom and compatible with the international obligations applicable to the member countries of the European Community and the Council of Europe.'

6.11 We have no doubt that the measure incorporating the European Convention into domestic law should apply to the United Kingdom as a whole rather than to Northern Ireland alone. . . .

Note: See also House of Lords, *Report of the Select Committee on a Bill of Rights.* H.L.(176). 1978.

CHAPTER 4

FREEDOM OF RELIGION AND CONSCIENCE

BLASPHEMY (AND RELATED OFFENCES)

Further Reading

O'Higgins, pp. 20–24; Smith & Hogan, pp. 708–10; Street, pp. 195–200.

H. Bradlaugh Bonner, *Penalties Upon Opinion* (Walls, 1912); E. S. P. Haynes, *Religious Persecution* (Duckworth, 1904); G. D. Nokes, *A History of the Crime of Blasphemy* (Sweet & Maxwell, 1928); R. S. W. Pollard, *Abolish the Blasphemy Laws* (Society for the Abolition of Blasphemy Laws, 1957); and Sir James FitzJames Stephen, *History of the Criminal Law* (MacMillan, 1883), Vol. 2, pp. 396–497.

C. S. Kenny, "Evolution of the Crime of Blasphemy," (1923) 1 *C.L.J.* 127–42; Sir John MacDonnell, "Blasphemy and the Common Law," 33 *Fortnightly Review* (1883) 776–89; P. O'Higgins, "Blasphemy in Irish Law," (1960) 23 *M.L.R.* 151–66; Sir James FitzJames Stephen, "Blasphemy and Blasphemous Libel," (1884) 35 *Fortnightly Review* 288–318; *ibid.* "The Laws of England as to the Expression of Religious Opinion," (1874–1875) 25 *Contemporary Review* 446–75.

See also comments on *Reg.* v. *Pooley* (1857) (p. 64) by H. T. Buckle in his review of Mill's *On Liberty* in (1859) 59 *Fraser's Magazine* 533 *et seq.* reprinted in H. Taylor, *Miscellaneous and Posthumous Works of H. T. Buckle* (Longmans, 1872), Vol. 1, pp. 20–70 (esp. pp. 57–62). This led J. D. Coleridge, who had prosecuted an undefended and demented Pooley on a charge of blasphemy before his father Coleridge J., to a very indignant defence of the proceedings (59 *Fraser's Magazine* 435 *et seq.*). This in turn led to Buckle's pamphlet *Letter to a Gentleman respecting Pooley's Case* (London, 1859, reprinted in *Miscellaneous Works*), Vol. 1, pp. 71–81), which included the challenge: "In this great warfare between liberty and repression Sir John Coleridge has chosen his side and I have chosen mine" (p. 79). J. D. Coleridge as Lord Chief Justice many years later was to preside in *Reg.* v. *Ramsay and Foote* (see p. 66).

Note: The continued survival of the offence of blasphemy must be a matter for astonishment to twentieth century liberals, but its survival has practical repercussions. Sir Ivor Jennings wrote in 1933:

". . . The wide definitions of treason, sedition, and blasphemy remain, and it is possible for any Government to use the judicial machinery to

put down opinion unfavourable to itself. Little of that law has been enforced during the past fifty years. But the moral of *A-G. v. Bradlaugh*
(1883) 15 Cox C.C. 355 [prosecution for blasphemy] surely is that sleeping laws, like sleeping dogs, are potentially dangerous. They are most
easily killed when they are asleep."—"Bradlaugh and the Law" in *Cham-
pion of Liberty: Charles Bradlaugh* (London, 1933), at p. 314.

Attempts on a number of occasions to secure the repeal of the offence of
blasphemy have failed, although both in 1914 and in 1929 the then Home
Secretaries of the day promised that there would be no government
prosecutions during their tenure of office. See *The Blasphemy Laws: Verbatim
Report of the Deputation to the Home Secretary on April 16, 1924* (London, 1924),
and Mark De Wolfe (ed.), *Holmes-Laski Letters: The Correspondence of Mr.
Justice Holmes and Harold J. Laski, 1916–1935* (2 vols, London, 1953), vol.2,
p. 1198.

The precise rationale in the modern world of the offence of blasphemy
remains obscure. Is it to prevent certain people from having their religious
feelings wounded or is it because it is necessary to protect Christian beliefs
which are seen in some sense as essential to the preservation of society? The
latter justification may draw some support from those who share Lord
Denning's view that "Without religion there can be no morality: and
without morality there can be no law"—*The Changing Law* (London, 1953) at
p. 99. As regards the first view see *Reg. v. Pooley* (1857). See below.

A particular problem with respect to blasphemy is the relationship
between the common law crime and the statutory crime of blasphemy.

There are other offences closely related to blasphemy, such as profanity
(see pp. 22 and 95) and riotous or indecent behaviour in church (see p. 95).

BLASPHEMY ACT 1697

1. . . . [I]f any Person or Persons having been educated in or at any time
having made Profession of the Christian Religion within this Realm shal by
writing printing teaching or advised speaking [deny any one of the Persons in
the Holy Trinity to be God or shal] assert or maintain there are more Gods
than One or shal deny the Christian Religion to be true or the Holy Scriptures
of the Old and New Testament to be of Divine Authority and shal . . . be
thereof lawfully convicted . . . such Person or Persons for the First Offence
shal be adjudged incapable and disabled in Law to all Intents and Purposes
whatsoever to have or enjoy any Office or Offices Imployment or
Imployments Ecclesiastical Civil or Military or any Part in them or any Profit
or Advantage appertaining to them or any of them.

Note: Words in square brackets were repealed by 53 Geo 3.c.160, s.2. The
whole Act was repealed by the Criminal Law Act 1967, s.13, Sched. 4, Part
1.

Reg. v. Pooley (1857) 8 St.Tr.N.S. 1381

Bodmin Assizes

Pooley, a well-sinker, chalked on a gate the words "Duloe stinks with the
monster Christ's Bible" and had advised people "If they would burn their

Bibles, and use the ashes for dressing the land, it would get rid of potato disease." He was tried on several counts of blasphemy, and was sentenced to six months' imprisonment for the words chalked on the gate; a further six months for the advice as to the avoidance of potato blight, and when he expostulated indignantly at these sentences he was sentenced to a further nine months' imprisonment. He was subsequently found to be insane. According to Mr. Justice Stephen in his *Digest of Criminal Law* (5th ed.), p. 125 Lord Coleridge, L.C.J., allowed him to say that the ruling of Coleridge, J. in this case was in accordance with the alternative definition of blasphemy in Article 179 of that *Digest:*

"Every publication is said to be blasphemous which contains matter relating to God, Jesus Christ, the Bible, or the Book of Common Prayer, and intended to wound the feelings of mankind, or to excite contempt and hatred against the church by law established or to promote immorality. Publications intended in good faith to propagate opinions on religious subjects which the person who publishes them regards as true are not blasphemous within the meaning of this definition merely because their publication is likely to wound the feelings of those who believe such opinions to be false, or because their general adoption might lead to alterations in the constitution of the church established by law."

Gathercole's Case (1838) 2 Lewin 237

York Summer Assizes

The Rev. Michael Gathercole was charged with a number of counts of libelling the Roman Catholic Church, in general, and the Scorton Nunnery in Yorkshire in particular, on account of his publishing certain pamphlets, the general flavour of which can be gathered from a short extract:

"Pope Hildebrand, who first prohibited the marriages of the clergy, kept a harlot named Matilda, who left her husband to live with the old wretch. Pope Sergius the Third had a harlot named Marozia, who had great power in governing the church. She brought the old pope a son, and afterwards got him to be pope, as John the Eleventh. John the Twelfth was accused before a synod, of wickedness with the widow of Rainecius, and with Stephana, his father's concubine; and with a widow named Anna, and her niece. Pope Benedict the Twelfth bought a beautiful young woman for a large sum of money. Pope Sextus the Fourth built a brothel (query nunnery) at Rome, and provided shoes covered with pearls for his concubine Tyresia. Pope Innocent the Eighth, innocently enough, became the father of eight sons and as many daughters."

ALDERSON B.:
The point is, whether this is only a libel on the whole Roman Catholic Church generally, or on Scorton Nunnery? In the former case, the defendant is entitled to an acquittal.

If it be a libel on Scorton Nunnery generally, then the defendant must be found guilty as to the charge on the 4th count. It may be on Scorton Nunnery generally, and on the inmates named in particular. In that case the defendant is liable to be convicted on all the counts.

A person may, without being liable to prosecution for it, attack Judaism, or Mahomedanism, or even any sect of the Christian Religion (save the established religion of the country); and the only reason why the latter is in a different situation from the others is, because it is the form established by law, and is therefore a part of the constitution of the country. In like manner, and for the same reason, any general attack on Christianity is the subject of criminal prosecution, because Christianity is the established religion of the country. The defendant here has a right to entertain his opinions, to express them, and to discuss the subject of the Roman Catholic religion and its institutions; but he has no right to say of a particular body of persons (*e.g.* the inhabitants of Scorton Nunnery), that the place they inhabit is 'a brothel of prostitution'; for in doing that he is attacking the individual characters of the body of whom Scorton Nunnery consists.

This indictment charges the defendant with intending to injure the character of the prosecutors; and every man, if he be a rational man, must be considered to intend that which must necessarily follow from what he does. For example if he cuts off the head he must intend to kill; if he puts out an eye, to maim. You will, therefore, have to say, whether it was not the necessary consequence of this defendant's act, that an injury would be inflicted on individual character, and on the reputation of the Lady Abbess, and the other particular persons composing the Nunnery at Scorton.

In considering this question, you will further observe, that a great portion of this libel consists of insinuations. Now, if a man insinuates a fact in asking a question, meaning thereby to assert it, it is the same thing as if he asserted it in terms.

If you think, therefore, that the defendant, by asking the questions, here meant to insinuate and to state, that 'infants are born in the Nunnery at Scorton, and that holy fathers bring them up or murder the innocents,' then it is a libel on those persons. Consider, therefore, whether what you have heard read was intended by the defendant as a mere illustration of his general opinion expressed with regard to the Roman Catholic Church, or whether it was his intention to impute specifically to the individuals at Scorton, the conduct which the language of his publication suggests.

If it was merely an attack upon the Roman Catholic Church, and in no respect an attack on Scorton Nunnery, then he is entitled to an acquittal, otherwise you must find him guilty.

Note: Verdict, Guilty.

Reg. v. Ramsay and Foote (1883) 15 Cox C.C. 231

Queens Bench Division

The defendants were tried for publishing blasphemous libels.

LORD COLERIDGE, L.C.J.: . . . Are these passages within the meaning of the law blasphemous libels? Now that is a matter entirely for you. You have the responsibility of judging, looking at and reading these passages, whether they are blasphemous libels. My duty is to explain to you what is the law on the subject, after which it is for you absolutely to determine the question. Now, according to the old law, or the *dicta* of the judges in old times, these passages would undoubtedly be blasphemous libels, because they asperse the truth of Christianity. But, as I said in the former trial, and now repeat, I think that these old cases can no longer be taken to be a statement of the law at the present day. It is no longer true in the sense in which it was true when these *dicta* were uttered, that "Christianity is part of the law of the land." Nonconformists and Jews were then under penal laws, and were hardly allowed civil rights. But now, so far as I know the law, a Jew might be Lord Chancellor (*a.*) Certainly he might be Master of the Rolls; and the great Judge whose loss we have all had to deplore (*b*) might have had to try such a case, and if the view of the law supposed be correct, he would have had to tell the jury, perhaps partly composed of Jews, that it was blasphemy to deny that Jesus Christ was the Messiah, which he himself did deny, and which Parliament had allowed him to deny, and which it was part of "the law of the land" that he might deny. Therefore, to asperse the truth of Christianity cannot *per se* be sufficient to sustain a criminal prosecution for blasphemy. And on the ground that in the sense understood by the judges in former times that Christianity is part of "the law of the land" to suppose so is in my judgment to forget that law grows. The principles of law remain, and it is the great advantage of the common law that its principles do remain; but then they have to be applied to the changing circumstances of the times. This may be called by some retrogression, but I should rather say it is progression—the progress of human opinion. Therefore to maintain that merely because the truth of Christianity is denied without more, that, therefore, a person may be indicted for blasphemous libel is, I venture to think, absolutely untrue. It is a view of the law which cannot be historically justified. Parliament, the supreme authority as to old law, has passed Acts which render the *dicta* of the judges in former times no longer applicable. And it is no disparagement to their authority to say that observations which were made under one state of the law are no longer applicable under a different state of things. As I observed on the last occasion, and I put it as a *reductio ad absurdum* that if it was enough to say that "Christianity was part of the law of the land," then there could be no discussion on any part of "the law of the land," and it would be impossible, for example, to discuss, in a grave argumentative way, the question of a monarchical form of Government, as Harrington discussed it in his "Oceana," without being liable to be indicted for a seditious libel. I was not aware that what I then put as a *reductio ad absurdum* had been judicially held, and that a man had actually been convicted of a seditious libel (*Rex v. Bedford*, Gilbert's Rep. 297) for discussing such a question. His work containing, as the report states, "no reflection whatever upon the existing Government." No judge, or jury, in our day would convict a man of seditious libel in such a case; it would be regarded as monstrous. I have no doubt, therefore, that the mere denial of the truth of Christianity is not enough to constitute the offence of blasphemy. It is my duty to lay down the law on the subject as I find it laid down in the best books of authority, and in "Starkie on Libel" (599, 4th edit.), it is there laid down as, I believe, correctly:

"There are no questions of more intense and awful interest than those which concern the relations between the Creator and the beings of His creation; and though, as a matter of discretion and prudence, it might be better to

(a) Certainly Lord Chief Justice.
(b) Sir George Jessel.

leave the discussion of such matters to those who, from their education and habits, are most likely to form correct conclusions; yet it cannot be doubted that any man has a right, not merely to judge for himself on such subjects, but also, legally speaking, to publish his opinion for the benefit of others. When learned and acute men enter upon those discussions with such laudable motives, their very controversies, even where one of the antagonists must necessarily be mistaken, so far from producing mischief, must in general tend to the advancement of truth, and the establishment of religion on the firmest and most stable foundations. The very absurdity and folly of an ignorant man, who professes to teach and enlighten the rest of mankind, are usually so gross as to render his errors harmless; but, be this as it may, the law interferes not with his blunders, so long as they are honest ones, justly considering that society is more than compensated for the partial and limited mischief which may arise from the mistaken endeavours of honest ignorance, by the splendid advantages which result to religion and truth from the exertions of free and unfettered minds. It is the mischievous abuse of this state of intellectual liberty which calls for penal censure. The law visits not the honest errors, but the malice of mankind. A wilful intention to pervert, insult, and mislead others, by means of licentious and contumelious abuse applied to sacred subjects, or by wilful misrepresentations or wilful sophistry, calculated to mislead the ignorant and unwary, is the criterion and test of guilt. A malicious and mischievous intention, or what is equivalent to such an intention, in law, as well as morals—a state of apathy and indifference to the interests of society—is the broad boundary between right and wrong."

Now that I believe to be a correct statement of the law; and it is worthy of notice that the learned writer quotes a passage from Michaelis to show that it may be that some sort of protection for the consituted religion of the country may be a good thing even for those who differ from it; for otherwise ill consequences might follow to them. It is not such a very long time ago in our history when a Birmingham mob wrecked the house of Dr. Priestley, one of the most distinguished and excellent of men. So that it is not quite clear that some sort of law against blasphemy may not be advantageous. However, the law is, I conceive, rightly laid down by Mr. Starkie; and I am not satisfied from my study of the cases on the subject that the law was ever laid down differently. I have taken three cases, about seventy or eighty years apart, and I find the law laid down in them was exactly the same. The first was the case of *Rex v. Taylor* (Vent. 293) before Lord Hale. The law laid down in any case must be taken in connection with the facts of the case, and in that case the information contained these expressions: "That Jesus Christ was a bastard, an imposter, and a cheat," and that he, the defendant, "feared neither God nor devil." These were the words to which Lord Hale had to apply the law, and as to which he said that "such kind of wicked and blasphemous words were not only an offence to God, but a crime against the laws, and punishable by the courts." He did not say that a grave argument against the truth of the Christian religion was punishable, but such kind of wicked and blasphemous words were the offence. That was Lord Hale's view of the law, and that is one of the cases on the subject. There are expressions in it which may seem to go further, but these must be looked at with reference to the subject-matter before Lord Hale, and as to which if it were before me now I should certainly hold that it was a blasphemous libel. So that I take it that ruling is a correct statement of the law as it is at present. The next case is that of *R. v. Woolston* (Strange, 834; and better reported in Fitzgibbon), where the defendant was convicted of blasphemous discourses on the miracles of our Lord and "the court desired him to take notice that they laid stress on the charge of 'general and indecent attacks,' and did not intend to include disputes between men on controversial points." Such was the law as laid down by Lord Raymond. Then came the case which has been commonly cited as bringing the law down to our own times; that was the case of *Rex* v. *Waddington* (1 B. & C. 26) tried before Lord Tenterden. There the words of the libel were "That Jesus Christ was an impostor, and a murderer, and a fanatic." The Lord Chief Justice laid it down that that was a libel. A juror asked him whether a work which denied the divinity of our Saviour was a libel. The answer of Lord Tenterden (a most cautious judge) was "that a work speaking of Jesus Christ in the language used in that publication was a libel." It is true he went on to say that Christianity was part of the law of the land, but his ruling was that a work speaking of Jesus Christ in the language used in the publication before him was a libel. The case came before the court, constituted of Tenterden, C.J., Bayley, J., Holroyd, J., and Best, J. The Lord Chief Justice said: "I told the jury that any publication in which our Saviour was spoken of in the language used in the publication was a libel, and I have no doubt whatever that it is a libel to publish of him that he was an impostor and a murderer." Bayley J. said: "It appears to me that the direction of the Lord Chief Justice was perfectly right. There can be no doubt that a work which does not merely deny the Godhead of Jesus Christ, but which states him to have been an impostor and a murderer was at common law, and still is, a libel." Holroyd, J. said: "I have no doubt whatever that any publication in which Jesus Christ is spoken of in the language used in this publication is a libel, and the direction was perfectly right in point of law." Best, J. said: "It is not necessary for me to say whether it be libellous to argue from Scripture against the Divinity of Chirst; that is not what the defendant has done. The Legislature has not altered the law in that respect, nor can it ever do so while the Christian religion is considered the basis of law." That is the only authority for the proposition that gravely to dispute the truth of Christianity would be an offence, because "Christianity is part of the law of the land." It is for that proposition this case is sometimes (by persons surely who never can have read it) cited as authority! The cases therefore are consistent on the subject, and I doubt whether the law as laid down in the older cases has ever been overruled, and whether the law as laid down in those cases, looked at with reference to the facts on which they were decided, was ever so illiberal as it has been the fashion to represent.

Still, whatever the older cases may have been, the fact remains that Parliament has altered the law as to religion. It is no longer the law that none but believers in Christianity can hold office in the State. Nonconformists are tolerated just as much as members of the Church of England. The state of things is no longer the same as when these judgments were pronounced, which, however, have been strained, I think, beyond what they will justly warrant. It is a comfort to think that the law has been altered as to disabilities and penalties for religious belief or non-belief, and though Lord Eldon in *The Attorney-General v. Pearson* (3 Merivale's Reports, 353) expressed a doubt whether some portions of the Act of 9 & 10 Will. 3 (directed against those who expressed disbelief in the Trinity, &c.) might not still be in force, I hope those doubts may never have to be brought to a solution in a court of law. (a)

(a) They were so in the case of Lady Henley's Charity (*Shore v. Wilson*, 9 Clarke & Finelly's Reports, 355), in which the judges were consulted, and held that the Act no longer raised a difficulty as to Unitarian endowments.

Such, however, are the rules or principles of law by which you are to judge whether these publications are blasphemous libels.

You have heard a great deal as to the expediency of these laws, and as to the expediency of enforcing them, and it has been truly said that, unless carried to an extent no longer possible in this country, they are not likely to be effectual. But all this has nothing to do with what we have to consider here. The defendant Foote has admitted that these publications were intended to be attacks on Christianity and on the Hebrew Scriptures, and he has cited a number of passages from approved writers which he says are to the same effect, and that may be so, and I think that some of them are not only similar in matter, but in style and manner; and he urged that, as these never were prosecuted, the law cannot be, as supposed, on the part of the prosecution, for it could not be that the offence consisted only in the style or taste of the publications, and that what was blasphemy in a penny paper was not so in more costly publications. Now, as to this, let me say that, as I understand, it is, and I believe always has been, the law; and at all events I now lay it down as law, that, if the decencies of controversy are observed, even the fundamentals of religion may be attacked without the writer being guilty of blasphemy. But no one can fail to see the difference between the works of the writers who have been quoted and the language used in the publications now before us; and I am obliged to say that it is a difference not only in degree, but in kind and nature. There is a grave and earnest tone, a reverent—perhaps I might even say a religious—spirit about the very attacks on Christianity itself which we find in the authors referred to, which shows that what they aimed at was not insult to the opinions of the majority of mankind nor to Christianity itself; but real, quiet, earnest pursuit of truth. And if the truth at which they have arrived is not that which you and I have been taught, or at which perhaps we might now arrive, so it is not because their conclusions differ from ours that they are to be deemed fit subject for criminal prosecution. Therefore, as to many of these authors whose writings have been quoted by the defendant, I think that they are within the protection of the law as laid down by Mr. Starkie in that passage I have cited as containing a correct statement of the law. As to some of the others, I confess I have a difficulty in distinguishing them from the publications now incriminated. They do appear to me to be open to the same complaint as those before you; and I should make no distinction in the application of the law between such authors and the defendant. So far as I can judge, some of them used strong and coarse expressions of contempt and hatred for the recognised truths of Christianity, and for the Hebrew Scriptures. But this is no argument in favour of the defendant, who has to show that he himself has not violated the law; not that others are guilty, but that he is not so. It is no defence for him to bring forward cases, some of which cannot be distinguished from his own. His case is before us, and we have to deal with it according to law. If these libels—now before you—are in your opinion permissible attacks upon religious belief, then find the defendants not guilty. But if they are such as do not come within the most liberal view of the law as I have laid it down to you, then your duty is to find the defendants guilty. Take these publications in your hands, and say whether in your judgment the defendants are or are not guilty of publishing blasphemous libels.

Note: The jury disagreed. Before the case came on again for hearing the private prosecutor applied to the Attorney-General for leave to enter a *nolle prosequi*. Sir James FitzJames Stephen was very critical of the judgment of Lord Coleridge. In his view Lord Coleridge by liberalising a bad law had preserved it. "My only objection to it is that I fear that its merits may be transferred illogically to the law which it expounds and lays down, and that then a humane and enlightened judgment may tend to perpetuate a bad law by diverting public attention from its defects. The law I regard as essentially and fundamentally bad." Stephen also took the view that Coleridge was wrong in his view of the relevance of the Blasphemy Act 1698. "No lapse of time or change of feeling affects the legal force of any statute."—35 *Fortnightly Review* (1884) 288 *et seq.*

Bowman v. Secular Society Ltd. [1917] A.C. 406

House of Lords

The Secular Society Ltd. was a registered company limited by guarantee. Under clause 3 (A) of its memorandum of association its main object was "to promote, in such ways as may from time to time be determined, the principle that human conduct should be based upon natural knowledge, and not upon super-natural belief, and that human welfare in this world is the proper end of all thought and action." The issue arose as to the validity of a bequest to the Society.

LORD DUNEDIN:

I agree with what I understand is the unanimous opinion of your Lordships, that as to what is necessary to constitute the crime of blasphemy at common law the dicta of Erskine J., Lord Denman C.J., and Lord Coleridge C.J. in the cases of *Shore* v. *Wilson* (1), *Reg.* v. *Hetherington* (2), and *Reg* v. *Ramsay* (3) respectively are correct, and I adopt the reasoning of the Lord Chancellor and Lord Buckmaster. Further, I agree with the Lord Chancellor that, on a fair construction, paragraph 3 (A) of the memorandum of association of the respondent company expresses the dominating purpose of the company; and that the other matters are mentioned not as independent, but only as subsidiary aims. I agree with him in thinking that teaching in accordance with 3 (A) is inconsistent with and to that extent subversive of the Christian religion—by which expression, without attempting definition, I mean all such forms of religion as have for a common basis belief in the Godhead of the Lord Jesus Christ.

It is said for the appellants that the Court will not lend its assistance for the furtherance of an illegal object, and that money given to the society must needs be illegally applied, because it certainly can only be used for objects in terms of the memorandum, and such objects are illegal, because the Christian religion is part of the law of the land. Now if money was laid out in either procuring publications or lectures in terms of the objects of the memorandum such publications or lectures need not be couched in scurrilous language and so need not be such as would constitute the crime of blasphemy at common law. Nor need they be criminal under the Blasphemy Act; for here I agree

(1) 9 Cl. & F. 355, 524.
(2) 4 St. Tr. (N.S.) 563.
(3) 15 Cox, C. C. 231.

with Lord Buckmaster that the Act is so framed as to make its penalties only apply when there has been what may be termed apostasy. It would not, I think, be safe to found any argument on the fact—but it is a fact sufficiently curious to be mentioned—that the Scottish Parliament two years before the Blasphemy Act passed an Act in similar terms, but omitting the words "having been educated in or at any time having made profession of the Christian religion, &c." In the repealing Act, 50 Geo. 3, c. 160, this and another older Scottish Act are repealed in toto, while the Blasphemy Act was allowed to stand. How innocuous it was on a true construction may be surmised from the fact that there seem to have been no prosecutions under it.

Criminal liability being negatived, no one has suggested any statute in terms of which it—by which I mean the supposed use of the money—is directly prohibited. There is no question of offence against what may be termed the natural moral sense. Neither has it been held, I think, as being against public policy, as that phrase is applied in the cases that have been decided on that head. Now if this is so, I confess I cannot bring myself to believe that there is still a terra media of things illegal, which are not criminal, not directly prohibited, not contra bonos mores, and not against public policy. Yet that, I think, is the result of holding that anything inconsistent with Christianity as part of the law of England cannot in any way be assisted by the action of the Courts.

LORD PARKER OF WADDINGTON:

My Lords, I will next proceed to consider whether a trust for the first object specified in the memorandum would be a valid trust. The society's first object is "to promote . . . , the principle that human conduct should be based upon natural knowledge and not upon super-natural belief, and that human welfare in this world is the proper end of all thought and action." A trust to promote or advocate this principle would certainly not be a trust for the benefit of individuals. But could it be established as a charitable trust? It is certainly not within the preamble of the statute 43 Eliz. c. 4. This is not conclusive, though the Courts have taken such preamble as their guide in determining what is or is not charitable. It is not a religious trust, for it relegates religion to a region in which it is to have no influence on human conduct. The principle may have its attractions for certain types of mind, but on analysis it appears to be extremely vague and ambiguous. The first branch does not prescribe the end to which human conduct is to be directed. It merely says that whatever aim a man has in view he is to base his conduct on natural knowledge rather than on supernatural belief. This may merely mean that if, for example, we desire to defeat our enemies we should avail ourselves of all known scientific means, and not rest idle in the belief that there is a special providence looking after our interests. The meaning intended must necessarily be obscure until the terms "natural knowledge" and "supernatural belief" are more narrowly defined. Passing to the second branch of the principle, it is, I think, equally obscure. It lays down dogmatically what ought to be the end of all human thought and action, "so think and act as to secure human welfare in this world." No hint is given as to what constitutes human welfare, a point on which there is the widest difference of opinion, or as to why any one should act on the precept unless it be assumed that altruism is merely enlightened egoism. It would in my opinion be quite impossible to hold that a trust to promote a principle so vague and indefinite was a good charitable trust. Even if the principle to be promoted were as definite as Kant's categoric imperative, I doubt whether a trust for its promotion would be charitable.

My Lords, it remains to consider the question (which formed the chief topic of argument at your Lordships' Bar) whether the promotion of the principle specified as the society's first object is either illegal or against the policy of the law. A trust for the promotion of the principle being unenforceable on other grounds, this question could only arise on a criminal prosecution for blasphemy or in an action to enforce a contract entered into for the purpose of promoting the principle. In discussing it I shall assume that the principle involves a denial of or an attack upon some of the fundamental doctrines of the Christian religion.

Mr Lords, on the subject of blasphemy I have had the advantage of reading, and I entirely agree with, the conclusions arrived at by my noble and learned friends the Lord Chancellor and Lord Buckmaster. In my opinion to constitute blasphemy at common law there must be such an element of vilification, ridicule, or irreverence as would be likely to exasperate the feelings of others and so lead to a breach of the peace. I cannot find that the common law has ever concerned itself with opinion as such, or with expression of opinion, so far as such expression is compatible with the maintenance of public order. Indeed there is express authority that heresy as such is outside the cognizance of a criminal Court unless the heretic by setting up conventicles or otherwise endangers the peace: see Hawkins' Pleas of the Crown, vol. 1, p. 354. The contrary view appears to be based on various dicta (I do not think they are more than dicta) to the effect that Christianity is part of the law of the land, the suggested inference being that to attack or deny any of its fundamental doctrines must therefore be unlawful. The inference of course depends on some implied major premise. If the implied major premise be that it is an offence to speak with contumely or even to express disapproval of existing law, it is clearly erroneous. If, on the other hand, the implied major premise is that it is an offence to induce people to disobey the law, the premise may be accepted, but to avoid a non sequitur it would be necessary to modify the minor premise by asserting that it is part of the law of the land that all must believe in the fundamental doctrines of Christianity, and this again is inadmissible. Christianity is clearly not part of the law of the land in the sense that every offence against Christianity is cognizable in the Courts.

A good deal of stress was laid in this connection upon the Blasphemy Act (9 & 10 Will. 3, c. 32), and its provisions undoubtedly give rise to certain difficulties. I think, however, for reasons which will appear later, that this Act should be construed as imposing, in the case of persons educated in or who have at any time professed the Christian religion, certain additional penalties for the common law offence rather than as creating a new statutory offence. The fact that there has, so far as can be discovered, never been a prosecution for an offence under the Act points to this view having been generally accepted.

My Lords, on the question whether the promotion of the principle in question is against public policy as opposed to being illegal in the criminal sense the appellants relied principally on two authorities—namely, *Cowan* v. *Milbourn* (1) and *Briggs* v. *Hartley*. (2) In the former case the Court, consisting of

(1) L. R. 2 Ex. 230.
(2) 19 L. J. (Ch.) 416.

Kelly C.B., Martin B., and Bramwell B., refused to enforce a contract for the hire of rooms, the purpose of the hirer being to use the rooms for certain lectures, one of which, as advertised, was to be on "The Character and Teachings of Christ; the former Defective, the latter Misleading," and another on "The Bible shown to be no more Inspired than any other Book." Kelly C.B. was of opinion that the first of these lectures could not be delivered without blasphemy. He referred especially to the fact that Christianity was part of the law of the land. Martin B. agreed. Bramwell B. quoted the Blasphemy Act, and said that the rooms were clearly intended to be used for a purpose declared by the statute to be unlawful. It appears, therefore, that all three judges considered that the purpose was unlawful in the strict sense, though Bramwell B. referred to the distinction between things actually unlawful in the sense of being punishable and things unlawful in the sense of being contrary to the policy of the law. This, however, appears to have been unnecessary for the decision. The Court refused to enforce the contract. In the case of *Briggs* v. *Hartley* the testator had created a trust to provide a prize for the best essay on natural theology, treated as a science, and sufficient when so treated to constitute a true, perfect, and philosophical system of universal religion. Shadwell V.-C. held the trust void as inconsistent with Christianity. In my opinion the first of these cases might possibly be supported on the footing that the lectures intended to be given would involve vilification, ridicule, or irreverence likely to lead to a breach of the peace. In so far as it decided that any denial of or attack upon the fundamental doctrines of Christianity was in itself blasphemous either at common law or under the statute, I think it was wrong. The second case, however, appears to be a direct authority on the point at issue, for the trust was clearly a good charity unless it could be held contrary to the policy of the law.

My Lords, I desire to call the attention of the House to certain general considerations and to certain authorities which have led me to the conclusion that *Briggs* v. *Hartley* was wrongly decided and that there is nothing contrary to the policy of the law in an attack on or a denial of the truth of Christianity or any of its fundamental doctrines, provided such attack or denial is unaccompanied by such an element of vilification, ridicule, or irreverence as is necessary for the common law offence of blasphemy. In the first place I desire to say something as to the history of religious trusts.

LORD SUMNER:

If the respondents are an anti-Christian society, is the maxim that Christianity is part of the law of England true, and, if so, in what sense? If Christianity is of the substance of our law, and if a Court of law must, nevertheless, adjudge possession of its property to a company whose every action seeks to subvert Christianity and bring that law to naught, then by such judgment it stultifies the law. So it was argued, and if the premise is right, I think the conclusion follows.

It is not enough to say with Lord Coleridge C.J. in *Ramsay's Case* (1) that this maxim has long been abolished, or with my noble and learned friend the

(1) 48 L. T. 733, 735; 15 Cox, C. C. 231, 235

Master of the Rolls in the Court below that "the older view," based on this maxim, "must now be regarded as obsolete." If that maxim expresses a positive rule of law, once established, though long ago, time cannot abolish it nor disfavour make it obsolete. The decisions which refer to such a maxim are numerous and old, and although none of them is a decision of this House, if they are in agreement and if such is their effect, I apprehend they would not now be overruled, however little Reason might incline your Lordships to concur in them. In what sense, then, was it ever a rule of law that Christianity is part of the law?

The legal material is fourfold: (1.) statute law; (2.) the criminal law of blasphemy; (3.) general civil cases; (4.) cases relating to charitable trusts. From statute law little is to be gleaned. During the sixteenth century many Acts were passed to repress objectionable doctrines, but plainly statutes were not needed if the common law possessed an armoury for the defence of Christianity as part and parcel of itself. Indeed, who but the King in Parliament could then say whether the Christianity, which for the time being formed part of the common law, was the Christianity of Rome or of Geneva or of Wittenberg? Certainly the Courts could not.

After the Revolution of 1688 there were passed the Toleration Act to give "some ease to scrupulous consciences in exercise of religion," which, upon conditions, relieved certain dissenters (Papists and those who denied the Trinity excepted) from the operation of various existing statutes, and the Blasphemy Act, which recites that "many persons have of late years openly avowed and published many blasphemous and impious opinions, contrary to the doctrines and principles of the Christian religion . . . . and may prove destructive to the peace and welfare of this kingdom." That the Blasphemy Act simply added new penalties for the common law offence of blasphemy, when committed under certain conditions, was held by Lord Hardwicke in *De Costa* v. *De Paz* (1) and by the Court of King's Bench in *Richard Carlile's Case* (2), and Lord Eldon in *Attorney-General* v. *Pearson* (3) said that the Toleration Act left the common law as it was and only exempted certain persons from the operation of certain statutes. Such, indeed, is the clear language of the statutes, nor can the fact that persons are singled out for special punishments who deny the Godhead of the Three Persons of the Trinity, the truth of the Christian religion, and the Divine authority of the Holy Scriptures, or who maintain that there be more gods than one, be accepted as showing that the common law offence of blasphemy consists in such denials and assertions and in nothing else. Later Acts have relieved various religious confessions from the burthen of the Blasphemy Act and other statutes, but, except in so far as they deal with charitable trusts for the purposes of such confessions, on which I do not now dwell, they seem to carry the present matter no further. . . . .

My Lords, with all respect for the great names of the lawyers who have used it, the phrase "Christianity is part of the law of England" is really not law; it is rhetoric, as truly so as was Erskine's peroration when prosecuting Williams: "No man can be expected to be faithful to the authority of man, who revolts against the Government of God." One asks what part of our law may Christianity be, and what part of Christianity may it be that is part of our law? Best C.J. once said in *Bird* v. *Holbrook* (4) (a case of injury by setting a spring-gun): "There is no act which Christianity forbids, that the law will not reach:

(1) 2 Swanst. 487, note (a); Amb. 228.   (2) 3 B. & Al. 161.
(3) (1817) 3 Mer. 353, 398, 399.   (4) (1828) 4 Bing. 628, 641.

if it were otherwise, Christianity would not be, as it has always been held to be, part of the law of England"; but this was rhetoric too. Spring-guns, indeed, were got rid of, not by Christianity, but by Act of Parliament. "Thou shalt not steal" is part of our law. "Thou shalt not commit adultery" is part of our law, but another part. "Thou shalt love thy neighbour as thyself" is not part of our law at all. Christianity has tolerated chattel slavery; not so the present law of England. Ours is, and always has been, a Christian State. The English family is built on Christian ideas, and if the national religion is not Christian there is none. English law may well be called a Christian law, but we apply many of its rules and most of its principles, with equal justice and equally good government, in heathen communities, and its sanctions, even in Courts of conscience, are material and not spiritual.

LORD BUCKMASTER:

The Act known as the Blasphemy Act (9 & 10 Will. 3, c. 32) is really an Act directed against apostates from the Christian faith, and that Act again provides certain penalties, cumulative and severe on second conviction, for any person who, having been educated in, or at any time having made profession of, the Christian religion within this realm, shall by writing or advised speaking deny any one of the Persons of the Holy Trinity to be God, or who shall assert that there are more gods than one, or shall deny the Christian religion to be true. This is a disabling statute still unrepealed, imposing penalties so severe that it is said no prosecution has ever been instituted under its provisions. Its terms, therefore, demand the narrowest and most jealous scrutiny. The fact that it has only incidentally been brought under judicial notice may explain the loose and, as I think, erroneous references made to its effect, as for example by Lord Lyndhurst in *Shore* v. *Wilson* (1), where he says that "those persons who by preaching denied the doctrine of the Trinity . . . . are subject to the penalties of the Act," and again by Bramwell B. in *Cowan* v. *Milbourn*. (2) This is not accurate; only those persons who had been educated in, or had at any time made profession of, the Christian religion within the realm could incur the statutory penalties.

Note: Lord Finlay, L.C., agreed with the others that mere denial of the truths of Christianity did not constitute the crime of blasphemy, but dissented from the others who overruled *Briggs* v. *Hartley* (1850) 19 L.J. 416 and *Cowan* v. *Milbourn* (1867) L.R. 2 Ex. 230.

R. v. Gott (1922) 16 Cr. App.R. 87

Court of Criminal Appeal

Gott was convicted for the fourth time on a charge of publishing a blasphemous libel in that he offered for sale certain freethinking periodicals

(1) 9 Cl. & F. 355,397.
(2) L. R. 2 Ex. 230.

and pamphlets in Stratford Broadway. One member of the public had said "You ought to be ashamed of yourself," another "Disgusting, disgusting!" Nothing further untoward occurred. In the course of his trial the Judge, **AVORY, J.**, summed up as follows:

The words 'lead to a breach of the peace' do not mean and do not involve even the idea that there must be evidence of the peace having been broken at the time when the publication actually takes place. The principle is exactly the same as in the case of an ordinary defamatory libel upon an individual . . . the only ground upon which it has been laid down that it may be made the subject of an indictment is that the publication of a defamatory libel upon an individual is calculated to provoke a breach of the peace. You must put it to yourself, supposing you received by post some abominable libel upon yourself, not written anonymously as so many of them are, generally, what is your first instinct? Is not the instinct of every man who is worthy the name of a man—the instinct is to thrash the man or the woman who has written a libel on him? and that is why the law says that it is calculated to provoke a breach of the peace. . . What you have to ask yourselves in this case is whether these words which are published, these matters which are published in these two pamphlets are, in your opinion, indecent and offensive attacks on Christianity or the Scriptures or sacred persons or objects, calculated to outrage the feelings of the general body of the community and so lead, possibly—not inevitably, but so lead, possibly, to a breach of the peace. You must ask yourselves if a person of strong religious feelings had stopped to read this pamphlet whether his instinct might not have been to go up to the man who was selling it and give him a thrashing, or, at all events, to use such language to him that a breach of the peace might be likely to be occasioned, because that would be quite sufficient to satisfy this definition. . .

. . . You must not turn your attention to one passage only but look at the whole of these passages . . . and ask yourselves whether, looked at as a whole, this is anything more than vilification, ridicule, or irreverence of the Christian religion and of the Scriptures. Is it in any sense argument? Is it in any sense within the bounds of decent controversy on religious subjects? Is it anything more than . . . vilification of sacred subjects and contemptuous—contemptuous and insulting?

Gott appealed unsuccessfully to the Court of Criminal Appeal. Lord **TREVITHIN, L.C.J.**, speaking for the Court:

The appellant has been three times before convicted of publishing blasphemous libels, and he had ample knowledge of what he was doing. It does not require a person of strong religious feelings to be outraged by a description of Jesus Christ entering Jerusalem "like a circus clown on the back of two donkeys." There are other passages in the pamphlets equally offensive to anyone in sympathy with the Christian religion, whether he be a strong Christian, or a lukewarm Christian, or merely a person sympathizing with their ideals. Such a person might be provoked to a breach of the peach.

There was no misdirection in the summing up.

Whitehouse v. Lemon; Whitehouse v. Gay News Ltd. [1979] 2 W.L.R. 281

House of Lords

The appellants were the editor and publishers of *Gay News* whose readership consisted largely of homosexuals. In June 1976 *Gay News* contained a poem in which a Roman soldier expresses homosexual love for Christ. Mrs. Whitehouse initiated a private prosecution of the appellants. The issue before the House of Lords was whether the Court of Appeal had been correct in holding that it was not necessary for the Crown to establish any further intention on the part of the defendants beyond an intention to publish material which constituted a blasphemous libel. Lord Diplock and Lord Edmund-Davies were in the minority in believing that the prosecution had to establish an intention "to blaspheme".

LORD DILHORNE:

The only question to be decided in this appeal is what mens rea has to be established to justify conviction of the offence of publishing a blasphemous libel. The choice does not, in my opinion, lie between regarding the offence as one of strict liability or as one involving mens rea, for, as was said by Stephen in 1883 in his *History of the Criminal Law of England,* vol. II, p. 351:

> "It is undoubtedly true that the definition of libel, like the definitions of nearly all other crimes, contains a mental element the existence of which must be found by a jury before a defendant can be convicted, but the important question is, What is that mental element? What is the intention which makes the act of publishing criminal? Is it the mere intention to publish written blame [sic], or is it an intention to produce by such a publication some particular evil effect?"

He said, at p. 353, that he knew of no authority for saying that the presence of any specific intention other than the intent to publish was necessary before Fox's Libel Act 1792. During the course of the proceedings in Parliament on the Bill which became that Act, a number of questions were put to the judges. In their answer to one of them they said (see Stephen's *History of the Criminal Law of England,* vol. II, p. 344):

> "The crime consists in publishing a libel. A criminal intention in the writer is no part of the definition of libel at the common law. 'He who scattereth firebrands, arrows, and death,' which, if not a definition, is a very intelligible description of a libel, is ea ratione criminal; it is not incumbent on the prosecutor to prove his intent, and on his part he shall not be heard to say, 'Am I not in sport?' "

In *Rex* v. *Dean of St. Asaph (Rex* v. *Shipley)* (1783) 21 St.Tr. 847 Erskine had argued that it had to be proved that the Dean had had a seditious intent. That argument was rejected in that case as it was by the judges in their answer to Parliament. Prior to 1792 on a charge of publishing a seditious libel, the only questions left to the jury were (1) did the matter published bear the meaning ascribed to it in the indictment or information? and (2) was it published by the defendant? It was for the judges to rule whether the matter published, bearing the sense ascribed to it, was seditious, that being regarded as a question of law (see *Rex* v. *Dean of St. Asaph*). I do not doubt that the same procedure was followed when the charge was of publishing any other form of criminal libel.

It thus appears that prior to 1792 the specific intent of the accused was not an ingredient of the offence. Why was that? It is, I think, only explicable on the ground that the evil sought to be prevented by treating the publication of a libel as a criminal offence was the dissemination of libels. The mischief lay in the scattering of firebrands in the form of libels, and if what was published was held to be seditious, the person who published it or was responsible for its publication was guilty. It mattered not, if what had been published was seditious, that he had had no seditious intent (see *Rex* v. *Dean of St. Asaph*).

The next question for consideration is, was the definition of a criminal libel altered later, either by Fox's Libel Act 1792 or in the course of the development of the common law, so that, on a charge of publishing a seditious or a blasphemous libel, proof that the defendant had a seditious or blasphemous intent, as the case might be, was essential to establish guilt? . . .

I can see nothing in this Act "to remove doubts respecting the functions of juries" to justify the conclusion that it made a change in the definition of the offence of publishing a criminal libel. It does not mention intent, and if it had been the desire of Parliament to give statutory authority to the argument of Erskine in *Rex* v. *Dean of St. Asaph*, 21 St.Tr. 847 and to reject the opinion of the judges as to the ingredients of the offence, I regard it as inconceivable that the Act would have taken the form it did. Stephen, however (*History of the Criminal Law of England*, vol. II, p. 359), regarded it as "having enlarged the old definition of seditious libel by the addition of a reference to the specific intention of the libeller—to the purpose for which he wrote . . ." and said that the Act assumed that the specific intentions of the defendant were material. I must confess my inability to find in the Act any basis for either conclusion. Professor Holdsworth in his *History of English Law*, 2nd ed. (1937) (vol. VIII, p. 342) recognised that the view that "the crime was, not so much the intentional publication of matter bearing the seditious or defamatory meaning . . . as its publication with a seditious or malicious intent" began to appear in the 18th century. He did not attribute this to Fox's Libel Act but to the practice of filling indictments "with averments of every sort of bad intention on the part of the defendant," averments which in Stephen's opinion were surplusage.

The conclusion to which I have come is that if any change in the definition of the offence occurred after 1792, it did not result from Fox's Libel Act.

Stephen also asserted that since that Act the law had ever since been administered upon the supposition that the specific intentions of the defendant were material (*History of the Criminal Law of England*, vol. II, p. 359). My examination of the cases since 1792 leads me to think that that is not so and Professor Holdsworth said that the view that the publication had to be with a seditious or malicious intent was "not . . . finally got rid of till the 19th century" (vol. VIII, p. 342). I infer from what he said that he thought that that view was erroneous.

It was not until 1967 by the Criminal Justice Act, section 8, that it was enacted that a court or jury should not be bound in law to infer that an accused intended or foresaw a result of his actions by reason only of its being a natural and probable result of those actions but that whether he intended or foresaw that result had to be decided by reference to all the evidence drawing such inferences from the evidence as appeared proper. If the conclusion was reached that a particular publication was blasphemous and it was proved that the defendant had published it, it could be presumed under the old law that he had done so with intent to blaspheme. In many cases it may be that the existence of such an intent was undeniable but the fact that a man might be presumed to have such an intent or had that intent does not in my opinion lead to the conclusion that the existence of such an intent was an essential element in the crime, though it may account for a reference being made in some cases in the course of a summing up to the accused's intent: see, for instance, *The Three Trials of William Hone* published by William Hone in 1818; *Rex v. Carlile (Richard)* (1819) 1 St.Tr.N.S. 1387; *Reg v. Moxon* (1841) 4 St.Tr.N.S. 693; *Reg v. Holyoake* (1842) 4 St.Tr.N.S. 1381.

In this appeal we are not, as I see it, concerned with how such an intent is to be established or its existence rebutted but whether it is an element in the offence. So with great respect to my noble and learned friend, Lord Diplock, I do not think that the terms of the Criminal Evidence Act 1898 and of section 8 of the Criminal Justice Act 1967 have any relevance to the question to be decided. If in a prosecution for the publication of a blasphemous libel, the accused's intent to blaspheme has to be proved, the Act of 1898 enables him to give evidence that he had no such intent and the Act of 1967 gives guidance as to the proof of such an intent.

What I regard as of great significance is that in none of what I regard as the leading cases on the publication of a blasphemous libel is there to be found any direction to the jury telling them that it had to be proved that the defendant intended to blaspheme, and I have not found in any decided case any criticism of the omission to do so . . .

[In 1843] . . . Parliament changed the law, not by enacting that proof of such an intent was necessary for a conviction but, by section 7 of Lord Campbell's Act 1843, providing that, on a trial for the publication of a libel where the publication was by the act of a person other than the defendant but with his authority, it was competent for the defendant to prove that the publication was made without his authority, consent or knowledge, and that the publication did not arise from want of care or caution on his part. As Stephen observes (*History of the Criminal Law of England,* vol. II, pp. 361-362) by virtue of this Act the "negligent publication of a libel by a bookseller who is ignorant of its contents" suffices to render him guilty and the fact that he may be found guilty if negligent is wholly inconsistent with the existence of any necessity to show that he intended to blaspheme. Again it may be noted that the intention of the person actually responsible for the publication was not relevant. If proof of such an intent was and is necessary, this Act did not serve any useful purpose.

I now come to the first of the two cases which I regard as the leading cases in this field. Prior to *Reg. v. Bradlaugh* (1883) 15 Cox C.C. 217 there had been very considerable controversy about what constituted blasphemy. In the 18th century and before, it appears to have been thought that any attack or criticism, no matter how reasonably expressed, on the fundamental principles of the Christian religion and any discussion hostile to the inspiration and perfect purity of the Scriptures was against the law. That was Stephen's view (*History of the Criminal Law of England,* vol. II, pp. 473 et seq.) but in this case it was rejected by Lord Coleridge C.J., who told the jury that he thought the law had been accurately stated in *Starkie's Slander and Libel,* 4th ed., p. 599, in the following terms, at p. 226:

" 'A wilful intention to pervert, insult, and mislead others, by means of licentious and contumelious abuse offered to sacred subjects, or by wilful misrepresentations or artful sophistry, calculated to mislead the ignorant and unwary, is the criterion and test of guilt. A malicious and mischievous intention, or what is equivalent to such an intention, in law, as well as morals,—a state of apathy and indifference to the interests of society,—is the broad boundary between right and wrong.' "

At first sight the citation of this passage by Lord Coleridge C.J. might appear to give support to the view that such an intent on the part of the accused had to be proved but it is to be noted that Lord Coleridge C.J. began his summing up by telling the jury that there were two questions to be considered, first, whether the publications in question were blasphemous libels, and, secondly, whether, assuming them to be so, Mr. Bradlaugh was guilty of publishing them. He did not at any time tell the jury that they had to consider Mr. Bradlaugh's intent, an astonishing omission if he regarded it necessary to prove that he had a blasphemous intent, and the passage he cited from *Starkie's Slander and Libel,* 4th ed., p. 599, was cited by him as providing the test for determining whether or not the publication itself was blasphemous.

This, to my mind, is shown beyond doubt by the fact that, after citing *Starkie,* he said, at p. 226:

"That I apprehend to be a correct statement of the law, and if you think the broad boundary between right and wrong that is laid down in the passage, has been overpast in the articles which are the subject matter of this indictment, then it will be your duty to answer the first question . . . against the defendant"

and by his saying at the end of his summing up, at pp. 230-231:

"It is a question, first of all, whether these things are not in any point of view blasphemous libels, whether they are not calculated and intended to insult the feelings and the deepest religious convictions of the great majority of the persons amongst whom we live; and if so they are not to be tolerated any more than any other nuisance is tolerated. We must not do things that are outrages to the general feeling of proprietry among the persons amongst whom we live. That is the first thing. Then the second thing is: Is Mr. Bradlaugh made out to have joined in the publication of these?"

"To say that the crime lies in the manner and not in the matter appears to me an attempt to evade and explain away a law which has no doubt ceased to be in harmony with the temper of the times" was Stephen's view (*History of the Criminal Law of England,* vol. II, p. 475) but since 1883 it has been accepted that it is the manner in which they are expressed that may constitute views expressed in a publication a blasphemous libel and this passage from *Starkie's Slander and Libel,* 4th ed., p. 599, has been relied on as providing the test for determining whether the publication exceeds that which is permissible. It is the intention revealed by the publication that may lead to its being held to be blasphemous. There was nothing in Lord Coleridge C.J.'s summing up to support the view that there was a third question for the jury to consider, namely the intent of the accused.

This case was followed by *Reg.* v. *Ramsay and Foote,* 48 L.T. 733, a case greatly relied on by the appellants, a case of great importance and also tried by Lord Coleridge C.J. Again he told the jury that there were two questions for them to consider:

> "First, are these publications in themselves blasphemous libels? Secondly, if they are so, is the publication of them traced home to the defendants so that you can find them guilty?" (p. 734.)

... While it may be that the development of the law as to seditious libel has now taken a different course, in *Rex* v. *Aldred* (1909) 22 Cox C.C. 1 in the course of his summing up on a charge of publishing a seditious libel, Coleridge J. told the jury that the accused could not plead the innocence of his motive as a defence to the charge, telling them, at p. 3, that:

> "The test is not either the truth of the language or the innocence of the motive with which he published it, but the test is this: was the language used calculated, or was it not, to promote public disorder or physical force or violence in a matter of state?"

and if the language was calculated to promote public disorder,

> "... then, whatever his motives, whatever his intentions, there would be evidence on which a jury might, on which I think a jury ought, and on which a jury would decide that he was guilty of a seditious publication ..." (p. 4.)

This direction was not followed in *Rex* v. *Caunt* (unreported), November 17, 1947, a seditious libel case tried in 1947. The transcript of that case shows that counsel agreed that a man published a seditious libel if he did so with a seditious intent and Birkett J. so directed the jury.

It is not necessary in this appeal to decide whether Birkett J.'s direction was right or unduly favourable to the accused and whether *Rex* v. *Aldred,* 22 Cox C.C. 1 was rightly decided for we are only concerned with blasphemous libel.

The last case to which I need refer is *Rex* v. *Gott,* reported in "The Freethinker" of January 8, 1922. Avory J. in his summing up cited the passage I have cited from the end of Lord Coleridge C.J.'s summing up in *Reg.* v. *Bradlaugh,* 15 Cox C.C. 217. He did not tell the jury that it was necessary to prove that the defendant had a blasphemous intent. He said nothing about the accused's intent. The case went to appeal but his omission to do so was not a ground of appeal or the subject of adverse comment by the Court of Criminal Appeal.

In the light of the authorities to which I have referred and for the reasons I have stated, I am unable to reach the conclusion that the ingredients of the offence of publishing a blasphemous libel have changed since 1792. Indeed, it would, I think, be surprising if they had. If it be accepted, as I think it must, that that which it is sought to prevent is the publication of blasphemous libels, the harm is done by their intentional publication, whether or not the publisher intended to blaspheme. To hold that it must be proved that he had that intent appears to me to be going some way to making the accused judge in his own cause. If Mr. Lemon had testified that he did not regard the poem and drawing as blasphemous, that he had no intention to blaspheme, and, it might be, that his intention was to promote the love and affection of some homosexuals of Our Lord, the jury properly directed would surely have been told that unless satisfied beyond reasonable doubt that he intended to blaspheme they should acquit, no matter how blasphemous they thought the publication. Whether or not they would have done so on such evidence is a matter of speculation on which views may differ.

The question we have to decide is a pure question of law and my conclusions thereon do not, I hope, evince any distrust of juries. The question here is what is the proper direction to give to them, not how they might act on such a direction; and distrust, which I do not have, of the way a jury might act, does not enter into it.

My Lords, for the reasons I have stated in my opinion the question certified should be answered in the affirmative. Guilt of the offence of publishing a blasphemous libel does not depend on the accused having an intent to blaspheme but on proof that the publication was intentional (or, in the case of a bookseller, negligent (Lord Campbell's Act 1843)) and that the matter published was blasphemous.

LORD EDMUND DAVIES:

By far the principal contest during the hearing of this appeal was that which gave rise to the certified question. The actus reus of the offence charged was said to be that the published poem and illustration vilified Christ, and in the course of a summing up which, apart from its treatment of the contested matter of intent, has rightly been regarded as a model of its kind, the learned judge correctly directed the jury on the matter of obscenity and vilification. By their verdict they found that the publication, objectively considered, was in fact blasphemous. It followed that, as Roskill L.J. emphasised [1979] Q.B. 10, 14, any quashing of the convictions

". . . would not in any way involve overturning the conclusions implicit in the jury's verdict of guilty that the allegedly offending poem and drawing was obscene in the ordinary meaning of that word, or that it 'vilified Christ in His life and crucifixion' in the ordinary meaning of that phrase."

But was that enough to justify the verdicts of guilty? The Court of Appeal though it was, despite the strong contrary submission of defendants' counsel. Now, although the certified question of law related solely to mens rea, it cannot be answered without regard being had to the actus reus of blasphemous libel. Nor should one over look the fact that seditious libel, blasphemous libel, obscene libel and defamatory libel all had their common origin in the Star Chamber, which (in the words of J. R. Spencer [1977] Crim. L.R. 383),

". . . regarded with the deepest suspicion the printed word in general, and anything which looked like criticism of the established institutions of Church or State in particular."

It was on the abolition of the Star Chamber in 1641 that the Court of King's Bench inherited its criminal jurisdiction, and shortly after the Restoration it tried the dramatist Sir Charles Sedley for indecency and blasphemy (*Rex* v. *Sedley* (1663) 17 St.Tr. 155; *Pepys' Diary*, (July 1, 1663). For centuries thereafter

". . . a published attach on a high state official . . . might be prosecuted as either a seditious or a defamatory libel, and an attack on the Church or its doctrine might be prosecuted as either a blasphemous or a seditious libel. What the attack in question was called seems to have depended largely on the taste in vituperative epithet of the man who drafted the indictment or information. Thus in one case a man was prosecuted for seditious rather than blasphemous libel when he published a book contrary to the teaching of the Church of England: *Rex* v. *Keach* (1665) 6 St.Tr. 701."

As to the actus reus, at first all open expressions of a disbelief in Christianity were punishable, the bench repeatedly laying down the plain principle that the public importance of the Christian religion was so great that no one was to be allowed to deny its truth; just as in *Reg.* v. *Bedford* (early 18th century, noted in *Bacon's Abridgement,* 7th ed. (1832), vol. 5, p. 200) a man was convicted of the kindred offence of seditious libel simply for discussing, civilly and gravely and "without any reflection whatever upon any part of the then existing government," the respective advantages of hereditary and elective monarchies. As late as 1841 the Commissioners on Criminal Law reported that "The law distinctly forbids *all* denial of the Christian religion," but nevertheless added that in actual practice ". . . the course has been to withhold the application of the penal law unless insulting language is used." These last words mark the second stage in the development of the actus reus of blasphemy, and echo the ruling of Lord Denman C.J. a year earlier in *Reg.* v. *Hetherington,* 4 St.Tr.N.S. 563, 590 that criminality lies ". . . not altogether [on] a matter of opinion, but that it must be, in a great degree, a question as to the tone, and style, and spirit, . . ."

My Lords, during the long years when the actus reus of blasphemy was constituted by the mere denial (however decently expressed) of the basic tenets of Christianity or, later, the couching of that denial in scurrilous language, there was no necessity to explore the intention of the accused, for his words were regarded as revealing in themselves what that intention was. And that was so notwithstanding the fact that indictments for blasphemy habitually contained assertions regarding the defendant's intention. Let me illustrate. One finds in the 7th edition of *Archbold's Pleading and Evidence* (1838), p. 501, an indictment charging that the accused

> ". . . wickedly and profanely devising and intending to bring the Holy Scriptures and the Christian religion into disbelief and contempt among the people of this kingdom . . . unlawfully and wickedly did compose, print, and publish . . . a certain scandalous, impious, blasphemous, and profane libel . . ."

The appended note gives a cross-reference to an indictment for seditious libel, and, notwithstanding an allegation in the latter of "intending to stir up and excite discontents and seditions amongst His Majesty's subjects," the author observed:

> "Whether the defendant really intended, by his publication, to alienate the affections of the people from the Government is . . . immaterial; if the publication be calculated to have that effect, it is a seditious libel. *Rex* v. *Burdett* (1820) 4 B. & Ald. 95; *Rex* v. *Harvey and Chapman* (1823) 2 B. & C. 257."

Such an assertion in such a book affords a good illustration of the laxity of language employed, certainly up to Lord Campbell's Libel Act of 1843. And it is worthwhile considering at some little length the two cases cited in support of the author's proposition that seditious libel was regarded, in effect, as a crime of strict liability, in order to determine whether in reality they did anything of the sort. In my judgment, they were, if anything, authorities for the directly contrary proposition. Thus, in *Rex* v. *Burdett,* 4 B. & Ald. 95 Best J. directed the jury regarding an allegedly seditious libel

"... that the question whether it was published with the intention alleged in the information, was peculiarly for their consideration; but I added, that the intention was to be collected from the paper itself, unless the import of the paper were explained by the mode of publication, or any other circumstances. I added that if it appeared that the contents of the paper were likely to excite sedition and disaffection, the defendant must be presumed to intend that which his act was likely to produce. I told them further, that if they should be of opinion that such was the intention of the defendant, then it was my duty to declare that, in my opinion, such a paper, published with such an intent, was a libel; leaving it, however, to them ... to find whether it was a libel or not."

Now that direction (later upheld by a full court of four judges on a motion for a new trial) in no sense brushed aside as irrelevant the intention of the accused publisher. On the contrary, it stressed the importance of his intention, while at the same time instructing the jury, in effect, that (as Lord Ellenborough C.J. had recently said in *Rex* v. *Dixon* (1814) 3 M. & S. 11, 15), it is a

"universal principle, that when a man is charged with doing an act, of which the probable consequence may be highly injurious, the intention is an inference of law resulting from doing the act. . . ."

A similar comment can properly be made regarding the second case cited by *Archbold, Rex* v. *Harvey and Chapman,* 2 B. & C. 257, where the proprietor, printer and publisher of a newspaper were charged in relation to a statement that they had good authority for asserting that King George IV laboured under mental infirmity. The defendants admitted that it was false to say that they had good authority for making the assertion, but urged that they nevertheless believed it to be true, in the light of widely prevalent rumours. Having directed the jury that, in his opinion, the publication was a libel calculated to vilify His Majesty, Abbott C.J. added, at p. 258 (as Fox's Libel Act 1792 required him to do): "But you have a right to exercise your own judgment upon the publication, and I invite you so to do." After a retirement, the jury returned and asked for the Lord Chief Justice's opinion whether or not it was necessary that there should be a malicious intention to constitute a libel. They were thereupon told, at p. 259:

"The man who publishes slanderous matter, in its nature calculated to defame and vilify another, must be presumed to have intended to do that which the publication is calculated to bring about, *unless he can show the contrary;* and it is for him to show the contrary."

Subsequently, on the hearing of an unsuccessful motion for a new trial on the ground of misdirection, Bayley and Best JJ., at pp. 261, 268 made similar observations in upholding Abbott C.J.'s direction.

... Between *Reg.* v. *Ramsay and Foote,* 15 Cox C.C. 231 and *Rex* v. *Gott* (1922, unreported save briefly in 16 Cr.App.R. 87) there were very few blasphemy prosecutions, and none thereafter until the present trial. Of the intervening cases, the direction of Phillimore J. in *Rex* v. *Boulter,* 72 J.P. 188 is, despite the misleadingly emphatic headnote, equivocal as to the necessity for intention, and the same is true of Avory J.'s direction in *Rex* v. *Gott* itself ("The Freethinker," January 8, 1922, p. 28). But it was the latter decision which sparked off Professor Kenny's survey of the relevant law, which led him to the conclusion that

> ". . . in criminal proceedings, guilt can only arise where the offensive matter was published with full knowledge of its contents and with readiness to offend. 'Wilful intention,' as Professor Starkie said, 'is the criterion and test of guilt' " (1922) 1 C.L.J. 127, 140.

My Lords, we have seen that sedition and blasphemy were in origin twin types of criminal libel, the latter consisting in its earliest stage as *any* attack upon the Christian Church, as part of the state, and Lord Hale C.J. declaring in *Taylor's case* (1676) 1 Vent. 293 that "Christianity is parcel of the laws of England." I understood the respondents to this appeal to accept that, in relation to *sedition,* the intention of the defendant is an essential ingredient, and such cases as *Reg.* v. *Burns* (1886) 16 Cox C.C. 355, 360 and *Rex* v. *Caunt* (unreported) proceeding upon that basis. It would be inexplicable were intention relevant in the one case but not in the other. *Reg.* v. *Burns* is also important as illustrating the lessening respect paid, as the 19th century progressed, to the presumption as to intention, Cave J. saying, at p. 364:

> "In order to make out the offence of speaking seditious words there must be a criminal intent upon the part of the accused, they must be words spoken with a seditious intent; and, although it is a good working rule, to say that a man must be taken to intend the natural consequences of his acts, and it is very proper to ask a jury to infer, if there is nothing to show the contrary, that he did intend the natural consequences of his acts, yet, if it is shown from other circumstances that he did not actually intend them, I do not see how you can ask a jury to act upon what has then become a legal fiction."

My Lords, allow me to summarise. This appeal raises the questions whether it is sufficient for conviction that the defendants intended to *publish* the blasphemous words for which they were indicted, as the learned trial judge held. Or was it necessary that they should have also known of their offensive character and have intended to offend, alternatively that they published with reckless indifference to the consequences of publication? Different answers to these questions were called for at different stages in the evolution of the law of blasphemy. In the earliest stage it was clearly a crime of strict liability and consisted merely of any attack upon the Christian Church and its tenets. In the second stage the original harshness of the law was ameliorated, and the attack was not punishable unless expressed in intemperate or scurrilous language. In the third stage, opinions were mixed. Some judges held that the subjective intention of author or publisher was irrelevant, others that it was of the greatest materiality. . . .

. . . [T]o treat as irrelevant the state of mind of a person charged with blasphemy would be to take a backward step in the evolution of a humane code. Unfortunately, despite the exemplary care taken by the learned trial judge, lacking as he did the prolonged and patient probing into the law of which this House has had the benefit, I am afraid that that is what has happened in this case. Accordingly, despite my strong feelings of revulsion over this deplorable publication, I find myself most reluctantly compelled to answer the certified question in the negative and to hold that these appeals against conviction should be allowed.

For the sake of completeness, and so as to show that I have not overlooked the point, I should add that I am at one with the Court of Appeal in upholding as "faultless" the learned judge's outright rejection of a further submission for some of the appellants that, in order to justify a conviction for blasphemous libel, the publication, when objectively considered, must tend to lead to a breach of the peace.

LORD RUSSELL OF KILLOWEN:

My Lords, it must be made at the outset absolutely clear that it is accepted by the appellants that the publication of a blasphemous libel is still a criminal offence; it is no part of your Lordships' function in this case to hold the contrary. Moreover, if the only ingredient of the offence is the knowing publication of matter which will in fact shock and outrage the feelings of ordinary Christians it must equally be made clear that, as the jury found, this publication was a blasphemous libel. It is not for your Lordships to agree or disagree with that finding: though speaking for myself as an ordinary Christian, I found the publication quite appallingly shocking and outrageous.

There is in this case one question only: whether an intention in the publisher to shock and outrage, or an indifference to a recognised possibility that it will do so, is a necessary ingredient of the offence. If it is such an ingredient, then the refusal of the trial judge to allow Mr. Lemon to give evidence of his subjective intention was an error in law: and however much one may doubt, as I do, that Mr. Lemon would have been able to persuade a jury that he did not think that the publication was likely to shock and outrage, yet if the direction was thus erroneous in law I would not consider that the conviction should be supported under the proviso [to section 2 (1) of the Criminal Appeal Act 1968].

It should be noted that the only evidence which could be said to be erroneously excluded was that of Mr. Lemon's state of mind. Of this only he could speak. "Expert" evidence would surely have been irrelevant, on any footing. I do not doubt that he had a *motive* in making this publication which seemed to him to justify it; supposedly (though I am guessing) that those of his usual readers who were active or passive homosexuals should not feel that they were for that reason excluded from the fellowship of Christianity. But whether intention is or is not an ingredient of the offence, motive is certainly not a defence.

So I return to the question of intent. The authorities embrace an abundance of apparently contradictory or ambivalent comments. There is no authority in your Lordships' House on the point. The question is open for decision. I do not, with all respect to the speech of my noble and learned friend Lord Diplock, consider that the question is whether this is an offence of strict liability. It is necessary that the editor or publisher should be aware of that which he publishes. Indeed that was the function of Lord Campbell's Act (1843), which assumed the law to be that an intention in the accused to blaspheme was not an ingredient of the offence, since it removed by statute a vicarious liability for an act of publication done by another without authority.

Why then should this House, faced with a deliberate publication of that which a jury with every justification has held to be a blasphemous libel, consider that it should be for the prosecution to prove, presumably beyond reasonable doubt, that the accused recognised and intended it to be such or regarded it as immaterial whether it was? I see no ground for that. It does not to my mind make sense: and I consider that sense should retain a function in our criminal law. The reason why the law considers that the publication of a blasphemous libel is an offence is that the law considers that such publication should not take place. And if it takes place, and the publication is deliberate, I see no justification for holding that there is no offence when the publisher is incapable for some reason particular to himself of agreeing with a jury on the true nature of the publication.

Accordingly I would answer the certified question of law in the affirmative and dismiss the appeal, and order the respondent's costs to be paid out of public funds.

LORD SCARMAN: . . . Mr Lords, I do not subscribe to the view that the common law offence of blasphemous libel serves no useful purpose in the modern law. On the contrary, I think that there is a case for legislation extending it to protect the religious beliefs and feelings of non-Christians. The offence belongs to a group of criminal offences designed to safeguard the internal tranquility of the kingdom. In an increasingly plural society such as that of modern Britain it is necessary not only to respect the differing religious beliefs, feelings and practices of all but also to protect them from scurrility, vilification, ridicule and contempt. Professor Kenny in his brilliant article on "The Evolution of the Law of Blasphemy" (1922) 1 C.L.J. 127 gives two quotations which are very relevant to British society today. When the Home Secretary (Mr. Shortt) was pressed to remit the sentence on Gott after the dismissal of his appeal (*Rex* v. *Gott,* 16 Cr.App.R. 87), he wrote:

> " 'The common law does not interfere with the free expression of bona fide opinion. But it prohibits, and renders punishable as a misdemeanour, the use of coarse and scurrilous ridicule on subjects which are sacred to most people in this country. Mr. Shortt could not support any proposal for an alteration of the common law which would permit such outrages on the feelings of others as those of which Gott was found to be guilty' " ((1922) 1 C.L.J. 127).

When nearly a century earlier Lord Macaulay protested in Parliament against the way the blasphemy laws were then administered, he added (*Speeches,* p. 116): "If I were a judge in India, I should have no scruple about punishing a Christian who should pollute a mosque" (1922) C.L.J. 127, 135. When Macaulay became a legislator in India, he saw to it that the law protected the religious feelings of all. In those days India was a plural society: today the United Kingdom is also.

I have permitted myself these general observations at the outset of my opinion because, my Lords, they determine my approach to this appeal. I will not lend my voice to a view of the law relating to blasphemous libel which would render it a dead letter, or diminish its efficacy to protect religious feeling from outrage and insult. My criticism of the common law offence of blasphemy is not that it exists but that it is not sufficiently comprehensive. It is shackled by the chains of history.

While in my judgment it is not open to your Lordships' House, even under the Lord Chancellor's policy announcement of July 26, 1966 (H.L. Debates, July 26, 1966, col. 677) [Practice Statement (Judicial Precedent) [1966] 1 W.L.R. 1234], to extend the law beyond the limits recognised by the House in *Bowman* v. *Secular Society Ltd.* [1917] A.C. 406, or to make by judicial decision the comprehensive reform of the law which I believe to be beneficial, this appeal does offer your Lordships the opportunity of stating the existing law in a form conducive to the social conditions of the late 20th century rather than to those of the 17th, 18th, or even the 19th century. This is, my Lords, no mere opportunity: it is a duty. As Lord Sumner said in his historic speech in *Bowman's* case, at pp. 446-467:

> "The words, as well as the acts, which tend to endanger society differ from time to time in proportion as society is stable or insecure in fact, or is believed by its reasonable members to be open to assault. In the present day meetings or processions are held lawful which 150 years ago would have been deemed seditious, and this is not because the law is weaker or has changed, but because, the times having changed, society is stronger than before. In the present day reasonable men do not apprehend the dissolution or the downfall of society because religion is publicly assailed by methods not scandalous. Whether it is possible that in the future irreligious attacks, designed to undermine fundamental institutions of our society, may come to be criminal in themselves, as constituting a public danger, is a matter that does not arise. The fact that opinion grounded on experience has moved one way does not in law preclude the possibility of its moving on fresh experience in the other; nor does it bind succeeding generations, when conditions have again changed. After all, the question whether a given opinion is a danger to society is a question of the times, and is a question of fact. I desire to say nothing that would limit the right of society to protect itself by process of law from the dangers of the moment, whatever right may be, but only to say that, experience having proved dangers once thought real to be now negligible, and dangers once very possibly imminent to have now passed away, there is nothing in the general rules as to blasphemy and irreligion, as known to the law, which prevents us from varying their application to the particular circumstances of our time in accordance with that experience."

The point of law certified by the Court of Appeal as of general public importance upon which the House gave leave to appeal is in these terms:

> 'Was the learned trial judge correct (as the Court of Appeal held) first in ruling and then in directing the jury that in order to secure the conviction of the appellants for publishing a blasphemous libel: (1) it was sufficient if the jury took the view that the publication complained of vilified Christ in His life and crucifixion: and (2) it was not necessary for the Crown to establish any further intention on the part of the appellants beyond an intention to publish that which in the jury's view was a blasphemous libel?''

The appellants' case is that it was necessary for the Crown to establish a further specific intention, and their counsel formulated the intention as follows:

> '. . . the intention to attack the Christian religion so violently or scurrilously as to insult the adherents of the Christian religion to such an extent that a breach of the peace is likely.'

The Crown led no evidence to prove any intention other than the intention to publish the words complained of: and the judge directed the jury in effect that any such evidence would be irrelevant. If, therefore, the appellants are correct in law that an intention beyond that of publication must be proved, it matters not whether their counsel have accurately formulated the specific intention required. Their convictions must be quashed.

. . . Upon appeal, the Court of Appeal upheld the convictions.
. . . The Court of appeal reached the conclusion that for a defendant to be guilty of publishing a blasphemous libel it was not necessary for the Crown to prove an intent other than an intent to publish the words of which complaint was made. It was enough, the court held, to prove that the defendant intended to publish that which offended.

In your Lordships' House it was recognised that no challenge could effectually be made against the finding of the jury that the poem and illustration were blasphemous. Equally it has to be recognised that no intention to insult or outrage has been established by the modern criteria of English law. No doubt because the judge ruled that any intention other than an intention to publish was irrelevant, Mr. Lemon did not give evidence. Had he given evidence, I have little doubt that he would have said, and truly said, that he had no intention to shock Christian believers but that he published the poem not to offend Christians but to comfort practising homosexuals by encouraging them to feel that there was room for them in the Christian religion. I am prepared to assume the honesty and sincerity of his motives.

The "actus reus" of the offence of blasphemy consists of the publication of words spoken or written. In the 17th century words challenging or questioning the doctrines of the established church were regarded as blasphemy: for ". . . Christianity is parcel of the laws of England; and therefore to reproach the Christian religion, is to speak in subversion of the law," as Sir Mathew Hale put it in *Taylor's case,* 1 Vent. 293. His view was accepted in 1729 in *Rex* v. *Woolston* (Fitzg. 64, 66), though Raymond C.J. did add: "we do not meddle with any differences of opinion—. . . we interpose only when the very root of Christianity itself is struck at."

Nevertheless in almost all the reported cases (including *Taylor's case* and *Rex* v. *Woolston*) the words complained of were scurrilous, insulting, or offensive: indeed Ventris reports Hale as saying expressly that "contumelious reproaches of the established religion are punishable here." And in one famous case, that of *Rex* v. *Dean of St. Asaph,* 21 St.Tr. 847, in which there was no element of scurrility, the defendant was ultimately acquitted.

The watershed between the old and the modern law comes with the cases of *Reg.* v. *Hetherington,* 4 St.Tr.N.S. 563 and *Reg.* v. *Ramsay and Foote,* 15 Cox C.C. 231. Lord Denman C.J.'s summing up in *Reg.* v. *Hetherington* contains the remarkable passage quoted by the Court of Appeal in this case. Its importance is such that I make no apology for quoting it again (pp. 590-591):

> "Now, gentlemen, upon the question whether it is blasphemous or not I have this general observation to make, which I have often heard from Lord Tenterden in cases of this description, namely, that the question is not altogether a matter of opinion, but that it must be, in a great degree, a question as to the tone, and style, and spirit, in which such inquiries are conducted. Because, a difference of opinion may subsist, not only as between different sects of Christians, but also with regard to the great doctrines of Christianity itself; and I have heard that great judge declare,

that even discussions upon that subject may be by no means a matter of criminal prosecution, but, if they be carried on in a sober and temperate and decent style, even those discussions may be tolerated, and may take place without criminality attaching to them; but that, if the tone and spirit is that of offence, and insult, and ridicule, which leaves the judgment really not free to act, and, therefore, cannot be truly called an appeal to the judgment, but an appeal to the wild and improper feelings of the human mind, more particularly in the younger part of the community, in that case the jury will hardly feel it possible to say that such opinions, so expressed, do not deserve the character which is affixed to them in this indictment. With that general observation, I leave the question of libel to you. Is it, or is it not, a blasphemous libel which the defendant appears to have published in his shop?"

In *Reg.* v. *Ramsay and Foote,* 15 Cox C.C. 231, Lord Coleridge C.J. finally dispelled any further possibility of a mere denial of the truth of the Christian religion being treated as a blasphemous libel. The "attack" on Christianity or the Scriptures must be, he directed the jury, "calculated to outrage the feelings of the general body of the community."

Since *Reg.* v. *Ramsay and Foote,* the modern law has been settled and in 1917 it received the accolade of this House's approval. "What the law censures or resists is not the mere expression of anti-Christian opinion" said Lord Sumner in *Bowman* v. *Secular Society Ltd.* [1917] A.C. 406, 460. The words must constitute, as it is put by *Odgers, Libel and Slander,* 6th ed. (1929), p. 404, an interference with our religious feelings, creating a sense of insult and outrage "by wanton and unnecessary profanity."

This is an appropriate moment to mention two points made on behalf of the appellants, albeit in the context of the intention to be proved. It was said that to constitute a blasphemous libel the words must contain an *attack* (emphasis supplied) upon religion and must tend to provoke a breach of the peace, and that the accused must so intend. The plausibility of the first point drives from the undoubted fact that, as a matter of history, most of the reported cases are of attacks upon the doctrines, practice, or beliefs, of the Christian religion. Since *Reg.* v. *Hetherington,* 4 St.Tr.N.S. 563 it has been clear, however, that the attack is irrelevant: what does matter is the manner in which "the feelings of the general body of the community" have been treated. If the words are an outrage upon such feelings, the opinion or argument they are used to advance or destroy is of no moment. In the present case, had the argument for acceptance and welcome of homosexuals within the loving fold of the Christian faith been advanced "in a sober and temperate . . . style" (*Reg.* v. *Hetherington,* at p. 590), there could have been no criminal offence committed. But the jury (with every justification) rejected this view of the poem and drawing.

The trial judge and the Court of Appeal effectually dealt with the second point. I would only add that it is a jejune exercise to speculate whether an outraged Christian would feel provoked by the words and illustration in this case to commit a breach of peace. I hope, and happen to believe, that most, true to their Christian principles, would not allow themselves to be so provoked. The true test is whether the words are calculated to outrage and insult the Christian's religious feelings: and in the modern law the phrase "a tendency to cause a breach of peace" is really a reference to that test. The use of the phrase is no more than a minor contribution to the discussion of the subject.

It does remind us that we are in the field where the law seeks to safeguard public order and tranquillity.

What, then, is the "mens rea" required by law to constitute the crime? No one has suggested that blasphemy is a crime of strict liability. The issue is as to the nature of the intention which has to be proved. As Eveleigh L.J. is reported to have put it in argument in this case [1979] Q.B. 10, 16:

> "must the defendants have had an intention to offend in the manner complained of, or is it enough that he or they intended to publish that which offends?"

Bowman v. *Secular Society Ltd.* [1917] A.C. 406 throws no light upon the point. The history of the law is obscure and confused. The point is, therefore, open for your Lordships' decision as a matter of principle. And in deciding the point your Lordships are not saying what the law was in the past or ought to be in the future but what is required of it in the conditions of today's society. As Lord Sumner said in *Bowman* v. *Secular Society Ltd.,* at p. 467:

> "The fact that opinion grounded on experience has moved one way does not in law preclude the possibility of its moving on fresh experience in the other; nor does it bind succeeding generations, when conditions have again changed."

The history of the law affords little guidance for a number of reasons. First, the nature of an indictment was, until the reforms in criminal procedure of the last 100 years, more an exercise in an advocate's skill in vituperation than a temperate formulation of the legal ingredients of the offence charged. Secondly, it was not until the enactment of the Criminal Evidence Act 1898 that an accused could give evidence in his own behalf. He was not, therefore, always heard in his own defence: and his intention had to be gathered from the words he had used. (One may mention, in passing, that persons accused of blasphemy very often defended themselves and so enabled the jury to form a view as to their intention. Richard Carlile at his trial read to the jury the whole of Paine's *Age of Reason: Rex* v. *Carlile (Richard)* 1 St.Tr.N.S. 1387.) Thirdly, it was not until the enactment of section 8 of the Criminal Justice Act 1967 that courts finally put away the notion that a man must be presumed to have intended the natural consequences of his acts.

The combined influence of these three factors was to obscure the distinction between the meaning and effect of the words and the intention of the accused. The words, as interpreted and understood—by the judge before Fox's Libel Act 1792 and by the jury after that Act—were the best, perhaps the only, indication of the accused's intention. And the high rhetoric to be found in the indictment charging the accused with devising and intending ("machinans et intendens," in the old cases) all manner of wickedness and evil against the Church and State was not traversable at trial. Indeed the more outrageous the rhetoric of the indictment the more likely I suspect it was that the crime being charged was one of "strict liability." Certainly poor Taylor in his case (*Taylor's Case,* 1 vent. 293) got nowhere with the defence that he did not mean the words in the sense "they ordinarily bear."

My Lords, I agree with the historical analysis of the case law to be found in the judgement of the Court of Appeal and in the speech of my noble and learned friend, Viscount Dilhorne. Lord Denman C.J. stated the law correctly as it was in his time when in *Reg.* v. *Hetherington,* 4 St.Tr.N.S. 563, 593 he told the jury that the only question for them to decide was a matter of fact and of opinion: "Aye or no, is this in your opinion a blasphemous publication, and has the defendant . . . issued it knowingly and wilfully?" In context his adverb "wilfully" meant no more than "deliberately." As Holt commented in his work on *The Law of Libel,* 2nd ed., p. 47, "Malice, in legal understanding, implies no more than wilfulness" and the first inquiry of a court is to see if there is present the mark of a voluntary act. He then quotes, at p. 48, the advice of the judges to the House of Lords on April 27, 1792:

> "The crime consists in publishing a libel; . . . He who scatters firebrands, arrows, and death (which, if not an accurate definition, is a very intelligible description of a libel), is ea ratione criminal.—It is not incumbent in the prosecutor to prove his intent; and, on his part, he shall not be heard to say, 'Am I not in sport?' "

Was the law changed by the famous summing-up of Lord Coleridge C.J. in *Reg.* v. *Ramsay and Foote,* 15 Cox C.C. 231? For the reasons given by the Court of Appeal and developed by my noble and learned friend, Viscount Dilhorne, I do not think it was. There was never any doubt, or issue, in that case as to the accused's intention. Lord Coleridge C.J. drew upon the passage in Professor Starkie's famous work *(Starkie's Slander and Libel,* 4th ed., p. 599) to explain not the mens rea but the nature of the "actus reus" of blasphemy. "Mens rea" not being an issue in the case, I do not think it legitimate to read the direction as an authority upon the nature of the "mens rea" required to establish the offence.

Neither Lord Denman C.J. *(Reg.* v. *Hetherington,* 4 St.Tr.N.S. 563) nor *Stephen's Digest of Criminal Law,* 7th ed., art. 231 and *Draft Code of the Criminal Law (Report of the Royal Commission Appointed to Consider the Law relating to Indictable Offences* (1879) (C.2345), Appendix), section 141 nor the subsequent case law supports Starkie's view *(Starkie's Slander and Libel,* 4th ed., p. 599) quoted by Lord Coleridge C.J. in *Reg.* v. *Ramsay and Foote,* 15 Cox C.C. 231, 236 that a "wilful intention to pervert, insult, and mislead others . . . is the criterion and test of guilt." Indeed, if Starkie's view of the law on this point were correct, it is inconceivable that Avory J. could have summed up in *Rex* v. *Gott* as he did, or that the Court of Criminal Appeal could have affirmed him, as they did, 16 Cr.App.R. 87. Your Lordships have had the opportunity of seeing the full report of the summing-up in *Rex* v. *Gott* published in the issue of "The Freethinker" of January 8, 1922. The whole weight of the summing-up was directed to the question: were the words complained of ". . . anything more than vilification and ridicule of the Christian religion and of the Scriptures" (p. 28)?

For these reasons I am of the opinion that historically the law has required no more than an intention to publish words found by the jury to be blasphemous. Yet I recognise that another view, such as that developed by my noble and learned friend Lord Edmund-Davies, has great persuasive force. Indeed, it has the formidable support of my noble and learned friend Lord Diplock.

The issue is, therefore, one of legal policy in the society of today. There is some force in the lawyer's conceptual argument that in the matter of "mens rea" all four species of criminal libel (seditious, blasphemous, obscene and defamatory) should be the same. It is said that an intention to stir up sedition is necessary to constitute the crime of seditious libel. I am not sure that it is or ought to be: contrast *Rex* v. *Aldred,* 22 Cox C.C. 1 with Birkett J.'s direction in *Rex* v. *Caunt* (un-reported). Prior to the enactment of the Obscene

Publications Act 1959 it was not necessary to establish an intention to deprave and corrupt in order to prove an obscene libel: *Reg.* v. *Hicklin* (1868) L.R. 3 Q.B. 360. At worst, the common law may be said to have become fragmented in this area of public order offences: at best, it may be said (as I believe to be true) to be moving towards a position in which people who know what they are doing will be criminally liable if the words they choose to publish are such as to cause grave offence to the religious feelings of some of their fellow citizens or are such as to tend to deprave and corrupt persons who are likely to read them.

The movement of the law is illustrated by recent statutes. The Obscene Publications Act 1959 focuses attention upon the words or article published, not the intention of the author or publisher. The test of obscenity depends on the article itself. Section 5 of the Public Order Act 1936 has been significantly amended by the addition of a new section, 5A. The Race Relations Act 1976, section 70 (2), by providing that section 5A be added, has made it unnecessary to prove an intention to provoke a breach of the peace in order to secure a conviction for incitement to racial hatred. All this makes legal sense in a plural society which recognises the human rights and fundamental freedoms of the European Convention [Convention for the Protection of Human Rights and Fundamental Freedoms (1950) (Cmd. 8969)]. Article 9 provides that every one has the right to freedom of religion, and the right to manifest his religion in worship, teaching, practice and observance. By necessary implication the article imposes a duty on all of us to refrain from insulting or outraging the religious feelings of others. Article 10 provides that every one shall have the right to freedom of expression. The exercise of this freedom "carries with it duties and responsibilities" and may be subject to such restrictions as are presented by law and are necessary "for the prevention of disorder or crime, for the protection of health or morals, for the protection of the reputation or rights of others . . ." It would be intolerable if by allowing an author or publisher to plead the excellence of his motives and the right of free speech he could evade the penalties of the law even though his words were blasphemous in the sense of constituting an outrage upon the religious feelings of his fellow citizens. This is no way forward for a successful plural society. Accordingly, the test of obscenity by concentrating attention on the words complained of is, in my judgment, equally valuable as a test of blasphemy. The character of the words published matter; but not the motive of the author or publisher.

For these reasons as well as for those developed in the speeches of my noble and learned friends, Viscount Dilhorne and Lord Russell of Killowen, with both of which I agree, I would dismiss these appeals. In my judgment the modern law of blasphemy is correctly formulated in article 214 of *Stephen's Digest of the Criminal Law,* 9th ed. (1950):

> "Every publication is said to be blasphemous which contains any con-temptuous, reviling, scurrilous or ludicrous matter relating to God, Jesus Christ, or the Bible, or the formularies of the Church of England as by law established. It is not blasphemous to speak or publish opinions hostile to the Christian religion, or to deny the existence of God, if the publication is couched in decent and temperate language. The test to be applied is as to the manner in which the doctrines are advocated and not as to the substance of the doctrines themselves.
>
> "Everyone who publishes any blasphemous document is guilty of the [offence] of publishing a blasphemous libel.

"Everyone who speaks blasphemous words is guilty of the [offence] of blasphemy."

TOWN POLICE CLAUSES ACT 1847

1 Incorporation with special Act

This Act shall extend only to such towns or districts in England or Ireland as shall be comprised in any Act of Parliament hereafter to be passed which shall declare that this Act shall be incorporated therewith; and all the clauses of this Act, save so far as they shall be expressly varied or excepted by any such Act, shall apply to the town or district which shall be comprised in such Act, and to the commissioners appointed for improving and regulating the same, so far as such clauses shall be applicable thereto respectively, and shall, with the clauses of every other Act which shall be incorporated therewith, form part of such Act, and be construed therewith as forming one Act . . .

28. Penalty on persons committing any of the offences herein named

Every person who in any street, to the obstruction, annoyance, or danger of the residents or passengers, commits any of the following offences, shall be liable to a penalty not exceeding forty shillings for each offence, or, in the discretion of the justice before whom he is convicted, may be committed to prison, there to remain for a period not exceeding fourteen days; and any officer appointed by virtue of this or the special Act or any constable shall take into custody, without warrant, and forthwith convery before a justice, any person who within his view commits any such offence; (that is to say,)

Every person who wilfully and indecently exposes his person:
Every person who publicly offers for sale or distribution, or exhibits to public view any profane, indecent, or obscene book, paper, print, drawing, painting, or representation, or sings any profane or obscene song or ballad, or uses any profane or obscene language:

Note: Proceedings under this provision provide the authorities with an alternative to a prosecution for blasphemy (or obscenity under the Obscene Publications Acts 1959 and 1964). It has been suggested that no charge of profanity under section 28 was brought before T. A. Jackson was charged with profanity at Leeds in April 1912; it is certain there have been a number of other cases since then. See Ernest Pack, *The Trial and Imprisonment of J. W. Gott for Blasphemy* (Bradford, c.1913), especially p. 76.

ECCLESIASTICAL COURTS JURISDICTION ACT 1860

2. Penalty on persons guilty of riotous behaviour, etc., in churches, chapels certified under the Places of Worship Registration Act, 1855 (c. 81), etc., churchyards, or burial grounds

Any person who shall be guilty of riotous, violent, or indecent behaviour in England or Ireland in any cathedral church, parish or district church or chapel of the Church of England *and Ireland,* or in any chapel of any religious denomination, or in England in any place of religious worship duly certified under the provisions of the Places of Worship Registration Act, 1855, whether during the celebration of divine service or at any other time, or in any churchyard or burial ground, or who shall molest, let, disturb, vex, or trouble, or by any other unlawful means disquiet or misuse any preacher duly authorized to preach therein, or any clergyman in holy orders ministering or celebrating any sacrament, or any divine service, rite, or office, in any cathedral, church, or chapel, or in any churchyard or burial ground, shall, on conviction thereof before two justices of the peace, be liable to a penalty of not more than *five pounds* for every such offence, or may, if the justices before whom he shall be convicted think fit, instead of being subjected to any pecuniary penalty, be committed to prison for any time not exceeding two months.

Abrahams and Others v. Cavey [1968] 1 Q.B. 479

Queens Bench Division

LORD PARKER C.J.:
This is an appeal by way of case stated from a decision of Brighton justices who convicted all eight defendants of having on October 2, 1966, been guilty of indecent behaviour in the Dorset Gardens Methodist Church during the celebration of divine service, contrary to section 2 of the Ecclesiastical Courts Jurisdiction Act, 1860.

The short facts were that on that day a Labour Party conference was in progress at Brighton, and a service for that day had been publicised. The service was attended by leaders of the party, including a number of Ministers. Whilst divine service was being celebrated, and indeed after the first lesson had been read, the defendant Walter interrupted, so the magistrates find, by shouting "Oh, you hypocrites, how can you use the word of God to justify your policies?" He was then escorted from the church and took no further part in the interrupting. The service proceeded, and about the time of the reading of the second lesson there were further interruptions by several persons, and the defendants Anderson and Radford joined in by standing and addressing the congregation from their pews in the body of the church. This intervention prevented the second lesson from being read. It was in this general disturbance that each of the other defendants participated, and certain of them were removed from the church.

The magistrates find that the theme of the interruptions was a protest against government members' active participation in the service against the background of alleged support for the United States policies in Vietnam. The justices held that the interruption of divine service by the defendants was an act that offended against the recognised standards of propriety, and accordingly convicted the defendants. The question for this court is whether on those findings they were entitled to hold that it amounted to indecent behaviour within the meaning of section 2 of the Act in question.

The Act in question, the Ecclesiastical Courts Jurisdiction Act, 1860, by section 2 provides, so far as it is material:

"Any person who shall be guilty of riotous, violent, or indecent behaviour . . . in any place of religious worship duly certified under the provisions of the eighty-first chapter of the statute passed in the session of Parliament of the eighteenth and nineteenth years of the reign of her present Majesty . . ."—and pausing there, the Dorset Gardens Methodist Church was so certified—". . . whether during the celebration of divine service or at any other time . . . shall on conviction thereof before two justices of the peace be liable to a penalty . . ."

I have omitted words which Mr. Brownlie on behalf of all the defendants except Mr. Walter (who has appeared in person) agreed were irrelevant, words which go on to make it an offence to "molest, let, distrub, vex or trouble or by any other unlawful means disquiet or misuse" any preacher or clergyman in Holy Orders whilst celebrating the service.

The sole question here is whether the behaviour of these defendants acting jointly could be said to be "indecent behaviour" within the meaning of that statute. Were it not for the great industry of Mr. Brownlie in this case, I for my part should have thought this was completely unarguable. He refers to the fact that "indecent" has a number of meanings, both dictionary meanings and meanings that can be ascertained from the cases. But the true meaning in any particular statute must naturally depend upon the context. It is quite clear here that indecency is not referring to anything in the nature of tending to corrupt or deprave; it is quite clearly used not with any sexual connotation whatsoever, but it is used in the context of "riotous, violent or indecent behaviour," to put it quite generally, within the genus of creating a disturbance, in a sacred place.

What is more, the cases (in so far as it is necessary to refer to cases on this matter) are all against Mr. Brownlie. It is very striking that in *Girt* v. *Fillingham*, a quarter sessions case at Bury St. Edmunds in 1900,[1] a clergyman himself was convicted under this section. He had gone to a neighbouring church with some 40 or 50 persons for the purpose of making protests against the conduct of services in that church, and during the prayer of consecration he cried out "Idolatry! Protestants, leave this House of Baal!" and thereupon they left. It was there held that he was properly convicted, and [2]

"It was pointed out, on the authority of Sir John Nicholl in *Palmer* v. *Roffey*,[3] that the sacredness of the place was the object of the protecting law, and that controversial matters could not be dealt with in Church without a violation of the statute."

As I have said, that was a case at quarter sessions, but it so happened that it came up and was in effect reviewed by the Chancellor of the Consistory Court of St. Albans.[4] In that case the Chancellor had no hesitation in confirming that the disturbance did amount to indecent behaviour within the statute.[5]

Again in *Jones* v. *Catterall*,[6] this court had before them a case in which it was said that the respondent had been guilty of indecent behaviour in that he had called out "Idolatry" at divine service. The matter came before this court after the refusal of justices to convict. I am not myself clear whether it was really

[1] (1900) 64 J.P. 457; [1901] P. 176.
[2] Ibid.
[3] (1824) 2 Add. 141.
[4] [1901] P. 176.
[5] Ibid. 184, 185.
[6] (1902) 18 T.L.R. 367.

asking for the case to go back to the justices, but Lord Alverstone C.J. acceded to the argument of counsel in these terms:

> "It was impossible that 'Idolatry' could be called out during the service in anything but an indecent manner. At least it must be indecent if addressed to the congregation or the Minister,"

and the Chief Justice said

> "that he had a great deal of sympathy with the view pressed by Mr. Duke, and from nothing that he said must it be thought that he countenanced anybody being justified in using loud expressions or interfering with the proper and orderly conduct of the service by expressions indicating his own disapproval. On such things being proved ordinary tribunals ought to hold that it was indecent behaviour."

The appeal however was dismissed because it became quite clear that the reason that the magistrates had failed to convict was that they were not satisfied so as to feel sure that the word in question had been uttered in a loud voice and otherwise than merely as an aside. It seems to me that not only as a matter of common sense were the justices bound to convict in the present case, but that all the authorities that there are support that view.

The only argument adduced, and one which I can understand, comes from Mr. Walter himself, who says:

> "What difference does it make that it is a church? If I had shouted out these words in the street towards the members in question, no longer being a congregation of the church, I would not have committed an offence; what difference does it make that it is in a church?"

The answer, of course, is that it makes all the difference because you are dealing with a sacred place and when a service is taking place. Even if this court felt that there was any doubt in the matter or wished to accede to Mr. Walter's argument, it is quite clear from the case that Mr. Worsley has referred to, *Worth v. Terrington*,[7] that it makes all the difference. Baron Parke there said:

> "If what is afterwards alleged is construed with reference to its being done on a weekday, or without any reference to the celebration of divine service, the question is totally altered; for it is clear that an act done in a church during divine service might be highly indecent and improper, which would not be so at another time."

As I have said, the justices in my judgment came to a correct decision and I would dismiss this appeal.

Diplock, L. J., and Widgery, J., agreed.

Questions

1. What elements are necessary to establish liability for the crime of blasphemous libel?

[7](1845) 13 M. & W. 781,795.

2. .... "[I]t appears to me that the whole of the law which can possibly be applied to the punishment of the expression of religious opinion should be abolished"—James FitzJames Stephen, 25 *Contemporary Review* (1874–5) at 474. Discuss.

DISABILITIES AND PRIVILEGES ON ACCOUNT OF RELIGION

De Smith, pp. 288; 461–2; Street, pp. 201–10; Wade & Phillips, p. 139. See also pp. 434 and 436.

GOVERNMENT OF IRELAND ACT 1920

5. Prohibition of laws interfering with religious equality, taking property without compensation, etc.

(1) In the exercise of their power to make laws under this Act *neither the Parliament of Southern Ireland nor* the Parliament of Northern Ireland shall make a law so as either directly or indirectly to establish or endow any religion, or prohibit or restrict the free exercise thereof, or give a preference, privilege, or advantage, or impose any disability or disadvantage, on account of religious belief or religious or ecclesiastical status, or make any religious belief or religious ceremony a condition of the validity of any marriage, or affect prejudicially the right of any child to attend a school receiving public money without attending the religious instruction at that school, or alter the constitution of any religious body except where the alteration is approved on behalf of the religious body by the governing body thereof, or divert from any religious denomination the fabric of cathedral churches, or, except for the purpose of roads, railways, lighting, water, or drainage works, or other works of public utility upon payment of compensation, any other property, . . .

Any law made in contravention of the restrictions imposed by this subsection shall, so far as it contravenes those restrictions, be void.

(2) Any existing enactment by which any penalty, disadvantage, or disability is imposed on account of religious belief or on a member of any religious order as such shall, as from the appointed day, cease to have effect in Ireland.

Note: This has now been repealed by the Northern Ireland Constitution Act 1973, Schedule 6. See also p. 436. The effect of this provision was to repeal any law then in force *in Ireland* (but not the rest of the United Kingdom) which conferred any privilege or imposed any disadvantage on account of religious belief or status. There is no law in the rest of the United Kingdom making discrimination on grounds of religion unlawful. See St. John A. Robilliard, "Should Parliament Enact a Religious Discrimination Act?" *Public Law* [1978] 379-90. See also *Londonderry County Council v. M'Glade* [1929] N.I. 47.

ROMAN CATHOLIC RELIEF ACT 1829

Note: Section 5 of the Government of Ireland Act 1920 (above) has the effect of repealing so far as Ireland is concerned the discriminatory provisions below.

11. Roman Catholics not exempted from taking any oaths required from other persons on admissions to offices

Provided always, . . . that nothing herein contained shall be construed to exempt any person professing the Roman Catholic religion from the necessity of taking any oath or oaths, or making any declaration, not herein-before mentioned, which are or may be by law required to be taken or subscribed by any person on his admission into any such office or place of trust or profit as aforesaid.

12. This Act not to enable Roman Catholics to hold certain offices

Provided also, . . . that nothing herein contained shall extend or be construed to extend to enable any person or persons professing the Roman Catholic religion to hold or exercise the office of guardians and justices of the United Kingdom, or of regent of the United Kingdom, under whatever name, style, or title such office may be constituted; nor to enable any person, otherwise than as he is now by law enabled, to hold or enjoy the office of lord high chancellor, lord keeper or lord commissioner of the great seal of Great Britain . . . ; or the office of lord lieutenant of Ireland; or his Majesty's high commissioner to the general assembly of the Church of Scotland.

15. Roman Catholic members of corporations not to vote in ecclesiastical appointments

Provided nevertheless, . . . that nothing herein contained shall extent to authorise or empower any of his Majesty's subjects professing the Roman Catholic religion, and being a member of any lay body corporate, to give any vote at or in any manner to join in the election, presentation, or appointment of any person to any ecclesiastical benefice whatsoever, or any office or place belonging to or connected with United Church of England and Ireland or the Church of Scotland, being in the gift, patronage, or disposal of such lay corporate body.

16. This Act not to extend to offices, etc., in the established churches, etc. nor to presentations to benefices

Provided also, . . . that nothing in this Act contained shall be construed to enable any persons, otherwise than as they are now by law enabled, to hold, enjoy, or exercise any office, place, or dignity, of, in, or belonging to the United Church of England and Ireland, or the Church of Scotland, or any place or office whatever of, in, or belonging to any of the ecclesiastical courts of judicature of England and Ireland respectively, or any court of appeal from or review of the sentences of such courts, or of, in, or belonging to the commissary court of Edinburgh, or of, in, or belonging to any cathedral or collegiate or ecclesiastical establishment or foundation: or any office or place whatever of, in, or belonging to any of the universities of this realm; or any office or place whatever, and by whatever name the same may be called, or, in, or belonging to any of the colleges or halls of the said universities, or the colleges of Eton, Westminster, or Winchester, or any college or school within this realm; or to repeal, abrogate, or in any manner to interfere with any local statute, ordinance, or rule, which is or shall be established by competent authority within any university, college, hall, or school, by which Roman

Catholics shall be prevented from being admitted thereto, or from residing or taking degrees therein: Provided also, that nothing herein contained shall extend or be construed to extend to enable any person, otherwise than as he is now by law enabled, to exercise any right of presentation to any ecclesiastical benefice whatsoever; or to repeal, vary, or alter in any manner the laws now in force in respect to the right of presentation to any ecclesiastical benefice.

17. Proviso for presentations to benefices connected with offices held by Roman Catholics

Provided always, . . . that where any right of presentation to any ecclesiastical benefice shall belong to any office in the gift or appointment of his Majesty, and such office shall be held by a person professing the Roman Catholic religion, the right of presentation shall devolve upon and be exercised by the archbishop of Canterbury for the time being.

18. No Roman Catholic to advise the Crown in the appointment to offices in the established churches

. . . It shall not be lawful for any person professing the Roman Catholic religion directly or indirectly to advise his Majesty, or any person or persons holding or exercising the office of guardians of the United Kingdom, or of regent of the United Kingdom, under whatever name, style or title such office may be constituted, or the lord lieutenant of Ireland, touching or concerning the appointment to or disposal of any office or preferment in the United Church of England and Ireland, or in the Church of Scotland; and if any such person shall offend in the premises he shall, being thereof convicted by due course of law, be deemed guilty of a high misdemeanor, and disabled for ever from holding any office, civil or military, under the Crown.

23. No other oaths necessary to be taken by Roman Catholics for holding property other than those required from other subjects

. . . No oath or oaths shall be tendered to or required to be taken by his Majesty's subjects professing the Roman Catholic religion, for enabling them to hold or enjoy any real or personal property, other than such as may by law be tendered to and required to be taken by his Majesty's other subjects . . .

24. Titles to sees, etc., not to be assumed by Roman Catholics in England or Ireland

And whereas the Protestant Episcopal Church of England and Ireland, and the doctrine, discipline, and government thereof, and likewise the Protestant Presbyterian Church of Scotland, and the doctrine, discipline and government thereof, are by the respective Acts of Union of England and Scotland, and of Great Britain and Ireland, established permanently and inviolably: And whereas the right and title of archbishops to their respective provinces, of bishops to their sees, and of deans to their deaneries, as well in England as in Ireland, have been settled and established by law: Be it therefore enacted, that if any person, other than the person thereunto authorized by law, shall assume or use the name, style, or title, of archbishop of any province, bishop of any bishoprick, or dean of any deanery, in England or Ireland, he shall for every such offence forfeit and pay the sum of one hundred pounds.

OFFENCES AGAINST THE PERSON ACT 1861

Assaults

36. Obstructing or assaulting a clergyman or other minister in the discharge of his duties in place of worship or burial place, or on his way thither

Whosoever shall, by threats or force, obstruct or prevent or endeavour to obstruct or prevent, any clergyman or other minister in or from celebrating divine service or otherwise officiating in any church, chapel, meeting house, or other place of divine worship, or in or from the performance of his duty in the lawful burial of the dead in any churchyard or other burial place, or shall strike or offer any violence to, or shall, upon any civil process, or under the pretence of executing any civil process, arrest any clergyman or other minister who is engaged in, or to the knowledge of the offender is about to engage in, any of the rites or duties in this section aforesaid, or who to the knowledge of the offender shall be going to perform the same or returning from the performance thereof, shall be guilty of a misdemeanor, and being convicted thereof shall be liable, at the discretion of the court, to be imprisoned for any term not exceeding two years, with or without hard labour.

EDUCATION ACT 1944

Religious Education in County and Voluntary Schools

25. General provisions as to religious education in county and in voluntary schools

(1) Subject to the provisions of this section, the school day in every county school and in every voluntary school shall begin with collective worship on the part of all pupils in attendance at the school, and the arrangements made therefor shall provide for a single act of worship attended by all such pupils unless, in the opinion of the local education authority or, in the case of a voluntary school, of the managers or governors thereof, the school premises are such as to make it impracticable to assemble them for that purpose.

(2) Subject to the provisions of this section, religious instruction shall be given in every county school and in every voluntary school.

(3) It shall not be required, as a condition of any pupil attending any county school or any voluntary school, that he shall attend or abstain from attending any Sunday school or any place of religious worship.

(4) If the parent of any pupil in attendance at any county school or any voluntary school requests that he be wholly or partly excused from attendance at religious worship in the school, or from attendance at religious instruction in the school, or from attendance at both religious worship and religious instruction in the school, then, until the request is withdrawn, the pupil shall be excused from such attendance accordingly.

(5) Where any pupil has been wholly or partly excused from attendance at religious worship or instruction in any school in accordance with the provisions of this section, and the local education authority are satisfied:—

    (*a*) that the parent of the pupil desires him to receive religious instruction of a kind which is not provided in the school during the periods during which he is excused from such attendance;

(b) that the pupil cannot with reasonable convenience be sent to another county or voluntary school where religious instruction of the kind desired by the parent is provided; and

(c) that arrangements have been made for him to receive religious instruction during school hours elsewhere,

the pupil may be withdrawn from the school during such periods as are reasonably necessary for the purpose of enabling him to receive religious instruction in accordance with the arrangements:

Provided that the pupil shall not be so withdrawn unless the local education authority are satisfied that the arrangements are such as will not interfere with the attendance of the pupil at school on any day except at the beginning or end of the school session on that day.

(6) No directions shall be given by the local education authority as to the secular instruction to be given to pupils in attendance at a voluntary school so as to interfere with the provision of reasonable facilities for religious instruction in the school during school hours; and no such direction shall be given so as to prevent a pupil from receiving religious instruction in accordance with the provisions of this section during the hours normally set apart for that purpose, unless arrangements are made whereby the pupil shall receive such instruction in the school at some other time.

(7) Where the parent of any pupil who is a boarder at a county school or at a voluntary school requests that the pupil be permitted to attend worship in accordance with the tenets of a particular religious denomination on Sundays or other days exclusively set apart for religious observance by the religious body to which his parent belongs, or to receive religious instruction in accordance with such tenets outside school hours, the managers or governors of the school shall make arrangements for affording to the pupil reasonable opportunites for so doing and such arrangements may provide for affording facilities for such worship or instruction on the school premises, so however that such arrangements shall not entail expenditure by the local education authority.

26. Special provisions as to religious education in county schools

Subject as hereinafter provided, the collective worship required by subsection (1) of the last foregoing section shall not, in any county school, be distinctive of any particular religious denomination, and the religious instruction given to any pupils in attendance at a county school in conformity with the requirements of subsection (2) of the said section shall be given in accordance with an agreed syllabus adopted for the school or for those pupils and shall not include any catechism or formulary which is distinctive of any particular religious denomination:

Provided that, where a county secondary school is so situated that arrangements cannot conveniently be made for the withdrawal of pupils from the school in accordance with the provisions of this Act to receive religious instruction elsewhere, then, if the local education authority are satisfied:—

(a) that the parents of pupils in attendance at the school desire them to receive religious instruction in the school in accordance with the tenets of a particular religious denomination; and

(b) that satisfactory arrangements have been made for the provision of such instruction to those pupils in the school, and for securing that the cost of providing such instruction to those pupils in the school will not fall upon the authority;

the authority shall, unless they are satisfied that owing to any special circumstances it would be unreasonable so to do, provide facilities for the carrying out of those arrangements.

27. Special provisions as to religious education in controlled schools

(1) Where the parents of any pupils in attendance at a controlled school request that they may receive religious instruction in accordance with the provisions of the trust deed relating to the school, or where provision for that purpose is not made by such a deed in accordance with the practice observed in the school before it became a controlled school, the foundation managers or foundation governors shall, unless they are satisfied that owing to special circumstances it would be unreasonable so to do, make arrangements for securing that such religious instruction is given to those pupils at the school during not more than two periods in each week.

(2) Without prejudice to the duty to make such arrangements as aforesaid whatever the number of the teaching staff of the school, where the number of the teaching staff of a controlled school exceeds two the teaching staff shall include persons (hereinafter referred to as "reserved teachers") selected for their fitness and competence to give such religious instruction as is required to be given under such arrangements and specifically appointed to do so:

Provided that the number of reserved teachers in any controlled school shall not exceed one-fifth of the number of the teaching staff of the school including the head teacher, so, however, that where the number of the teaching staff is not a multiple of five it shall be treated for the purposes of this subsection as if it were the next higher multiple thereof.

(3) The head teacher of a controlled school shall not, while holding that position, be a reserved teacher, but before appointing any person to be the head teacher of such a school the local education authority shall inform the managers or governors of the school as to the person whom they propose to appoint and shall consider any representations made by the managers or governors with respect to the proposed appointment.

(4) Where the local education authority propose to appoint any person to be a reserved teacher in a controlled school, the authority shall consult the foundation managers or foundation governors of the school, and, unless the said managers or governors are satisfied as to that person's fitness and competence to give such religious instruction as is required in pursuance of such arrangements as aforesaid the authority shall not appoint that person to be a reserved teacher.

(5) If the foundation managers or foundation governors of a controlled school are of opinion that any reserved teacher has failed to give such religious instruction as aforesaid efficiently and suitably, they may require the authority to dismiss him from employment as a reserved teacher in the school.

(6) Subject to any arrangements made under subsection (1) of this section, the religious instruction given to the pupils in attendance at a controlled school shall be given in accordance with an agreed syllabus adopted for the school or for those pupils.

28. Special provisions as to religious education in aided schools and in special agreement schools

(1) The religious instruction given to the pupils in attendance at an aided school or at a special agreement school shall be under the control of the

managers or governors of the school and shall be in accordance with any provisions of the trust deed relating to the school, or, where provision for that purpose is not made by such a deed, in accordance with the practice observed in the school before it became a voluntary school:

Provided that where the parents of pupils in attendance at the school desire them to receive religious instruction in accordance with any agreed syllabus adopted by the local education authority and cannot with reasonable convenience cause those pupils to attend any school at which that syllabus is in use, then, unless the authority are satisfied that owing to any special circumstances it would be unreasonable so to do, arrangements shall be made for religious instruction in accordance with that syllabus to be given to those pupils in the school during the times set apart for the giving of religious instruction therein, and such arrangements shall be made by the managers or governors of the school, so, however, that if the local education authority are satisfied that the managers or governors are unwilling to make such arrangements, the arrangements shall be made by the authority.

(2) If a teacher appointed to give in an aided school religious instruction, other than instruction in accordance with an agreed syllabus, fails to give such instruction efficiently and suitably, he may be dismissed on that ground by the managers or governors of the school without the consent of the local education authority.

(3) Where the special agreement made with respect to any special agreement school provides for the employment of reserved teachers, the local education authority shall, when they propose to appoint any person to be such a teacher in the school, consult the foundation managers or foundation governors of the school, and unless the said managers or governors are satisfied as to that person's fitness and competence to give such religious instruction as aforesaid, the authority shall not appoint that person to be such a teacher.

(4) If the foundation managers or foundation governors of a special agreement school are of opinion that any such reserved teacher as aforesaid has failed to give, efficiently and suitably, such religious instruction as he was appointed to give, they may require the authority to dismiss him from employment as a reserved teacher in the school.

29. Provisions as to religious instruction in accordance with agreed syllabus

(1) The provisions of the Fifth Schedule to this Act shall have effect with respect to the preparation, adoption, and reconsideration, of an agreed syllabus of religious instruction.

(2) A local education authority shall have power to constitute a standing advisory council on religious education to advise the authority upon matters connected with the religious instruction to be given in accordance with an agreed syllabus and, in particular, as to methods of teaching, the choice of books, and the provision of lectures for teachers.

(3) The method of appointment of the members of any council constituted under the last foregoing subsection and the term of office and conditions of retirement of the members thereof shall be such as may be determined by the local education authority.

(4) A local education authority shall have regard to any unanimous recommendations which may be made to them by any conference convened in accordance with the provisions of the said Fifth Schedule with respect to the

expediency of constituting such an advisory council as aforesaid or with respect to the method by which or the terms and conditions upon which members of any such council shall be appointed.

30. Saving as to position of teachers

Subject as hereinafter provided, no person shall be disqualified by reason of his religious opinions, or of his attending or omitting to attend religious worship, from being a teacher in a county school or in any voluntary school, or from being otherwise employed for the purposes of such a school; and no teacher in any such school shall be required to give religious instruction or receive any less emolument or be deprived of, or disqualified for, any promotion or other advantage by reason of the fact that he does or does not give religious instruction or by reason of his religious opinions or of his attending or omitting to attend religious worship:

Provided that, save in so far as they require that a teacher shall not receive any less emolument or be deprived of, or disqualified for, any promotion or other advantage by reason of the fact that he gives religious instruction or by reason of his religious opinions or of his attending religious worship, the provisions of this section shall not apply with respect to a teacher in an aided school or with respect to a reserved teacher in any controlled school or special agreement school.

Note: See Brigid Brophy, *Religious Education in State Schools* (Fabian Tract no. 374, London, 1967).

Ahmad v. Inner London Education Authority [1977] I.C.R. 490

Court of Appeal

The facts appear from the judgments.
LORD DENNING M.R.:

Mr. Ahmad is a schoolteacher. He was employed by the Inner London Education Authority ("I.L.E.A.") as a full-time teacher. This meant that he had to attend the school and teach the children on the five days, Monday to Friday, inclusive each week, with a break each day for luncheon from 12.30 p.m. to 1.30 p.m.

But Mr. Ahmad was not only a schoolteacher. He was a devout Muslim. By his religion it was his duty every Friday to attend prayers at the nearest mosque. The time for these prayers was 1 p.m. to 2 p.m. and the mosque was about 15 to 20 minutes away. So when he went to the prayers he did not get back at 1.30 p.m. in time to teach his class. He only got back at 2.15 p.m. or 2.20 p.m. This meant that he missed about three-quarters of an hour of his teaching duty every Friday. One of the headmasters—at the school for maladjusted children—did his best to help and made arrangements to cope with his absence. But other headmasters in ordinary schools could not do so. His absence disrupted the classes too much. They could not fit it in with the rest of the work. But still he went to his Friday prayers. He said that he was entitled to do so and, notwithstanding his absences, he was entitled to full pay, just the same as if he had worked for the full five days.

There was a provision in the staff code which allowed teachers to have time off for special days in their religion when no work was to be done, such as Good Friday for Christians, or the Day of Atonement for Jews, and Ramadan for Muslims. But that provision did not apply to working days, like Fridays. The other members of the staff thought it was unfair for Mr. Ahmad to have Friday afternoon off each week on full pay. So the issue was referred to the I.L.E.A. They took the view that, if he desired to take time off on Fridays for his prayers, he could only be fitted in as a part-time teacher, doing $4\frac{1}{2}$ days a week and being paid for $4\frac{1}{2}$ days: but they would see that his pension rights and so forth were not prejudiced. He was unwilling to accept this proposal. He resigned in protest. He gave as his reason: "I was exploited and humiliated by the I.L.E.A." He put in a claim for unfair dismissal, saying that his employers' conduct "forced me to resign."

Now, if his resignation was brought about by the employers' conduct, he was entitled to treat it as a dismissal (see the Trade Union and Labour Relations Act 1974, Schedule 1, paragraph 5 (2) (c)); but the question whether it was a fair or unfair dismissal would depend on whether the employers "in the circumstances . . . acted reasonably . . .": see paragraph 6 (8) of that Schedule.

The industrial tribunal found unanimously that the employers were not being unreasonable. The Employment Appeal Tribunal [1976] I.C.R. 461 affirmed their decision, again unanimously, but gave leave to appeal.

On the appeal, Mr. Ahmad relied much on section 30 of the Education Act 1944. It was a section inserted so as to safeguard the position of teachers. It said:

". . . no teacher . . . shall be required to give religious instruction or receive any less emolument or be deprived of, or disqualified for, any promotion or other advantage by reason of the fact that he does or does not give religious instruction or by reason of his religious opinions or of his attending or omitting to attend religious worship: . . ."

If the words were read literally without qualification, they would entitle Mr. Ahmad to take time off every Friday afternoon for his prayers without loss of pay. I cannot think this was ever intended. The school time-table was well known to Mr. Ahmad when he applied for the teaching post. It was for the usual teaching hours from Monday to Friday, inclusive. If he wished to have every Friday afternoon off for his prayers, *either* he ought not to have applied for this post: *or* he ought to have made it clear at the outset and entered into a $4\frac{1}{2}$-day engagement only. This was the sensible thing for him to do. Instead he undertook full-time work without making any disclosure that he wanted Friday afternoon off for prayers.

I think that section 30 can be applied to the situation perfectly well by reading it as subject to the qualification "if the school time-table so permits." So read, it means that he is to be entitled to attend for religious worship during the working week if it can be arranged consistently with performing his teaching duties under his contract of employment. It has been so interpreted by the great majority of Muslim teachers in our schools. They do not take time off for their prayers. Nor should Mr. Ahmad if he wants to get his full pay for a five-day week. The industrial tribunal said:

". . . none of the other education authorities has ever received such a request from Muslim staff and the problem would seem to be unique to the applicant, Mr. Ahmad."

I have no doubt that all headmasters will try to arrange their time-table so as to accommodate devout Muslims like Mr. Ahmad: but I do not think they should be compelled to do so, if it means disrupting the work of the school and the well-being of the pupils.

During the argument Scarman L.J. drew attention to article 9 of the European Convention on Human Rights (Convention for the Protection of Human Rights and Fundamental Freedoms, Cmd. 8969), to which this country has subscribed. It says:

> "(1) Everyone has the right to freedom of thought, conscience and religion; this right includes freedom to change his religion or belief and freedom, either alone or in community with others and in public or private, to manifest his religion or belief in worship, teaching, practice and observance. (2) Freedom to manifest one's religion or beliefs shall be subject only to such limitations as are prescribed by law and are necessary in a democratic society in the interests of public safety, for the protection of public order, health or morals, or for the protection of the rights and freedoms of others."

The convention is not part of our English law, but, as I have often said, we will always have regard to it. We will do our best to see that our decisions are in conformity with it. But it is drawn in such vague terms that it can be used for all sorts of unreasonable claims and provoke all sorts of litigation. As so often happens with high-sounding principles, they have to be brought down to earth. They have to be applied in a work-a-day world. I venture to suggest that it would do the Muslim community no good—or any other minority group no good—if they were to be given preferential treatment over the great majority of the people. If it should happen that, in the name of religious freedom, they were given special privileges or advantages, it would provoke discontent, and even resentment among those with whom they work. As, indeed, it has done in this very case. And so the cause of racial integration would suffer. So, whilst upholding religious freedom to the full, I would suggest that it should be applied with caution, especially having regard to the setting in which it is sought. Applied to our educational system, I think that Mr. Ahmad's right to "manifest his religion in practice and observance" must be subject to the rights of the education authorities under the contract and to the interests of the children whom he is paid to teach. I see nothing in the European Convention to give Mr. Ahmad any right to manifest his religion on Friday afternoons in derogation of his contract of employment: and certainly not on full pay.

I find myself in agreement with the industrial tribunal and the Employment Appeal Tribunal. I would dismiss the appeal.

Orr. L.J. delivered a concurring judgment.

SCARMAN, L.J., dissenting:

The true construction of section 30 of the Education Act 1944 is at the heart of this case. [For text see p. 106] . . .

It has, so far as I am aware, never been considered by the courts. The reasons for its 30 years of immunity from judicial interpretation are not hard to see. First, and foremost, local education authorities, like the I.L.E.A. in this case, have treated it as no more than of negative intent—forbidding discrimination on the ground of religion in the selection and employment of teachers, but not obliging them to ensure that religious minorities are represented amongst their teachers. The I.L.E.A., we have been told, have sought to comply with the section by not asking questions, the theory being that, if you do not know a man's religion, you cannot discriminate against him on that ground. Secondly, there were until recently no substantial religious groupings in our country which fell outside the broad categories of Christian and Jew. So long as there was no discrimination between them, no problem was likely to arise. The five-day school week, of course, takes care of the Sabbath and of Sunday as days of special religious observance. But with the advent of new religious groups in our society section 30 assumes a new importance. Is it an infringement of section 30 for a local education authority to refuse a Muslim time off to go to the mosque on Friday unless he accepts less pay than a full-time teacher earns?

When the section was enacted, the negative approach to its interpretation was, no doubt, sufficient. But society has changed since 1944: so also has the legal background. Religions, such as Islam and Buddhism, have substantial followings among our people. Room has to be found for teachers and pupils of the new religions in the educational system, if discrimination is to be avoided. This system must be made sufficiently flexible to accommodate their beliefs and their observances: otherwise, they will suffer discrimination—a consequence contrary to the spirit of section 30, whatever the letter of that law. The change in legal background is no less momentous. Since 1944 the United Kingdom has accepted international obligations designed to protect human rights and freedoms, and has enacted a series of statutes designed for the same purpose in certain critical areas of our society. These major statutes include the Trade Union and Labour Relations Act 1974, the Employment Protection Act 1975, the Sex Discrimination Act 1975, and the race relations legislation.

They were enacted after the United Kingdom had ratified the European Convention on Human Rights (signed November 1950: in force since September 3, 1953) and in the light of our obligations under the Charter of the United Nations. Today, therefore, we have to construe and apply section 30 not against the background of the law and society of 1944 but in a multiracial society which has accepted international obligations and enacted statutes designed to eliminate discrimination on grounds of race, religion, colour or sex. Further, it is no longer possible to argue that because the international treaty obligations of the United Kingdom do not become law unless enacted by Parliament our courts pay no regard to our international obligations. They pay very serious regard to them: in particular, they will interpret statutory language and apply common law principles, wherever possible, so as to reach a conclusion consistent with our international obligations: see *Salomon* v. *Customs and Excise Commissioners* [1967] 2 Q.B. 116 (particularly *per* Diplock L.J. at p. 143) and *Post Office* v. *Estuary Radio Ltd.* [1968] 2 Q.B. 740.

With these general considerations in mind, I conclude that the present case, properly considered, begins but does not end with the law of contract. It ends with a very difficult problem—the application to the particular circumstances of this appellant of the new law associated with the protection of the individual's human rights and fundamental freedoms.

Mr. Ahmad's contract of employment is to be found in the I.L.E.A.'s letter of May 30, 1968, offering him a full-time appointment, and his written acceptance of June 2, 1968. He was required to give full-time service exclusively in the capacity of a teacher: his terms and conditions relating to hours of work were not specified, but particular provisions were included in the staff code. In effect, he was to be available for duty as a teacher during school hours. He was to be entitled to leave with pay for religious observance on days of special obligation. This was provided for by clause 9 of the staff code, which I quote:

> "Religious observance: teachers (other than supply teachers) in any establishment aided and maintained by the authority who, for reasons of conscience, have objections to working on a particular day in term time, it being a day of special obligation in their religion, shall be allowed to leave with pay on the understanding that such leave shall be restricted to the days which are generally recognised in their religion as days when no work may be done."

It is accepted that, so far as relevant, section 30 of the Education Act 1944 was incorporated into his contract, and overrides any contractual provision inconsistent with it.

It was, therefore, a contract whereby the teacher undertook to be at school and available for teacher's duty during school hours subject to his right to leave with pay on days recognised as of special religious obligation "when no work may be done" and subject to his rights under section 30 to be protected from discrimination on the ground of his religion. In Islam Friday is not recognised as a day when no work may be done: on the contrary, it is a man's religious duty to work on Friday as well as to go to the mosque to pray. Clause 9 of the staff code, therefore, does not assist Mr. Ahmad, save indirectly as showing the intention of the parties to adjust their contract so far as is reasonable to accommodate the religious obligations of the teacher. Mr. Ahmad has, therefore, to rely on section 30.

The section protects certainly two classes of person: the candidate for a job, and an employed teacher. Mr. Ahmad was an employed teacher. The statutory words applicable to him are:

> "... no teacher in any such school shall be required to give religious instruction or receive any less emolument or be deprived of, or disqualified for, any promotion or other advantage by reason of the fact that he does or does not give religious instruction or by reason of his religious opinions or of his attending or omitting to attend religious worship ..."

The I.L.E.A. recognises that the section is essentially concerned with non-discrimination, but submits that the reference to "attending or omitting to attend religious worship" is a reference to the act of worship in school for which this part of the Education Act 1944, i.e. the set of sections 25 to 30, makes provision. Accordingly, the authority submits that the section imposes no obligation upon them to give a full-time teacher leave to attend religious worship outside school during school hours. The authority submits that it cannot be in breach of its contractual or statutory obligation merely because the appellant chose to accept a contractual obligation inconsistent with his religious duty.

The Employment Appeal Tribunal [1976] I.C.R. 461 accepted this submission. But, in my judgment, it begs the question. If section 30 means what Mr. Ahmad says it means, he made a contract which put upon the I.L.E.A. the obligation to make reasonable adjustments to his school time-table so as to avoid discrimination against him because of his Friday attendance at a mosque to worship.

The question is what the contract, which admittedly incorporates section 30, means. Is the section to be given a broad or a narrow construction? I have already referred to the narrow construction in outlining the I.L.E.A.'s submission.

The broad construction, for which Mr. Ahmad contends, is as follows. The section, it is submitted, is concerned quite generally with the religious opinions and practice of the teacher: he is to suffer no financial or career disadvantage by reason of his religion. No problem arises either in respect of the teacher's religious opinions or in respect of religious instruction. Opinions are not capable of spatial or temporal limitation. Contrariwise, it is obvious that the reference to giving religious instruction is a reference to something occurring at school in school hours. The words "by reason . . . of his attending or omitting to attend religious worship" are clearly also a reference to an event occurring in school hours. Are they also limited to "a single act of worship" with which the school day is to begin? See section 25 (1) of the Act. There is no such express limitation in the section. Is it, then, necessary to read it into the section?

The I.L.E.A. submits that because of its context, coming as it does as a final saving for the position of teachers at the end of a set of sections dealing with religious education in schools, the section is to be read as limited to attending, or omitting to attend worship in school. Further, the authority submits, it would be unfair on the teacher's colleagues, who will have to stand in for him while away, to read the section otherwise.

Although I see the force of the submission, I reject it; because fundamentally a narrow construction of the section is in conflict with the developments in our society to which I have already referred—developments which are protected by the statutes to which I have also referred. A narrow construction of the section would mean that a Muslim, who took his religious duty seriously, could never accept employment as a full-time teacher, but must be content with the lesser emoluments of part-time service. In modern British society, with its elaborate statutory protection of the individual from discrimination arising from race, colour, religion or sex, and against the background of the European Convention, this is unacceptable, inconsistent with the policy of modern statute law, and almost certainly a breach of our international obligations. Unless, therefore, the language of section 30 forces one to adopt the narrow construction, I would think it wrong to do so. But it does not: the section, linguistically speaking, can be construed broadly or narrowly. No doubt, Parliament in 1944 never addressed its mind to the problem of this case. But, if the section lends itself, as successful human rights or consitutional legislation must lend itself, to judicial interpretation in accordance with the spirit of the age, there is nothing in this point, save for the comment that Parliament by refusing to be too specific was wiser than some of us have subsequently realised. The choice of construction, while it must be exercised judicially, is ours: for the reasons which have attempted to formulate, the decision must be in favour of the broad construction.

Prais v. Council for the European Communities [1977] I.C.R. 284

European Court of Justice

The facts appear from the following extract from the judgment:

1. Whereas, by application registered in the Registry of the court on December 23, 1975, the applicant, of British nationality, a candidate in open competition "Council/LA/108," with a view to recruiting a linguistic expert (translator) of English mother tongue and to create a reserve list, seeks: (a) the annulment of the decision, contained in a letter dated September 29, 1975, from the Secretary-General of the Council, rejecting the applicant's complaint lodged on July 14, 1975; (b) the annulment of the Council's decision of May 5, 1975, refusing the applicant's request made by letter of April 25, 1975, for an alternative date for the written test in the competition; (c) the annulment of the results of the competition in so far as they may have been affected by that refusal; and (d) the award of damages.

2. By letter of April 25, 1975, the applicant informed the Council that, being of Jewish religion, and Friday May 16, 1975—the date fixed by the Council for the written test in the competition, which should take place simultaneously in Brussels and London—being the first day of the Jewish feast of Shavuot (Pentecost), during which it is not permitted to travel or to write, she would be unable to undergo the test on that day, and asked the Council to fix another day for the test.

3. By letter of May 5, 1975, the Council replied to the applicant that it could not fix another date, since it was essential that all candidates should be examined on tests taken on the same date.

4. By application inscribed on the register of the court on April 7, 1976, Mr. David Grant Lawrence, a person recruited as a result of the competition, sought to intervene in this case, which was permitted by order of the court (First Chamber) on May 21, 1976.

5. During the oral hearing, the applicant abandoned her complaint concerning the annulment of the results of the competition in question, while maintaining that the costs of the intervention should not be borne by her.

6. The applicant claims first that the refusal of her request had as a result that by reason of her religious convictions she was prevented from taking part in the competition, in contravention of article 27, second paragraph, of the Staff Regulations, which provides that officials shall be selected without reference to race, creed or sex.

7. In addition the applicant claims that religious discrimination is prohibited by community law as being contrary to the fundamental rights of the individual, respect for which the court is bound to ensure.

8. The applicant also relies on article 9 of the European Convention for the Protection of Human Rights and Fundamental Freedoms, paragraph (2) of which provides:

> "Freedom to manifest one's religion or beliefs shall be subject only to such limitations as are prescribed by law and are necessary in a democratic society in the interests of public safety, for the protection of public order, health or morals, or for the protection of the rights and freedoms of others."

Since the European Convention has been ratified by all the member states the rights enshrined in it are, according to the applicant, to be regarded as included in the fundamental rights to be protected by community law.

9. The applicant claims that article 27 of the Staff Regulations is to be interpreted in such a manner that the Council should so arrange the dates of tests for competitions to enter its service as to enable every candidate to take part in the tests, whatever his religious circumstances. Alternatively the right of freedom of religion guaranteed by the European Convention so requires.

10. The Council does not deny that article 27 of the Staff Regulations requires that officials shall be selected without reference to race, creed or sex, nor does it seek to suggest that the right of freedom of religion as embodied in the European Convention does not form part of the fundamental rights recognised in community law, but says that neither the Staff Regulations nor the European Convention are to be understood as according to the applicant the rights she claims.

11. The Council submits that such an obligation would force it to set up an elaborate administrative machinery. Article 27 does not limit its application to any particular creeds by enumerating them, and it would be necessary to ascertain the details of all religions practised in any member state in order to avoid fixing for a test a date or a time which might offend against the tenets of any such religion and make it impossible for a candidate of that religious persuasion to take part in the test.

12. The Staff Regulations envisage that when a vacant post is being filled, and it is decided not to fill it by promotion or transfer, the selection of the candidate to be appointed shall, in general, be made by following the procedure of competition which may be on the basis of qualifications or of tests or of both qualifications and tests.

13. When the competition is on the basis of tests, the principle of equality necessitates that the tests shall be on the same conditions for all candidates, and in the case of written tests the practical difficulties of comparison require that the written tests for all candidates should be the same.

14. It is therefore of great importance that the date of the written tests should be the same for all candidates.

15. The interest of participants not to have a date fixed for the test which is unsuitable must be balanced against this necessity.

16. If a candidate informs the appointing authority that religious reasons make certain dates impossible for him the appointing authority should take this into account in fixing the date for written tests, and endeavour to avoid such dates.

17. On the other hand if the candidate does not inform the appointing authority in good time of his difficulties, the appointing authority would be justified in refusing to afford an alternative date, particularly if there are other candidates who have been convoked for the test.

18. If it is desirable that an appointing authority informs itself in a general way of dates which might be unsuitable for religious reasons, and seeks to avoid fixing such dates for tests, nevertheless, for the reasons indicated above, neither the Staff Regulations nor the fundamental rights already referred to can be considered as imposing on the appointing authority a duty to avoid a conflict with a religious requirement of which the authority has not been informed.

19. In so far as the Council, if informed of the difficulty in good time, would have been obliged to take reasonable steps to avoid fixing for a test a date which would make it impossible for a person of a particular religious persuasion to undergo the test, it can be said that the Council in the present case was not informed of the unsuitability of certain days until the date for the

test had been fixed, and the Council was in its discretion entitled to refuse to fix a different date when the other candidates had already been convoked.

20. For these reasons the applicant's claim should be rejected.

OATHS ACT 1888

1. When affirmation may be made instead of oath

Every person upon objecting to being sworn, and stating, as the ground of such objection, either that he has no religious belief, or that the taking of an oath is contrary to his religious belief, shall be permitted to make his solemn affirmation instead of taking an oath in all places and for all purposes where an oath is or shall be required by law, which affirmation shall be of the same force and effect as if he had taken the oath; . . .

2. Form of affirmation

Every such affirmation shall be as follows:

"I, A.B., do solemnly, sincerely, and truly declare and affirm," and then proceed with the words of the oath prescribed by law, omitting any words of imprecation or calling to witness.

3. Validity of oath not affected by absence of religious belief

Where an oath has been duly administered and taken, the fact that the person to whom the same was administered had, at the time of taking such oath, no religious belief, shall not for any purpose affect the validity of such oath.

4. Form of affirmation in writing

Every affirmation in writing shall commence "I,————, of————, do solemnly and sincerely affirm," and the form in lieu of jurat shall be "Affirmed at————, this———— day of————, 18——. Before me."

5. Swearing with uplifted hand

If any person to whom an oath is administered desires to swear with uplifted hand, in the form and manner in which an oath is usually administered in Scotland, he shall be permitted so to do, and the oath shall be administered to him in such form and manner without further question.

MOTOR-CYCLE CRASH-HELMETS (RELIGIOUS EXEMPTION) ACT 1976

An Act to exempt turban-wearing followers of the Sikh religion from the requirement to wear a crash-helmet when riding a motor-cycle.

Amendment of Road Traffic Act 1972

1. In section 32 of the Road Traffic Act 1972 there shall be inserted after subsection (2) the following new subsection:—

"(2A) A requirement imposed by regulations under this section (whenever made) shall not apply to any follower of the Sikh religion while he is wearing a turban."

THE LORD CHANCELLOR (TENURE OF OFFICE AND DISCHARGE OF ECCLESIASTICAL FUNCTIONS) ACT 1974

An Act to declare the law relating to the tenure of the office of Lord Chancellor by Roman Catholics and to make provision for the exercise of ecclesiastical functions during any tenure of the Office of Lord Chancellor by Roman Catholics.

1. Declaratory provision as to office of Lord Chancellor

For the avoidance of doubt it is hereby declared that the office of Lord Chancellor is and shall be tenable by an adherent of the Roman Catholic faith.

2. Provision for alternative exercise of functions normally performed by Lord Chancellor

In the event of the office of Lord Chancellor being held by an adherent of the Roman Catholic faith it shall be lawful for Her Majesty in Council to make provision for the exercise of any or all the visitational or the ecclesiastical functions normally performed by the Lord Chancellor, and any patronage to livings normally in the gift of the Lord Chancellor, to be performed by the Prime Minister or any other Minister of the Crown.

Note: Some uncertainty has been expressed as to whether Jews or Roman Catholics (Muslims? Atheists?) were eligible to hold the office of Lord Chancellor—See *Halsbury's Laws of England* (4th ed.), Vol. 8, Constitutional Law, para. 1171. There is good reason to believe that this doubt lacked foundation—See W. S. Lilly and J. E. P. Wallis, *A Manual of the Law Specially affecting Catholics* (London, 1893), pp. 36-43 (note especially the Opinion of the Attorney-General, Sir John Coleridge, in 1872, reproduced as an Appendix, at pp. 181-3). Be that as it may the view has been authoritatively expressed by Mr. W. E. Gladstone in introducing a Bill to remove certain religious disabilities that "it is quite plain that no person charged by Her Majesty with the solemn duty of forming a government in this country could venture to recommend to Her Majesty this or that individual for either of these great offices [Lord Chancellor and Lord Lieutenant of Ireland—the latter was dealt with specifically in the Government of Ireland Act 1920, s. 37 (1)] while there was the smallest doubt attaching to the law which would place the validity of his acts in question." The occasion for Gladstone's attempt to open up the Chancellorship was that a Catholic, Sir William Russell seemed a possible candidate for the post—in fact he was made a Lord of Appeal, as Lord Russell of Killowen, and later Lord Chief Justice. The enactment of the 1974 Act may similarly have been with a particular individual in mind. To the question why did the 1974 Act not simply provide that "the Office of Lord Chancellor is and shall be tenable by an adherent of any faith or of no faith?" the answer may be that, that is not the way the official mind works. It seems, therefore, that before a Jew (or a member of any non-Christian group) is appointed as Lord Chancellor legislation will probably be felt to be necessary.

SHOPS ACT 1950

Part IV Sunday Trading

General provisions in England and Wales

47. Closing of shops on Sunday

Every shop shall, save as otherwise provided by this Part of this Act, be closed for the serving of customers on Sunday:

53. Persons observing the Jewish Sabbath

(1) Subject to the provisions of this section, the occupier of any shop who is a person of the Jewish religion shall be entitled, upon making to the local authority an application in accordance with the provisions of this section, to have the shop registered under this section by the local authority, and so long as the shop is so registered then—

> (a) the shop shall be closed for all purposes connected with trade or business on Saturday; and
>
> (b) the provisions of this Part of this Act requiring the shop to be closed for the serving of customers on Sunday shall not apply until two o'clock in the afternoon; and
>
> (c) there shall be kept conspicuously placed in the shop a notice stating that it will be closed on Saturday and, if the shop will be open for the serving of customers on Sunday after two o'clock in the afternoon for the purposes of any transaction for which it is permitted under this Part of this Act to be so open, specifying the hours during which, and the purposes for which, it will be so open.

(2) Any application for the registration of a shop under this section shall be in the prescribed form and shall be accompanied—

> (a) by a statutory declaration made by the occupier of the shop in such form as may be prescribed declaring that he conscientiously objects on religious grounds to carrying on trade or business on the Jewish Sabbath; and
>
> (b) by such further statutory or other declarations and certificates, if any, made by such persons, and in such form, as may be prescribed.

(3) For the purposes of this section, a shop occupied by a partnership or company shall be deemed to be occupied by a person of the Jewish religion if the majority of partners or of the directors, as the case may be, are persons of that religion, but not otherwise, and such a shop shall not be registered under this section unless the statutory declaration required by paragraph (a) of the last foregoing subsection is made by the majority of partners or directors and specifies the names and addresses of all the other partners or directors.

(4) If for the purpose of procuring the registration of any shop under this section any person knowingly or recklessly makes an untrue statement or untrue representation, he shall be liable, on summary conviction, to imprisonment for a term not exceeding three months or to a fine not exceeding fifty pounds, or to both such imprisonment and fine.

(7) If upon representations made to them it appears to the local authority that there is reason to believe—

(a) that the occupier of any shop registered under this section is not a person of the Jewish religion; or

(b) that a conscientious objection on religious grounds to carrying on business on the Jewish Sabbath is not genuinely held by the occupier of the shop, or in the case of a shop occupied by a partnership or company by the majority of the partners or of the directors, as the case may be,

the local authority may furnish particulars of the case to such tribunal as may, after consultation with the London Committee of Deputies of the British Jews, be prescribed, and if that tribunal, after considering the case in accordance with such rules as may be prescribed, report to the local authority that in their opinion the occupier of the shop is not a person of the Jewish religion or that such a conscientious objection is not so held as aforesaid, the local authority shall revoke the registration of the shop, and upon the revocation thereof the registration under this section of all other shops occupied by the same occupier, whether in the area of that local authority or elsewhere, shall be deemed to be also revoked.

(12) This section shall apply to persons who are members of any religious body regularly observing the Jewish Sabbath as it applies to persons of the Jewish religion, and references therein to persons of the Jewish religion shall be construed accordingly as including any person who is a member of such a body, and in the application of this section to such persons this section shall have effect as if for the reference therein to the London Committee of Deputies of the British Jews there were substituted a reference to such body as appears to the Secretary of State to represent such persons.

(13) As respects any shop which is for the time being registered under this section, this Act shall have effect as if—

(a) in subsection (1) of section one and subsection (1) of section seventeen, the references to weekdays were construed as references to weekdays other than Saturdays;

62. Exemption as respects Jewish retail dealers in meat

(1) Notwithstanding anything in this or any other Act prohibiting the carrying on of business on Sunday, any person of the Jewish religion may carry on the business of a retail dealer in Kosher meat and may keep open a shop for the serving of customers for the purpose of that business on Sunday, on condition that he complies with the following provisions, that is to say—

(a) he must be licensed for the sale of Kosher meat by the local Board of Shechita, or in the absence of any such Board by a committee appointed for the purpose by the local Jewish congregation established in accordance with Jewish law;

(b) he shall not carry on the business either of a retail dealer in Kosher meat or of a retail dealer in butchers' meat on Saturday and, if he carries on the business in a shop, he shall not keep open the shop for the purpose of the business on Saturday;

(c) he shall previously give notice to the local authority of his intention to carry on the business of a retail dealer in Kosher meat on Sunday; and

(d) if he carries on the business in any shop, he shall cause to be kept conspicuously posted in the shop a notice stating that it is open on Sunday for the purposes of retail dealing in Kosher meat, but is not open on Saturday.

(2) As respects any shop in which any such person carries on the said business on Sunday in compliance with the provisions of this section, this Act shall have effect as if—

(a) in subsection (1) of section one and subsection (1) of section seventeen, the references to weekdays were construed as references to weekdays other than Saturdays;

(b) . . .

Note: See similar provisions in Factories Act 1961, s. 109.

Ostreicher v. Secretary of State for the Environment and Another [1978] 1 W.L.R. 810

Court of Appeal

The applicant and her husband, Mr. and Mrs. Ostreicher, owned houses in respect of which the local authority had made a compulsory purchase order. In the light of an objection lodged by the applicants the Secretary of State decided to hold a public inquiry, and in a letter of February 5, 1976 the applicant's surveyors were informed that the inquiry would be held on April 21, 1976. On April 1 the surveyors wrote to the Secretary of State informing him that due to religious reasons they [the applicant and her husband] are totally unable to attend the hearing in respect of the proposed compulsory purchase order . . ." The surveyors, therefore, requested that the applicants should be permitted to "have a special hearing at a time and place to be arranged as they should not be penalised for not being able to attend through religious reasons." The Department of Environment declined either to postpone the hearing or to arrange for a special hearing, but informed the applicant that the Department's inspector would take account of the written objections already submitted and that in any case they could arrange to be represented in their absence. The hearing went ahead without the presence of the Ostreichers or their representative and the compulsory purchase order was confirmed. Mrs. Ostreicher moved to have the order quashed on the grounds *inter alia* of a breach of natural justice. Sir Douglas Frank, Q.C. sitting as a deputy judge in the Queen's Bench Division dismissed the application holding *inter alia*, that in his judgment "Article 9 of the European Convention of Human Rights and Fundamental Freedoms is of little assistance because it does not apply and moreover it is in vague terms." The applicant appealed.

LORD DENNING, M.R.: Now Sarah and Jacob Ostreicher are devout Jews. They observe the Sabbath in accordance with the Fourth Commandment in the Book of Exodus, and in accordance with the Talmud which is their holy book, they likewise observe other holy days: and these include the seventh day of the Passover. In accordance with the injuction in their holy book, they do no manner of work themselves, nor do they permit any of their servants to work, "nor the stranger that is within thy gates." That is their religious belief. No doubt many other people in Hackney share it. It is an area in which there is a large Jewish community.

Mr. and Mrs. Ostreicher instructed their surveyors to look after the matter for them. They were the firm of Philip Fisher & Co. These surveyors put in objections. So did the owners of the other properties in the area. The Secretary of State for the Environment decided to hold a public inquiry. It is provided for by Schedule 3 to the Housing Act 1957. The minister had to fix a day. Reading between the lines it is pretty plain what happened. The men at the ministry looked at their diaries. This was in January 1976. They had to give at least six weeks' notice to all objectors (that is provided for by rule 4 (2) of the Compulsory Purchase by Local Authorities (Inquiries Procedure) Rules 1962). They had to give notice to the public by advertisements and so forth 14 days before the hearing. So they had to arrange the day of the hearing some considerable time ahead.

In this particular case they decided to give 10 or 11 weeks' notice in advance of the inquiry. Looking at their diaries in January 1976, they decided that April would be a suitable month in which to hold the inquiry. Mid-April would not be suitable because Good Friday fell on April 16, 1976, and Easter Monday would be on April 19. Those dates not being suitable, the men at the ministry decided that Wednesday, April 21, 1976, would be a suitable day. Most people would think that would be a very suitable day for an inquiry, the Wednesday after the Easter bank holiday. No doubt the ministry consulted Hackney council about it. The council did not think the date was unsuitable. So that date was chosen. All the objectors were notified that the inquiry was to be held on April 21. A room was booked at Hackney Town Hall.

On March 8 (some weeks before the inquiry) the local council sent to the surveyors for Mr. and Mrs. Ostreicher's particulars about the houses which were unfit. Having received those particulars, the surveyors started their preparations. But, lo and behold, just three weeks before the inquiry was to be held, the surveyors for Mr. and Mrs. Ostreicher, no doubt on their clients' instructions, said that Wednesday, April 21, would not suit them because it was the seventh day of the Passover; and people of the Jewish faith were not allowed to work on that day: and no one was allowed to do anything on their behalf. On April 1, the surveyors wrote to the Secretary of State . . .

Just consider the ministry's position. The inquiry had been fixed for April 21. The local council had been making their preparations. The other objectors and the lessees and so on had been making their arrangements. The ministry felt that, after making all those preparations, they could not change the date of the inquiry. Accordingly, on April 7, 1976, the Department of the Environment sent this reply to the surveyors:

". . . Unfortunately it is not possible for the department to consider either a deferment of the current inquiry date or any form of special hearing into a compulsory purchase order at this stage. In the event of your client not appearing at the inquiry arranged for April 21, 1976, you may be assured that the department's inspector will take full account of your written objection before submitting his findings to the Secretary of State for consideration. Should your clients deem it necessary they are open of course to arrange to be represented at the inquiry in their absence."

In that letter the ministry referred to the "written objection" which the surveyors had already submitted: and told them that they would be taken fully into account: and added that Mr. and Mrs. Ostreicher could be represented if they wished. That seems to me to be a very sensible suggestion so as to solve the problem..

Unfortunately the surveyors did not reply to that letter at all. April 21 arrived. The inspector went to the town hall. Many of the objectors were represented there. The inspector held the inquiry. He had Mr. and Mrs. Ostreicher's papers before him stating their case. He noted down that no one was there to represent them. He made a note in his report that "owing to reasons of religion" Mr. and Mrs. Ostreicher "were unable to appear at the inquiry to enlarge upon their written grounds of objection" which he summarised. He inspected the premises. He eventually made his report with his various recommendations. He recommended that the order should be affirmed with some variations as to individual houses. One of Mr. and Mrs. Ostreicher's houses came out well. It was no. 16 Rushmore Road. That house was lifted up. Instead of being taken at site value, that house was found to be in a sufficiently good condition for the inspector to recommend that it be put into the grey category and taken at market value. But as to the rest of the houses, he recommended that they were unfit for human habitation and should be purchased at site value.

The inspector made that report to the minister on July 21, 1976. On October 26, 1976, the minister wrote his decision letter confirming the order and carrying out the inspector's recommendations.

When that decision was received by the surveyors of Mr. and Mrs. Ostreicher, they took objection . . .

Looking at this particular case, it seems to me that the men at the department acted perfectly reasonably in what they did. First, they acted reasonably in arranging the date of April 21, the Wednesday after Easter Monday. That would seem to all ordinary people to be quite a suitable day. I cannot think that even in Hackney it would be wrong for the minister to give that date as a suitable date for the inquiry. Indeed no objection was ever taken to it by anyone until two or three months later when this letter of April 1, 1976, was written on behalf of Mr. and Mrs. Ostreicher. In that letter the surveyors do not say that they could not attend themselves or that anyone else could not attend on behalf of Mr. and Mrs. Ostreicher to look after their interests. Moreover that letter only refers to one house, no. 16. It only says: ". . . our clients and their solicitors say that due to religious reasons they are totally unable to attend." The minister's representative wrote back quite reasonably. He said: "Should your clients deem it necessary they are open of course to arrange to be represented at the inquiry in their absence." That was a reasonable suggestion from the department "Send your surveyor if you wish." There was no reply to that letter. If Mr. and Mrs. Ostreicher or their representative thought that there ought to be a postponement or an adjournment, so far as their houses were concerned, they could have written back and said so. They did not ask for an adjournment.

Secondly, the inspector acted reasonably in going on with the inquiry as he did. No representative turned up on behalf of Mr. and Mrs. Ostreicher. It seems to me that the inspector could well have understood from what had happened that they were content to leave the position as it was on the papers. Their objection had been put forward in writing. It appeared as if they left it to the inspector, after the inspection, to come to his decision. I see no want of natural justice whatever in what the inspector did either at the inquiry or later on in making his report.

Shaw and Waller, L.JJ. agreed.

EMPLOYMENT PROTECTION (CONSOLIDATION) ACT 1978

Dismissal relating to trade union membership:

58.—(3) Dismissal of an employee by an employer shall be regarded as fair . . . if—

(a) it is the practice, in accordance with a union membership agreement, for employees for the time being of the same class as the dismissed employee to belong to a specified independent trade union, or to one of a number of specified independent trade unions; and

(b) the reason for the dismissal was that the employee was not a member of the specified union or one of the specified unions, or had refused or proposed to refuse to become or remain a member of that union or one of those unions;

but subject to subsections (3A) to (3C).

(3A) The dismissal of an employee in the circumstances set out in subsection (3) shall be regarded as unfair if he objects on grounds of conscience or other deeply-held personal conviction to being a member of any trade union whatsoever or of a particular trade union.

(3B) The dismissal of an employee by an employer in the circumstances set out in subsection (3) shall be regarded as unfair if the employee—

(a) has been among those employees of the employer who belong to the class to which the union membership agreement relates since before the agreement had the effect of requiring them to be or become members of a trade union, and

(b) has not at any time while the agreement had that effect been a member of a trade union in accordance with the agreement.

(3C) Where a union membership agreement takes effect after the commencement of section 6 of the Employment Act 1980 in relation to the employees of any class of an employer, and an employee of that class is dismissed by the employer in the circumstances set out in subsection (3), the dismissal shall be regarded as unfair if—

(a) the agreement has not been approved in relation to those employees in accordance with section 58A, or

(b) it has been so approved through a ballot in which the dismissed employee was entitled to vote, but he has not at any time since the day on which the ballot was held been a member of a trade union in accordance with the agreement.

Note: s. 58, (3A)–(3C) inserted by Employment Act 1980.

Saggers v. British Railways Board [1977] I.C.R. 809

Saggers v. British Railways Board (No. 2) [1978] I.C.R. 1111

Employment Appeal Tribunal

Saggers after 20 years' membership of the National Union of Railwaymen left it in 1958 as a result of a dispute over arrears of union dues. At that time he had for some time been a Jehovah's Witness, a sect which permitted membership of a trade union. In 1974 British Rail and the N.U.R. entered into a union membership agreement, establishing a closed shop. Saggers wrote to his employer saying that his religious convictions did not allow him to join the N.U.R. as required by the union membership agreement. He was subsequently dismissed and then brought a claim for unfair dismissal to an industrial tribunal, which failed. He appealed.

ARNOLD, J. delivered the judgment of the Employment Appeal Tribunal: There are a number of matters arising on construction [of para. 6 (5) of Schedule 1, Trade Union and Labour Relations Act 1974, as amended in 1976, and now re-enacted as s. 58 (3) of the Employment Protection (Consolidation) Act 1978]. The first arises not so much on the language of this particular paragraph, but upon that language taken in comparison with the predecessor provision in the Industrial Relations Act 1971. That Act contained the corresponding provisions in section 9.

It is not necessary to read the whole of that section. The corresponding phrase appears in section 9 (1) (b) which relates to a worker who objects on grounds of conscience to being a member of a trade union. That was translated, when this provision of the Act of 1971, in common with many other provisions relating to dismissal, was re-enacted in Schedule 1 to the Act of 1974, from the language of section 9 to the differing language of paragraph 6 (5) and in particular for grounds of conscience one finds grounds of religious belief. The industrial tribunal said in its decision that it attached importance to that fact, and that view certainly contributed to the tribunal's conclusion.

There is much to be said for the view that, at any rate in very many cases, perhaps the overwhelming majority of cases, there will not in fact be any distinction between conscience as a factor forbidding or grounding an objection to belonging to a trade union or indeed doing anything else, and religious belief providing that ground. Indeed, in a case as long ago as 1941, *Newell* v. *Gillingham Corporation* [1941] 1 All E.R. 552, a case concerning the word "conscientious" as used in the phrase "conscientious objector," Atkinson J., referring to the problem which he had to consider, whether the plaintiff in that case was a conscientious objector or not, said, at p. 553:

> "It is perfectly plain that the plaintiff was not a conscientious objector in the true sense. He was a political conscientious objector. A true conscientious objector which is what Parliament had in mind, is one who upon religious grounds thinks it wrong to kill and to resist force by force. He thinks that is the teaching of Christ . . ."

That seems to suggest two things: first of all, that in a proper context one can have someone who is not a religious conscientious objector nevertheless described as a conscientious objector—in that case, a political conscientious objector; but secondly, that in the ordinary way, if one is to describe someone as a conscientious objector, one would expect to find a religious basis for his objection.

In *Hynds* v. *Spillers-French Baking Ltd.* (1974) 9 I.T.R. 261, which came before the National Industrial Relations Court, where it was heard by Lord Thomson and two other members of the court, in the judgment in that case—which was a judgment in which the expression "grounds of conscience " as used in section 9, in the passage which I have quoted from the Industrial Relations Act 1971, was under consideration—the court said, at p. 265:

> "In our opinion 'grounds of conscience' necessarily points to and involves a belief or conviction based on religion in the broadest sense as contrasted with personal feeling, however strongly held, or intellectual creed."

Of course, if that is right, if it necessarily points to and involves a religious belief or religious conviction—and as between those two we see no distinction—the change of language from "grounds of conscience" to the phrase used in the Act of 1974 would not be of significance, because every ground of conscience would equate to a ground of religious belief and it could hardly be suggested that there would be some ground of religious belief which validly founded an objection which did not constitute itself a ground of conscience. But with the greatest respect to the court which decided the *Hynds* case we find it impossible to go the whole way with that dictum. We can conceive, rare though they may be, that there may well be cases in which conscience directs or forbids a certain course of action, be it joining a trade union or anything else, having been brought to that point of conviction by moral or ethical considerations which do not possess a religious content. An obvious example might be provided by a consideration of an acknowledged atheist who is nevertheless a man of strong moral principle, whose mind is possessed by a conviction that it would be ethically wrong to do such-and-such an act; and it seems to us that it could fairly be said that to do that act would be against his conscience. Yet there is, by definition, no religious motivation or causation involved in that conclusion or the formulation of that conviction. One can conceive, perhaps more probably, of a man who, whilst a religious man in that he is a convinced believer in religious dogma or creed or idiosyncratic religious convictions, forms a moral objection to a particular course of action for reasons other than those which inform his religious life. If that is the right view, then there is significance in a general way in the change of language as between the statute of 1971 and the statute of 1974 in that it would not be any objection based on grounds of conscience which after the substitution of the Act of 1974 would justify the refusal, but only such objections based on grounds of conscience as could be discerned to be based also on religious grounds. There would, to put it another way, be some conscientious objection which did not qualify. That would be a matter of importance in a case in which at the material time there was some reason to suppose that considerations other than religious considerations operated upon the mind of the claimant, the refuser, so as to cause him to refuse to join the union or to insist on leaving the union. It would not be an important distinction in a case in which the only moral factors which informed his conscience could be religious factors. That would be a matter for evidence in each case. That is the first point of construction which has been argued, and that is our conclusion upon that point.

The next matter for consideration has been this. In many cases—one might perhaps go so far as to say in almost all cases—a man's religious belief is identifiable with the accepted belief within a religious organisation to which he adheres. It therefore follows that in almost every case, in order to determine what is the religious belief of the subject of the inquiry, it will be sufficient to inquire what is the body of religious belief which is accepted within the denomination or sect to which he belongs. The question is whether that is always and necessarily so. That question falls to be answered by a consideration of the language which is used in paragraph 6 (5) of Schedule 1 to the Act of 1974 in the context of what common sense tells one are the available possibilities.

The language which is used is this: "the employee genuinely objects on grounds of religious belief." The objection which has to be taken into consideration quite simply must be the objection of the employee. Then one has to consider upon what that objection is grounded; that is, religious belief. The word "belief," first of all, seems to us to suggest that which is believed by the person whose belief is under consideration; and for that reason it seems to us that the word more naturally describes the content of intellectual acceptance by the person under consideration than an established body of creed or dogma appertaining to himself as well as a number of other persons. In almost every case, no doubt, the two are identical. In many cases it will not be easily credible that a faithful adherent to a particular organisation has developed a body of belief which can truly and accurately be described as religious and which differs from that generally accepted within that body. But it seems to us that if, perhaps in the exceptional case, the industrial tribunal, having considered the evidence of what the body generally believes, and having considered the evidence of what the employee claims to believe, is convinced that in spite of differences between the two the employee's claim is truly and genuinely justified as being that which the tribunal is convinced that he does really and truly believe, then there is no conceptual impossibility about accepting that that is indeed his religious belief. But, of course, it cannot be sufficiently stressed that these are practical matters to be decided by practical men. A very strong pointer, no doubt, to the question what his religious belief really and truly extends to, will in almost every case be assisted with insight by establishing what is the body of belief commonly held by the sect or demonination to which he belongs . . .

From those general considerations we proceed to an examination of the details of this appeal. What happened here was this, that about 1938, fairly early in the very long service which the employee had on the railway, he joined the National Union of Railwaymen, and he remained a member of that union for 20 years. In 1958, by which time he had for some time already been a member of the denomination—if that is the right word to use—to which he now belongs (that of the Watch Tower Society, otherwise Jehovah's Witnesses), he fell out with the union over matters which had nothing whatever to do with ethical, moral or religious considerations; it was all about how much his arrears of subscription were when he was transferred from one branch to another. And he left the union for those reasons. Later on, after he had been away from the union for quite a time, in the run-up, it is fair to say, to the enactment of the Act of 1971 the question of a closed shop was being discussed. It is unnecessary to go into any greater detail than that. In January 1971, the employee had an interview with the branch secretary of the union in the relevant area. He was accompanied by Mr. Lindars, who was a personnel officer of the employers, and at the end of a discussion, in which it was made plain that the employee had no intention of becoming a member of any trade union, he was instructed by Mr. Lindars, on behalf of his employers, either to join the recognised trade union or to apply for exemption. And he did apply for exemption by letter of January 25, 1971, in which he said, shortly put, that he was so busy promoting the Christian faith—that was in the context of membership of the Watch Tower Society—that he had no time to devote to other matters and that that was why he was unwilling to join the union; and he wished to claim exemption from joining it on that account. That was an indication of a refusal or unwillingness to join the union, with religious connections; but it is not claimed, and could not be claimed, that that was an objection on the grounds of religious belief. Thus stood the matter in 1971.

Then there came into operation the Act of 1974 which, for various reasons which it is not necessary to describe, made the proceeding of the union and employers to a closed shop situation more likely and more immediate. In that context the matter of the employee's continuing non-membership of the union came up again. On October 14, 1975, the employee wrote to the area signal manager at Brighton, Mr. Tubb, obviously referring to what had happened in 1971, saying he thought the matter to be settled on the basis, in effect, that he would pay the equivalent of his dues to a charitable organisation, and ending up with these words: "With my Christian convictions as they are, my conscience does not permit my joining any union or political organisation." That created a problem which could only be solved by a conclusion as to whether he could be persuaded to change his mind, or should be dismissed. The matter was reported through the usual channels within the British Railways organisation, and in due course an internal body was set up —referred to as a "panel"—consisting of representatives of the employers and the relevant unions, to consider what the position really and truly was with regard to the employee. That panel sat on March 18, 1976. Five days before that, on March 13, 1976, the employee again wrote about the matter. He said this, in exactly the same terms as the previous letter, so far as material:

> "I therefore wish to be excused from joining. My Christian convictions as they are, my conscience does not permit my joining any union or political organisation."

On March 18 the panel sat and the employee appeared before it to explain the position. A note is before the appeal tribunal, recorded by Mr. Baldock, a manpower officer from regional headquarters of the employers, in terms which are not challenged as being an accurate record of what passed. This is what Mr. Baldock wrote down:

> "The employee is a member of Jehovah's Witnesses. He confirmed: (a) his religion does not proscribe trade union membership and he thought some Jehovah's Witnesses were also trade union members; (b) but for a mix-up some years back which resulted in loss of trade union membership [that was 1958] he might still be a trade union member today."

The formal minute of that meeting, which is also in evidence, confirms those two items.

The conclusion which was reached by that panel was that exemption from joining an appropriate trade union could not be granted in respect of the employee and accordingly he had to be dismissed. And dismissed he was, with effect from some date in the following August, but his last participation in the events which led up to his dismissal was his attitude as displayed on March 18 when he appeared before the panel . . .

All those matters in the 1938-1958 history, the 1958 departure from the union, the letter of 1971, the two letters of 1975 and 1976, the hearing before the panel in March 1976, and the cross-examination of the employee before the industrial tribunal, were in the minds of the members of the tribunal when they made their decision. In that decision there is no specific conclusion as to whether or not the employee's objection was really grounded on religious belief. The form which the decision took was this, that the majority of the membership of the industrial tribunal apparently reached the conclusion that religious belief had to be an idenfiable belief shared by the employee whose refusal was under consideration and by the other persons with whom he was religiously associated. The dissenting member took the view that religious belief was personal to the man concerned and did not refer to the religious belief of the organisation. We have indicated our acceptance of that dissenting view of the law. But because that was the way in which the matter was decided, there is no specific finding whether or not the employee's idiosyncratic conclusion of conscience was or was not one which was grounded in an idiosyncratic religious belief. We are invited on behalf of the employee, on the one hand, to say that there is enough material in the findings of the industrial tribunal to enable us to say upon those findings that had they taken the view of the law which we have taken they would be bound to have said. "Yes, this refusal of the employee was grounded upon religious belief." We are urged on behalf of the employers to say that, looking at the matter in general, in relation to the findings, in relation to the primary material which the industrial tribunal had before it, we could safely adopt the opposite conclusion and say that this was a case in which the industrial tribunal must have said that they were not satisfied that the objection was grounded on religious belief. We have little difficulty in rejecting the latter course. In the course of their findings, after mentioning the content of the letter of October 1975—"With my Christian convictions as they are, my conscience does not permit my joining any union"—the industrial tribunal proceeded:

> "There were obviously discussions and the usual procedures were gone through"—between October and March—regarding [the employee] but [he] maintained his position and may we add here that we accept without question the genuineness and sincerity of the attitude adopted by him."

That included an expression of attitude that, his Christian convictions being what they were, his conscience did not permit him to join any union. It seems impossible in the face of that fact to say that, whatever exactly they meant by that passage—and it is not very clear what they did mean—there is sufficient material to say with confidence that they would not have accepted the view that his objection was grounded on religious belief. On the other hand, we think that, given the varying attitude demonstrated by the history which we have recounted, given that the industrial tribunal's acceptance of the genuineness and sincerity of the employee's attitude was not pin-pointed in relation to any particular expression of that attitude and did not proceed from any examination in the context of that statement of what are to some extent inconsistencies in the history, we equally do not feel that we can with confidence ourselves supply the conclusion which is not arrived at by the industrial tribunal, that this is a case in which the employee had demonstrated the accuracy of the proposition that his objections were grounded upon religious belief. There is therefore, as we think, no alternative—unattractive as this is—to sending the matter back for a new conclusion by the industrial tribunal upon the basis of the guidance on the law which we have done our best to lay down.

The tribunal found that his scruples against joining the N.U.R. were not based on religious belief and dismissed his claim. Saggers again appealed on a question of law to the Employment Appeal Tribunal.

KILNER BROWN J. delivered the judgment of the Tribunal:

Now the case comes before us on a fourth hearing because the employee has appealed again. It is all most unfortunate. However no less than nine members of tribunals have all found it a most troublesome case. As will emerge, three members are in favour of the employee, three are against him and three found that they were not able to make a subjective assessment of the man's beliefs on the information before them. Two of us today recognise the force of the viewpoint of the member of this tribunal, Mr. Goff. He founds his conclusion on two factors, one, that the employee ceased to be a member of the National Union of Railwaymen for reasons which had nothing to do with religion and, two, that membership of the Watch Tower Society in no way inhibited a believer from remaining or becoming a member of a trade union. Moreover the employee was a faithful adherent of the sect, did not reject their views, nor did he claim to establish a religion of his own with different objectives and different standards. As Mr. Goff puts it, he finds it difficult to accept that people can shelter within a recognised religion or sect which enables them to claim genuine religious beliefs and then tack on personal riders such as a refusal to join a trade union. The remaining two of us do not consider that we can dismiss the appeal on that basis. It does not do justice to the industrial tribunal's findings of fact.

The majority of us begin our approach to this case by reminding ourselves that an appeal can only succeed on a point of law and that we are bound by the findings of fact and the tribunal's assessment of the witnesses. It is in the latter context that we consider we are driven to adopt a course different from that which appealed to Mr. Goff and the majority of the industrial tribunal. At the first hearing the reasons contain these sentences:

> "We accept without question the genuineness and sincerity of the attitude adopted by the employee. We also accepted him as a witness of truth when giving evidence."

At the second hearing they recognised that these findings restricted a fresh approach and they made these comments:

> "We said in our original decision that we accepted the sincerity and genuineness of his attitude. That is still our opinion, and we do not think that anyone who has seen [the employee] in the witness box could come to any other conclusion. But we should explain what we mean by that. We meant, and still mean, that he is honest in his belief that he is entitled to object to trade union membership because of his religious beliefs. He honestly believes that what he repeatedly calls his conscientious scruples arise from his religious beliefs. His objection is not bogus."

The majority then went on to say that despite these findings as his religious beliefs had not changed and he had once accepted trade unionism his objection was not due to genuine religious belief but to a conscientious objection. It seems to the majority of us that this amounts to a revision of their original finding of fact and their original assessment of the man. This is what the employee said in evidence and which the industrial tribunal on the first occasion specifically accepted as true:

> "With my growth of faith I became more convinced that I could not join a trade union. If I could have squared my religious beliefs with membership of a trade union I would have joined. My conscience stems from my religion."

When cross-examined he added:

> "My faith is showing me the way more clearly. There has been a continuous process of my thought. I do not think that a Christian can be a trade unionist. This is my personal opinion."

The majority of us in this appeal tribunal are firmly of the view that if all that was accepted as true there was only one answer and that was, as the minority member of the industrial tribunal concluded, the employee had clearly established an objection due to religious belief. This means that we are driven to say by a majority that the majority decision was on the facts as found by them one that no reasonable tribunal could have reached. It is not necessary to go so far as to say it was perverse though some would find it to be so. This amounts to an error on a point of law and by a majority the appeal is allowed.

In re Lysaght, Decd. Hill and Another v. Royal College of Surgeons and Others [1966] 1 Ch.191

Chancery Division

Mrs Morris Lysaght having long intended to found studentships for the advancement of medical education and research by her will sought to set up a trust fund to be managed by the Royal College of Surgeons for the establishment of studentships, which by clause 11(D) of her will were to be held only by students who were British born "and not of the Jewish or Roman Catholic Faith." The Royal College of Surgeons informed the trustees that they were unable to accept the bequest on terms which specifically excluded Jewish or Roman Catholic students as such a limitation was "so invidious and so alien to the spirit of the College's work as to make the gift inoperable in its present form." The College indicated that they would be willing to accept the bequest if this limitation were to be deleted. The trustees of the will took out a summons asking, *inter alia*, (i) whether, on the true construction of the will, and in the events which had happened, the trust to pay £5,000 out of the trust fund to the Royal College of Surgeons was a valid trust for charitable purposes or whether it failed for uncertainty; (ii) if it was a valid charitable trust, whether the trustees ought to pay the £5,000 to the Royal College of Surgeons on the footing that the exclusion by the will from the objects of the trust of persons of the Jewish or Roman Catholic faiths was not valid or whether the £5,000 ought to be applied *cy-près;* and (iii) if necessary that a scheme for the application of the £5,000 might be established.

BUCKLEY J.:

I think that the Attorney-General is justified in his submission that clause 11 (D) is not an essential part of the primary and paramount object of the testatrix in respect of the endowment fund. . . .

Are, then, the circumstances such as to justify the court in permitting the trusts of the endowment fund to be administered without regard to so much of clause 11 (D) as requires religious discrimination?

In *Clayton* v. *Ramsden,*[1] a condition subsequent under which a beneficiary was to forfeit a benefit in the event of her marrying a person not of Jewish parentage and of the Jewish faith was held void for uncertainty, but different considerations apply in this respect to a forfeiture provision from those applicable to a condition precedent or a qualification to take a benefit: *In re Allen.*[2] In the one case the person liable to suffer a forfeiture must be able to

[1] [1943] A.C. 320.
[2] [1953] Ch. 116; [1953] 2 W.L.R. 244; [1953] 1 All E.R. 308. [1953] Ch. 810; [1953] 3 W.L.R. 637; [1953] 2 All E.R. 898, C.A.

know with certainty what will cause a forfeiture: in the other all that any person claiming to benefit has to do is to establish that the condition and qualification is satisfied in his particular case. The fact that someone else might have difficulty in demonstrating this with certainty does not prevent someone who clearly satisfies the appropriate test from claiming to be entitled or eligible to benefit. In the present case there would be a wide field open to any trustee of the endowment fund for the selection of students who manifestly satisfy the qualification of being neither of the Jewish nor of the Roman Catholic faith. Accordingly, I do not think that this part of the trust is affected by the vice of uncertainty. Nor, in my judgment, is it contrary to public policy, as Mr. Balcombe suggests. I accept that racial and religious discrimination is nowadays widely regarded as deplorable in many respects and I am aware that there is a Bill dealing with racial relations at present under consideration by Parliament, but I think that it is going much too far to say that the endowment of a charity, the beneficiaries of which are to be drawn from a particular faith or are to exclude adherents to a particular faith, is contrary to public policy. The testatrix's desire to exclude persons of the Jewish faith or of the Roman Catholic faith from those eligible for the studentship in the present case appears to me to be unamiable, and I would accept Mr. Clauson's suggestion that it is undesirable, but it is not, I think, contrary to public policy.

I do not understand the college to assert that it would be legally incapable of accepting the trusts of the endowment and giving them effect with due regard to the provision for religious discrimination. It is not suggested that this would be ultra vires the college. What I understand from their solicitor's letter which is in evidence and from what counsel has stated in court is that on account of the character of the college and of the purposes which it exists to serve, the college would be unalterably opposed to accepting and administering a trust containing any provision for religious discrimination.

Obviously a trustee will not normally be permitted to modify the terms of his trust on the ground that his own opinions or convictions conflict with them. If the conscience will not allow him to carry out the trust faithfully in accordance with its terms, he must make way for a trustee who can and will do so. But how, if the identity of the trustee selected by the settlor is essential to his intention? If it is of the essence of a trust that the trustees selected by the settlor and no one else shall act as the trustees of it and those trustees cannot or will not undertake the office, the trust must fail: *In re Lawton*[3] and see *Reeve* v. *Attorney-General,*[4] and Tudor on Charities, 5th ed., (1929), p. 128. I have already reached the conclusion that it is an essential part of the testatrix's intention that the college should be the trustee of the endowment fund. The college is, as I have said, unalterably opposed to accepting the trust if any provision for religious discrimination is an effective part of it. That part of paragraph (D) which requires religious discrimination, if it is to be insisted upon, will consequently defeat the testatrix's intention entirely for in that case the college must disclaim the trust with the result that it will fail.

The impracticability of giving effect to some inessential part of the testatrix's intention cannot, in my judgment, be allowed to defeat her paramount charitable intention.

[3] [1936] 3 All E.R. 378.
[4] (1843) 3 Hare 191, 197.

In *In re Robinson*,[5] P.O. Lawrence J. had to deal with a fund bequeathed many years earlier for the endowment of a church of an evangelical character to which conditions were attached, including what was called an "abiding" condition that a black gown should be worn in the pulpit unless this should become illegal. The evidence showed that in 1923 the wearing of a black gown in the pulpit, though not illegal, would be detrimental to the teaching and practice of evangelical doctrines and services in the church in question. Lawrence J. had to determine whether a scheme could properly be sanctioned dispensing with the observance of this condition. He said[6]:

> "The contention on behalf of the petitioner is that the condition as to the wearing of a black gown in the pulpit is impracticable, but that it is subsidiary to the main purpose of the bequest, and that the present case falls within that class of cases when the main charitable purpose is practicable, but a subsidiary purpose is impracticable. If that contention be correct, I am satisfied that the court, on assuming the execution of the charitable trusts declared by the testatrix, has ample jurisdiction to execute those trusts cy-près and to sanction a scheme, modifying the trusts by dispensing with the subsidiary purpose, so as to carry out, as nearly as possible, the main charitable intentions of the testatrix. In my judgment, the contention that the condition as to the black gown is subsidiary to the main purpose of the bequest is sound. The dominant charitable intention of the testatrix, as expressed in her will, was to provide a fund towards the endowment of a proposed evangelical church at Bournemouth, the right of patronage and presentation to the living of which should be vested in the trustee of a deed of November 24, 1877. This main purpose can be fully carried into effect apart altogether from the condition as to wearing a black gown in the pulpit. In these circumstances the wearing of the black gown in the pulpit, although expressly insisted upon by the testatrix as a condition of her bequest, is a purpose which is subsidiary to the main purpose of the bequest. Consequently, the court, if satisfied that the condition is impracticable, can properly sanction a scheme dispensing with it."

The judge held on the evidence that the effect of insisting upon the condition would be to defeat the main intention of the testatrix. He held that, although compliance with the condition was not impossible in an absolute sense, it was impracticable and ought to be dispensed with.

In that case compliance with the condition relating to the black gown was not impracticable at the inception of the trust in 1889, but had become so by 1923. In the present case, if the trust is impracticable, this is due to an initial difficulty, not to any change of circumstances. Since *In re Robinson*[7] was decided it has been recognised that different considerations govern the application of the cy-près doctrine when impracticability supervenes after a charitable trust has once taken effect from those which apply in cases of initial impracticability. In cases of supervening impracticability it matters not whether the original donor had or had not a general charitable intention (see *In re Wright*[8]). It was not, however, on any such ground as this that the decision in *In re Robinson*[9]

[5] [1923] 2 Ch. 332; 39 T.L.R. 509.
[6] [1923] 2 Ch. 332, 336.
[7] [1923] 2 Ch. 332.
[8] [1954] Ch. 347, 362; [1954] 2 W.L.R. 972; [1954] 2 All E.R. 98, C.A.
[9] [1923] 2 Ch. 332.

was based. The passage which I have read from the judgment of P.O. Lawrence J. makes it clear that he decided as he did because, in his opinion, the testatrix's dominant intention was to endow a church and that the condition as to wearing a black gown was not an essential part of that intention but merely subsidiary.

If I am right in the view that I have formed, that it was an essential part of the testatrix's intention in the present case that the College should be the trustee of the endowment fund, then I think that the reasoning in *In re Robinson*[10] is precisely applicable to the present case. Just as insistence on the black gown condition would in *In re Robinson* have defeated the paramount intention of the testatrix, so insistence on the provision for religious discrimination would defeat the paramount intention of the testatrix in the present case: indeed it would destroy the trust, for it would result in the College disclaiming the trusteeship, which would occasion the failure of the trust.

Accordingly, in my judgment, the court can and should enable the College to carry the trust into effect without any element of religious discrimination.

Blathwayt v. Baron Cawley and Others [1976] A.C. 397

House of Lords

By clause 6 of his will a testator who died in 1936 settled certain property upon trust for the benefit of certain persons. By clause 9 it was provided that if any person who became entitled as tenant for life or tenant in tail male to possession of the estate should "be or become a Roman Catholic . . . the estate hereby limited to him shall cease and determine and be utterly void and my principal estate shall thereupon go to the person next entitled . . . ." An issue having arisen before the courts as to how the trust property should be held one of the issues that had to be considered was the validity of the forfeiture clause.

LORD WILBERFORCE:

On the question whether the forfeiture clause, in so far as it relates to being or becoming a Roman Catholic is void for uncertainty. I am clearly of opinion that it is not. Clauses relating in one way or another to the Roman Catholic Church, or faith, have been known and recognised for too many years both in Acts of Parliament (e.g., the Bill of Rights and the Act of Settlement ("Popish religion") and Roman Catholic Relief Acts of 1791 and 1829) and in wills and settlements for it now to be possible to avoid them on this ground. I am of course aware that the present clause is a condition subsequent (or resolutive condition) and I need not quarrel with the accepted doctrine of English law derived from Lord Cranworth's words in *Clavering* v. *Ellison* (1859) 7 H.L.Case. 707, 725 which requires a greater degree of certainty in advance as to the scope of such conditions than is needed when the condition is precedent (or suspensive). I can respect this distinction for the purposes of this case without renouncing the right, which I conceive judges have, to judge the degree of certainty with some measure of common sense and knowledge and

---

[10][1923] 2 Ch. 332.

without excessive astuteness to discover ambiguities. The decisions which have been given, in relation to clauses as to Roman Catholicism, as well as those in which such clauses have passed scrutiny sub silentio, are, with rare exception, one way. They include: *In re May* [1917] 2 Ch. 126; *In re May* (No. 2) [1932] 1 Ch. 99; *In re Wright* (1937) 158 L.T. 368; *In re Morrison's Will Trusts* [1940] Ch. 102; *In re Evans* [1940] Ch. 629; *In re McKenna* [1947] I.R. 277; *McCausland* v. *Young* [1948] N.I. 72; [1949] N.I. 49. As decision the other way is *In re Borwick* [1933] Ch. 657, but there the condition was composite: "be or become a Roman Catholic or not be openly or avowedly Protestant." The balance of authority is strongly in favour of validity and the contrary would be barely arguable but for the views expressed in this House in *Clayton* v. *Ramsden* [1943] A.C. 320. The condition there was composite "not of Jewish parentage and of the Jewish faith." It was held by all members of the House that the first limb (and therefore on this ground the whole condition) was void for uncertainty and by four of their Lordships that the second limb, was void on the same ground. Lord Wright took the opposite view on the second limb, as had Lord Greene M.R. delivering the judgment of the Court of Appeal.

My Lords, I have no wish to whittle away decisions of this House by fine distinctions; but accepting, as I fully do, the opinions of the majority of their Lordships as regards the religious part of this condition, I do not consider myself obliged, or, indeed justified, in extending the conclusion there reached, as to uncertainty, to other clauses relating to other religions or branches of religions. The judgment of Lord Greene M.R. in the Court of Appeal (sub nom. *In re Samuel* [1942] Ch. 1) contains a very full account of decisions relating to the Roman Catholic faith, to the Protestant religion and the Church of England (amongst which he cited *Clavering* v. *Ellison*, 7 H.L.Cas. 707, and to which could be added the *Church Property Trustees of the Diocese of Newcastle* v. *Ebbeck* (1960) 104 C.L.R. 394) and the Lutheran religion (*Patton* v. *Toronto General Trusts Corporation* [1930] A.C. 629). All of these cases must, from a reading of that judgment, and from their Lordships' own experience, have been present to their minds. The absence of any reference to them in the speeches in this House refutes any suggestion that a new general principle was being laid down as to the invalidity on ground of uncertainty of all subsequent conditions whatsoever relating to all varieties of religious belief. It confirms that the decision in *Clayton* v. *Ramsden* [1943] A.C. 320 was a particular decision on a condition expressed in a particular way about one kind of religious belief or profession. I do not think it right to apply it to Roman Catholicism.

2. Finally, as to public policy. The argument under this heading was put in two alternative ways. First, it was said that the law of England was now set against discrimination on a number of grounds including religious grounds, and appeal was made to the Race Relations Act 1968 which does not refer to religion and to the European Convention of Human Rights of 1950 which refers to freedom of religion and to enjoyment of that freedom and other freedoms without discrimination on ground of religion. My Lords, I do not doubt that conceptions of public policy should move with the times and that widely accepted treaties and statutes may point the direction in which such conceptions, as applied by the courts, ought to move. It may well be that conditions such as this are, or at least are becoming, inconsistent with standards now widely accepted. But acceptance of this does not persuade me that we are justified, particularly in relation to a will which came into effect as long ago as 1936 and which has twice been the subject of judicial consideration, in in-

troducing for the first time a rule of law which would go far beyond the mere avoidance of discrimination on religious grounds. To do so would bring about a substantial reduction of another freedom, firmly rooted in our law, namely that of testamentary disposition. Discrimination is not the same thing as choice: it operates over a larger and less personal area, and neither by express provision nor by implication has private selection yet become a matter of public policy.

LORD CROSS OF CHELSEA:

Before the decision of this House in *Clayton* v. *Ramsden* [1943] A.C. 320 few if any Chancery practitioners would have thought it seriously arguable that a condition subsequent forfeiting a life interest on the life tenant becoming a Roman Catholic was void. The decision in *Clayton* v. *Ramsden* turned primarily on a condition for forfeiture on the beneficiary marrying a person "not of Jewish parentage" but four of the members of the House expressed the view that a condition against marriage with a person "not of the Jewish faith" was also void for uncertainty. If that be so then it is certainly arguable that a condition for forfeiture on the beneficiary becoming a Roman Catholic is void. That point was not however taken on behalf of Mark on the hearing of the summons taken out after his birth in 1949. That proceeded on the footing that Christopher forfeited his life interest in 1939 and that the only point to be determined was whether the interest in the income to which Justin then became entitled in possession had come to an end on Mark's birth. Your Lordships refused Mark leave to raise the issue of Christopher's forfeiture on this appeal, but the question whether the condition is or is not void emerges again in its application to Mark's estate tail. In agreement, I believe, with all your Lordships, I am clearly of opinion that the condition was not and is not void either for uncertainty or, as applied to a person of full age at the date of the will, on grounds of public policy. I accept, of course, that by the law of England a stricter test of certainty is applied to a condition subsequent than to a condition precedent but I agree with the judges both in the Irish Republic and in Northern Ireland that it would be an affront to common sense to hold that a condition for forfeiture if the beneficiary should become a Roman Catholic is open to objection on the ground of uncertainty: see *in re McKenna* [1947] I.R. 277 and *McCausland* v. *Young* [1948] N.I. 72; [1949] N.I. 49. If I had been a member of the House which heard *Clayton* v. *Ramsden*, I might well have agreed with Lord Wright that a condition for forfeiture on marriage with a person "not of the Jewish faith" was valid. But it is a vaguer conception than being or not being a Roman Catholic and acceptance of the view of the majority does not involve the consequence that a condition of forfeiture on becoming a Roman Catholic is open to objection on the score of uncertainty. Turning to the question of public policy, it is true that it is widely thought nowadays that it is wrong for a government to treat some of its citizens less favourably than others because of differences in their religious beliefs; but it does not follow from that that it is against public policy for an adherent of one religion to distinguish in disposing of his property between adherents of his faith and those of another. . . .

Note: Lord Simon of Glaisdale, Lord Edmund Davies and Lord Fraser of Tullybelton were in agreement on the validity of the forfeiture condition.

Administrative action taken against the Church of Scientology

On 25 July 1968 Mr. Robinson, Minister of Health made the following announcement in the House of Commons by way of written answer to a Parliamentary question:–

"During the past two years, Her Majesty's Government have become increasingly concerned at the spread of Scientology in the United Kingdom. Scientology is a pseudo-philosophical cult introduced into this country some years ago from the United States and has its world headquarters in East Grinstead. It has been described by its founder, Mr. L. Ron Hubbard, as 'the world's largest mental health organisation.

On 6th March 1967 scientology was debated in the House on a Motion for the Adjournment, when I made it clear that my Rt. Hon. Friend the Home Secretary and I considered the practice of scientology to be potentially harmful. Since the Anderson Report on Scientology (published in 1965 in the State of Victoria, Australia), coupled with the evidence already available in this country, sufficiently established the general undesirability and potential dangers of the cult, we took the view that there was little point in holding another enquiry.

Although this warning received a good deal of public notice at the time, the practice of scientology has continued, and indeed expanded, and Government Departments, Members of Parliament and local authorities have received numerous complaints about it.

The Government are satisfied, having reviewed all the available evidence, that scientology is socially harmful. It alienates members of families from each other and attributes squalid and disgraceful motives to all who oppose it; its authoritarian principles and practice are a potential menace to the personality and well-being of those so deluded as to become its followers; above all, its methods can be a serious danger to the health of those who submit to them. There is evidence that children are now being indoctrinated.

There is no power under existing law to prohibit the practice of scientology; but the Government have concluded that it is so objectionable that it would be right to take all steps within their power to curb its growth.

It appears that scientology has drawn its adherents largely from overseas, though the organisation is now making intensive efforts to recruit residents of this country. Foreign nationals come here to study scientology and to work at the so-called College in East Grinstead. The Government can prevent this under existing law (the Aliens Order), and have decided to do so. The following steps are being taken with immediate effect:

   (*a*) The Hubbard College of Scientology, and all other scientology establishments, will no longer be accepted as educational establishments for the purposes of Home Office policy on the admission and subsequent control of foreign nationals;

   (*b*) Foreign nationals arriving at United Kingdom ports who intend to proceed to Scientology establishments will no longer be eligible for admission as students;

   (*c*) Foreign nationals who are already in the United Kingdom, for example as visitors, will not be granted student status for the purpose of attending a scientology establishment;

(d) Foreign nationals already in the United Kingdom for study at a scientology establishment will not be granted extensions of stay to continue these studies;

(e) Work permits and employment vouchers will not be issued to foreign nationals (or Commonwealth citizens) for work at a scientology establishment;

(f) Work permits already issued to foreign nationals for work at a scientology establishment will not be extended.

My Rt. Hon. Friend the Home Secretary and I have amassed a considerable body of evidence about the activities of the cult in this country, in particular its effects on the mental health of a number of its clients, and its treatment of those who attempt to leave the movement or who oppose it in any way. We shall continue to keep a close watch on the situation and are ready to consider other measures, should they prove necessary".[1]

In January 1969 Sir John Foster, K.B.E., Q.C., M.P., was appointed by the Secretary of State for Social Services, Mr. Crossman, to "enquire into the practice and effects of Scientology, and to report." He reported, *inter alia*, with respect to certain forms of administrative discrimination against Scientologists, as follows:

193. By far the most important of all the Scientologists' complaints to me relates to the current Home Office policy of refusing leave to land to Scientologists from overseas who wish to enter the United Kingdom to study or work at Scientology establishments, and especially the exclusion from this country of Mr. Hubbard and his wife Mary Sue, and to the related policy of refusing extensions of permissions to stay here to those foreign and Commonwealth Scientologists who were already lawfully in the country. The scope of these policies was, it will be remembered, announced in the House of Commons on 25th July 1968 by Mr. Kenneth Robinson, M.P. (the then Minister of Health) in terms which I have already recited in paragraph 14 of this Report.

194. In fact, I have reason to think that the conduct of Immigration Officers at our ports of entry has been even more stringent than the letter of these measures. For example,

(a) not only foreign nationals, but also a number of Commonwealth citizens, have been refused leave to land when they disclosed themselves as Scientologists, although the relevant paragraph was expressed to refer only to foreigners;

(b) some Scientologists of foreign nationality have been turned away despite the fact that they came neither to study nor to work (these being the only categories mentioned in the relevant paragraphs).

210. Against the background, it seems to me wrong in principle for the Secretary of State for Home Affairs to use his wide powers of exclusion against those Scientologists who happen to be foreigners or Commonwealth citizens, when there is no law which prevents their colleagues holding U.K. citizenship from believing in their theories or carrying on their practices here. If the practices of Scientology are thought to constitute a danger to our society sufficiently grave to warrant prohibition or control under the law, then it is for Parliament to make such a law and for the Executive to apply it impartially

[1] 769 *H.C. Deb.*, Cols. *189-91.*

to Britons and foreigners alike within the confines of this country. But so long as none of our laws are being infringed, the classification of *foreign* Scientologists as "undesirable aliens" so that they are forbidden entry through our ports, while the accident of birth permits those Scientologists who happen to be citizens of the United Kingdom to process and be processed here with impunity, seems to me to constitute a use of this discretionary power which is quite contrary to the traditional policy followed by successive Home Secretaries over many years.

211. I draw some comfort from the fact that, in another connection, the Home Office itself seems to share this view. When the present Home Secretary, in a letter to Mr. Michael Foot, M.P. dated 25th August 1970, explained why he was not willing to extend the stay of Mr. Rudi Dutschke, he said this:–

> "I think it is wrong in principle that people who come to this country should do so on the basis that they refrain from any activities which are lawful for the ordinary citizen."[2]

If that is right—and of course I agree—then *a fortiori* it must be wrong in principle to exclude people from this country altogether on the sole ground that they intend to carry out here "activities which are lawful for the ordinary citizen".

212. In the view which I take, therefore, there is no reason why Scientologists of foreign or Commonwealth nationality should not henceforth be admitted to this country as visitors on precisely the same footing as other people. This would normally entitle them, under current policy set out in paragraph 14 of the Instructions to Immigration Officers, to a stay of up to three months at a time.

213. Again, foreign or Commonwealth Scientologists who wish to come and work here should in my view be granted or refused a work permit on precisely the same criteria as everyone else, and the fact that they or their proposed employers are Scientologists should be regarded as irrelevant.

214. The position of students is somewhat different. Under present Home Office policy, they form a privileged class in that they are normally given leave to stay for up to 12 months in the first instance, that is four times as long as an ordinary visitor. One of the necessary conditions for this is acceptance for a course of full-time study at a "bona fide educational establishment" and I am bound to say that on the evidence before me I am not satisfied that Scientology establishments as now organised can be said to fall within that description. However, as appears from the next Chapter of this Report, I recommend the passing of certain legislation for the organisation of psychotherapy as a profession, and if Parliament accepts this recommendation there will in due course be a professional body which will have, amongst its other functions, the duty to approve or disapprove courses of training leading to registration as a practitioner under its jurisdiction. If and when the time arrives where Scientology training receives the approval of this body, foreign or Commonwealth students wishing to take it should be admitted on the same considerations as all other bona fide students. Until that time, however, I see no objection to the continuance of the present Home Office Policy in this respect only: foreign or Commonwealth Scientologists wishing to come here for study at a Scientologist establishment should be admitted as visitors only, and not as students.

[2] *The Times*, 16th September 1970.

[Enquiry into the Practice and Effects of Scientology: Report by Sir John G. Foster, K.B.E., Q.C., M.P. Ordered by The House of Commons to be printed December 21, 1971.]

Van Duyn v. Home Office [1975] 1 Ch. 358

European Court of Justice

Yvonne Van Duyn a member of the Church of Scientology and a Dutch national was refused entry to the United Kingdom. She brought an action in the Chancery Division of the High Court for declarations that she was entitled to accept an offer of employment as a secretary by the Church of Scientology at East Grinstead, Sussex, and that she was entitled to enter and stay in the United Kingdom for the purpose of employment. Pennycuick V.–C., pursuant to Article 177 of the Rome Treaty, ordered a reference to the European Court of Justice for a preliminary ruling on the interpretation of Article 48 of the Treaty and Article 3 of Directive 64/221 concerning the movement of nationals of members states within the Community. The Court delivered the following judgment:

FACTS

The order for reference and the written observations submitted pursuant to article 20 of the Protocol on the Statute of the Court of Justice of the E.E.C. may be summarised as follows:

I. *Facts and procedure*

1. The Church of Scientology is a body established in the United States of America, which functions in the United Kingdom through a college at East Grinstead, Sussex. The British Government regards the activities of the Church of Scientology as contrary to public policy. On July 25, 1968, the Minister of Health stated in the House of Commons that the government was satisfied that scientology was socially harmful. The statement included the following remarks:

> "Scientology is a pseudo-philosophical cult . . . The government are satisfied having reviewed all the available evidence that scientology is socially harmful. It alienates members of families from each other and attributes squalid and disgraceful motives to all who oppose it; its authoritarian principles and practice are a potential menace to the personality and well being of those so deluded as to become its followers; above all its methods can be a serious danger to the health of those who submit to them. There is evidence that children are now being indoctrinated. There is no power under existing law to prohibit the practice of scientology; but the government have concluded that it is so objectionable that it would be right to take all steps within their power to curb its growth . . . Foreign nationals come here to study scientology and to work at the so-called 'college' in East Grinstead. The government can prevent this under existing law . . . and have decided to do so. The following steps are being taken with immediate effect . . . (e) Work permits and employment vouchers will not be issued to foreign nationals . . . for work at a scientology establishment."

No legal restrictions are placed upon the practice of scientology in the United Kingdom nor upon British nationals (with certain immaterial exceptions) wishing to become members of or take employment with the Church of Scientology.

2. Miss Van Duyn is a Dutch national. By a letter dated May 4, 1973, she was offered employment as a secretary with the Church of Scientology at its college at East Grinstead. With the intention of taking up that offer she arrived at Gatwick Airport on May 9, 1973, where she was interviewed by an immigration officer and refused leave to enter the United Kingdom. It emerged in the course of the interview that she had worked in a scientology establishment in Amsterdam for six months, that she had taken a course in the subject of scientology, that she was a practising scientologist and that she was intending to work at a scientology establishment in the United Kingdom.

The ground of refusal of leave to enter which is stated in the document entitled "Refusal of leave to enter" handed by the immigration officer to Miss Van Duyn reads:

> "You have asked for leave to enter the United Kingdom in order to take employment with the Church of Scientology but the Secretary of State considers it undesirable to give anyone leave to enter the United Kingdom on the business of or in the employment of that organisation . . ."

The power to refuse entry into the United Kingdom is vested in immigration officers by virtue of section 4 (1) of the Immigration Act 1971. Leave to enter was refused by the immigration officer acting in accordance with the policy of the government and with rule 65 of the relevant Immigration Rules for Control of Entry which Rules have legislative force. Rule 65 reads:

> "Any passenger except the wife or child under 18 of a person settled in the United Kingdom may be refused leave to enter on the ground that his exclusion is conducive to the public good, where—(a) the Secretary of State has personally so directed, or (b) from information available to the immigration officer it seems right to refuse leave to enter on that ground—if, for example, in the light of the passenger's character, conduct or associations it is undesirable to give him leave to enter."

3. Relying on the community rules on freedom of movement of workers and especially on article 48 of the E.E.C. Treaty, Regulation 1612/68 and article 3 of Directive 64/221, Miss Van Duyn claims that the refusal of leave to enter was unlawful and seeks a declaration from the High Court that she is entitled to stay in the United Kingdom for the purpose of employment and to be given leave to enter the United Kingdom.

Before deciding further, the High Court has stayed the proceedings and requested the Court of Justice, pursuant to article 177 of the E.E.C. Treaty, to give a preliminary ruling on the following questions. 1. Whether article 48 of the Treaty establishing the European Economic Community is directly applicable so as to confer on individuals rights enforceable by them in the court of a member state. 2. Whether Directive 64/221 adopted on February 25, 1964, in accordance with the Treaty establishing the European Economic Community is directly applicable so as to confer on individuals rights enforceable by them in the courts of a member state. 3. Whether upon the proper interpretation of article 48 of the Treaty establishing the European Economic Community and article 3 of Directive 64/221/EEC a member state in the performance of its duty to base a measure taken on grounds of public policy exclusively on the personal conduct of the individual concerned is entitled to take into account as matters of personal conduct (a) the fact that the individual is or has been associated with some body or organisation the activities of which the member state considers contrary to the public good but which are not unlawful in that state, (b) the fact that the individual intends to take employment in the member state with such a body or organisation, it being the case that no restrictions are placed upon nationals of the member state who wish to take similar employment with such a body or organisation.

4. The order of the High Court of March 1, 1974, was registered at the court on June 13, 1974. Written observations have been submitted on behalf of Miss Van Duyn by Alan Newman, on behalf of the United Kingdom by W. H. Godwin and on behalf of the Commission by its legal adviser, A. McClellan. Having heard the report of the Judge-Rapporteur and the opinion of the Advocate-General, the court decided to open the oral procedure without any preparatory inquiry.

On the second question

Miss Van Duyn submits that article 3 of Directive 64/221 is directly applicable. She observes that the court has already held that, in principle, directives are susceptible of direct application. She refers to the judgments of the court of October 6, 1970, in *Grad* v. *Finanzamt Traunstein* (Case 9/70) (1970) XVL Recueil 825 and of December 17, 1970, in *S.A.C.E.* v. *Italian Ministry of Finance* (Case 33/70) (1970) XVI Recueil 1213; [1971] C.M.L.R. 123. She submits that the criterion as to whether a directive is directly applicable is identical with the criterion adopted in the case of articles in the Treaty itself, and she observes that the court has not felt itself constrained to hold that a given article in the Treaty is not directly applicable merely because in its formal wording it imposes an obligation on a member state. She refers to the judgments of the court of December 19, 1968, in *Salgoil S.p.A.* v. *Italian Ministry of Foreign Trade* (Case 13/68) (1968) XIV Recueil 661 and of June 16, 1966, in *Alfons Lütticke G.m.b.H.* v. *Hauptzollamt Sarrelouis* (Case 57/65) (1966) XII Recueil 293. Miss Van Duyn further submits that a directive which directly affects an individual is capable of creating direct rights for that individual where its provisions are clear and unconditional and where, as to the result to be achieved, it leaves no substantial measure of discretion to the member state. Provided that these criteria are fulfilled it does not matter (a) whether the provision in the directive consists of a positive obligation to act or of a negative prohibition, or (b) that the member state has a choice of form and methods to be adopted in order to achieve the stated result. As to (a), it is implicit in the court's judgments in the cases of *Lütticke* and *Salgoil* (already cited) that an article of the Treaty which imposes a positive obligation on a member state to act is capable of direct applicability and the same reasoning is valid in relation to directives. As to (b), she notes that article 189 of the Treaty expressly draws a distinction in relation to directives between the binding effect of the result to be achieved and the discretionary nature of the methods to be adopted.

She contends that the provisions of article 3 fulfill the criteria for direct applicability. She refers to the preamble to the Directive which envisages a direct applicability when it states:

"whereas, in each member state, nationals of other member states should have adequate legal remedies available to them in respect of the administration in such matters . . ."

(i.e. when a member state invokes grounds of public policy, public security or public health in matters connected with the movement or residence of foreign nationals).

The only "adequate legal remedy" available to an individual is the right to invoke the provisions of the Directive before the national courts. A decision to this effect would undoubtedly strengthen the legal protection of individual citizens in the national courts.

The Commission submits that a provision in a directive is directly applicable when it is clear and unambiguous. It refers to the judgments in the *Grad* and *S.A.C.E.* cases (already cited).

The Commission observes that a community regulation has the same weight with immediate effect as national legislation whereas the effect of a directive is similar to that of those provisions of the Treaty which create obligations for the member states. If provisions of a directive are legally clear and unambiguous, leaving only a discretion to the national authorities for their implementation, they must have an effect similar to those Treaty provisions which the court has recognised as directly applicable.

It therefore submits that (a) the executive of a member state is bound to respect community law; (b) if a provision in a directive is not covered by an identical provision in national law, but left, as to the result to be achieved, to the discretion of the national authority, the discretionary power of that authority is reduced by the community provision; (c) in these circumstances and given that to comply with a directive it is not always indispensable to amend national legislation it is clear that the private individual must have the right to prevent the national authority concerned from exceeding its powers under community law to the detriment of that individual.

According to the Commission, article 3 is one of the provisions of Directive 64/221 having all the characteristics necessary to have direct effect in the member state to which it is addressed. And it further recalls that the difficulty of applying the rules in a particular case does not derogate from their general application. In this context the Commission examines the judgment of October 7, 1968, of the Belgian Conseil d'Etat in the *Corveleyn* case (CE 1968, no. 13.146 arrêt 7.10.1968, p. 710).

As the British authorities have not adopted the wording of article 3 of the Directive to achieve the required result, the Commission submits, by virtue of article 189 of the Treaty and in the light of the case of the court, that article 3 is a directly applicable obligation which limits the wide discretion given to immigration officers under rule 65 in the "Statement of Immigration Rules." The Commission proposes the following answer to the question: where a provision is legally clear and unambiguous as is article 3 of Directive 64/221, such a provision is directly applicable so as to confer on individuals rights enforceable by them in the courts of a member state.

The United Kingdom recalls that article 189 of the E.E.C. Treaty draws a clear distinction between regulations and directives, and that different effects are ascribed to each type of provision. It therefore submits that prima facie the Council in not issuing a regulation must have intended that the Directive should have an effect other than that of a regulation and accordingly should not be binding in its entirety and not be directly applicable in all member states.

The United Kingdom submits that neither the *Grad* nor the *S.A.C.E.* decision is authority for the proposition that it is immaterial whether or not a provision is contained in a regulation, directive or decision. In both cases the purpose of the directive in question was merely to fix a date for the implementation of clear and binding obligations contained in the Treaty and instruments made under it. Those cases show that in special circumstances a limited provision in a directive could be directly applicable. The provisions of the Directive in the present case are wholly different. Directive 64/221 is far broader in scope. It gives comprehensive guidance to member states as to all measures taken by them affecting freedom of movement for workers and it was expressly contemplated in article 10 that member states would put into force the measures necessary to comply with the provisions of the Directive. Indeed the very terms of article 3 (1) itself contemplate the taking of measures.

The United Kingdom examines the only four cases in which national courts to its knowledge have considered the question of the direct applicability of the Directive. It submits that little assistance can be obtained from these cases. Inter alia it points out that the true effect of the *Corveleyn* case (already cited) has been the subject of considerable debate among Belgian jurists and the better view appears to be that the Conseil d'Etat did not decide that the Directive was directly applicable but applied the Belgian concept of public order which itself required international obligations of Belgium to be taken into account.

On the third question

Miss Van Duyn points out that the first part of the question assumes a situation where an organisation engages in activities which are lawful in the state. The question does not necessarily assume that the individual concerned intends to continue this association. It is sufficient that he has in the past been associated. In this respect Miss Van Duyn recalls that even if the individual had been associated with an illegal organisation and, by virtue of his activities therein, had been convicted of a crime, that circumstance would not, by virtue of the provisions of article 3, paragraph 2, of Directive 64/221, in itself be sufficient grounds for the member state to take measures based on public policy to exclude the individual.

Merely belonging to a lawful organisation, without necessarily taking part in its activities, cannot, in her submission, amount to "conduct." Conduct implies "activity." Moreover, the activities of the organisation in question are not, merely because the individual is or has been a passive member, "personal" to the individual concerned. To hold otherwise would mean that a member state could exclude an individual merely because, in the distant past, he had for a brief period perfectly lawfully belonged to a somewhat extreme political or religious organisation in his own member state.

In regard to the second part of the question, Miss Van Duyn recalls that freedom of movement of persons is one of the fundamental principles established by the Treaty and that discrimination on grounds of nationality is prohibited in article 7. Exemptions to these fundamental principles must be interpreted restrictively.

She points out that the question assumes discrimination on grounds of nationality and that it assumes a situation where an individual whose past activity has been blameless seeks entry into a member state in order to work for an organisation in whose employment the nationals of the member state are perfectly free to engage. She submits that if an organisation is deemed contrary to the public good the member state is faced with a simple choice: either to ban everyone, including its own nationals, from engaging in employment with that organisation, or to tolerate nationals of other member states as it tolerates its own nationals engaging in such employment.

The Commission asserts that the concepts "public policy" and "personal conduct" contained in article 48, paragraph 3, of the Treaty and article 3 of Directive 64/221 are concepts of community law. They must first be interpreted in the context of community law and national criteria are only relevant to its application.

In practice, if each member state could set limits to the interpretation of public policy the obligations deriving from the principle of freedom of movement of workers would take a variety of forms in different member states. It is only possible for this freedom to be maintained throughout the community on the basis of uniform application in all the member states. It would be inconsistent with the Treaty if one member state accepted workers from another member state while its own workers did not receive uniform treatment as regards the application of the rules in respect of public order in that other state.

The Commission submits that the discrimination by a member state on grounds of public policy against nationals of another member state for being employed by an organisation the activities of which it considers contrary to the public good when it does not make it unlawful for its own nationals to be employed by such organisation is contrary to article 48, paragraph 2, of the Treaty. Article 3 (1) of the Directive is precise in stating that measures taken on grounds of public policy shall be based exclusively on the personal conduct of the individual concerned. Personal conduct which is acceptable when exercised by a national of one member state cannot be unacceptable, under community law, when exercised by a national of another member state.

It is for consideration that article 3 precludes a member state, as a general contingency against some potential harm to society, from invoking public policy as a ground for refusing entry when the personal conduct of the individual is or was not contrary to public policy in the member states concerned. It is not denied that membership of a militant organisation proscribed in the host member state would be an element to be taken into account in assessing personal conduct for the purpose of justifying a refusal of entry on grounds of public policy or public security.

As to the first part of the question the United Kingdom deals with three problems.

The first problem is whether an individual's past or present association with an organisation can be regarded as an aspect of his personal conduct. The United Kingdom asserts that it is of importance that a member state in relation to public policy should be entitled to consider a person's associations with a body or organisation. The member state should be entitled to exclude that person in appropriate cases, i.e. if the organisation is considered sufficiently undesirable from the viewpoint of public policy and the association by that person with that organisation is sufficiently close.

Secondly the United Kingdom submits that a measure which is taken on grounds of public policy and which provides for the exclusion from a member state of an individual on the ground of that individual's association with an organisation is compatible with the requirement of article 3 (1). It accepts that the intention underlying that article must have been to exclude collective expulsions and to require the consideration by the national authorities of the personal circumstances of each individual in each case. Nevertheless it is not inconsistent with that intention for a member state to take into account an individual's association with an organisation and, in appropriate cases, to exclude the individual by reason of that association. Whether, in any case, such exclusion is justified will depend on the view that the member state takes of the organisation.

As a practical matter the processes of admitting persons to enter a member state must be administered by a large number of officials. Such officials cannot be expected to know all that the government may know about a particular organisation and it is inevitable that such officials must act in accordance with directions given by the government and laying down broad principles on which the officials are to act. It is inevitable also that such directions may relate to particular organisations which a government may consider contrary to the public good.

Thirdly the United Kingdom submits that the fact that the activities of the organisation are not unlawful in a member state though considered by the member state to be contrary to the public good does not disentitle the member state from taking into account the individual's association with the organisation. It must be a matter for each state to decide whether it should make activities of an organisation, or the organisation itself, illegal. Only that state is competent to make such evaluation and it will do so in the light of the particular circumstances of that state. Thus, as is common knowledge, the United Kingdom practises a considerable degree of tolerance in relation to organisations within the United Kingdom. In the case of scientology the reasons why the United Kingdom regards the activities of the scientologists as contrary to public policy were explained in the statement made in Parliament on July 25, 1968. The scientologists still have their world headquarters in the United Kingdom so that scientology is of particular concern to the United Kingdom.

The United Kingdom notes that two problems arise in connection with the matter referred to in sub-paragraph (b) of the question.

The first problem is whether the fact that an individual intends to take employment with such an organisation is an aspect of that individual's personal conduct. It is submitted that such an intention is a very material aspect of the individual's personal conduct.

The second problem is whether the fact that no restrictions are placed upon nationals of the member state who wish to take similar employment with such an organisation disentitles the member state from taking this intention into account.

The United Kingdom points out that it is inevitable that in respect of the entry into a state of persons, there must be some discrimination in favour of the nationals of that state. For a national, however undesirable and potentially harmful his entry may be, cannot be refused admission into his own state. A state has a duty under international law to receive back its own nationals. The United Kingdom refers, inter alia, to article 5 (b) (ii) of the Universal Declaration of Human Rights which states: "Everyone has the right to leave any country, including his own, and to return to his country." It observes that, for example, a member state would be justified in refusing to admit a drug addict who is a national of another state even though it would be obliged to admit a drug addict who was one of its own nationals.

Miss Van Duyn, represented by Alan Newman, the United Kingdom, represented by Peter Gibson, and the Commission represented by Anthony McClellan, submitted oral observations at the hearing on October 23, 1974.

The Advocate-General delivered his opinion at the hearing on November 13, 1974.

LAW

1. By order of Pennycuick V.-C., of March 1, 1974, lodged at the court on June 13, the Chancery Division of the High Court of Justice of England, referred to the court, under article 177 of the E.E.C. Treaty, three questions relating to the interpretation of certain provisions of community law concerning freedom of movement for workers.

2. These questions arise out of an action brought against the Home Office by a woman of Dutch nationality who was refused leave to enter the United Kingdom to take up employment as a secretary with the "Church of Scientology."

3. Leave to enter was refused in accordance with the policy of the Government of the United Kingdom in relation to the said organisation, the activities of which it considers to be socially harmful.

First question

4. By the first question, the court is asked to say whether article 48 of the E.E.C. Treaty is directly applicable so as to confer on individuals rights enforceable by them in the courts of a member state.

5. It is provided, in article 48 (1) and (2), that freedom of movement for workers shall be secured by the end of the transitional period and that such freedom shall entail:

> "the abolition of any discrimination based on nationality between workers of member states as regards employment, remuneration and other conditions of work and employment."

6. These provisions impose on member states a precise obligation which does not require the adoption of any further measure on the part of either of the community institutions or of the member states and which leaves them, in relation to its implementation, no discretionary power.

7. Paragraph 3, which defines the rights implied by the principle of freedom of movement for workers, subjects them to limitations justified on grounds of public policy, public security or public health. The application of these limitations is, however, subject to judicial control, so that a member state's right to invoke the limitations does not prevent the provisions of article 48, which enshrine the principle of freedom of movement for workers, from conferring on individuals rights which are enforceable by them and which the national courts must protect.

8. The reply to the first question must therefore be in the affirmative.

Second question

9. The second question asks the court to say whether Council Directive 64/221 of February 25, 1964, on the co-ordination of special measures concerning the movement and residence of foreign nationals which are justified

on grounds of public policy, public security or public health is directly applicable so as to confer on individuals rights enforceable by them in the courts of a member state.

10. It emerges from the order making the reference that the only provision of the Directive which is relevant is that contained in article 3 (1) which provides:

"Measures taken on grounds of public policy or public security shall be passed exclusively on the personal conduct of the individual concerned."

11. The United Kingdom observes that, since article 189 of the Treaty distinguishes between the effects ascribed to regulations, directives and decisions, it must therefore be presumed that the Council, in issuing a directive rather than making a regulation, must have intended that the directive should have an effect other than that of a regulation and accordingly that the former should not be directly applicable.

12. If, however, by virtue of the provisions of article 189 regulations are directly applicable and, consequently, may by their very nature have direct effects, it does not follow from this that other categories of acts mentioned in that article can never have similar effects. It would be incompatible with the binding effect attributed to a directive by article 189 to exclude, in principle, the possibility that the obligation which it imposes may be invoked by those concerned. In particular, where the community authorities have, by directive, imposed on member states the obligation to pursue a particular course of conduct, the useful effect of such an act would be weakened if individuals were prevented from relying on it before their national courts and if the latter were prevented from taking it into consideration as an element of community law. Article 177, which empowers national courts to refer to the court questions concerning the validity and interpretation of all acts of the community institutions, without distinction, implies furthermore that these acts may be invoked by individuals in the national courts. It is necessary to examine, in every case, whether the nature, general scheme and wording of the provision in question are capable of having direct effects on the relations between member states and individuals.

13. By providing that measures taken on grounds of public policy shall be based exclusively on the personal conduct of the individual concerned, article 3 (1) of Directive 64/221 is intended to limit the discretionary power which national laws generally confer on the authorities responsible for the entry and expulsion of foreign nationals. First, the provision lays down an obligation which is not subject to any exception or condition and which, by its very nature, does not require the intervention of any act on the part either of the institutions of the community or of member states. Secondly, because member states are thereby obliged, in implementing a clause which derogates from one of the fundamental principles of the Treaty in favour of individuals, not to take account of factors extraneous to personal conduct, legal certainty for the persons concerned requires that they should be able to rely on this obligation even though it has been laid down in a legislative act which has no automatic direct effect in its entirety.

14. If the meaning and exact scope of the provision raise questions of interpretation, these questions can be resolved by the courts, taking into account also the procedure under article 177 of the Treaty.

15. Accordingly, in reply to the second question, article 3 (1) of Council Directive 64/221 of February 25, 1964, confers on individuals rights which are

enforceable by them in the courts of a member state and which the national courts must protect.

Third question

16. By the third question the court is asked to rule whether article 48 of the Treaty and article 3 of Directive 64/221 must be interpreted as meaning:

> "a member state, in the performance of its duty to base a measure taken on grounds of public policy exclusively on the personal conduct of the individual concerned, is entitled to take into account as matters of personal conduct: (a) the fact that the individual is or has been associated with some body or organisation the activities of which the member state considers contrary to the public good but which are not unlawful in that state; (b) the fact that the individual intends to take employment in the member state with such a body or organisation it being the case that no restrictions are placed upon nationals of the member state who wish to take similar employment with such a body or organisation."

17. It is necessary, first, to consider whether association with a body or an organisation can in itself constitute personal conduct within the meaning of article 3 of Directive 64/221. Although a person's past association cannot, in general, justify a decision refusing him the right to move freely within the community, it is nevertheless the case that present association, which reflects participation in the activities of the body or of the organisation as well as identification with its aims and its designs, may be considered a voluntary act of the person concerned and, consequently, as part of his personal conduct within the meaning of the provision cited.

18. This third question further raises the problem of what importance must be attributed to the fact that the activities of the organisation in question, which are considered by the member state as contrary to the public good, are not however prohibited by national law. It should be emphasised that the concept of public policy in the context of the community and where, in particular, it is used as a justification for derogating from the fundamental principle of freedom of movement for workers, must be interpreted strictly, so that its scope cannot be determined unilaterally by each member state without being subject to control by the institutions of the community. Nevertheless, the particular circumstances justifying recourse to the concept of public policy may vary from one country to another and from one period to another, and it is therefore necessary in this matter to allow the competent national authorities an area of discretion within the limits imposed by the Treaty.

19. It follows from the above that where the competent authorities of a member state have clearly defined their standpoint as regards the activities of a particular organisation and where, considering it to be socially harmful, they have taken administrative measures to counteract these activities, the member state cannot be required, before it can rely on the concept of public policy, to make such activities unlawful, if recourse to such a measure is not thought appropriate in the circumstances.

20. The question raises finally the problem whether a member state is entitled, on grounds of public policy, to prevent a national of another member state from taking gainful employment within its territory with a body or organisation, it being the case that no similar restriction is placed upon its own nationals.

21. In this connection, the Treaty, while enshrining the principle of freedom of movement for workers without any discrimination on grounds of nationality, admits, in article 48 (3), limitations justified on grounds of public policy, public security or public health to the rights deriving from this principle. Under the terms of the provision cited above, the right to accept offers of employment actually made, the right to move freely within the territory of member states for this purpose, and the right to stay in a member state for the purpose of employment are, among others all subject to such limitations. Consequently, the effect of such limitations, when they apply, is that leave to enter the territory of a member state and the right to reside there may be refused to a national of another member state.

22. Furthermore, it is a principle of international law, which the E.E.C. Treaty cannot be assumed to disregard in the relations between member states, that a state is precluded from refusing its own nationals the right of entry or residence.

23. It follows that a member state, for reasons of public policy, can, where it deems necessary, refuse a national of another member state the benefit of the principle of freedom of movement for workers in a case where such a national proposes to take up a particular offer of employment even though the member state does not place a similar restriction upon its own nationals.

24. Accordingly, the reply to the third question must be that article 48 of the E.E.C. Treaty and article 3 (1) of Directive 64/221 are to be interpreted as meaning that a member state, in imposing restrictions justified on grounds of public policy, is entitled to take into account, as a matter of personal conduct of the individual concerned, the fact that the individual is associated with some body or organisation the activities of which the member state considers socially harmful but which are not unlawful in that state, despite the fact that no restriction is placed upon nationals of the said member state who wish to take similar employment with these same bodies or organisations.

25. . . . . On those grounds, the court in answer to the questions referred to it by the High Court of Justice, by order of that court, dated March 1, 1974, hereby rules:

(1) Article 48 of the E.E.C. Treaty has a direct effect in the legal orders of the member states and confers on individuals rights which the national courts must protect.

(2) Article 3 (1) of Council Directive No. 64/221 of February 25, 1964, on the co-ordination of special measures concerning the movement and residence of foreign nationals which are justified on grounds of public policy, public security or public health confers on individuals rights which are enforceable by them in the national courts of a member state and which the national courts must protect.

(3) Article 48 of the E.E.C. Treaty and article 3 (1) of Directive 64/221 must be interpreted as meaning that a member state, in imposing restrictions justified on grounds of public policy, is entitled to take into account as a matter of personal conduct of the individual concerned, the fact that the individual is associated with some body or organisation the activities of which the member state considers socially harmful but which are not unlawful in that state, despite the fact that no restriction is placed upon nationals of the said member state who wish to take similar employment with the same body or organisation.

Questions

1. What privileges are conferred by law upon the Church of England and its members? What justification is there for these privileges?

2. What are the practical and legal disabilities or disadvantages to which religious minorities (including non-believers) may be subject in the United Kingdom. See *Halsbury's Laws of England* (4th ed.), Vol. 14, Ecclesiastical Law, paras. 352–60; 1388–1435; Vol. 15, Elections, para. 622, and H.S.Q. Henriques, *The Jews and the English Law* (Bibliophile Press, 1908).

Chapter 5

FREEDOM OF EXPRESSION AND COMMUNICATION

Further Reading

De Smith, Chap. 21; Dicey, Chap. 6; Street, Chap. 3, 4 & 5; Wade & Phillips, Chap. 27.

D. Humphrey, *The Cricket Conspiracy* (Cobden Trust, 1975), G. Marshall, *Constitutional Theory* (O.U.P., 1971), Chap. 8.

See also Chapters 4, 9 and 11.

1. *CENSORSHIP OF BOOKS AND PUBLISHING*

Books and publishing

O'Higgins, pp. 62–74.

Alec Craig, *Above all Liberties* (Allen & Unwin, 1942); Alec Craig, *The Banned Books of England and other Countries: A Study of the Conception of Literary Obscenity* (London, 1962); L. Kuper, "Censorship by Proxy," (1975) 4(3) *Index on Censorship* pp. 48–50; Stephen Parks (ed.), *The English Book Trade 1660–1853, 156 Titles relating to the early history of English Publishing, Bookselling, the Struggle for Copyright and the Freedom of the Press, Reprinted in 42 Volumes* (New York and London, 1974); C. H. Rolph, *Books in the Dock* (Andre Deutsch, 1969); D. Thomas, *A Long Time Burning: The History of Literary Censorship in England* (Routledge, 1969); Wayland Young, "The Adventures of Eros Denied," (1966) 2(2) *Censorship* pp. 2–13.

Censorship

O'Higgins, *passim*.

P. Lloyd, *Not for Publication* (Bow Group, 1968); Jonathan Millar, *Censorship and the Limits of Permission* (London, 1973); National Council of Civil Liberties, *Against Censorship* (N.C.C.L., 1972); Jean Straker (ed.), *Censorship in the Arts* (London, 1966); D. Tribe, *Questions of Censorship* (Allen & Unwin, 1973).

2. *CONTEMPT OF COURT*

Sunday Times Case (1979)

European Court of Human Rights

Distillers Co. (Biochemicals) Ltd. manufactured and marketed thalidomide, which caused a number of women who had taken the drug during pregnancy to give birth to children with severe deformities. Arising out of these facts, parents of children with deformities at various dates issued writs against Distillers. In 1972 at a time when some parents had settled but the majority were still considering terms of an offer of settlement from Distillers the *Sunday Times* on September 24, 1972 published an article criticising the terms offered by Distillers.

It was indicated that in a later article the *Sunday Times* would trace how the tragedy occurred. In November a Divisional Court granted an application by the Attorney-General for an injunction to restrain publication of this future article on the ground that it would constitute contempt of court. On appeal to the Court of Appeal, it discharged the injunction but an appeal by the Attorney-General to the House of Lords was unanimously allowed and the Divisional Court was directed to grant an injunction against the *Sunday Times*. The editor of the *Sunday Times* and other journalists lodged an application with the Commission who in 1975 decided by eight votes to five that there had been a breach of Article 10 of the Convention. The Commission then referred the case to the court. Considering the question whether there had been a violation of Article 10 by reason of the judgment of the House of Lords the court said:

44. Originally, the injunction in question was granted by the Divisional Court and concerned only the draft *Sunday Times* article (see paragraph 21 above). It was discharged by the Court of Appeal (see paragraph 24 above) but the House of Lords restored it and considerably widened its scope by directing the Divisional Court to order

> "That . . . Times Newspapers Ltd., by themselves, their servants, agents or otherwise, be restrained from publishing, or causing or authorising or procuring to be published or printed, any article or matter which prejudges the issues of negligence, breach of contract or breach of duty, or deals with the evidence relating to any of the said issues arising in any actions pending or imminent against Distillers . . . in respect of the development, distribution or use of the drug 'thalidomide'."

45. It is clear that there was an "interference by public authority" in the exercise of the applicants' freedom of expression which is guaranteed by paragraph 1 of Article 10. Such an interference entails a "violation" of Article 10 if it does not fall within one of the exceptions provided for in paragraph 2 (Handyside judgment of 7 December 1976, Series A no. 24, p. 21, § 43). The Court therefore has to examine in turn whether the interference in the present case was "prescribed by law", whether it had an aim or aims that is or are legitimate under Article 10 § 2 and whether it was "necessary in a democratic society" for the aforesaid aim or aims.

A. *Was the interference "prescribed by law"?*

46. The applicants argue, *inter alia*, that the law of contempt of court, both before and after the decision of the House of Lords, was so vague and uncertain and the principles enunciated by that decision so novel that the restraint imposed cannot be regarded as "prescribed by law". The Government maintain that it suffices, in this context, that the restraint was in accordance with the law; they plead, in the alternative, that on the facts of the case the restraint

was at least "roughly foreseeable". This latter test had been referred to by the Commission in its report, although there it merely proceeded on the assumption that the principles applied by the House of Lords were "prescribed by law". However, at the hearing on 25 April 1978, the Commission's Principal Delegate added that, in view of the uncertainties of the law, the restraint was not "prescribed by law", at least when the injunction was first granted in 1972.

47. The Court observes that the word "law" in the expression "prescribed by law" covers not only statute but also unwritten law. Accordingly, the Court does not attach importance here to the fact that contempt of court is a creature of the common law and not of legislation. It would clearly be contrary to the intention of the drafters of the Convention to hold that a restriction imposed by virtue of the common law is not "prescribed by law" on the sole ground that it is not enunciated in legislation: this would deprive a common-law State which is Party to the Convention of the protection of Article 10 § 2 and strike at the very roots of the State's legal system.

In fact, the applicants do not argue that the expression "prescribed by law" necessitates legislation in every case; their submission is that legislation is required only if—as in the present case—the common-law rules are so uncertain that they do not satisfy what the applicants maintain is the concept enshrined in that expression, namely the principle of legal certainty.

48. The expression "prescribed by law" appears in paragraph 2 of Articles 9, 10 and 11 of the Convention, the equivalent in the French text being in each case "*prévues par la loi*". However, when the same French expression appears in Article 8 § 2 of the Convention, in Article 1 of Protocol No. 1 and in Article 2 of Protocol No. 4, it is rendered in the English text as "in accordance with the law", "provided for by law" and "in accordance with law", respectively. Thus confronted with versions of a law-making treaty which are equally authentic but not exactly the same, the Court must interpret them in a way that reconciles them as far as possible and is most appropriate in order to realise the aim and achieve the object of the treaty (see the Wemhoff judgment of 27 June 1968, Series A no. 7, p 23, § 8, and Article 33 § 4 of the Vienna Convention of 23 May 1969 on the Law of Treaties).

49. In the Court's opinion, the following are two of the requirements that flow from the expression "prescribed by law". Firstly, the law must be adequately accessible: the citizen must be able to have an indication that is adequate in the circumstances of the legal rules applicable to a given case. Secondly, a norm cannot be regarded as a "law" unless it is formulated with sufficient precision to enable the citizen to regulate his conduct: he must be able—if need be with appropriate advice—to foresee, to a degree that is reasonable in the circumstances, the consequences which a given action may entail. Those consequences need not be foreseeable with absolute certainty: experience shows this to be unattainable. Again, whilst certainty is highly desirable, it may bring in its train excessive rigidity and the law must be able to keep pace with changing circumstances. Accordingly, many laws are inevitably couched in terms which, to a greater or lesser extent, are vague and whose interpretation and application are questions of practice.

50. In the present case, the question whether these requirements of accessibility and foreseeability were satisfied is complicated by the fact that different principles were relied on by the various Law Lords concerned. The Divisional Court had applied the principle that a deliberate attempt to influence the settlement of pending proceedings by bringing public pressure to

bear on a party constitutes contempt of court (the "pressure principle"; see paragraph 23 above). Certain members of the House of Lords also alluded to this principle whereas others preferred the principle that it is contempt of court to publish material which prejudges, or is likely to cause public prejudgment of, the issues raised in pending litigation (the "prejudgment principle"; see paragraphs 29 to 33 above).

51. The applicants do not claim to have been without an indication that was adequate in the circumstances of the "pressure principle". Indeed, the existence of this principle had been recognised by counsel for Times Newspapers Ltd. who is reported as saying before the Divisional Court: "Even if it applies pressure to a party, the article is not contempt at all because [the higher public interest] overcomes any question of wrongdoing. Alternatively, if the article is prima facia contempt, the higher public interest provides a defence against what would otherwise be contempt." Again, Lord Justice Phillimore in the Court of Appeal referred to "the mass of authority . . . showing that an attempt to stir up public feeling against a party is a serious contempt".

The Court also considers that there can be no doubt that the "pressure principle" was formulated with sufficient precision to enable the applicants to foresee to the appropriate degree the consequences which publication of the draft article might entail. In *Vine Products Ltd.* v. *Green* (1966), Mr. Justice Buckley had formulated the law in this way: "It is a contempt of this court for any newspaper to comment on pending legal proceedings in any way which is likely to prejudice the fair trial of the action. That may arise in various ways. It may be that the comment is one which is likely in some way or other to bring pressure to bear upon one or other of the parties to the action, so as to prevent that party from prosecuting or from defending the action, or encourage that party to submit to terms of compromise which he otherwise might not have been prepared to entertain, or influence him in some other way in his conduct in the action, which he ought to be free to prosecute or to defend, as he is advised, without being subject to such pressure."

52. The applicants contend, on the other hand, that the prejudgment principle was novel and that they therefore could not have had an adequate indication of its existence. Support for this view is to be found in several authorities cited by the applicants, including the Phillimore report which stated that the House of Lords "formulated a rather different test" (see paragraph 18 above). Nevertheless, the Court has also noted the following:

> in the applicants' memorial it is submitted (paragraph 2.54): "the 'prejudgment principle' as applied by the House of Lords to the facts of the present case has never before constituted the 'ratio' of an English judicial decision *in a comparable case*" (emphasis added);
>
> in 1969 the Interdepartmental Committee on the Law of Contempt as it affects Tribunals of Inquiry (see paragraph 36 above) stated in paragraph 26 of its report: "There is no reported case of anyone being found guilty of contempt of court in respect of comment made about the subject matter of a trial before a judge alone . . . There are however dicta which support the view that such comment may amount to contempt.";
>
> the third edition (current in 1972) of *Halsbury's Laws of England* (vol. 8, pp. 7 *et seq.*, paragraphs 11–13) contains the following passages which are accompanied by references to previous case-law: ". . . writings . . . prejudicing the public for or against a party are contempts . . . there [is

nothing] of more pernicious consequence than to prejudice the minds of the public against persons concerned as parties in causes before the cause is finally heard . . . It is a contempt to publish an article in a newspaper commenting on the proceedings in a pending . . . civil action . . . In such cases the mischievous tendency of a trial by the newspapers when a trial by one of the regular tribunals of the country is going on is to be considered . . . On the other hand, the summary jurisdiction [to punish contempt] ought only to be exercised when it is probable that the publication will substantially interfere with a fair trial."

As regards the formulation of the "prejudgment principle", the Court notes that reference was made in the House of Lords to various authorities and, in particular, to *Hunt* v. *Clarke* (1889), where Lord Justice Cotton had stated the law in this way: "If any one discusses in a paper the rights of a case or the evidence to be given before the case comes on, that, in my opinion, would be a very serious attempt to interfere with the proper administration of justice. It is not necessary that the court should come to the conclusion that a judge or a jury will be prejudiced, but if it is calculated to prejudice the proper trial of a cause, that is a contempt, and would be met with the necessary punishment in order to restrain such conduct." Moreover, the editor of *The Sunday Times* said in his affidavit filed in the Divisional Court proceedings: ". . . I was given legal advice that the [proposed] article . . . was in a category different from that of the articles published hitherto in that in addition to presenting information which strengthened the moral argument for a fairer settlement it included evidence which related to the issue of liability in the pending thalidomide proceedings."

To sum up, the Court does not consider that the applicants were without an indication that was adequate in the circumstances of the existence of the "prejudgment principle". Even if the Court does have certain doubts concerning the precision with which that principle was formulated at the relevant time, it considers that the applicants were able to foresee, to a degree that was reasonable in the circumstances, a risk that publication of the draft article might fall foul of the principle.

53. The interference with the applicants' freedom of expression was thus "prescribed by law" within the meaning of Article 10 § 2.

B. *Did the interference have aims that are legitimate under Article 10 § 2?*

54. In the view of the applicants, the Government and the minority of the Commission, the law of contempt of court serves the purpose of safeguarding not only the impartiality and authority of the judiciary but also the rights and interests of litigants.

The majority of the Commission, on the other hand, whilst accepting that the law of contempt has the general aim of securing the fair administration of justice and that it thereby seeks to achieve purposes similar to those envisaged in Article 10 § 2 where it speaks of maintaining the authority and impartiality of the judiciary, considered that it was not called upon to examine separately whether that law has the further purpose of protecting the rights of others.

55. The Court first emphasises that the expression "authority and impartiality of the judiciary" has to be understood "within the meaning of the Convention" (see, *mutatis mutandis*, the König judgment of 28 June 1978, Series A no. 27, pp. 29–30, § 88). For this purpose, account must be taken of the central position occupied in this context by Article 6 which reflects the

fundamental principle of the rule of law (see, for example, the Golder judgment of 21 February 1975, Series A no. 18, p. 17, § 34).

The term "judiciary" ("*pouvoir judiciaire*") comprises the machinery of justice or the judicial branch of government as well as the judges in their official capacity. The phrase "authority of the judiciary" includes, in particular, the notion that the courts are, and are accepted by the public at large as being, the proper forum for the ascertainment of legal rights and obligations and the settlement of disputes relative thereto; further, that the public at large have respect for and confidence in the courts' capacity to fulfil that function.

It suffices, in this context, to adopt the description of the general purpose of the law of contempt given by the Phillimore report. As can be seen from paragraph 18 above, the majority of the categories of conduct covered by the law of contempt relate either to the position of the judges or to the functioning of the courts and of the machinery of justice: "maintaining the authority and impartiality of the judiciary" is therefore one purpose of that law.

56. In the present case, the Court shares the view of the majority of the Commission that, insofar as the law of contempt may serve to protect the rights of litigants, this purpose is already included in the phrase "maintaining the authority and impartiality of the judiciary": the rights so protected are the rights of individuals in their capacity as litigants, that is as persons involved in the machinery of justice, and the authority of that machinery will not be maintained unless protection is afforded to all those involved in or having recourse to it. It is therefore not necessary to consider as a separate issue whether the law of contempt has the further purpose of safeguarding "the rights of others".

57. It remains to be examined whether the aim of the interference with the applicants' freedom of expression was the maintenance of the authority and impartiality of the judiciary.

None of the Law Lords concerned based his decision on the ground that the proposed article might have an influence on the "impartiality" of the judiciary. This ground was also not pleaded before the Court and can be left out of account.

The reasons why the draft article was regarded as objectionable by the House of Lords (see paragraphs 29 to 33 above) may be briefly summarised as follows:

> by "prejudging" the issue of negligence, it would have led to disrespect for the processes of the law or interfered with the administration of justice;
> it was of a kind that would expose Distillers to public and prejudicial discussion of the merits of their case, such exposure being objectionable as it inhibits suitors generally from having recourse to the courts;
> it would subject Distillers to pressure and to the prejudices of prejudgment of the issues in the litigation and the law of contempt was designed to prevent interference with recourse to the courts;
> prejudgment by the press would have led inevitably in this case to replies by the parties, thereby creating the danger of a "trial by newspaper" incompatible with the proper administration of justice;
> the courts owe it to the parties to protect them from the prejudices of prejudgment which involves their having to participate in the flurries of pre-trial publicity.

The Court regards all these various reasons as falling within the aim of maintaining the "authority . . . of the judiciary" as interpreted by the Court in the second sub-paragraph of paragraph 55 above.

Accordingly, the interference with the applicants' freedom of expression had an aim that is legitimate under Article 10 § 2.

C. *Was the interference "necessary in a democratic society" for maintaining the authority of the judiciary?*

58. The applicants submit and the majority of the Commission are of the opinion that the said interference was not "necessary" within the meaning of Article 10 § 2. The Government contend that the minority of the Commission was correct in reaching a contrary conclusion and rely, in particular, on the margin of appreciation enjoyed by the House of Lords in the matter.

59. The Court has already had the occasion in its above-mentioned Handyside judgment to state its understanding of the phrase "necessary in a democratic society", the nature of its functions in the examination of issues turning on that phrase and the manner in which it will perform those functions.

The Court has noted that, whilst the adjective "necessary", within the meaning of Article 10 § 2, is not synonymous with "indispensable", neither has it the flexibility of such expressions as "admissible", "ordinary", "useful", "reasonable" or "desirable" and that it implies the existence of a "pressing social need" (p. 22, § 48).

In the second place, the Court has underlined that the initial responsibility for securing the rights and freedoms enshrined in the Convention lies with the individual Contracting States. Accordingly, "Article 10 § 2 leaves to the Contracting States a margin of appreciation. This margin is given both to the domestic legislator . . . and to the bodies, judicial amongst others, that are called upon to interpret and apply the laws in force" (p. 22, § 48).

"Nevertheless, Article 10 § 2 does not give the Contracting States an unlimited power of appreciation": "The Court . . . is empowered to give the final ruling on whether a 'restriction' . . . is reconcilable with freedom of expression as protected by Article 10. The domestic margin of appreciation thus goes hand in hand with a European supervision" which "covers not only the basic legislation but also the decision applying it, even one given by an independent court" (*ibid.*, p. 23, § 49).

The Court has deduced from a combination of these principles that "it is in no way [its] task to take the place of the competent national courts but rather to review under Article 10 the decisions they delivered in the exercise of their power of appreciation" (*ibid.*, p. 23, § 50).

This does not mean that the Court's supervision is limited to ascertaining whether a respondent State exercised its discretion reasonably, carefully and in good faith. Even a Contracting State so acting remains subject to the Court's control as regards the compatibility of its conduct with the engagements it has undertaken under the Convention. The Court still does not subscribe to the contrary view which, in essence, was advanced by the Government and the majority of the Commission in the Handyside case (pp. 21-22, § 47).

Again, the scope of the domestic power of appreciation is not identical as regards each of the aims listed in Article 10 § 2. The Handyside case concerned the "protection of morals". The view taken by the Contracting States of the "requirements of morals", observed the Court, "varies from time to time and from place to place, especially in our era", and "State authorities are in principle in a better position than the international judge to give an opinion on the exact content of these requirements" (p. 22, § 48). Precisely the same cannot be said of the far more objective notion of the "authority" of the judiciary. The domestic law and practice of the Contracting States reveal a fairly substantial measure of common ground in this area. This is reflected in a number of provisions of the Convention, including Article 6, which have no equivalent as far as "morals" are concerned. Accordingly, here a more extensive European supervision corresponds to a less discretionary power of appreciation.

In the different, but to a certain extent comparable, contexts of Articles 5 § 3 and 6 § 1, the Court has on occasion reached conclusions different from those of the national courts on matters in respect of which the latter were also competent and qualified to make the initial assessment (Neumeister judgment of 27 June 1968, Series A no. 8, pp. 9-15 and 38-40; Stögmüller judgment of 10 November 1969, Series A no. 9, pp. 11-24, 39 and 43-44; Ringeisen judgment of 16 July 1971, Series A no. 13, pp. 24-34 and 42-44; König judgment of 28 June 1978, Series A no. 27, pp. 16 *in fine*, 22, 23-24 and 33-40).

60. Both the minority of the Commission and the Government attach importance to the fact that the institution of contempt of court is peculiar to common-law countries and suggest that the concluding words of Article 10 § 2 were designed to cover this institution which has no equivalent in many other member States of the Council of Europe.

However, even if this were so, the Court considers that the reason for the insertion of those words would have been to ensure that the general aims of the law of contempt of court should be considered legitimate aims under Article 10 § 2 but not to make that law the standard by which to assess whether a given measure was "necessary". If and to the extent that Article 10 § 2 was prompted by the notions underlying either the English law of contempt of court or any other similar domestic institution, it cannot have adopted them as they stood: it transposed them into an autonomous context. It is "necessity" in terms of the Convention which the Court has to assess, its rôle being to review the conformity of national acts with the standards of that instrument.

In addition, the Court exercises its supervision in the light of the case as a whole (above-mentioned Handyside judgment, p. 23, § 50). Accordingly, it must not lose sight of the existence of a variety of reasoning and solutions in the judicial decisions summarised at paragraphs 22 to 35 above, of extensive debates in England on the law of contempt of court and of proposals for reform. As regards the latter, the Court observes that, although the Government Green Paper sets out arguments for and against certain of the recommendations of the Phillimore Committee, it does not call in question the suggestion that the "prejudgment" test referred to in the House of Lords should be reconsidered (see paragraph 37 above).

61. Again, the Court cannot hold that the injunction was not "necessary" simply because it could or would not have been granted under a different legal system. As noted in the judgment of 9 February 1967 in the "Belgian Linguistic" case, the main purpose of the Convention is "to lay down certain international standards to be observed by the Contracting States in their relations with persons under their jurisdiction" (Series A no. 5, p. 19). This does not mean that absolute uniformity is required and, indeed, since the

Contracting States remain free to choose the measures which they consider appropriate, the Court cannot be oblivious of the substantive or procedural features of their respective domestic laws (see, *mutatis mutandis*, judgment of 23 July 1968 in the "Belgian Linguistic" case, Series A no. 6, pp. 34-35).

62. It must now be decided whether the "interference" complained of corresponded to a "pressing social need", whether it was "proportionate to the legitimate aim pursued", whether the reasons given by the national authorities to justify it are "relevant and sufficient under Article 10 § 2" (above-mentioned Handyside judgment, pp. 22-24, §§ 48-50). In this connection, the Court has examined the subject-matter of the injunction, then the state of the thalidomide case at the relevant time and, finally, the circumstances surrounding that case and the grant of the injunction.

63. The injunction, in the form ordered by the House of Lords, was not directed against the draft *Sunday Times* article alone (see paragraph 44 above). The applicants allege that it also prevented them from passing the results of their research to certain Government committees and to a Member of Parliament and from continuing their research, delayed plans for publishing a book and debarred the editor of *The Sunday Times* from commenting on the matter or replying to criticism aimed at him. In fact, the injunction was couched in terms wide enough to cover such items; its very breadth calls for a particularly close scrutiny of its "necessity".

The draft article was nonetheless the principal subject-matter of the injunction. It must therefore be ascertained in the first place whether the domestic courts' views as to the article's potential effects were relevant in terms of the maintenance of the "authority of the judiciary".

One of the reasons relied on was the pressure which the article would have brought to bear on Distillers to settle the actions out of court on better terms. However, even in 1972, publication of the article would probably not have added much to the pressure already on Distillers (see paragraph 29, second sub-paragraph, above). This applies with greater force to the position obtaining in July 1973, when the House of Lords gave its decision: by that date, the thalidomide case had been debated in Parliament and had been the subject not only of further press comment but also of a nationwide campaign (see paragraphs 13 and 14 above).

The speeches in the House of Lords emphasised above all the concern that the processes of the law may be brought into disrespect and the functions of the courts usurped either if the public is led to form an opinion on the subject-matter of litigation before adjudication by the courts or if the parties to litigation have to undergo "trial by newspaper". Such concern is in itself "relevant" to the maintenance of the "authority of the judiciary" as that expression is understood by the Court (see paragraph 55 above). If the issues arising in litigation are ventilated in such a way as to lead the public to form its own conclusion thereon in advance, it may lose its respect for and confidence in the courts. Again, it cannot be excluded that the public's becoming accustomed to the regular spectacle of pseudo-trials in the news media might in the long run have nefarious consequences for the acceptance of the courts as the proper forum for the settlement of legal disputes.

Nevertheless, the proposed *Sunday Times* article was couched in moderate terms and did not present just one side of the evidence or claim that there was only one possible result at which a court could arrive; although it analysed in detail evidence against Distillers, it also summarised arguments in their favour and closed with the words "There appears to be no neat set of answers . . .".

In the Court's opinion, the effect of the article, if published, would therefore have varied from reader to reader. Accordingly, even to the extent that the article might have led some readers to form an opinion on the negligence issue, this would not have had adverse consequences for the "authority of the judiciary", especially since, as noted above, there had been a nationwide campaign in the meantime.

On the other hand, publication of the proposed article might well have provoked replies. However, the same is true, to a greater or lesser extent, of any publication that refers to the facts underlying or the issues arising in litigation. As items in that category do not inevitably impinge on the "authority of the judiciary", the Convention cannot have been intended to permit the banning of all of them. Moreover, although this particular reason for the injunction might possibly have been "relevant" under Article 10 § 2, the Court cannot decide whether it was "sufficient" without examining all the surrounding circumstances.

64. At the time when the injunction was originally granted and at the time of its restoration, the thalidomide case was at the stage of settlement negotiations. The applicants concur with the Court of Appeal's view that the case was "dormant" and the majority of the Commission considers it unlikely that there would have been a trial of the issue of negligence. For the Government and the minority of the Commission, on the other hand, such a trial was a real possibility.

An assessment of the precise status of the case during the relevant period is not needed for the Court's decision: preventing interference with negotiations towards the settlement of a pending suit is a no less legitimate aim under Article 10 § 2 than preventing interference with a procedural situation in the strictly forensic sense. The same applies to the procedure for judicial approval of a settlement (see paragraph 9 above). What is to be retained is merely that negotiations were very lengthy, continuing for several years, and that at the actual moment when publication of the article was restrained the case had not reached the stage of trial.

Nevertheless, the question arises as to how it was possible to discharge the injunction in 1976—by reference, incidentally, to the "pressure principle" rather than the "prejudgment principle" (see paragraph 35 above). At that time, there were still outstanding not only some of the parents' actions but also an action between Distillers and their insurers involving the issue of negligence; the latter action, moreover, had been set down for trial (see paragraph 16 above). Discharge of the injunction in these circumstances prompts the question whether the injunction was necessary in the first place.

65. The Government's reply is that it is a matter of balancing the public interest in freedom of expression and the public interest in the fair administration of justice; they stress that the injunction was a temporary measure and say that the balance, on being struck again in 1976 when the situation had changed, fell on the other side.

This brings the Court to the circumstances surrounding the thalidomide case and the grant of the injunction.

As the Court remarked in its Handyside judgment, freedom of expression constitutes one of the essential foundations of a democratic society; subject to paragraph 2 of Article 10, it is applicable not only to information or ideas that are favourably received or regarded as inoffensive or as a matter of indifference, but also to those that offend, shock or disturb the State or any sector of the population (p. 23, § 49).

These principles are of particular importance as far as the press is concerned. They are equally applicable to the field of the administration of justice, which serves the interests of the community at large and requires the co-operation of an enlightened public. There is general recognition of the fact that the courts cannot operate in a vacuum. Whilst they are the forum for the settlement of disputes, this does not mean that there can be no prior discussion of disputes elsewhere, be it in specialised journals, in the general press or amongst the public at large. Furthermore, whilst the mass media must not overstep the bounds imposed in the interests of the proper administration of justice, it is incumbent on them to impart information and ideas concerning matters that come before the courts just as in other areas of public interest. Not only do the media have the task of imparting such information and ideas: the public also has a right to receive them (see, *mutatis mutandis*, the Kjeldsen, Busk Madsen and Pedersen judgment of 7 December 1976, Series A no. 23, p. 26, § 52).

To assess whether the interference complained of was based on "sufficient" reasons which rendered it "necessary in a democratic society", account must thus be taken of any public interest aspect of the case. The Court observes in this connection that, following a balancing of the conflicting interests involved, an absolute rule was formulated by certain of the Law Lords to the effect that it was not permissible to prejudge issues in pending cases: it was considered that the law would be too uncertain if the balance were to be struck anew in each case (see paragraphs 29, 32 and 33 above). Whilst emphasising that it is not its function to pronounce itself on an interpretation of English law adopted in the House of Lords (see, *mutatis mutandis*, the Ringeisen judgment of 16 July 1971, Series A no. 13, p. 40, § 97), the Court points out that it has to take a different approach. The Court is faced not with a choice between two conflicting principles but with a principle of freedom of expression that is subject to a number of exceptions which must be narrowly interpreted (see, *mutatis mutandis*, the Klass and others judgment of 6 September 1978, Series A no. 28, p. 21, § 42). In the second place, the Court's supervision under Article 10 covers not only the basic legislation but also the decision applying it (see the Handyside judgment, p. 23, § 49). It is not sufficient that the interference involved belongs to that class of the exceptions listed in Article 10 § 2 which has been invoked; neither is it sufficient that the interference was imposed because its subject-matter fell within a particular category or was caught by a legal rule formulated in general or absolute terms: the Court has to be satisfied that the interference was necessary having regard to the facts and circumstances prevailing in the specific case before it.

66. The thalidomide disaster was a matter of undisputed public concern. It posed the question whether the powerful company which had marketed the drug bore legal or moral responsibility towards hundreds of individuals experiencing an appalling personal tragedy or whether the victims could demand or hope for indemnification only from the community as a whole; fundamental issues concerning protection against and compensation for injuries resulting from scientific developments were raised and many facets of the existing law on these subjects were called in question.

As the Court has already observed, Article 10 guarantees not only the freedom of the press to inform the public but also the right of the public to be properly informed (see paragraph 65 above).

In the present case, the families of numerous victims of the tragedy, who were unaware of the legal difficulties involved, had a vital interest in knowing all the underlying facts and the various possible solutions. They could be deprived of this information, which was crucially important for them, only if it appeared absolutely certain that its diffusion would have presented a threat to the "authority of the judiciary".

Being called upon to weigh the interests involved and assess their respective force, the Court makes the following observations:

In September 1972, the case had, in the words of the applicants, been in a "legal cocoon" for several years and it was, at the very least, far from certain that the parents' actions would have come on for trial. There had also been no public enquiry (see paragraph 14 above).

The Government and the minority of the Commission point out that there was no prohibition on discussion of the "wider issues", such as the principles of the English law of negligence, and indeed it is true that there had been extensive discussion in various circles especially after, but also before, the Divisional Court's initial decision (see paragraphs 11, 12 and 14 above). However, the Court considers it rather artificial to attempt to divide the "wider issues" and the negligence issue. The question of where responsibility for a tragedy of this kind actually lies is also a matter of public interest.

It is true that, if the *Sunday Times* article had appeared at the intended time, Distillers might have felt obliged to develop in public, and in advance of any trial, their arguments on the facts of the case (see paragraph 63 above); however, those facts did not cease to be a matter of public interest merely because they formed the background to pending litigation. By bringing to light certain facts, the article might have served as a brake on speculative and unenlightened discussion.

67. Having regard to all the circumstances of the case and on the basis of the approach described in paragraph 65 above, the Court concludes that the interference complained of did not correspond to a social need sufficiently pressing to outweigh the public interest in freedom of expression within the meaning of the Convention. The Court therefore finds the reasons for the restraint imposed on the applicants not to be sufficient under Article 10 § 2. That restraint proves not to be proportionate to the legitimate aim pursued; it was not necessary in a democratic society for maintaining the authority of the judiciary.

Accordingly, by 11 votes to 9, the Court decided that there had been a breach of Article 10.

3. REFORM OF CONTEMPT OF COURT

Further Reading

De Smith, pp. 361–362; O'Higgins, pp. 40–43; Smith & Hogan, pp. 737–749; Street, pp. 166–187; Wade & Phillips, pp. 323–330.

G. Borrie and N. Lowe, *The Law of Contempt* (Butterworth, 1973); Sir John C. Fox, *The History of Contempt of Court* (Clarendon Press, 1927); Justice, *Contempt of Court* (1959); C. J. Miller, *Contempt of Court* (Elek, 1976).

Summary of conclusions and recommendations of the Report of the Committee on Contempt of Court [the "Phillimore Report"], Cmnd. 5794, 1974.

General

1. The law of contempt in England and Wales and in Scotland is required as a means of:—

(a) maintaining the rights of the citizen to a fair and unimpeded system of justice; and

(b) protecting the orderly administration of the law.

2. The operation of the law of contempt should be confined to circumstances where the achievement of its objectives requires the application of a swift and summary procedure.

3. In essentials the law of contempt, especially as it affects the press, should be the same in England and Wales and in Scotland so far as procedural differences allow.

4. The law as it stands contains uncertainties which impede and restrict reasonable freedom of speech. It should be amended and clarified by statute so as to allow as much freedom of speech as is consistent with the basic purposes of the law of contempt.

5. A particular area of uncertainty concerns the period of operation of the law of contempt, as to whether publications are at risk when proceedings are "imminent" and, if so, what period that expression covers.

Unintentional contempts out of court

6. Strict liability for contempt (that is, liability even though the contempt was unintentional) should apply only to *publications* (including for this purpose any speech, writing, broadcast or other communication, in whatever form, which is addressed to the public at large), and not to any other conduct.

7. A publication should give rise to strict liability for contempt only if it creates a risk that the course of justice in particular proceedings will be seriously impeded or prejudiced, and this definition of contempt should be provided by statute.

8. In *criminal proceedings,* strict liability for publications should apply in England and Wales only when the accused person is charged or a summons served (instead of when proceedings are imminent, as at present), and in Scotland when he is publicly charged on petition or otherwise, or at the first calling in court of a summary complaint (instead of when a crime is known to have been committed).

9. In *civil proceedings,* strict liability for publications should apply, not as at present from the commencement of the proceedings, but in England and Wales when the case has been set down for trial and in Scotland when proof or jury trial has been ordered, or the equivalent stage in other civil proceedings in which those stages do not occur. (This recommendation was subject to a note by Mr. Robin Day, who recommended that liability should not apply until shortly (say one or two weeks) before the trial, with the publication of a special *sub judice* list to show which cases have reached this stage).

10. Strict liability for publications should cease when the judgment, sentence or other order of the court is given; but in a criminal case in England and Wales, if the jury fails to agree, strict liability should continue to apply until it is clear that no retrial is to be ordered; in the event of a new trial it should apply as before.

11. The existing defence of innocent publication and distribution under section 11 of the Administration of Justice Act 1960 (which protects a person

who publishes prejudicial matter if, having taken reasonable care, he did not know and had no reason to suspect that legal proceedings which might be prejudiced were pending or imminent) should be retained in England and Wales and extended to Scotland.

12. It should also be a defence to an allegation of contempt that the publication was a fair and accurate report of legal proceedings in open court published contemporaneously and in good faith.

13. It should further be a defence to an allegation of contempt that the publication formed part of a legitimate discussion of matters of general public interest and that it only incidentally and unintentionally created a risk of serious prejudice to particular proceedings.

14. A general defence that a publication, though prejudicial, is in the public interest should *not* be introduced into the law.

15. The existing law governing editorial and corporate responsibility for publications should be retained, with necessary modifications in regard to broadcasting and television organisations.

Intentional contempts out of court

16. Any conduct, including publication, which is *intended* to prevent or obstruct the course of justice in particular proceedings should continue to be capable of being dealt with as contempt of court, but:—

(a) only if the proceedings in question have started and have not yet been finally settled or concluded; and, in any event,

(b) such conduct should normally be dealt with as a criminal offence unless there are compelling reasons requiring it to be dealt with as a matter of urgency by means of summary contempt procedures.

17. In Scotland, it should continue to be a contempt of court to publish the content of the written pleadings before the record is closed.

18. It should be provided by statute that bringing influence or pressure to bear upon a party to proceedings shall not be held to be a contempt unless it amounts to intimidation or unlawful threats to his person, property or reputation.

19. It should no longer be a contempt to take or threaten reprisals against a witness or juror after the conclusion of legal proceedings with the intention of punishing him for his part in them. Instead, such conduct should be made an indictable offence, with provision for the victim to recover compensation for any loss or damage he may have suffered.

20. "Scandalising the court" should cease to be part of the law of contempt. Instead, it should be made an indictable offence both in England and Wales and in Scotland to defame a judge in such a way as to bring the administration of justice into disrepute. Proof that the allegations were true *and* that publication was for the public benefit should be a defence. In England and Wales this offence should be made a branch of the law of criminal libel.

21. All distinctions between 'civil' and 'criminal' contempts in England and Wales should be abolished, so that breach of a court order is not treated differently from other forms of contempt.

Contempts in court

22. Contempt in the face of the court should continue to be dealt with by the judge himself, in accordance with the present practice, but:—

(a) the judge should always ensure that the contemnor is in no doubt about the nature of the conduct complained of, and give him an opportunity of explaining or denying his conduct, and of calling witnesses;

(b) before any substantial penalty is imposed there should be a short adjournment, with power to remand the contemnor in custody. The judge should have power to obtain a background report on the contemnor, and the contemnor should be entitled to speak in mitigation of sentence;

(c) for the purposes of defending himself and of making a plea in mitigation the contemnor should be entitled to legal representation, and the court should have power to grant legal aid immediately for the purpose where appropriate; and

(d) if the contempt also amounts to a criminal offence, the judge should consider referring it to the prosecuting authorities to be dealt with under the ordinary criminal law, and should so refer it in serious cases unless reasons of urgency or convenience require that it be dealt with summarily.*

23. Magistrates in England and Wales should be given power to impose penalties for contempt in the face of the court (subject to the limits proposed in recommendations 34 and 35 below).

24. Bankruptcy Registrars in the High Court in England should be given the same powers as county court judges to punish contempts in the face of the court.

25. For the purposes of section 41 of the Criminal Justice Act 1925 (prohibition on use of cameras in courts and their precincts) a map or plan should be displayed wherever practicable indicating the boundaries of the precincts of the court.

26. Regulations should be made governing the unofficial use of tape-recorders in court, and of recordings obtained thereby. Breach of the regulations in court should be punishable as a contempt.

Procedure, appeals, sentences, etc.

27. The right of private individuals to initiate proceedings for contempt both in England and Wales and in Scotland should continue, without prejudice to the power of either the Attorney General or the Lord Advocate to take proceedings at his own instance should he consider it proper to do so in the public interest.

28. In all contempt proceedings which a private individual seeks to institute, other than those for the enforcement of a court order made in his favour, he should be required to serve notice of those proceedings on the Attorney General or the Lord Advocate as the case may be.

29. *Ex parte* committal orders in England and Wales should in any case include a direction that the contemnor is to be brought up before the judge making the order (or another judge if he is not available) at the earliest opportunity.

30. There should be created a right of appeal to the Court of Criminal Appeal in Scotland by way of Note of Appeal from a finding of contempt in a criminal trial on indictment.

*In Scotland these recommendations were largely put into effect by a memorandum to judges and sheriffs from the Lord Justice General issued in August 1975. Similar guidance to courts in England and Wales was given by the Court of Appeal in *Balogh* v. *St. Alban's Crown Court* [1975] 1 Q.B. 73.

31. All sentences of imprisonment for contempt of court in England and Wales should be for fixed terms (as they already are in Scotland), but the power to review a case and order release before the full sentence is served should be retained. Exercise of the Royal prerogative of mercy should not be advised in any case of contempt.

32. In superior courts both in England and Scotland the power to fine for contempt should remain unlimited but the power to imprison should be limited to a maximum period of two years. All courts should in addition have appropriate powers to deal with mentally disordered offenders.

33. The powers of judges of county courts (in England and Wales) and sheriffs (in Scotland) to punish for contempt should be increased and reduced respectively to a maximum fine of £150 or three months' imprisonment.

34. Both in England and Scotland, magistrates and justices of the peace should have power to impose a fine of up to £20 or imprisonment for up to seven days for contempt in the face of the court.

35. Powers of both sheriffs and magistrates in Scotland and of magistrates in England to certify more serious cases of contempt in the face of the court to the High Court of Justiciary or the Inner House of the Court of Session and the Divisional Court respectively should be given or confirmed, as the case may be.

36. Prison regulations in England and Wales should be amended to require notification to be given to the Official Solicitor of prisoners committed for contempt by county courts for fixed terms of less than six weeks, in the same way as for other contempt prisoners.

37. The machinery for the enforcement of fines for contempt in the High Court and Restrictive Practices Court in England and Wales should be replaced by a system on the lines of that provided by the Criminal Justice Act 1967.

[See also *Contempt of Court: A Discussion Paper,* Cmnd. 7145, 1978.]

4. *REFORM OF CRIMINAL LIBEL*

Further Reading

Smith & Hogan, pp. 793–795.

J. R. Spencer, "Criminal Libel in Action—The Snuffing of Mr. Wicks," (1979) 38 *Cambridge Law Journal* pp. 60–78; *ibid.* "Criminal Libel—A Skeleton in the Cupboard," (1977) Crim. L.R. pp. 383–394; pp. 465-474.

Report of the Committee on Defamation, Cmnd. 5909, 1975

Recommendations

448. We *recommend* the following slight alterations to the existing law, namely:—

    (*a*) criminal libel should apply to broadcasting, in addition to matter in permanent form;

    (*b*) courts of summary jurisdiction should be empowered to try cases of criminal libel with the consent of the defendant and to impose a sentence of imprisonment not exceeding 9 months or a fine not exceeding £500 or both;

(c) privilege and comment should be declared to be defences subject to rebuttal as in civil actions.

(d) a civil action for defamation should be declared to be no bar to a prosecution for criminal libel (whether or not such an action has been concluded);

(e) the protection given by section 8 of the Law of Libel Amendment Act 1888 should be extended to include the following persons:—

the proprietors, publishers, editors of periodical publications or any other person responsible for the publication of such periodicals and contributors thereto (whether or not employed) and all broadcasting authorities and person paid to present or contribute to the programmes of such authorities (whether or not employed).

5. OBSCENITY

Further Reading

De Smith, pp. 478–483; O'Higgins, pp. 24–31; Smith & Hogan, pp. 691–708; Street, pp. 128–156; Wade & Phillips, pp. 478–483.

D. F. Barber, *Pornography and Society* (Skitton, 1972); A. Burns (ed.) *To Deprave and Corrupt* (Davis-Paynter, 1972); A. Calder-Marshall, *Lewd, Blasphemous and Obscene* (Hutchinson, 1962); J. Chandos (ed.), *"To Deprave and Corrupt . . ."* (Souvenir Press, 1962); B. Crick, *Crime, Rape and Gin: Reflections on Contemporary Attitudes to Violence, Pornography and Addiction* (Elek/Pemberton, 1974); L. Grant, *Civil Liberty: The N.C.C.L. Guide to Your Rights* (Penguin, 1978) pp. 311–318; D. Holbrook (ed.) *The Case against Pornography* (Tom Stacey, 1972); Law Commission, *Report on Conspiracy and Criminal Law Reform,* H.C. 176, 1976; Lord Longford, *Pornography: The Longford Report* (Coronet Books, 1972); E. J. Mishan, *Making the World Safe for Pornography* (Alcone Press, 1973); *The Obscenity Laws: A Report by the Working Party set up by a Conference convened by the Chairman of the Arts Council of Great Britain* (Andre Deutsch, 1969); Geoffrey Robertson, *Obscenity* (Weidenfeld & Nicholson, 1979); C. H. Rolph (ed.), *Does Obscenity Matter?* (London, 1961); Society of Conservative Lawyers, *The Pollution of the Mind* (London, 1971); N. St. John Stevas, *Obscenity and the Law* (Secker & Warburg, 1956).

See also Home Office, *Report of the Committee on Obscenity and Film Censorship, Chairman: Bernard Williams,* Cmnd. 7772, 1979.

VAGRANCY ACT 1838

2.—Persons exposing obscene prints, etc., in shop windows liable on conviction to punishment

. . . Every person who shall wilfully expose or cause to be exposed to public view in the window or other part of any shop or other building situate in any street, road, highway, or public place, any obscene print, picture, or other indecent exhibition, shall be deemed to have wilfully exposed such obscene print, picture, or other indecent exhibition to public view within the intent and meaning of the said Act, and shall accordingly be liable to be proceeded against, and on conviction to be punished, under the provisions of the said Act.

METROPOLITAN POLICE ACT 1839

54. Penalty on persons committing in thoroughfares the offences herein mentioned

. . . Every person shall be liable to a penalty not more than forty shillings, who, within the limits of the metropolitan police district, shall in any thoroughfare or public place, commit any of the following offences; (that is to say,)

12. Every person who shall sell or distribute or offer for sale or distribution, or exhibit to public view, any profane, indecent, or obscene book, paper, print, drawing, painting or representation, or sing any profane, indecent, or obscene song or ballad, or write or draw any indecent or obscene word, figure, or representation, or use any profane, indecent or obscene language to the annoyance of the inhabitants or passengers:

13. Every person who shall use any threatening, abusive, or insulting words or behaviour with intent to provoke a breach of the peace, or whereby a breach of the peace may be occasioned:

CUSTOMS CONSOLIDATION ACT 1876

42. Prohibitions and restrictions

The goods enumerated and described in the following table of prohibitions and restrictions inwards are hereby prohibited to be imported or brought into the United Kingdom, save as thereby excepted . . .

A TABLE OF PROHIBITIONS AND RESTRICTIONS INWARDS

Goods prohibited to be imported

Indecent or obscene prints, paintings, photographs, books, cards, lithographic or other engravings, or any other indecent or obscene articles.

POST OFFICE ACT 1953

11. Prohibition on sending by post of certain articles

(I) A person shall not send or attempt to send or procure to be sent a postal packet which—
   (a) save as the authority may either generally or in any particular case allow, encloses any explosive, dangerous, noxious or deleterious substance, any filth, any sharp instrument not properly protected, any noxious living creature, or any creature, article or thing whatsoever which is likely to injure either other postal packets in course of conveyance or a person engaged in the business of the authority; or
   (b) encloses any indecent or obscene print, painting, photograph, lithograph, engraving, cinematograph film, book, card or written communication, or any indecent or obscene article whether similar to the above or not; or

(c) has on the packet, or on the cover thereof, any words, marks or designs which are grossly offensive or of an indecent or obscene character.

CHILDREN AND YOUNG PERSONS
(HARMFUL PUBLICATIONS) ACT 1955

An Act to prevent the dissemination of certain pictorial publications harmful to children and young persons

1. Works to which this Act applies
This Act applies to any book, magazine or other like work which is of a kind likely to fall into the hands of children or young persons and consists wholly or mainly of stories told in pictures (with or without the addition of written matter), being stories portraying—
   (a) the commission of crimes; or
   (b) acts of violence or cruelty; or
   (c) incidents of a repulsive or horrible nature;
in such a way that the work as a whole would tend to corrupt a child or young person into whose hands it might fall.

2. Penalty for printing, publishing, selling, etc., works to which this Act applies
(1) A person who prints, publishes, sells or lets on hire a work to which this Act applies, or has any such work in his possession for the purpose of selling it or letting it on hire, shall be guilty of an offence and liable, on summary conviction, to imprisonment for a term not exceeding four months or to a fine not exceeding one hundred pounds or to both:

Provided that, in any proceedings taken under this subsection against a person in respect of selling or letting on hire a work or of having it in his possession for the purpose of selling it or letting it on hire, it shall be a defence for him to prove that he had not examined the contents of the work and had no reasonable cause to suspect that it was one to which this Act applies.

(2) A prosecution for an offence under this section shall not, in England or Wales, be instituted except by, or with the consent of, the Attorney General.

3. Power to search for, and dispose of, works to which this Act applies and articles for printing them
(1) Where, upon an information being laid before a justice of the peace that a person has, or is suspected of having, committed an offence under the last foregoing section with respect to a work (hereafter in this subsection referred to as "the relevant work"), the justice issues a summons directed to that person requiring him to answer to the information or issues a warrant to arrest that person, that or any other justice, if satisfied by written information substantiated on oath that there is reasonable ground for suspecting that the said person has in his possession or under his control—
   (a) any copies of the relevant work or any other work to which this Act applies; or
   (b) any plate prepared for the purpose of printing copies of the relevant work or any other work to which this Act applies or any photographic film prepared for that purpose;
may grant a search warrant authorising any constable named therein to enter (if necessary by force) any premises specified in the warrant and any vehicle or stall used by the said person for the purposes of trade or business and to

search the premises, vehicle or stall and seize any of the following things which the constable finds therein or thereon, that is to say:–

   (i) any copies of the relevant work and any copies of any other work which the constable has reasonable cause to believe to be one to which this Act applies; and

   (ii) any plate which the constable has reasonable cause to believe to have been prepared for the purpose of printing copies of any such work as is mentioned in paragraph (i) of this subsection and any photographic film which he has reasonable cause to believe to have been prepared for that purpose.

(2) The court by or before which a person is convicted of an offence under the last foregoing section with respect to a work may order any copies of that work and any plate prepared for the purpose of printing copies of that work or photographic film prepared for that purpose, being copies which have, or a plate or film which has, been found in his possession or under his control, to be forfeited:

Provided that an order made under this subsection by a magistrates' court or, on appeal from a magistrates' court, by a court of quarter sessions shall not take effect until the expiration of the ordinary time within which an appeal in the matter of the proceedings in which the order was made may be lodged (whether by giving notice of appeal or applying for a case to be stated for the opinion of the High Court) or, where such an appeal is duly lodged, until the appeal is finally decided or abandoned.

4. Prohibition of importation of works to which this Act applies and articles for printing them

The importation of—

   (a) any work to which this Act applies; and

   (b) any plate prepared for the purpose of printing copies of any such work and any photographic film prepared for that purpose;

is hereby prohibited.

OBSCENE PUBLICATIONS ACT 1959

1. Test of obscenity

(1) For the purposes of this Act an article shall be deemed to be obscene if its effect or (where the article comprises two or more distinct items) the effect of any one of its items is, if taken as a whole, such as to tend to deprave and corrupt persons who are likely, having regard to all relevant circumstances, to read, see or hear the matter contained or embodied in it.

(2) In this Act "article" means any description of article containing or embodying matter to be read or looked at or both, any sound record, and any film or other record of a picture or pictures.

(3) For the purposes of this Act a person publishes an article who—

   (a) distributes, circulates, sells, lets on hire, gives, or lends it, or who offers it for sale or for letting on hire; or

   (b) in the case of an article containing or embodying matter to be looked at or a record, shows, plays or projects it:

Provided that paragraph (b) of this subsection shall not apply to anything done in the course of television or sound broadcasting.

2. Prohibition of publication of obscene matter

(1) Subjects as hereinafter provided, any person who, whether for gain or not publishes an obscene article [or who has an obscene article for publication for gain (whether gain to himself or gain to another)] shall be liable—

    (a) on summary conviction to a fine not exceeding one hundred pounds or to imprisonment for a term not exceeding six months;

    (b) on conviction on indictment to a fine or to imprisonment for a term not exceeding three years or both.

(2) Notwithstanding anything in section one hundred and four of the Magistrates' Courts Act, 1952, summary proceedings for an offence against this section may be brought at any time within twelve months from the commission of the offence; and paragraph 16 of the First Schedule to the Magistrates' Courts Act, 1952 (under which an offence at common law of publishing, exhibiting or selling obscene articles may be tried summarily) is hereby repealed.

(3) A prosecution on indictment for an offence against this section shall not be commenced more than two years after the commission of the offence.

(3A) Proceedings for an offence under this section shall not be instituted except by or with the consent of the Director of Public Prosecutions in any case where the article in question is a moving picture film of a width of not less than sixteen millimetres and the relevant publication or the only other publication which followed or could reasonably have been expected to follow from the relevant publication took place or (as the case may be) was to take place in the course of a cinematograph exhibition; and in this subsection 'the relevant publication' means—

    (a) in the case of any proceedings under this section for publishing an obscene article, the publication in respect of which the defendant would be charged if the proceedings were brought; and

    (b) in the case of any proceedings under this section for having an obscene article for publication for gain, the publication which, if the proceedings were brought, the defendant would be alleged to have had in contemplation.

(4) A person publishing an article shall not be proceeded against for an offence at common law consisting of the publication of any matter contained or embodied in the article where it is of the essence of the offence that the matter is obscene.

(4A) Without prejudice to subsection (4) above, a person shall not be proceeded against for an offence at common law—

    (a) in respect of a cinematograph exhibition or anything said or done in the course of a cinematograph exhibition, where it is of the essence of the common law offence that the exhibition or, as the case may be, what was said or done was obscene, indecent, offensive, disgusting or injurious to morality; or

    (b) in respect of an agreement to give a cinematograph exhibition or to cause anything to be said or done in the course of such an exhibition where the common law offence consists of conspiring to corrupt public morals or to do any act contrary to public morals or decency.

(5) A person shall not be convicted of an offence against this section if he proves that he had not examined the article in respect of which he is charged and had no reasonable cause to suspect that it was such that his publication of it would make him liable to be convicted of an offence against this section.

(6) In any proceedings against a person under this section the question whether an article is obscene shall be determined without regard to any publication by another person unless it could reasonably have been expected that the publication by the other person would follow from publication by the person charged.

3. Powers of search and seizure

(1) If a justice of the peace is satisfied by information on oath that there is reasonable ground for suspecting that, in any premises in the petty sessions area for which he acts, or on any stall or vehicle in that area, being premises or a stall or vehicle specified in the information, obscene articles are, or are from time to time, kept for publication for gain, the justice may issue a warrant under his hand empowering any constable to enter (if need be by force) and search the premises, or to search the stall or vehicle, within fourteen days from the date of the warrant, and to seize and remove any articles found therein or thereon which the constable has reason to believe to be obscene articles and to be kept for publication for gain.

(2) A warrant under the foregoing subsection shall, if any obscene articles are seized under the warrant, also empower the seizure and removal of any documents found in the premises or, as the case may be, on the stall or vehicle which relate to a trade or business carried on at the premises or from the stall or vehicle.

(3) Any articles seized under subsection (1) of this section shall be brought before a justice of the peace acting for the same petty sessions area as the justice who issued the warrant, and the justice before whom the articles are brought may thereupon issue a summons to the occupier of the premises or, as the case may be, the user of the stall or vehicle to appear on a day specified in the summons before a magistrates' court for that petty sessions area to show cause why the articles or any of them should not be forfeited; and if the court is satisfied, as respects any of the articles, that at the time when they were seized they were obscene articles kept for publication for gain, the court shall order those articles to be forfeited:

Provided that if the person summoned does not appear, the court shall not make an order unless service of the summons is proved.

Provided also that this subsection does not apply in relation to any article seized under subsection (1) of this section which is returned to the occupier of the premises or, as the case may be, to the user of the stall or vehicle in or on which it was found.

(4) In addition to the person summoned, any other person being the owner, author or maker of any of the articles brought before the court, or any other person through whose hands they had passed before being seized, shall be entitled to appear before the court on the day specified in the summons to show cause why they should not be forfeited.

(5) Where an order is made under this section for the forfeiture of any articles, any person who appeared, or was entitled to appear, to show cause against the making of the order may appeal to quarter sessions; and no such order shall take effect until the expiration thereof notice of appeal is duly given or application is made for the statement of a case for the opinion of the High Court, until the final determination or abandonment of the proceedings on the appeal or case.

(6) If as respects any articles brought before it the court does not order forfeiture, the court may if it thinks fit order the person on whose information the warrant for the seizure of the articles was issued to pay such costs as the court thinks reasonable to any person who has appeared before the court to show cause why those articles should not be forfeited; and costs ordered to be paid under this subsection shall be enforceable as a civil debt.

(7) For the purposes of this section the question whether an article is obscene shall be determined on the assumption that copies of it would be published in any manner likely having regard to the circumstances in which it was found, but in no other manner.

(8) The Obscene Publications Act, 1857, is hereby repealed, without prejudice, however, to the execution of any warrant issued thereunder before the commencement of this Act or to the taking of any proceedings in pursuance of a warrant so issued.

4. Defence of public good

(1) Subject to subsection (1A) of this section a person shall not be convicted of an offence against section two of this Act, and an order for forfeiture shall not be made under the foregoing section, if it is proved that publication of the article in question is justified as being for the public good on the ground that it is in the interests of science, literature, art or learning, or of other objects of general concern.

(1A) Subsection (1) of this section shall not apply where the article in question is a moving picture film or soundtrack but—

(a) a person shall not be convicted of an offence against section 2 of this Act in relation to any such film or soundtrack, and

(b) an order for forfeiture of any such film or soundtrack shall not be made under section 3 of this Act,

if it is proved that publication of the film or soundtrack is justified as being for the public good on the ground that it is in the interests of drama, opera, ballet or any other art, or of literature or learning.

(2) It is hereby declared that the opinion of experts as to the literary, artistic, scientific or other merits of an article may be admitted in any proceedings under this Act either to establish or to negative the said ground.

(3) In this section "moving picture soundtrack" means any sound record designed for playing with a moving picture film, whether incorporated with the film or not.

CRIMINAL JUSTICE ACT 1967

25. Restrictions on issue of search warrants under Obscene Publications Act 1959.

A justice of the peace shall not issue a warrant under section 3(1) of the Obscene Publications Act 1959 (search for and seizure of obscene articles) except on an information laid by or on behalf of the Director of Public Prosecutions or by a constable.

OBSCENE PUBLICATIONS ACT 1964

1. Obscene articles intended for publication for gain

(1) In section 2 (1) of the Obscene Publications Act 1959 (under which it is an offence punishable on summary conviction or on indictment to publish an

obscene article, whether for gain or not) after the words "any person who, whether for gain or not, publishes an obscene article" there shall be inserted the words "or who has an obscene article for publication for gain (whether gain to himself or gain to another)".

(2) For the purpose of any proceedings for an offence against the said section 2 a person shall be deemed to have an article for publication for gain if with a view to such publication he has the article in his ownership, possession or control.

(3) In proceedings brought against a person under the said section 2 for having an obscene article for publication for gain the following provisions shall apply in place of subsections (5) and (6) of that section, that is to say,—

(a) he shall not be convicted of that offence if he proves that he had not examined the article and had no reasonable cause to suspect that it was such that his having it would make him liable to be convicted of an offence against that section; and

(b) the question whether the article is obscene shall be determined by reference to such publication for gain of the article as in the circumstances it may reasonably be inferred he had in contemplation and to any further publication that could reasonably be expected to follow from it, but not to any other publication.

(4) Where articles are seized under section 3 of the Obscene Publications Act 1959 (which provides for the seizure and forfeiture of obscene articles kept for publication for gain), and a person is convicted under section 2 of that Act of having them for publication for gain, the court on his conviction shall order the forfeiture of those articles:

Provided that an order made by virtue of this subsection (including an order so made on appeal) shall not take effect until the expiration of the ordinary time within which an appeal in the matter of the proceedings in which the order was made may be instituted or, where such an appeal is duly instituted, until the appeal is finally decided or abandoned; and for this purpose—

(a) an application for a case to be stated or for leave to appeal shall be treated as the institution of an appeal; and

(b) where a decision on appeal is subject to a further appeal, the appeal shall not be deemed to be finally decided until the expiration of the ordinary time within which a further appeal may be instituted or, where a further appeal is duly instituted, until the further appeal is finally decided or abandoned.

(5) References in section 3 of the Obscene Publications Act 1959 and this section to publication for gain shall apply to any publication with a view to gain, whether the gain is to accrue by way of consideration for the publication or in any other way.

2. Negatives, etc. for production of obscene articles

(1) The Obscene Publications Act 1959 (as amended by this Act) shall apply in relation to anything which is intended to be used, either alone or as one of a set, for the reproduction or manufacture therefrom of articles containing or embodying matter to be read, looked at or listened to, as if it were an article containing or embodying that matter so far as that matter is to be derived from it or from the set.

(2) For the purposes of the Obscene Publications Act 1959 (as so amended) an article shall be deemed to be had or kept for publication if it is had or kept

for the reproduction or manufacture therefrom of articles for publication; and the question whether an article so had or kept is obscene shall—

  (a) for purposes of section 2 of the Act be determined in accordance with section 1 (3) (b) above as if any reference there to publication of the article were a reference to publication of articles reproduced or manufactured from it; and

  (b) for purposes of section 3 of the Act be determined on the assumption that articles reproduced or manufactured from it would be published in any manner likely having regard to the circumstances in which it was found, but in no other manner.

Reg. v. Commissioner of Police of the Metropolis, Ex parte Blackburn and Another (No. 3) [1973] 2 W.L.R. 43

Court of Appeal

The Divisional Court dismissed an application for an order of *mandamus* directed to the Commissioner of the Police of the Metropolis to secure the enforcement of the law against the publication and sale of pornographic literature. The applicant appealed to the Court of Appeal.

LORD DENNING M.R.:

The procedure of the police

We were told of the procedure of the Metropolitan Police to enforce the law under the Act of 1959. It is this: the police get to know—by their own inspection or by information from others—that pornographic material is on sale at a certain shop. They report it to the Obscene Publications Squad at New Scotland Yard. They are 14 officers who are especially assigned to investigate obscenity. One of this squad goes to the shop. If he thinks the material is obscene, he goes to a magistrate and asks for a warrant. Armed with the warrant, he searches the shop and seizes all obscene material he finds there. Having seized it, he submits it to the Director of Public Prosecutions. The director then considers whether it is obscene or not. If he thinks it is obscene, he then gives his opinion, whether the occupier should be prosecuted, or not: or whether the lesser course should be taken of submitting it to the courts for a destruction order. If he advises a prosecution, the director himself undertakes the prosecution. If he advises the lesser course, he leaves it to the police to issue a summons and get the material destroyed. In many cases the police do not take the matter to the court. They caution the occupier and invite him to sign a "disclaimer" disclaiming any interest in the material. They then destroy it. The commissioner has given figures to show the activities of the police under this procedure. He did so in a letter of July 10, 1972, and in the affidavit he put before the court. These figures are impressive. For instance, in the first nine and a half months of 1972 the Metropolitan Police made 166 searches and seized 871,468 items. Some of these were large-scale operators. At one address in Watford on September 21, 1972, the police seized 219,600 copies of *Men Only* at an estimated value of £100,000. At other addresses large quantities of obscene material were seized of much value. But impressive as those figures are, they seem to have made little impact on the trade. It remains very large. Next, the figures for Soho. They are not nearly so impressive. The commissioner gave them for the first nine and a half months of 1972. In Soho the police searched 45 shops. In 10 of them, they searched two, three or four times. But in the remaining 35, they searched once only in each shop. Out of these 35, eight shops gave a negative result, 27 resulted in a caution, four resulted in a prosecution. The remaining three await a decision, presumably by the director.

Mr. Blackburn criticised the police severely on their search procedure. He gave evidence that he went to three shops where the police searches proved "negative." He found there obscene material readily on sale. He bought them and produced them to us. He also said that the procedure by way of caution or "disclaimer" was quite ineffective: because the shops continued to sell their obscene material just the same. He asked us to infer that the police were not carrying out their duty of enforcing the law. Why were not the searches and seizures made every week, instead of once a year? That would, he suggested, bring the trade in hard pornography rapidly to a close. He also asked why the Director of Public Prosecutions should be consulted in every case? Many of these publications are obvious pornography. Why not proceed at once? Why should not the station commander himself take action? These are pertinent questions which require an answer. He submitted correspondence in which the commissioner acknowledges, quite frankly, that the practice was to consult the director, and go by his advice.

The legal position

Mr. Blackburn's principal point was a legal one. He said that there was no legal justification for the police referring all cases to the director. It causes delay. They can and should act at once without his advice. I have, therefore, looked into the law: and I find that Mr. Blackburn has a point worthy of serious consideration.

The powers of the police to search and seize are contained in section 3 of the Obscene Publications Act 1959, as amended by section 25 of the Criminal Justice Act 1967. Under it the police must first lay an information on oath before a magistrate and get a warrant to search and seize. If they find obscene articles and seize them, they must, as I read the statute, bring them before a magistrate and he can then order their destruction. But, instead of taking the articles before a magistrate, the police have adopted in many cases the practice of accepting disclaimers. I must describe this, because it goes back to a time before the Act was passed. It is described in the proceedings before the Select Committee in 1957 (*Report from the Select Committee on Obscene Publications*, H.C. Paper 123–1, Session 1957–1958). It was this: when the police searched premises and found articles which might be considered obscene, they submitted the articles to the Director of Public Prosecutions. In some cases the director would advise a prosecution. In other cases, he would instruct the officer to take steps to have the material destroyed. The officer would then go to the shopkeeper and ask him if he disputed the case. If he did not dispute it, the officer invited him to sign a disclaimer in this form: "I do hereby disclaim ownership to the above items seized from my bookshop." On getting that disclaimer the officer destroyed the material. That practice was in use for many years before 1957. It had the advantage of saving time. No summons was issued. There was no hearing before a magistrate, and no examination of documents by a magistrate.

The Select Committee in 1957, however, regarded that practice as *undesirable*, and for this reason. It enabled the alleged obscene matter to be destroyed without reference to the courts (see their report, paragraph 30); whereas, the Select Committee thought it desirable that the material should be brought before the courts. When the Act was passed in 1959, it would appear that Parliament accepted the view of the Select Committee. It enacted that when the police, under the authority of a warrant, search premises and seize articles, they *must* bring the articles before a magistrate. As I read section 3 (3) it is mandatory. It says: "Any articles seized shall be brought before a justice of the peace." The magistrate may then issue a summons to the occupier to show cause why the articles should not be forfeited.

Notwithstanding that enactment, it appears that the police of the metropolis still continue the practice of accepting disclaimers. When the police search premises and seize articles, they do not submit them in the first instance to the courts. They submit them to the Director of Public Prosecutions. Then, after consultation with him and on his authority—I use the commissioner's own words—they do one of these things: (i) they may return the articles to the occupier; or (ii) they may caution him and accept a disclaimer to the property; or (iii) they may summons the occupier before the court and seek a forfeiture order under section 3. That appears from the commissioner's affidavit, paragraphs 4 and 5.

I can see the practical advantages of the procedure adopted by the police. There is a great deal to be said for it. The attitude of the courts is so unpredictable and the time and trouble so excessive, that the practice of accepting "disclaimers" is far more convenient and effective. It is similar to the practice of the customs authorities who can seize obscene or indecent articles, and destroy them, without reference to the courts, unless the owners contest the issue. But the customs authorities have wider powers than the police. There is no provision in the Customs Acts similar to section 3 (3) of the Act of 1959.

The Commissioner of Police, in justification of his practice, relies on the regulations relating to the prosecution of offences [the Prosecution of Offences Regulations 1946, (S.I. 1946, No. 1467 (L. 17))]. These were made in 1946 long before the Act of 1959. Regulation 6 (2) (*d*) says that the chief officer of police *shall* report to the Director of Public Prosecutions "cases of obscene or indecent libels, exhibitions or publications, in which it appears to the chief officer of police that there is a prima facie case for prosecution." I can see the reason for this regulation. It is because it is often difficult to know whether a book or magazine comes within the test of obscenity. It is also desirable to apply a uniform standard throughout the country. So, whenever there is a prima facie case for prosecution, it should be reported to the director. So far so good. But I do not think the regulation is a complete answer to Mr. Blackburn's point. Accepting that cases should be reported to the director, nevertheless, the police are not bound to hold their hand pending his advice. On the contrary, the Act of 1959, as I read it, requires the articles to be brought before the magistrate for him to decide whether the occupier should be summoned, or not. Under the present practice, this is not done. In many cases, the articles are never brought before the magistrate. They are put before the director, and he advises whether the occupier be summoned, or not. This may be a very convenient and sensible procedure: but I cannot forbear from asking the question: Is it in accordance with the statute? And I would add: Is it as effective as a summons issued by the court? A pornographic trader might take little notice of a caution, but much of a summons for destruction, especially if it was coupled with a summons for an offence.

Conclusion

In *Reg.* v. *Commissioner of Police of the Metropolis Ex parte Blackburn* [1968] 2 Q.B. 118, 136, 138, 148–149, we made it clear that, in the carrying out of their duty of enforcing the law, the police have a discretion with which the courts will not interfere. There might, however, be extreme cases in which he was not carrying out his duty. And then we would. I do not think this is a case for our interference. In the past the commissioner has done what he could under the existing system and with the available manpower. The new commissioner is doing more. He is increasing the number of the Obscene Publications Squad to 18 and he is reforming it and its administration. No more can reasonably be expected.

The plain fact is, however, that the efforts of the police have hitherto been largely ineffective. Mr. Blackburn amply demonstrated it by going out from this court and buying these pornographic magazines—hard and soft—at shops all over the place. I do not accede to the suggestion that the police turn a blind eye to pornography or that shops get a "tip-off" before the police arrive. The cause of the ineffectiveness lies with the system and the framework in which the police have to operate. The Obscene Publications Act 1959 does not provide a sound foundation. It fails to provide a satisfactory test of obscenity: and it allows a defence of public good which has got out of hand. There is also considerable uncertainty as to the powers and duties of the police when they seize articles.

If the people of this country want pornography to be stamped out, the legislature must amend the Obscene Publications Act 1959 so as to make it strike unmistakeably at pornography: and it must define the powers and duties of the police so as to enable them to take effective measures for the purpose. The police may well say to Parliament: "Give us the tools and we will finish the job." But, without efficient tools, they cannot be expected to stamp it out. Mr. Blackburn has served a useful purpose in drawing the matter to our attention: but I do not think it is a case for mandamus. I would, therefore dismiss the appeal.

Phillimore and Roskill, L.JJ. agreed with the course proposed by Lord Denning, M.R. but for varying reasons. **PHILLIMORE** L.J. had this to say about police procedure:

Police orders have set up an Obscene Publications Squad in Scotland Yard. If in any division it is thought that "porn," and in particular "hard porn," is being peddled in any shop, that division is required to inform the squad. An officer from the squad will then investigate and if he sees confirmation of the report when visiting the premises he will obtain a warrant authorising him to enter, search the premises and seize any material he thinks obscene.

It appears that thereafter he will either invite a disclaimer, by which the occupier states that he has no interest in the material, and if the disclaimer is signed the police proceed with the destruction of the material. As already described by Lord Denning M.R. this is an undesirable and possibly illegal procedure and enables the shopkeeper to avoid any further proceeding. If he refuses the disclaimer (euphemistically described as a "caution") a report will go to the Director of Public Prosecutions pursuant to regulation 6 (2) (*d*) of the Prosecution of Offences Regulations 1946 with a view to his advice on whether the case merits prosecution.

Question

1. Is the disclaimer procedure lawful or desirable? Is the description given of the disclaimer procedure by Phillimore L.J. the same as that given by Lord Denning, M.R.?

Handyside Case (1976)

European Court of Human Rights

The applicant, proprietor of a publishing firm, was summarily convicted in 1971 in Lambeth Magistrates' Court, of having in his possession an obscene book, *The Little Red Schoolbook*, for publication for gain. At the same time the court made a forfeiture order for the destruction of copies of the book by the police. Handyside petitioned the Commission alleging violation of the European Convention. The Commission decided that there had been no violation of Article 10 of the Convention or of Article 1 of the First Protocol. The Commission referred the case to the Court requesting it to judge whether there had been a violation of these provision of the Convention and its Protocol. The Court said:

I. *On the alleged violation of Article 10 of the Convention*

43. The various measures challenged—the applicant's criminal conviction, the seizure and subsequent forfeiture and destruction of the matrix and of hundreds of copies of the Schoolbook—were without any doubt, and the Government did not deny it, "interferences by public authority" in the exercise of his freedom of expression which is guaranteed by paragraph 1 of the text cited above. Such interferences entail a "violation" of Article 10 if they do not fall within one of the exceptions provided for in paragraph 2, which is accordingly of decisive importance in this case.

44. If the "restrictions" and "penalties" complained of by Mr. Handyside are not to infringe Article 10, they must, according to paragraph 2, in the first place have been "prescribed by law". The Court finds that this was the case. In the United Kingdom legal system, the basis in law for the measures in question was the 1959/1964 Acts (paragraphs 14–18, 24–25 and 27–34 above). Besides, this was not contested by the applicant who further admitted that the competent authorities had correctly applied those Acts.

45. Having thus ascertained that the interferences complained of satisfied the first of the conditions in paragraph 2 of Article 10, the Court then investigated whether they also complied with the others. According to the Government and the majority of the Commission, the interferences were "necessary in a democratic society", "for the protection of . . . morals".

46. Sharing the view of the Government and the unanimous opinion of the Commission, the Court first finds that the 1959/1964 Acts have an aim that is legitimate under Article 10 § 2, namely, the protection of morals in a democratic society. Only this latter purpose is relevant in this case since the object of the said Acts—to wage war on "obscene" publications, defined by their tendency to "deprave and corrupt"—is linked far more closely to the

protection of morals than to any of the further purposes permitted by Article 10 § 2.

47. The Court must also investigate whether the protection of morals in a democratic society necessitated the various measures taken against the applicant and the Schoolbook under the 1959/1964 Acts. Mr. Handyside does not restrict himself to criticising these Acts as such: he also makes—from the viewpoint of the Convention and not of English law—several complaints concerning their application in his case.

The Commission's report and the subsequent hearings before the Court in June 1976 brought to light clear-cut differences of opinion on a crucial problem, namely, how to determine whether the actual "restrictions" and "penalties" complained of by the applicant were "necessary in a democratic society", "for the protection of morals". According to the Government and the majority of the Commission, the Court has only to ensure that the English courts acted reasonably, in good faith and within the limits of the margin of appreciation left to the Contracting States by Article 10 § 2. On the other hand, the minority of the Commission sees the Court's task as being not to review the Inner London Quarter Sessions judgment but to examine the Schoolbook directly in the light of the Convention and of nothing but the Convention.

48. The Court points out that the machinery of protection established by the Convention is subsidiary to the national systems safeguarding human rights (judgment of 23 July 1968 on the merits of the "Belgian Linguistic" case, Series A no. 6, p. 35, § 10 *in fine*). The Convention leaves to each Contracting State, in the first place, the task of securing the rights and liberties it enshrines. The institutions created by it make their own contribution to this task but they become involved only through contentious proceedings and once all domestic remedies have been exhausted (Article 26).

These observations apply, notably, to Article 10 § 2. In particular, it is not possible to find in the domestic law of the various Contracting States a uniform European conception of morals. The view taken by their respective laws of the requirements of morals varies from time to time and from place to place, especially in our era which is characterised by a rapid and far-reaching evolution of opinions on the subject. By reason of their direct and continuous contact with the vital forces of their countries, State authorities are in principle in a better position than the international judge to give an opinion on the exact content of these requirements as well as on the "necessity" of a "restriction" or "penalty" intended to meet them. The Court notes at this juncture that, whilst the adjective "necessary", within the meaning of Article 10 § 2, is not synonymous with "indispensable" (cf., in Articles 2 § 2 and 6 § 1, the words "absolutely necessary" and "strictly necessary" and, in Article 15 § 1, the phrase "to the extent strictly required by the exigencies of the situation"), neither has it the flexibility of such expressions as "admissible", "ordinary" (cf. Article 4 § 3), "useful" (cf. the French text of the first paragraph of Article 1 of Protocol No. 1), "reasonable" (cf. Articles 5 § 3 and 6 § 1) or "desirable". Nevertheless, it is for the national authorities to make the initial assessment of the reality of the pressing social need implied by the notion of "necessity" in this context.

Consequently, Article 10 § 2 leaves to the Contracting States a margin of appreciation. This margin is given both to the domestic legislator ("prescribed by law") and to the bodies, judicial amongst others, that are called upon to interpret and apply the laws in force (Engel and others judgment of 8

June 1976, Series A no. 22, pp. 41–42, § 100; cf., for Articles 8 § 2, De Wilde, Ooms and Versyp judgment of 18 June 1971, Series A no. 12, pp. 45–46, § 93, and the Golder judgment of 21 February 1975, Series A no. 18, pp. 21–22, § 45).

49. Nevertheless, Article 10 § 2 does not give the Contracting States an unlimited power of appreciation. The Court which, with the Commission, is responsible for ensuring the observance of those States' engagements (Article 19), is empowered to give the final ruling on whether a "restriction" or "penalty" is reconcilable with freedom of expression as protected by Article 10. The domestic margin of appreciation thus goes hand in hand with a European supervision. Such supervision concerns both the aim of the measure challenged and its "necessity"; it covers not only the basic legislation but also the decision applying it, even one given by an independent court. In this respect, the Court refers to Article 50 of the Convention ("decision or . . . measure taken by a legal authority or any other authority") as well as to its own case-law (Engel and others judgment of 8 June 1976, Series A no. 22, pp. 41–42, § 100).

The Court's supervisory functions oblige it to pay the utmost attention to the principles characterising a "democratic society". Freedom of expression constitutes one of the essential foundations of such a society, one of the basic conditions for its progress and for the development of every man. Subject to paragraph 2 of Article 10, it is applicable not only to "information" or "ideas" that are favourably received or regarded as inoffensive or as a matter of indifference, but also to those that offend, shock or disturb the State or any sector of the population. Such are the demands of that pluralism, tolerance and broadmindedness without which there is no "democratic society". This means, amongst other things, that every "formality", "condition", "restriction" or "penalty" imposed in this sphere must be proportionate to the legitimate aim pursued.

From another standpoint, whoever exercises his freedom of expression undertakes "duties and responsibilities" the scope of which depends on his situation and the technical means he uses. The Court cannot overlook such a person's "duties" and "responsibilities" when it enquires, as in this case, whether "restrictions" or "penalties" were conducive to the "protection of morals" which made them "necessary" in a "democratic society".

50. It follows from this that it is in no way the Court's task to take the place of the competent national courts but rather to review under Article 10 the decisions they delivered in the exercise of their power of appreciation.

However, the Court's supervision would generally prove illusory if it did no more than examine these decisions in isolation; it must view them in the light of the case as a whole, including the publication in question and the arguments and evidence adduced by the applicant in the domestic legal system and then at the international level. The Court must decide, on the basis of the different data available to it, whether the reasons given by the national authorities to justify the actual measures of "interference" they take are relevant and sufficient under Article 10 § 2 (cf., for Article 5 § 3, the Wemhoff judgment of 27 June 1968, Series A no. 7, pp. 24–25, § 12, the Neumeister judgment of 27 June 1968, Series A no. 8, p. 37, § 5, the Stögmüller judgment of 10 November 1969, Series A no. 9, p. 39, § 3, the Matznetter judgment of 10 November 1969, Series A no. 10, p. 31, § 3, and the Ringeisen judgment of 16 July 1971, Series A no. 13, p. 42, § 104).

51. Following the method set out above, the Court scrutinized under Article 10 § 2 the individual decisions complained of, in particular, the judgment of the Inner London Quarter Sessions.

The said judgment is summarised in paragraphs 27–34 above. The Court reviewed it in the light of the case as a whole; in addition to the pleadings before the Court and the Commission's report, the memorials and oral explanations presented to the Commission between June 1973 and August 1974 and the transcript of the proceedings before the Quarter Sessions were, *inter alia*, taken into consideration.

52. The Court attaches particular importance to a factor to which the judgment of 29 October 1971 did not fail to draw attention, that is, the intended readership of the Schoolbook. It was aimed above all at children and adolescents aged from about twelve to eighteen. Being direct, factual and reduced to essentials in style, it was easily within the comprehension of even the youngest of such readers. The applicant had made it clear that he planned a widespread circulation. He had sent the book, with a press release, to numerous daily papers and periodicals for review or for advertising purposes. What is more, he had set a modest sale price (thirty pence), arranged for a reprint of 50,000 copies shortly after the first impression of 20,000 and chosen a title suggesting that the work was some kind of handbook for use in schools.

Basically the book contained purely factual information that was generally correct and often useful, as the Quarter Sessions recognised. However, it also included, above all in the section on sex and in the passage headed "Be yourself" in the chapter on pupils (paragraph 32 above), sentences or paragraphs that young people at a critical stage of their development could have interpreted as an encouragement to indulge in precocious activities harmful for them or even to commit certain criminal offences. In these circumstances, despite the variety and the constant evolution in the United Kingdom of views on ethics and education, the competent English judges were entitled, in the exercise of their discretion, to think at the relevant time that the Schoolbook would have pernicious effects on the morals of many of the children and adolescents who would read it.

However, the applicant maintained, in substance, that the demands of the "protection of morals" or, to use the wording of the 1959/1964 Acts, of the war against publications likely to "deprave and corrupt', were but a pretext in his case. The truth of the matter, he alleged, was that an attempt had been made to muzzle a small-scale publisher whose political leanings met with the disapproval of a fragment of public opinion. Proceedings were set in motion, said he, in an atmosphere little short of "hysteria", stirred up and kept alive by ultra-conservative elements. The accent in the judgment of 29 October 1971 on the anti-authoritarian aspects of the Schoolbook (paragraph 31 above) showed, according to the applicant, exactly what lay behind the case.

The information supplied by Mr. Handyside seems, in fact, to show that letters from members of the public, articles in the press and action by Members of Parliament were not without some influence in the decision to seize the Schoolbook and to take criminal proceedings against its publisher. However, the Government drew attention to the fact that such initiatives could well have been explained not by some dark plot but by the genuine emotion felt by citizens faithful to traditional moral values when, towards the end of March 1971, they read in certain newspapers extracts from the book which was due to appear on 1 April. The Government also emphasised that the proceedings ended several months after the "campaign" denounced by the applicant and that he did not claim that it had continued in the intervening period. From this the Government concluded that the "campaign" in no way impaired dispassionate deliberation at the Quarter Sessions.

For its part the Court finds that the anti-authoritarian aspects of the Schoolbook as such were not held in the judgment of 29 October 1971 to fall foul of the 1959/1964 Acts. Those aspects were taken into account only insofar as the appeal court considered that, by undermining the moderating influence of parents, teachers, the Churches and youth organisations, they aggravated the tendency to "deprave and corrupt" which in its opinion resulted from other parts of the work. It should be added that the revised edition was allowed to circulate freely by the British authorities despite the fact that the anti-authoritarian passages again appeared there in full and even, in some cases, in stronger terms (paragraph 35 above). As the Government noted, this is hard to reconcile with the theory of a political intrigue.

The Court thus allows that the fundamental aim of the judgment of 29 October 1971, applying the 1959/1964 Acts, was the protection of the morals of the young, a legitimate purpose under Article 10 § 2. Consequently, the seizures effected on 31 March and 1 April 1971, pending the outcome of the proceedings that were about to open, also had this aim.

53. It remains to examine the "necessity" of the measures in dispute, beginning with the said seizures.

If the applicant is right, their object should have been at the most one or a few copies of the book to be used as exhibits in the criminal proceedings. The Court does not share this view since the police had good reasons for trying to lay their hands on all the stock as a temporary means of protecting the young against a danger to morals on whose existence it was for the trial court to decide. The legislation of many Contracting States provides for a seizure analogous to that envisaged by section 3 of the English 1959/1964 Acts.

54. A series of arguments which merit reflection was advanced by the applicant and the minority of the Commission concerning the "necessity" of the sentence and the forfeiture at issue.

Firstly, they drew attention to the fact that the original edition of the Schoolbook was the object of no proceedings in Northern Ireland, the Isle of Man and the Channel Islands and of no conviction in Scotland and that, even in England and Wales, thousands of copies circulated without impediment despite the judgment of 29 October 1971.

The Court recalls that section 5 (3) of the 1959/1964 Acts provides that they shall not extend to Scotland or to Northern Ireland (paragraph 25 *in fine* above). Above all, it must not be forgotten that the Convention, as is shown especially by its Article 60, never puts the various organs of the Contracting States under an obligation to limit the rights and freedoms it guarantees. In particular, in no case does Article 10 § 2 compel them to impose "restrictions" or "penalties" in the field of freedom of expression; it in no way prevents them from not availing themselves of the expedients it provides for them (cf. the words "*may* be subject"). The competent authorities in Northern Ireland, the Isle of Man and the Channel Islands may, in the light of local conditions, have had plausible reasons for not taking action against the book and its publisher, as may the Scottish Procurator Fiscal for not summonsing Mr. Handyside to appear in person in Edinburgh after the dismissal of the complaint under Scottish law against Stage 1 in respect of the revised edition (paragraph 19 above). Their failure to act — into which the Court does not have to enquire and which did not prevent the measures taken in England from leading to revision of the Schoolbook—does not prove that the judgment of 29 October 1971 was not a response to a real necessity, bering in mind the national authorities' margin of appreciation.

These remarks also apply, *mutatis mutandis*, to the circulation of many copies in England and Wales.

55. The applicant and the minority of the Commission also stressed that the revised edition, albeit little different in their view from the first, was not the object of proceedings in England and Wales.

The Government charged them with minimising the extent of the changes made to the orginal text of the Schoolbook: although the changes were made between the conviction at first instance on 1 July 1971 and the appeal judgment of 29 October 1971, they were said to relate to the main passages cited by the Quarter Sessions as showing particularly clearly a tendency to "deprave and corrupt". The Government claimed that the Director of Public Prosecutions must have taken the view that the changes dispensed him from invoking the 1959/1964 Acts again.

In the Court's view, the absence of proceedings against the revised edition, which differed fairly extensively from the original edition on the points at issue (paragraphs 22-23 and 35 above), rather suggests that the competent authorities wished to limit themselves to what was strictly necessary, an attitude in conformity with Article 10 of the Convention.

56. The treatment meted out to the Schoolbook and its publisher in 1971 was, according to the applicant and the minority of the Commission, all the less "necessary" in that a host of publications dedicated to hard core pornography and devoid of intellectual or artistic merit allegedly profit by an extreme degree of tolerance in the United Kingdom. They are exposed to the gaze of passers-by and especially of young people and are said generally to enjoy complete impunity, the rare criminal prosecutions launched against them proving, it was asserted, more often than not abortive due to the great liberalism shown by juries. The same was claimed to apply to sex shops and much public entertainment.

The Government countered this by the remark, supported by figures, that the Director of Public Prosecutions does not remain inactive nor does the police, despite the scanty manpower resources of the squad specialising in this field. Moreover, they claim that, in addition to proceedings properly so called, seizures were frequently made at the relevant time under the "disclaimer/ caution procedure" (paragraph 26 above).

In principle it is not the Court's function to compare different decisions taken, even in apparently similar circumstances, by prosecuting authorities and courts; and it must, just like the respondent Government, respect the independence of the courts. Furthermore and above all, the Court is not faced with really analogous situations: as the Government pointed out, the documents in the file do not show that the publications and entertainment in question were aimed, to the same extent as the Schoolbook (paragraph 52 above), at children and adolescents having ready access thereto.

57. The applicant and the minority of the Commission laid stress on the further point that, in addition to the original Danish edition, translations of the "Little Book" appeared and circulated freely in the majority of the member States of the Council of Europe.

Here again, the national margin of appreciation and the optional nature of the "restrictions" and "penalties" referred to in Article 10 § 2 prevent the Court from accepting the argument. The Contracting States have each fashioned their approach in the light of the situation obtaining in their respective territories; they have had regard, *inter alia*, to the different views prevailing there about the demands of the protection of morals in a democratic society. The fact that most of them decided to allow the work to be distributed does not mean that the contrary decision of the Inner London Quarter Sessions was a breach of Article 10. Besides, some of the editions published outside the United Kingdom do not include the passages, or at least not all the passages, cited in the judgment of 29 October 1971 as striking examples of a tendency to "deprave and corrupt".

58. Finally, at the hearing on 5 June 1976, the delegate expounding the opinion of the minority of the Commission maintained that in any event the respondent State need not have taken measures as Draconian as the initiation of criminal proceedings leading to the conviction of Mr. Handyside and to the forfeiture and subsequent destruction of the Schoolbook. The United Kingdom was said to have violated the principle of proportionality, inherent in the adjective "necessary", by not limiting itself either to a request to the applicant to expurgate the book or to restrictions on its sale and advertisement.

With regard to the first solution, the Government argued that the applicant would never have agreed to modify the Schoolbook if he had been ordered or asked to do so before 1 April 1971: was he not strenuously disputing its "obscenity"? The Court for its part confines itself to finding that Article 10 of the Convention certainly does not oblige the Contracting States to introduce such prior censorship.

The Government did not indicate whether the second solution was feasible under English law. Neither does it appear that it would have been appropriate in this case. There would scarcely have been any sense in restricting to adults sales of a work destined above all for the young; the Schoolbook would thereby have lost the substance of what the applicant considered to be its *raison d'être*. Moreover, he did not advert to this question.

59. On the strength of the data before it, the Court thus reaches the conclusion that no breach of the requirements of Article 10 has been established in the circumstances of the present case.

II. *On the Alleged Violation of Article 1 of Protocol No. 1*

60. The applicant in the second place alleges the violation of Article 1 of Protocol No. 1 which provides:

> "Every natural or legal person is entitled to the peaceful enjoyment of his possessions. No one shall be deprived of his possessions except in the public interest and subject to the conditions provided for by law and by the general principles of international law.
> The preceding provisions shall not, however, in any way impair the right of a State to enforce such laws as it deems necessary to control the use of property in accordance with the general interest or to secure the payment of taxes or other contributions or penalties."

61. The complaint concerns two distinct measures, namely, the seizure on 31 March and 1 April 1971 of the matrix and of hundreds of copies of the Schoolbook, on the one hand, and their forfeiture and subsequent destruction following the judgment of 29 October 1971, on the other. Both measures interfered with Mr. Handyside's right "to the peaceful enjoyment of his possessions". The Government do not contest this but, in agreement with the majority of the Commission, maintain that justification for the measures is to be found in the exceptions attached by Article 1 of the Protocol to the principle enunciated in its first sentence.

62. The seizure complained of was provisional. It did no more than prevent the applicant, for a period, from enjoying and using as he pleased possessions of which he remained the owner and which he would have recovered had the proceedings against him resulted in an acquittal.

In these circumstances, the Court thinks that the second sentence of the first paragraph of Article 1 does not come into play in this case. Admittedly the expression "deprived of his possessions", in the English text, could lead one to think otherwise but the structure of Article 1 shows that that sentence, which originated moreover in a Belgian amendment drafted in French (Collected Edition of the "*travaux préparatoires*", document H (61) 4, pp. 1083, 1084, 1086, 1090, 1105, 1110-1111 and 1113-1114), applies only to someone who is "deprived of ownership" ("*privé de sa propriété*").

On the other hand the seizure did relate to "the use of property" and thus falls within the ambit of the second paragraph. Unlike Article 10 § 2 of the Convention, this paragraph sets the Contracting States up as sole judges of the "necessity" for an interference. Consequently, the Court must restrict itself to supervising the lawfulness and the purpose of the restriction in question. It finds that the contested measure was ordered pursuant to section 3 of the 1959/1964 Acts and following proceedings which it was not contested were in accordance with the law. Again, the aim of the seizure was "the protection of morals" as understood by the competent British authorities in the exercise of their power of appreciation (paragraph 52 above). And the concept of "protection of morals", used in Article 10 § 2 of the Convention, is encompassed in the much wider notion of the "general interest" within the meaning of the second paragraph of Article 1 of the Protocol.

On this point the Court thus accepts the argument of the Government and the opinion of the majority of the Commission.

63. The forfeiture and destruction of the Schoolbook, on the other hand, permanently deprived the applicant of the ownership of certain possessions. However, these measures were authorised by the second paragraph of Article 1 of Protocol No. 1, interpreted in the light of the principle of law, common to the Contracting States, whereunder items whose use has been lawfully adjudged illicit and dangerous to the general interest are forfeited with a view to destruction.

The court held by 13 votes to 1 that there had been no breach of Article 10, and held unanimously that there had been no breach of Article 1 of the First Protocol (Nor of Articles 14 and 18 of the Convention, to which the Court also adverted). Judge **MOSLER** was the sole dissentient on Article 10, on the grounds that the restriction imposed upon Handyside in derogation of Article 10 had not been proved to be *necessary*. He said:

What is "necessary" is not the same as what is indispensable (paragraph 48 of the judgment). Such a definition would be too narrow and would not correspond to the usage of this word in domestic law. On the other hand, it is beyond question that the measure must be appropriate for achieving the aim. However, a measure cannot be regarded as inappropriate, and hence not "necessary", just because it proves ineffectual by not achieving its aim. A measure likely to be effectual under normal conditions cannot be deprived of its legal basis after the event by failure to attain the success which it might have had in more favourable circumstances.

The greater part of the first edition of the book circulated without impediment. The measures taken by the competent authorities and confirmed by the Inner London Quarter Sessions prevented merely the distribution of under 10 per cent of the impression. The remainder, that is about 90 per cent, reached the public including probably, to a large extent, the adolescents meant to be protected (cf. the address of Mr. Thornberry at the hearing on 7 June 1976). The measures in respect of the applicant had thus so little success that they must be taken as ineffectual in relation to the aim pursued. In fact young people were not protected against the influence of the book that had been qualified as likely to "deprave and corrupt" them by the authorities, acting within their legitimate margin of appreciation.

The ineffectualness of the measures would in no way prevent their being considered appropriate if it had been due to circumstances beyond the influence and control of the authorities. However, that was not the case. Certainly it cannot be presumed that the measures were not taken in good faith and with the genuine intention of preventing the book's circulation. Above all, the carefully reasoned judgment of the Inner London Quarter Sessions excludes such a presumption. Nevertheless, from an objective point of view, the measures actually taken against the book's circulation could never have achieved their aim without being accompanied by other measures against the 90 per cent of the impression. Yet nothing in the case file, in particular in the addresses of those appearing before the Court, shows that action of this kind was attempted.

Under Article 10 § 2, the authorities' action in certain respects and their lack of action in others must be viewed as a whole. The aim, legitimate under Article 10 § 2, of restricting freedom of expression in order to protect the morals of the young against The Little Red Schoolbook, is one and indivisible. The result of the authorities' action as well as of their inaction must be attributed to the British State. It is responsible for the application of measures that were not appropriate with regard to the aim pursued because they covered only one small part of the object of the prosecution without taking the others into account.

Accordingly the measures chosen by the authorities were, by their very nature, inappropriate.

Furthermore some attendant facts must be reviewed.

I leave aside the fact, apparently not disputed between the State, the Commission and the applicant, that publications far more "obscene" than The Little Red Schoolbook were readily accessible to anyone in the United Kingdom. Assuming this to be correct, it does not prevent the authorities from having recourse to measures of prohibition against a book intended in particular for schoolchildren.

On the other hand, the diversity of the approaches adopted in different regions of the United Kingdom (paragraph 19 of the judgment) raises doubts about the necessity of the measures taken in London. Undoubtedly the Convention does not compel the Contracting States to pass uniform legislation for all the territory under their jurisdiction. Nevertheless, it does oblige them to act in such a way that the level of protection guaranteed by the Covention is maintained throughout the whole of that territory. In this case it is difficult to understand why a measure that was not thought necessary outside England and Wales was deemed to be so in London.

There remains the question whether the application of the contested measures, which were inappropriate from an objective point of view, fell within the margin left to the domestic institutions to choose between different measures having a legitimate aim and to assess their potential effectualness. In my view, the reply must be negative because of the clear lack of proportion between that part of the impression subjected to the said measures and that whose circulation was not impeded. Admittedly the result of the action taken was the punishment of Mr. Handyside in accordance with the law, but this result does not by itself justify measures that were not apt to protect the young against the consequences of reading the book.

3. It must follow that the action complained of was not "necessary", within the meaning of Article 10 § 2, with regard to the aim pursued. Such a measure is not covered by the exceptions to which freedom of expression can be subjected, even if the aim is perfectly legitimate and if the qualification of what is moral in a democratic society remained within the framework of the State's margin of appreciation.

The right enshrined in Article 10 § 1 is so valuable for every democratic society that the criterion of necessity, which, when combined with other criteria, justifies an exception to the principle, must be examined from every aspect suggested by the circumstances.

It is only for this reason that I have regretfully voted against paragraph 1 of the operative provisions. As for paragraph 2, concerning Article 1 of Protocol No. 1 and two other Articles, I have rejoined the majority as I was bound by the prior decision on Article 10 and, on this basis, was quite able to accept the Court's reasons.

PROTECTION OF CHILDREN ACT 1978

An Act to prevent the exploitation of children by making indecent photographs of them; and to penalise the distribution, showing and advertisement of such indecent photographs.

1.—(1) It is an offence for a person—
  (a) to take, or permit to be taken, any indecent photograph of a child (meaning in this Act a person under the age of 16); or
  (b) to distribute or show such indecent photographs; or
  (c) to have in his possession such indecent photographs, with a view to their being distributed or shown by himself or others; or
  (d) to publish or cause to be published any advertisement likely to be understood as conveying that the advertiser distributes or shows such indecent photographs, or intends to do so.

(2) For purposes of this Act, a person is to be regarded as distributing an indecent photograph if he parts with possession of it to, or exposes or offers it for acquisition by, another person.

(3) Proceedings for an offence under this Act shall not be instituted except by or with the consent of the Director of Public Prosecutions.

(4) Where a person is charged with an offence under subsection (1) (*b*) or (*c*), it shall be a defence for him to prove—

(*a*) that he had a legitimate reason for distributing or showing the photographs or (as the case may be) having them in his possession; or

(*b*) that he had not himself seen the photographs and did not know, nor had any cause to suspect, them to be indecent . . .

6.—(1) Offences under this Act shall be punishable either on conviction on indictment or on summary conviction.

(2) A person convicted on indictment of any offence under this Act shall be liable to imprisonment for a term of not more than three years, or to a fine or to both.

(3) A person convicted summarily of any offence under this Act shall be liable—

(*a*) to imprisonment for a term not exceeding six months; or

(*b*) to a fine not exceeding the prescribed sum for the purposes of section 28 of the Criminal Law Act 1977 (punishment on summary conviction of offences triable either way: £1,000 or other sum substituted by order under that Act), or to both.

7.—(1) The following subsections apply for the interpretation of this Act.

(2) References to an indecent photograph include an indecent film, a copy of an indecent photograph or film, and an indecent photograph comprised in a film.

(3) Photographs (including those comprised in a film) shall, if they show children and are indecent, be treated for all purposes of this Act as indecent photographs of children.

(4) References to a photograph include the negative as well as the positive version.

(5) 'Film' includes any form of video-recording.

Questions

1. "The law concerning pornography raises no issue concerning freedom of speech, as it is not a means of controlling or restricting the communication of information or ideas. Pornography is intended purely to titillate and arouse sexual feelings." Discuss.

2. "But is manifestly untrue to assert that there is, in the plural societies of the West, any censorship on the expression of views, however radical"—E. J. Mishan, 1973.

3. "There are two main ways of dealing with the problem of the definition of 'obscenity'; either one must admit the futility of any attempt at a definition, or one must admit that the only practicable definition is that embodied on the Obscene Publications Act 1959." Discuss.

6. *MINSTERIAL MEMOIRS*

Report of the Committee of Privy Counsellors on Ministerial Memoirs, Cmnd. 6386, 1976

56. We are able to extract from the considerations as to confidentiality that we have now laid out three working rules as to the reticence due from an ex-Minister. We will phrase them as follows:

(a) In dealing with the experience that he has acquired by virtue of his official position, he should not reveal the opinions or attitudes of colleagues as to the Government business with which they have been concerned. That belongs to their stewardship, not to his. He may, on the other hand, describe and account for his own.

(b) He should not reveal the advice given to him by individuals whose duty it has been to tender him their advice or opinions in confidence. If he wishes to mention the burden or weight of such advice, it must be done without attributing individual attitudes to identifiable persons. Again, he will need to exercise a continuing discretion in any references that he makes to communications received by him in confidence from outside members of the public.

(c) He should not make public assessments or criticisms, favourable or unfavourable, of those who have served under him or those whose competence or suitability for particular posts he has had to measure as part of his official duties.

57. These obligations of reticence are not owed merely or even primarily to the individuals whose opinions, advice or qualifications are involved. They are public duties. They cannot therefore be released by the consent of such persons. The rules themselves and the general principle of which they are only the exponent are far-reaching and their application to the needs of particular sets of circumstances will often prove to be matter of debate and will call for sympathetic adjustment. How best to approach the question of securing their observance is something which belongs to Part III.

64. There are three considerations arising from this Judgment's* exposition of the law which we will set out briefly below, because they seem to us to be critical for the purposes of our own inquiry.

(a) The common law does extend so far as to be capable of prohibiting an ex-Minister or his inheritors from publishing in his memoirs information which he has received in confidence by virtue of his office. He is not merely under "a gentleman's agreement to refrain from publication". But to enable a Court of law to intervene the threatened disclosure must be "improper"; and this description is evidently intended to describe some more particular combination of circumstances than the bare fact that the Crown's permission has not been obtained (as prescribed by Mr. Morrison) or that the material to be used is itself an account of some proceedings of the Cabinet or one of its Committees.

(b) The impropriety of disclosure which the Court needs to find in order to justify its intervention must be proved before it by evidence in each case. With regard to "public secrets" there cannot be "a single rule governing the publication of such a variety of matters". While the basic confidentiality of Cabinet proceedings or discussions itself creates secrets the necessity of protecting which a Court can recognise, the restriction imposed must not go beyond the "strict requirement of public need" on the facts of the case before it. The Judge indeed may hold that there are "other facets of the public interest contradictory of and more compelling than" the maintenance of the inviolability of Cabinet confidence. An example suggested is the importance of maintaining freedom of speech. While the disclosure of individual opinions

*Att.-Gen. v. Jonathan Cape Ltd. [1975] 3 W.L.R. 608.

expressed by Ministers in the course of Cabinet discussions does involve the sort of breach of confidence which a Court of law has the power to restrain, the Judge must be satisfied by demonstration that the confidentiality continues at the time when he is asked to give relief. In the case of Volume 1 of the Crossman Diaries, which was the subject of the recent litigation, the Lord Chief Justice, after reading the book, refused to hold that the material disclosed after what has become a gap of some ten years retained a sufficient element of confidentiality to call for legal remedy.

(c) The categories of information described as (1) advice given by senior Civil Servants to their Ministers and (2) observations made by Ministers on the capacity of individual senior Civil Servants and their suitability for specific appointments do not, it seems, qualify for legal protection from disclosure on the ground of any intrinsic confidentiality. The Judgment does not enter in any detail into the considerations which are thought to distinguish material of this kind from other forms of confidential discussion belonging to the internal processes of government and we are left in uncertainty how far to treat the Court's refusal of relief as based on general principles or on a mere allowance for the time factor involved in the particular case.

69. In our view legislation does not offer the right solution. Theoretically, no doubt, a set of principles could be declared by Act of Parliament to have the status of law; a scheme could be set up under the Act, prescribing time limits, procedures and, perhaps, a tribunal or commission to arbitrate on disputed points. There would have to be penalties, a fine or imprisonment or both, since we do not envisage the creation of statutory duties without the attachment of statutory sanctions for their breach. But we cannot persuade ourselves that an Act of Parliament is the appropriate instrument for protecting the State's interest in these Ministerial revelations. Presumably that category which relates to any form of national security will always carry its own criminal sanction, under either the existing Official Secrets Acts or some new and more restricted version of the same. That is not the point. What we have to concern ourselves with more particularly is the broad but never precisely definable area of Government confidentiality. While we are satisfied that the public interest calls for some workable restrictions in this field, they seem to us remote from any true connection with the concepts of criminal law. It is to be remembered that in all we are speaking of the occasional and limited activities of a small number of persons; and those persons men or women who *ex hypothesi* have held high office under the Crown and responsible positions in public life. They should be able, surely, to conduct themselves properly and recognise their obligations without the creation of statutory offences or statutory penalties. To be driven to suggest otherwise would be to acknowledge a sad decline in the prestige of modern government. We do not think that things have come to such a pass. There can indeed be no guarantee that there will never be anything to complain of in the future if the burden of compliance is left to rest on the free acceptance of an obligation of honour. There may well be an occasional rebel or an occasional breach; but so long as there remains a general recognition of the practical necessity of some rules and the importance of observing them, we do not think that such transgressions, even though made the subject of sensational publicity, should be taken as having shattered the fabric of a sensible system. In the result we do

not recommend legislation. But we wish to emphasise that the arguments for avoiding that course do not in any way weaken the view which we have already expressed in paragraph 51 that the breaches of confidence which we have described are injurious to good government.

70. We must now describe what arrangements we think are needed to secure observance of the principles that we have recommended. If a statutory code is not to be resorted to and if litigation at common law does not offer itself as a satisfactory instrument for general guidance, it becames important to try to devise some working procedure that will be both widely understood and easy to operate. That much is, we think, due to the intending author of memoirs who may find when he has retired that his path is somewhat beset by rules and conditions to which he has given no active attention during his Ministerial life.

71. The first thing seems to be therefore that every Minister on taking office should have his attention drawn explicitly to the obligations with regard to the future that he is assuming by virtue of that office. Exactly how this is to be done must be for each Prime Minister to decide as part of the good order of his administration. But it has been the practice of successive Prime Ministers in the past to circulate to each incoming colleague a confidential document drawing his attention to the general principles of Ministerial conduct and some other matters of Ministerial procedure. A Minister on first appointment is required also to sign a declaration that his attention has been drawn to the provisions of the Official Secrets Acts. We should like to see a system instituted, if the principles of our Report commend themselves, under which each Minister would be furnished at the start with a separate memorandum abstrating the substance of this Report and asked to sign a declaration similar to that which he signs with reference to the Official Secrets Acts. No doubt a simpler arrangement would be to add to the list of general rules of conduct with which he is furnished a section reproducing the wording of the several specific rules that we have recommended. We are conscious ourselves however that the force of those rules and their intelligent application depend much upon some understanding of the historic practices upon which they are based and the arguments which assert their continuing validity. The rules barely stated by themselves might seem arbitrary and jejune. It is this consideration that makes us suggest the reproduction of the substance of the Report, or rather so much of it as may be accepted as official policy.

72. It is not the practice to allow a Minister on leaving office to retain in his possession the confidential document on procedure that we have mentioned. To apply that rule to our Report, which is designed to prescribe for the conduct of the Minister after he has vacated office, would be to defeat its utility. We recommend that at any rate at that point he should be given a copy of it. But his first formal introduction to his future obligations should not be deferred until then. He should be conscious of them from the start. Awareness of them may influence the nature of any notes or diaries he keeps or any provisions he makes for later publication.

73. We recommend that, having regard to the considerations that we have advanced in paragraph 44, every ex-Minister who wishes to make public an account bearing on his Ministerial life should make it his business to let the Secretary of the Cabinet see in advance the full text of what he proposes to say. We emphasise this because we realise that some of the issues that are involved in deciding how much is premature in the disclosure of what is basically confidential matter are not only difficult in themselves but also capable of being

of major public importance, and it is right that such material should pass under the inspection of a critical and objective eye before it is released for general consumption. It is also the fact that only by regular observance of this procedure can Ministers as a whole gain the assurance that each who wishes to write will find his work scrutinised according to a consistent set of working principles.

81. It has been suggested to us on various occasions that, if there should be irreconcilable differences between the Cabinet Secretary and an author in this class of case relating to the confidentialities of government, there might be brought into the dispute some commission or tribunal of reference, formed, say, from members of the Privy Council, who could be asked to consider the matter and give a verdict or render an opinion. Certainly, there are attractions in the idea. Such a reference could take a controversy out of the area of immediate confrontation; and it would bring to bear upon it the objective judgments of a number of persons with political or judicial experience of affairs. On the whole, however, we do not advocate a formal proceeding of this kind. If on any particular occasion the Prime Minister should wish to bring into consultation and take the advice of any one or more such persons, there is nothing to prevent him from doing so. But we think that it would be a mistake to institute any such regular practice.

The time factor

82. The more we have had to consider the various problems raised by 'secrecy' considerations, the more clearly it has been borne in upon us that the time factor is the critical element. There may be some things that have come to the ex-Minister's knowledge that should never be recorded in any measurable period of time. Even they probably depend upon questions of personal taste or discretion. But, generally speaking, what we are talking about are the underlying constituents of public affairs, knowledge of which is value to the accumulating stock of historical, social and political information. At some point of time the secrets of one period must become the common learning of another. How then to find any working rule for the ex-Minister author which will do justice to the proper claims of governmental and administrative life on the one side and to the demands of genuine historical inquiry on the other?

83. Reviewing the various categories of restriction that we have recommended, we see that the time factor has not the same significance for all of them. In this respect questions of national security and international relations impose their own time limits simply by virtue of their own special circumstances. Certain facts bear upon them and certain considerations arise out of those facts. When those considerations have ceased to import a danger to national security or international confidence the 'secret' itself ends its life. That life may cover only a few months or the need for reticence or silence may persist over a period of years. The only thing that matters for this purpose is that the intending author should always clear his material through the Cabinet Secretary before he offers it to the public.

84. But the problem is fundamentally different for those issues which we have classed as Confidential Relationships. Essentially they do not depend upon the special circumstances of individual cases; they arise from the general assurance or expectation of confidentiality which is owed to the efficient conduct of Government business. The 'secrecy' which it enjoins has no need to be

permanent in order to be effective; and we are led to the conclusion that a fixed time limit, at the expiry of which the restrictions proposed under this heading of Confidential Relationships will be lifted, is the only satisfactory way of reconciling the interests of the State, the needs of the author, and the demands of the interested public.

85. Any such time limit must necessarily be arbitrary and general. It does not admit of any reasoned process of measurement. We take into account the desirability of a man who thinks that he has something important to say being able to give his account publicly during his own lifetime. We think it advantageous too that what he has to say should be said during the probable lifetime of others who may be involved in his account. These considerations persuade us that a period of 30 years analogous to the present moratorium on the availability of public records is altogether too long for the purpose. Nor do we think a period of that length is needed to satisfy the basic requirements of confidentiality. Controversies die down and issues become stale. What we propose for the time limit is a period of 15 years. That, after all, is sufficient to cover the maximum life span of three successive Parliaments. What we mean to secure by it is that, while in dealing with incidents or affairs or matters which are less than 15 years ago at the date of intended publication an author should regard himself as bound by the approved rules and procedures governing Confidential Relationships, he can, if he so wishes, take his own unrestricted line in dealing with any subject of an earlier date. The matter lies then wholly at the decision of his own taste and judgment.

86. We must note however that there is one principle which we have outlined earlier which cannot be adequately covered by the observance of a simple time limit. That is the rule that an ex-Minister should not reveal the advice given to him in confidence by those in the Service whose duty it has been to advise him. If he gives the weight of it, it must be given without attributing it to any identifiable persons (see paragraphs 54 and 56(b)). It is a rule that, according to our recommendation, should be adhered to during the whole period of the adviser's Service life, not just for the sake of his own protection but also because successive Governments have accepted a convention that neither the views of predecessors in office nor the advice tendered to them by their departmental officers should be made available to their successors. It is quite possible however that the expiry of 15 years will find some such advisers still in the Service, and the principle of the rule will be violated if the ex-Minister can thereupon come forward with a discussion of their former opinions and advice. In such cases, admittedly special ones, the period of restriction should be regarded as 15 years or the remainder of the Service life of the adviser, whichever be the longer. The same principle should be applied to the assessments and criticisms to which we have referred in paragraph 56(c).

87. Before we leave this subject we think it worthwhile to point out that the rules we have proposed in no way preclude the writing by former Ministers of memoirs and other such works before the expiry of 15 years, provided only that the memorialist keeps within the limitations we have outlined. In relation to the whole of his Ministerial experience they leave him a wide latitude for the writing of an account of his stewardship.

CHAPTER 6

FREEDOM OF ASSOCIATION

Further Reading

De Smith, pp. 484–485; Street, Chap. 9 and pp. 267–268; Wade & Phillips, pp. 489–490.

See also Chapter 7.

POLICE ACT 1964

47. Membership of trade unions

(1) Subject to the provisions of this section, a member of a police force shall not be a member of any trade union, or of any association having for its objects, or one of its objects, to control or influence the pay, pensions or conditions of service of any police force:

Provided that where a person was a member of a trade union before becoming a member of a police force, he may, with the consent of the chief officer of police, continue to be a member of that union during the time of his service in the police force.

(2) If any question arises whether any body is a trade union or an association to which this section applies, the question shall be determined by the chief registrar of friendly societies.

(3) This section applies to police cadets as it applies to members of a police force, and references to a police force or to service in a police force shall be construed accordingly.

(4) Nothing in this section applies to membership of the Police Federations, or of any body recognised by the Secretary of State for the purposes of this section as representing members of police forces who are not members of those Federations.

EMPLOYMENT PROTECTION (CONSOLIDATION) ACT 1978

Trade union membership and activities

Trade union membership and activities

23.—(1) Subject to the following provision of this section, every employee shall have the right not to have action (short of dismissal) taken against him as an individual by his employer for the purpose of—

    (*a*) preventing or deterring him from being or seeking to become a member of an independent trade union, or penalising him for doing so; or

(b) preventing or deterring him from taking part in the activities of an independent trade union at any appropriate time, or penalising him for doing so; or

(c) compelling him to be or become a member of a trade union which is not independent.

(2) In this section "appropriate time", in relation to an employee taking part in any activities of a trade union, means time which either—

(a) is outside his working hours, or

(b) is a time within his working hours at which, in accordance with arrangements agreed with, or consent given by his employer, it is permissible for him to take part in those activities;

and in this subsection "working hours", in relation to an employee, means any time when, in accordance with his contract of employment, he is required to be at work.

(3) The provisions of subsection (4) shall have effect in relation to an employee—

(a) of the same class as employees for whom it is the practice in accordance with a union membership agreement to belong to a specified independent trade union or to one of a number of specified independent trade unions; or

(b) not of the same class as described in paragraph (a) but of the same grade or category as such employees as are referred to in that paragraph.

(4) In relation to such an employee the right conferred by subsection (1) (b) in relation to the activities of an independent trade union shall extend to activities on the employer's premises only if that union is a specified union.

(5) For the purposes of this section a trade union—

(a) shall be taken to be specified for the purposes of, or in relation to, a union membership agreement if it is specified in the agreement or is accepted by the parties to the agreement as being the equivalent of a union so specified; [and

(b) shall also be treated as so specified if—

(i) the Advisory, Conciliation and Arbitration Service has made a recommendation for recognition of that union covering the employee in question which is operative within the meaning of section 15 of the Employment Protection Act 1975; or

(ii) the union has referred a recognition issue covering that employee to the Advisory, Conciliation and Arbitration Service under section 11 of the said Act of 1975 and the Service has not declined to proceed on the reference under section 12 of that Act, the union has not withdrawn the reference, or from the reference, and the issue has not been settled or reported on under that section.]

[(6) An employee who genuinely objects on grounds of religious belief to being a member of any trade union whatsoever shall have the right not to have action (shortof dismissal) taken against him by his employer for the purpose of compelling him to belong to a trade union.]

(7) In this section, unless the context otherwise requires, references to a trade union include references to a branch or section of a trade union.

Note: Words in square brackets are proposed to be deleted by Employment Bill, 1979, which proposes a new section 23 (b): An employee who objects on grounds of conscience or other deeply-held personal conviction to being a member of any trade union whatsoever or of a particular trade union shall have the right not to have action (short of dismissal) taken against him by his employer for the purpose of compelling him to belong to a trade union or, as the case may be, that particular trade union.

Question

1. Brown is employed as a senior manager by Green & Co. Under the terms of his contract of employment he has agreed that so long as he continues to be employed by Green & Co., (*a*) he will not stand for any public elected office; (*b*) he will not write for any periodical on any subject or give interviews to the press: (*c*) he will not join the Conservative, Labour or Liberal parties; (*d*) he will not practice any religion other than Christianity; (*e*) he will not join the Transport & General Workers' Union.

In what circumstances and before what bodies could Brown challenge these promises? Are there circumstances in which Green & Co. could "penalise" Brown for breach of any of these promises, or otherwise enforce them?

CHAPTER 7

FREEDOM OF ASSEMBLY

Further Reading

De Smith, Chap. 22; Dicey, Chap. 6; Smith & Hogan, pp. 759–771; Street, Chap. 2; Wade & Phillips, Chap. 28.

R. Benewick & T. Smith (ed.), *Direct Action and Democratic Politics* (London, 1972); V. T. Bevan, "Protest and Public Order" [1979] *Public Law* pp. 163–187; W. Birtles, "The Common Law Power of the Police to Control Public Meetings," (1973) 34 *Modern Law Review* pp. 587–599; I. Brownlie, *The Law Relating to Public Order* (Butterworth, 1968); A. Crew, *The Law Relating to Public Meetings and Processions* (Pitman, 1937); A. L. Goodhart, "Public Meetings and Processions," (1937) 6 *Cambridge Law Journal* pp. 161–174; L. Grant, *et al.,* (ed.) *Civil Liberty: The NCCL Guide to Your Rights* (Penguin, 1978) Chap. 4; E. C. S. Wade, "Police Powers and Public Meetings" (1937) 6 *Cambridge Law Journal* pp.175–200; D. G. T. Williams, *Keeping the Peace: The Police and Public Order* (Hutchinson, 1967); G. Wilson, *Cases and Materials on Constitutional and Administrative Law* (2nd ed., C.U.P., 1976) Chap. XIV.

METROPOLITAN POLICE ACT 1839

52. Commissioners may make regulations for the route of carriages, and persons, and for preventing obstruction of the streets during public processions, etc., or in the neighbourhood of public buildings, etc.

. . . It shall be lawful for the commissioners of police from time to time, and as occasion shall require, to make regulations for the route to be observed by all carts, carriages, horses, and persons, and for preventing obstruction of the streets and thoroughfares within the metropolitan police district, in all times of public processions, public rejoicings, or illuminations, and also to give directions to the constables for keeping order and for preventing any obstruction of the thoroughfares in the immediate neighbourhood of her Majesty's palaces and the public offices, the High Court of Parliament, the courts of law and equity, the police courts, the theatres, and other places of public resort, and in any case when the streets or thoroughfares may be thronged or may be liable to be obstructed.

Note: See *Papworth* v. *Coventry* [1967] 2 All E.R. 41. *For an Order made under section 52 Metropolitan Police Act 1839.* See over page.

PROHIBITION OF CERTAIN MEETINGS AND PROCESSIONS DURING THE SITTING OF PARLIAMENT

By virtue of the powers conferred upon me by section 52 of the Metropolitan Police Act 1839 and in furtherance of the following Sessional Orders:

House of Lords

"ORDERED, by the Lords Spiritual and Temporal, in Parliament assemble, That the Commissioner of Police of the Metropolis do take care that during the Session of Parliament the passages through the streets leading to this House be kept free and open; and that no obstruction be permitted to hinder the passage of the Lords to and from this House; and that no disorder be allowed in Westminster Hall, or in the passages leading to this House during the sitting of Parliament; and that, there be no annoyance therein and thereabouts; and that the Gentleman Usher of the Black Rod attending this House do communicate this Order to the Commissioner aforesaid."

House of Commons

"ORDERED, That the Commissioner of Police of the Metropolis do take care that during the Session of Parliament the passages through the streets leading to this House be kept free and open and that no obstruction be permitted to hinder the passage of Members to and from this House, during the Sitting of Parliament, and that there be no annoyance therein or thereabouts; and that the Serjeant at Arms attending this House do communicate this Order to the Commissioner aforesaid."

I, the undersigned Commissioner of Police of the Metropolis, do hereby give the following Directions to all Constables:

(1) That they shall disperse all assemblies or processions of persons causing or likely to cause obstruction or disorder on any day on which Parliament is sitting within the area specified hereunder:

South side of the River Thames between Waterloo and Vauxhall Bridges, Vauxhall Bridge Road, Victoria Street (between Vauxhall Bridge Road and Buckingham Palace Road), Grosvenor Gardens, Grosvenor Place, Piccadilly, Coventry Street, New Coventry Street, Leicester Square (north side), Cranbourn Street, Long Acre, Bow Street, Wellington Street, crossing Strand and Victoria Embankment to Waterloo Bridge. Provided that procession may be routed along the thoroughfares named except Victoria Embankment west of Waterloo Bridge.

(2) That they shall prevent or remove any other cause of obstruction within the said area so that every facility shall be afforded for the free passage of Peers and Members to and from the Houses of Parliament on any day on which Parliament is sitting.

[Signed: David McNee]
Commissioner of Police of the Metropolis.

Metropolitan Police Office,
New Scotland Yard, SW1H 0BG
May 15, 1979.

HYDE PARK

POLICY AND PROCEDURE FOR THE USE OF HYDE PARK FOR SPECIAL EVENTS, JULY 1969

1. a. Applications may be considered from any organisation (religious, political or otherwise) for permission to hold assemblies and events in Hyde Park. Normally, the Speakers Corner/Reformer's Tree areas will be used for assemblies/rallies, but for special events other areas are permissible (e.g. Cockpit, Serpentine Road etc.).
    b. There will be no discrimination on religious, political or other grounds but ALL applications for assembly/rally must be referred first to the Metropolitan Police for their comments. Similarly, all political events and any others likely to provoke controversy, must be approved by the Secretary of State for the Environment. When necessary the Home Office will be consulted.
    c. The Department must reserve the right to refuse any request without giving reasons.
2. a. With the exception of certain special and/or annual events, bookings will not be made more than six months before the day of the event and will be on a first come first served basis.
    b. Generally, permission will be given for only one event to take place at any one time. If more than one event is requested at the same time, the Metropolitan Police must be consulted.
3. a. The Parks Regulations must be strictly observed on all occasions.
    b. Only one banner or placard giving the name of the organisation and the event will be permitted to be displayed in the Park. Others must not be unfurled and may have to be left outside the Park.
    c. Music and amplification may be allowed on application; but the sound level must be kept to the minimum—sufficient to reach only the audience within the Park.
    d. No money may be collected in the Park.
4. a. The distribution of leaflets, programmes etc. will be strongly discouraged as this creates litter.
    b. In all cases, the organiser/s of the event will be advised beforehand that they will be liable for the cost of clearing any litter caused by, or because of, their assembly.
5. a. Any services provided by the Department, such as the supply of electricity, additional toilets, roping, barriers etc. will be charged to the organisers.
    b. Such charges will be realistic and will include "on-costs". Payment should normally be made in advance.
6. a. All arrangements for the event, including the proposed siting, entry and exit points, must be agreed in advance with the Superintendent, Central Royal Parks and the Chief Inspector Hyde Park Police.
    b. No vehicles will be allowed entry into areas normally restricted unless previously authorised by both the Park Superintendent and Hyde Park Police.
7. a. The Department's conditions of use will be written into the letter of authorisation for the event issued by the Royal Parks Division. A copy must be signed and returned to the Department by the organiser/s before the date.

b. The organiser/s will be required to indemnify the Department against any claims for damage to persons or property resulting for their use of the Park.

[*Supplied by Department of the Environment, Royal Parks Division.*]

THE PUBLIC MEETINGS ACT 1908

An Act to prevent disturbance of Public Meetings

1. Penalty on endeavour to break up public meeting

(1) Any person who at a lawful public meeting acts in a disorderly manner for the purpose of preventing the transaction of the business for which the meeting was called together shall be guilty of an offence . . .

(2) Any person who incites others to commit an offence under this section shall be guilty of a like offence.

(3) If any constable reasonably suspects any person of committing an offence under the foregoing provisions of this section, he may if requested so to do by the chairman of the meeting require that person to declare to him immediately his name and address and, if that person refuses or fails so to declare his name and address or gives a false name and address he shall be guilty of an offence under this subsection and liable on summary conviction thereof to a fine not exceeding forty shillings, and if he refuses or fails so to declare his name and address or if the constable reasonably suspects him of giving a false name and address the constable may without warrant arrest him.

Burden v. Rigler [1911] 1 K.B. 337

Divisional Court

Justices dismissed an information brought against the defendants alleging that they had unlawfully, contrary to the Public Meetings Act 1908, acted in a disorderly manner for the purpose of preventing the transaction of business by a lawful public meeting. They did so on the ground that the meeting being held on the highway was not a lawful meeting. On an appeal **LORD ALVERSTONE,** C.J. said:

In this case proceedings were taken in respect of interference with a meeting held on June 20, 1910, on a public highway. The evidence in support of the charge having been partly given, the justices declined to proceed further with the summons on the ground that the meeting, being held on a highway, was ipso facto an unlawful meeting. That ruling goes much too far. I express no opinion as to whether or not there was an obstruction; that depends upon the facts. The justices ought to entertain the summons, and if any point arises upon the evidence as to an obstruction or otherwise, it can be reserved, if necessary, for the consideration of this Court, but the justices had no right to assume that, simply because the meeting was held on a highway, it could be interrupted notwithstanding the provisions of the Public Meeting Act, 1908. The appeal must be allowed, and the case remitted to the justices to be further dealt with.

Avory and Pickford JJ. agreed.

Public Order Act 1936

1. Prohibition of uniforms in connection with political objects

(1) Subject as hereinafter provided, any person who in any public place or at any public meeting wears uniform signifying his association with any political organisation or with the promotion of any political object shall be guilty of an offence:

Provided that, if the chief officer of police is satisfied that the wearing of any such uniform as aforesaid on any ceremonial, anniversary, or other special occasion will not be likely to involve risk of public disorder, he may, with the consent of a Secretary of State, by order permit the wearing of such uniform on that occasion either absolutely or subject to such conditions as may be specified in the order.

(2) Where any person is charged before any court with an offence under this section, no further proceedings in respect thereof shall be taken against him without the consent of the Attorney-General except such as the court may think necessary by remand (whether in custody or on bail) or otherwise to secure the due appearance of the person charged, so, however, that if that person is remanded in custody he shall, after the expiration of a period of eight days from the date on which he was so remanded, be entitled to be discharged from custody on entering into a recognisance without sureties unless within that period the Attorney-General has consented to such further proceedings as aforesaid.

2. Prohibition of quasi-military organisations

(1) If the members or adherents of any association of persons, whether incorporated or not, are—

(a) organised or trained or equipped for the purpose of enabling them to be employed in usurping the function of the police or of the armed forces of the Crown; or

(b) organised and trained or organised and equipped either for the purpose of enabling them to be employed for the use or display of physical force in promoting any political object, or in such manner as to arouse reasonable apprehension that they are organised and either trained or equipped for that purpose;

then any person who takes part in the control or management of the association, or in so organising or training as aforesaid any members or adherents thereof, shall be guilty of an offence under this section:

Provided that in any proceedings against a person charged with the offence of taking part in the control or management of such an association as aforesaid it shall be a defence to that charge to prove that he neither consented to nor connived at the organisation, training, or equipment of members or adherents of the association in contravention of the provisions of this section.

(2) No prosecution shall be instituted under this section without the consent of the Attorney-General.

(3) If upon application being made by the Attorney-General it appears to the High Court that any association is an association of which members or adherents are organised, trained, or equipped in contravention of the provisions of this section, the Court may make such order as appears

necessary to prevent any disposition without the leave of the Court of property held by or for the association and in accordance with rules of court may direct an inquiry and report to be made as to any such property as aforesaid and as to the affairs of the association and make such further orders as appear to the Court to be just and equitable for the application of such property in or towards the discharge of the liabilities of the association lawfully incurred before the date of the application or since that date with the approval of the Court, in or towards the repayment of moneys to persons who became subscribers or contributors to the association in good faith and without knowledge of any such contravention as aforesaid, and in or towards any costs incurred in connection with any such inquiry and report as aforesaid or in winding-up or dissolving the association, and may order that any property which is not directed by the Court to be so applied as aforesaid shall be forfeited to the Crown.

(4) In any criminal or civil proceedings under this section proof of things done or of words written, spoken or published (whether or not in the presence of any party to the proceedings) by any person taking part in the control or management of an association or in organising, training or equipping members or adherents of an association shall be admissible as evidence of the purposes for which, or the manner in which, members or adherents of the association (whether those persons or others) were organised, or trained, or equipped.

(5) If a judge of the High Court is satisfied by information on oath that there is reasonable ground for suspecting that an offence under this section has been committed, and that evidence of the commission thereof is to be found at any premises or place specified in the information, he may, on an application made by an officer of police of a rank not lower than that of inspector, grant a search warrant authorising any such officer as aforesaid named in the warrant together with any other persons named in the warrant and any other officers of police to enter the premises or place at any time within one month from the date of the warrant, if necessary by force, and to search the premises or place and every person found therein, and to seize anything found on the premises or place or on any such person which the officer has reasonable ground for suspecting to be evidence of the commission of such an offence as aforesaid:

Provided that no woman shall, in pursuance of a warrant issued under this subsection, be searched except by a woman.

(6) Nothing in this section shall be construed as prohibiting the employment of a reasonable number of persons as stewards to assist in the preservation of order at any public meeting held upon private premises, or the making of arrangements for that purpose or the instruction of the persons to be so employed in their lawful duties as such stewards, or their being furnished with badges or other distinguishing signs.

3. Powers for the preservation of public order on the occasion of processions

(1) If the chief officer of police, having regard to the time or place at which and the circumstances in which any public procession is taking place or is intended to take place and to the route taken or proposed to be taken by the procession, has reasonable ground for apprehending that the procession may occasion serious public disorder, he may give directions imposing upon the persons organising or taking part in the procession such conditions as appear

to him necessary for the preservation of public order, including conditions prescribing the route to be taken by the procession and conditions prohibiting the procession from entering any public place specified in the directions:

Provided that no conditions restricting the display of flags, banners, or emblems shall be imposed under this subsection except such as are reasonably necessary to prevent risk of a breach of the peace.

(2) If at any time the chief officer of police is of opinion that by reason of particular circumstances existing in any borough or urban district or in any part thereof the powers conferred on him by the last foregoing subsection will not be sufficient to enable him to prevent serious public disorder being occasioned by the holding of public processions in that borough, district or part, he shall apply to the council of the borough or district for an order prohibiting for such period not exceeding three months as may be specified in the application the holding of all public processions or of any class of public procession so specified either in the borough or urban district or in that part thereof, as the case may be, and upon receipt of the application the council may, with the consent of a Secretary of State, make an order either in terms of the application or with such modifications as may be approved by the Secretary of State.

This subsection shall not apply within the City of London as defined for the purposes of the Acts relating to the City police or within the Metropolitan police district.

(3) If at any time the Commissioner of the City of London police or the Commissioner of police of the Metropolis is of opinion that, by reason or particular circumstances existing in his police area or in any part thereof, the powers conferred on him by subsection (1) of this section will not be sufficient to enable him to prevent serious public disorder being occasioned by the holding of public processions in that area or part, he may, with the consent of the Secretary of State, make an order prohibiting for such period not exceeding three months as may be specified in the order the holding of all public processions or of any class of public procession so specified either in the police area or in that part thereof, as the case may be.

(4) Any person who knowingly fails to comply with any directions given or conditions imposed under this section, or organises or assists in organising any public procession held or intended to be held in contravention of an order made under this section or incites any person to take part in such a procession, shall be guilty of an offence.

4. Prohibition of offensive weapons at public meetings and processions

(1) Any person who, while present at any public meeting or on the occasion of any public procession, has with him any offensive weapon, otherwise than in pursuance of lawful authority, shall be guilty of an offence.

(2) For the purposes of this section, a person shall not be deemed to be acting in pursuance of lawful authority unless he is acting in his capacity as a servant of the Crown or of either House of Parliament or of any local authority or as a constable or as a member of a recognised corps or as a member of a fire brigade [or as a member of a visiting force within the meaning of any of the provisions of Part I of the Visiting Forces Act 1952 or of a headquarters or organisation designated for the purposes of the International Headquarters and Defence Organisations Act 1964].

5. Prohibition of offensive conduct conducive to breaches of the peace

Any person who in any public place or at any public meeting—
  (a) uses threatening, abusive or insulting words or behaviour, or
  (b) distributes or displays any writing, sign or visible representation which
       is threatening, abusive or insulting,
with intent to provoke a breach of the peace or whereby a breach of the peace
is likely to be occasioned, shall be guilty of an offence.

5A. Incitement to racial hatred

(1) A person commits an offence if—
  (a) he publishes or distributes written matter which is threatening, abusive
       or insulting; or
  (b) he uses in any public place or at any public meeting words which are
       threatening, abusive or insulting,
in a case where having regard to all the circumstances, hatred is likely to be
stirred up against any racial group in Great Britain by the matter or words in
question.
  (2) Subsection (1) above does not apply to the publication or distribution
of written matter consisting of or contained in—
  (a) a fair and accurate report of proceedings publicly heard before any
       court or tribunal exercising judicial authority, being a report which is
       published contemporaneously with those proceedings or, if it is not
       reasonably practicable or would be unlawful to publish a report of
       them contemporaneously, is published as soon as publication is
       reasonably practicable and (if previously unlawful) lawful; or
  (b) a fair and accurate report of proceedings in Parliament.
  (3) In any proceedings for an offence under this section alleged to have
been committed by the publication or distribution of any written matter, it
shall be a defence for the accused to prove that he was not aware of the content of the written matter in question and neither suspected nor had reason to
suspect it of being threatening, abusive or insulting.
  (4) Subsection (3) above shall not prejudice any defence which it is open to
a person charged with an offence under this section to raise apart from that
subsection.
  (5) A person guilty of an offence under this section shall be liable—
  (a) on summary conviction, to imprisonment for a term not exceeding six
       months or to a fine not exceeding £400, or both;
  (b) on conviction on indictment, to imprisonment for a term not exceeding
       two years or to a fine, or both;
but no prosecution for such an offence shall be instituted in England and
Wales except by or with the consent of the Attorney General.
  (6) In this section—
'publish' and 'distribute' mean publish or distribute to the public at large
       or to any section of the public not consisting exclusively of members of
       an association of which the person publishing or distributing is a
       member;
'racial group' means a group of persons defined by reference to colour,
       race, nationality or ethnic or national origins, and in this definition
       'nationality' includes citizenship;
'written matter' includes any writing, sign or visible representation.

7. Enforcement

(1) Any person who commits an offence under setion two of this Act shall be liable on summary conviction to imprisonment for a term not exceeding six months or to a fine not exceeding one hundred pounds, or to both such imprisonment and fine, or, on conviction on indictment, to imprisonment for a term not exceeding two years or to a fine not exceeding five hundred pounds, or to both such imprisonment and fine.

(2) Any person guilty of any offence under this Act other than an offence under section 2 or section 5 or 5A shall be liable on summary conviction to imprisonment for a term not exceeding three months or to a fine not exceeding fifty pounds, or to both such imprisonment and fine.

(3) A constable may without warrant arrest any person reasonably suspected by him to be committing an offence under section one, four or five of this Act.

9. Interpretation, etc.

(1) In this Act the following expressions have the meanings hereby respectively assigned to them, that is to say:—
   "Meeting" means a meeting held for the purpose of the discussion of matters of public interest or for the purpose of the expression of views on such matters;
   "Private premises" means premises to which the public have access (whether on payment or otherwise) only by permission of the owner, occupier, or lessee of the premises;
   "Public meeting" includes any meeting in a public place and any meeting which the public or any section thereof are permitted to attend, whether on payment or otherwise;
   "Public place" includes any highway and any other premises or place to which at the material time the public have or are permitted to have access, whether on payment or otherwise".
   "Public procession" means a procession in a public place;
   "Recognised corps" means a rifle club, miniature rifle club or cadet corps approved by a Secretary of State under the Firearms Acts, 1920 to 1936, for the purposes of those Acts.

(2) The powers conferred by this Act on the Attorney-General may, in the event of a vacancy in the office or in the event of the Attorney-General being unable to act owing to illness or absence, be exercised by the Solicitor-General.

(3) Any order made under this Act by the council of any borough or urban district or by a chief officer of police may be revoked or varied by a subsequent order made in like manner.

(4) The powers conferred by this Act on any chief officer of police may, in the event of a vacancy in the office or in the event of the chief officer of police being unable to act owing to illness or absence, be exercised by the person duly authorised in accordance with directions given by a Secretary of State to exercise those powers on behalf of the chief officer of police.

Note: Section 5A added by Race Relations Act 1976, s. 70.

ORDER UNDER PUBLIC ORDER ACT 1936, S.3 (1)

PUBLIC ORDER ACT 1936

WHEREAS I, David Blackstock McNee, Commissioner of Police of the Metropolis, am of the opinion that, by reason of particular circumstances existing in my police area, the powers conferred on me by sub-section (1) of section 3 of the Public Order Act, 1936, will not be sufficient to enable me to prevent serious public disorder being occasioned by the holding of public processions in the Metropolitan Police District.

Now I, David Blackstock McNee, Commissioner of Police of the Metropolis, with the consent of the Secretary of State, in pursuance of the powers conferred on me by sub-section (3) of Section 3 of the said Act hereby by this order prohibit for the period of 2 months from 6 a.m. on Friday, 24th February, 1978 the holding of the following class of public processions, that is to say all public processions other than those of a religious, educational, festive or ceremonial character customarily held within the Metropolitan Police District.

[signed David McNee]
Commissioner of Police of the Metropolis

Dated this 22nd day of February, 1978
New Scotland Yard,
London, SW1H 0BG.

I hereby certify that the above Order has been made by the Commissioner of Police with my consent.

[signed Merlyn Rees]
Secretary of State for the Home Department

REPRESENTATION OF THE PEOPLE ACT 1949

Election meetings

Right to use certain schools and halls for meetings at parliamentary elections.

82.—(1) Subject to the provisions of this section, a candidate at a parliamentary election shall be entitled for the purpose of holding public meetings in furtherance of his candidature to the use at reasonable times between the receipt of the writ and the date of the poll of—

(a) a suitable room in the premises of any school to which this section applies;

(b) any meeting room to which this section applies.

(2) This section applies—

(a) in England and Wales, to county schools and voluntary schools of which the premises are situated in the constituency or an adjoining constituency; and

(b) in Scotland, to any school of which the premises are so situated, not being an independent school within the meaning of the Education (Scotland) Act, 1946;

but a candidate shall not be entitled under this section to the use of a room in school premises outside the constituency if there is a suitable room in other premises in the constituency which are reasonably accessible from the same parts of the constituency as those outside and are premises of a school to which this section applies.

(3) This section applies to meeting rooms situated in the constituency, the expense of maintaining which is payable wholly or mainly out of public funds or out of any rate, or by body whose expenses are so payable.

(4) Where a room is used for a meeting in pursuance of the rights conferred by this section, the person by whom or on whose behalf the meeting is convened—

　　(a) may be required to pay for the use of the room a charge not exceeding the amount of any actual and necessary expenses incurred in preparing, warming, lighting and cleaning the room and providing attendance for the meeting and restoring the room to its usual condition after the meeting; and

　　(b) shall defray any damage done to the room or the premises in which it is situated, or to the furniture, fittings or apparatus in the room or premises.

(5) A candidate shall not be entitled to exercise the rights conferred by this section except on reasonable notice; and this section shall not authorise any interference with the hours during which a room in school premises is used for educational purposes, or any interference with the use of a meeting room either for the purposes of the person maintaining it or under a prior agreement for its letting for any purpose.

(6) The provisions of the Seventh Schedule to this Act shall have effect with respect to the rights conferred by this section and the arrangements to be made for their exercise.

(7) For the purposes of this section (except those of paragraph (b) of subsection (4) thereof), the premises of a school shall not be taken to include any private dwelling house, and in this section—

　　(a) the expression "meeting room" means any room which it is the practice to let for public meetings; and

　　(b) the expression "room" includes a hall, gallery or gymnasium.

(8) This section shall not apply to Northern Ireland.

Right to use certain schools and rooms for meetings at local government elections.

83.—(1) Subject to the provisions of this section, a candidate at a local government election shall be entitled for the purpose of holding public meetings in furtherance of his candidature to use free of charge, at all reasonable times, during the period commencing on the day on which the notice of election is given, and ending on the day preceding the day of election,—

　　(a) in England or Wales, any suitable room in the premises of a county or voluntary school situated in the electoral area for which he is a candidate, or, except in London, in a parish in part comprised in that electoral area;

　　(b) in Scotland; any suitable room in the premises of any school (not being an independent school within the meaning of the Education (Scotland) Act, 1946) situated in the electoral area for which his is a candidate (or, if there is no such school in the area, in any such school in an adjacent electoral area) or any suitable room the expense of maintaining which is payable by a district council.

(2) Where a room is used for a meeting in pursuance of the rights conferred by this section, the person by whom or on whose behalf the meeting is convened shall defray any expense incurred by the persons having control over the room or any damage done to the school premises or to the furniture, fittings or apparatus therein.

(3) A candidate shall not be entitled to exercise rights conferred by this section except on reasonable notice; and this section shall not authorise the use of any room used as part of a private dwelling house or any interference with the hours during which the school premises are used for educational purposes.

(4) Any question arising under this section as to what is reasonable or suitable shall be determined in England or Wales by the Minister of Education and in Scotland, where the question arises in relation to a room in the premises of a school by the persons having control of the school and, in the case of a room maintained by a district council, by that council.

Disturbances at election meetings.

84.—(1) Any person who at a lawful public meeting to which this section applies acts, or incites others to act, in a disorderly manner for the purpose of preventing the transaction of the business for which the meeting was called together shall be guilty of an illegal practice.

(2) This section applies to—
(a) a political meeting held in any constituency between the date of the issue of a writ for the return of a member of Parliament for the constituency and the date at which a return to the writ is made;
(b) a meeting held with reference to a local government election in the electoral area for that election on, or within three weeks before, the day of election.

(3) If any constable reasonably suspects any person of committing an offence under subsection (1) of this section, he may if requested so to do by the chairman of the meeting require that person to declare to him immediately his name and address and, if that person refuses or fails so to declare his name and address or gives a false name and address he shall be liable on summary conviction to a fine not exceeding forty shillings, and if he refuses or fails so to declare his name and address or if the constable reasonably suspects him of giving a false name and address, the constable may without warrant arrest him.

This subsection shall not apply in Northern Ireland.

Effect on rateability of premises of holding election meeting.

85.—The use of any premises for the holding of public meetings in furtherance of any person's candidature at a parliamentary or local government election shall not render any person liable to be rated or to pay any rate for the premises.

Note: See also Schedule 7 of this Act.

THE CONSPIRACY, AND PROTECTION OF PROPERTY ACT 1875
(38 & 39 Vict. c. 86)

7. Penalty for intimidation or annoyance by violence or otherwise

Every person who, with a view to compel any other person to abstain from doing or to do any act which such other person has a legal right to do or abstain from doing, wrongfully and without legal authority,—

1. Uses violence to or intimidates such other person or his wife or children, or injures his property; or
2. Persistently follows such other person about from place to place; or,
3. Hides any tools, clothes, or other property owned or used by such other person, or deprives him of or hinders him in the use thereof; or,
4. Watches or besets the house or other place where such other person resides, or works, or carries on business, or happens to be, or the approach to such house or place; or,
5. Follow such other person with two or more other persons in a disorderly manner in or through any street or road,

shall, on conviction thereof by a court of summary jurisdiction, or on indictment as herein-after mentioned, be liable either to pay a penalty not exceeding twenty pounds, or to be imprisoned for a term not exceeding three months, with or without hard labour . . .

HIGHWAYS ACT 1959

Obstruction of highways and streets

121. Penalty for wilful obstruction

(1) If a person, without lawful authority or excuse, in any way wilfully obstructs the free passage along a highway he shall be guilty of an offence and shall be liable in respect thereof to a fine not exceeding forty shillings.

(2) A constable may arrest without warrant any person whom he sees committing an offence against this section.

TRADE UNION AND LABOUR RELATIONS ACT 1974

15. Peaceful picketing

It shall be lawful for one or more persons in contemplation or furtherance of a trade dispute to attend at or near—

(a) a place whether another person works or carries on business; or
(b) any other place where another person happens to be, not being a place where he resides,

for the purpose only of peacefully obtaining or communicating information, or peacefully persuading any person to work or abstain from working.

Note: The Employment Bill, 1979, clause 14 proposes a radical change in this section.

Duncan v. Jones [1936] 1 K.B. 218

Divisional Court

A number of people, including Mrs. Duncan, collected to hold a meeting in a street outside the entrance to an unemployed training centre. Inspector

Jones told Mrs. Duncan, of the National Unemployed Workers' Movement, that the meeting could not be held opposite the training centre but that it could be held in another street, 175 yards away. Mrs. Duncan could see no justification with this interference with her "right" to freedom of speech and accordingly commenced the meeting. She was immediately arrested. She was subsequently convicted of the offence of obstructing a policeman in the execution of his duty under the Prevention of Crimes Act 1871, s. 12 (now replaced by the Police Act 1964, s. 51). A case was stated, after an unsuccessful appeal to quarter sessions. The appeal was dismissed by the Divisional Court.

LORD HEWART C.J.:

There have been moments during the argument in this case when it appeared to be suggested that the Court had to do with a grave case involving what is called the right of public meeting. I say 'called', because English law does not recognize any special right of public meeting for political or other purposes. The right of assembly, as Professor Dicey puts it (Dicey's *Law of the Constitution,* 8th ed., p. 499), is nothing more than a view taken by the Court of the individual liberty of the subject. If I thought that the present case raised a question which has been held in suspense by more than one writer on constitutional law—namely, whether an assembly can properly be held to be unlawful merely because the holding of it is expected to give rise to a breach of the peace on the part of persons opposed to those who are holding the meeting—I should wish to hear much more argument before I expressed an opinion. The case, however, does not even touch that important question.

Our attention has been directed to the somewhat unsatisfactory case of *Beatty* v. *Gillbanks* (1882), 9 Q.B.D. 308. The circumstances of that case and the charge must be rememberd, as also must the important passage in the judgment of Field J., in which Cave J. concurred. Field J. said (Ibid. 314): 'I entirely concede that every one must be taken to intend the natural consequences of his own acts, and it is clear to me that if this disturbance of the peace was the natural consequence of acts of the appellants they would be liable, and the justices would have been right in binding them over. But the evidence set forth in the case does not support this contention; on the contrary, it shows that the disturbances were caused by other people antagonistic to the appellants, and that no acts of violence were committed by them.' Our attention has also been directed to other authorities where the judgments in *Beatty* v. *Gillbanks* (1882), 9 Q.B.D. 308, have been referred to, but they do not carry the matter any further, although they more than once express a doubt about the exact meaning of the decision, In my view, *Beatty* v. *Gillbanks* is apart from the present case. No such question as that which arose there is even mooted here.

The present case reminds one rather of the observations of Bramwell B. in *Reg.* v. *Prebble* (1858), 1 F. & F. 325, 326, where, in holding that a constable, in clearing certain licensed premises of the persons thereon, was not acting in the execution of his duty, he said: 'It would have been otherwise had there been a nuisance or disturbance of the public peace, or any danger of a breach of the peace.'

The case stated which we have before us indicates clearly a casual connection between the meeting of May, 1933, and the disturbance which occurred after it—that the disturbance was not only post the meeting but was also propter the meeting. In my view, the deputy-chairman was entitled to come to the conclusion to which he came on the facts which he found and to hold that the conviction of the appellant for wilfully obstructing the respondent when in the execution of his duty was right. This appeal should, therefore, be dismissed.

HUMPHREYS J.:

I agree. I regard this as a plain case. It has nothing to do with the law of unlawful assembly. No charge of that sort was even suggested against the appellant. The sole question raised by the case is whether the respondent, who was admittedly obstructed, was so obstructed when in the execution of his duty.

It does not require authority to emphasize the statement that it is the duty of a police officer to prevent apprehended breaches of the peace. Here it is found as a fact that the respondent reasonably apprehended a breach of the peace. It then, as is rightly expressed in the case, became his duty to prevent anything which in his view would cause that breach of the peace. While he was taking steps so to do he was wilfully obstructed by the appellant. I can conceive no clearer case with in the statutes than that.

SINGLETON J.:

On the facts stated in the case I am satisfied that the respondent at the material time was doing that which it was his duty to do, and that, therefore, the obstruction of him by the appellant constituted obstruction of him when in the execution of his duty. Authorities in other branches of the law do not carry the matter any further. I agree that the appeal should be dismissed.

Note: In *Wershof* v. *Commissioner of Police for the Metropolis* [1978] 3 All E.R. 540, May J. said at p. 550: "I hold that the position in law is that a police constable may only arrest without a warrant anyone who wilfully obstructs him in the execution of his duty if the nature of that obstruction is such that he actually causes, or is likely to cause, a breach of the peace or is calculated to prevent the lawful arrest or detention of another."

Hubbard and Others v. Pitt and Others [1976] 1 Q.B.142

Court of Appeal

Members of the Islington Tenants Campaign, believing that estate agents assisting property developers were acting improperly, picketed on the pavement outside the offices of Prebble & Co., an Islington estate agent. The plaintiffs, partners in the firm of Prebble & Co. sought an interim injunction against the defendants to restrain the defendants from picketing. Forbes J. granted an inerlocutory injunction. The defendants appealed.

LORD DENNING, M.R.:

To solve the problem, it is necessary to inquire what are the restrictions placed by the law on such activities as these.

1. *The law of libel*

By the placards and leaflets, the defendants are undoubtedly casting serious slurs on the plaintiffs. If the words are untrue, the defendants can be restrained from repeating them. But the defendants assert that they are true and that they are ready to prove it. In such a situation the courts never grant an interim injunction before the trial. Quite recently we had a case where a man was angry because some builders had, he thought, made his front door very badly. So he took it off its hinges, put it on the front of his Rolls-Royce motor car, and drove it round the roads. It bore words saying: "This door is typical of the poor materials used. Be warned." We refused to grant an interim injunction: see *Crest Homes Ltd.* v. *Ascott*, February 4, 1975, Bar Library Transcript No. 52B of 1975. The principle on which we go was stated many years ago by a very strong Court of Appeal consisting of Lord Coleridge C.J., Lord Esher M.R., Lindly L.J., Bowen L.J., and Lopes L.J. in *Bonnard* v. *Perryman* [1891] 2 Ch. 269, 284:

> "The right of free speech is one which it is for the public interest that individuals should possess, and, indeed, that they should exercise without impediment, so long as no wrongful act is done; and, unless an alleged libel is untrue, there is no wrong committed; but, on the contrary, often a very wholesome act is performed in the publication and repetition of an alleged libel."

Now the right of protest is one aspect of the right of free speech. It is the right which the defendants claim here. They say that the words are true and that the matter is of public concern. They think that tenants should be warned against the activities of Prebble & Co. They have chosen their offices as the most effective place at which to make their protest. I see nothing in the law of libel to stop them—at any rate, not until there is a trial of the issue whether the words were true, or not.

2. *The law of highways*

(i) *The magistrates.* If the defendants had been guilty of wrongful obstruction of the pavement, the police could have intervened and taken them before the magistrates. This is provided by section 121 of the Highways Act 1959, which says:

> "(1) If a person, without lawful authority or excuse, in any way wilfully obstructs the free passage along a highway he shall be guilty of an offence . . . (2) A constable may arrest without warrant any person whom he sees committing an offence against this section."

In order to be an offence under this section, it has been authoritatively said:

> "there must be proof that the use in question was an unreasonable use . . . It depends upon all the circumstances, including the length of time the obstruction continues, the place where it occurs, the purpose for which it is done, and of course whether it does in fact cause an actual obstruction as opposed to a potential obstruction":

see *Nagy* v. *Weston* [1965] 1 W.L.R. 280, 284 by Lord Parker C.J.

In the present case the police evidently thought there was no breach of this law. The presence of these half a dozen people on Saturday morning for three hours was not an unreasonable use of the highway. They did no interfere with the free passage of people to and fro. Of course, if there had been any fear of a breach of the peace, the police could have interfered: see *Duncan* v. *Jones* [1936] 1 K.B. 218. But there was nothing of that kind.

(ii) *Public nuisance.* If the defendants had been guilty of an unreasonable obstruction on the highway, they could have been restrained by an action on the relation of the Attorney-General: or by an adjoining occupier who suffered particular damage: see *Harper* v. *G. N. Haden and Sons Ltd.* [1933] Ch. 298, 304 and *Dwyer* v. *Mansfield* [1946] K.B. 437. But there was nothing in the nature of a public nuisance here. No crowds collected. No queues were formed. No obstruction caused. No noises. No smells. No breaches of the peace. Nothing for which an indictment would lie, nor an action on the relation of the Attorney-General. And if there was no public nuisance, there can be no question of any individual suing for particular damage therefrom.

(iii) *Trespass to the highway.* The public have a right of passage over a highway: but the soil may belong to someone else. The owner of the soil may sue if a person abuses the right of passage so as to use it for some other and unreasonable purpose. Such as where a racing tout walked up and down to note the trials of the race horses: see *Hickman* v. *Maisey* [1900] 1 Q.B. 752. But those cases do not give Prebble & Co. a cause of action here: because Prebble & Co. do not own the pavement. It is a highway. The surface is vested in the local authority and they have not complained. Nor could they, since no wrong has been done to them or their interest.

(iv) *Conspiracy.* In the action Prebble & Co. charge the defendants with conspiracy: but there is no evidence of this, at any rate not such as to warrant an interim injunction. The predominant purpose of the defendants was to warn the tenants and not to injure Prebble & Co.: see *Crofter Hand Woven Harris Tweed Co. Ltd.* v. *Veitch* [1942] A.C. 435.

(v) *Private nuisance.* As the argument developed, the plaintiffs placed their chief reliance on the tort of private nuisance. The conduct of the defendants was actionable, they said, on the principle, stated by Sir Nathaniel Lindley M.R. in *J. Lyons & Sons* v. *Wilkins* [1899] 1 Ch. 255, 267:

> "The truth is that to watch or beset a man's house with a view to compel him to do or not to do what is lawful for him not to do or to do is wrongful and without lawful authority unless some reasonable justification for it is consistent with the evidence."

That statement has not stood the test of time. Later authority shows that there is no such tort as "watching or besetting" a "man's house" even though it is done with a view to compel, etc. Watching or besetting is only wrongful if it is combined with other conduct (for example, obstruction or violence) such that the whole conduct amounts to a nuisance. It was so decided by this court seven years after *J. Lyons* v. *Wilkins.* The case is *Ward, Lock and Co. Ltd.* v. *Operative Printers' Assistants' Society* (1906) 22 T.L.R. 327. It aroused much interest at the time. It was reported day by day in "The Times" newspaper, both at the trial before Darling J. and in the Court of Appeal. The Court of Appeal reserved their decisions. Their judgments are only to be found in the Times Law Reports, but they are well worth studying both for the actual decision and the reasons given for it. They have been quoted and followed in later cases. In particular in *Fowler* v. *Kibble* [1922] 1 Ch. 487–493 by Lord Sterndale M.R. and p. 497 by Warrington L.J. . . . .

Seeing that there were six days of continuous picketing, that decision is a direct authority that picketing a person's premises (even if done with a view to compel or persuade) is not unlawful unless it is associated with other conduct such as to constitute the whole conduct a nuisance at common law. Picketing is not a nuisance in itself. Nor is it a nuisance for a group of people to attend at or near the plaintiffs' premises in order to obtain or to communicate information or in order peacefully to persuade. It does not become a nuisance unless it is associated with obstruction, violence intimidation, molestation, or threats.

The root question in the present case is: were the defendants in this case guilty of a common law nuisance? There was no obstruction, no violence, no intimidation, no molestation, no noise, no smells, nothing except a group of six or seven people standing about with placards and leaflets outside the plaintiffs' premises, all quite orderly and well-behaved. That cannot be said to be a nuisance at common law. This question can be tested by supposing that the placards and leaflets contained nothing derogatory of the plaintiffs, but commended them and their services. No one could suggest that there was a nuisance at common law. This shows that the real grievance of the plaintiffs is that the words on the placards and leaflets were defamatory of them. Their real cause of action, if it exists, is for libel and not for nuisance.

3. *Generally as to picketing*

The judge held that picketing was unlawful. He said ante, p. 161A:

"The sole issue before me has been whether or not the use of the highway for picketing which is not in contemplation or furtherance of a trade dispute is a lawful operation. I have concluded that it is not."

This ruling is of such significance that I do not think it should be allowed to stand. I see no valid reason for distinguishing between picketing in furtherance of a trade dispute and picketing in furtherance of other causes. Why should workers be allowed to picket and other people not? I do not think there is any distinction drawn by the law save that, in the case of a trade dispute, picketing is governed by statutory provisions: and, in the case of other causes, it is left to the common law. But, broadly speaking, they are in line the one with the other. Picketing is lawful so long as it is done merely to obtain or communicate information, or peacefully to persuade; and is not such as to submit any other person to any kind of constraint or restriction of his personal freedom: see *Hunt v. Broome* [1974] A.C. 587, 597 by Lord Reid.

4. *The grant of an interlocutory injunction*

The plaintiffs placed much reliance on the recent decision of the House of Lords in *American Cyanamid Co.* v. *Ethicon Ltd.* [1975] A.C. 396. It was suggested that it had revolutionised our approach to interlocutory injunctions: and that henceforward we were not to consider the strength of each party's case, but only the balance of convenience. And that in general the balance of convenience was to maintain the status quo. That would mean, in this case, and most cases, granting an interlocutory injunction.

There has since been another case in this court differently constituted in which again the same point was made. It is *Fellowes* v. *Fisher* [1976] Q.B. 122, about a covenant in restraint of trade. I have tried there to reconcile the authorities. I will not repeat it here. All I would say is that I think this case does not come within the ruling in the *American Cyanamid* case. In the first place this is one of the "individual" cases in which there are special factors to be taken into consideration. So much so that the court should assess the relative strength of each party's case before deciding whether to grant an injunction. The plaintiffs should not be granted an interlocutory injunction unless they can make out a prima facie case. In the second place there are "uncompensatable disadvantages" which are so evenly balanced that is appropriate to have regard to the strength of each party's case.

My reasons are these: first, on the facts, so far as the picketing is concerned, there is virtually no dispute. The only dispute on the facts is on the issue of libel, that is, whether the words on the placards and leaflets can be justified, or not.

Second: If an interlocutory injunction is granted, it will virtually decide the whole action in favour of the plaintiffs: because the defendants will be restrained until the trial (which may mean two years, or more) from picketing the plaintiffs' premises, by which time the campaign will be over. It is true that the plaintiffs will have to give an undertaking in damages, but that will be of no use to the defendants, seeing that they will not suffer any pecuniary damages, but only be prevented from continuing their campaign in this way.

Finally, the real grievance of the plaintiffs is about the placards and leaflets. To restrain these by an interlocutory injunction would be contrary to the principle laid down by the court 85 years ago in *Bonnard* v. *Perryman* [1891] 2 Ch. 269, and repeatedly applied ever since. That case spoke of the right of free speech. Here we have to consider the right to demonstrate and the right to protest on matters of public concern. These are rights which it is in the public interest that individuals should possess; and, indeed, that they should exercise without impediment so long as no wrongful act is done. It is often the only means by which grievances can be brought to the knowledge of those in authority—at any rate with such impact as to gain a remedy. Our history is full of warnings against suppression of these rights. Most notable was the demonstration at St. Peter's Fields, Manchester, in 1819 in support of universal suffrage. The magistrates sought to stop it. At least 12 were killed and hundreds injured. Afterwards the Court of Common Council of London affirmed "the undoubted right of Englishmen to assemble together for the purpose of deliberating upon public grievances." Such is the right of assembly. So also is the right to meet together, to go in procession, to demonstrate and to protest on matters of public concern. As long as all is done peaceably and in good order, without threats or incitement to violence or obstruction to traffic, it is not prohibited: see *Beatty* v. *Gillbanks* (1882) 9 Q.B.D. 308. I stress the need for peace and good order. Only too often violence may break out: and then it should be firmly handled and severely punished. But so long as good order is maintained, the right to demonstrate must be preserved. In his recent inquiry on the Red Lion Square disorders, Scarman L.J. was asked to recommend that "a positive right to demonstrate should be enacted." He said that it was unnecessary: "The right, of course exists, subject only to limits required by the need for good order and the passage of traffic": The Red Lion Square Disorders of 15 June, 1974 (1975) (Cmnd. 5919), p. 38. In the recent report on Contempt of Court (1974) (Cmnd. 5794), the committee considered the campaign of the "Sunday Times" about thalidomide and said that the issues were "a legitimate matter for public comment": p. 28, line 7. It recognised that it was important to maintain the "freedom of protest on issues of public concern": p. 100, line 5. It is time for the courts to recognise this too. They should not interfere by interlocutory injunction with the right to demonstrate and to protest any more than they interfere with the right of free speech; provided that everything is done peaceably and in good order. That is the case here. The only thing of which complaint can legitimately be made is the placards and leaflets. If it turned out at the trial that the words on the placards and leaflets were untrue, then an injunction should be granted. But not at present—when, for aught we know, the words may be true and justifiable. And, if true, it may be very wholesome for the truth to be made known. The defendant Pitt is ready to give an undertaking not to obstruct, molest or intimidate anyone: and not to attend at or near the plaintiffs' premises save for the purposes of communicating information. The other defendants, I presume, will give a like undertaking. On these undertakings being given, I would allow the appeal and discharge the injunction.

ORR, L.J.:

... The judge heard the application on affidavit evidence and at the defendants' request delivered a judgment in open court in which he dealt fully with the law as to picketing and highways but, although he referred to it in general terms, expressed no conclusion on an alternative claim of the plaintiffs that the activities of the defendants had amounted to a watching or besetting of the plaintiffs' premises with a view to compelling the plaintiffs not to do acts which it was lawful for them to do, and that, on the authority of this court in *J. Lyons & Sons* v. *Wilkins* [1899] 1 Ch. 255, such action is capable in law of amounting to a private nuisance. On the other side of the dividing line is the decision of this court in *Ward, Lock & Co. Ltd.* v. *Operative Printers' Assistants' Society* (1906) 22 T.L.R. 327, that picketing, without violence, obstruction, annoyance or molestation, in the vicinity of the plaintiff's business premises with a view to persuading the plaintiffs' employees to become members of a union, does not amount to a nuisance. A crucial question in the present case is on which side of this dividing line the facts lie, and this issue, it must be assumed, will in due course, either alone or in conjunction with other issues, come on for trial on evidence including that to which Stamp L.J. has referred, and probably also oral evidence, which will be of great importance, as to the defendants' intention and state of mind. In these circumstances I think it undesirable to say anything more at this stage as to that issue or any other issue which may arise at the trial, and I return to the *Cyanamid* case.

On the authority of that case the first question which the judge had to ask himself in deciding whether an interlocutory injunction should be granted was not whether, on no other evidence than he had before him, the plaintiffs' claim would succeed in the action, nor even whether it was more likely to succeed than to fail, but simply whether there was a serious question to be tried in the sense that the claim was not frivolous or vexatious. I have no doubt that this requirement was satisfied in the present case. It is true that certain criticisms have been made of the judgment of Forbes J., and I am content for the present purposes to assume that these may turn out to be well founded, but there is clearly, in my judgment, a serious issue to be tried at least on the *J. Lyons & Sons* v. *Wilkins* [1899] 1 Ch. 255 issue.

The next question to be asked is whether, if the plaintiffs were to succeed at the trial, they would be adequately compensated for the interim continuance of the defendants' activities. In my judgment, the answer is that they plainly would not, because such continuance might well cause very serious damage to their business, and the judge was entitled, on this issue, to have regard to any doubts he might have felt as to the defendants' ability to satisfy any award of damages made against them. Mr. Turner-Samuels has claimed that it would be wrong to do so in the absence of any evidence that the defendants would be unable to pay; but I think that the boot was on the other foot and that in the absence of any evidence as to ability to pay what could amount to very substantial damages the judge would have been entitled to put in the balance any doubts he may have felt as to that matter.

The next question to be asked is the converse question whether if the defendants were to succeed at the trial they would be adequately compensated for the interim restriction on their activities which the grant of an interlocutory injunction would have imposed. I have no doubt that they would be, since the only restriction imposed by the injunction would be in respect of activities in front of the plaintiffs' premises, leaving the defendants free to conduct their campaign by lawful means elsewhere and if, as some at least of the defendants assert and as I am for the present purposes prepared to assume, their object has not been to damage the plaintiffs but simply to impart information, it seems to me that the disadvantage involved would be minimal, and in any event I see no reason to suppose that the plaintiffs would be unable to pay any damages properly recoverable.

On this basis, on the authority of the *Cyanamid* case, it was appropriate for the judge to consider balance of convenience, and, if the relevant factors were evenly balanced, to grant an interlocutory injunction which would maintain the status quo; that being in the context of this case the situation which existed prior to the commencement, very shortly before the issue of the writ, of the activities complained of. In reality, however, the factors relating to balance of convenience were, in my judgment, for the reasons already given, quite plainly not evenly balanced but heavily weighted in favour of the grant of the injunction and in this respect the facts of the present case differ radically from those involved in the recent case of *Fellowes & Son* v. *Fisher* [1976] Q.B. 122 to which I have already referred.

It follows, in my judgment, that the defendants' case against the grant of an interlocutory injunction fails at each of the four stages indicated in the *Cyanamid* case. . . .

Stamp, L.J. agreed with Orr L.J. in dismissing the appeal for substantially the same reasons.

Note: See Peter Wallington, "Injuctions and the 'Right to Demonstrate'," 35 *Cambridge Law Journal* [1976] 82–111.

"A RIGHT TO DEMONSTRATE"?

The Red Lion Square Disorders of June 15, 1974; Report of an Inquiry by the Rt. Hon. Lord Justice Scarman, O.B.E. Cmnd. 5919, 1975

First principles

5. Amongst our fundamental human rights there are, without doubt, the rights of peaceful assembly and public protest and the right to public order and tranquility. Civilised living collapses—it is obvious—if public protest becomes violent protest or public order degenerates into the quietism imposed by successful oppression. But the problem is more complex than a choice between two extremes—one, a right to protest whenever and wherever you will and the other, a right to continuous calm upon our streets unruffled by the noise and obstructive pressure of the protesting procession. A balance has to be struck, a compromise found that will accommodate the exercise of the right to protest within a framework of public order which enables ordinary citizens, who are not protesting, to go about their business and

pleasure without obstruction or inconvenience. The fact that those who at any one time are concerned to secure the tranquillity of the streets are likely to be the majority must not lead us to deny the protesters their opportunity to march: the fact that the protesters are desperately sincere and are exercising a fundamental human right must not lead us to overlook the rights of the majority.

6. This Inquiry has been concerned to discover where the balance should be struck, and the role of the police in maintaining it. Indiscipline amongst demonstrators, heavy-handed police reaction to disorder are equally mischievous: for each can upset the balance. Violent demonstrators by creating public disorder infringe a fundamental human right which belongs to the rest of us: excessively violent police reaction to public disorder infringes the rights of the protesters. The one and the other are an affront to civilised living.

The role of the police

7. The police are not to be required in any circumstances to exercise political judgment. Their role is the maintenance of public order—no more, and no less. When the National Front marches, the police have no concern with their political message; they will intervene only if the circumstances are such that a breach of the peace is reasonably apprehended. Even if the message be "racist", it is not for the police to "ban the march" or compel it to disperse unless public order is threatened. If, of course, the message appears to infringe the race relations legislation, the police have a duty to report the facts so that consideration may be given to subsequent prosecution: moreover in such circumstances a senior police officer, accompanying the march, might think it wise to warn the organisers of the march that, if it proceeds with its slogans, he will report the fact. But it is vital, if the police are to be kept out of political controversy, that in a public order situation their sole immediate concern is, and is seen to be, with public order.

Demonstrations and the public highway

122. Little attention was given in argument before me to one of the more important reconciliations that the law has to effect in this field. There is a conflict of interest between those who seek to use the streets for the purpose of passage and those who seek to use them for the purpose of demonstration. English law recognises as paramount the right of passage: a demonstration which obstructs passage along the highway is unlawful. The paramount right of passage is, however, subject to the reasonable use of the highway by others. A procession, therefore, which allows room for others to go on their way is lawful: but it is open to question whether a public meeting held on a highway could ever be lawful, for it is not in any way incidental to the exercise of the right of passage. Most certainly a "mass picket" such as the IMG contemplated in Red Lion Square would be unlawful: see Hubbard v Pitt (Times Newspaper 12 November 1974), where the law is reviewed.

123. I think the priority that the law gives to the right of passage is sound. Free movement between place and place and access to premises may seem workaday matters when compared with such rights as those of demonstration and protest: but society could grind to a halt if the law adopted any other priority. There is, therefore, a case, as was suggested by one party, for the specific provision of public meeting-places in our towns and cities. Public meeting-places, whether they be a speaker's corner in the centre of a great city

or a village green, are as essential to civilised life as is priority for the right of passage along our highways.

Reform of the law

124. Only those who completely distrusted the established authorities criticised in the course of the Inquiry the principle of the law. I fancy from what they said about the rights of the National Front that they would like the law to contain more prohibitions than it does, to be less liberal and more restrictive. In my opinion, the principle of the law and the balance that it strikes between freedom, public order and the right of passage have not been shown by these disorders to be unsound: and I do not recommend any fundamental reform.

125. The statute law does, however, call for scrutiny. Section 6 of the Race Relations Act is merely an embarrassment to the police. Hedged about with restrictions (proof of intent, requirement of the Attorney-General's consent) it is useless to a policeman on the street. The police made no report of any infringement of the section by the National Front: and I think they were right. I very much doubt whether a case could have been proved—particularly when one recollects that the general public appeared to have treated the National Front march with indifference. And it was only the thought that the National Front were marching, not their visible appearance, which could be said to have played any part in the causation of the disorders. The section needs radical amendment to make it an effective sanction, particularly, I think, in relation to its formulation of the intent to be proved before an offence can be established.

126. Sections 3, 4 and 5 of the Public Order Act are directly concerned with demonstrations and public processions. The first point to note is that the Act does not oblige the organisers of a public procession to give notice to the police of their intention to demonstrate—though some local acts do impose the requirement in some places, eg the Warley Corporation Act 1969, Section 82, the Wolverhampton Corporation Act 1969, Section 102, and the Kidderminster Corporation Act 1969, Section 73.

127. The Commissioner of Police of the Metropolis, in a submission to the Inquiry, recommended that the law should be changed so as to include a requirement of seven clear days' notice. His proposal is that:

"No person shall organise, arrange or advertise any public procession unless, within seven clear days before the holding of the said procession, notice has been given to the Superintendent of Police for the district or districts in which the same is to be held, of the proposed route, purpose and arrangements for the control of the said procession, and the numbers expected to take part therein, provided that the period of seven days may be reduced to one of twenty-four hours if notice is given to the chief officer of police of the matters hereinbefore referred to and he consents to the holding of the said procession."

Under his proposal, a public procession taking place without the appropriate notice having been given would not be unlawful: but its organisers, by their omission, would have committed an offence. The proposal envisages a shortened period of notice in the event of the need for an immediate or early demonstration, eg outside the embassy of a state threatening to execute somebody believed not to merit execution.

128. The law of most Western European states (including France, West Germany, Italy and Holland) contains a requirement of notice: it is difficult, therefore, to argue that it represents an unacceptable encroachment upon liberty. But I do not think the need for it has been established: and it does present really insuperable difficulty for the urgently called demonstration. Certainly the lack of any such requirement played no part in the causation of these disorders: for the police had all the notice they needed.

129. It cannot be said too often that our law assumes that people will be tolerant, self-disciplined, and willing to co-operate with the police. The assumption is still sound: that is why the police go unarmed, and also why, with no legal requirement of notice, the police are in fact notified in at least 80 per cent of the cases. There are some who—law or no law—would never give notice: but they are on the very fringe of our society and should not, I suggest, force upon the law a largely unnecessary requirement, which can at times be an embarrassment to law-abiding citizens. In the few instances where no notification is given, the police have so far experienced no difficulty in finding out that a demonstration is planned. An effective demonstration needs a degree of advance publicity: the police, therefore, are seldom ignorant of what is planned. I do not, therefore, recommend this change in the law.

130. In the present instance the police did fail to make proper use of the notice that they had. Their failure to make clear to Liberation the route to be followed when entering Red Lion Square did not provide any excuse for the rioting: but it did afford a pretext which will continue to be regarded as sufficient by those who wish to exculpate themselves—at least in their own opinion. It was suggested that the police should be required to give notice in writing of the route to be taken by a march. A legal requirement to such effect is, in my judgment, undesirable. But I recommend that in planning for major demonstrations and in other suitable cases the police should confirm in writing the route agreed or acceptable to them—always provided that it is made clear that at any time thereafter, even in the course of the demonstration itself, the police retain the right to change the route if they consider it necessary.

131. Section 3(1) of the Public Order Act, which confers power, subject to certain conditions, upon a chief officer of police to give directions, is obscurely drafted. Undoubtedly it confers a power to give directions before the procession takes place: but it is doubtful whether it confers any effective power once the procession has started. For this reason the Commissioner proposed that the law should be amended so as to make it an offence to disobey the directions of a police constable when taking part in a public procession. This, I think, goes too far but it is of critical importance that the law should be clarified. It should not be possible to challenge a route direction given by a senior police officer to a procession that is under way. I think it likely that a police officer already has the power to direct a procession *en route* if a breach of the peace is reasonably apprehended, or if it is required by the exigencies of traffic exercising its right of passage. I recommend that the statute be amended so as to confer upon the senior officer present a power to give a direction as to the route to be taken, if he thinks it necessary in the interests of public order.

132. The Commissioner also proposed that:

"When a public procession is taking place a constable may direct that any article which in his opinion is likely to provoke a breach of the peace may not be carried or worn by any person taking part in the said procession."

I appreciate the difficulty under the existing law of proving that a weapon is offensive. It is obvious that a heavy banner pole or a flag pole with a metal tip may appear an innocent thing when carried in a procession and yet a few minutes later may be used as an offensive weapon. But it would, I think, cause trouble rather than lead to the maintenance of peace if at an early stage, before the threat of trouble, a police officer intervened to direct that such articles may not be carried in the procession. Though I sympathise with the police in the difficulty which prompted this proposal, I think it would be unwise to extend the law in the way proposed.

155. Finally, I would emphasise that demonstration is only one of several purposes to which our streets may be put: and, perhaps, not the most important. It is a means of protest, not a substitute for political discussion or parliamentary debate. The streets are not the place for carrying on the discussion necessary for democratic government, though they can accommodate the voice of protest provided public order and the right of passage are not endangered.

[*The Red Lion Square Disorders of June 15, 1974; Report of an Inquiry by the Rt. Hon. Lord Justice Scarman, O.B.E.,* Cmnd. 5919, 1975.]

Questions

1. In what sense does there exist a right to demonstrate in British law?
Cf. I. Brownlie, *The Law Relating to Public Order* (Butterworths, 1968), pp. 139-47.

2. Members of the Free Ulster Movement conduct a propaganda walkabout in a public park in Oxbridge. Under the Oxbridge City byelaws political meetings may not be held in the park and anybody holding such a meeting is liable to a fine of £5. Members of the Free Ulster Movement walk in Indian file round and round the park carrying banners on which are written the words "British Troops Do Not Shoot Brothers." The demonstrators all wear dark glasses. When park-keepers approach the demonstrators they are frightened away by walking-sticks which are waved in the air by the demonstrators.

For which offences, if any, may the demonstrators be liable?

Project

Draft, with explanatory memorandum, a bill regulating to right to demonstrate, paying particular attention to the role of the police, the place in which demonstrations may take place, the responsibility of the organisers for disorder, as well as issues such as notice to hold the demonstration, etc.

CHAPTER 8

LIBERTY OF THE PERSON

Further Reading

De Smith, Chap. 20; Dicey, Chap. 5; Wade & Phillips, pp. 442–460.

G. Wilson, *Cases and Materials on Constitutional and Administrative Law* (2nd ed., C.U.P., 1976) Chap. XIII.

See also Chapter 10.

HABEAS CORPUS

De Smith, pp. 452–456; Dicey, pp. 213–237; Street, pp. 38–40; Wade & Phillips, pp. 455–461.

R. G. Sharpe, *The Law of Habeas Corpus* (O.U.P., 1976).

HABEAS CORPUS ACT 1679

[1.] Sheriff, etc., within three days after service of habeas corpus, with the exception of treason and felony, as and under the regulations herein mentioned, to bring up the body before the court to which the writ is returnable; and certify the true causes of imprisonment

Whensoever any person or persons shall bring any habeas corpus directed unto any sheriffe or sheriffes goaler minister or other person whatsoever for any person in his or their custody and the said writt shall be served upon the said officer or left at the gaole or prison with any of the under officers under-keepers or deputy of the said officers or keepers that the said officer or officers his or their under officers under-keepers or deputyes shall within three dayes after the service thereof as aforesaid (unlesse the committment aforesaid were for treason . . . plainely and specially expressed in the warrant of committment) upon payment or tender of the charges of bringing the said prissoner to be ascertained by the judge or court that awarded the same and endorsed upon the said writt not exceeding twelve pence per mile and upon security given by his owne bond to pay the charges of carrying backe the prisoner if he shall bee remanded by the court or judge to which he shall be brought according to the true intent of this present Act and that he will not make any escape by the way make returne of such writt [or] bring or cause to be brought the body of the partie soe committed or restrained unto or before the lord chauncelior or lord keeper of the great seale of England for the time being or the judges or barons of the said court from whence the said writt shall issue or unto and before such other person [and] persons before whome the said writt is made returnable according to the command thereof, and shall [likewise then] certifie the true causes of his detainer or imprisonment unlesse the committment of the said partie be in any place beyond the distance of twenty miles from the place or places where such court or person is or shall be resideing and if beyond the distance of twenty miles and not above one hundred miles then within the space of ten dayes and if beyond the distance of one hundred miles then within the space of twenty dayes after such delivery aforesaid and not longer.

2. How writs to be marked—Persons committed, except for treason and felony, etc., may appeal to the lord chancellor, etc.—Habeas corpus may be awarded; and upon service thereof the officer to bring up the prisoners as before mentioned; and thereupon within two days lord chancellor, etc., may discharge upon recognizance; and certify the writ with the return and recognizance—Proviso for process not bailable

And to the intent that noe sheriffe gaoler or other officer may pretend ignorance of the import of any such writt bee it enacted by the authoritie aforesaid that all such writts shall be marked in this manner Per statutum tricesimo primo Caroli Secundi Regis and shall be signed by the person that awards the same And if any person or persons shall be or stand committed or detained as aforesaid for any crime unlesse for treason . . . plainely expressed in the warrant of committment in the vacation time and out of terme it shall and may be lawfull to and for the person or persons soe committed or detained (other then persons convict or in execution) by legall processe or any one [in] his or their behalfe to appeale or complaine to the lord chauncellour or lord keeper or any one of his Majestyes justices [either] of the one bench or of the other or the barons of the Exchequer of the degree of the coife and the said lord chauncellor lord keeper justices or barons or any of them upon view of the copy or copies of the warrant or warrants of committment and detainer or otherwise upon oath made that such copy or copyes were denyed to be given by such person or persons in whose custody the prisoner or prisoners is or are detained are hereby authorized and required [upon request made in writeing by such person or persons or any on his her or their behalfe attested and subscribed by two witnesses [that] were present at the delivery of the same] to award and grant an habeas corpus under the seale of such court whereof he shall then be one of the judges to be directed to the officer or officers in whose custodie the party soe committed or detained shall be returnable immediate before the said [lord chauncellor or] lord keeper or such justice baron or any other justice or baron of the degree of the coife of any of the said courts and upon service thereof as aforesaid the officer or officers his or their under-officer or under officers under keeper or under keepers or [their] deputy in whose custodie the partie is soe committed or detained shall within the times respectively before limitted [bring such prisoner or prisoners] before the s̃d lord chauncellor or lord keeper or such justices barons or one of them [before whome the said writt is made returnable and in case of his absence before any of them] with the returne of such writt and the true causes of the committment and detainer and thereupon within two dayes after the partie shall committment and detainer and thereupon within two dayes after the partie shall be brought before them the said lord chauncellor or lord keeper or such justice or baron before whome the prisoner shall be brought as aforesaid shall discharge the said prisoner from his imprisonment takeing his or their recognizance with one or more suretie or sureties in any summe according to their discretions haveing reguard to the quality of the prisoner and nature of the offence for his or their appearance in the Court of Kings Bench the terme following or at the next assizes sessions or generall goale-delivery of and for such county city or place where the committment was or where the offence was committed or in such other court where the said offence is properly cognizable as the case shall require and then shall certifie the said writt with the returne thereof and the said recognizance or recognizances into the said court where such appearance is to be made unlesse it shall appeare unto the said lord chauncellor or lord keeper or justice or justices [or] baron or barons that the party soe committed is detained upon a legall processe order or warrant out of some court that hath jurisdiction of criminall matters or by some warrant signed and sealed with the hand and seale of any of the said justices or barons or some justice or justices of the peace for such matters or offences for the which by the law the prisoner is not baileable.

3. Habeas corpus not granted in vacation to prisoners who have neglected to pray the same

Provided always and bee it enacted that if any person shall have wilfully neglected by the space of two whole termes after his imprisonment to pray a habeas corpus for his enlargement such person soe wilfully neglecting shall not have any habeas corpus to be granted in vacation time in pursuance of this Act.

4. Officer neglecting, etc., to make the said returns, etc., or upon demand to deliver a copy of warrant of commitment; first offence, penalty £100, second offence, £200 and incapacity—Judgment at suit of party sufficient conviction

And . . . if any officer or officers his or their under-officer or under-officers under-keeper or under-keepers or deputy shall neglect or refuse to make the returnes aforesaid or to bring the body or bodies of the prisoner or prisoners according to the command of the said writt within the respective times aforesaid or upon demand made by the prisoner or person in his behalfe shall refuse to deliver or within the space of six houres after demand shall not deliver to the person soe demanding a true copy of the warrant or warrants of committment and detayner of such prisoner, which he and they are hereby required to deliver accordingly all and every the head goalers and keepers of such prisons and such other person in whose custodie the prisoner shall be detained shall for the first offence forfeite to the prisoner or partie grieved the summe of one hundred pounds and for the second offence the summe of two hundred pounds and shall and is hereby made incapeable to hold or execute his said office, the said penalties to be recovered by the prisoner or partie grieved his executors or administrators against such offender his executors or administrators by any action of debt suite bill plaint or information in any of the Kings courts at Westminster wherein noe . . . injunction . . . or stay of prosecution by non vult ulterius prosequi or otherwise shall bee admitted or allowed . . ., and any recovery or judgment at the suite of any partie grieved shall be a sufficient conviction for the first offence and any after recovery or judgement at the suite of a partie grieved for any offence after the first judge-ment shall bee a sufficient conviction to bring the officers or person within the said penaltie for the second offence.

5. Proviso as to imprisonment of party after having been set at large upon habeas corpus—Unduly recommitting such discharged persons or assisting therein; penalty to the party, £500

And for the prevention of unjust vexation by reiterated committments for the same offence bee it enacted by the authoritie aforesaid that noe person or persons which shall be delivered or sett at large upon any habeas corpus shall at any time hereafter bee againe imprisoned or committed for the same offence by any person or persons whatsoever other then by the legall order and processe of such court wherein he or they shall be bound by recognizance to appeare or other court haveing jurisdiction of the cause and if any other person or persons shall knowingly contrary to this Act recommitt or imprison or knowingly procure or cause to be recommitted or imprisoned for the same offence or pretended offence any person or persons delivered or sett at large as aforesaid or be knowingly aiding or assisting therein then he or they shall forfeite to the prisoner or party grieved the summe of five hundred pounds any colourable pretence or variation in the warrant or warrants of committment notwithstanding to be recovered as aforesaid.

6. If persons committed for high treason or felony plainly expressed in warrant shall not on petition be indicted as herein mentioned, judges, etc., may discharge upon bail; proviso; and if not indicted and tried as herein mentioned then to be discharged

Provided alwayes . . . that if any person or persons shall be committed for high treason . . . plainely and specially expressed in the warrant of committment upon his prayer or petition in open court the first weeke of the terme or first day of the sessions of oyer and terminer or generall goale delivery to be brought to his tryall shall not be indicted sometime in the next terme sessions of oyer and terminer or generall goale delivery after such committment it shall and may be lawfull to and for the judges of the Court of Kings Bench and justices of oyer and terminer or generall goale delivery and they are hereby required upon motion to them made in open court the last day of the terme sessions or goale-delivery either by the prisoner or any one in his behalfe to sett at liberty the prisoner upon baile unlesse it appeare to the judges and justices upon oath made that the witnesses for the King could not be produced the same terme sessions or generall goal-delivery. And if any person or persons committed as aforesaid upon his prayer or petition in open court the first weeke of the terme or first day of the sessions of oyer and terminer or generall goale delivery to be brought to his tryall shall not be indicted and tryed the second terme sessions of oyer and terminer or generall goale delivery after his committment or upon his tryall shall be acquitted he shall be discharged from his imprisonment.

7. Proviso respecting persons charged in debt, etc.

Provided alwayes that nothing in this Act shall extend to discharge out of prison any person charged in debt or other action or with processe in any civill cause but that after he shall be discharged of his imprisonment for such his criminall offence he shall be kept in custodie according to law for such other suite.

8. Persons committed for criminal matter not to be removed but by habeas corpus or other legal writ—Unduly making out, etc., warrant for removal; penalty

Provided alwaies . . . that if any person or persons subject of this realme shall be committed to [any] prison or in custodie of any officer or officers whatsoever for any criminall or supposed criminall matter that the said person shall not be removed from the said prison and custody into the custody of any other officer or officers unlesse it be by habeas corpus or some other legall writt or where the prisoner is delivered to the constable or other inferiour officer to carry such prisoner to some common goale [or where any person is sent by order of any judge of assize or justice of the peace to any common worke-house or house of correction or where the prisoner is removed from one prison or place to another within the same county in order to his or her tryall or discharge in due course of law or in case of suddaine fire or infection or other necessity] and if any person or persons shall after such committment aforesaid make out and signe or countersigne any warrant or warrants for such removeall aforesaid contrary to this Act as well he that makes or signes or countersignes such warrant or warrants as the officer or officers that obey or execute the same shall suffer and incurr the paines and forfeitures in this Act before-mentioned both for the first and second offence respectively to be recovered in manner aforesaid by the partie grieved.

9. Proviso for application for and granting habeas corpus in vacation time—Lord chancellor, etc., unduly denying writ; penalty to party, £500

Provided alsoe . . . that it shall and may be lawfull to and for any prisoner and prisoners as aforesaid to move obtaine his or their habeas corpus as well out of the High Court of Chauncery or Court of Exchequer as out of the courts of Kings Bench or Common Pleas or either of them and if the said lord chauncellor or lord keeper or any judge or judges baron or barons for the time being of the degree of the coife of any of the courts aforesaid in the vacation time upon view of the copy or copies of the warrant or warrants of committment or detainer or upon oath made that such copy or copyes were denied as aforesaid shall deny any writt of habeas corpus by this Act required to be granted being moved for as aforesaid they shall severally forfeite to the prisoner or partie grieved the summe of five hundred pounds to be recovered in manner aforesaid.

10. Habeas corpus may be directed into counties palatine, etc.

And . . . an habeas corpus according to the true intent and meaning of this Act may be directed and runn into any county palatine the cinque ports or other priviledged places within the kingdome of England dominion of Wales or towne of Berwicke upon Tweede and the islands of Jersey or Guernsey any law or usage to the contrary notwithstanding.

11. No subject to be sent prisoner into Scotland, etc., or any parts beyond the seas—Persons so imprisoned may maintain action against the person committing or otherwise acting in respect thereof, as herein mentioned; treble costs and damages; and the person so committing or acting disabled from office, and incur premunire, and be incapable of pardon

And for preventing illegall imprisonments in prisons beyond the seas bee it further enacted by the authoritie aforesaid that noe subject of this realme that now is or hereafter shall be an inhabitant or resiant of this kingdome of England dominion of Wales or towne of Berwicke upon Tweede shall or may be sent prisoner into Scotland Ireland Jersey Gaurnsey Tangeir or into any parts garrisons islands or places beyond the seas which are or at any time hereafter [shall be] within or without the dominions of his Majestie his heires or successors and that every such imprisonment is hereby enacted and adjudged to be illegall and that if any of the said subjects now is or hereafter shall bee soe imprisoned [every such person and persons soe imprisoned] shall and may for every such imprisonment maintaine by vertue of this Act an action or actions of false imprisonment in any of his Majestyes courts of record against the person or persons by whome he or she shall be soe committed detained imprisoned sent prisoner or transported contrary to the true meaning of this Act and against all or any person or persons that shall frame contrive write seale or countersigne any warrant or writeing for such committment detainer imprisonment or transportation or shall be adviseing aiding or assisting in the same or any of them and the plaintiffe in every such action shall have judgement to recover his . . . costs besides damages which damages soe to be given shall not be lesse than five hundred pounds in which action noe delay stay or stopp of proceeding by rule order or command nor noe injunction . . . whatsoever . . . shall be allowed [excepting such rule of the court wherein the action shall depend made in open court as shall bee thought in justice necessary for speciall cause to be expressed in the said rule] and the person or persons who shall knowingly frame contrive write seale or countersigne any warrant for such committment detainer or transportation or shall soe committ detaine imprison or transport any person or persons contrary to this Act or be any wayes adviseing aiding or assisting therein being lawfully convicted thereof shall be disabled from thenceforth to beare any office of trust or proffitt within the said realme of England dominion of Wales or towne of Berwicke upon Tweede or any of the islands territories or dominions thereunto belonging and [be liable to imprisonment for life] and be incapeable of any pardon from the King his heires or successors of the said . . . disabilities or any of them.

15. Proviso for sending persons to be tried in places where any capital offence committed

Provided alsoe that if any person or persons at any time resiant in this realme shall have committed any capitall offence in Scotland or Ireland or any of the islands or forreigne plantations of the King his heires or successors where he or she ought to be tryed for such offence such person or persons may be sent to such place there to receive such tryall in such manner as the same might have beene used before the makeing of this Act any thing herein contained to the contrary notwithstanding.

16. Limitation of prosecution for offences against this Act

Provided alsoe . . . that noe person or persons shall be sued impleaded molested or troubled for any offence against this Act unlesse the partie offending be sued or impleaded for the same within two yeares at the most after such time wherein the offence shall be committed [in case the partie grieved shall not be then in prison and if he shall be in prison then within the space of two yeares] after the decease of the person imprisoned or his or her delivery out of prison which shall first happen.

17. After assizes proclaimed, no person to be removed from common gaol upon habeas corpus, but brought before judge or assize

And to the intent noe person may avoid his tryall at the assizes or generall goale-delivery by procureing his removeall before the assizes at such time as he cannot be brought backe to receive his tryall there bee it enacted that after the assizes proclaimed for that county where the prisoner is detained noe person shall be removed from the common goale upon any habeas corpus granted in pursuance of this Act but upon any such habeas corpus shall be brought before the judge of assize in open court who is thereupon to doe what to justice shall appertaine.

18. After assizes person detained may have habeas corpus

Provided neverthelesse that after the assizes are ended any person or persons detained may have his or her habeas corpus according to the direction and intention of this Act.

ADMINISTRATION OF JUSTICE ACT 1960

14. Procedure on application for habeas corpus

(1) On a criminal application for habeas corpus an order for the release of the person restrained shall be refused only by a Divisional Court of the Queen's Bench Division, whether the application is made in the first instance to such a court or to a single judge in accordance with rules of court.

(2) Notwithstanding anything in any enactment or rule of law, where a criminal or civil application for habeas corpus has been made by or in respect of any person, no such application shall again be made by or in respect of that person on the same grounds, whether to the same court or judge or to any other court or judge, unless fresh evidence is adduced in support of the application; and no such application shall in any case be made to the Lord Chancellor.

15. Appeal in habeas corpus proceedings

(1) Subject to the provisions of this section, an appeal shall lie, in any proceedings upon application for habeas corpus, whether civil or criminal, against an order for the release of the person restrained as well as against the refusal of such an order.

(2) No appeal shall lie by virtue of this section from an order made by a single judge on a criminal application for habeas corpus.

Question

"All the other freedoms of the most generous bill of rights may stand destitute of meaning, as long as individuals can be detained indefinitely by police action without appeal"—Arnold Brecht (1942).

"This one human right to habeas corpus is the safeguard of most other human rights"—E. Chaffe, Jr. (1951).

"The Habeas Corpus is the single advantage our government has over that of other countries"—Dr Johnson (1769).

Discuss.

Project

Take either the All England Reports or the Weekly Law Reports for the last few years, and working through the reported cases list all those in which the writ of habeas corpus was applied for or used. How often was the writ used during the years reviewed and for what purposes? Is anything to be learnt for the extent of the use of habeas corpus over these years and from the purposes for which it was used?

CHAPTER 9

POLITICAL OFFENCES

Further Reading

De Smith, pp. 469–474; Smith & Hogan, Chap. 21; Street, pp. 211–234; Wade & Phillips, pp. 474–476.

I. Brownlie, *The Law Relating to Public Order* (Butterworths, 1968), Chap. 8; L. H. Leigh, "Law Reform and the Law of Treason and Sedition" (1978) *Public Law* pp. 128–148; D. G. T. Williams, "Offences against the State 1964–1973," [1974] Crim. L.R. pp. 634–641.

See also pp. 393, 424 and p. 439.

1. *TREASON*

TREASON FELONY ACT 1848

3. Offences herein mentioned declared to be felonies

. . . If any person whatsoever shall, within the United Kingdom or without, compass, imagine, invent, devise, or intend to deprive or depose our Most Gracious Lady the Queen . . . from the style, honour, or royal name of the imperial crown of the United Kingdom, or of any other of her Majesty's dominions and countries, or to levy war against her Majesty, . . . within any part of the United Kingdom, in order by force or constraint to compel her . . . to change her . . . measures or counsels, or in order to put any force or constraint upon or order to intimidate or overawe both Houses or either House of Parliament, or to move or stir any foreigner or stranger with force to invade the United Kingdom or any other of her Majesty's dominions or countries under the obeisance of her Majesty, . . . and such compassings, imaginations, inventions, devices, or intentions, or any of them, shall express, utter, or declare, by publishing any printing or writing, . . . or by any overt act or deed, every person so offending shall be guilty of felony, and being convicted thereof shall be liable, . . . to be transported beyond the seas for the term of his or her natural life . . .

6. Saving as to 25 Edw. 3 stat. 5 c.2

Provided always, . . . that nothing herein contained shall lessen the force of or in any manner affect any thing enacted by the Treason Act, 1351.

7. Indictments for felony valid, though the facts may amount to treason

Provided also, . . . that if the facts or matters alleged in an indictment for any felony under this Act shall amount in law to treason, such indictment shall not by reason thereof be deemed void, erroneous, or defective; and if the facts or matters proved on the trial of any person indicted for any felony under this Act shall amount in law to treason, such person shall not by reason thereof be entitled to be acquitted of such felony; but no person tried for such felony shall be afterwards prosecuted for treason upon the same facts.

Note: This Act was enacted to remove the "martyr's crown" from Irish rebels who might otherwise have been convicted of and hanged for treason.

2. *INCITEMENT TO DISAFFECTION*

De Smith, pp. 470–471; Smith & Hogan, pp. 807–880; Street, pp. 215–220.

L. Grant, "Incitement to Disaffection," 3(3) *Index on Censorship* (1974) pp. 3–10; W. Ivor Jennings, *The Sedition Bill Explained* (New Statesman & Nation, 1934); Thom Young and M. Kettle, *Incitement to Disaffection* (NCCL, 1976).

INCITEMENT TO DISAFFECTION ACT 1934

An Act to make better provision for the prevention and punishment of endeavours to seduce members of His Majesty's forces from their duty or allegience

1. Penalty on persons endeavouring to seduce members of His Majesty's forces from their duty or allegiance

If any person maliciously and advisedly endeavours to seduce any member of His Majesty's forces from his duty or allegiance to His Majesty, he shall be guilty of an offence under this Act.

2. Provisions for the prevention and detection of offences under this Act

(1) If any person, with intent to commit or to aid, abet, counsel, or procure the commission of an offence under section one of this Act, has in his possession or under his control any document of such a nature that the dissemination of copies thereof among members of His Majesty's forces would constitute such an offence, he shall be guilty of an offence under this Act.

(2) If a judge of the High Court is satisfied by information on oath that there is reasonable ground for suspecting that an offence under this Act has been committed, and that evidence of the commission thereof is to be found at any premises or place specified in the information, he may, on an application made by an officer of police of a rank not lower than that of inspector, grant a search warrant authorising any such officer as aforesaid named in the warrant together with any other persons named in the warrant and any other officers of police to enter the premises or place at any time within one month

from the date of the warrant, if necessary by force, and to search the premises or place and every person found therein, and to seize anything found on the premises or place or on any such person which the officer has reasonable ground for suspecting to be evidence of the commission of such an offence as aforesaid:

Provided that—

(a) a search warrant shall only be issued in respect of an offence suspected to have been committed within the three months prior to the laying of the information thereof; and

(b) if a search warrant under this Act has been executed on any premises, it shall be the duty of the officer of police who has conducted or directed the search to notify the occupier that the search has taken place, and to supply him with a list of any documents or other objects which have been removed from the premises, and where any documents have been removed from any other person to supply that person with a list of such documents.

(3) No woman shall, in pursuance of a warrant issued under the last foregoing subsection, be searched except by a woman.

(4) Anything seized under this section may be retained for a period not exceeding one month, or if within that period proceedings are commenced for an offence under this Act until the conclusion of those proceedings, and subject as aforesaid, and to the provisions of this Act conferring powers on courts dealing with offences, the Police (Property) Act, 1897 (which makes provision with respect to the disposal of property in the possession of the police), shall apply to property which has come into the possession of the police under this section as it applies to property which has come into the possession of the police in the circumstances mentioned in that Act.

3. Provisions as to punishment of offences

(1) A person guilty of an offence under this Act shall be liable, on conviction on indictment to imprisonment for a term not exceeding two years or to a fine not exceeding two hundred pounds, or on summary conviction to imprisonment for a term not exceeding four months or to a fine not exceeding twenty pounds, or (whether on conviction on indictment or on summary conviction) to both such imprisonment and fine.

(2) No prosecution in England under this Act shall take place without the consent of the Director of Public Prosecutions.

(3) Where a prosecution under this Act is being carried on by the Director of Public Prosecutions, a court of summary jurisdiction shall not deal with the case summarily without the consent of the Director.

(4) Where any person is convicted of an offence under this Act, the court dealing with the case may order any documents connected with the offence to be destroyed or dealt with in such other manner as may be specified in the order, but no documents shall be destroyed before the expiration of the period within which an appeal may be lodged, and if an appeal is lodged no document shall be destroyed until after the appeal has been heard and decided.

Note: For a recent example of the invocation of this Act see *R.* v. *Arrowsmith* [1975] Q.B. 678. See also Police Act 1964, s. 53.

Question

"Unless one believes that freedom includes the right to persuade British soldiers to desert or mutiny, the conclusion must be that although the original Bill conferred unreasonably wide powers on the executive to interfere with the citizen, the Act, despite some objectionable features, is not now a serious threat to liberty."—Street. Discuss.

POLICE ACT 1964

53. Causing disaffection

(1) Any person who causes, or attempts to cause, or does any act calculated to cause, disaffection amongst the members of any police force, or induces or attempts to induce, or does any act calaculated to induce, any member of a police force to withhold his services or to commit breaches of discipline, shall be guilty of an offence and liable;
  (a) on summary conviction, to imprisonment for a term not exceeding six months or to a fine not exceeding £100, or to both;
  (b) on conviction on indictment, to imprisonment for a term not exceeding two years or to a fine or to both.

3. *EXTRADITION*

EXTRADITION ACT 1870

3. Restrictions on surrender of criminals

The following restriction shall be observed with respect to the surrender of fugitive criminals:
  (1) A fugitive criminal shall not be surrendered if the offence in respect of which his surrender is demanded is one of a political character, or if he prove to the satisfaction of the police magistrate or the court before whom he is brought on habeas corpus, or to the Secretary of State, that the requisition for his surrender has in fact been made with a view to try or punish him for an offence of a political character:
  (2) A fugitive criminal shall not be surrendered to a foreign state unless provision is made by the law of that state, or by arrangement that the fugitive criminal shall not, until he has been restored or had an opportunity of returning to Her Majesty's dominions, be detained or tried in that foreign state for any offence committed prior to his surrender other than the extradition crime proved by the facts on which the surrender is grounded:
  (3) A fugitive criminal who has been accused of some offence within English jurisdiction not being the offence for which his surrender is asked, or is undergoing sentence under any conviction in the United Kingdom, shall not be surrendered until after he has been discharged, whether by acquittal or on expiration of his sentence or otherwise:
  (4) A fugitive criminal shall not be surrendered until the expiration of fifteen days from the date of his being committed to prison to await his surrender.

BACKING OF WARRANTS (REPUBLIC OF IRELAND) ACT 1965

1. Endorsement of warrants issued in Republic of Ireland

(1) Where—
- (a) a warrant has been issued by a judicial authority in the Republic of Ireland (in this Act referred to as the Republic) for the arrest of a person accused or convicted of an offence against the laws of the Republic, being an indictable offence or an offence punishable on summary conviction with imprisonment for six months; and
- (b) an application for the endorsement of the warrant is made to a justice of the peace in the United Kingdom by a constable who produces the warrant and states on oath that he has reason to believe the person named or described therein to be within the area for which the justice acts;

then, subject to the provisions of this section, the justice shall endorse the warrant in the prescribed form for execution within the part of the United Kingdom comprising the area for which he acts.

(2) A warrant for the arrest of a person accused of an offence which under the laws of the Republic is not an indictable offence but is punishable on summary conviction with imprisonment for six months shall not be endorsed under this section unless—
- (a) he has failed to appear in answer to a summons issued by or on behalf of a court in the Republic requiring his presence before the court for the trial of the offence and, not less than fourteen days before the date names in the summons for his appearance, the summons was served on him personally in the Republic or a notice of the issue of the summons, together with a copy of the summons, was served on him personally in the United Kingdom; or
- (b) having entered into a recognizance for his appearance before a court in the Republic for the trial of the offence, he has failed to appear in pursuance of the recognizance; or
- (c) having appeared before a court in the Republic for the trial of the offence, he has subsequently failed to appear on any date to which the proceedings were adjourned.

(3) A warrant for the arrest of a person convicted of any offence against the laws of the Republic shall not be endorsed under this section unless the purpose of the arrest is to enable him—
- (a) to be brought before a court in the Republic for sentence in respect of the conviction; or
- (b) to be taken to a place where he is to undergo imprisonment under such a sentence, not being imprisonment in default of the payment of a fine or other sum.

2. Proceedings before magistrates' court

(1) So soon as is practicable after a person is arrested under a warrant endorsed in accordance with section 1 of this Act, he shall be brought before a magistrates' court and the court shall, subject to the following provisions of this section, order him to be delivered at some convenient point of departure from the United Kingdom into the custody of a member of the police force (Garda Síochána) of the Republic, and remand him until so delivered.

(2) An order shall not be made under subsection (1) of this section if it appears to the court that the offence specified in the warrant does not correspond with any offence under the law of the part of the United Kingdom in which the court acts which is an indictable offence or is punishable on summary conviction with imprisonment for six months; nor shall such an order be made if it is shown to the satisfaction of the court—

(a) that the offence specified in the warrant is an offence of a political character, or an offence under military law which is not also an offence under the general criminal law, or an offence under an enactment relating to taxes, duties or exchange control; or

(b) that there are substantial grounds for believing that the person named or described in the warrant will, if taken to the Republic, be prosecuted or detained for another offence, being an offence of a political character or an offence under military law which is not also an offence under the general criminal law.

(3) In the case where the court does not make an order under subsection (1) of this section, the court shall order the person named or described in the warrant to be discharged.

SUPPRESSION OF TERRORISM ACT 1978

An Act to give effect to the European Convention on the Suppression of Terrorism; to amend the law relating to the extradition of criminals and the obtaining of evidence for criminal proceedings outside the United Kingdom; to confer jurisdiction in respect of certain offences committed outside the United Kingdom; and for connected purposes.

Cases in which certain offences are not to be regarded as of a political character

1.—(1) This section applies to any offence of which a person is accused or has been convicted outside the United Kingdom if the act constituting the offence, or the equivalent act, would, if it took place in any part of the United Kingdom or, in the case of an extra-territorial offence, in corresponding circumstances outside the United Kingdom, constitute one of the offences listed in Schedule 1 to this Act.

(2) For the purposes mentioned in subsection (3) below—

(a) no offence to which this section applies shall be regarded as an offence of a political character; and

(b) no proceedings in respect of an offence to which this section applies shall be regarded as a criminal matter of a political character or as criminal proceedings of a political character.

(3) Those purposes are—

(a) the purposes of the Extradition Act 1870 in relation to any requisition for the surrender of a fugitive criminal made on behalf of a convention country after the coming into force of this paragraph;

(b) the purposes of the Fugitive Offenders Act 1967 in relation to any request for the return of a person under that Act made on behalf of a convention country after the coming into force of this paragraph;

(c) the purposes of the Backing of Warrants (Republic of Ireland) Act 1965 in relation to any warrant issued in the Republic of Ireland to which this paragraph applies by virtue of an order under subsection (4) below; and (*d*) the purposes of section 5 of the Extradition Act 1873 (evidence for foreign criminal matters) and section 5 of the Evidence (Proceedings in Other Jurisdictions) Act 1975 (evidence for criminal proceedings outside the United Kingdom) in relation to—

(i) any criminal proceedings instituted in a convention country (not being the Republic of Ireland) after the coming into force of this subparagraph; and

(ii) any criminal proceedings in the Republic of Ireland to which this subparagraph applies by virtue of an order under subsection (4) below.

(4) The Secretary of State may by order direct that subsection (3) (*c*) above shall apply to warrants of the kind mentioned in section 1 (1) (*a*) of the said Act of 1965 issued while the order is in force, and that subsection (3) (*d*) (ii) above shall apply to criminal proceedings instituted in the Republic of Ireland while the order is in force.

(5) On the revocation of an order made under subsection (4) above—

(*a*) subsection (3) (*c*) above shall cease to apply to any warrant issued while the order was in force; and

(*b*) subsection (3) (*d*) (ii) above shall cease to apply to any criminal proceedings instituted while the order was in force,

but without prejudice to the validity of anything done while the order was in force.

Restrictions on return of criminal under Extradition Act 1870, or to Republic of Ireland, in certain cases

2.—(1) In relation to any requisition for the surrender of a fugitive criminal made as mentioned in section 1 (3) (*a*) above in respect of an offence to which section 1 above applies, the Extradition Act 1870 shall have effect as if at the end of paragraph (1) of section 3 (which prohibits the surrender of a criminal if he proves as there mentioned that the requisition for his surrender has in fact been made with a view to try to punish him for an offence of a political character) there were added the words "or with a view to try or punish him on account of his race, religion, nationality, or political opinions, or that he might, if surrendered, be prejudiced at his trial or punished, detained or restricted in his personal liberty by reason of his race, religion, nationality or political opinions:".

(2) In relation to any warrant issued in the Republic of Ireland which specifies an offence to which section 1 above applies, being a warrant to which paragraph (*c*) of subsection (3) of that section applies as mentioned in that paragraph, the Backing of Warrants (Republic of Ireland) Act 1965 shall have effect as if at the end of section 2 (2), as amended by the Criminal Jurisdiction Act 1975, (cases where warrant from Republic of Ireland is not to be executed) there were added the following words—

"or

(*e*) that there are substantial grounds for believing—

(i) that the warrant was in fact issued in order to secure the return of the person named or described in it to the Republic for the purpose of prosecuting or punishing him on account of his race, religion, nationality or political opinions; or

(ii) that he would, if returned there, be prejudiced at his trial or punished, detained or restricted in his personal liberty by reason of his race, religion, nationality or political opinions.".

Extraditable offences

3.—(1) There shall be deemed to be included in the list of extradition crimes contained in Schedule 1 to the Extradition Act 1870—

 (*a*) any offence under the Explosive Substances Act 1883;

 (*b*) any indictable offence under the Firearms Act 1968; and

 (*c*) any attempt to commit any of the crimes in that list (including crimes added to it after the passing of this Act).

(2) There shall be deemed to be included among the descriptions of offences set out in Schedule 1 to the Fugitive Offenders Act 1967—

 (*a*) any indictable offence under the Offences against the Person Act 1861;

 (*b*) any offence under the Explosive Substances Act 1883; and

 (*c*) any indictable offence under the Firearms Act 1968.

Jurisdiction in respect of offences committed outside United Kingdom

4.—(1) If a person, whether a citizen of the United Kingdom and Colonies or not, does in a convention country any act which, if he had done it in a part of the United Kingdom, would have made him guilty in that part of the United Kingdom of—

 (*a*) an offence mentioned in paragraph 1, 2, 4, 5, 10, 11, 12, 13, 14 or 15 of Schedule 1 to this Act; or

 (*b*) an offence of attempting to commit any offence so mentioned,

he shall, in that part of the United Kingdom, be guilty of the offence or offences aforesaid of which the act would have made him guilty if he had done it there.

(2) If a person, whether a citizen of the United Kingdom and Colonies or not, does in a convention country any act to or in relation to a protected person which, if he had done it in a part of the United Kingdom, would have made him guilty in that part of the United Kingdom of—

 (*a*) an offence mentioned in paragraph 3, 6, 8 or 9 of Schedule 1 to this Act; or

 (*b*) an offence of attempting to commit any offence so mentioned,

he shall, in that part of the United Kingdom, be guilty of the offence or offences aforesaid of which the act would have made him guilty if he had done it there.

For the purposes of this subsection it is immaterial whether a person knows that another person is a protected person.

(3) If a person who is a national of a convention country but not a citizen of the United Kingdom and Colonies does outside the United Kingdom and that convention country any act which makes him in that convention country guilty of an offence and which, if he had been a citizen of the United Kingdom and Colonies, would have made him in any part of the United Kingdom guilty of an offence mentioned in paragraph 1, 2 or 13 of Schedule 1 to this Act, he shall, in any part of the United Kingdom, be guilty of the offence or offences aforesaid of which the act would have made him guilty if he had been such a citizen.

(4) Proceedings for an offence which would not be an offence apart from this section shall not be instituted—

 (*a*) in Northern Ireland, except by or with the consent of the Attorney General for Northern Ireland; or

(b) in England and Wales, except by or with the consent of the Attorney General;

and references to a consent provision in Article 7 (3) to (5) of the Prosecution of Offences (Northern Ireland) Order 1972 (which relates to consents to prosecutions) shall include so much of this subsection as precedes paragraph (b).

(5) Without prejudice to any jurisdiction exercisable apart from this subsection, every sheriff court in Scotland shall have jurisdiction to entertain proceedings for an offence which would not be an offence in Scotland apart from this section.

(6) In this section "a protected person" means, in relation to any such act as is mentioned in subsection (2) above, any of the following, namely—

(a) a person who at the time of the act is a Head of State, a member of a body which performs the functions of Head of State under the constitution of the State, a Head of Government or a Minister for Foreign Affairs and is outside the territory of the State in which he holds office;

(b) a person who at the time of the act is a representative or an official of a State or an official or agent of an international organisation of an intergovernmental character, is entitled under international law to special protection from attack on his person, freedom or dignity and does not fall within the preceding paragraph;

(c) a person who at the time of the act is a member of the family of another person mentioned in either of the preceding paragraphs and—

  (i) if the other person is mentioned in paragraph (a) above, is accompanying him, or

  (ii) if the other person is mentioned in paragraph (b) above, is a member of his household;

and if in any proceedings a question arises as to whether a person is or was a protected person, a certificate issued by or under the authority of the Secretary of State and stating any fact relating to the question shall be conclusive evidence of that fact.

(7) For the purposes of this section any act done—

(a) on board a ship registered in a convetion country, being an act which, if the ship had been registered in the United Kingdom, would have constituted an offence within the jurisdiction of the Admiralty; or

(b) on board an aircraft registered in a convention country while the aircraft is in flight elsewhere than in or over that country; or

(c) on board a hovercraft registered in a convention country while the hovercraft is in journey elsewhere than in or over that country,

shall be treated as done in that convention country; and section 7 (2) of the Tokyo Convention Act 1967 (meaning of "in flight" or, as applied to hovercraft, "in journey") shall apply for the purposes of this sub-section as it applies for the purposes of section 1 of that Act.

Power to apply provisions of Act to non-convention countries

5.—(1) In the case of any country which, not being a convention country, is either—

(a) a designated Commonwealth country within the meaning of the Fugitive Offenders Act 1967; or

(b) a foreign state with which there is in force an arrangement of the kind described in section 2 of the Extradition Act 1870 with respect to the surrender to that state of fugitive criminals; or

(c) a United Kingdom dependency within the meaning of the Fugitive Offenders Act 1967,

the Secretary of State may by order direct—

(i) in the case of a country within paragraph (a) or (b) above, that all or any of the provisions of this Act which would, apart from this section, apply only in relation to convention countries shall apply in relation to that country (subject to such exceptions, if any, as may be specified in the order) as they apply in relation to a convention country; or

(ii) in the case of a country within paragraph (c) above, that the provisions of section 4 above shall so apply in relation to that country;

and while such an order is in force in the case of any country, the provisions in question shall apply in relation to it accordingly.

(2) The Secretary of State may, at any time when the Republic of Ireland is not a convention country, by order direct that section 4 above shall apply in relation to the Republic as if it were a convention country; and while such an order is in force, that section shall apply in relation to the Republic accordingly.

(3) An order under subsection (2) above shall, unless previously revoked, cease to have effect if the Republic of Ireland subsequently becomes a convention country.

Amendment of Criminal Jurisdiction Act 1975, Sch. 3

6.—(1) For paragraph 2 (2) of Schedule 3 to the Criminal Jurisdiction Act 1975 (postponement of operation of order for return to Republic of Ireland of person accused of extra-territorial offence where he is serving a sentence imposed for any other offence) there shall be substituted—

"(2) If at the time when the order under this paragraph is made the accused stands charged with or convicted of an offence other than the extra-territorial offence, so much of the order as directs him to be delivered as aforesaid shall not take effect until the conclusion of the proceedings (including any appeal or retrial) in respect of that other offence and of any sentence of imprisonment or detention imposed in those proceedings.".

(2) This section shall extend to Northern Ireland only.

Extension to Channel Islands, Isle of Man and other countries

7.—(1) Subject to subsection (2) below, this Act shall extend to the Channel Islands and the Isle of Man, and shall have effect as if each of them were part of the United Kingdom.

(2) Her Majesty may by Order in Council direct that this Act shall, in its application to any of the said islands, have effect subject to such exceptions, adaptations or modifications as may be specified in the Order.

(3) Her Majesty may by Order in Council make provision for extending any provisions of this Act, with such exceptions, adaptations or modifications as may be specified in the Order, to any colony, other than a colony for whose external relations a country other than the United Kingdom is responsible, or any country outside Her Majesty's dominions in which Her Majesty has jurisdiction in right of the government of the United Kingdom.

(4) An Order in Council under subsection (3) above shall be subject to annulment in pursuance of a resolution of either House of Parliament.

(5) An Order in Council under subsection (2) or (3) above may be varied or revoked by a subsequent Order in Council under that subsection.

Provisions as to interpretation and orders

8.—(1) In this Act—

"act" includes omission;

"convention country" means a country for the time being designated in an order made by the Secretary of State as a party to the European Convention on the Suppression of Terrorism signed at Strasbourg on the 27th January 1977;

"country" includes any territory;

"enactment" includes an enactment of the Parliament of Northern Ireland, a Measure of the Northern Ireland Assembly, and an Order in Council under the Northern Ireland (Temporary Provisions) Act 1972 or the Northern Ireland Act 1974.

(2) Except so far as the context otherwise requires, any reference in this Act to an enactment is a reference to it as amended by or under any other enactment, including this Act.

(3) For the purpose of construing references in this Act to other Acts, section 38 (1) of the Interpretation Act 1889 shall apply in cases of repeal and re-enactment by a Measure of the Northern Ireland Assembly or by an Order in Council under the Northern Ireland Act 1974 as it applies in cases of repeal and re-enactment by an Act.

(4) Any power to make an order conferred on the Secretary of State by any provision of this Act—

(a) shall be exercisable by statutory instrument; and

(b) shall include power to revoke or vary a previous order made under that provision.

(5) No order shall be made—

(a) under section 1 (4) above at a time when the Republic of Ireland is not a convention country; or

(b) under section 5 above at any time,

unless a draft of the order has been laid before Parliament and approved by a resolution of each House of Parliament.

(6) Any statutory instrument containing an order made under section 1 (4) above at a time when the Republic of Ireland was a convention country or an order made under subsection (1) above shall be laid before Parliament after being made.

Short title, repeals and commencement

9.—(1) This Act may be cited as the Suppression of Terrorism Act 1978.

(2) The enactments specified in Schedule 2 to this Act (which contains provisions superseded by section 3 above) are hereby repealed to the extent specified in the third column of that Schedule.

(3) This Act shall come into force on such day as the Secretary of State may by order appoint, and different days may be so appointed for different purposes.

SCHEDULE 1

List of Offences

Common law offences

1. Murder.
2. Manslaughter or culpable homicide.
3. Rape
4. Kidnapping, abduction or plagium.
5. False imprisonment.
6. Assault occasioning actual bodily harm or causing injury.
7. Wilful fire-raising.

Offences against the person

8. An offence under any of the following provisions of the Offences against the Person Act 1861—
   (a) section 18 (wounding with intent to cause grievous bodily harm);
   (b) section 20 (causing grievous bodily harm);
   (c) section 21 (attempting to choke etc. in order to commit or assist in the committing of any indictable offence);
   (d) section 22 (using chloroform etc. to commit or assist in the committing of any indictable offence);
   (e) section 23 (maliciously administering poison etc. so as to endanger life or inflict grievous bodily harm);
   (f) section 24 (maliciously administering poison etc. with intent to injure etc.);
   (g) section 48 (rape).
9. An offence under section 1 of the Sexual Offences Act 1956 (rape).

Abduction

10. An offence under any of the following provisions of the Offences against the Person Act 1861—
   (a) section 55 (abduction of unmarried girl under 16);
   (b) section 56 (child-stealing or receiving stolen child).
11. An offence under section 20 of the Sexual Offences Act 1956 (abduction of unmarried girl under 16).

Explosives

12. An offence under any of the following provisions of the Offences against the Person Act 1861—
   (a) section 28 (causing bodily injury by gunpowder);
   (b) section 29 (causing gunpowder to explode etc. with intent to do grievous bodily harm);
   (c) section 30 (placing gunpowder near a building etc. with intent to cause bodily injury).

13. An offence under any of the following provisions of the Explosive Substances Act 1883—
(a) section 2 (causing explosion likely to endanger life or property);
(b) section 3 (doing any act with intent to cause such an explosion, conspiring to cause such an explosion, or making or possessing explosive with intent to endanger life or property).

Firearms

14. The following offences under the Firearms Act 1968—
(a) an offence under section 16 (possession of firearm with intent to injure);
(b) an offence under subsection (1) of section 17 (use of firearm or imitation firearm to resist arrest) involving the use or attempted use of a firearm within the meaning of that section.

15. The following offences under the Firearms Act (Northern Ireland) 1969—
(a) an offence under section 14 consisting of a person's having in his possession any firearm or ammunition (within the meaning of that section) with intent by means thereof to endanger life, or to enable another person by means thereof to endanger life;
(b) an offence under subsection (1) of section 15 (use of firearm or imitation firearm to resist arrest) involving the use or attempted use of a firearm within the meaning of that section.

Offences against property

16. An offence under section 1 (2) of the Criminal Damage Act 1971 (destroying or damaging property intending to endanger life or being reckless as to danger to life).

17. An offence under Article 3 (2) of the Criminal Damage (Northern Ireland) Order 1977 (destroying or damaging property intending to endanger life or being reckless as to danger to life).

Offences in relation to aircraft

18. An offence under the Hijacking Act 1971.
19. An offence under Part I of the Protection of Aircraft Act 1973.

Attempts

20. An offence of attempting to commit any offence mentioned in a preceding paragraph of this Schedule.

Question

"There are no political crimes, no political prisoners, no political trials in Britain. Perhaps there ought to be." Discuss.

4. *OFFICIAL SECRECY*

Further Reading

De Smith, pp. 471–473; O'Higgins, pp. 36–40; Chap. 6; Smith & Hogan, pp. 808–812; Street, pp. 221–249; Wade & Phillips, pp. 523–527.

J. Aitken, *Officially Secret* (London, 1971); W. Birtle, "Big Brother Knows Best; The Franks Report and Section 2 of the Official Secrets Act," [1973] *Public Law* pp. 100–122; Barbara de Smith, "The right to information about the activities of the Government," in *Fundamental Rights* (J. W. Bridge, *et al.* ed.) (1973), pp. 137–149; J. Hayward, "The Crossman Diaries," (1975) 5(4) *Index on Censorship* pp. 26–30; J. Michael, "Britain: Secrecy in Government," (1978) 7(1) *Index on Censorship* pp. 9–15; A. Nicol, "Official Secrets and Jury Vetting," (1979) Crim. L.R. pp. 284–291; Outer Circle Policy Unit, *An Official Information Act* (London, 1977); Chapman Pincher, *Inside Story* (Sidgwick & Jackson, 1978); Paul Smith, "Secrecy in Local Government," (1966) 2(2) *Censorship* pp. 18–21; D. G. T. Williams, *Not in the Public Interest* (London, 1965); G. Wilson, *Cases and Materials on Constitutional and Administrative Law* (2nd ed., Cambridge, 1976) pp. 435–472; H. Young, *The Crossman Affair* (Hamish Hamilton/Jonathan Cape, 1976).

See also: *Security Procedures in the Public Service,* Cmnd. 1681 (1962); *Lord Denning's Report,* Cmnd. 2152 (1963); *The "D" Notice System,* Cmnd. 3312 (1967); *Report of the Committee of Privy Counsellors appointed to inquire into 'D' notice matters,* Cmnd. 3309 (1967).

OFFICIAL SECRETS ACTS 1911

1. Penalties for spying

(1) If any person for any purpose prejudicial to the safety or interests of the State—

(a) approaches inspects, passes over or is in the neighbourhood of, or enters any prohibited place within the meaning of this Act; or

(b) makes any sketch, plan, model, or note which is calculated to be or might be or is intended to be directly or indirectly useful to an enemy; or

(c) obtains, collects, records, or publishes, or communicates to any other person any secret official code word, or pass word, or any sketch, plan, model, article, or note, or other document or information which is calculated to be or might be or is intended to be directly or indirectly useful to an enemy;

he shall be guilty of felony . . .

(2) On a prosecution under this section, it shall not be necessary to show that the accused person was guilty of any particular act tending to show a purpose prejudicial to the safety or interests of the State, and, notwithstanding that no such act is proved against him, he may be convicted if, from the circumstances of the case, or his conduct, or his known character as proved, it appears that his purpose was a purpose prejudicial to the safety or interests of the State; and if any sketch, plan, model, article, note, document, or information relating to or used in any prohibited place within the meaning of this Act, or anything in such a place or any secret official code word or pass word, is made, obtained, collected, recorded, published, or communicated by any person other than a person acting under lawful authority, it shall be deemed

to have been made, obtained, collected, recorded, published or communicated for a purpose prejudicial to the safety or interests of the State unless the contrary is proved.

2. Wrongful communication, etc., of information

(1) If any person having in his possession or control any secret official code word, or pass word, or any sketch, plan, model, article, note, document, or information which relates to or is used in a prohibited place or anything in such a place, or which has been made or obtained in contravention of this Act, or which has been entrusted in confidence to him by any person holding office under His Majesty or which he has obtained or to which he has had access owing to his position as a person who holds or has held office under His Majesty, or as a person who is or has been employed under a person who holds or has held such an office or contract,—

    (a) communicates the code word, pass word, sketch, plan, model, article, note, document, or information to any person, other than a person to whom he is authorised to communicate it, or a person to whom it is in the interest of the State his duty to communicate it, or,

    (aa) Uses the information in his possession for the benefit of any foreign power or in any other manner prejudicial to the safety or interests of the State;

    (b) retains the sketch, plan, model, article, note, or document in his possession or control when he has no right to retain it or when it is contrary to his duty to retain it or fails to comply with all directions issued by lawful authority with regard to the return or disposal thereof or

    (c) fails to take reasonable care of, or so conducts himself as to endanger the safety of the sketch, plan, model, article, note, document, secret official code or pass word or information:

that person shall be guilty of a misdemeanour.

(1A) If any person having in his possession or control any sketch, plan, model, article, note, document, or information which relates to munitions of war, communicates it directly or indirectly to any foreign power, or in any other manner prejudicial to the safety or interests of the State, that person shall be guilty of a misdemeanour;

(2) If any person receives any secret official code word, or pass word, or sketch, plan, model, article, note, document, or information, knowing, or having reasonable ground to believe, at the time when he receives it, that the code word, pass word, sketch, plan, model, article, note, document, or information is communicated to him in contravention of this Act, he shall be guilty of a misdemeanour, unless he proves that the communication to him of the code word, pass word, sketch, plan, model, article, note, document, or information was contrary to his desire.

3. Definition of prohibited place

For the purpose of this Act, the expression "prohibited place" means—

    (a) Any work of defence, arsenal, naval or air force establishment or station, factory, dockyard, mine, minefield, camp, ship, or aircraft belonging to or occupied by or on behalf of His Majesty, or any telegraph, telephone, wireless or signal station, or office so belonging or occupied, and any place belonging to or occupied by or on behalf of

His Majesty and used for the purpose of building, repairing, making, or storing any munitions of war, or any sketches, plans, models, or documents relating thereto, or for the purpose of getting any metals, oil, or minerals of use in time of war; and

(b) any place not belonging to His Majesty where any munitions of war, or any [sketches, models, plans] or documents relating thereto, are being made, repaired, gotten or stored under contract with, or with any person on behalf of, His Majesty, or otherwise on behalf of His Majesty; and

(c) any place belonging to or used for the purpose of His Majesty which is for the time being declared [by order of a Secretary of State] to be a prohibited place for the purposes of this section on the ground that information with respect thereto, or damage thereto, would be useful to an enemy; and

(d) any railway, road, way, or channel, or other means of communication by land or water (including any works or structures being part thereof or connected therewith), or any place used for gas, water, or electricity works or other works for purposes of a public character, or any place where any munitions of war, or any sketches, models, plans or documents relating thereto, are being made, repaired, or stored otherwise than on behalf of His Majesty, which is for the time being declared by order of a Secretary of State to be a prohibited place for the purposes of this section, on the ground that information with respect thereto, or the destruction or obstruction thereof, or interference therewith, would be useful to any enemy.

6. Power to arrest

Any person who is found committing an offence under this Act . . . or who is reasonably suspected of having committed, or having attempted to commit, or being about to commit, such an offence, may be apprehended and detained . . .

7. Penalty for harbouring spies

If any person knowingly harbours any person whom he knows, or has reasonable grounds for supposing, to be a person who is about to commit or who has committed an offence under this Act, or knowlingly permits to meet or assemble in any premises in his occupation or under his control any such persons, or if any person having harboured any such person, or permitted to meet or assemble in any premises in his occupation or under his control any such persons, wilfully omits or refuses to disclose to a superintendent of police any information which it is in his power to give in relation to any such person he shall be guilty of a misdemeanour . . .

8. Restriction on prosecution

A prosecution for an offence under this Act shall not be instituted except by or with the consent of the Attorney-General:

Provided that a person charged with such an offence may be arrested, or a warrant for his arrest may be issued and executed, and any such person may be remanded in custody or on bail, notwithstanding that the consent of the Attorney-General to the institution of a prosecution for the offence has not been obtained, but no further or other proceedings shall be taken until that consent has been obtained.

9. Search warrants

(1) If a justice of the peace is satisfied by information on oath that there is reasonable ground for suspecting that an offence under this Act has been or is about to be committed, he may grant a search warrant authorising any constable named therein to enter at any time any premises or place named in the warrant, if necessary, by force, and to search the premises or place and every person found therein, and to seize any sketch, plan, model, article, note, or document, or anything of a like nature or anything which is evidence of an offence under this Act having been or being about to be committed, which he may find on the premises or place or on any such person, and with regard to or in connexion with which he has reasonable ground for suspecting that an offence under this Act has been or is about to be committed.

(2) Where it appears to a superintendent of police that the case is one of great emergency and that in the interest of the State immediate action is necessary, he may be a written order under his hand give to any constable the like authority as may be given by the warrant of a justice under this section.

OFFICIAL SECRETS ACT 1920

4. Power to require the production of telegrams

(1) Where it appears to a Secretary of State that such a course is expedient in the public interest, he may by warrant under his hand, require any person who owns or controls any telegraphic cable or wire, or any apparatus for wireless telegraphy, used for the sending or receipt of telegrams to or from any place out of the United Kingdom, to produce to him, or to any person named in the warrant, the originals and transcripts, either of all telegrams, or of telegrams of any specified class or description, or of telegrams sent from or addressed to any specified person or place, sent or received to or from any place out of the United Kingdom by means of any such cable, wire, or apparatus, and all other papers relating to any such telegram as aforesaid.

(2) Any person who, on being required to produce any such original or transcript or paper as aforesaid, refuses or neglects to do so shall be guilty of an offence under this Act and shall, for each offence, be liable on conviction under the Summary Jurisdiction Acts to imprisonment with or without hard labour for a term not exceeding three months, or to a fine not exceeding fifty pounds, or to both such imprisonment and fine.

(3) In this section the expression "telegram" shall have the same meaning as in the Telegraph Act, 1869, and the expression "wireless telegraphy" shall have the same meaning as in the Wireless Telegraphy Act, 1904.

6. (1) Where a chief officer of police is satisfied that there is reasonable ground for suspecting that an offence under section one of the principal Act has been committed and for believing that any person is able to furnish information as to the offence or suspected offence, he may apply to a Secretary of State for permission to exercise the powers conferred by this subsection and, if such permission is granted, he may authorise a superintendent of police, or any police officer not below the rank of inspector, to require the person believed to be able to furnish information to give any information in his power relating to the offence or suspected offence, and, if so required and on tender of his reasonable expenses, to attend at such reasonable time and place as may be specified by the superintendent or other officer; and if a person required in pursuance of such an authorisation to give information, or to attend as aforesaid, fails to comply with any such requirement or knowingly gives false information, he shall be guilty of a misdemeanour.

(2) Where a chief officer of police has reasonable grounds to believe that the case is one of great emergency and that in the interest of the State immediate action is necessary, he may exercise the powers conferred by the last foregoing subsection without applying for or being granted the permission of a Secretary of State, but if he does so shall forthwith report the circumstances to the Secretary of State.

(3) References in this section to a chief officer of police shall be construed as including references to any other officer of police expressly authorised by a chief officer of police to act on his behalf for the purposes of this section when by reason of illness, absence, or other cause he is unable to do so.

Reform of the Official Secrets Act, s. 2

The General Effect of Our Proposals

275 Our main conclusion is that the present law is unsatisfactory, and that it should be changed so that criminal sanctions are retained only to protect what is of real importance.

276 Section 2 of the Official Secrets Act 1911 should be repealed, and replaced by a new statute, called the Official Information Act, which should apply only to official information which—

a. is classified information relating to defence or internal security, or to foreign relations, or to the currency or to the reserves, the unauthorised disclosure of which would cause serious injury to the interests of the nation; *or*

b. is likely to assist criminal activities or to impede law enforcement; *or*

c. is a Cabinet document; *or*

d. has been entrusted to the Government by a private individual or concern.

The Act should contain safeguards relating to the classification of information of the kinds mentioned in a. above.

277 It should be an offence under the Official Information Act—

a. for a Crown servant to communicate information to which the Act applies, contrary to his official duty;

b. for a Government contractor or a person entrusted with official information in confidence to communicate information of one of the kinds in paragraph 276 a., b. and c., otherwise than for the purposes of the contract or for which it was entrusted;

c. for any person to communicate information of one of the kinds in paragraph 276 a., b. and c., which he knows, or has reasonable ground to believe, has reached him as the result of a contravention of the Official Information Act;

d. to communicate or use official information of any kind for purposes of private gain.

Prosecutions should require the consent of the Attorney General in the case of information of the kinds mentioned in paragraph 276 a., c. and d., and of the Director of Public Prosecutions in the case of b. and of private gain.

[*Departmental Committee on Section 2 of the Official Secrets Act 1911*, Chairman: Lord Franks, Vol. 1: Report of the Committee, Cmnd. 5104, 1972.]

Note: See also *Reform of section 2 of the Official Secrets Act 1911*, Cmnd. 7285, 1978.

Questions

1. "The Franks Committee's inquiry was of curiously limited scope; its recommendations, even if fully implemented, will make little difference." Discuss.

2. "What is needed is not a reform of the Official Secrets Act but rather its repeal and the enactment of a statute conferring a legal right on members of the public to have access to information concerning the activities of governmental and other public bodies." Discuss.

3. Is the broad range of offences created by the Official Secrets Act 1911 compatible with the United Kingdom's obligations under the European Convention on Human Rights?

Further Reading

De Smith, Chaps. 17 and 20; Street, Chap. 1; Wade & Phillips, pp. 442–455.

Carol Ackroyd, K. Margolis, J. Rosenhead, T. Shalice, *The Technology of Political Control* (Penguin, 1977); I. Brownlie, *The Law Relating to Public Order* (Butterworth, 1968), Chaps. 2 and 3; Tony Bunyan, *The History and Practice of the Political Police in Britain* (revised ed., J. Friedmann, 1977); Barry Cox, J. Shirley, M. Short, *The Fall of Scotland Yard* (Penguin 1977); T. C. Daintith, "Disobeying a Policeman: A Fresh Look at *Duncan* v. *Jones*," (1966) *Public Law* p. 248; Hilary Draper, *Private Police* (Penguin, 1978); A. L. Goodhart, "*Thomas* v. *Sawkins*: A Constitutional Innovation," (1936) 6 *Cambridge Law Journal* pp. 23–30; L. Grant, *et al., Civil Liberty: The NCCL Guide to your Rights* (Penguin, 1978), Chap. 1; P. Hain (ed.), *Policing the Police* (J. Calder, 1979); L. H. Leigh, *Police Powers in England and Wales* (Butterworth, 1975); R. Mark, *Policing a Perplexed Society* (Allen & Unwin, 1977); *ibid. In the Office of Constable* (Collins, 1978); G. Marshall, *Police and Government* (Methuen, 1965); C. Price and J. Caplan, *The Confait Confession* (Boyars, 1977); Geoffrey Robertson, *Reluctant Judas: The Life and Death of the Special Branch Informer Kenneth Lennon* (M. T. Smith, 1976); E. C. S. Wade, "Police Search," (1934) 50 *Law Quarterly Review* pp. 354–367; D. G. T. Williams, *Keeping the Peace: The Police and Public Order* (Hutchinson, 1967); G. Wilson, *Cases and Materials on Constitutional and Administrative Law* (2nd ed., C.U.P., 1976), Chap. XIII.

THE JUDGES' RULES

From Home Office Circular No. 89/1978.

Appendix A

RULES

I. When a police officer is trying to discover whether, or by whom, an offence has been committed he is entitled to question any person, whether suspected or not, from whom he thinks that useful information may be obtained. This is so whether or not the person in question has been taken into custody so long as he has not been charged with the offence or informed that he may be prosecuted for it.

II. As soon as a police officer has evidence which would afford reasonable grounds for suspecting that a person has committed an offence, he shall caution that person or cause him to be cautioned before putting to him any questions, or further questions, relating to that offence.

The caution shall be in the following terms:—

> "You are not obliged to say anything unless you wish to do so but what you say may be put into writing and given in evidence:"

When after being cautioned a person is being questioned, or elects to make a statement, a record shall be kept of the time and place at which any such questioning or statement began and ended and of the persons present.

III. (a) Where a person is charged with or informed that he may be prosecuted for an offence he shall be cautioned in the following terms:—

> "Do you wish to say anything? You are not obliged to say anything unless you wish to do so but whatever you say will be taken down in writing and may be given in evidence."

(b) It is only in exceptional cases that questions relating to the offence should be put to the accused person after he has been charged or informed that he may be prosecuted. Such questions may be put where they are necessary for the purpose of preventing or minimising harm or loss to some other person or to the public or for clearing up an ambiguity in a previous answer or statement.

Before any such questions are put the accused should be cautioned in these terms:—

> "I wish to put some questions to you about the offence with which you have been charged (or about the offence for which you may be prosecuted). You are not obliged to answer any of these questions, but if you do the questions and answers will be taken down in writing and may be given in evidence."

Any questions put and answers given relating to the offence must be contemporaneously recorded in full and the record signed by that person or if he refuses by the interrogating officer.

(c) When such a person is being questioned, or elects to make a statement, a record shall be kept of the time and place at which any questioning or statement began and ended and of the persons present.

IV. All written statements made after caution shall be taken in the following manner:—

(a) If a person says that he wants to make a statement he shall be told that it is intended to make a written record of what he said. He shall always be asked whether he wishes to write down himself what he wants to say; if he says that he cannot write or that would like someone to write it for him, a police officer shall, before starting, ask the person making the statement to sign, or make his mark to, the following:—

> "I, ... , wish to make a statement. I want someone to write down what I say. I have been told that I need not say anything unless I wish to do so and that whatever I say may be given in evidence."

(b) Any person writing his own statement shall be allowed to do so without any prompting as distinct from indicating to him what matters are material.

(c) The person making the statement, if he is going to write it himself, shall be asked to write out and sign before writing what he wants to say, the following:—

> "I make this statement of my own free will. I have been told that I need not say anything unless I wish to do so and that whatever I say may be given in evidence."

(d) Whenever a police officer writes the statement, he shall take down the exact words spoken by the person making the statement, without putting any questions other than such as may be needed to make the statement coherent, intelligible and relevant to the material matters; he shall not prompt him.

(e) When the writing of a statement by a police officer is finished the person making it shall be asked to read it and to make any corrections, alterations or additions he wishes. When he has finished reading it he shall be asked to write and sign or make his mark on the following Certificate at the end of the statement:—

> "I have read the above statement and I have been told that I can correct, alter or add anything I wish. This statement is true. I have made it of my own free will."

(f) If the person who has made a statement refuses to read it or to write the above mentioned Certificate at the end of it or to sign it, the senior police officer present shall record on the statement itself and in the presence of the person making it, what has happened. If the person making the statement cannot read, or refuses to read it, the officer who has taken it down shall read it over to him and ask him whether he would like to correct, alter or add anything and to put his signature or make his mark at the end. The police officer shall then certify on the statement itself what he has done.

V. If at any time after a person has been charged with, or has been informed that he may be prosecuted for an offence a police officer wishes to bring to the notice of that person any written statement made by another person who in respect of the same offence has also been charged or informed that he may be prosecuted, he shall hand to that person a true copy of such written statement, but nothing shall be said or done to invite any reply or comment. If that person says that he would like to make a statement in reply, or starts to say something, he shall at once be cautioned or further cautioned as prescribed by Rule III(a).

VI. Persons other than police officers charged with the duty of investigating offences or charging offenders shall, so far as may be practicable, comply with these Rules.

Appendix B

ADMINISTRATIVE DIRECTIONS ON INTERROGATION AND THE TAKING OF STATEMENTS

1. *procedure generally*

(a) When possible statements of persons under caution should be written on the forms provided for the purpose. Police officers' notebooks should be used for taking statements only when no forms are available.

(b) When a person is being questioned or elects to make a statement, a record should be kept of the time or times at which during the questioning or making of a statement there were intervals or refreshment was taken. The nature of the refreshment should be noted. In no circumstances should alcoholic drink be given.

(c) In writing down a statement, the words used should not be translated into "official" vocabulary; this may give a misleading impression of the genuineness of the statement.

(d) Care should be taken to avoid any suggestion that the person's answers can only be used in evidence against him, as this may prevent an innocent person making a statement which might help clear him of the charge.

2. Record of interrogation

Rule II and Rule III(c) demand that a record should be kept of the following matters:—

(a) when, after being cautioned in accordance with Rule II, the person is being questioned or elects to make a statement—of the time and place at which any such questioning began and ended and of the persons present;

(b) when, after being cautioned in accordance with Rule III(a) or (b) a person is being questioned or elects to make a statement—of the time and place at which any questioning and statement began and ended and of the persons present.

In addition to the records required by these Rules full records of the following matters should additionally be kept:—

(a) of the time or times at which cautions were taken, and

(b) of the time when a charge was made and/or the person was arrested, and

(c) of the matters referred to in paragraph 1(b) above.

If two or more police officers are present when the questions are being put or the statement made, the records made should be countersigned by the other officers present.

3. Comfort and refreshment

Reasonable arrangements should be made for the comfort and refreshment of persons being questioned. Whenever practicable both the person being questioned or making a statement and the officers asking the questions or taking the statement should be seated.

4. Interrogation of children and young persons

As far as practicable children and young persons under the age of 17 years (whether suspected of crime or not) should only be interviewed in the presence of a parent or guardian, or in their absence, some person who is not a police officer and is of the same sex as the child. A child or young person should not be arrested, nor even interviewed, at school if such action can possibly be avoided. Where it is found essential to conduct the interview at school, this should be done only with the consent, and in the presence, of the head teacher, or his nominee.

4A. *Interrogation of mentally handicapped persons*

(a) If it appears to a police officer that a person (whether a witness or a suspect) whom he intends to interview has a mental handicap which raises a doubt as to whether the person can understand the questions put to him, or which makes the person likely to be especially open to suggestion, the officer should take particular care in putting questions and accepting the reliability of answers. As far as practicable, and where recognised as such by the police, a mentally handicapped adult (whether suspected of crime or not) should be interviewed only in the presence of a parent or other person in whose care, custody or control he is, or of some person who is not a police officer (for example a social worker).

(b) So far as mentally handicapped children and young persons are concerned, the conditions of interview and arrest by the police are governed by Administrative Direction 4 above.

(c) Any document arising from an interview with a mentally handicapped person of any age should be signed not only by the person who made the statement, but also by the parent or other person who was present during the interview. Since the reliability of any admission by a mentally handicapped person may even then be challenged, care will still be necessary to verify the facts admitted and to obtain corroboration where possible.

5. *Statements in languages other than English*

In the case of a person making a statement in a language other than English:

(a) The interpreter should take down the statement in the language in which it is made.

(b) An official English translation should be made in due course and be proved as an exhibit with the original statement.

(c) The person making the statement should sign that at (a).

Apart from the question of apparent unfairness, to obtain the signature of a suspect to an English translation of what he said in another language can have little or no value as evidence if the suspect disputes the accuracy of this record of his statement.

6. *Supply to accused persons of written statement of charges*

(a) The following procedure should be adopted whenever a charge is preferred against a person arrested without warrant for any offence:—

As soon as a charge has been accepted by the appropriate police officer the accused person should be given a written notice containing a copy of the entry in the charge sheet or book giving particulars of the offence with which he is charged. So far as possible the particulars of the charge should be stated in simple language so that the accused person may understand it, but they should also show clearly the precise offence in law with which he is charged. Where the offence charged is a statutory one, it should be sufficient for the latter purpose to quote the section of the statute which created the offence.

The written notice should include some statement on the lines of the caution given orally to the accused person in accordance with the

Judges' Rules after a charge has been preferred. It is suggested that the form of notice should begin with the following words:—

"You are charged with the offence(s) shown below. You are not obliged to say anything unless you wish to do so, but whatever you say will be taken down in writing and may be given in evidence."

(b) Once the accused person has appeared before the court it is not necessary to serve him with a written notice of any further charges which may be preferred. If, however, the police decide, before he has appeared before a court, to modify the charge or to prefer further charges, it is desirable that the person concerned should be formally charged with the further offence and given a written copy of the charge as soon as it is possible to do so having regard to the particular circumstances of the case. If the accused person has then been released on bail, it may not always be practicable or reasonable to prefer the new charge at once, and in cases where he is due to surrender to his bail within forty-eight hours or in other cases of difficulty it will be sufficient for him to be formally charged with the further offence and served with a written notice of the charge after he has surrendered to his bail and before he appears before the court.

7. *Facilities for defence*

(a) A person in custody should be supplied on request with writing materials.

Provided that no hindrance is reasonably likely to be caused to the processes of investigation or the administration of justice:

(i) he should be allowed to speak on the telephone to his solicitor or to his friends;

(ii) his letters should be sent by post or otherwise with the least possible delay;

(iii) telegrams should be sent at once, at his own expense.

(b) Persons in custody should not only be informed orally of the rights and facilities available to them, but in addition notices describing them should be displayed at convenient and conspicuous places at police stations and the attention of persons in custody should be drawn to these notices.

Appendix C

POLICE INQUIRIES INVOLVING DEAF PERSONS

When, in the course of police inquiries, it becomes necessary to ask questions of a deaf person, there is sometimes difficulty in arranging for the proceedings to be interpreted with sufficient clarity, especially when such persons have no useful hearing and can only communicate manually by means of finger-spelling and signing. In these circumstances the services of competent interpreters for the deaf may be required. It has been agreed with the Association of Directors of Social Services and the Royal National Institute for the Deaf that Directors of Social Services will, on request, designate points of contact (which may, depending on local circumstances, be an office of the local authority or of a voluntary organisation) through which arrangements for securing the services of interpreters can be made. Chief officers of police are therefore requested to get in touch with Directors of Social Services locally so that arrangements for designating a point of contact can be made.

In cases of difficulty The Royal National Institute for the Deaf, 105 Gower Street, London WC1E 6AH (telephone number 01-387 8033) will be glad to advise.

[*Judges' Rules and Administrative Directions to the Police,* H.M.S.O., 1978.]

SOME POLICE PRACTICES

120. . . . it has long been the practice of the Police to search the dwelling of a person for whose arrest a warrant has been issued, and, in cases of arrest without warrant, to search premises as well as the arrested person in cases of serious crime where it appears that material evidence is likely to be obtained.

We are informed that there is no specific statutory sanction for this practice, although the view was expressed by the representatives of the Home Office that it had, by long use, become part of the common law. Various decided cases have been brought to our notice but we find it difficult to deduce from them any very definite conclusion. On the other hand, whilst the Courts have recognised the practice, and cases can be cited in which the action of the Police has been upheld, actions against the Police for trespass have sometimes been successful. For instance, our attention has been drawn to a case in which damages of £100 were awarded (in 1926) against a Policeman in Liverpool who had searched the premises of a person arrested on a charge of warehouse-breaking.

121. We are satisfied that the existing practice of the Police as to the search of premises is, in the main, necessary and proper in the interests of justice and cannot be regarded as in any way an undue infringement of the rights and liberties of the subject. It is, however, a matter of some concern to us that the Police, in the discharge of their essential duties, should have to rely upon powers of which the legality seems doubtful or obscure. As a matter of principle, the Police should never exceed their legal powers and consequently the powers necessary to enable them to investigate crimes and offences should be clearly defined and should rest upon unimpeachable authority.

We therefore recommend that the practice of the Police as regards the search of premises should be regularised by a statute authorising them to search without a warrant the premises of persons who have been arrested.

Arrest on a Minor Charge, pending Inquiries into a Major Crime.

159. Our attention has been directed to the fact that in cases of serious crime the suspected culprit is sometimes arrested on a minor charge, on which the Court is asked to remand him, whilst (though this may not be admitted) the case against him in connection with the major crime is being followed up. This practice is recognised by the Metropolitan Police, who regard themselves as free to question the man on the major crime, after his arrest on the minor charge, under Nos. (1) and (3) of the Judges' Rules. The main object of this procedure, if deliberately employed, is, no doubt, to keep the suspect safely under lock and key during the investigation into the major crime. The Director of Public Prosecutions in oral evidence gave it as his view that "from the point of view of the public it is a first-rate procedure."

160. We think that any deliberate recourse to this practice, which contains elements of subterfuge, is on principle to be deprecated. There is a special risk of unfairness when the minor charge on which the man is arrested is itself of an undefined character, such as "loitering with intent to commit a felony." . . .

Facilities to be Afforded to Persons in Custody.

178. We are in complete agreement with the views expressed by the late Right Hon. J. F. P. Rawlinson, K.C., in his Report* on the case of Major Sheppard, with regard to the facilities which ought to be afforded at once to all persons in custody. In particular they ought, immediately on arrival at the Police station, to be allowed to consult their legal advisers, and also their friends unless there is strong reason to anticipate improper disclosures to confederates.

[*Report of the Royal Commission on Police Powers and Procedure,* Cmd. 3297, 1929.]

MAGISTRATES' COURTS ACT 1952

91. Binding over to keep the peace or be of good behaviour

(1) The power of a magistrates' court on the complaint of any person to adjudge any other person to enter into a recognizance, with or without sureties, to keep the peace or to be of good behaviour towards the complainant shall be exercised by order on complaint.

(2) Where a complaint is made under this section, the power of the court to remand the defendant under subsection (5) of section forty-seven of this Act shall not be subject to the restrictions imposed by subsection (6) of that section.

(3) If any person ordered by a magistrates' court under subsection (1) of this section to enter into a recognizance, with or without sureties, to keep the peace or to be of good behaviour fails to comply with the order, the court may commit him to custody for a period not exceeding six months or until he sooner complies with the order.

POLICE ACT 1964

51. Assaults on constables

(3) Any person who resists or wilfully obstructs a constable in the execution of his duty, or a person assisting a constable in the execution of his duty shall be guilty of an offence and liable on summary conviction to imprisonment for a term not exceeding one month or to a fine not exceeding £20, or to both.

THE CRIMINAL LAW ACT 1967

2. Arrest without warrant

(1) The powers of summary arrest conferred by the following subsections shall apply to offences for which the sentence is fixed by law or for which a

*Cmd. 2497, 1925.

person (not previously convicted) may under or by virtue of any enactment be sentenced to imprisonment for a term of five years, and to attempts to commit any such offence; and in this Act, including any amendment made by this Act in any other enactment, "arrestable offences" means any such offence or attempt.

(2) Any person may arrest without warrant anyone who is, or whom he, with reasonable cause, suspects to be, in the act of committing an arrestable offence.

(3) Where an arrestable offence has been committed, any person may arrest without warrant anyone who is, or whom he, with reasonable cause, suspects to be, guilty of the offence.

(4) Where a constable, with reasonable cause, suspects that an arrestable offence has been committed, he may arrest without warrant anyone whom he, with reasonable cause, suspects to be guilty of the offence.

(5) A constable may arrest without warrant any person who is, or whom he, with reasonable cause, suspects to be, about to commit an arrestable offence.

(6) For the purpose of arresting a person under any power conferred by this section a constable may enter (if need be, by force) and search any place where that person is or where the constable, with reasonable cause, suspects him to be.

The Firearms Act 1968

Part III

Law Enforcement and Punishment of Offences

46. Power of search with warrant

(1) If a justice of the peace or, in Scotland, the sheriff or any magistrate (by whatever named called) officiating under the provisions of a general or local Police Act, is satisfied by information on oath that there is reasonable ground for suspecting that an offence relevant for the purposes of this section has been, is being, or is about to be committed, he may grant a search warrant authorising a constable named therein—

    (*a*) to enter at any time any premises or place named in the warrant, if necessary by force, and to search the premises or place and every person found there;

    (*b*) to seize and detain any firearm or ammunition which he may find on the premises or place, or on any such person, in respect of which or in connection with which he has reasonable ground for suspecting that an offence relevant for the purposes of this section has been, is being or is about to be committed; and

    (*c*) if the premises are those of a registered firearms dealer, to examine any books relating to the business.

(2) The offences relevant for the purposes of this section are all offences under this Act except an offence under section 22 (3) or an offence relating specifically to air weapons.

47. Powers of constables to stop and search

(1) A constable may require any person whom he has reasonable cause to suspect—

(a) of having a firearm, with or without ammunition, with him in a public place; or

(b) to be committing or about to commit, elsewhere than in a public place, an offence relevant for the purposes of this section.

to hand over the firearm or any ammunition for examination by the constable.

(2) It is an offence for a person having a firearm or ammunition with him to fail to hand it over when required to do so by a constable under subsection (1) of this section.

(3) If a constable has reasonable cause to suspect a person of having a firearm with him in a public place, or to be committing or about to commit, elsewhere than in a public place, an offence relevant for the purposes of this section, the constable may search that person and may detain him for the purpose of doing so.

(4) If a constable has reasonable cause to suspect that there is a firearm in a vehicle in a public place, or that a vehicle is being or is about to be used in connection with the commission of an offence relevant for the purposes of this section elsewhere than in a public place, he may search the vehicle and for that purpose require the person driving or in control of it to stop it.

(5) For the purpose of exercising the powers conferred by this section a constable may enter any place.

(6) The offences relevant for the purpose of this section are those under sections 18 (1) and (2) and 20 of this Act.

Garfinkel and Others v. Metropolitan Police Commissioner [1972] Crim. L.R. 44

Queen's Bench Vacation Court

On the authority of a search warrant granted under the Explosive Substances Acts 1875 and 1883, police officers searched premises occupied by one of the plaintiffs. No substances to which the warrant related were found, but the officers did find and remove a large number of leaflets, etc., of which the plaintiffs claimed to be in possession. The plaintiffs sought an interim injunction for the return of the documents.

Held, dismissing the application, that where police officers found goods showing a person to be implicated in some crime other than that to which their warrant was directed, they could remove them provided they acted reasonably and detained them no longer than necessary. The defendant contended that the documents had been seized as evidence of a criminal act, *e.g.* conspiracy to pervert the course of justice, and submitted to the Director of Public Prosecutions to consider the institution of proceedings. There was material which merited that consideration and, accordingly, the defendant was acting reasonably and detaining the documents no longer than necessary.

Elias and Others v. Pasmore and Others [1934] 2 K.B. 164

King's Bench Division

The defendants, policemen, armed with a warrant for the arrest of one Hannington, National Organiser of the National Unemployed Workers'

Movement, entered the headquarters of the Movement, the plaintiffs' premises. While on the premises they siezed and took away (a) documents which were subsequently used in the trial of Elias (referred to in the judgment below as bundle "2 (A)"); (b) a document found on Hannington and subsequently used at his trial, and (c) other documents which were not subsequently used in any legal proceedings. Subsequently the documents were returned with the exception of bundle "2(A)". The plaintiffs claimed damages for trespass to the premises and the return of the documents in bundle "2 (A)" and damages for their detention.

HORRIDGE J.: . . .

It was not contended before me that there was any general right of search or seizure, but it was submitted that in certain circumstances there was a right to seize and detain documents; but this contention, if correct, did not in any way justify the seizure and removal of the documents and goods which have already been returned, and I will deal later on in my judgment with the remedy which the plaintiffs have in respect of such seizure and removal.

The propositions put forward with regard to the removal of the remaining documents in bundle 2 (A) were: (1) that there was a right to search the person arrested; (2) that the police may take all articles which were in the possession or control of the person arrested and which may be or are material on a charge against him or any other person; (3) that the police, having lawfully entered, are protected if they take documents which subsequently turn out to be relevant on a charge of a criminal nature against any person whatever; (4) that the police are entitled to retain property taken until the conclusion of any charge on which the articles are material.

In dealing with these different propositions, I only propose to deal with the authorities which seem to me to be the most relevant to this enquiry, although others have been cited to me. (1): As to the right to search on arrest. This right seems to be clearly established by the footnote to *Bessell* v. *Wilson*[1] in the report in the *Law Times*, where Lord Campbell clearly lays down that this right exists, but this right does not seem to me to authorize what was done in this case, namely, to seize and take away large quantities of documents and other property found on premises occupied by persons other than the person of whom the arrest was made.

As to the second contention, I think the case of *Dillon* v. *O'Brien*[2] clearly lays down that constables are entitled upon a lawful arrest by them of a person charged to take and detain property found in his possession which will form material evidence on his prosecution for that crime, and I think, for the reasons hereinafter stated with regard to the third contention, that that would include property which would form material evidence on the prosecution of any criminal charge. This, however, would not justify the seizure of the documents in this case with the exception of the letter signed 'P.C.', a copy of which was found on Hannington, and which is in the bundle 2 (A).

In support of the third contention, the Attorney-General relied on the case of *Pringle* v. *Bremner and Stirling*[3] . . .

[1] 20 L.T.(O.S.) 233; 1 E. & B. 489; E.R. 518.
[2] 20 L.R.Ir. 300, 316.
[3] 5 M.(H.L.) 55.

That case seems to me to show that in the opinion of the Lord Chancellor and Lord Colonsay, though the seizure of documents was originally wrongful, if it in fact turned out that the documents seized were documents which might be properly used in a prosecution against any one, then the seizure would become excused. This, however, is a Scotch case, and must not be taken to have been decided on the law of England, and it becomes necessary therefore to consider whether in principle the same doctrine can be applied to a seizure of documents in England. There was no direct authority cited to me in support of the proposition in English law.

In examining the case of *Dillon* v. *O'Brien* (1) and the judgment of Palles C.B., it seems to me that the principle on which he held that there was a right to detain property in the possession of the person arrested is that the interest of the State in the person charged being brought to trial in due course necessarily extends as well to the preservation of material evidence of his guilt or innocence as to his custody for the purpose of trial, and in dealing with the case of *Entick* v. *Carrington* (2) he says (3): "The question there was as to the legality of a warrant, not only to seize and apprehend the plaintiff and bring him before a Secretary of State, but also to seize his books and papers. In that case there was no allegation of the plaintiff's guilt, nor that there was reasonable and probable cause for believing him to be guilty, not that a crime had, in fact, been committed by any one, nor that he had in his possession anything that was evidence of (or that there were reasonable grounds for believing might be evidence of) a crime committed by him or any one else."

In the case of *Crozier* v. *Cundey* (4), where a constable having a warrant to search for certain specific goods alleged to have been stolen found and took away these goods and certain others also supposed to have been stolen but which were not mentioned in the warrant and which were not likely to be of use in substantiating the charge of stealing the goods mentioned in the warrant, it was held that the constable was liable to an action of trespass. Abbott C.J. says (5): "If those others had been likely to furnish evidence of the identity of the articles stolen and mentioned in the warrant, there might have been reasonable ground for seizing them, although not specified in the warrant." He also said: "I have expressed myself in this manner in order to prevent the supposition, that a constable seizing articles not mentioned in the warrant under which he acts, is necessarily a trespasser." It therefore seems to me that the interests of the State must excuse the seizure of documents, which seizure would otherwise be unlawful, if it appears in fact that such documents were evidence of a crime committed by any one, and that so far as the documents in this case fall into this category, the seizure of them is excused.

The documents coming within this description were all the documents contained in bundle 2 (A) which were marked as exhibits and which were used at the trial of Elias. It was admitted by counsel for the plaintiffs that these documents were capable of being evidence in the case against Elias, who was convicted of unlawfully soliciting and inciting Emrys Glunf Llewellyn and Walter Hannington to commit the crime of sedition. In my opinion the seizure of these exhibits was justified, because they were capable of being and were used as evidence in this trial. If I am right in the above view, the original

(1) 20 L. R. Ir. 300.
(2) 19 How. S. T. 1029.
(3) 20 L. R. Ir. 318.
(4) 6 B. & C. 232.
(5) Ibid. 233.

seizure of these exhibits, though improper at the time, would therefore be excused.

As to the fourth proposition, that the police are entitled to retain property the taking of which is excused until the conclusion of any charge on which the articles are material, Wright J. says in the case of *Reg.* v. *Lushington, Ex parte Otto*: 'In this country I take it that it is undoubted law that it is within the power of, and is the duty of, constables to retain for use in Court things which may be evidences of crime, and which have come into the possession of the constables without wrong on their part. I think it is also undoubted law that when articles have once been produced in Court by witnesses it is right and necessary for the Court, or the constable in whose charge they are placed (as is generally the case), to preserve and retain them, so that they may be always available for the purposes of justice until the trial is concluded.' In this case, however, both the trials of Hannington and Elias have been concluded and I think there is no answer now to the claim for their detention after demand and for the £10 claimed as damages for their detention.

The Attorney-General stated that for the purposes of this case only he did not intend to contend that the plaintiffs, because these documents were of a seditious character, could have no property in the exhibits which had been used on the charge against Elias . . .

There will therefore be judgment for the plaintiffs for £20 damages for trespass [i.e. as regards the documents which were taken but not used at either trial], an order for the return of the documents comprised in 2 (A), £10 damages for detention of those documents, and the defendants must pay the costs of the action.

Chic Fashions (West Wales) Ltd. v. Jones [1968] 2 Q.B. 299

Court of Appeal

The defendant was sued for damages as Chief Constable of the Carnarvonshire and Cardiganshire Constabulary. Members of his force armed with a warrant to search for goods stolen from "Ian Peters Ltd." entered the plaintiffs' premises. They did not find any of the "Ian Peters" goods specified in the warrant but they seized other similar goods believing them to be stolen. This belief turned out to be mistaken and the goods were returned to the plaintiffs. A county court judgment was given in favour of the plaintiffs. The defendant appealed to the Court of Appeal.

LORD DENNING M.R.:

It comes to this, therefore: the police officers held a search warrant entitling them to enter the shop to search for ladies' garments which had been recently stolen from the factory of Ian Peters Ltd. When the police entered the shop and searched it, they found none of the goods that had been stolen from Ian Peters Ltd. But they found 65 items of clothing, not mentioned in the warrant, which they believed upon reasonable grounds were stolen and would form material evidence on a criminal charge. The question is: were the police entitled to seize goods not mentioned in the warrant but which they believed on reasonable grounds to have been stolen?

You might have thought that this question would have been settled long ago. But, strangely enough, there is very little authority upon it . . .

[Lord Denning then considered the cases (*Entick* v. *Carrington* (1765) 19 St. Tr. 1029; *Price* v. *Messenger* (1800) 2 Bos. & P. 158; *Crozier* v. *Cundey* (1827) 6 B. & C. 232; *Dillon* v. *O'Brien* (1887) 16 Cox C.C. 245, and *Elias* v. *Pasmore* [1934] 2 K.B. 164, principally.]

Such are the cases. They contain no broad statement of principle: but proceed, in our English fashion, from case to case until the principle emerges. Now the time has come when we must endeavour to state it. We have to consider, on the one hand, the freedom of the individual. The security of his home is not to be broken except for the most compelling reason. On the other hand, we have to consider the interest of society at large in finding out wrongdoers and repressing crime. In these present times, with the ever-increasing wickedness there is about, honest citizens must help the police and not hinder them in their efforts to track down criminals. I look at it in this way: So far as a man's individual liberty is concerned, the law is settled concerning powers of arrest. A constable may arrest him and deprive him of his liberty, if he has reasonable grounds for believing that a felony (now an "arrestable offence") has been committed and that he is the man. I see no reason why goods should be more sacred than persons. In my opinion, when a constable enters a house by virtue of a search warrant for stolen goods, he may seize not only the goods which he reasonably believes to be covered by the warrant, but also any other goods which he believes on reasonable grounds to have been stolen and to be material evidence on a charge of stealing or receiving against the person in possession of them or anyone associated with him. Test it this way: Suppose the constable does not find the goods mentioned in the warrant but finds other goods which he reasonably believes to be stolen. Is he to quit the premises and go back to the magistrate and ask for another search warrant to cover these other goods? If he went away, I should imagine that in nine cases out of ten, by the time he came back with a warrant, these other goods would have disappeared. The true owner would not recover them. The evidence of the crime would have been lost. That would be to favour thieves and to discourage honest men. Even if it should turn out that the constable was mistaken and that the other goods were not stolen goods at all, nevertheless so long as he acted reasonably and did not retain them longer than necessary, he is protected. The lawfulness of his conduct must be judged at the time and not by what happens afterwards. I know that at one time a man could be made a trespasser ab initio by the doctrine of relation back. But that is no longer true. The *Six Carpenters' Case*[16] was a by-product of the old forms of action. Now that they are buried, it can be interred with their bones.

In this case, on the agreed facts, the police had reasonable ground for believing the 65 items of clothing to have been stolen and to be material evidence on a criminal charge against the plaintiff company or its officers. So they seized them. On investigation they found out that they were not stolen and they returned them. On the principles I have stated they are not liable.

I would allow this appeal and give judgment to the defendant.

[16] 8 Co. Rep. 146a.

SALMON L.J.: . . .

On the facts of this case I would hold that the defendant has a good defence at common law. I go no further. In particular I wish to make it plain that I incline to the view that if a policeman finds property which he reasonably believes to be stolen in the possession of a person whom he has no reasonable grounds to believe is criminally implicated, the policeman has no common law right to seize the property. If, for example, a policeman is admitted to a house, and whilst there sees some silver on the sideboard which he reasonably believes is stolen property but which he has no reason to suppose was dishonestly acquired by the householder, he cannot take it away without the householder's consent. Nor do I think that, in practice, magistrates would or should issue a warrant under section 42 (1) of the Larceny Act, 1916, enabling the police to enter the house of a respectable citizen and search for and seize stolen goods of which the householder is thought to be innocently in possession after having acquired them in good faith.

I agree, however, that on the facts of the present case the plaintiff company's goods were lawfully seized and the appeal should accordingly be allowed.

Diplock L.J. delivered a judgment also allowing the appeal.

Ghani and Others v. Jones [1970] 1 Q.B. 693

Court of Appeal

LORD DENNING, M.R.:

Police officers inquiring into a woman's disappearance searched, without a warrant, the house of her father-in-law. At their request he handed to them documents including the passports of himself, his wife and daughter, the plaintiffs living in the house. The plaintiffs, who were Pakistanis, later asked for the return of the passports and documents as they wished to visit Pakistan. The police refused to return them. The plaintiffs brought an action against the defendant, a senior police officer, for a mandatory order for the delivery up of the passports and documents, an injunction restraining their detention and damages for detinue.

On the plaintiffs' interlocutory application, the police gave affidavit evidence of their belief that the woman had been murdered and that they would apprehend those concerned. They said that in the event of charges being preferred some of the documents would be of evidential value and others of potential evidential value. The defendant said that the plaintiffs could help the police inquiries and that if they left the United Kingdom they might not return. No one had been arrested or charged with the murder. Talbot J. ordered the return of the documents and passports.

The first thing to notice is that the police officers had *no search warrant*. The reason is simple. No magistrate—no judge even—has any power to issue a search warrant for murder. He can issue a search warrant for stolen goods and for some statutory offences, such as coinage. But not for murder. Not to dig for the body. Nor to look for the axe, the gun or the poison dregs. The police have to get the consent of the householder to enter if they can: or, if not, do it by stealth or by force. Somehow they seem to manage. No decent person refuses them permission. If he does, he is probably implicated in some way or other. So the police risk an action for trespass. It is not much risk.

The second thing to notice is that the police officers kept the passports and letters *without the consent of the holders.* Mr. Leonard suggested that they took them with consent. This is a little far-fetched. Here were two police officers asking a Pakistani for the passports of himself and his wife. Of course he handed them to them. It would look bad for him if he did not. He bowed to their authority. Even if he consented to their looking at the passports, he did not consent to their *keeping* them. Even if he did consent to their *keeping* them, it was only for a while; and he could withdraw it at any time. As in fact he did. So it is all the same. They detain the passports *without his consent.*

The third thing to notice is that *no one has been arrested* for the murder or *charged* with it. The police officers believe that the woman has been murdered. They say so. In addition, although they do not say so, they must, I think, suspect that these three *may* in some way be implicated in it. Otherwise they would not hold on to the passports or papers as they do. But they have not arrested anyone or charged anyone. I can understand it. It would not be right for them to make an arrest or lay a charge unless the grounds were pretty strong.

So we have a case where the police officers, in investigating a murder, have seized property without a warrant and without making an arrest and have retained it without the consent of the party from whom they took it. Their justification is that they believe it to be of "evidential value" on a prosecution for murder. Is this a sufficient justification in law? . . .

. . . We have to consider, on the one hand, the freedom of the individual. His privacy and his possessions are not to be invaded except for the most compelling reasons. On the other hand, we have to consider the interest of society at large in finding out wrongdoers and repressing crime. Honest citizens should help the police and not hinder them in their efforts to track down criminals. Balancing these interests, I should have thought that, in order to justify the taking of an article, when no man has been arrested or charged, these requisites must be satisfied:

First: The police officers must have reasonable grounds for believing that a serious offence has been committed—so serious that it is of the first importance that the offenders should be caught and brought to justice.

Second: The police officers must have reasonable grounds for believing that the article in question is either the fruit of the crime (as in the case of stolen goods) or is the instrument by which the crime was committed (as in the case of the axe used by the murderer) or is material evidence to prove the commission of the crime (as in the case of the car used by a bank raider or the saucer used by a train robber).

Third: The police officers must have reasonable grounds to believe that the person in possession of it has himself committed the crime, or is implicated in it, or is accessory to it, or at any rate his refusal must be quite unreasonable.

Fourth: The police must not keep the article, nor prevent its removal, for any longer than is reasonably necessary to complete their investigations or preserve it for evidence. If a copy will suffice; it should be made and the original returned. As soon as the case is over, or it is decided not to go on with it, the article should be returned.

Finally: The lawfulness of the conduct of the police must be judged at the time, and not by what happens afterwards.

Tested by these criteria, I do not think the police officers are entitled to hold on to these passports or letters. They may have reasonable grounds for believing that the woman has been murdered. But they have not shown reasonable grounds for believing that these passports and letters are material evidence to prove the commission of the murder. All they say is that they are of "evidential value", whatever that may mean. Nor have they shown reasonable grounds for believing that the plaintiffs are in any way implicated in a crime, or accessory to it. In any case, they have held them quite long enough. They have no doubt made photographs of them, and that should suffice.

Edmund Davies, L.J. and Sir Gordon Wilmer agreed with Lord Denning in dismissing the appeal.

Note: See J. W. Bridge, "Search and Seizure: An Antipodean View of *Ghani* v. *Jones* [1974] Crim. L.R. 218-22.

Questions

1. "There is an urgent need for a codification of police powers of arrest, search and seizure and for more stringent control over the possibility of abuse of such powers." Discuss.

2. Two plainclothes police officers, Nod and Plod, are conducting house to house inquiries in pursuit of a suspected murderer. They call at Quelch's house, but on knocking receive no answer. Hearing the sound of gun shots inside the house, Nod and Plod break down the door and discover Quelch and a neighbour, Raymond, watching a 'western' on television. Raymond bears a resemblance to the wanted man, and Nod immediately seizes him, saying 'Murdering swine—you're the one we want.' Raymond resists the seizure but is eventually carried off and transported to the police station. Plod returns to search Quelch's house, and despite Quelch's protests ransacks the house and eventually takes away a quantity of magazines published by an extremist organization, Quelch's address book, and a television set, for which Quelch has been unable to produce either a receipt or a licence.

Raymond is kept in custody for three days. He is then released and subsequently charged with assaulting the police in the execution of their duty.

Advise Quelch and Raymond.

Project

Draft a Bill, together with accompanying Explanatory Memorandum, to govern the law of arrest, search, and seizure of property, by the police. The Bill should indicate the sanctions to be available in case of police violation of their statutory powers.

CHAPTER 11

THE MEDIA

Further Reading

Wade & Phillips, pp. 483–487.

T. C. Hartley and J. A. G. Griffith, Government and Law (Weidenfeld & Nicolson, 1975), Chap. 13; P. Hartmann and C. Husband, *Racism and the Mass Media* (Davis-Poynter, 1974); P. Hansford Johnson, *On Inquity* (MacMillan, 1967); Labour Party, *The People and the Media* (London, 1974); C. Macey (ed.), *The Arts in a Permissive Society* (Pemberton, 1970); C. Seymour Ure, *The Political Impact of the Mass Media* (Constable, 1974); J. Whale, *The Politics of the Media* (Manchester U.P., 1977).

See also Chapter 4.

1. *ADVERTISING*

O'Higgins, pp. 99–104; Street, pp. 107–127.

Labour Party, *Report of a Commission of Enquiry into Advertising* (London, 1966); J. Todd, *The Big Sell* (Lawrence & Wishart, 1961).

BRITISH CODE OF ADVERTISING PRACTICE

I. INTRODUCTION

The British Code of Advertising Practice adapts, for use in the United Kingdom, the rules of the International Chamber of Commerce's International Code of Advertising Practice, 1973.

The Code has a dual purpose. First, it sets out in detail the rules which advertising men and women agree to follow. Second, it indicates to those outside the advertising business the steps that are taken to ensure, through self-imposed regulations, that advertisements can be trusted.

The Code's rules form the basis for adjudication whenever there may be conflicting views about the acceptability of an advertisement, whether it is challenged from within or from outside the advertising business. Both the general public and an advertiser's competitors have an equal right to expect the content of advertisements to be presented fairly, intelligibly, and responsibly, and without unnecessary offence.

> *The Code binds advertiser, advertising agency and media owner, but the principal responsibility for observing its terms lies with the advertiser . . .*

The Control System

The system of control by means of which the Code is enforced has four levels. The majority of the decisions which ensure conformity with the Code are taken at the level of the individual advertiser, advertising agency or medium; hence the description of the system as self-regulatory. The role of media is particularly important. Media check the acceptability of all advertisement copy submitted to them for publication.

The second level is that of the trade associations in membership of the CAP Committee. These bring together advertisers with shared interests, the various kinds of media and advertising agencies. The associations are responsible for co-ordinating their members' actions over enforcement matters, for ensuring that they are kept up to date with changes in the Code and for giving advice to them on compliance with the Code. The work of the associations themselves is co-ordinated by the Code of Advertising Practice Committee and the whole system is over-seen by the Advertising Standards Authority.

The Code of Advertising Practice Committee (The CAP Committee or CAP)

The CAP Committee is the third tier of the control system. It is the body which, under the general supervision of ASA, co-ordinates the executive actions of the system. It consists of persons nominated by the 20 trade and professional associations listed on the inside front cover. It is responsible for ensuring that the Code is kept up-to-date and, through the co-operation of its member organisations, for seeing that everybody in advertising is aware of the Code's rules and abides by them. Members of the CAP Committee, unlike those of the ASA Council, serve as representatives of the organisations which appoint them. In four particularly complex areas—financial advertising, mail order advertising, health and nutrition claims and sales promotion—the CAP Committee is assisted by standing sub-Committees which include specialist advisers. The services of these expert Committees are also available to ASA, and an ASA Council representative sits upon each of them. Complaints from within the advertising business are dealt with by CAP.

The CAP Committee and its Sales Promotion sub-Comittee are responsible for the implrementation of the British Code of Sales Promotion Practice.

The Advertising Standards Authority (ASA)

ASA is the top tier of the control system. It is an independent body, financed by a surcharge on display advertising, set up by the advertising business to en-sure that its system of self-regulation works effectively in the public interest. The Authority has an independent Chairman. He appoints the Authority's twelve Council members, two-thirds of whom are independent of any adver-tising interest. All Council members—whether independents or advertising specialists—serve as individuals, not as representatives of any other body or section of the public.

The Authority investigates complaints about advertisements which are made from outside the advertising business. It publishes regular Case Reports giv-ing the results of its investigations. These constitute a major source of advice and guidance. It conducts a continuous programme of monitoring, checking that the vast majority of advertisements which are not the subject of any public complaint conform to the Code. The outcome of the Authority's monitoring investigations is also made public.

The Authority is responsible for publicising the existence of the self-regulatory system and for ensuring that its own role as an independent adjudicator upon public complaints is both widely known and generally accepted. The Authority retains a panel of independent consultants to help in assessing substantiation for technical, scientific and other claims where expert knowledge is required.

The Copy Panel

Individual advertisements about the acceptability of which there is doubt may be remitted for consideration to the Copy Panel. Each week, one of five sections of the Copy Panel is available to deal with pre- or post-publication problems on the interpretation of the Code. Matters may be referred to the Panel by the CAP Committee or ASA, though in the latter case, final judgment is reserved to the ASA Council. Each section of the Panel consists of five persons nominated by CAP member organisations and one independent member of the ASA Council. Consistency between the judgments of the different sections is ensured by regular meetings of the Chairmen of the sections. Subject to the Chairmen of ASA and the CAP Committee agreeing that a point of substance arises, a panel decision on a matter referred by CAP may be remitted to the ASA Council for final determination . . .

Pre-publication clearance by CAP

Pre-publication clearance is required for advertisements for the following—
    (i) Cigarettes and their components.
    (ii) Pregnancy testing and counselling services, pregnancy termination (abortion), vasectomy and sterilisation . . .

Sanctions

If an advertiser or agency does not agree to amend or withdraw an advertisment :-
    (i) Adverse publicity will be given in ASA's Case Reports.
    (ii) Advertising space or time can be withheld from the advertiser.
    (iii) The Advertising agency's trading privileges may be withdrawn.
    (iv) Other consumer protection agencies may be notified . . .

II GENERAL RULES

All advertisements should be legal, decent, honest and truthful.

Legality

    1.1 Advertisements should contain nothing which is in breach of the law, nor omit anything which the law requires.
    1.2 Advertisements should not encourage or condone defiance of the law.

Decency

    2 Advertisements should contain nothing which is likely, in the light of generally prevailing standards of decency and propriety, to cause grave or widespread offence.

2.1 The purpose of the Code is to control the content of advertisements, not to hamper the sale of products which may be found offensive, for whatever reason, by some people. Provided, therefore, that advertisements for such products are not themselves offensive, there will normally be no ground for objection to them in terms of this section of the Code (Cf. II 4.2.2 and 4.2.6).

Honesty

3 Advertisements should not be so framed as to abuse the trust of consumers or exploit their lack of experience or knowledge.

Truthful presentation

4.1 All descriptions, claims and comparisons which relate to matters of objectively ascertainable fact should be capable of substantiation. **Advertisers and advertising agencies are required to hold such substantiation ready for production immediately to the CAP Committee or the Advertising Standards Authority.** They should compile a statement outlining substantiation and have it available *before* offering an advertisement for publication.

4.2 **Advertisements should not contain statements or visual presentations which, directly or by implication, by omission, ambiguity, or exaggeration, are likely to mislead the consumer about the product advertised, the advertiser, or about any other product or advertiser . . .**

Contraceptives, birth control

D.6.1 There is no objection under the Code to the advertising of contraceptive methods, either in general or particular, provided that such advertisements conform to this Code and that a reference is made in appropriate cases to the fact that certain methods are available only on prescription.

D.6.2 The effectiveness or safety of particular methods in comparison with others should not be exaggerated. Attention is also drawn to the provisions relating to spermicidal contraceptives contained in Schedule 3 of the Medicines (Labelling and Advertising to the Public) Regulations, 1978 . . .

[*The British Code of Advertising Practice,* (6th ed.), pp. 7-11, 14, 44 (1979)]

Advertising Standards Authority

Note: The Advertising Standards Authority Ltd. (or ASA) is a company limited by guarantee, under whose Memorandum its object principally is:

(A) The promotion and enforcement throughout the United Kingdom of the highest standards of advertising in all media so as to ensure in co-operation with all concerned that no advertising contravenes or offends against these standards, having regard *inter alia* to the British Code of Advertising Practice and the British Code of Standards in Relation to the Advertising of Medicines and Treatments.

Paragraph 6 provides for members of the Authority:

6. (i) There shall be three classes of members of the Authority:—
    (A) The Chairman
    (B) Independent Members
    (C) Advertising Members

(ii) The Chairman of the Authority shall be appointed by the Advertising Standards Board of Finance Limited, for such period and upon such terms as may be thought fit, after consultation with the members of the Council of the Authority, and with the Advertising Association subject to the power of the Advertising Standards Board of Finance Limited with the agreement of the Council of the Authority to vary or revoke such appointment. The Chairman shall not be engaged in the business of advertising.

(iii) The Independent Members and the Advertising Members shall be appointed by the Chairman. None of the Independent Members shall be engaged in the business of advertising. Each of the Advertising Members shall be persons experienced in the business of advertising and together they shall have experience in the businesses of advertisers, media owners and advertising agents.

(iv) The number of members shall not be less than nine, excluding the Chairman, of whom not less than one third shall be Advertising Members.

(v) Any member may withdraw from the Authority by giving not less than three months' prior written notice to the Council.

"ASA at Work"

This month, two Council members, Patricia Mann and the Reverend Paul Flowers, describe work of the Council as they see it.

First, however, who are Patricia Mann and Paul Flowers? She works for an advertising agency, is a copywriter by trade, and is also a Council member of the Institute of Practitioners in Advertising and its Professional Standards Committee. The objectivity which is necessary in these capacities she also employs to notable effect in the Council of the ASA. Indeed, Lord Thomson has observed that members of the industry often take a stronger and more critical line about offending advertisements than the lay members, since they are more experienced in advertising practice and prouder and more sensitive about the professional reputation of the advertising business. Paul Flowers, a young Methodist minister, sits as an independent with the advantage of possessing a valuable grass-roots knowledge of men and women in their day to day lives.

The twelve Council members are all appointed by the ASA Chairman. Patricia Mann remarks: "Eight are independent of any advertising interest and four are from the advertising industry—two of them work for advertising agencies, one for an advertiser and one for an advertising medium. For my part, I think the size is exactly right. It enables everyone to contribute and come to a consensus opinion that is founded not only on the range of specialist knowledge and varied experience that we represent but also on the fact that every member—independent or not—serves as an individual and *not* as a representative of a particular body or interest. I suppose the most important qualifications are common sense, commitment and a determination to see to it that the Code of Advertising Practice is observed in the spirit as well as the letter."

Paul Flowers speculates on the part he, as an independent, has to play as a member of the Council. "Just what," he wonders, "is a young Methodist minister doing on the Council of the ASA, looking at, among other things, pictures of bare bosoms and trying to decide whether or not they are tasteful or decent? The answer, of course, is that the work of the Council goes far beyond such occasional decisions of propriety. We have to look at the advertising brought before us in the light of the social, ethical and practical tenets embodied in the Code and to judge sometimes how people are likely to react to this or that advertisement. And, as a minister, I'm in the fortunate position of being constantly in touch with the people in my area so that helps me to sense their feelings about the attitudes some advertisements represent."

There is a not uncommon feeling, says Patricia Mann, that members of a Council which meets formally only once a month can do little more than "rubber stamp" Secretariat decisions. She scotches this firmly: "In the case of the ASA, this is far from the truth. No ASA investigation is concluded without Council approval."

And Paul Flowers also has something to say about the "rubber stamp" misconception. ". . . the Council during the past year has reversed a number of the conclusions recommended by the Secretariat . . . it is indicative of the general care that the Council takes to arrive at conclusions that *they* believe are right and not always the ones that the Secretariat feels are appropriate."

Council briefing and procedure is described by Patricia Mann. "Each week, every Council member receives for comment a progress report. At the front is a breakdown of all the complaints received and the action taken. Complaints about broadcast commercials are automatically referred to the Independent Broadcasting Authority. Others may be outside the ASA's remit, concerned with packaging or instruction manuals, for example. A further group of complaints is listed as "not pursued", with a detailed analysis: these complaints may have misread or misinterpreted the advertisement concerned, or taken a peculiarly idiosyncratic view, or have objections to a particular product or service, rather than to its advertising. Council members are able to check the list and may ask for any of the complaints to be investigated further.

The bulk of the progress report, however, concerns individual complaints. For each there is a photocopy of the advertisement concerned, a summary of the complaint or complaints against it and a suggested conclusion. Each Council member is then responsible for endorsing, amending or rejecting the suggested conclusion or, if necessary, asking for further information.

Comments are circulated prior to Council meetings and any disparity of views is resolved by Council discussion.

Considerable efforts are made to ensure that complaints are processed quickly. Each complaint is dated, so that any untoward delays are recorded. The complaints are also anonymous. The only indication of their source is the identification of the complainant's home town. In certain instances, names may be revealed with the complainant's consent, but this is the exception.

Questions of taste and decency tend to be referred directly to Council meetings, as do posters and other advertisements which it is inconvenient to circulate. Background information concerning any appeals against ASA or CAP decisions is circulated in advance but the appeal is discussed by the Council. Whilst this may seem an elaborate system, it works very well in ensuring that all Council members have an opportunity to comment on every single case investigated and that no conclusion is reached without the approval of a substantial majority.

Independent Council members also sit on CAP copy panels, where they contribute to pre-publication advice and the resolution of complaints from within the advertising industry. This helps to ensure consistency between CAP and ASA judgements on the Code's interpretation."

[Extract from "The Council at Work," *ASA Case Report* 45, January 1979]

CONSIDERATION OF COMPLAINT BY ASA

MONITOR PRESS
89 Portland Road London W11 4LN

Basis of complaint: A Consumer Protection Officer objected to an advertisement for the book "Consumer Law Statutes" which described it as having, "For the first time, all the consumer law statutes . . . brought together in one volume". The complainant maintained that a number of important consumer law statutes e.g. the Weights and Measures Act and the Food and Drugs Act had been omitted. (Section II, 4.1)
Conclusion: Complaint upheld. The advertisers agreed that by strict definition the book did not contain all the Consumer Law Statutes. It was noted that no further advertising was planned but the advertisers were asked to ensure that in the event of any future advertising the copy would be modified.

Complaint from: London N15

[*ASA Case Report*, July 1979, p. 10.]

INDEPENDENT BROADCASTING AUTHORITY'S CODE
OF ADVERTISING STANDARDS AND PRACTICE

Preamble

1 The general principle which will govern all broadcast advertising is that it should be legal, decent, honest and truthful. It is recognised that this principle is not peculiar to broadcasting, but is one which applies to all reputable advertising in other media in this country. Nevertheless, broadcasting, and particularly television, because of its greater intimacy within the home, gives rise to problems which do not necessarily occur in other media and it is essential to maintain a consistently high quality of broadcast advertising.

2 Advertisements must comply in every respect with the law, common or statute.

3 The detailed rules set out below are intended to be applied in the spirit as well as the letter and should be taken as laying down the minimum standards to be observed.

4 The word 'advertisement' has the meaning implicit in the Independent Broadcasting Authority Act 1973, i.e. any item of publicity inserted in the programmes broadcast by the Authority in consideration of payment to a programme contractor or to the Authority.

Programme Independence

5 No advertisement may include anything that states, suggests or implies, or could reasonably be taken to state, suggest or imply, that any part of any programme broadcast by the Authority has been supplied or suggested by any advertiser.

Identification of Advertisements

6 An advertisement must be clearly distinguishable as such and recognisably separate from the programmes.

'Subliminal' Advertising

8 No television advertisement may include any technical device which, by using images of very brief duration or by any other means, exploits the possibility of conveying a message to, or otherwise influencing the minds of, members of an audience without their being aware, or fully aware, of what has been done.

Politics, Industrial and Public Controversy

9 No advertisement may be inserted by or on behalf of any body, the objects whereof are wholly or mainly of a political nature, and no advertisement may be directed towards any political end. No advertisement may have any relation to any industrial dispute.
No advertisement may show partiality as respects matters of political or industrial controversy or relating to current public policy.

Religion

10 No advertisement may be inserted by or on behalf of any body, the objects of which are wholly or mainly of a religious nature, and no advertisement may be directed towards any religious end.

Charities

11 No advertisement may give publicity to the needs or objects of any association or organisation conducted for charitable or benevolent purposes.
(This does not preclude advertisements which are confined to the giving of necessary details of flag days, fêtes, lotteries permitted under the Lotteries and Amusements Act 1976 other events organised by such associations or organisations or publications of general interest.)

Good Taste

12 No advertisement should offend against good taste or decency or be offensive to public feeling.

Gifts or Prizes

13 No advertisement may include an offer of any prize or gift of significant value, being a prize or gift which is available only to television viewers or radio listeners or in relation to which any advantage is given to viewers or listeners.

Stridency

14 Audible matter in advertisements must not be excessively noisy or strident.

Appeals to Fear

15   Advertisements must not without justifiable reason play on fear.

Superstition

16   No radio or television advertisement should exploit the superstitious.

Unacceptable Products or Services

17   Advertisements for products or services coming within the recognised character of, or specifically concerned with, the following are not acceptable:
  (a) breath-testing devices and products which purport to mask the effects of alcohol;
  (b) matrimonial agencies and correspondence clubs;
  (c) fortune-tellers and the like;
  (d) undertakers or others associated with death or burial;
  (e) unlicensed employment services, registers or bureaux;
  (f) organisations/companies/persons seeking to advertise for the purpose of giving betting tips;
  (g) betting (including pools): (*this does not preclude lotteries permitted under the Lotteries and Amusements Act 1976 but such advertisements shall be limited to an announcement of the event and necessary details.*)
  (h) cigarettes and cigarette tobacco;
  (i) private investigation agencies;
  (j) privately owned advisory services related to personal or consumer problems.
N.B. An advertisement for an acceptable product or service may be unacceptable should it see to the Authority that its main purpose would be to publicise indirectly, the unacceptable product.

[Extracts from *IBA Code of Advertising Standards and Practice* (1979).]

VENEREAL DISEASE ACT 1917

An Act to prevent the treatment of Venereal Disease otherwise than by duly qualified medical Practitioners, and to control the supply of Remedies therefor; and for other matters connected therewith.

2. Restriction on advertisements, etc.

(1) A person shall not by any advertisement or any public notice or announcement treat or offer to treat any person for venereal disease, or prescribe or offer to prescribe any remedy therefor, or offer to give or give any advice in connection with the treatment thereof.

5. Short title

This Act may be cited as the Venereal Disease Act, 1917.
  Provided that nothing in this section shall apply to any advertisement notification, announcement, recommendation, or holding out made or

published by any local or public authority, or made or published with the sanction of the Local Government Board, or in Scotland and Ireland the Local Government Board for Scotland and Ireland respectively, or to any publication sent only to duly qualified medical practitioners or to wholesale or retail chemists for the purposes of their business.

METROPOLITAN STREETS ACT 1867

9. Prohibition of carriage of advertisements, except those approved by Commissioner of Police

No picture, print, board, placard, or notice, except in such form and manner as may be approved of by the Commissioner of Police, shall, by way of advertisement, be carried or distributed in any street within the general limits of this Act by any person riding in any vehicle, or on horseback, or being on foot.

Any person doing any act in contravention of this section shall be liable for each offence to a penalty not exceeding ten shillings.

This section shall not apply to the sale of newspapers.

Note. By section 4 the "general limits of this Act" are defined as such parts of the City of London as are enclosed in a circle of which the centre is Charing Cross and of which the radius is six miles.

INDECENT ADVERTISEMENTS ACT 1889

3. Summary proceedings against persons affixing, etc., indecent or obscene pictures or printed or written matter

Whoever affixes to or inscribes on any house, building, wall, hoarding, gate, fence, pillar, post, board, tree, or any other thing whatsoever so as to be visible to a person being in or passing along any street, public highway, or footpath, and whoever affixes to or inscribes on any public urinal, or delivers or attempts to deliver, or exhibits, to any inhabitant or to any person being in or passing along any street, public highway, or footpath, or throws down the area of any house, or exhibits to public view in the window of any house or shop, any picture or printed or written matter which is of an indecent or obscene nature, shall, on summary conviction in manner provided by the Summary Jurisdiction Acts, be liable to a penalty not exceeding forty shillings, or, in the discretion of the Court, to imprisonment for any term not exceeding one month, with or without hard labour.

4. Summary proceedings against persons sending others to do the acts punishable under s. 3

Whoever gives or delivers to any other person any such pictures, or printed or written matter mentioned in section three of this Act, with the intent that the same, or some one or more thereof, should be affixed, inscribed, delivered, or exhibited as therein mentioned, shall, on conviction in manner provided by the Summary Jurisdiction Acts, be liable to a penalty not exceeding five pounds, or, in the discretion of the Court, to imprisonment for any term not exceeding three months with or without hard labour.

5. Certain advertisements declared indecent

Any advertisement relating to syphilis, gonorrhoea, nervous debility, or other complaint or infirmity arising from or relating to sexual intercourse, shall be deemed to be printed or written matter of an indecent nature within the meaning of section three of this Act, if such advertisement is affixed to or inscribed on any house, building, wall, hoarding, gate, fence, pillar, post, board, tree, or other thing whatsoever, so as to be visible to a person being in or passing along any street, public highway, or footpath, or is affixed to or inscribed on any public urinal, or is delivered or attempted to be delivered to any person being in or passing along any street, public highway, or footpath.

6. Constables may arrest on view of offence

Any constable or other peace officer may arrest without warrant any person whom he shall find committing any offence against this Act.

THE INDECENT ADVERTISEMENTS (AMENDMENT) ACT 1970

1. Amendment of Indecent Advertisements Act 1889

At the end of section 5 of the Indecent Advertisements Act 1889 (under which advertisements relating to certain venereal diseases or other matters are to be regarded for purposes of that Act as indecent if affixed or inscribed so as to be visible in the street, or affixed or inscribed in public urinals, or handed out in the street) there shall be added the following proviso:—

> "Provided that this section shall not apply to advertisements affixed or inscribed as aforesaid by reason of their relating to any venereal disease, if they are so affixed or inscribed for a local or public authority or for a person publishing them with the sanction of the Secretary of State."

2. *THE CINEMA*

De Smith, pp. 466–467; O'Higgins, pp. 78–90; Street, pp. 67–77; Wade & Phillips, p. 484.

S. Brody, *Screen Violence and Film Censorship* (HMSO, 1977); N. M. Hunnings, *Film Censors and the Law* (Allen & Unwin, 1967); D. Knowles, *The Censor, The Drama and the Film 1900-1934* (London, 1934), Part II; G. Phelps, *Film Censorship* (Allen & Unwin, 1975); J. Trevelyan, *What the Censor Saw* (Michael Joseph, 1973); E. Wistrich, '*I Don't Mind the Sex, It's the Violence: Film Censorship Explored*' (M. Boyars, 1978).

THE CINEMATOGRAPH ACT 1952

1. Extension of 9 Edw. 7. c. 30 to cinematograph exhibitions using non-inflammable films or television, etc.

Subject to the provisions of section seven of the Act of 1909 and to the exemptions hereinafter provided, the said Act and (except so far as they otherwise provide) any regulations made thereunder shall apply as respects all cinematograph exhibitions, whether given by means involving the use of inflammable films or non-inflammable films, or by means not involving the use of films.

2. Scope of Secretary of State's regulations

(1) The matters for which provision may be made by the regulations of the Secretary of State under the Act of 1909 shall be the following:—

   (a) safety, in connection with the giving of cinematograph exhibitions (including the keeping and handling, in premises where other entertainments are being given or meetings held, of cinematograph film used or to be used for the purposes of cinematograph exhibitions or other articles or equipment so used or to be used);

   (b) the health and welfare of children in relation to attendance at cinematograph exhibitions.

(2) Any statutory instrument containing such regulations as aforesaid shall be subject to annulment in pursuance of a resolution of either House of Parliament.

3. Provisions as to conditions in licences

(1) It shall be the duty of the licensing authority, in granting a licence under the Act of 1909 as respects any premises,—

   (a) to impose conditions or restrictions prohibiting the admission of children to cinematograph exhibitions involving the showing of works designated, by the licensing authority or such other body as may be specified in the licence, as works unsuitable for children; and

   (b) to consider what (if any) conditions or restrictions should be imposed as to the admission of children to other cinematograph exhibitions involving the showing of works designated by the authority or such other body as aforesaid as of such other descriptions as may be specified in the licence.

(2) Neither the last foregoing section nor subsection (1) of this section shall be construed as derogating from the generality of the power of the licensing authority, as respects any premises, to impose conditions or restrictions.

4. Control of cinematograph exhibitions for children

(1) Subject to the provisions of this Act, no premises shall be used, except with the consent of the licensing authority, for a cinematograph exhibition organised wholly or mainly as an exhibition for children.

(2) Subject to the regulations of the Secretary of State under the Act of 1909, and without prejudice to any conditions or restrictions imposed by the licensing authority on the granting of a licence, the authority may impose special conditions or restrictions on the granting of any consent under this section.

(3) Subsections (2) to (5) of section two of the Act of 1909 (which contain supplemental provisions as to licences) shall with the necessary modifications apply for the purposes of this section as they apply for the purposes of the said section two; and sections three and four of that Act (which impose penalties and confer powers of entry for purposes of inspection) shall have effect as if references to that Act included references to this section and references to licences included references to consents.

5. Exemptions for non-commercial exhibitions

(1) The following exemptions shall have effect in the case of cinematograph exhibitions (hereinafter referred to as "exempted exhibitions") to which the public are not admitted or to which the public are admitted without payment, that is to say:—

(a) a licence under the Act of 1909 shall not be required by reason only of the giving of an exempted exhibition, and for the purposes of subsection (2) of section seven of that Act (which exempts premises used only occasionally for cinematograph exhibitions) the giving in any premises of an exempted exhibition shall be disregarded;

(b) section four of this Act shall not apply to an exempted exhibition;

(c) regulations made by the Secretary of State under the Act of 1909, being regulations made by virtue of paragraph (b) of subsection (1) of section two of this Act, shall not apply in relation to an exempted exhibition, and regulations made by the Secretary of State under that Act, being regulations made by virtue of paragraph (a) of the said subsection (1), shall not apply in relation to an exempted exhibition unless given in premises in respect of which a licence under the Act of 1909 is in force;

(d) in connection with the giving of an exempted exhibition in premises in respect of which a licence under the Act of 1909 is in force no condition or restriction on or subject to which the licence was granted shall apply except in so far as it relates to the matters specified in paragraph (a) of subsection (1) of section two of this Act;

Provided that (without prejudice to the operation of paragraph (d) of this subsection) paragraph (a) thereof shall not have effect in the case of exhibitions where the pictures are produced by means specified by regulations of the Secretary of State under the Act of 1909 as means involving risk such that it is inexpedient that the said paragraph (a) should have effect.

(2) For the purposes of this section an exhibition shall not be treated as an exempted exhibition if organised wholly or mainly as an exhibition for children who are members of a club, society or association the principal object of which is attendance at cinematograph exhibitions, so however that this subsection shall not apply to any exhibition given in a private dwelling-house or any exhibition given as part of the activities of an educational or religious institution.

(3) Subject to the provisions of the last foregoing subsection an exhibition given by an exempted organisation in any premises shall be treated for the purposes of this section as an exempted exhibition, notwithstanding payment for admission thereto:

Provided that an exhibition shall not be treated for those purposes as an exempted exhibition by virtue of this subsection if on more than three out of the last preceding seven days the premises in question were used for the giving of a cinematograph exhibition which fell to be treated as an exempted exhibition by virtue of this subsection.

(4) In the last foregoing subsection the expression "exempted organisation" means a society, institution, committee or other organisation as respects which there is in force at the time of the exhibition in question a certificate of the Commissioners of Customs and Excise certifying that the Commissioners are satisfied that the organisation is not conducted or established for profit.

9. Interpretation

(1) In this Act the following expressions have the meanings hereby assigned to them respectively, that is to say:—

"Act of 1909" means the Cinematograph Act, 1909;
"child" means a person under the age of sixteen;
"cinematograph exhibition" means an exhibition of moving pictures produced on a screen by means which include the projection of light;
"licensing authority", in relation to any premises, means the authority which for the time being has power to grant licences for the premises under section two of the Act of 1909.

(2) Except where the context otherwise requires, references in this Act to any enactment shall be construed as references to that enactment as amended by or under any other enactment, including this Act.

Note: See also Local Government Act 1972, ss. 204 (5), 272 and Schedule 30.

REFORM OF FILM CENSORSHIP

Home Office: Report of the Committee on Obscenity and Film Censorship, Chairman, Bernard Wilson, Cmnd. 7772, 1979

34. Censorship imposed by local authorities on the basis of their powers to licence cinemas should be ended (paragraph 12.20).

35. A statutory board should be set up to take over the censorship powers of local authorities and the functions now exercised by the British Board of Film Censors, but the responsibility for licensing cinemas should continue to rest with local authorities (paragraph 12.29).

36. The Board should be known as the Film Examining Board and should comprise about twelve members chosen to represent a range of interests, including the film industry and local government, and relevant expertise (paragraph 12.30).

37. The Board should be non-profit making and so far as possible self-supporting from the fees charged for examining films; but provision should be made for some financial assistance from public funds (paragraph 12.32).

38. The functions of the Board members should be

(a) to establish the policy and principles of film censorship within the criteria laid down by statute;
(b) to appoint a Chief Examiner of Films and, on the recommendation of the Chairman and Chief Examiner, a small staff of film examiners to take decisions on individual films;
(c) to prescribe procedures for the censorship of films, the fees to be charged and to decide on the waiver of fees where appropriate;
(d) to hear appeals against the decisions of the examiners (paragraph 12.31).

39. When the decision of the examiners is the subject of an appeal by the applicant for a certificate, the Board should be required to view the film before determining the appeal (paragraph 12.31).

40. It should be open to any person to appeal against a particular decision of the examiners, but in the case of an appeal by a person other than the applicant the Board should have power to reach a decision either after seeing the film or after deciding that the written reasons for the appeal do not justify their taking steps to see it (paragraph 12.31).

41. The Board's examiners should allocate each film examined to one of the following six categories:

(U) ; Suitable for all ages
(11A) Children under the age of eleven should be accompanied by a responsible adult
(16) No person under the age of sixteen to be admitted
(18) No person under the age of eighteen to be admitted
(18R) For restricted exhibition only. No person under the age of eighteen to be admitted.
Certificate refused
(paragraphs 12.41–43).

42. The category of a film, in the form of an encircled symbol, should be clearly shown in any advertisements for it, at the entrance to the cinema and on the screen immediately before the film is shown (paragraph 12.49).

43. The Board should give to the applicant on request a statement of reasons why a film is refused a certificate or allocated to a particular category, giving sufficient indication of any changes that might be required for it to qualify for a certificate, or for a less restrictive certificate (paragraph 12.45).

44. In formulating its policy on the control of film content, the Board should be required to have regard to the following guidelines:

(a) the issue of certificates indicating a film's suitability or unsuitability for persons under eighteen should take account of the protection of children and young persons from influences which may be disturbing or harmful to them, or from material whose unrestricted availability to them would be unacceptable to responsible parents.
(b) a film should be classified for restricted exhibition only if its visual content and the manner in which it deals with violence, cruelty or horror, or sexual, faecal or urinary functions or genital organs is such that in the judgment of the examiners it is appropriate that the film should be shown only under restricted conditions.

(c) a film should be refused a certificate only if, in the judgment of the examiners, it is unfit for public exhibition. A film unfit for public exhibition should be one that either

(i) contains material prohibited by law; or

(ii) having regard to the importance of allowing the development of artistic expression and of not suppressing truth or reality, is nevertheless unacceptable because of the manner in which it depicts violence or sexual activity or crime. (paragraph 12.45).

45. A film classified for restricted exhibitions should not be shown for gain other than in a cinema designated by the local cinema licensing authority as suitable for the showing of such films. The local authority should have absolute discretion whether or not to approve an application for designation and its decision should be final (paragraph 12.38).

46. An auditorium in a multi-screen cinema complex should be eligible for designation as suitable for the showing of restricted films (paragraph 12.38).

47. A designated cinema should be free to show any film granted a certificate by the Film Examining Board (paragraph 12.39).

48. When exhibiting a restricted film, a designated cinema should be required to make no pictorial display outside the cinema and to display in the foyer a brief synopsis or description of the film prepared by the Film Examining Board (paragraph 12.39).

49. Steps should be taken to bring commercial cinema clubs within the scope of the censorship system by providing an exemption only for film exhibitions not promoted for private gain (paragraph 12.40).

50. A film intended for exhibition in this country should not be seized on importation as a prohibited import without being referred to the Film Examining Board for advice and for decision as to whether, in a cut form, it could qualify for a certificate (paragraph 12.47).

51. It should be an offence to exhibit for private gain any film not possessing a certificate issued by the Film Examining Board (paragraph 12.46).

52. It should be an offence to exhibit any film for private gain other than in accordance with the requirements of the certificate issued to it (paragraph 12.49).

53. It should not be an offence for a person under the age of eighteen to seek to gain entry to a film designated as unsuitable for persons of that age (paragraph 12.51).

54. It should be an offence to advertise a film or exhibit it without complying with the requirements to specify the category of certificate granted to it (paragraph 12.49).

55. The Board should not have a responsibility for prosecuting offenders nor should any individual be free to institute proceedings; prosecutions should be brought by the police or by or with the consent of the Director of Public Prosecutions (paragraph 12.49).

56. Offences concerned with film censorship should be triable only by magistrates. Showing uncertificated films should be punishable by fines of up to £1,000 and imprisonment of up to six months; other offences should be punishable by fines of up to £500 (paragraph 12.49).

LOCAL AUTHORITY CONDITIONS

CAMBRIDGESHIRE COUNTY COUNCIL

CINEMATOGRAPH ACTS 1909 AND 1952

General conditions imposed by Cambridgeshire County Council (hereinafter called "The Council") in connection with the granting of Cinematograph licence as agents for the Licensing Authority. [Extract]

(Regulations)

1. These conditions shall supplement the Regulations of the Secretary of State made under the Cinematograph Acts 1909 and 1952 which must be exhibited in the licensed premises so that they can easily be seen by members of staff.

(Hours of opening and closing)

2. The licensed premises shall not be opened for exhibition purposes before twelve-thirty o'clock in the afternoon, nor continue open after eleven o'clock in the evening on any week-day, except with the special permission of the Council.

(Sunday, Christmas Day and Good Friday opening)

3. No cinematograph exhibition shall be given in the licensed premises on any Sunday, Christmas Day, or Good Friday, without permission first having been obtained from the Council.

(Films which may be shown)

4. No film shall be exhibited unless:–
   (a) it has received a "U", "A", "AA" or "X" certificate of the British Board of Film Censors, or
   (b) it is a current news-reel which has not been submitted to the British Board of Film Censors.

Notwithstanding anything contained in (a) or (b) above no film shall be exhibited whether or not it has received a certificate of the British Board of Film Censors if the Council consider it to be unsuitable for exhibition and give notice to the Licensee that they consider the said film to be unsuitable for exhibition.

(Admission of persons)

5. No person apparently under the age of eighteen years shall be admitted to any exhibition at which there is to be shown any film which has received an "X" certificate from the British Board of Film Censors, except that this condition shall not apply to employees of a cinema provided the written consent of their parents or guardians is obtained and produced to the Council on request.

6. No person apparently under the age of fourteen years shall be admitted to any exhibition at which there is to be shown any film which has received an "AA" certificate from the British Board of Film Censors.

(Exhibition of Film by consent of the Council)

7. Notwithstanding the conditions hereinbefore contained, a film may be exhibited, or persons, or any class of persons, may be admitted thereto, if the permission of the Council is first obtained, and any conditions of such permission are complied with.

(Exhibition of certificate of British Board of Film Censors)

8. A representation or written statement of the terms of any certificate given by the British Board of Film Censors shall be shown on the screen immediately before the showing of any film to which it relates and the representation or statement shall be shown for long enough and in a form large enough for it to be read from any seat in the auditorium.

(Exhibition of notice as to category of Films)

9. There shall be prominently exhibited at each public entrance whenever the premises are open to the public a notice indicating in tabular form and in clear bold letters and figures:–
  (a) the title of each film to be shown on that day, other than trailers and films of less than five minutes duration;
  (b) the aproximate times of commencement of each such film;
  (c) whether each such film has received a "U", "A", "AA" or "X" certificate from the British Board of Film Censors;
  (d) the effect of such "U", "A", "AA" or "X" certificates in relation to the admission of persons under the age of eighteen years, such effect to be stated in the following manner:-

CATEGORY "U"	Passed for general exhibition.
CATEGORY "A"	Passed for general exhibition but parents/guardians are advised that the film contains material they might prefer children under fourteen years not to see.
CATEGORY "AA"	Passed as suitable only for exhibition to persons of fourteen years and over. When a programme includes an "AA" film no persons under fourteen years can be admitted.
CATEGORY "X"	Passed as suitable only for exhibition to adults. When a programme includes an "X" film no persons under eighteen years can be admitted.

(Exhibition of Films to the Council if required)

10. When films have been examined by the Council they shall be exhibited exactly, in the form in which they were passed for exhibition, without any alteration or additions, unless the consent of the Council to such alteration or addition has previously been obtained.

(Objectionable advertisements)

11. Where the Council have given notice in writing to the Licensee of the premises objecting to an advertisement on the ground that, if displayed, it would offend against good taste or decency or be likely to encourage or incite crime or to lead to disorder or to be offensive to public feeling that advertisement shall not be displayed at the licensed premises except with the consent in writing of the Council.

(Contents of advertisements)

12. The nature of any certificate received in respect of a film from the British Board of Film Censors shall be clearly indicated by the letter "U", "A", "AA" or "X" in any advertisement of the film displayed at the premises. This rule shall also apply in respect of any advertisement of a film other than at the premises.

13. No advertisement displayed at the premises of a film to be exhibited at the premises shall depict as a scene or incident in the film any scene or incident which is not included in the film as certified by the British Board of Film Censors or approved for exhibition by the Council, as the case may be. This rule shall also apply in respect of any advertisement of a film other than at the premises.

(Objectionable films)

14. Where the Council have given notice in writing to the licensee of the premises prohibiting the exhibition of a film on the ground that it contains matter which, if exhibited, would offend against good taste or decency or would be likely to encourage or incite to crime or to lead to disorder or to be offensive to public feeling, that film shall not be exhibited in the licensed premises except with the consent in writing of the Council.

Reg. v. G.L.C. Ex. p. Blackburn and Another [1976] 1 W.L.R. 550

Court of Appeal

A number of ratepayers sought a prohibition against the G.L.C. to prevent them from exercising their censorship powers by applying the statutory test of obscenity rather than by the common law test of gross indecency and from delegating their powers of censorship to the British Board of Film Censors. Other relevant facts appear below. The Divisional Court refused the applications. An appeal was brought to the Court of Appeal.

LORD DENNING M.R.:

Mr. Raymond Blackburn comes before us once again. This time he draws to our attention the pornographic films which are being shown openly in cinemas in London, and elsewhere. They are grossly indecent. They are an offence against the common law of England. Yet the Greater London Council, the licensing authority, are doing nothing to stop them. On the contrary, he says, they are virtually permitting them. The rules of the Greater London Council are framed in such limited terms that films get through which are grossly indecent. He gives a striking instance. Last year they gave their consent to a film called "More about the Language of Love." Afterwards the exhibitors were prosecuted on the ground that it was an outrage to public decency. The jury convicted the exhibitors. They had no doubt about it, retiring only for 20 minutes. The judge said to them: "Thank you in the name of the public." The case raises important questions on the censorship of films.

1. *The powers of the Greater London Council*

There are only two statutes which give the council control over cinemas. The first is the Cinematograph Act 1909. It was passed in the early days and was concerned with the safety in cinemas, not with censorship. The title states that it is "An Act to make better provision for securing safety." It gave the county councils the power to grant licences—no doubt with a view to safety—but this power was expressed in such wide terms that it was afterwards interpreted so as to give a power of censorship. It says in section 2 (1):

> "A county council may grant licences to such persons as they think fit to use the premises . . . on such terms and conditions and under such restrictions as . . . the council may by the respective licences determine."

Although the Act was concerned with safety, nevertheless the courts two years later held that a county council could impose conditions which related to other matters, so long as they were not unreasonable. So in 1911 the courts held that a condition saying that the premises should not be opened on Sundays was valid: see *London County Council* v. *Bermondsey Bioscope Co. Ltd.* [1911] 1 K.B. 445. Soon aftertwards the county councils began to insert a condition that no film shown should be of a licentious or indecent character. Such a condition was accepted as valid, but it did not permit any censorship beforehand. Next, the county council tried to insert a power of censorship by delegating it to three justices. This was held to be invalid: see *Rex* v. *Burnley Justices* (1916) 32 T.L.R. 695. Once again they tried. They sought to hand over all power of censorship to the British Board of Film Censors: but this was held invalid because the county councils were not allowed to delegate their powers: see *Ellis* v. *Dubowski* [1921] 3 K.B. 621. But in 1924 there was a breakthrough. The courts gave a decision which allowed censorship by the British Board of Film Censors provided that that body did not have the final say, but was subject to review by the county council itself: see *Mills* v. *London County Council* [1925] 1 K.B. 213. That decision has held the field since that time and must, I think, be accepted as good law. It was recognised as such by Parliament itself in 1952 when it made it compulsory for conditions to be imposed for the protection of children: see section 3 of the Cinematograph Act 1952. Under that section the county council are under a duty to impose conditions so as to ensure that, if a film is designated as unsuitable for children, then children are not to be admitted to see it. Such designation is to be done "by the licensing authority or such other body as may be specified in the licence." In speaking of "such other body" Parliament no doubt had in mind the British Board of Film Censors. To that extent, therefore, the board has Parliamentary approval.

2. *The British Board of Film Censors*

The British Board of Film Censors is not a legal entity. It has no existence known to the law. It is but a name given to the activities of a few persons, but it goes back for 60 years. There is a president, at present Lord Harlech, who is responsible for broad policy. There is a secretary, Mr. James Ferman, who makes executive decisions. There are four film examiners, who work full-time. These work in pairs, viewing films on three days each week. They put films into four categories, according to their suitability for various age groups: U, A, AA and X. U for everyone. X for those over 18. They sometimes required cuts before giving a certificate. The examiners are recruited from outside the film industry. They are paid salaries. The money is provided by the manufacturers of films through the Incorporated Association of Kinematograph Manufacturers.

The extent of their work is shown by what they did last year—1975. They saw 417 feature films. They passed 400 and refused 17. But of those 17, they passed five after cuts had been made. They passed 73 documentary films.

Although the board is not a body known to the law, it is, I think, a "body" within section 3 (1) of the Act of 1952. I do not think the county councils can delegate the whole of their responsibilities to the board: see section 5 of the Act of 1909 (repealed in 1972) and *Ellis* v. *Dubowski* [1921] 3 K.B. 621, 625: but they can treat the board as an advisory body whose views they can accept or reject; provided that the final decision—aye or nay—rests with the county council. If the exhibitor—or any member of the public—brings the film up before the county council, they ought themselves to review the decision of the British Board of Film Censors and exercise their own judgment on it. That is, I think, the right way to interpret *Mills* v. *London County Council* [1925] 1 K.B. 213. When the board issues a certificate permitting the exhibition of a film—and the county council takes no objection to it—that is equivalent to a permission by the county council itself. When the board refuses a certificate, the exhibitor can appeal to the county council. The county council can then give their consent to the exhibition, and from their decision there is no appeal.

The upshot of it all is this. The county council are in law the body which have the power to censor films for exhibition in cinemas: but in practice it is the British Board of Film Censors which carries out the censorship, subject to review by the county council.

3. *The tests to be applied*

The next question is: what tests are the county council to apply when they exercise censorship powers? Are they to apply the tests laid down in the Obscene Publications Act 1959? Or the tests laid down by the common law?

(i) *The Obscene Publications Act 1959*

In 1959 Parliament passed the Obscene Publications Act 1959. I remember it well. I attended the debates, and took part. Its object was to strengthen the law against pornography. It contained a test of obscenity which was to be applied to publications. An article was to be deemed obscene if its effect, taken as a whole, was "such as to tend to deprave and corrupt persons" likely to read it. Unfortunately that legislation mis-fired. I explained the reasons in *Reg.* v. *Commissioner of Police of the Metropolis, Ex parte Blackburn (No. 3)* [1973] Q.B. 241. One reason was because of the inadequacy of the definition of obscenity. It did not stop gross indecency. An article might be so indecent as to shock the readers: but yet it might not tend to deprave and corrupt them. Another reason was because of the defence of public good. The courts used to allow so-called experts to come forward and say that pornography is good for those who take pleasure in it. Fortunately this court, only a week or two ago, held that the evidence on those lines was inadmissible: see *Reg.* v. *Staniforth* [1976] 2 W.L.R. 849. But still the fact remains that the test itself is inadequate.

(ii) *The common law test*

It has been established for centuries that it is an offence at common law to show in public an indecent exhibition. There was a case 100 years ago in which two showmen kept on Epsom Downs a booth in which a grossly indecent exhibition took place. The Court for Crown Cases Reserved held that "those facts are abundant to prove a common law offence": see *Reg.* v. *Saunders* (1875) 1 Q.B.D. 15, 19.

This common law offence was clearly recognised by the House of Lords in *Reg.* v. *Knuller (Publishing , Printing and Promotions) Ltd.* [1973] A.C. 435. Lord Reid said, at p. 458, in this context that indecency "includes anything which an ordinary decent man or woman would find to be shocking, disgusting and revolting": and Lord Simon of Glaisdale said, at p. 493, that "the authorities establish a common law offence of conduct which outrages public decency."

This common law offence has proved to be a far better stop upon pornography than the Act of 1959. For this simple reason: pornography shocks and disgusts decent people, but it does not tend to deprave or corrupt them. They revolt from it and turn away from it. If asked, they will be quite ready to say that it is grossly indecent, but far less ready to say that it tends to deprave or corrupt.

The proof of the pudding is in the eating. The customs authorities and Post Office apply the simple test: "Is this indecent?" They have no difficulty in condemning millions of magazines on that account, without their decision being questioned. But when jurors are asked to apply the test: "Does this tend to deprave or corrupt?," they have been known to allow the most indecent articles to get into circulation.

I notice that the Law Commission in its Report *Criminal Law: Report on Conspiracy and Criminal Law Reform* (Law Com. No. 76), March 17, 1976, recommends that the common law offence (where the test is gross indecency) should be abolished (see paragraph 3.138, p. 120); and that instead the statutory offence (where the test is to tend to deprave or corrupt) should be made to apply to films (see paragraph 3.150 (a), p. 123). I hope that Parliament will look closely into this recommendation before it is adopted and made law. Some may think that the common law offence is capable of being far more effective in stopping pornography—and is much easier for juries to understand and apply—than the stautory offence.

(iii) *Cinematograph films*

Parliament expressly said that the provisions of the Act of 1959 were not to apply to cinematograph films shown in public. It did so by the proviso to section 1 (3) (b). Why did Parliament do this? I propose to look at *Hansard* to find out. I know that we are not supposed to do this. But the Law Commission looked at *Hansard*: see their Report, paragraph 3.46, p. 88. So did Lord Diplock in *Knuller's* case [1973] A.C. 435, 480. So I have looked at *Hansard* to refresh my memory. In the Lords Viscount Kilmuir L.C. referred to the four forms of publication which were excepted from the Bill. First, the live performance of stage plays; secondly, the cinema; thirdly, television; and fourthly, broadcasting. He said that the promoters of the Bill—it was a private member's Bill—desired to leave those four out of the Bill and to allow the common law to apply to them. The government were content that this should be so. The Lord Chancellor said that they "have in practice not been

prosecuted in the past and . . . are most unlikely, so far as can be contemplated, to be prosecuted in the future": see *Hansard* (House of Lords),
June 22, 1959, vol. 217, col. 74. In the Commons the Solicitor-General added
that those four forms "are subject, in fact, to censorship either by public
authority or internal control by the Lord Chamberlain, the Board of Film
Censors, or whatever it may be": see *Hansard* (House of Commons), July 22,
1959, vol. 609, col. 1446.

So we have the reason why cinematograph films were omitted. It was
because they could be left to the common law and the existing means of
censorship.

No doubt those reasons seemed sufficient in 1959. But they are no longer
valid today. During the last two or three years pornographic films have been
imported from Sweden. I believe, in large numbers—and no doubt at much
expense. They have been exhibited in cinemas in London to the shame of its
decent citizens. The existing censorship has proved totally ineffective to stop
it. This was brought vividly into the open by *Reg.* v. *Jacey (London) Ltd.* decided
at the Central Criminal Court on June 5, 1975, and reported as news in "The
Times," June 6, 1975. A film called "More about the Language of Love" was
refused a certificate by the British Board of Film Censors: but the exhibitors
appealed to the Greater London Council. The council granted consent to it
being shown. It was shown at a public cinema. The redoubtable Mr.
Blackburn brought it to the notice of Sir Robert Mark, the Commissioner of
Police. A prosecution was brought on the ground that it offended against
common law. The owners and manager of the cinema were charged with
showing a film which was grossly indecent. The jury found them guilty. The
judge fined the two companies £500 apiece and the manager £50.

Why did the Greater London Council grant their consent to the showing of
that film—which was found by the jury to be grossly indecent—and which
was, therefore, unlawful? The answer is because they have been applying the
wrong test. They have applied the test of "tendency to deprave or corrupt"
under the Act of 1959, instead of the test of "indecency" under the common
law.

The tests laid down by the Greater London Council

The Greater London Council at present accept responsibilities as censor of
films to be shown in London. They have laid down rules [*Greater London: Rules
of Management for Places of Entertainment*] which are incorporated as conditions
of every licence issued by the council. These are the material rules:

"108. No film shall be exhibited at the premises unless—(*a*) it is a 'flash'
or current news-reel; (*b*) it has been passed by the British Board of Film
Censors as a U, A, AA or X film; or (*c*) the council has expressly consented to the exhibition of the film.

"111 If the council does not agree with the category in which any film
passed by the British Board of Film Censors is placed it shall if it thinks fit
alter such category and . . . the film thereafter shall be treated as having
been placed in the altered category . . .

"112 Any special conditions which the council may impose in respect
of the exhibition of any film shall, after notice thereof by the council to
the licensee, be complied with.

"116"—quite an important one—"No film shall be exhibited at the
premises—(1) which is likely— (*a*) to encourage or to incite to crime: or

(*b*) to lead to disorder; or (*c*) to stir up hatred against any section of the public in Great Britain on grounds of colour, race or ethnic or national origins; or (2) the effect of which is, if taken as a whole, such as to tend to deprave and corrupt persons who are likely to see it.

"If the licensee is notified by the council in writing that it objects to the exhibition of a film on any of the grounds, such film shall not be exhibited."

It is to be noticed that, so far as obscenity is concerned, those rules, in rule 116 (2) adopt the test laid down by section 1 of the Obscene Publications Act 1959, which I may abbreviate as "tendency to deprave and corrupt." And there is overwhelming evidence to show that that is the test which the county council themselves apply when their viewing committee exercises their power of censorship. For instance, the chairman of their film viewing board gave an interview which was published in "Cinema T.V. Today" on March 1, 1975. He was described as "Phil Bassett, now GLC censor" and reported as saying: "We just have to ask ourselves the question of whether the films are likely to deprave or corrupt anyone." On July 16, 1975, the Arts Committee, in a report to the council, set out rule 116, containing the "tendency to deprave and corrupt" and said: "This condition . . . has provided the council's film censorship criteria since [1965]." On October 23, 1975, the solicitor to the Greater London Council said in an affidavit:

"Since the enactment of the Obscene Publications Act in 1959, it is, I submit, appropriate for the council to consider whether the effect of a film taken as a whole as to tend to deprave and corrupt persons who are likely to see it. The test . . . is, I submit, the very test which Parliament in 1959 expected and hoped cinematograph licensing authorities would apply."

Much further evidence was also put before us by Mr. Blackburn. It shows conclusively that the council apply the test in the Act of 1959, and not the common law test.

4. *The validity of the G.L.C. rules*

Those rules made by the G.L.C. prohibit a film which is such as to "tend to deprave and corrupt": but they do not prohibit a film which is grossly indecent. Test it this way: if the British Board of Film Censors *pass* a film which is grossly indecent, the G.L.C. cannot stop it being shown. There is nothing in their rules which enables them to do so. If the British Board of Film Censors *reject* a film which is grossly indecent, the licensee can apply to the G.L.C. for their consent to the exhibition of the film: and they will give their consent (as they did in the *Jacey* case) so long as it does not tend to deprave or corrupt.

By making these rules and so applying them, it follows that a film which is unlawful (as being grossly indecent) may, nevertheless, be shown in London cinemas with the sanction of the Greater London Council, as happened in the *Jacey* case. In other words, the The Greater London Council, have made rules which permit films to be shown, even though their exhibition is contrary to law. This is, to my mind, a misuse of the licensing power which they have assumed. It is wrong for a licensing authority to give their consent to that which is unlawful. That is shown by *Rex* v. *London County Council, Ex parte Entertainments Protection Association Ltd.* [1931] 2 K.B. 215. The L.C.C. there made a condition that a cinema should not be opened on Sundays, but announced that they would take no action if £35 was paid to charity for each Sunday opening. Now Sunday opening was a plain breach of the Sunday Observance Act 1780. This court held that the L.C.C. had acted illegally. They had purported to sanction the doing of something which was contrary to law—to dispense with the law—a thing which cannot be done by anyone, not even by the London County Council.

5. *Locus standi*

It was suggested that Mr. Blackburn has no sufficient interest to bring these proceedings against the G.L.C. It is a point which was taken against him by the Commissioner of Police: see *Reg.* v. *Commissioner of Police of the Metropolis, Ex parte Blackburn* [1968] 2 Q.B. 118, 137, 149: and against the late Mr. McWhirter of courageous memory by the Independent Broadcasting Authority: see *Attorney-General ex rel. McWhirter* v. *Independent Broadcasting Authority* [1973] Q.B. 629, 648-649. On this point, I would ask: Who then can bring proceedings when a public authority is guilty of a misuse of power? Mr. Blackburn is a citizen of London. His wife is a ratepayer. He has children who may be harmed by the exhibition of pornographic films. If he has no sufficient interest, no other citizen has. I think he comes within the principle which I stated in *McWhirter's* case [1973] Q.B. 629, 649, which I would recast today so as to read:

> "I regard it as a matter of high constitutional principle that if there is good ground for supposing that a government department or a public authority is transgressing the law, or is about to transgress it, in a way which offends or injures thousands of Her Majesty's subjects, then any one of those offended or injured can draw it to the attention of the courts of law and seek to have the law enforced, and the courts in their discretion can grant whatever remedy is appropriate."

The applications by Mr. Blackburn and Mr. McWhirter did much good. They show how desirable such a principle is. One remedy which is always open, by leave of the court, is to apply for a prerogative writ, such as certiorari, mandamus or prohibition. These provide a discretionary remedy and the discretion of the court extends to permitting an application to be made by any member of the public: see *Reg.* v. *Thames Magistrates' Court, Ex parte Greenbaum* (1975) 55 L.G.R. 129, and especially what was said by Parker L.J.; and *Reg.* v. *Hereford Corporation, Ex parte Harrower* [1970] 1 W.L.R. 1424; though it will refuse it to a mere busybody who is interfering in things which do not concern him: see *Reg.* v. *Paddington Valuation Officer, Ex parte Peachey Property Corporation Ltd.* [1966] 1 Q.B. 380, 401. Another remedy open likewise is by asking for a declaration: see *Dyson* v. *Attorney-General* [1911] 1 K.B. 410; *Prescott* v. *Birmingham Corporation* [1955] Ch. 210 and *Thorson* v. *Attorney-General of Canada* (1975) 1 S.C.R. 138, where Laskin C.J. and his colleagues notably expanded the scope of the remedy. Also by injunction, as in *Bradbury* v. *Enfield London Borough Council* [1967] 1 W.L.R. 1311.

The remedy

There is nothing in the statute which compels the G.L.C. to exercise powers of censorship over films to be shown to adults. They are under a duty to censor films which are unsuitable for children (under the Act of 1952), but not those for adults. If the G.L.C. think it right no longer to act as censors for adults, there is nothing to stop them. But they would have to amend their existing rules before they could do so. Alternatively, they could amend their rules so as to make sure that they prohibit the exhibition of any film which is grossly indecent contrary to the common law. Unless they do one or other of these things, I think that this court has power to prohibit them from continuing their present procedure, and should do so. The prerogative writ of prohibition has, in the past, usually been exercised so as to prohibit judicial tribunals from exceeding their jurisdiction. But just as the scope of certiorari has been extended to administrative authorities, so also with prohibition. It is available to prohibit administrative authorities from exceeding their powers, or misusing them. In particular, it can prohibit a licensing authority from making rules or granting licences which permit conduct that is contrary to law.

Conclusion

In my opinion, therefore, Mr. Blackburn has made out his case, He has shown that the G.L.C. have been exercising their censorship powers in a manner which is unlawful: because they have been applying a test which is bad in law. If they continue with their present wrong test and in consequence give their consent to films which are grossly indecent, they may be said to be aiding and abetting a criminal offence. In these circumstances this court can and should issue an order of prohibition to stop them. But I do not think we should issue the order today. We should give the Greater London Council time to mend their ways either by applying the proper test or no longer exercising censorship. They have already suspended their viewing of films. They suspended it on July 22, 1975, after the decision in the *Reg.* v. *Jacey*, "The Times," June 6, 1975, case. It may be that, as a result of our decision today, they will discontinue film viewing altogether and give up any responsibility for the censorship of films save in regard to children. If they should do this, it will be imperative for Parliament itself to take action: so as to place the censorship of films on a proper footing.

I would allow the appeal so as to award Mr. Blackburn his costs here and below, and give him leave to apply later if necessary for prohibition.

Stephenson and Bridges L.JJ. delivered judgments which reached the same conclusion, and the appeal was allowed. **BRIDGES** L.J. however added:
Although the conclusions I have reached on the questions of law involved in this appeal seem to me inescapable as the law stands, I cannot say I feel any enthusiasm for the result. The statutory test of obscenity has been much criticised, and with good reason. But I don't know how many people today would accept as an appropriate test of criminality what is "shocking, disgusting and revolting." There are profound differences of opinion as to what are the appropriate standards in relation to such matters which the law ought to be designed to maintain. Some want the law to move one way, some another, but surely no one can be content for it to stand still. The one proposition which I imagine nearly everybody would assent to is that the law in its present state is so full of anomalies and operates so uncertainly and unevenly that some rationalisation is urgently needed. If our decision has the result, as seems probable, that many authorities will abandon altogether the thankless task of censoring films for adults, perhaps that may emphasise the urgency of some reforming legislation.

3. *THE PRESS*

Further Reading

De Smith, pp. 462–465; O'Higgins, pp. 104–122; Street, pp. 97–107;
Wade & Phillips, pp. 470–473, 484–485.

D. Astor, "How the British Press Censors itself," (1977) 6(1) *Index on Censorship* pp. 3–9; John Beavan, *The Press and the Public* (1971) Fabian Tract no. 338; M. Beloff, *Freedom under Foot* (M. T. Smith, 1976); Peter Benenson, *A Free Press* (1961) Fabian Research ser. no. 223, 1961; H. Evans, *et al., The Freedom of the Press* (Granada Guildhall Lectures, Hart-Davis, MacGibbon, 1974); N. Herbert, "The British Press and the Closed Shop," (1975) 4(2) *Index on Censorship* pp. 12–15; Justice and International Press Institute, *The Law and the Press* (London, 1965); R. Kidd, *The Fight for a Free Press* (NCCL, 1942); H. P. Levy, *The Press Council* (MacMillan, 1967); W. Moonman (ed.), *The Press: A Case for Commitment* (1969) Fabian Tract no. 391; G. Scott, "A Press Charter for Britain," (1977) 6(1) *Index on Censorship* pp. 9–16; J. Tunstoll, *The Westminster Lobby Correspondents* (Routledge & Kegan Paul, 1970); J. Whale, *Journalism and Government: A British View* (MacMillan, 1972); W. H. Wickwar, *The Struggle for the Freedom of the Press, 1819–1932* (Allen & Unwin, 1928); C. Wintour, *Pressures on the Press* (Deutsch, 1972); M. Withers, "A Closed Shop for Journalists," (1975) 1 *Poly Law Review* pp. 34–35; R. Winsbury, *Government and the Press* (1968) Fabian Tract no. 379, 1968.

NEWSPAPER LIBEL AND REGISTRATION ACT 1881

*An Act to amend the Law of Newspaper Libel, and to provide for
Registration of Newspaper Proprietors*

1. Interpretation

In the construction of this Act, unless there is anything in the subject or context repugnant thereto, the several words and phrases herein-after mentioned shall have and include the meanings following; (that is to say,)

The word "newspaper" shall mean any paper containing public news, intelligence, or occurrences, or any remarks or observations therein printed for sale, and published in England or Ireland periodically, or in parts or numbers at intervals not exceeding twenty-six days between the publication of any two such papers, parts or numbers.

Also any paper printed in order to be dispersed, and made public weekly or oftener, or at intervals not exceeding twenty-six days, containing only or principally advertisements.

4. Inquiry as to libel being for public benefit or being true

A court of summary jurisdiction, upon the hearing of a charge against a proprietor, publisher, or editor, or any person responsible for the publication of a newspaper, for a libel published therein, may receive evidence as to the publication being for the public benefit, and as to the matters charged in the libel being true, and as to the report being fair and accurate, and published without malice, and as to any matter which under this or any other Act, or otherwise, might be given in evidence by way of defence by the person charged on his trial on indictment, and the court, if of opinion after hearing such evidence that there is a strong or probable presumption that the jury on the trial would acquit the person charged, may dismiss the case.

7. Registration of the names of only a portion of the proprietors of a newspaper

Where, in the opinon of the Board of Trade, inconvenience would arise or be caused in any case from the registry of the names of all the proprietors of the newspaper (either owing to minority, coverture, absence from the United Kingdom, minute subdivision of shares, or other special circumstances), it shall be lawful for the Board of Trade to authorise the registration of such newspaper in the name or names of some one or more responsible "representative proprietors."

8. Register of newspaper proprietors to be established

A register of the proprietors of newspapers as defined by this Act shall be established under the superintendence of the registrar.

9. Annual Returns

It shall be the duty of the printers and publishers for the time being of every newspaper to make or cause to be made to the Registry Office . . . in the month of July in every year, a return of the following particulars according to the Schedule A hereunto annexed; that is to say,

  (a) The title of a newspaper:
  (b) The names of all the proprietors of such newspaper together with their respective occupations, places of business (if any), and places of residence.

Law of Libel Amendment Act 1888

3. Newspaper reports of proceedings in court privileged

A fair and accurate report in any newspaper of proceedings publicly heard before any court exercising judicial authority shall, if published contemporaneously with such proceedings, be privileged: Provided that nothing in this section shall authorise the publication of any blasphemous or indecent matter.

8. Order of Judge required for prosecution of newspaper proprietor, etc.

. . . No criminal prosecution shall be commenced against any proprietor, publisher, editor, or any person responsible for the publication of a newspaper for any libel published therein without the order of a Judge at Chambers being first had and obtained.

Such application shall be made on notice to the person accused, who shall have an opportunity of being heard against such application.

Defamation Act 1952

7. Qualified privilege of newspapers

(1) Subject to the provisions of this section, the publication in a newspaper of any such report or other matter as is mentioned in the Schedule to this Act shall be privileged unless the publication is proved to be made with malice.

(2) In an action for libel in respect of the publication of any such report or matter as is mentioned in Part II of the Schedule to this Act, the provisions of this section shall not be a defence if it is proved that the defendant has been requested by the plaintiff to publish in the newspaper in which the original publication was made a reasonable letter or statement by way of explanation or contradiction, and has refused or neglected to do so, or has done so in a manner not adequate or not reasonable having regard to all the circumstances.

(3) Nothing in this section shall be construed as protecting the publication of any matter the publication of which is prohibited by law, or of any matter which is not of public concern and the publication of which is not for the public benefit.

(4) Nothing in this section shall be construed as limiting or abridging any privilege subsisting (otherwise than by virtue of section four of the Law of Libel Amendment Act, 1888) immediately before the commencement of this Act.

(5) In this section the expression "newspaper" means any paper containing public news or observations thereon, or consisting wholly or mainly of advertisements, which is printed for sale and is published in the United Kingdom either periodically or in parts or numbers at intervals not exceeding thirty-six days.

8. Extent of Law of Libel Amendment Act, 1888, s. 3

Section three of the Law of Libel Amendment Act, 1888 (which relates to contemporary reports of proceedings before courts exercising judicial authority) shall apply and apply only to courts exercising judicial authority within the United Kingdom.

SCHEDULE

Newspaper Statements Having Qualified Privilege

Part I

Statements Privileged Without Explanation or Contradiction

1. A fair and accurate report of any proceedings in public of the legislature of any part of Her Majesty's dominions outside Great Britain.

2. A fair and accurate report of any proceedings in public of an international organisation of which the United Kingdom or Her Majesty's Government in the United Kingdom is a member, or of any international conference to which that government sends a representative.

3. A fair and accurate report of any proceedings in public of an international court.

4. A fair and accurate report of any proceedings before a court exercising jurisdiction throughout any part of Her Majesty's dominions outside the United Kingdom, or of any proceedings before a court-martial held outside the United Kingdom under the Naval Discipline Act, the Army Act, 1955 or the Air Force Act, 1955.

5. A fair and accurate report of any proceedings in public of a body or person appointed to hold a public inquiry by the government or legislature of any part of Her Majesty's dominions outside the United Kingdom.

6. A fair and accurate copy of or extract from any register kept in pursuance of any Act of Parliament which is open to inspection by the public, or of any other document which is required by the law of any part of the United Kingdom to be open to inspection by the public.

7. A notice or advertisement published by or on the authority of any court within the United Kingdom or any judge or officer of such a court.

Part II

Statements Privileged Subject to Explanation or Contradiction

8. A fair and accurate report of the findings or decision of any of the following associations, or of any committee or governing body thereof, that is to say—

(a) an association formed in the United Kingdom for the purpose of promoting or encouraging the exercise of or interest in any art, science, religion or learning, and empowered by its constitution to exercise control over or adjudicate upon matters of interest or concern to the association, or the actions or conduct of any person subject to such control or adjudication;

(b) an association formed in the United Kingdom for the purpose of promoting or safeguarding the interests of any trade, business, industry or profession, or of the persons carrying on or engaged in any trade, business, industry or profession, and empowered by its constitution to exercise control over or adjudicate upon matters connected with the trade, business, industry or profession, or the actions or conduct of those persons;

(c) an association formed in the United Kingdom for the purpose of promoting or safeguarding the interests of any game, sport or pastime to the playing or exercise of which members of the public are invited or admitted, and empowered by its constitution to exercise control over or adjudicate upon persons connected with or taking part in the game, sport or pastime,

being a finding or decision relating to a person who is a member of or is subject by virtue of any contract to the control of the association.

9. A fair and accurate report of the proceedings at any public meeting held in the United Kingdom, that is to say, a meeting bona fide and lawfully held for a lawful purpose and for the furtherance or discussion of any matter of public concern, whether the admission to the meeting is general or restricted.

10. A fair and accurate report of the proceedings at any meeting or sitting in any part of the United Kingdom of—

(a) any local authority or committee of a local authority or local authorities;

(*b*) any justice or justices of the peace acting otherwise than as a court exercising judicial authority;

(*c*) any commission, tribunal, committee or person appointed for the pusposes of any inquiry by Act of Parliament, by Her Majesty or by a Minister of the Crown;

(*d*) any person appointed by a local authority to hold a local inquiry in pursuance of any Act of Parliament;

(*e*) any other tribunal, board, committee or body constituted by or under, and exercising functions under, an Act of Parliament,

not being a meeting or sitting admission to which is denied to representatives of newspapers and other members of the public.

11. A fair and accurate report of the proceedings at a general meeting of any company or association constituted, registered or certified by or under any Act of Parliament or incorporated by Royal Charter, not being a private company within the meaning of the Companies Act, 1948.

12. A copy or fair and accurate report or summary of any notice or other matter issued for the information of the public by or on behalf of any government department, officer of state, local authority or chief officer of police.

Part III

Interpretation

13. In this Schedule the following expressions have the meanings hereby respectively assigned to them, that is to say:—

"Act of Parliament" includes an Act of the Parliament of Northern Ireland, and the reference to the Companies Act, 1948, includes a reference to any corresponding enactment of the Parliament of Northern Ireland;

"government department" includes a department of the Government of Northern Ireland;

"international court" means the International Court of Justice and any other judicial or arbitral tribunal deciding matters in dispute between States;

"legislature", in relation to any territory comprised in Her Majesty's dominions which is subject to a central and a local legislature, means either of those legislatures;

"local authority" means any authority or body to which the Public Bodies (Admission to Meetings) Act, 1960, or the Local Government (Ireland) Act, 1902, as amended by any enactment of the Parliament of Northern Ireland, applies;

"part of Her Majesty's dominions" means the whole of any territory within those dominions which is subject to a separate legislature.

14. In relation to the following countries and territories, that is to say, India, the Republic of Ireland, and protectorate, protected state or trust territory within the meaning of the British Nationality Act, 1948, any territory administered under the authority of a country mentioned in subsection (3) of section one of that Act, the Sudan and the New Hebrides, the provisions of this Schedule shall have effect as they have effect in relation to Her Majesty's dominions, and references therein to Her Majesty's dominions shall be construed accordingly.

PUBLIC BODIES (ADMISSION TO MEETINGS) ACT 1960

1. Admission of public to meetings of local authorities and other bodies

(1) Subject to subsection (2) below, any meeting of a local authority or other body exercising public functions, being an authority or other body to which this Act applies, shall be open to the public.

(2) A body may, by resolution, exclude the public from a meeting (whether during the whole or part of the proceedings) whenever publicity would be prejudicial to the public interest by reason of the confidential nature of the business to be transacted or for other special reasons stated in the resolution and arising from the nature of that business or of the proceedings; and where such a resolution is passed, this Act shall not reuire the meeting to be open to the public during proceedings to which the resolution applies.

(3) A body may under subsection (2) above treat the need to receive or consider recommendations or advice from sources other than members, committees or sub-committees of the body as a special reason why publicity would be prejudicial to the public interest, without regard to the subject or purport of the recommendations or advice; but the making by this subsection of express provision for that case shall not be taken to restrict the generality of subsection (2) above in relation to other cases (including in particular cases where the report of a committee or sub-committee of the body is of a confidential nature).

(4) Where a meeting of a body is required by this Act to be open to the public during the proceedings or any part of them, the following provisions shall apply, that is to say,—

   (a) public notice of the time and place of the meeting shall be given by posting it at the offices of the body (or, if the body has no offices, then in some central and consipicuous place in the area with which it is concerned) three clear days at least before the meeting or, if the meeting is convened at shorter notice, then at the time it is convened;

   (b) there shall, on request and on payment of postage or other necessary charge for transmission, be supplied for the benefit of any newspaper a copy of the agenda for the meeting as supplied to members of the body (but excluding, if thought fit, any item during which the meeting is likely not to be open to the public), together with such further statements or particulars, if any, as are necessary to indicate the nature of the items included or, if thought fit in the case of any item, with copies of any reports or other documents supplied to members of the body in connection with the item;

   (c) while the meeting is open to the public, the body shall not have power to exclude members of the public from the meeting and duly accredited representatives of newspapers attending for the purpose of reporting the proceedings for those newspapers shall, so far as practicable, be afforded reasonable facilities for taking their report and, unless the meeting is held in premises not belonging to the body or not on the telephone, for telephoning the report at their own expense.

(5) Where a meeting of a body is required by this Act to be open to the public during the proceedings or any part of them, and there is supplied to a member of the public attending the meeting, or in pursuance of paragraph (b) of subsection (4) above there is supplied for the benefit of a newspaper, any such copy of the agenda as is mentioned in that paragraph, with or without

further statements or particulars for the purpose of indicating the nature of any item included in the agenda, the publication thereby of any defamatory matter contained in the agenda or in the further statements or particulars shall be privileged, unless the publication is proved to be made with malice.

(6) When a body to which this Act applies resolves itself into committee, the proceedings in committee shall for the purposes of this Act be treated as forming part of the proceedings of the body at the meeting.

(7) Any reference in this section to a newspaper shall apply also to a news agency which systematically carries on the business of selling and supplying reports or information to newspapers, and to any organisation which is systematically engaged in collecting news for sound or television broadcasts; but nothing in this section shall require a body to permit the taking of photographs of any proceedings, or the use of any means to enable persons not present to see or hear any proceedings (whether at the time or later), or the making of any oral report on any proceedings as they take place.

(8) The provisions of this section shall be without prejudice to any power of exclusion to suppress or prevent disorderly conduct or other misbehaviour at a meeting.

Note: The Act applies (by s. 2) to bodies listed in the Schedule or added thereto by ministerial order; it applies not only to these bodies but also to any committee consisting of or including all the members of that body. The Schedule is as follows:

SCHEDULE

Bodies to which this Act Applies

1. The bodies to which in England and Wales this Act applies are—
   (a) local authorities within the meaning of the Local Government Act, 1933 . . . the Common Council of the City of London and the Council of the Isles of Scilly, and joint boards or joint committees constituted to discharge functions of any two or more of those bodies;
   (b) the parish meetings of rural parishes;
   (c) the Metropolitan Water Board, and joint boards and joint committees constituted by or under any Act for the purposes of water supply, and consisting of or including representatives of local authorities within the meaning of the Local Government Act, 1933;
   (d) education committees (including joint education committees) constituted under Part II, and divisional executives constituted under Part III of the First Schedule to the Education Act, 1944;
   (e) bodies constituted in accordance with regulations made under subsection (4) of section twenty-two of the National Health Service Act, 1946;
   (f) regional hospital boards constituted under section eleven of the said Act of 1946;
   (g) executive councils constituted under section thirty-one of the said Act of 1946, but only so far as regards the exercise of their executive functions;

(*h*) bodies not mentioned above but having, within the meaning of the Public Works Loans Act, 1875, power to levy a rate (other than police authorities).

Note: The Act does not apply to Northern Ireland. There is a separate list of applicable bodies for Scotland.

FAIR TRADING ACT 1973

Part V

Mergers

Newspaper merger references

57. Meaning of "newspaper", "transfer of newspaper or of newspaper assets" and related expressions

(1) In this Part of this Act—

> (*a*) "newspaper" means a daily, Sunday or local (other than daily or Sunday) newspaper circulating wholly or mainly in the United Kingdom or in a part of the United Kingdom;
>
> (*b*) "newspaper proprietor" includes (in addition to an actual proprietor of a newspaper) any person having a controlling interest in a body corporate which is a newspaper proprietor, and any body corporate in which a newspaper proprietor has a controlling interest;

and any reference to the newspapers of a newspaper proprietor includes all newspapers in relation to which he is a newspaper proprietor and, in the case of a body corporate, all newspapers in relation to which a person having a controlling interest in that body corporate is a newspaper proprietor.

(2) In this Part of this Act "transfer of a newspaper or of newspaper assets" means any of the following transactions, that is to say—

> (*a*) any transaction (whether involving a transfer or not) by virtue of which a person would become, or would acquire the right to become, a newspaper proprietor in relation to a newspaper;
>
> (*b*) any transfer of assets necessary to the continuation of a newspaper as a separate newspaper (including goodwill or the right to use the name of the newspaper);
>
> (*c*) any transfer of plant or premises used in the publication of a newspaper, other than a transfer made without a view to a change in the ownership or control of the newspaper or to its ceasing publication;

and "the newspaper concerned in the transfer", in relation to any transaction falling within paragraph (*a*), paragraph (*b*) or paragraph (*c*) of this subsection, means the newspaper in relation to which (as mentioned in that paragraph) the transaction is or is to be effected.

(3) In this Part of this Act "average circulation per day of publication" in relation to a newspaper, means its average circulation for the appropriate period, ascertained by dividing the number of copies to which its circulation

amounts for that period by the number of days on which the newspaper was published during that period (circulation being calculated on the basis of actual sales in the United Kingdom of the newspaper as published on those days); and for the purposes of this subsection "the appropriate period"—

    (a) in a case in which an application is made for consent under the next following section, means the period of six months ending six weeks before the date of the application, or

    (b) in a case in which a transfer or purported transfer is made without any such application for consent, means the period of six months ending six weeks before the date of the transfer or purported transfer.

(4) For the purposes of this section a person has a controlling interest in a body corporate if (but only if) he can, directly or indirectly, determine the manner in which one-quarter of the votes which could be cast at a general meeting of the body corporate are to be cast on matters, and in circumstances, not of such a description as to bring into play any special voting rights or restrictions on voting rights.

58. Prohibition of certain newspaper mergers

(1) Subject to the following provisions of this section, a transfer of a newspaper or of newspaper assets to a newspaper proprietor whose newspapers have an average circulation per day of publication amounting, together with that of the newspaper concerned in the transfer, to 500,000 or more copies shall be unlawful and void, unless the transfer is made with written consent given (conditionally or unconditionally) by the Secretary of State.

(2) Except as provided by subsections (3) and (4) of this section and by section 60(3) of this Act, the consent of the Secretary of State under the preceding subsection shall not be given in respect of a transfer until after the Secretary of State has received a report on the matter from the Commission.

(3) Where the Secretary of State is satisfied that the newspaper concerned in the transfer is not economic as a going concern and as a separate newspaper, then—

    (a) if he is also satisfied that, if the newspaper is to continue as a separate newspaper, the case is one of urgency, he may give his consent to the transfer without requiring a report from the Commission under this section;

    (b) if he is satisfied that the newspaper is not intended to continue as a separate newspaper, he shall give his consent to the transfer, and shall give it unconditionally, without requiring such a report.

(4) If the Secretary of State is satisfied that the newspaper concerned in the transfer has an average circulation per day of publication of not more than 25,000 copies, he may give his consent to the transfer without requiring a report from the Commission under this section.

(5) The Secretary of State may by order made by statutory instrument provide, subject to any transitional provisions contained in the order, that for any number specified in subsection (1) or subsection (4) of this section (whether as originally enacted or as previously varied by an order under this subsection) there shall be substituted such other number as is specified in the order.

(6) In the section "satisfied" means satisfied by such evidence as the Secretary of State may require.

59. Newspaper merger reference

(1) Where an application is made to the Secretary of State for his consent to a transfer of a newspaper or of newspaper assets, the Secretary of State, subject to the next following subsection, shall, within one month after receiving the application, refer the matter to the Commission for investigation and report.

(2) The Secretary of State shall not make a reference to the Commission under the preceding subsection in a case where—

  (a) by virtue of subsection (3) of section 58 of this Act he is required to give his consent unconditionally without requiring a report from the Commission under this section, or

  (b) by virtue of subsection (3) or subsection (4) of that section he has power to give his consent without requiring such a report from the Commission, and determines to exercise that power,

or where the application is expressed to depend on the operation of subsection (3) or subsection (4) of that section.

(3) On a reference made to them under this section (in this Act referred to as a "newspaper merger reference") the Commission shall report to the Secretary of State whether the transfer in question may be expected to operate against the public interest, taking into account all matters which appear in the circumstances to be relevant and, in particular, the need for accurate presentation of news and free expression of opinion.

60. Time-limit for report on newspaper merger reference

(1) A report of the Commission on a newspaper merger reference shall be made before the end of the period of three months beginning with the date of the reference or of such further period (if any) as the Secretary of State may allow for the purpose in accordance with the next following subsection.

(2) The Secretary of State shall not allow any further period for a report on such a reference except on representations made by the Commission and on being satisfied that there are special reasons why the report cannot be made within the original period of three months; and the Secretary of State shall allow only one such further period on any one reference, and no such further period shall be longer than three months.

(3) If on such a reference the Commission have not made their report before the end of the period specified in subsection (1) or of any further period allowed under subsection (2) of this section, the Secretary of State may, without waiting for the report, give his consent to the transfer to which the reference relates.

61. Report on newspaper merger reference

(1) In making their report on a newspaper merger reference, the Commission shall include in it definite conclusions on the questions comprised in the reference, together with—

  (a) such an account of their reasons for those conclusions, and

  (b) such a survey of the general position with respect to the transfer of a newspaper or of newspaper assets to which the reference relates, and of the developments which have led to that position,

as in their opinion are expedient for facilitating a proper understanding of those questions and of their conclusions.

(2) Where on such a reference the Commission find that the transfer of a newspaper or of newspaper assets in question might operate against the

public interest, the Commission shall consider whether any (and, if so, what) conditions might be attached to any consent to the transfer in order to prevent the transfer from so operating, and may, if they think fit, include in their report recommendations as to such conditions.

62. Enforcement provisions relating to newspaper mergers

(1) Any person who is knowingly concerned in, or privy to, a purported transfer of a newspaper or of newspaper assets which is unlawful by virtue of section 58 of this Act shall be guilty of an offence.

(2) Where under that section the consent of the Secretary of State is given to a transfer of a newspaper or of newspaper assets, but is given subject to one or more conditions, any person who is knowingly concerned in, or privy to, a breach of that condition, or of any of those conditions, as the case may be, shall be guilty of an offence.

(3) A person guilty of an offence under this section shall be liable, on conviction on indictment, to imprisonment for a term not exceeding two years or to a fine or to both.

(4) No proceedings for an offence under this section shall be instituted—

(a) in England or Wales, except by, or with the consent of, the Director of Public Prosecutions, or

(b) in Northern Ireland, except by, or with the consent of, the Director of Public Prosecutions for Northern Ireland.

TRADE UNION AND LABOUR RELATIONS ACT 1974

Charter on freedom of the press

1A.—(1) If before the end of the period of twelve months beginning with the passing of the Trade Union and Labour Relations (Amendment) Act 1976, there is agreed among parties including employers of journalists (or employers' associations representing such employers), editors (or editors' organisations) and trade unions representing journalists, a charter containing practical guidance for employers, trade unions and editors and other journalists on matters relating to the freedom of the press, the Secretary of State shall lay before both Houses of Parliament a draft of that charter.

(2) For the purposes of subsection (1) above, practical guidance on matters relating to the freedom of the press must include guidance on the avoidance of improper pressure to distort or suppress news, comment, or criticism, the application of union membership agreements to journalists (and in particular the right of editors to discharge their duties and to commission and to publish any article) and the question of access for contributors.

(3) If no such charter has been agreed as mentioned above, or if a draft charter laid before Parliament (under subsection (1) above or this subsection) is not approved by resolution of each House of Parliament as mentioned in subsection (6) below, the Secretary of State shall after consultation with the Press Council and such of the parties referred to in subsection (1) above, such organisations representing workers and such organisations representing employers, as he thinks fit, prepare in draft a charter, as follows:—

(a) where, or so far as, there appears to the Secretary of State to be agreement among the parties referred to in subsection (1) above on any matter relating to the freedom of the press, he shall incorporate in the draft charter such practical guidance as he thinks appropriate to give effect to that agreement;

(*b*) where, so far as there appears to the Secretary of State to be no such agreement on any of the particular matters referred to in subsection (2) above, he shall incorporate in the draft charter such practical guidance on that matter as he thinks fit,

and the Secretary of State shall lay the draft charter before both Houses of Parliament.

(4) A charter agreed as mentioned in subsection (1) above, or prepared by the Secretary of State in accordance with subsection (3) above, shall define its field of operation.

(5) A charter agreed as mentioned in subsection (1) above, or prepared by the Secretary of State in accordance with subsection (3) above, shall provide for the constitution of a body which shall have the functions of—

(*a*) hearing any complaint by a person aggrieved by a failure on the part of any other person to observe any provision of the charter;

(*b*) issuing to the parties a declaration as to whether such a complaint is well-founded; and

(*c*) securing the publication of its decision.

(6) If a draft laid under subsection (1) or (3) above is approved by a resolution of each House of Parliament, the Secretary of State shall issue the charter in the form of the draft.

(7) A charter for the time being in force under this section may be revised from time to time by agreement between such parties as are referred to in subsection (1) above, and the Secretary of State shall lay a draft of the revised charter before both Houses of Parliament.

(8) If a draft laid under subsection (7) above is approved by a resolution of each House of Parliament, the Secretary of State shall issue the revised charter in the form of the draft.

(9) On issuing charter or revised charter under subsection (6) or (8) above the Secretary of State shall make by statutory instrument an order specifying the date on which the charter or revised charter is to come into effect.

(10) A failure on the part of any person to observe any provision of a charter which is for the time being in force under this section shall not of itself render him liable to any proceedings, but in any proceedings—

(*a*) Any such charter shall be admissible in evidence, and

(*b*) any provision of such a charter which appears to the court or tribunal to be relevant to any question arising in those proceedings shall be taken into account by the court or tribunal in determining that question.

Note: Employment Bill 1979, cl. 16 proposes repeal of this provision.

THE PRESS COUNCIL

Articles of Constitution of The Press Council approved by The Newspaper Publishers' Association Ltd., The Newspaper Society, Periodical Publishers Association Ltd., The Scottish Daily Newspaper Society, Scottish Newspaper Proprietors' Association, The Institute of Journalists, the National Union of Journalists and The Guild of British Newspaper Editors hereinafter referred to as the constituent bodies.

1 Foundation—The Press Council, hereinafter called the Council, is voluntarily constituted on and from the first day of July, 1953, in the designation

"The General Council of the Press". The Council revokes that style and title on and from the first day of July, 1963, but accepts responsibility for all acts performed by The General Council of the Press as though they had been done by The Press Council.

2 Objects—The Objects of the Council are:

(i) To preserve the established freedom of the British Press.

(ii) To maintain the character of the British Press in accordance with the highest professional and commercial standards.

(iii) To consider complaints about the conduct of the Press or the conduct of persons and organisations towards the Press; to deal with these complaints in whatever manner might seem practical and appropriate and record resultant action.

(iv) To keep under review developments likely to restrict the supply of information of public interest and importance.

(v) To report publicly on developments that may tend towards greater concentration or monopoly in the Press (including changes in ownership, control and growth of Press undertakings) and to publish statistical information relating thereto.

(vi) To make representations on appropriate occasions to the Government, organs of the United Nations and to Press organisations abroad.

(vii) To publish periodical reports recording the Council's work and to review from time to time, developments in the Press and the factors affecting them.

3 Membership—The Council shall consist of:

(i) A Chairman who shall be a person otherwise unconnected with the Press.

(ii) Eighteen members nominated by the following bodies in the proportions indicated:

The Newspaper Publishers' Association Ltd.	3

At least one of whom shall be an editorial—as distinct from managerial—nominee.

The Newspaper Society	3

At least one of whom shall be an editorial nominee.

Periodical Publishers Association Ltd. including one editorial nominee	2
The Scottish Daily Newspaper Society	1
Scottish Newspaper Proprietors' Association	1
The Guild of British Newspaper Editors	2
National Union of Journalists	4
The Institute of Journalists	2

(iii) Representatives of the Public who, excluding the Chairman, shall amount to one half of the Council's total membership entitled to vote   18

(iv) Additionally each constituent body may nominate one of its officials to attend meetings of the Council in a consultative capacity. Such nominees may speak but not vote. Constituent bodies may change these nominees by giving seven days' notice to the Director of the Council.

4 Methods of appointment

(i) The Chairman shall be invited to accept office on such terms as shall be agreed mutually by him and the Council.

(ii) Members nominated within the provisions of Article 3 (ii) shall be persons who at the time of appointment, are full-time directors of newspapers, periodicals, news agencies supplying a daily service of news to newspapers in Great Britain and/or overseas or full-time editorial or managerial employees on the staffs of such organisations. Editorial qualification shall include also full-time professional free-lance journalists regularly engaged in supplying news and/or articles to recognised newspapers, periodicals or news agencies. A member ceasing to be so qualified shall notify the Director of the Council in writing within one calendar month and his membership shall terminate within three calendar months.

(iii) Representatives of the Public co-opted to the Council shall be selected by an Appointments Commission (as hereinafter provided) from a panel of candidates submitted to the Appointments Commission by the Council from time to time. These representatives shall rank equal with members nominated by the constituent bodies in the rights, privileges and duties inherent in membership of the Council other than qualification for election to the vice-chairmanship.

(iv) The Appointments Commission shall consist of up to five persons who shall be chosen by the Chairman and other members of the Council and shall be invited to accept office on such terms as shall be agreed mutually between them and the Council. The Director of the Council shall act as Secretary of the Commission.

5 Retirement

(i) On nomination to the Council a person, if qualified and except as provided in Clause (iii) of this Article, shall be entitled to membership for three consecutive years or until the termination of the third financial year of the Council following the nomination, whichever may be the longer.

(ii) At the end of such period of membership of the Council, a nominee in the group described in Article 3 (ii) above, if qualified, shall be eligible for renomination.

(iii) Of the first six members selected by the Appointments Commission under Article 4 (iii) above, except those who are re-selected for a second term, two shall retire at the end of the first year and a half of membership and a further four at the end of two and a half years' membership. The members so retiring shall be decided by lot. They will be eligible for renomination and thereafter the normal period of their membership of the Council and that of their successors shall be three years.

6 Casual Vacancies—A person filling a casual vacancy shall be appointed to membership in like manner to that by which the person whose vacancy he fills was appointed. On initial appointment he shall retain membership only for the unexpired portion of the period which remained to the person whose place in the Council he takes.

7 Procedure—The Council is empowered by the constituent bodies to regulate and control all its procedure and action for the furtherance and attainment of the objects defined in Article 2 hereof as the Council may decide. The Chairman and members shall each be entitled to cast one vote in any matter decided by them on a show of hands or by ballot, but if the division should result in an equal number of votes being cast for and against the

motion the chairman for the time being shall be entitled to exercise a casting vote.

8 Quorum—A quorum at a Council meeting shall be 18 members of whom not fewer than 9 shall be members in the group described in Article 3 (ii) above.

9 Vice-Chairman

(i) At its first meeting following the thirty-first day of December in each year the Council shall elect from its Press members nominated under the provision of Article 3 (ii) a vice-chairman who shall hold office until the first meeting of the Council in the following financial year.

(ii) In the event of a casual vacancy in the vice-chairmanship the election of a successor shall take place at the meeting of the Council next following the expiration of 14 days from the occurrence of the vacancy.

(iii) Members who have consented to be candidates for the vice-chairmanship shall be nominated and seconded in writing in advance of the meeting. If there is no written nomination, oral nominations may be received at the time of the election.

(iv) Subject to remaining qualified under Articles 3 (ii) and 4 (ii) a retiring vice-chairman shall be eligible for re-election. In the absence of any nomination the retiring vice-chairman shall be declared elected.

(v) Should the office of Chairman be vacant the vice-chairman shall fulfill all the functions of chairmanship. In the absence of the Chairman the vice-chairman shall preside at Council and Committee meetings.

10 Meetings—Meetings shall be held at least five times a year. The Chairman is empowered to call a special meeting, if, in his opinion, the business to be transacted warrants this action. A special meeting shall be convened by the Director on the requisition of not fewer than nine members. Such requisitions shall be addressed to the Director at the office of the Council for the time being. Not less than seven days' notice shall be given in writing of any meeting of the Council unless members agree to accept shorter notice.

16 Dissolution—The Council may at any time terminate its existence if it appears to the members that the Council's voluntary nature and independence are threatened. A resolution to dissolve the Council, to be binding, must be passed by a two-thirds majority of its members present and voting at a meeting specially called for the purpose, which two-thirds majority shall be not less than a simple majority of the membership of the Council. Not less than twenty-one days' notice shall be given of any such meeting and this shall give particulars of the purpose for which the meeting is called. The Council shall notify secretaries of the constituent bodies of such meeting at the time it summons members.

17 Alteration of Constitution—Alterations of these Articles of Constitution shall require the approval of a two-thirds majority of the members present and voting at a meeting, which two-thirds majority shall be not less than a simple majority of the membership of the Council. No alteration shall be effective unless at least 28 days' notice of a proposed alteration shall have been given to Council members and secretaries of the constituent bodies.

AN AJUDICATION BY THE PRESS COUNCIL

MP's privacy complaint rejected

A complaint by Ms Maureen Colquhoun, MP, that the *Daily Mail* had intruded into her privacy in a story in its gossip column was rejected. Nevertheless the Council decided that the identification of a woman friend in the story was a gross intrusion into privacy which could not be justified on the grounds of public interest. The Council considered the methods employed to obtain information from the friend constituted harassment of a serious kind, but ruled that there was no harassment in the case of Ms Colquhoun. The Council went on to make an important pronouncement on the privacy of MPs.

In its Diary the newspaper published a story saying that Ms Colquhoun had left her matrimonial home in Shoreham to share an East End house with a close woman friend. Subsequently the newspaper published two further reports on Ms Colquhoun. One concerned a burglary at the house and said it was a little hurtful that she had asked the local police not to give details of it to the *Daily Mail*. The other said the writer had been endeavouring to contact Ms Colquhoun who was trying to introduce a Bill on privacy, but she would not take the calls. "Can either action have anything to do with my report that Maureen had left her husband?," asked the report.

Two days before publication of the original article Ms Colquhoun wrote to the Editor complaining of harassment by his reporters, one of whom was Nigel Dempster, she said. She asked that it be stopped.

She told the Council that publication of items by the *Daily Mail* in three separate reports was an unjustified intrusion into her private life. The whole tone of the first article was one of leering innuendo and lip-smacking suggestion. Her friends and children of her friends were approached by a reporter and so were Labour councillors in her constituency of Northampton North. During the week following publication she, her friend, and friend's children were persistently badgered by reporters and photographers. To clear the air she issued a statement to her constituents telling them she had ceased to live with her husband; that they had been married for 26 years and it had been a happy, loving and faithful marriage and had resulted in three children who were leading useful and balanced lives. She and her husband had decided, in a civilised way, to go their separate ways.

Ms Colquhoun submitted a letter from her husband Keith telling her that Nigel Dempster had phoned him asking for a comment on the breakup of their marriage. When he declined to comment, he said Mr. Dempster became increasingly persistent and excited. He reported Nigel Dempster as saying:– "I am going to publish the story tomorrow anyway and your attitude will look very silly."

Daily Mail reporter Alison McInnes told the Council she had phoned Ms Colquhoun at the London house and that a child answered. She asked if Ms Colquhoun lived there and was told she did but was out. Miss McInnes said she felt no need to tell the child who she was. She phoned again, and as Ms Colquhoun was out asked for the woman friend's office address and telephone number. She called the friend's office several times and asked to speak to her. At all times she represented herself as a reporter on the *Daily Mail*. She phoned the press department of the friend's office and asked for a photograph. She then went to the house with a photographer, and to the House of Commons, but Ms Colquhoun refused to see her.

In a statement to the Council, Ms Colquhoun's friend said while she was engaged, her office had been phoned several times by *Mail* reporter Alison McInnes. When Miss McInnes spoke to her she asked if Maureen Colquhoun lived with her and the friend replied she had no comment. The following day Nigel Dempster repeatedly phoned her office. She told him she was not in the habit of discussing her family or friends with gossip columnists and she would be obliged if he would stop pestering her very busy office. He asked to meet her and when she refused said she would feel very differently when she saw her and her daughter's name in his column. He told her she would be well advised to meet him to prevent this and that he "knew all about her" but he was "really after Maureen Colquhoun who, as a Member of Parliament, accepted public money." He was rather sorry for her and again urged her to meet him for her own good. She repeated she had nothing to say and that she considered his tone grossly insulting.

The following morning she was told by officials at her office that they were being pestered by the *Daily Mail* for a photograph. Other acquaintances were also phoned and visited by the *Daily Mail* asking for a photograph of her. In the days that followed, her husband and children were constantly harassed by reporters phoning and ringing the doorbell. Her children became very frightened and upset.

Nigel Dempster told the Council he phoned the friend's office three times before he spoke to her. He told her he was making a courtesy call because he was writing a story concerning her domestic arrangements with Maureen Colquhoun and if there were any comments she wished to make he would be delighted to publish them. Mr. Dempster said she did not feel she could comment and he left the invitation open should she change her mind. His recollection was of a friendly conversation.

The Editor, Mr. David English, told the Council that the newspaper's inquiries into the breakup of Ms Maureen Colquhoun's marriage and the subsequent publication of the facts was a legitimate news story in the public interest. Such inquiries into the lives of public figures could not be held to be an invasion of privacy. He submitted a ten-page letter setting out his reasons.

The newspaper used three criteria to decide which matrimonial difficulties should be published and which ones ignored:-

(1) If the people are what might lossely be termed 'national or international personalities' . . .
(2) Where the circumstances of the breakup are significantly different to make news in themselves.
(3) Where the circumstances of the breakup might have a direct bearing on an individual's work or social-political attitudes; particularly where such a person is in the public eye and their work should be accountable to the public. For example, a politician representing many thousands of constituents.

He argued that the circumstances of Ms Colquhouns' matrimonial breakup were "in the public interest" on the basis of points two and three. In February

(1976) she had made a formal request to the Parliamentary Serjeant-at-Arms and the Speaker of the House of Commons not to call her Mrs., but to address her using the "American Women's Liberation appellation of Ms." Newspapers reported on 13 March that the Speaker had accepted Mrs. Colquhoun's request and made history by using the word Ms in front of her name when he called her to speak."

Mr. English stressed that the whole weight of the story and all the inquiries were directed towards a legitimate area of a woman MP who was becoming involved with the women's liberation movement and was moving into its more radical section. The newspaper wanted to talk at length to Ms Colquhoun on whether her strong involvement had caused her matrimonial breakup and whether it would affect her political and Parliamentary attitudes in the future.

He said Mr. Dempster had telephoned Mr. Colquhoun and was quite straightforward in asking whether he wanted to comment on the breakup of the marriage. Mr. Dempster rejected Mr. Colquhoun's recall of the conversation. Mr. English said that Mr. Dempster also rejected totally the woman friend's account of his telephone call to her.

Before the Council's Complaints Committee Mr. Dempster outlined the circumstances of his telephone call and said his memory of the conversation was that it lasted several minutes and at the end of it he felt he had been talking to a very restrained and courteous lady. He had made no notes. He used no form of harassment to make her do anything against her will and he did not bully or have a bullying tone in his voice. Mr. Dempster did not believe that asking an employer for a photograph of an employee was an infringement of that person's privacy. It was ordinary journalistic practice and an insurance policy against "future trouble."

He said there were parts of the Press Council's statement of principle on privacy with which he disagreed: he felt that anyone who entered public life forfeited their privacy.

The woman friend of Ms Colquhoun repeated in essence the written statement she had submitted to the Press Council and supported it with notes she had taken during the conversation.

The adjudication was: The Press Council recently declared that the publication of information about the private lives or concerns of individuals without their consent is only acceptable if there is a legitimate public interest overriding the right of privacy. The Council has emphasised that the public interest relied upon as a justification for publication or inquiries into such matters must be a legitimate and proper public interest and not only a prurient or morbid curiosity. In particular the Council has said that entry into public life does not disqualify an individual from a right to privacy about his private affairs save when the circumstances relating to the private life of an individual occupying a public position may be likely to affect the performance of his public duties or public confidence in him or his office.

What was published about the complainant in this case, both as fact and as innuendo, would undoubtedly have been an unacceptable invasion of the privacy to which a private individual is entitled. But Ms Colquhoun is not a private person. She is a Member of Parliament. If that had been all, the Press Council might not have considered that that fact alone entitled the *Daily Mail* to intrude upon her privacy any more than if she had been a private person: Members of Parliament are entitled to a degree of protection in their private lives. But it is not all, and the factor which in the opinion of the Council takes the case just over the border into what is permissible is that she is a Member of Parliament who has taken a very strong stand on feminist issues and has not been loath to publicise her views upon them. In the Press Council's view this brings the breakdown of her marriage and the fact that she had left what had been her matrimonial home to share a house with another woman into the area of those matters which the public is entitled to know as being capable of affecting the performance of her public duties or affecting public confidence in her views as a Member of Parliament.

The publication in the *Daily Mail* of two further references to Ms Colquhoun was the result in the one case of what the Council considers to have been a misguided effort to prevent information available to the rest of the Press being given to the *Daily Mail*, and in the other by her own activity in the attempted promotion of privacy legislation. Given that the original publication about her cannot be regarded as a breach of the Council's guidelines as to privacy, the Council does not feel able to condemn these further references.

Having regard to these considerations, the measures taken by the *Daily Mail* to make contact with Ms Colquhoun and to inquire into these matters were not unreasonable. The Council rejects the complaint that the *Daily Mail* unjustifiably intruded into Ms Colquhoun's private life and it rejects the complaint that the methods employed constituted harassment of her.

The woman friend with whom Ms Colquhoun shares a house is in a different position. The Press Council deplores her identification in the gossip column of the *Daily Mail* as being a gross intrusion into her privacy which cannot be justified on the grounds of public interest even in the terms set out by the Editor of the newspaper itself. The Council considers that the methods employed to obtain information from her and from Mr. Colquhoun constituted harassment of a serious kind. The Council upholds Ms Colquhoun's complaint in this respect.

The Council decided that Ms Colquhoun's woman friend should not be identified in its press release. (N 5158P).

Statement about amended press release

Four months later the Council issued a statement following a request by Ms Colquhoun that it should investigate the manner in which the *Daily Mail* published the adjudication and the subsequent leaders and comments by the Editor.

Ms Colquhoun asked why the newspaper was able to bring lawyers and threats of sueing upon the Council; why a second press release had been issued, mitigating in favour of the *Daily Mail*; and why it included a new paragraph saying: "The Council goes on to make an important pronouncement on the privacy of MPs."

The Complaints Committee noted that Mr. English had written to the Council that it was unfortunate that Mr. Dempster had stated on Capital Radio that the Council had revised its draft after a warning of legal action by the *Mail*. He had been rebuked for this. At no time, wrote Mr. English, did he or any member of his staff discuss the matter with their legal advisers nor did they issue any threat of legal action.

The Council's statement was: The manner in which the *Daily Mail* published the Press Council's adjudication on the complaint made by Ms Maureen

Colquhoun, MP, was noted by the Complaints Committee of the Press Council on the day of publication and the Director sent a letter to the Editor, Mr. David English, pointing out the omissions.

Mr. English replied expressing his distress. The following morning the *Daily Mail* published the paragraph that had been omitted and declared full acceptance of the Press Council's guidelines that the whole adjudication should always be published. Subsequently representatives of the newspaper met the Complaints Committee which accepted the newspaper's apology for what had occurred.

When advance copies of the press release were sent to the parties, the Press Council received representations from the *Daily Mail* that the narrative part of the press release lacked balance to the unreasonable prejudice of the newspaper. No representations were made by the *Daily Mail* in connection with the adjudication itself. The Director of the Council was satisfied that the press release was indeed out of balance and required editorial rearrangement. The language of the original press release was then changed, not by the *Daily Mail*, but by the Director in words of his own choice. The newspaper had nothing to do with the insertion of a new paragraph and was given no notice of it. As Ms Colquhoun subsequently agreed, the new paragraph was an accurate statement of fact.

At no time did Mr. English convey any threat of legal proceedings against the Press Council, nor did he nor any member of his staff discuss the matter with their legal advisers. The statement which was subsequently made on the radio on this point was untrue.

Two factual alterations were requested by Ms Colquhoun. They were discussed with her, the wording was agreed and the changes were made. A copy of the amended press release was posted to Ms Colquhoun on the day before publication. It cannot be established why she did not receive it.

The Press Council accepts the view that the unusual publicity given to the case in the *Daily Mail* reflected the importance of the matter from the point or view of the Press, and the Press Council agrees it was an important announcement. They found no impropriety in the action of the *Daily Mail* or of the Director of the Council. (O 5629).

[*The Press and the People, Twenty-fourth Annual Report of the Press Council, 1977* (London, 1979), pp. 72-80.]

Note: 48 M.P.'s signed a motion regretting the adjudication of the Press Council in this case. See also pp. 350 and 360.

Goldsmith v. Sperrings Ltd. and others [1977] 1 W.L.R. 478

Court of Appeal

Sir James Goldsmith considered that he had been libelled by *Private Eye,* a satirical magazine. He began civil actions against the publishers, the editor and the main distributors. He obtained leave to prosecute this group (the principals) for criminal libel. In addition he issued writs, 74 in number, against 37 secondary wholesale and retail distributors of the magazine. Sixteen of the distributors reached settlements with the plaintiff on terms that he would cease his action against them and they would cease to handle *Private Eye*. Seventeen distributors continued to handle the magazine.

Negotiations between the plaintiff and the principals for a settlement, but it was understood by all that if a settlement had been reached the plaintiff would have to agree not to impede sales of *Private Eye,* would discontinue his actions against the remaining distributors and would release from their undertaking not to handle Private Eye those distributors with whom he had already settled.

The remaining distributors applied for an order to stay the actions against them as an abuse of process of the court in that the plaintiff's purpose in pursuing actions against the distributors was said not to be to protect his reputation but the collateral purpose of destroying Private Eye by cutting off its retail outlets. A Master stayed the action, but Stocker, J. ordered that the stay be lifted. The distributors appealed.

LORD DENNING, M.R.:
The standard form of settlement

Sir James's solicitors actually prepared and used a standard form draft for distributors to sign on a settlement. It contains an undertaking by the distributors never to distribute "Private Eye" again: and for Sir James not to take proceedings in respect of the various issues, including that of December 12, 1975. This was the standard form letter for a distributor to sign. This was one signed by Twentieth Century Suppliers Ltd.:

> "Our clients . . . wish to apologise unreservedly to Mr. J. M. Goldsmith for any distress he may have been caused by their having distributed certain issues of 'Private Eye' containing statements considered to be defamatory of Mr. Goldsmith. Our clients recognise that 'Private Eye' is a contentious and controversial publication which appears to attract a fair number of libel writs. That being the case, they have decided to discontinue distributing the magazine and can assure Mr. Goldsmith that in consideration of him not proceeding further with Actions 1976 G Nos. 245 and 246 and not issuing further proceedings against them in connection with any distribution of 'Private Eye' which has occurred prior to today's date our clients for their part undertake not to distribute 'Private Eye' again. . . ."

The reply by Sir James's solicitors was an acceptance of that undertaking, repeating the same words.

. . . I see no *need* and no *justification* for Sir James to sue the subordinate distributors. There was no *need* to sue the distributors: for he had issued writs against the principals of "Private Eye" and could obtain in those proceedings everything to which he was entitled, namely, damages and an injunction against similar libels. There was no *justification* for him to sue the distributors. No one could suppose that they had been in any way negligent. Their only offence, if any, was that they had distributed "Private Eye": and I have yet to learn that that gave Sir James a cause of action against them: any more than it gave him a cause of action against the public libraries or others who distributed it.

Further, his actions have caused *irremediable damage* in advance of any judicial determination of wrong-doing. By no possibility could Sir James have obtained before trial an interim injunction against the principals of "Private Eye" themselves. Even if he had, he would have had to give an undertaking in damages in case he was wrong. Yet, by suing the distributors, he has achieved more than ever an injunction would have done. He has succeeded in obtaining a big reduction in the circulation of "Private Eye." It has dropped by more than 12,000 in every issue. That may affect its finances, even its continuance. This has come about because the distributors who were sued—and other distributors, too—feel that they dare not risk handling it any more. They fear that if they do, they may be sued for libel. This damage has been done by the use of legal process. I ask the question: is it right to allow legal process to be used so as to inflict irremediable damage of this sort? Damage which is different in kind and worse than a court of law could inflict. Namely, the reduction or extinction of its circulation. The significance of the issue is observed by a leader writer in a trade paper which was put in evidence before us. By issuing "frightening writs" against distributors—he puts it in inverted commas, like "gagging writs"—an individual may succeed in cutting the lifeline by which a periodical reaches its paying public—which would be a graver blow than any court case.

Not only was there no need for Sir James to sue the subordinate distributors so as to obtain redress. Just see the way he went about it. He, or his solicitors, must have gone through a list of newsagents who distribute newspapers and periodicals. There are a great many of them. They picked out 37 of them, with nothing to distinguish them from all the others except that they were the bigger firms with several shops and bookstalls. Why pick on these 37 only? They must have said to themselves, "Let us sue all the big firms." It was done so hastily that the list included three who had never handled "Private Eye" at all. The solicitors treated each one of the 37 with scant courtesy. They never wrote a letter before action. They never gave any of them the chance of explaining or apologising, or of making arrangements for the future.They never inquired whether they had used due care or not. Sir James, with the help of his solicitors, shot off his gun against each. A double-barrelled gun, too. Two writs against each, where one would do: 74 writs in all, when all could have been brought in one writ against all 37.

Was this the proper use of legal process? I do not think so. . . .

Conclusion

I would like to say that I appreciate to the full the indignation which Sir James justly and rightfully felt on account of the most hurtful campaign which "Private Eye" mounted against him. He was quite entitled to use every legal process available to hit the principals of "Private Eye" hard—as hard as he could within the limits allowed by law. Sometimes he has succeeded against them. Sometimes he has failed. But his indignation, I think, got the better of him when he went for the subordinate distributors also—at any rate, in the way he did it.

No doubt he thought that "Private Eye" was such a scurrilous magazine that it ought not to be published or distributed by anyone: and thought that a good way of stopping it, or reducing it, was to hit at the channels of distribution and shut them off. But that was a collateral purpose outside the legitimate scope of the legal process. The freedom of the press depends on keeping the channels of distribution open. If these are blocked so that a ban is placed on the distribution of even one periodical, that is an intrusion on the freedom of the press. Such a ban, whether reached by agreement, or otherwise, is not to be enforced by the law unless there are sufficient circumstances to justify it. I find no sufficient circumstances here to justify a ban on the distribution of "Private Eye." In so far as the object of these actions was to get it banned, it was an improper object: and the continuance of them would be oppressive. In my opinion, the courts should not allow the actions to continue. I would, therefore, be in favour of allowing the appeals and restoring the order of Master Warren.

SCARMAN L.J.:

Since I find myself in complete agreement with the judgment under appeal, delivered by Stocker J. in chambers on October 15, 1976, I shall be brief.

I dissent from Lord Denning M.R. with diffidence and very great respect: but at the end of the day, notwithstanding the persuasive eloquence of Mr. Comyn for the appellants, I take a different view of the facts from that which the Master of the Rolls has taken. As I see it, this appeal (for it is really one appeal, though there are several appellants, each of whom appeals in his own separate action) turns on a question of fact. The history of the matter is complex: but the question can be shortly put and answered. If Sir James Goldsmith's purpose in initiating or pursuing his actions against the secondary distributors be to destroy "Private Eye," namely, to use his wealth so as to suppress it, he is abusing the process of the court. Neither wealth nor power entitles a man to censor the press. If, however, his purpose be to vindicate and protect his reputation, the use of all remedies afforded him by the law for that purpose cannot be an abuse of the court's process. It is never easy to determine a man's purpose. Ordinarily this task of judgment is tackled only after trial. In the instant case, we are being asked to pass judgment on the respondent's purpose upon a preliminary application, the effect of which, if successful, will prevent him bringing to trial actions in each of which (it was admitted in argument) he is pleading a cause of action recognised by the law. It is right, therefore, that to obtain before trial the summary arrest of a plaintiff's proceedings as an abuse of the process of the court, the task of satisfying the court that a stay should be imposed is, and should be seen to be, a heavy one: see *Shackleton* v. *Swift* [1913] 2 K.B. 304, 311-312.

Unless the court is satisfied, a stay is a denial of justice by the court—a situation totally intolerable.

In the instant proceedings the defendants have to show that the plaintiff has an ulterior motive, seeks a collateral advantage for himself beyond what the law offers, is reaching out "to effect an object not within the scope of the process": *Grainger* v. *Hill* (1838) 4 Bing.(N.C.) 212, 221 *per* Tindal C.J. In a phrase, the plaintiff's purpose has to be shown to be not that which the law by granting a remedy offers to fulfil, but one which the law does not recognise as a legitimate use of the remedy sought: see *In re Majory* [1955] Ch. 600, 623. It was no doubt with these considerations in mind that at the outset of his argument for the plaintiff, Sir James Goldsmith, respondent in the appeal, Mr. Hawser submitted that the appellants cannot get their case off the ground unless they can satisfy the court that his client's purpose in starting or continuing his actions against the "secondary" distributors was to stifle the future publication of "Private Eye" by depriving it of its commercial outlets. The judge was not satisfied that this was Sir James Goldsmith's purpose. Neither am I. Sir James Goldsmith has asserted on his oath that it was not his purpose to shut off the channels of distribution of "Private Eye," and that he sued the distributors merely as participators in the publication of what he regarded as very grave and damaging libels: see his affidavit of September 22, 1976. In the same affidavit he described negotiations into which he entered between April 26 and May 11, 1976, with "the principal defendants," that is, the publishers, editor, and main distributors of the magazine, for the settlement of all pending litigation between them. He put forward terms of settlement which could in no way impede or obstruct the future publication of "Private Eye" and, according to his sworn word, it was understood by all who took part in the discussion that, if there was a settlement, he would not pursue the remaining actions against the secondary distributors. . . .

. . . If the true issue be, as upon the authorities it must be, what was (and is) the purpose of Sir James Goldsmith in pursuing the rights given him by law against the secondary distributors, Sir James Goldsmith is not putting the press in peril. If this purpose be illegitimate, his actions will be stayed. If it is not, he is exercising rights given him by law. If, therefore, there be in these proceedings a threat to press freedom, the threat comes, not from Sir James Goldsmith, but from the law itself, in that it provides a cause of action against distributors as well as publishers. That is a matter for Parliament, not the courts. So long as the cause of action exists, it may be invoked unless it can be shown that it is being used to secure a collateral advantage.

If the effect of the law is to diminish freedom of the press, Parliament will have to decide where the balance is to be struck between freedom and the protection of the defamed citizen. Some, no doubt, will argue against any restraint being imposed upon distributors of newspapers. Some may even wish to go so far as to call for a legal obligation to be imposed upon all newsagents and others engaged in the business of newspaper distribution to provide an outlet for all newspapers and periodicals, whatever they publish. Others, however, will argue that the existing law provides in the action against a secondary distributor a valuable additional remedy for an individual who is defamed by a scurrilous or financially dubious publication. We do not have to consider these questions.

My third, and final, comment on the argument to which we have listened is that decision in this appeal is not helped by reference to the wealth of Sir James Goldsmith. Wealth may well have afforded him the chance of invoking the law to protect his reputation in a way in which—alas!—a poorer man could not. If so, the inference is simply that this branch of the law is not, as it should be, available to poor men.

I would dismiss the appeals.

Bridge L.J. delivered a lengthy judgment agreeing with the judgments of Stocker J. and Scarman, L.J. The Appeal Committee of the House of Lords dismissed a petition by the distributors for leave to appeal.

Associated Newspapers Group Ltd. v. Wade [1979] I.R.L.R. 201

Court of Appeal

This was an appeal against an interlocutory injuction granted against Mr. Wade, General Secretary, and other officers of the National Graphical Association restraining them from organising a blacking of certain advertisements in the press. The N.G.A. was in dispute with the Nottingham

Evening Post over a claim for recognition. The N.G.A. sought to put pressure on the paper by dissuading companies and organisations from placing advertisements in the Post. When 16 organisations continued to advertise in the Post the N.G.A. instructed its members employed on other newspapers not to handle advertisements from these organisations. The purpose of this was to pressurise the organisations concerned to withdraw their advertisements from the Post. The Court of Appeal dismissed the appeal on a variety of grounds. In the course of his judgment, **LORD DENNING,** M.R. in considering the legality of the unions' action at common law had this to say concerning freedom of the press:

Running through all our cases you will find it implicitly accepted as a fundamental principle of our law that the press shall be free. It shall be at liberty to express opinions and to give news and information to the public at large without interference by anyone inside or outside their organisation: so long as they do not offend against the law of libel or confidential information or contempt of court or suchlike. The fact that the law has admitted those special exceptions proves the existence of the general principle: and I have stated it myself on several occasions, such as in *BBC* v. *Hearn* [1977] IRLR 273 and in *Slater* v. *Raw* (unreported).

In this respect our law corresponds with Article 10(1) of the European Convention of Human Rights which says: 'Everyone has the right to freedom of expression. This right includes freedom to hold opinions and to receive and impart information and ideas without interference by public authority and regardless of frontiers.'

If there is to be no interference by public authority, all the more so there should be no interference by private individuals.

Article 10(2) contains exceptions corresponding to those in our own law.

The same principle was specifically accepted by trade unions in the agreement which followed the General Strike of 1926 and confirmed in letters of 1956 and written into all agreements with the men. This is what was said: '(It is) the established and accepted practice in the industry that there shall be no interference with the contents of any newspaper, periodical, or other matter printed or published by members'.

It was suggested to us that the word 'contents' there only refers to editorial copy and not to advertisements. I do not agree with that interpretation. It is a piece of special pleading. 'Contents' obviously includes advertisements as well as editorial copy.

We were shown letters passing between Lord Goodman (the Chairman of the Newspaper Publishers Association) and Mr. Wade in July 1975 in which the NGA denied this principle. They said:

'In general, we do not normally seek to interfere with the contents of newspapers—either editorial or advertising; nor do we wish to attempt to impose any form of censorship. But we do reserve the right to give unqualified backing to our members in circumstances where they feel strongly about some comment or other which is directed against them or the interests of this union; and we do reserve the right to use our industrial strength in the general interests of the members of this Association'.

To my mind there is no such right. A trade union has no right to use its industrial strength to invade the freedom of the press. They have no right to interfere with the freedom of editors to comment on matters of public interest. They have no right to interfere with the freedom—and duty—of public authorities to recruit staff; or otherwise inform the public of matters of interest or concern to them. They have no right to interfere with the freedom of commercial firms to advertise their wares. These freedoms are so fundamental in our society that no trade union has any right to interfere with them. Interference with the freedom of the press is so contrary to the public interest that it is to be regarded as the employment of unlawful means: just as Lord Justice Russell regarded the boycott of the 'Daily Mirror' in *Daily Mirror Newspapers* v. *Gardner* (1968) 2 Queen's Bench 762 at page 785.

I do not mean to suggest by all this that men employed by newspapers cannot come out on strike for better wages or conditions: but this is because they are given statutory immunity in that respect. I am only concerned at the moment to state the common law as I understand it.

Questions

1. Jones is the proprietor of the *Daily Blurb*, a national newspaper. He strongly supports Brown, M.P. as the next leader of the Labour Party, but Green, M.P. who is extremely popular with his colleagues is the candidate most likely to replace the present leader at his retirement. Jones disapproves strongly of Green's left-wing tendencies. He therefore instructs White, the editor of the *Daily Blurb*, to publish nothing that is in any way favourable to Green in the columns of the *Daily Blurb*. He also instructs White to publish any "dirt" he can dig out about Green.

Hearing of Jone's action, the *Red Bull*, a left-wing weekly, publishes an article which attacks Jone's instruction to his editor and exposes Jone's own shady financial dealings. Jones issues a writ for defamation. Realising that they will be unable to justify what they have said concerning Jone's financial dealings because of the reluctance of certain key witnesses to appear in court, the *Red Bull* agree to settle the matter out of court on terms which include an undertaking that they will not in future publish any material defaming or critical of Jones.

What action can either Green or the *Red Bull* take to challenge the action taken against them and before whom?

2. "The liberty of the press consists in printing without previous licence, subject to the consequences of the law" — Lord Mansfield (1784).

"Freedom of the press today consists in the freedom of the three multi-national companies and six rich men, who control the nation's daily press, to publish what *they* choose"—Trade Unionist (1980).

Discuss.

3. What do you think freedom of the press should mean today? What legal or other changes would be necessary to implement your views.?

4.   RADIO AND TELEVISION

Further Reading

De Smith, pp. 465–466; O'Higgins, pp. 122–137; Street, pp. 77–96; Wade & Phillips, pp. 486–487.

J. Dearlove, "The BBC and the Politicians," (1974) 3(1) *Index on Censorship* pp. 23–34; (1966) 2(4) *Censorship, passim*; Sir Hugh Greene, *The Future of Broadcasting in Britain* (Hart-Davis, MacGibbon, 1972); J. D. Halloran (ed.), *The Effects of Mass Communication* (Leicester U.P., 1970); P. Schlesigner, *Putting 'Reality' Together* (Constable, 1978); A. Smith, *The Shadow in the Cave: The Broadcaster, the Audience and the State* (Allen & Unwin, 1973); *ibid*, "TV Coverage of Northern Ireland", (1972) 1(2) *Index on Censorship* pp. 15–32; M. Tracey, *The Production of Political Television* (Routledge, 1977); J. Whale, *The Half-Shut Eye: Television and Politics in Britain and America* (MacMillan, 1970); M. Whitehouse, *Cleaning-up TV* (Blandford, 1967); C. R. Munro, *Television Censorship & The Law* (Saxon House, 1979).

REPRESENTATION OF THE PEOPLE ACT 1969

9. Broadcasting during elections

(1) Pending a parliamentary or local government election it shall not be lawful for any item about the constituency or electoral area to be broadcast from a television or other wireless transmitting station in the United Kingdom if any of the persons who are for the time being candidates at the election takes part in the item and the broadcast is not made with his consent; and where an item about a constituency or electoral area is so broadcast pending a parliamentary or local government election there, then if the broadcast either is made before the latest time for delivery of nomination papers, or is made after that time but without the consent of any candidate remaining validly nominated, any person taking part in the item for the purpose of promoting or procuring his election shall be guilty of an illegal practice, unless the broadcast is so made without his consent.

(2) For purposes of subsection (1) above—

(a) a parliamentary election shall be deemed to be pending during the period ending with the close of the poll and beginning—

(i) at a general election, with the date of the dissolution of Parliament or any earlier time at which Her Majesty's intention to dissolve Parliament is announced; or

(ii) at a by-election, with the date of the issue of the writ for the election or any earlier date on which a certificate of the vacancy is notified in the Gazette in accordance with the Recess Elections Act 1784, the Election of Members during Recess Act 1858, the Bankruptcy (Ireland) Amendment Act 1872 or the Bankruptcy Act 1883.

BBC—METROPOLITAN POLICE AGREEMENT

Note: In the summer of 1979 an agreement was entered into between the BBC and the Metropolitan Police concerning the provision of facilities by the Police for programmes by the BBC. It is not uncommon for public bodies to lay down the conditions under which they are prepared to allow journalists and others facilities for the collection of information, etc. This particular agreement is unusual in its being written. Despite the fact that it is an agreement between two public bodies, requests to the BBC for a copy have been declined but the BBC refers enquirers to a report in *Broadcast* (July 1979):–

BBC answers back on Metropolitan Police "Charter"

AT A press conference last week, Dick Francis, director of BBC News and Current Affairs, said of the *Leveller's* disclosure of BBC internal discussions about relations with the police (see last week's *Broadcast*) that the new procedural arrangements merely codified what was normal practice with any institution which provided complex facilities.

The arrangements require producers to discuss and define a proposed programme area, put this in writing and secure police agreement, and to dicuss and obtain agreement on any change of plan.

A BBC spokesman described as "nonsense" the suggestion that the agreement undermined the editorial freedom of programme-makers. He insisted that the BBC would be happy to codify such arrangements with any institution which provided complex facilities, but it was only the agreement with the police which was in writing.

It was certainly not true, he said that the Metropolitan Police had the right to some deep level inquiry before the programme was made; if they took exception to a programme they had normal recourse to the law or to take the matter to the BBC Complaints Commission.

There was no way in which the BBC would have agreed to a contract, proposed by the police, which would give the "Met" the right to preview and censor programmes concerning police matters.

And the written procedures, which codified rights which had always existed informally, applied only to programmes which required special facilities, not to news items or straightforward current affairs features on police work.

Nor did they apply to drama. As far as dramatised documentaries, or "factions", were concerned, Dick Francis at the press conference had expressed his continued surprise that some people were unable to make the distinction between drama and documentary, although the BBC had gone to considerable pains to ensure that viewers knew when they were watching one or the other.

BBC employees' freedom of expression

28.8. We were disturbed at the extent of the restrictions which the BBC in particular find it necessary to impose upon their staff. For example, we were surprised to find that the BBC did not allow their staff to publish anything or speak in public about broadcasting generally, without seeking the BBC's permission. We consider this is an unnecessary restriction which in law would most likely be held against public policy. Nor should the restrictions continue to operate during the time when a person under contract, having been made redundant, receives his redundancy pay. The BBC have made a move to reduce the number of staff bound by restrictions and that is to the good. But we would go further and consider that the BBC should thoroughly overhaul their regulations and restore rights to individuals which they should never have been asked to surrender.

28.9. But we accept that some restrictions on political activities are essential if the broadcasters are to be accepted by the public as observing due impartiality in their programmes. We also accept that in common with most business concerns, the BBC and television and radio companies are entitled to write into staff contracts provisions forbidding them to disclose information relating to the business or affairs of the organisation gained during their employment, or to publish or speak in public about the organisation and its affairs. The BBC must also ensure that their staff do not associate themselves with commercial advertising. However, we consider that the restrictions on staff activities, both in the BBC and in other broadcasting organisations, should be limited to the minimum essential for safeguarding public confidence in any broadcasting service. We recommend accordingly.

[*Report of the Committee on the Future of Broadcasting,* Cmnd. 6753, 1977.]

BBC COMPLAINTS COMMISSION

Constitution and Terms of Reference

1 A Programmes Complaints Commission is hereby constituted to consider and review complaints against the BBC of the type hereinafter set out.

2 The Commission shall consist of three members who shall hold office for three years (one of whom shall act as Chairman). Provided always that any member:
  (i) may resign on giving three months' notice at any time;
  (ii) shall resign if for any reason he becomes unfitted to act as such member. In the case of any doubt or dispute as to such unfitness it shall be resolved by the President of the Law Society for the time being or by a person nominated by the President.

3 The Commissioners first appointed shall make recommendations to the BBC as to the mode of securing the appointment as their successors of persons of similar independent status.

4 The complaints which the Commission will consider and review are complaints from individuals or organisations claiming themselves to have been treated unjustly or unfairly in connection with a programme or a related series of programmes as broadcast. Unjust or unfair treatment shall include unwarrented invasion of privacy and misrepresentation.

5 Subject to the provision in Clause 13, the Commission shall consider and review complaints if:
  (i) a) the complaint has first been raised in writing with the BBC within thirty days of the transmission or the last transmission in a related series of transmissions to which the complaint refers, and the complainant in the event of dissatisfaction with the explanation of its conduct given by the BBC has referred the matter to the Commission within thirty days of the receipt of the BBC's explanation;
  or b) the complaint has been raised in writing with the Commission within thirty days of the transmission or the last transmission in a related series of transmissions to which the complaint refers;
  and (ii) the complainant shall have undertaken in writing not to have recourse to the courts of law in connection with his complaint. A complainant who chooses first to go to law over his complaint may subsequently lay a complaint before the Commission if it relates to aspects of the matter other than those disposed of in the courts.

Provided, however, that the Commission may consider and review a complaint notwithstanding that the conditions of (i) above may not have been fulfilled, if the Commission considers that there are special circumstances which make it proper to do so, and provided further that the Commission may decline to consider and review a complaint notwithstanding that the conditions of (i) and (ii) above have been fulfilled if the Commission considers that the complaint is frivolous or constitutes an abuse of the procedure for the review of complaints.

6　Complaints shall be treated as being laid against the BBC and not against individual members of the BBC's staff or its other contributors, although the details of complaints will often require to be accompanied by the names of individuals.

7　The Commission shall report its adjudication on any complaint to the BBC which undertakes to publish each adjudication in one of its journals. The Commission shall, when it seems to it appropriate, prepare its adjudication in a form suitable for broadcasting and require the Corporation to transmit the adjudication which the Corporation undertakes to do.

8　The BBC shall pay proper regard to the views expressed in each adjudication. It shall be free to comment thereon and to decide what subsequent action, if any, is called for.

9　The BBC undertakes to give every assistance to the Commission. In particular it shall make available to the Commission such recordings or transcripts as may exist of transmitted programmes about which complaints are laid. The BBC shall also, on request from the Commission, make available unused material gathered for programmes, if it still exists, such as the Commission, after consulting the BBC, feels necessary. The Commission shall not disclose any unused material provided to it by the BBC to other parties without permission from the BBC, and, where appropriate, any other copyright-holders involved.

10　The Commission shall undertake to deal with complaints within a reasonable time and the BBC shall undertake to publish adjudications not later than 30 days from the date of their delivery to the BBC.

11　In making adjudications, the Commission shall act collectively, although this should not exclude the possibility of the expression of a dissenting opinion. When one member is absent or declares himself to be disqualified by reason of a special interest in any adjudication, it shall be proper for complaints to be considered by only two members of the Commission.

12　The Commission will, from time to time, decide on its own practice and procedure. Unless otherwise decided, however,
  (i) Complaints will ordinarily be put forward in writing, although whenever the Commission in its discretion considers it necessary an oral hearing will be granted.
  (ii) Complaints will be heard in private.
  (iii) Complaints must bear their own costs.

13　The decision of the Commission that a complaint does not come within its jurisdiction shall be final.

Programmes

[BBC Complaints Commission, *Annual Report* 1978-79 (London, 1979), pp. 39-41.]

An Adjudication by the BBC Complaints Commission

Complaint by Salford City Council

On 12 July 1973 a film report on gypsies was broadcast in the *Nationwide* programme on BBC-1. This was intended to illustrate how the Caravan Sites Act of 1968 was working out in practice. In describing some of the problems which arise in the treatment of gypsies, the broadcast dealt at some length with the situation at Salford, where, it was said, the gypsies had been fighting a running war with the Corporation, the police and the people of the City themselves. A gypsy was shown describing how he and his family had been roughly ejected by the police, several times, from a site on private land; the gypsies, it was said, claimed that, as far as they are concerned, Salford Corporation was one of the worst local authorities in Britain. Salford City Council, though invited by the BBC to comment, had declined to do so.

Salford City Council complained to the BBC and thereafter to the Commission that they had been unfairly treated by this broadcast. The Commission viewed a recording of the *Nationwide* item and studied the correspondence which had passed between Salford City Council and the BBC. The Commission also received oral submissions separately from representatives of Salford City Council and representatives of the BBC.

Salford City Council's complaint covered two main issues. The first was concerned with the Council's reasons for refusing to take part in the programme or to make any comment. BBC staff who were making the programme pressed the Council for comment but the Council replied to the BBC, both verbally and in a telex message on 22 June, that Salford had applied for exemption from the duty to provide a caravan site, that the appropriate Minister was seised of this matter in a judicial capacity and that the Council had undertaken with the Minister not to comment to the Press. A further telex message was sent to the BBC on 12 July (the day of the broadcast) confirming that this was the Council's reason for not commenting and adding that outstanding cases before the courts also precluded the possibility of comment. The telex message ended with the request that if any comment was to be made in the programme on the position of Salford the full text of the telex message (which amounted to some 170 words) should be made known. In the event the words used in the broadcast itself were:

> 'Salford City Council wouldn't talk to us because they're still hoping to persuade the Department of the Environment for exemption from the Act, saying that comment now would jeopardise their case.'

The omission of their own explanation, the Council said, was misleading, and the wording used was inaccurate and false.

The second main issue in the Council's complaint was that the overall effect of the programme was knowingly to give a false and misleading impression of the situation in Salford. Particular criticism was expressed by the Council of the sentence, 'Since then the Corporation has been using the police to harass the gypsies off council land and off private land.' This, said the Council, was untrue and should be withdrawn. Subsequently to the hearing, Salford City Council supplied to the Commission a copy of a letter of 29 October 1973 from the Assistant Chief Constable of Manchester to the Gypsy Council about a police investigation of events in April which the Salford City Council consider to be corroboration of the view expressed in their complaint. The

Council representatives re-affirmed to the Commission their view that the overall effect of the programme as a whole was unfair to Salford City Council. The BBC in replying to Salford City Council's criticisms, said that they accepted without question the right of any individual or organisation not to take part in a programme but did not accept an obligation to broadcast a verbatim statement on their behalf. They had doubted the likelihood that the Minister had required an undertaking which prohibited the council from explaining its position in general terms in the context of the film, and they did not consider that the legal proceedings referred to by Salford City Council prevented the Council explaining, if it chose, its attitude to gypsies in the city. The reason given in the programme for the Council's refusal to comment, scripted in the light of various conversations between the film-makers and members of the Salford authority, was, in the BBC's view, fair reportage. As to the overall effect of the programme the BBC stood by their view that the programme was fair and balanced. They drew attention to various passages in which the reasons for the attitude adopted by Salford and other towns were explained and stressed that the broadcast had been based on a considerable amount of first-hand evidence.

Adjudication

The Commission, having viewed the film and considered the points made by the Salford City Council and the BBC, have reached the following conclusions.

We accept that Salford City Council have consistently stated, both to the BBC and to the Press generally, that they had undertaken to the Minister not to make public comment while their request for exemption was under consideration. Whether or not they could in this instance have obtained release from the undertaking, their representatives confirmed that they had not sought such release, and that it was because of the undertaking that they were not prepared to comment. We agree with the BBC that it was not obliged to quote the Salford City Council's statement in full, as telexed on 12 July, particularly as it only arrived shortly before the broadcast. But the earlier message of 22 June was available as an explanation as to why the Council was unwilling to make any public comment. We do not need to decide whether it would constitute unfair treatment if the BBC were to omit altogether any reference to the explanation given by a party for its refusal to take part or to comment. But we are satisfied that, if reference is to be made to the reasons given, a fair and accurate statement of any reasons put forward by the party should be made. That is so even if the BBC have doubts about the validity of the reasons given, though in such circumstances it would be legitimate for the BBC to add their own comments in relation to the reasons given. In the present case the reason alleged by the BBC to have been given was quite different from that which the Council had in fact given, and was worded in such a way that in the context of the programme it was prejudicial to the Salford City Council. We consider that this amounted to misrepresentation, and as such was unfair treatment. To this extent, the complaint is upheld.

On the general accuracy of the programme and in particular the sentence which Salford City Council said was untrue—'Since then the Corporation has been using the police to harass the gypsies off council land and off private land'—we are in no position to say exactly what the facts were in each of a number of incidents over a considerable period. We are, however, satisfied from the evidence which the BBC gave us that the BBC did not make this statement without careful consideration and that they believed that they had reliable information to justify the statement they made. In these circumstances, we do not consider that the inclusion of this statement in the broadcast amounted to unfair treatment of Salford City Council, given their unwillingness to make any comment.

There remains the complaint that the overall effect of the programme was unfair to Salford City Council by giving a false and misleading impression. The BBC has reminded us that the policy prescribed for the Corporation is to treat controversial subjects with due impartiality in the general field of programmes dealing with matters of public policy. At our request the BBC has also stated its policy when one party to a dispute which is the subject of a programme refuses to participate in the programme. The BBC confirmed that it recognises the right of anyone to refuse to take part in a programme, but cannot allow that right to be exercised to prevent discussion of a subject. In such circumstances, the BBC told us that it accepts a duty of ensuring that the case of the absent party does not go by default. We have no criticism of the policy as described by the BBC; provided that it is properly observed, we believe that it is well designed to avoid unfairness.

It may well be that if the Salford City Council had participated in the programme their arguments might have been put more fully and more effectively. But the programme did illustrate the reasons for the Salford City Council's attitude to gypsies. The BBC drew our attention to instances (which we ourselves) had noticed when we viewed the recording of the programme) where the BBC reporter had stated the case against the gypsies in such terms as: 'Gypsies live outside society . . . they're not part of us, yet they live among us . . . they scavenge for a living . . . they litter land with their debris . .' and 'A leading councillor explained that Salford simply didn't want gypsies, that the Council unanimously backed this decision and so did the people of the city'. The programme also made it clear that Salford's attitude was shared by some of the other towns referred to in the film.

Taking the programme as a whole we believe that the BBC sufficiently discharged its obligation to ensure that the case of Salford City Council did not go by default in their absence, and on this part of their complaint we do not uphold Salford City Council.

Edmund Compton
Maybray-King
H. A. P. Fisher

December 1973

[BBC Programmes Complaints Commission, *Annual Report 1973-74* (London, 1974), pp. 8-11.]

DEFAMATION ACT 1952

9. Extension of certain defences to broadcasting

(1) Section three of the Parliamentary Papers Act, 1840 (which confers protection in respect of proceedings for printing extracts from or abstracts of

parliamentary papers) shall have effect as if the reference to printing included a reference to broadcasting by means of wireless telegraphy.

(2) Section seven of this Act and section three of the Law of Libel Amendment Act, 1888, as amended by this Act shall apply in relation to reports or matters broadcast by means of wireless telegraphy as part of any programme or service provided by means of a broadcasting station within the United Kingdom, and in relation to any broadcasting by means of wireless telegraphy of any such report or matter, as they apply in relation to reports and matters published in a newspaper and to publication in a newspaper; and subsection (2) of the said section seven shall have effect in relation to any such broadcasting, as if for the words "in the newspaper in which" there were substituted the words "in the manner in which."

(3) In this section "broadcasting station" means any station in respect of which a licence granted by the Postmaster General under the enactments relating to wireless telegraphy is in force, being a licence which (by whatever form of words) authorises the use of the station for the purpose of providing broadcasting services for general reception.

INDEPENDENT BROADCASTING AUTHORITY ACT 1973

The Independent Broadcasting Authority

Constitution of Authority

1.—(1) There shall be an authority to be called the Independent Broadcasting Authority (in this Act referred to as "the Authority") which shall consist of a Chairman, a Deputy Chairman and such other members, not being less than five, as the Minister may from time to time determine.

(2) Unless and until the Minister otherwise determines by notice in writing to the Authority, a copy of which shall be laid before each House of Parliament, the number of the said other members shall be eight. . . .

Function and duties of Authority

2.—(1) The function of the Authority shall be to provide in accordance with the provisions of this Act, and until 31st July 1976, television and local sound broadcasting services, additional in each case to those of the British Broadcasting Corporation and of high quality, both as to the transmission and as to the matter transmitted, for so much of the United Kingdom, the Isle of Man and the Channel Islands as may from time to time be reasonably practicable.

(2) It shall be the duty of the Authority—

(a) to provide the television and local sound broadcasting services as a public service for disseminating information, education and entertainment;

(b) to ensure that the programmes broadcast by the Authority in each area maintain a high general standard in all respects, and in particular in respect of their content and quality, and a proper balance and wide range in their subject-matter, having regard both to the programmes as a whole and also to the days of the week on which, and the times of the day at which, the programmes are broadcast; and

(c) to secure a wide showing or (as the case may be) hearing for programmes of merit.

(3) Without prejudice to the powers conferred on the Authority by this Act, the programmes broadcast by the Authority shall, so far as may be consistently with the observance of the requirements of this Act, be provided not by the Authority but by persons (in this Act referred to as "programme contractors") who, under contracts with the Authority, have, in consideration of payments to the Authority and subject to the provisions of this Act, the right and the duty to provide programmes or parts of programmes to be broadcast by the Authority, which may include advertisements . . .

Central provisions with respect to content of programmes

4.—(1) It shall be the duty of the Authority to satisfy themselves that, so far as possible, the programmes broadcast by the Authority comply with the following requirements, that is to say—

(a) that nothing is included in the programmes which offends against good taste or decency or is likely to encourage or incite to crime or to lead to disorder or to be offensive to public feeling;

(b) that a sufficient amount of time in the programmes is given to news and news features and that all news given in the programmes (in whatever form) is presented with due accuracy and impartiality;

(c) that proper proportions of the recorded and other matter included in the programmes are of British origin and of British performance;

(d) that the programmes broadcast from any station or stations contain a suitable proportion of matter calculated to appeal specially to the tastes and outlook of persons served by the station or stations and, where another language as well as English is in common use among those so served, a suitable proportion of matter in that language;

(e) in the case of local sound broadcasting services, that the programmes broadcast from different stations for reception in different localities do not consist of identical or similar material to an extent inconsistent with the character of the services as local sound broadcasting services; and

(f) that due impartiality is preserved on the part of the persons providing the programmes as respects matters of political or industrial controversy or relating to current public policy.

In applying paragraph (f) of this subsection, a series of programmes may be considered as a whole.

(2) Without prejudice to the generality of subsection (1) of this section, it shall be the duty of the Authority to secure the exclusion from the programmes broadcast by them of all expressions of their own opinion as to any of the matters referred to in paragraph (f) of that subsection, or of the opinion as to any such matters—

(a) of any of their members or offices, or

(b) of any programme contractor, or

(c) in the case of a programme contractor being a firm, of any partner therein, or

(d) in the case of a programme contractor being a body corporate, of any director or officer thereof or person having control thereof.

(3) It shall be the duty of the Authority to satisfy themselves that the programmes broadcast by the Authority do not include, whether in an advertisement or otherwise, any technical device which, by using images of very brief duration or by any other means, exploits the possibility of conveying a

message to, or otherwise influencing the minds of, members of an audience without their being aware, or fully aware, of what has been done. . . .

(5) Except with the previous approval of the Authority, there shall not be included in any programme broadcast by the Authority—

(*a*) any religious service or any propaganda relating to matters of a religious nature;

(*b*) any item, whether an advertisement or not, which gives or is designed to give publicity to the needs or objects of any association or organisation conducted for charitable or benevolent purposes.

(6) For the purpose of maintaining supervisor and control over the programmes (including advertisements) broadcast by them the Authority may make visual and sound records of those programmes or any part thereof; and the making and use by the Authority of any such record exclusively for that purpose—

(*a*) shall not constitute an infringement of the copyright in any work, sound recording or cinematograph film; and

(*b*) shall not constitute an offence under any of the provisions of the Performers' Protection Acts 1958 and 1963.

Programmes other than advertisements

Code for programmes other than advertisements

5.—(1) The Authority—

(*a*) shall draw up, and from time to time review, a code giving guidance—

(i) as to the rules to be observed in regard to the showing of violence, and in regard to the inclusion in local sound broadcasts of sounds suggestive of violence, particularly when large numbers of children and young persons may be expected to be watching or listening to the programmes, and

(ii) as to such other matters concerning standards and practice for programmes (other than advertisements) broadcast by the Authority as the Authority may consider suitable for inclusion in the code,

and in considering what other matters ought to be included in the code in pursuance of sub-paragraph (ii) shall have special regard to programmes broadcast when large numbers of children and young persons may be expected to be watching or listening; and

(*b*) shall secure that the provisions of the code are observed in relation to all programmes (other than advertisements) broadcast by the Authority.

(2) The Authority may, in the discharge of their general responsibility for programmes other than advertisements, impose requirements as to standards and practice for such programmes which go beyond, or relate to matters not covered by, the provisions of the code; and the methods of control exercisable by the Authority for the purpose of securing that the provisions of the code are observed, and for the purpose of securing compliance with such requirements which go beyond, or relate to matters not covered by, the code, shall include a power to give directions to a programme contractor (or any other person providing such programmes) imposing prohibitions or restrictions as respects items of a specified class or description or as respects a particular item.

Advertisements

Advertisements

8.—(1) The programmes broadcast by the Authority may, so long as the provisions of this Act are complied with in relation thereto, include advertisements inserted therein in consideration of payments to the relevant programme contractor or, in the case of an advertisement included in a programme or part of a programme provided under section 3 (2) (*b*) of this Act, to the Authority.

(2) Orders for the insertion of the said advertisements may be received either through advertising or other agents or direct from the advertiser, but neither the Authority nor any programme contractor shall act as an advertising agent.

(3) It shall be the duty of the Authority to secure that the provisions of Schedule 2 to this Act are complied with in relation to the advertisements included in the programmes broadcast by the Authority.

(4) After consultation with the Authority the Minister may make regulations by statutory instrument amending, repealing, or adding to the provisions of the said Schedule.

(5) Without prejudice to any of the duties incumbent on the Authority otherwise than under this subsection in relation to advertisements, it shall be the duty of the Authority to consult from time to time with the Minister as to the classes and descriptions of advertisements which must not be broadcast and the methods of advertising which must not be employed, and to carry out any directions which he may give them in those respects. . . .

Code for advertisements

9.—(1) It shall be the duty of the Authority—
- (*a*) to draw up, and from time to time review, a code governing standards and practice in advertising and prescribing the advertisements and methods of advertising to be prohibited, or prohibited in particular circumstances; and
- (*b*) to secure that the provisions of the code are complied with as regards the advertisements included in the programmes broadcast by the Authority.

(2) The Authority may, in the discharge of their general responsibility for advertisements and methods of advertising, impose requirements as to advertisements and methods of advertising which go beyond the requirements imposed by the code; and the methods of control exercisable by the Authority for the purpose of securing that the provisions of the code are complied with, and for the purpose of securing compliance with requirements which go beyond the requirements of the code, shall include a power to give directions to a programme contractor with respect to the classes and descriptions of advertisements and methods of advertising to be excluded, or to be excluded in particular circumstances, or with respect to the exclusion of a particular advertisement, or its exclusion in particular circumstances. . . .

Government control over Authority as to certain other matters

22.—(1) The Minister or any other Minister of the Crown may, if it appears to him to be necessary or expedient to do so in connection with his functions as such, at any time by notice in writing require the Authority to broadcast, at such times as may be specified in the notice and from such of the stations used by them as may be so specified, any announcement so specified, with or without visual images of any picture, scene or object mentioned in the announcement, and it shall be the duty of the Authority to comply with the notice.

(2) Where the Authority broadcast any announcement in pursuance of a notice under the preceding subsection they may, if they think fit, announce that they are doing so in pursuance of such a notice.

(3) Subject to subsection (4) of this section, the Minister may at any time by notice in writing require the Authority to refrain from broadcasting any matter or classes of matter specified in the notice, and it shall be the duty of the Authority to comply with the notice.

(4) If under subsection (3) of this section the Minister by notice in writing requires the Authority to refrain from broadcasting anything, the Authority may, if they think fit, broadcast an announcement of the notice or of the revocation or expiration of the notice. . . .

SCHEDULE 2

RULES AS TO ADVERTISEMENTS

1.—(1) The advertisements must be clearly distinguishable as such and recognisably separate from the rest of the programme.

(2) Successive advertisements must be recognisably separate.

(3) Advertisements must not be arranged or presented in such a way that any separate advertisement appears to be part of a continuous feature.

(4) Audible matter in advertisements must not be excessively noisy or strident.

2. The standards and practice to be observed in carrying out the requirements of the preceding paragraph shall be such as the Authority may determine either generally or in particular cases.

3. The amount of time given to advertising in the programmes shall not be so great as to detract from the value of the programmes as a medium of information, education and entertainment.

4. Advertisements shall not be inserted otherwise than at the beginning or the end of the programme or in natural breaks therein. . . .

8. No advertisement shall be permitted which is inserted by or on behalf of any body the objects whereof are wholly or mainly of a religious or political nature, and no advertisement shall be permitted which is directed towards any religious or political end or has any relation to any industrial dispute.

IBA COMPLAINTS REVIEW BOARD

Note: The IBA has its own machinery to consider complaints from the public. The Board consists of the Deputy Chairman of the IBA (as Chairman of the Board, three members of the IBA's General Advisory Council, together with the Deputy Director General of the IBA. It meets quarterly and its mandate as laid down by the IBA is as follows:

The Board is concerned with complaints from the public or from persons appearing in programmes about the content of programmes transmitted or the preparation of programmes for transmission. Its functions are to:
(i) keep under review regular reports of complaints received and investigated by the Authority's staff;
(ii) consider specific complaints referred to it by the Authority or any member of the Authority through the Chairman of the Authority;
(iii) consider specific complaints when the complainant remains unsatisfied after investigation and reply by the Authority's staff.

The Board is empowered to investigate in depth complaints of the above kind and it may, at any time, select particular issues for further investigation when it considers that the issue has not been satisfactorily resolved by the normal procedures or that it would be inappropriate to attempt to resolve it through such procedures. It does not deal with advertising matters or with the business relations between programme companies and those appearing in programmes. In the case of matters which might give rise to a right of legal action, the Board will ask for a written undertaking that any such right will not be exercised in connection with the complaint.

Complaint considered by board

(iii) Yorkshire Television's programme THE GOOD, THE BAD AND THE INDIFFERENT, broadcast as a repeat in March 1977, gave rise to a complaint from a viewer who objected to a statement made in the programme that the Church of England had the lion's share of 4,000 hours a year of religious broadcasting in this country. The complainant contended that the real figure was nearer 1,000 hours.

The Authority's Religious Programmes Officer explained to the complainant that 4,000 hours was indeed accurate, the total given representing the combined religious output of all the BBC and IBA national and regional television and national and local radio. The complainant did not accept this explanation and wrote to his MP, who in turn wrote to the Chairman of the Authority, who confirmed that the Authority's view was that the figure of 4,000 hours was not misleading. The complainant had made various attempts, through his MP and through Yorkshire Television, to get a correction made in the opening announcement of a follow-up discussion programme the next week, but without success. He then asked for his complaint to be referred to the Board. In considering this complaint, the Board noted that the complainant had referred to the total of religious broadcasting available 'to any one listener or viewer'. The Board did not consider that the programme had suggested that the figure of 4,000 had been computed on this basis, and thought that, although the figure was a broad estimate only, it had not been incorrectly used in the context of the programme. The Board was satisfied that there was in fact a total of this order of different religious programmes broadcast on radio and television on the various services, national, regional and local, throughout the country. It noted that no other complaints on the matter had been received, and that there was no evidence that the statement in this programme had been misleading. It considered, therefore, that this complaint was not well founded.

[Independent Broadcasting Authority, *Annual Report and Accounts 1977-78* (London, 1979), pp. 105 and 108.]

Political broadcasting

Broadcasting on political issues began to be seriously developed in 1928 when the BBC was made free to broadcast on controversial matters. The importance of broadcasting as a medium for spreading political ideas and knowledge among a widening public was soon recognised by the parties. It proved difficult in the early years to secure agreement between them on the arrangement of balanced broadcasts on political issues—the General Election of 1931 was an example.

In 1935, when the record of the Corporation over its first 10 years came under review by the Ullswater Committee, political broadcasting was established as one of the important duties of the BBC. The Committee paid tribute to the BBC for its policy of holding the scales evenly between the political parties, and its recommendations were largely an endorsement of the BBC's practice as it had been built up in the early years. The Committee recommended that there should be co-operation and consultation between the BBC and the authorised spokesmen of the recognised political parties, but took care to point out that they were far from implying that all broadcast treatment of political questions should be controlled by the political party organisations.

Some years later, in 1947, an agreement was reached between the BBC, the Government and the Opposition, and recorded in an *Aide Mémoire,* which was published as an appendix to the Report of the Broadcasting Committee 1949. It established the subsequent pattern of political broadcasting after the war, and indeed for the next 25 years. Certain detailed amendments to the agreement were introduced in 1948 and one of its clauses was suspended in 1955 after debate in Parliament. In 1969 the agreement was reviewed be representatives of the main political parties and of the BBC, and certain agreed amendments were set out in a revised *Aide Mémoire* . . .

Party political broadcasts

As well as leaving the BBC free to produce programmes on political topics, the agreement provides for broadcasts by party spokesmen, and each year a limited amount of broadcasting time is offered by the BBC to the political parties.

The broadcasting authorities (the BBC and IBA) and representatives of the leading political parties agree annually on the detailed arrangements, the number and the length of broadcasts allocated to each party being determined by a formula based on the number of votes cast for the party at the previous general election. These broadcasts are known as party political broadcasts. The BBC has no editorial responsibility for their content; subjects, speakers and content are chosen by the parties and any party may if it wishes use one or more of its quota to reply to a previous broadcast. The broadcasts are arranged in two series, one given on television and one on radio. In addition to the series of national network broadcasts, the Scottish and Welsh national parties have since 1965 been allocated party political broadcasts in Scotland and Wales respectively.

Ministerial broadcasts

The agreement with parties also provides for a class of broadcasts known as Ministerial; these are broadcasts for which the initiative comes from the Government and in which the speaker is a minister of the crown.

There are now two categories of such broadcasts. The first relates to ministers wishing to explain legislation or administrative policies approved by Parliament, or to seek the co-operation of the public in matters where there is a general consensus of opinion. The BBC undertakes to provide suitable opportunities for such broadcasts within the regular framework of its programmes; there is no right of reply by the Opposition.

The second category relates to those occasions, when the Prime Minister, or one of his more senior cabinet colleagues designated by him, wishes to broadcast to the nation in order to provide information or explanation of events of prime national or international importance, or to enlist public co-operation.

In this second case the Opposition has an unconditional right of reply. This right, if exercised, leads to a third programme, a discussion, in which any party with electoral support comparable with that of the Liberal Party, at the time when the *Aide Mémoire* was revised, is entitled to be represented, together with the two main parties.

Budget broadcasts

For many years past, the BBC has offered time to the Chancellor of the Exchequer and to a spokesman nominated by the Opposition to broadcast on successive evenings in budget week. These budget broadcasts take place both on radio and television.

Other broadcasts by MPs

Over and above these relatively formal arrangements, the BBC takes steps to ensure that in radio and television a fair balance over a period is maintained between appearances in programmes by Members of Parliament of the political party in power and appearances by members of parties in opposition.

General elections: party election broadcasts

The arrangements for party election broadcasts during a general election are agreed beforehand by a committee comprising political parties and the broadcasting authorities (the BBC and IBA). At a general election broadcasting time is made available to the political parties for election broadcasts in radio and television. The committee decides how the time shall be allocated. Other parties not included in these arrangements may qualify for a broadcast if they have 50 or more candidates in the field on Nomination Day. The government of the day customarily speaks first and last.

Broadcasting and electoral law

The participation of parliamentary candidates in broadcast programmes is governed by electoral law. The Representation of the People Act, 1949, required candidates, or their agents, to include expenses incurred in broadcasting in their returns of electoral expenses. The law has since been revised, and under the Representation of the People Act, 1969, broadcasting is given the same exemption as the press in regard to electoral expenses. Under the new Act, however, a candidate is still guilty of an illegal practice at election time if for the purpose of promoting or procuring his election he takes part in a broadcast about his constituency in which any other rival candidate neither takes part nor consents to its going forward without his taking part. When the Bill was debated, it was stated in both Houses of Parliament that 'taking part' was intended to imply active and conscious participation. In practice the 1969 Act has not imposed any new legal restriction on straight political reporting and, by setting definite anterior time limits for all kinds of elections, it has removed any doubt about the length of an electoral period.

[*BBC Handbook 1979* (BBC London, 1979), pp. 185-6.]

Aide Mémoire, 1947

Note:—The "Aide-Mémoire" is the official record of the terms of the agreement reached in February, 1947, between the Government, the Opposition and the BBC.

(1) It is desirable that political broadcasts of a controversial character shall be resumed.

(2) In view of their responsibilities for the care of the nation the Government should be able to use the wireless from time to time for Ministerial broadcasts which, for example, are purely factual, or explanatory of legislation or administrative policies approved by Parliament; or in the nature of appeals to the nation to co-operate in national policies, such as fuel economy or recruiting, which require the active participation of the public. Broadcasts on State occasions also come in the same category.

It will be incumbent on Ministers making such broadcasts to be as impartial as possible, and in the ordinary way there will be no question of a reply by the Opposition. Where, however, the Opposition think that a Government broadcast is controversial it will be open to them to take the matter up through the usual channels with a view to a reply.

(i) As a reply if one is to be made should normally be within a very short period after the original broadcast, say three days, the BBC will be free to exercise its own judgment if no agreement is arrived at within that period.

(ii) Replies under this paragraph will not be included in the number of broadcasts provided for under paragraph 4.

(iii) Copies of the scripts of broadcasts under this paragraph shall be supplied to the leaders of each Party.

(iv) All requests for Ministerial broadcasts under this paragraph shall be canalized through the Minister designated for this purpose—at present the Postmaster General.

(3) "Outside" broadcasts, e.g. of speeches at Party Conferences which are in the nature of news items, shall carry no right of reply by the other side.

(4) A limited number of controversial party political broadcasts shall be allocated to the various parties in accordance with their polls at the last General Election. The allocation shall be calculated on a yearly basis and the total number of such broadcasts shall be a matter for discussion between the parties and the BBC.

(5) The Opposition parties shall have the right, subject to discussion through the usual channels, to choose the subjects for their own broadcasts. Either side will be free, if it wishes, to use one of its quota for the purpose of replying to a previous broadcast, but it will be under no necessity to do so. There will, of course, be no obligation on a party to use its whole quota.

(6) (i) Paragraphs (4) and (5) relate to controversial party political broadcasts on issues of major policy on bahalf of the leading political Parties. For the ensuing year the total number, excluding Budget broadcasts, shall be

12—divided as to Government 6, Conservative Opposition 5, Liberal Opposition 1. Reasonable notice will be given to the BBC.

(ii) The BBC reserve the right, after consultation with the party leaders, to invite to the microphone a member of either House of outstanding national eminence who may have become detached from any party.

(iii) Apart from these limited broadcasts on major policy the BBC are free to invite members of either House to take part in controversial broadcasts of a round-table character in which political questions are dealt with, provided two or more persons representing different sides take part in the broadcasts.

(iv) No broadcasts arranged by the BBC other than the normal reporting of Parliamentary proceedings are to take place on any question while it is the subject of discussion in either House.

(7) Where any dispute arises an effort shall be made to settle it through the usual channels. Where this is not possible, the BBC will have to decide the matter on its own responsibility.

(8) These arrangements shall be reviewed after a year, or earlier if any party to the conference so desires.

6th February, 1947

Notes: 1. The above agreement was revised in July, 1948, when Government and Opposition agreed with the BBC that 6 (iv) should be construed as:

(a) that the BBC will not have discussions or *ex parte* statements on any issues for a period of a fortnight before they are debated in either House;

(b) that while matters are subjects of legislation M.P.s will not be used in such discussions.

2. With regard to paragraph 6 (i), it was agreed with the BBC that, for the year 1950, if one of the Government or Conservative broadcasts should not be taken during a quarter, it should be forfeited.

[*Report of the Broadcasting Committee, 1949. Appendix H—Memoranda submitted to the Committee,* (Cmnd. 8117, 1951), pp. 109-10.]

Aide Mémoire, 1969

1. In view of its executive responsibilities the Government of the day has the right to explain events to the public, or seek co-operation of the public, through the medium of broadcasting.

2. Experience has shown that such occasions are of two kinds and that different arrangements are appropriate for each.

3. The first category relates to Ministers wishing to explain legislation or administrative policies approved by Parliament, or to seek the co-operation of the public in matters where there is a general consensus of opinion. The BBC will provide suitable opportunities for such broadcasts within the regular framework of their programmes; there will be no right of reply by the Opposition.

4. The second category relates to more important and normally infrequent occasions, when the Prime Minister or one of his most senior Cabinet colleagues designated by him wishes to broadcast to the nation in order to provide information or explanation of events of prime national or international importance, or to seek the co-operation of the public in connection with such events.

5. The BBC will provide the Prime Minister or Cabinet Minister with suitable facilities on each occasion in this second category. Following such an occasion they may be asked to provide an equivalent opportunity for a broadcast by a leading Member of the Opposition, and will in that event do so.

6. When the Opposition exercises this right to broadcast, there will follow as soon as possible, arranged by the BBC, a broadcast discussion of the issues between a Member of the Cabinet and a senior Member of the Opposition nominated respectively by the Government and Opposition but not necessarily those who gave the preceding broadcasts. An opportunity to participate in such a discussion should be offered to a representative of any other party with electoral support at the time in question on a scale not appreciably less than that of the Liberal Party at the date of this *Aide Mémoire*.

7. As it will be desirable that such an Opposition broadcast and discussion between Government and Opposition should follow the preceding broadcast with as little delay as possible, a request for the necessary facilities by the Opposition should reach the BBC before noon on the day following the Ministerial Broadcast. This will enable the BBC to arrange the Opposition broadcast and the discussion as soon as possible.

8. Copies of the scripts of these broadcasts will be supplied to the Leaders of the Government, the Opposition and of other parties when they participate.

9. These arrangements will be reviewed annually.

(With effect from 25 February, 1969)

[*BBC Handbook, 1979* (BBC, London, 1979) p. 186-7.]

5. THEATRES

Further Reading

O'Higgins, pp. 90–99; Street, pp. 65–67.

(1964–1965) 1(4) *Censorship, passim*; R. Findlater, *Banned! A Review of Theatrical Censorship in Britain* (London, 1967); *Joint Committee on Censorship of the Theatre: Report*, (1967) H.L. 255, H.C. 503; D. Knowles, *The Censor, The Drama and the Film 1900–1934* (Allen & Unwin, 1934), Part I; J. Palmer, *The Censor and the Theatres* (Fisher, Unwin, 1912); G. B. Shaw, Preface to *The Shewing-up Blanco Posnet* (London, 1910).

Theatres Act 1968

Abolition of censorship of the theatre

1. Abolition of censorship of the theatre

(1) The Theatres Act 1843 is hereby repealed; and none of the powers which were exercisable thereunder by the Lord Chamberlain of Her Majesty's Household shall be exercisable by or on behalf of Her Majesty by virtue of Her royal prerogative.

(2) In granting, renewing or transferring any licence under this Act for the use of any premises for the public performance of plays or in varying any of

the terms, conditions or restrictions on or subject to which any such licence is held, the licensing authority shall not have power to impose any term, condition or restriction as to the nature of the plays which may be performed under the licence or as to the manner of performing plays thereunder:

Provided that nothing in this subsection shall prevent a licensing authority from imposing any term, condition or restriction which they consider necessary in the interests of physical safety or health or any condition regulating or prohibiting the giving of an exhibition, demonstration or performance of hypnotism within the meaning of the Hypnotism Act 1952.

2. Prohibition of presentation of obscene performances of plays

(1) For the purposes of this section a performance of a play shall be deemed to be obscene if, taken as a whole, its effect was such as to tend to deprave and corrupt persons who were likely, having regard to all relevant circumstances, to attend it.

(2) Subject to sections 3 and 7 of this Act, if an obscene performance of a play is given, whether in public or private, any person who (whether for gain or not) presented or directed that performance shall be liable—

(a) on summary conviction, to a fine not exceeding £400 or to imprisonment for a term not exceeding six months;

(b) on conviction on indictment, to a fine or to imprisonment for a term not exceeding three years, or both.

(3) A prosecution on indictment for an offence under this section shall not be commenced more than two years after the commission of the offence.

(4) No person shall be proceeded against in respect of a performance of a play or anything said or done in the course of such a performance—

(a) for an offence at common law where it is of the essence of the offence that the performance or, as the case may be, what was said or done was obscene, indecent, offensive, disgusting or injurious to morality; or

(b) for an offence under section 4 of the Vagrancy Act 1824 consisting of wilfully exposing to public view an indecent exhibition, including such an offence under that section as applied to Scotland by section 15 of the Prevention of Crimes Act 1871; . . .

and no person shall be proceeded against for an offence at common law of conspiring to corrupt public morals, or to do any act contrary to public morals or decency, in respect of an agreement to present or give a performance of a play, or to cause anything to be said or done in the course of such a performance.

3. Defence of public good

(1) A person shall not be convicted of an offence under section 2 of this Act if it is proved that the giving of the performance in question was justified as being for the public good on the ground that it was in the interests of drama, opera, ballet or any other art, or of literature or learning.

(2) It is hereby declared that the opinion of experts as to the artistic, literary or other merits of a performance of a play may be admitted in any proceedings for an offence under section 2 of this Act either to establish or negative the said ground.

5. Incitement to racial hatred by means of public performance of a play

(1) Subject to section 7 of this Act, if there is given a public performance of a play involving the use of threatening, abusive or insulting words, any person who (whether for gain or not) presented or directed that performance shall be guilty of an offence under this section if—

 (a) he did so with intent to stir up hatred against any section of the public in Great Britain distinguished by colour, race or ethnic or national origins; and

 (b) that performance, taken as a whole, is likely to stir up hatred against that section on grounds of colour, race or ethnic or national origins.

 . . .

6. Provocation of breach of peace by means of public performance of a play

(1) Subject to section 7 of this Act, if there is given a public performance of a play involving the use of threatening, abusive or insulting words or behaviour, any person who (whether for gain or not) presented or directed that performance shall be guilty of an offence under this section if—

 (a) he did so with intent to provoke a breach of the peace; or

 (b) the performance, taken as a whole, was likely to occasion a breach of the peace.

(2) A person guilty of an offence under this section shall be liable—

 (a) on summary conviction, to a fine not exceeding £100 or to imprisonment for a term not exceeding three months, or both;

 (b) on conviction on indictment, to a fine not exceeding £500 or to imprisonment for a term not exceeding twelve months, or both.

7. Exceptions for performances given in certain circumstances

(1) Nothing in sections 2 to 4 of this Act shall apply in relation to a performance of a play given on a domestic occasion in a private dwelling.

(2) Nothing in sections 2 to 6 of this Act shall apply in relation to a performance of a play given solely or primarily for one or more of the following purpose, that is to say—

 (a) rehearsal; or

 (b) to enable—

  (i) a record or cinematograph film to be made from or by means of the performance; or

  (ii) the performance to be broadcast; or

  (iii) the performance to be transmitted to subscribers to a diffusion service;

but in any proceedings for an offence under section 2, 5 or 6 of this Act alleged to have been committed in respect of a performance of a play or an offence at common law alleged to have been committed in England and Wales by the publication of defamatory matter in the course of a performance of a play, if it is proved that the performance was attended by persons other than persons directly connected with the giving of the performance or the doing in relation thereto of any of the things mentioned in paragraph (b) above, the performance shall be taken not to have been given solely or primarily for one or more of the said purposes unless the contrary is shown.

(3) In this section—

> "broadcast" means broadcast by wireless telegraphy (within the meaning of the Wireless Telegraphy Act 1949), whether by way of sound broadcasting or television;
>
> "cinematograph film" means any print, negative, tape or other article on which a performance of a play or any part of such a performance is recorded for the purposes of visual reproduction;
>
> "record" means any record or similar contrivance for reproducing sound, including the sound-track of a cinematograph film;

and section 48 (3) of the Copyright Act 1956 (which explains the meaning of references in that Act to the transmission of a work or other subject-matter to subscribers to a diffusion service) shall apply for the purposes of this section as it applies for the purposes of that Act.

8. Restriction on institution of proceeedings

Proceedings for an offence under section 2, 5 or 6 of this Act or an offence at common law committed by the publication of defamatory matter in the course of a performance of a play shall not be instituted in England and Wales except by or with the consent of the Attorney-General.

Licensing of premises for public performance of plays

12. Licensing of premises for public performance of plays

(1) Subject to the following provisions of this Act, no premises, whether or not licensed for the sale of intoxicating or exciseable liquor, shall be used for the public performance of any play except under and in accordance with the terms of a licence granted under this Act by the licensing authority.

(2) A licence shall not be required for any premises under any enactment other than this Act by reason only of the public performance at those premises of a play.

(3) For the purposes of subsection (2) above any music played at any premises by way of introduction to, in any interval between parts of, or by way of conclusion of a performance of a play or in the interval between two such performances shall be treated as forming part of the performance or performances, as the case may be, if the total time taken by music so played on any day amounts to less than one quarter of the time taken by the performance or performances of the play or plays given at the premises on that day.

(4) Schedule 1 to this Act shall have effect with respect to licences under this Act.

18. Interpretation

(1) In this Act—

> "licensing authority" means—
>
> (a) as respects premises in Greater London, the Greater London Council;
>
> (b) as respects premises in a county or county borough in England and Wales, the council of that county or borough;
>
> (c) *(applies to Scotland);*
>
> "play" means—
>
> (a) any dramatic piece, whether involving improvisation or not, which is given wholly or in part by one or more persons actually present and

performing and in which the whole or a major proportion of what is done by the person or persons performing, whether by way of speech, singing or acting, involves the playing of a role; and

(b) any ballet given wholly or in part by one or more persons actually present and performing, whether or not it falls within paragraph (a) of this definition;

"police officer" means a member, or in Scotland a constable, of a police force;

"premises" includes any place;

"public performance" includes any performance in a public place within the meaning of the Public Order Act 1936 and any performance which the public or any section thereof are permitted to attend, whether on payment or otherwise;

"script" has the meaning assigned by section 9 (2) of this Act.

(2) For the purposes of this Act—

(a) a person shall not be treated as presenting a performance of a play by reason only of his taking part therein as a performer;

(b) a person taking part as a performer in a performance of a play directed by another person shall be treated as a person who directed the performance if without reasonable excuse he performs otherwise than in accordance with that person's direction; and

(c) a person shall be taken to have directed a performance of a play given under his direction notwithstanding that he was not present during the performance;

and a person shall not be treated as aiding or abetting the commission of an offence under section 2, 5 or 6 of this Act in respect of a performance of a play by reason only of his taking part in that performance as a performer.

CHAPTER 12

PRIVACY

Further Reading

De Smith, pp. 456–458; Street, pp. 262–265.

Sir John Foster and P. Sieghart, "Libel, privacy and English law," (1972) 1(3–4) *Index on Censorship* pp. 67–84; L. Grant, *et al., Civil Liberty: The NCCL Guide to Your Rights* (Penguin, 1978), Chap. 14; P. Hewitt, *Privacy: The Information Gatherers* (NCCL, 1977); Frits W. Hondius, *Emerging Data Protection in Europe* (North Holland Pub. Co., 1975); Mervyn Jones, (ed.), *Privacy* (David & Charles, 1974); Justice, *Privacy and the Law* (London, 1965); C. J. F. Kidd, "Freedom from Unwanted Publicity," in *Fundamental Rights* (J. W. Bridge, *et al.* ed.) at pp. 43–59; 31 *Law & Contemporary Problems* (1966) *passim*; Law Commission, Working Paper No. 85, *Breach of Confidence* (London, 1974); D. Madgwick, *Privacy under Attack* (NCCL, 1968); D. Madgwick & T. Smythe, *The Invasion of Privacy* (Pitman, 1974); A. P. Miller, *Assault on Privacy* (Ann Arbor University of Michigan Press, 1971); W. F. Pratt, "The Brandeis and Warren Argument for a Right to Privacy," (1975) *Public Law* pp. 161–190; Press Council, *Privacy, Press and Public* (London, 1971); *Report of the Committee on Computers and Privacy,* Cmnd. 6353 (1975); James B. Rule, *Private Lives and Public Surveillance* (A. Lane, 1973); Paul Sieghart, *Privacy and Computers* (Latimer New Dimensions, 1976); A. F. Westin, *Privacy and Freedom* (The Bodley Head, 1969).

See also p. 304.

Fraser v. Evans [1969] 1 Q.B. 349

Court of Appeal

The plaintiff, a public relations consultant to the Greek government under a contract expressly imposing on him a duty not to reveal any information about his work for the governement, made a written report to that government. A copy of the report came into the hands of *The Sunday Times,* whose reporters interviewed the plaintiff. The paper proposed to publish an article based on the interview and on the report prepared by the plaintiff for his client. The article it was admitted would have been defamatory to the plaintiff. He obtained an injunction *ex parte* to restrain publication on the grounds that it would be both in breach confidence and defamatory. The defendants appealed. The appeal was upheld.

LORD DENNING, M.R.:

"The Sunday Times" have told us quite frankly that the article will be defamatory of Mr. Fraser. They propose to print extracts from the report, to give some of the answers that he made at the interview, and to say what they think of them. In other words, to comment on what he has written and said. But they say that, although it will be defamatory of him, nevertheless if he should sue them for libel, their defence will be that the facts are true, that the comments which they make upon those facts will be fair comment made honestly on a matter of public interest. If the facts are not true, they say that Mr. Fraser cannot complain because they are only giving the facts as he told them.

One of the principal difficulties in dealing with this case is that we do not know what the article when published will contain. We do not know what the extracts will be. We do not know what facts will be stated or what comments will be made. Despite this ignorance, we have to deal with the case as best we can. I will take the various points in order.

First, *Libel*. In so far as the article will be defamatory of Mr. Fraser, it is clear he cannot get an injunction. The court will not restrain the publication of an article, even though it is defamatory, when the defendant says he intends to justify it or to make fair comment on a matter of public interest. That has been established for many years ever since *Bonnard v. Perryman*.[1] The reason sometimes given is that the defences of justification and fair comment are for the jury, which is the constitutional tribunal, and not for a judge. But a better reason is the importance in the public interest that the truth should out. As the court said in that case[2]:

"The right of free speech is one which it is for the public interest that individuals should possess, and, indeed, that they should exercise without impediment, so long as no wrongful act is done."

There is no wrong done if it is true, or if it is fair comment on a matter of public interest. The court will not prejudice the issue by granting an injunction in advance of publication.

Second, *Breach of Confidence*. Mr. Fraser says that the report was a confidential document and that the publication of it should be restrained on the principles enunciated in the cases from *Albert (Prince) v. Strange*[3] to *Argyll (Duchess) v. Argyll (Duke)*.[4] Those cases show that the court will in a proper case restrain the publication of confidential information. The jurisdiction is based not so much on property or on contract as on the duty to be of good faith. No person is permitted to divulge to the world information which he has received in confidence, unless he has just cause or excuse for doing so. Even if he comes by it innocently, nevertheless once he gets to know that it was originally given in confidence, he can be restrained from breaking that confidence. But the party complaining must be the person who is entitled to the confidence and to have it respected. He must be a person to whom the duty of good faith is owed. It is at this point that I think Mr. Fraser's claim breaks down. There is no doubt that Mr. Fraser himself was under an obligation of confidence to the Greek Government. The contract says so in terms. But there is nothing in the contract which expressly puts the Greek Government under any obligation of confidence. Nor, so far as I can see, is there any implied obligation. The Greek Government entered into no contract with Mr. Fraser to keep it secret. We have seen affidavits—one of them as late as this morning—which say that it was not the policy of the Greek Government to publish, or allow the

[1] [1891] 2 Ch. 269, C.A.
[2] Ibid. 284.
[3] (1849) 1 Mac. & G. 25.
[4] [1967] Ch. 302; [1965] 2 W.L.R. 790; [1965] 1 All E.R. 611.

publication, of any documents prepared by Mr. Fraser or his firm, and that they would, as matter of practice, keep them confidential. But that policy still leaves them free, in point of law, to circulate the documents or their contents to anyone whom they pleased. The information was obtained for them by Mr. Fraser under a contract with them. They paid for it. They were the people entitled to the information. They were the people to say aye or no whether it should be communicated elsewhere, or be published generally. It follows that they alone have any standing to complain if anyone obtains the information surreptitiously or proposes to publish it. And they did not complain of the publication now proposed. At any rate, they have not come to the court to complain. On this short point it seems to me that Mr. Fraser himself cannot proceed on breach of confidence so as in his own behalf to prevent "The Sunday Times" publishing the article.

Even if Mr. Fraser had any standing to complain, "The Sunday Times" say that in any event they have just cause or excuse for publishing. They rely on the line of authority from *Gartside* v. *Outram*[5] to the latest case, *Initial Services Ltd.* v. *Putterill*.[6] They quote the words of Woods V.-C. that[7] "there is no confidence as to the disclosure of iniquity." I do not look upon the word "iniquity" as expressing a principle. It is merely an instance of just cause or excuse for breaking confidence. There are some things which may be required to be disclosed in the public interest, in which event no confidence can be prayed in aid to keep them secret. I feel it might be difficult for "The Sunday Times" to make out that case here. We have Mr. Fraser's report before us, and, on reading of it, I doubt whether it is such as to enable them to make out this ground for publication.

Third. It was said: Seeing that no injunction should be granted in respect of the defamatory aspect of the article, likewise no injunction should be granted in respect of the breach of confidence. The plaintiff should not be able to avoid the salutary rule of law in libel by framing the case in breach of confidence. Reliance was placed on *Sim* v. *H. J. Heinz Co. Ltd.*[8] I do not think it necessary to rule on this point today. I can well see that there may be cases where it would be wrong to grant an injunction on breach of confidence when it would not be granted on libel: but I can equally well see that there are some cases of breach of confidence which are defamatory, where the court might intervene, even though the defendant says he intends to justify.

The final point is on copyright. There is no doubt that Mr. Fraser was the author of this report and is entitled to the literary copyright in it. But copyright does not subsist in the information contained in the report. It exists only in the literary form in which the information is dressed. If "The Sunday Times" were going to print this report in full, thus taking the entire literary form, it might well be a case for an injunction to restrain the infringement of copyright. But "The Sunday Times" say that they are going to do no such thing. They say that they are only going to print short extracts from it, followed up with some of the statements which Mr. Fraser made to them and their comments on it. They say that would be a "fair dealing" such as is permitted by section 6 (3) of the Copyright Act, 1956, which says that:

[5] (1856) 26 L.J.Ch. 113.
[6] [1968] 1 Q.B. 396; [1967] 3 W.L.R. 1032; [1967] 3 All E.R. 145, C.A.
[7] 26 L.J.Ch. 113, 114.
[8] [1959] 1 W.L.R. 313; [1959] 1 All E.R. 547, C.A.

"No fair dealing with a literary . . . work shall constitute an infringement of the copyright in the work if it is for the purpose of reporting current events—(a) in a newspaper . . ."

We have not seen what is going to be published. We cannot pre-judge the matter. We cannot say that there is going to be an unfair dealing when "The Sunday Times" say it is to be a fair dealing. So no injunction should be granted to prevent them publishing.

It all comes back to this. There are some things which are of such public concern that the newspapers, the Press, and indeed, everyone is entitled to make known the truth and to make fair comment on it. This is an integral part of the right of free speech and expression. It must not be whittled away. "The Sunday Times" assert that in this case there is a matter of public concern. They admit that they are going to injure Mr. Fraser's reputation, but they say that they can justify it; and that they are only making fair comment on a matter of public interest; and, therefore, they ought not to be restrained. We cannot prejudge this defence by granting an injunction against them. I think the injunction which has been granted should be removed. "The Sunday Times" should be allowed to publish the article at their risk. If they are guilty of libel or breach of confidence, or breach of copyright, that can be determined by an action hereafter and damages awarded against them. But we should not grant an interim injunction in advance of an article when we do not know in the least what it will contain. I would allow the appeal accordingly and discharge the injunction.

Davies and Widgery,L.JJ. agreed.

CONSUMER CREDIT ACT 1974

Credit reference agencies

Duty to disclose name etc. of agency

157.—(1) A creditor, owner or negotiator, within the prescribed period after receiving a request in writing to that effect from the debtor or hirer, shall give him notice of the name and address of any credit reference agency from which the creditor, owner or negotiator has, during the antecedent negotiations, applied for information about his financial standing.

(2) Subsection (1) does not apply to a request received more than 28 days after the termination of the antecedent negotiations, whether on the making of the regulated agreement or otherwise.

(3) If the creditor, owner or negotiator fails to comply with subsection (1) he commits an offence.

Duty of agency to disclose filed information

158.—(1) A credit reference agency, within the prescribed period after receiving,—

(a) a request in writing to that effect from any individual (the "consumer"), and
(b) such particulars as the agency may reasonably require to enable them to identify the file, and
(c) a fee of 25 new pence,

shall give the consumer a copy of the file relating to him kept by the agency.

(2) When giving a copy of the file under subsection (1), the agency shall also give the consumer a statement in the prescribed form of his rights under section 159.

(3) If the agency does not keep a file relating to the consumer it shall give him notice of that fact, but need not return any money paid.

(4) If the agency contravenes any provision of this section it commits an offence.

(5) In this Act "file", in relation to an individual, means all the information about him kept by a credit reference agency, regardless of how the information is stored, and "copy of the file", as respects information not in plain English, means a transcript reduced into plain English.

Correction of wrong information

159.—(1) A consumer given information under section 158 who considers that an entry in his file is incorrect, and that if it is not corrected he is likely to be prejudiced, may give notice to the agency requiring it either to remove the entry from the file or amend it.

(2) Within 28 days after receiving a notice under subsection (1), the agency shall by notice inform the consumer that it has—

  (a) removed the entry from the file, or

  (b) amended the entry, or

  (c) taken no action,

and if the notice states that the agency has amended the entry it shall include a copy of the file so far as it comprises the amended entry.

(3) Within 28 days after receiving a notice under subsection (2), or where no such notice was given, within 28 days after the expiry of the period mentioned in subsection (2), the consumer may, unless he has been informed by the agency that it has removed the entry from his file, serve a further notice on the agency requiring it to add to the file an accompanying notice of correction (not exceeding 200 words) drawn up by the consumer, and include a copy of it when furnishing information included in or based on that entry.

(4) Within 28 days after receiving a notice under subsection (3), the agency, unless it intends to apply to the Director under subsection (5), shall by notice inform the consumer that it has received the notice under subsection (3) and intends to comply with it.

(5) If—

  (a) the consumer has not received a notice under subsection (4) within the time required, or

  (b) it appears to the agency that it would be improper for it to publish a notice of correction because it is incorrect, or unjustly defames any person, or is frivolous or scandalous, or is for any other reason unsuitable,

the consumer or, as the case may be, the agency may, in the prescribed manner and on payment of the specified fee, apply to the Director, who may make such order on the application as he thinks fit.

(6) If a person to whom an order under this section is directed fails to comply with it within the period specified in the order he commits an offence.

Alternative procedure for business consumers

160.—(1) The Director, on an application made by a credit reference agency, may direct that this section shall apply to the agency if he is satisfied—

(a) that compliance with section 158 in the case of consumers who carry on a business would adversely affect the service provided to its customers by the agency, and

(b) that, having regard to the methods employed by the agency and to any other relevant factors, it is probable that consumers carrying on a business would not be prejudiced by the making of the direction.

(2) Where an agency to which this section applies receives a request, particulars and a fee under section 158 (1) from a consumer who carries on a business, and section 158 (3) does not apply, the agency, instead of complying with section 158, may elect to deal with the matter under the following subsections.

(3) Instead of giving the consumer a copy of the file, the agency shall within the prescribed period give notice to the consumer that it is proceeding under this section, and by notice give the consumer such information included in or based on entries in the file as the Director may direct, together with a statement in the prescribed form of the consumer's rights under subsections (4) and (5).

(4) If within 28 days after receiving the information given him under subsection (3), or such longer period as the Director may allow, the consumer—

(a) gives notice to the Director that he is dissatisfied with the information, and

(b) satisfies the Director that he has taken such steps in relation to the agency as may be reasonable with a view to removing the cause of his dissatisfaction, and

(c) pays the Director the specified fee,

the Director may direct the agency to give the Director a copy of the file, and the Director may disclose to the consumer such of the information on the file as the Director thinks fit.

(5) Section 159 applies with any necessary modifications to information given to the consumer under this section as it applies to information given under section 158.

(6) If an agency making an election under subsection (2) fails to comply · with subsection (3) or (4) it commits an offence.

YOUNGER COMMITTEE ON PRIVACY

Note: In May 1970 a committee under Mr. Kenneth Younger was set up to consider "whether legislation is needed to give further protection to the individual citizen and to commercial and industrial interests against intrusions into privacy by private persons and organisations, or by companies." Northern Ireland was excluded from their consideration as were invasions of privacy by public authorities.

WHAT IS PRIVACY?

Report of the Committee on Privacy, Cmnd. 5012, 1972

57 It might seem a prerequisite of our task that we should have agreed what privacy is and be able to say what we mean by it. The "Justice" Committee on Privacy said:

"In the course of our work, we have become increasingly aware of the difficulties which seem to beset any attempt to find a precise or logical formula which could either circumscribe the meaning of the word 'privacy' or define it exhaustively. We think that there are two underlying reasons for this. First and foremost, the notion of privacy has a substantial emotive content in that many of the things which we feel the need to preserve from the curiosity of our fellows are feelings, beliefs or matters of conduct which are themselves irrational. Secondly, the scope of privacy is governed to a considerable extent by the standards, fashions and mores of the society of which we form part, and these are subject to constant change, especially at the present time. We have therefore concluded that no purpose would be served by our making yet another attempt at developing an intellectually rigorous analysis. We prefer instead to leave the concept much as we have found it, that is as a notion about whose precise boundaries there will always be a variety of opinions, but about whose central area there will always be a large measure of agreement. At any given time, there will be certain things which almost everyone will agree ought to be part of the 'private' area which people should be allowed to preserve from the intrusion of others, subject only to the overriding interest of the community as a whole where this plainly outweighs the private right. Surrounding this central area there will always be a 'grey area' on which opinions will differ, and the extent of this grey area, as also that of the central one, is bound to vary from time to time."[7]

They concluded that this "central area" should be given a general protection under the law, yet when they were obliged to select its ingredients in order to define it in clause 9 of their draft Right of Privacy Bill,[8] they had to fall back on a list of examples of widely differing character.

58 The majority of us regard the "Justice" Committee's conclusion as one more indication, and a highly significant one, that the concept of privacy cannot be satisfactorily defined. We have looked at many earlier attempts, and mention some below, and have noted that there are important differences between them all. Either they go very wide, equating the right to privacy with the right to be let alone,[9] or they boil down to a catalogue of assorted values to which the adjective "private" or "personal" can reasonably, but not exclusively, be attached. We conclude from these manifold efforts that no useful purpose would be served by our also entering the lists with yet another attempt to formulate a precise and comprehensive definition of privacy.

59 If one abandons the attempt to find a single and comprehensive definition of privacy, as we have done, the next task is to try to decide what are the values in which privacy is a major element, and then to decide which deserve protection. We agree with the "Justice" Committee that there is an area of private matters about which there will always (if by that is meant: at any given time) be a large measure of agreement. We think that to describe this as a "central area" is liable to be misleading, since it is in fact a grouping of distinct, if sometimes closely linked, areas. We agree also that there is a fringe or "grey area" beyond this grouping on which opinions will differ. We agree further that opinions as to what are aspects of privacy will vary from time to time. Man, as the "Justice" Committee point out, is a social animal; his

[7]"Privacy and the Law" p.5, paragraph 18.

[8]Ibid., Appendix J (also as in Appendix F hereto).

[9]From Judge Cooley's "The Right to be Let Alone", Torts, second edition, 1888, which has been adopted by later authorities.

society evolves; and this evolution will alter from time to time the public's view on what needs to be dealt with by the law. This brings us to the various concepts of privacy that have been advanced in other studies of the problem.

60 Professor Alan Westin first[10] describes privacy as "the state of solitude or small group intimacy". The "Justice" Bill[11] speaks of a person's state of being "protected from intrusion upon himself, his home, his family, his relationships and communications with others, his property and his business affairs, including intrusion by spying, prying, watching and besetting [and] the unauthorised overhearing . . . of spoken words . . .". The Nordic Conference,[12] expanding on what they meant by the right of privacy (which they equated with the right to be let alone), spoke of a person's "private, family or home life" as the first area to be protected, but they also singled out as activities against which a person should be protected: "(b) interference with his physical . . . integrity . . . (g) spying, prying, watching and besetting; [and] (h) interference with his correspondence . . .".

61 The second of Professor Westin's definitions[13] is that "Privacy is the claim of individuals, groups or institutions to determine for themselves when, how and to what extent information about them is communicated to others". The "Justice" Bill[14] adds to a person's protection from the forms of intrusion mentioned above (paragraph 60): "including intrusion by . . . the unauthorised use or disclosure of confidential information, or facts (including his name, identity or likeness) calculated to cause him distress, annoyance or embarrassment, or to place him in a false light".[15]

62 We consider first the broadest interpretation of privacy: the state of being let alone. We take this to mean freedom from human interference by any means. Privacy would be an element in it, but there are other elements of equal importance: protection from physical harm and restraint, freedom from direction, and peaceful enjoyment of one's surroundings. The threats to these could take the form of injurious acts by other private persons, of public impositions or of man-made disasters or nuisances, and any one of these might threaten several of the elements which constitute the state of being let alone. A badly maintained factory chimney which falls on your family in your private house causes physical harm and interferes with the peaceful enjoyment of your surroundings; it also invades your privacy, but most people would not spontaneously make that the reason for being angry about it. Arbitrary arrest at home interferes with peaceful enjoyment and involves direction; it is also an invasion of privacy, but is unlikely to be condemned primarily on that score.

63 If there were to be a right of privacy under the law it should not, in our opinion, be synonymous with a right to be let alone. An unqualified right of this kind would in any event be an unrealistic concept, incompatible with the concept of society, implying a willingness not to be let entirely alone and a recognition that other people may be interested and consequently concerned about us. If the concept were to be embodied into a right, its adaptation to the dominant pressures of life in society would require so many exceptions that it

[10]"Privacy and Freedom", p.7.
[11]"Privacy and the Law", Appendix J, clause 9.
[12]Conclusions of the Nordic Conference of International Jurists on the Right of Privacy, Stockholm, 1967; at Appendix K hereto.
[13]"Privacy and Freedom", p.7.
[14]"Privacy and the Law", Appendix J, clause 9.
[15]These and other suggested definitions of privacy or of its elements are given in full in Appendix K.

would lose all coherence and hence any valid meaning. We have concluded therefore that the type of conduct against which legal protection might be afforded on the ground of intrusion on privacy should be confined to injurious or annoying conduct deliberately aimed at a particular person or persons where the invasion of privacy is the principal wrong complained of.

64 The evidence we have received indicates that the main concern about what is termed invasion of privacy involves the treatment of personal information. The "information" which we have been urged to protect is that in which a person should be regarded as having something in the nature of a proprietary interest, either, in most cases, because it relates personally to him or because he has been entrusted with it by the person to whom it relates, as in the case of a doctor, tutor, employer or friend of the family. If the information is passed to another recipient who is also acceptable, then that recipient in turn can be said to be entrusted with it.

65 It is not contended in all the evidence to us that the information concerned need be private, though if the information is also confidential its unauthorised handling is all the more objectionable. The unauthorised handling of information which may well be known or available through approved sources can also constitute a breach of privacy in certain circumstances. The most obvious example is where it is published at large to a far wider audience than would otherwise learn of it: the conduct of the mass information media is the main object of criticism under this heading. Another circumstance is where the information is directly used for commercial gain or other ulterior purpose without authority: use of a name or portrait in an advertisement is the most likely example, which shows how this circumstance may overlap with the first one of media publicity. A third circumstance is where the information is collated with other personal information so that a dossier is compiled on the individual concerned, which tells the compiler more than the isolated pieces could do—on the principle that the whole is greater than the sum of the parts.

66 The unauthorised use, by way of compilation, communication and dissemination, of personal information is not the whole extent of the concern about privacy and information. The means used to extract such information from its private domain may be at least equally offensive. This may involve none of the subsequent stages of handling the information, since it may have as its motive pure inquisitiveness or self-indulgence. A case in point would be the peeping Tom, who normally keeps the "information" very much to himself. Usually, however, those who go to the trouble of prying to get information do so with the object of using it: by passing it on to particular recipients, storing it for future reference or disseminating it. The common factor in all these is intrusion into the domain in which the information has hitherto been kept private.

67 The concept of intrusion implies some geographically private area, and this is commonly conceived of as the home and garden, extending to other forms of accommodation, whether owned or merely occupied, such as a place of business or a hotel room or lodging. But it goes further than that, involving also private, family or domestic activities away from owned or occupied property, which are not meant to be publicly observed though they may occur in what is legally a public place. It is possible that there could be deliberate intrusion without the object of acquiring information, but to provoke or inhibit a course of action. Ill-disposed neighbours might conduct a campaign of prying to induce people to move house, or otherwise annoy them. The law gives

specific protection against this only in the cases of landlords harassing tenants[16] and of the harassment of debtors.[17]

68 Keeping strictly in mind that we are concerned only with injurious or annoying conduct deliberately aimed at a particular person or group of persons, we think it right to give the following activities our particular attention: intrusive gathering and dissemination of information by the publicity media, handling of credit information, unwarrantable intrusion into personal matters at work and in education and medicine, prying by neighbours and landlords, intrusive sales methods, investigations by private detectives, and industrial espionage. We have also given special attention to certain modern technical developments which affect privacy: the technical surveillance devices and computers.

69 It has been suggested to us that there are two other constituents of privacy—freedom from interference with moral and intellectual integrity and freedom from being placed in a false light. These are both constituents of the Nordic Conference concept of the right to be let alone,[18] a concept we have already rejected as a whole in paragraph 63. But they occur elsewhere. As to the first, we received no serious evidence that subliminal influencing, sleep teaching, manipulative selection, group conditioning and other uses of the behavioural sciences to influence people's subconscious minds are a problem in this country or that special legal protection is needed against them.

70 Placing someone in a false light is one of the four torts into which Dean Prosser has analysed the United States law on privacy,[19] which seem to have influenced the Nordic Conference[20] and they in turn the "Justice" Bill.[21] We consider that placing someone in a false light is an aspect of defamation rather than of privacy.[22]

71 We do not support the view of those who argue that the publication of an untruth about a person should be treated by the law as an invasion of privacy rather than under the heading of defamation. In this connection we commend the warning by Professor Harry Kalven about the way in which the "false light" aspect of privacy has been used in the United States to extend the scope for actions of a defamation nature.[23] He says that any extensions of the

[16]Rent Act 1965, section 30.

[17]Administration of Justice Act 1970, section 40.

[18]Conclusions of the Nordic Conference of International Jurists on the Right of Privacy, Stockholm 1967; at Appendix K hereto.

[19]"Privacy", Dean William L Prosser, California Law Review, August 1960.

[20]Conclusions of the Nordic Conference of International Jurists on the Right of Privacy, Stockholm 1967; at Appendix K hereto, 2 (d) and (f).

[21]"Privacy and the Law", Appendix J, clause 9 (e) and (f).

[22]The law on defamation is under consideration by the Committee set up in May 1971 under the Chairmanship of Mr. Justice Faulks "to consider whether, in the light of the Defamation Act 1952, any changes are desirable in the law, practice and procedure relating to actions for defamation".

[23]"Privacy in Tort Law—Were Warren and Brandeis Wrong?" Law and Contemporary Problems, Chicago University 1966:

"... if the colonization of defamation by privacy does take place, it will only be because by the use of a fiction the courts have turned at last to reform of the law of defamation. It will not be because they have perceived that logically defamation is subsumed in privacy. They will simply be calling false statements by a new name ... one may wonder if this trend represents even good judicial statesmanship. The technical complexity of the law of defamation, which has shown remarkable stamina in the teeth of centuries of acid criticism, may reflect one useful strategy for a legal system forced against its ultimate better judgment to deal with dignitary harms ... In any event, it would be a notable thing if the right of privacy, having, as it were, failed in three-quarters of a century to amount to anything at home, went forth to take over the traditional torts of libel and slander."

law of defamation should be made openly as such, but he suggests also that the restrictions on the application of the law of defamation may reflect a wise caution about permitting its extension to the mollification of outraged dignity. We were interested in this connection to learn of the development of case law on defamation and "false light" in the decisions of the Federal Court of the Federal Republic of Germany: defamation has lost its identity there as a separate tort and become fused into the broader tort of infringment of the right of personality (Persönlichkeitsrecht).[24] To our mind there could be a real threat to freedom of speech if the safeguards for it that have been built into the law of defamation were to be put in jeopardy by the process of subsuming defamation into a wider tort which is implied by the doctrine of "false light".[25] We believe that the concepts of defamation and of intrusion into privacy should be kept distinct from one another.

72 Thus we find nothing to suggest that, in limiting ourselves to the headings set out in paragraph 68, we are omitting any substantial intrusions into privacy. We examine in Part II those activities which this analysis has led us to conclude potentially threaten the values in which privacy is a major element. But before we go on to do that, we survey the extent to which it is protected now and was protected in the past, and also attempt some assessment of how important it is.

73 In this Chapter we have concluded that we should not attempt a single and comprehensive definition of "privacy" or consequently "invasion of privacy" and "intrusion into privacy". However, these expressions not only appear in our terms of reference, but occur time and again in the evidence given to us, so that we repeat them where we mention the evidence. For the sake of brevity, we also use them elsewhere in this Report to mean generally the areas or activities which, as we have explained in this Chapter, we accept as those which we should examine.

Protection under the present law

137 Against physical intrusion into privacy by the press the law gives a remedy by way of damages or injunction, but only to the owner or tenant of any property that is trespassed upon. Both the civil and the criminal law of conspiracy might be invoked in rather limited circumstances, of which the essential one is that two or more offenders should be involved. If a newspaper reporter was caught using a wireless "bugging" device he could be prosecuted for offences under the Wireless Telegraph Acts. If he sent messages by telephone which caused annoyance, inconvenience or needless anxiety to another person he would commit an offence under section 78 of the Post Office Act 1969.

138 The civil law of defamation affords a strong protection against the publication of defamatory false statements about a person. The remedy is damages which take account of the injured feelings of the person defamed and which can be large. Certainly the press take the possibility of an action for defamation most seriously. Indeed some of their representatives labour under a sense of grievance that the law on this matter in this country is more severe than in others and regard its minatory character as a hindrance to the proper exercise of the liberties of the press. Be that as it may, it applies only where the

---

[24] Oral evidence of Professor Dr. Hein Kötz, 6 January 1972.

[25] See also the Report of the Porter Committee on the Law of Defamation, 1948, Cmd 7536, paragraphs 24–26, quoted at p. 41 below.

matter published cannot be proved to be true. Similar considerations apply in the limited circumstances in which an action for injurious falsehood might be brought.

139 If objection is taken to the publication of true private information, the law provides a possible protection in four circumstances only. First, if the information was obtained in confidence an action for damages or injunction may lie under the civil law on breach of confidence. The position is not entirely clear, however, and we examine it at some length in Appendix I (paragraphs 29-32). Nor can one give a definitive answer regarding one possible; important limitation on the action for breach of confidence. Suppose a newspaper in good faith buys a story, which has in fact been obtained in breach of confidence, has the person whose confidence has been betrayed an effective remedy against the paper? It would seem that the courts today regard the action to prevent by injunction a breach of confidence as resting essentially on the knowledge by the defendant of the confidential character of the information concerned. Hence it is probably that the paper could, as soon as it had been informed of the circumstances, be restrained from publishing the story.

140 The second circumstance is where publication of a true statement about a person involves, at least notionally, provocation to commit a breach of the peace, thus becoming a matter of concern to the public at large. A prosecution for criminal libel might then succeed, because the truth of the statement would not be a defence unless it could be proved that the publication was in the public interest. Cases of criminal libel are very rare and no prosecution may be initiated against a newspaper without leave of a Judge in Chambers. Thus, although criminal libel appears to provide a sanction against publication of defamatory statements, even if true, in practice these limitations have reduced its usefulness in situations where privacy is likely to be at stake. Moreover it is limited to England and Wales, there being no criminal libel in Scottish law.

141 The third set of circumstances in which true statements could lead to proceedings is in Scotland under the law of convicium. An action for damages for convicium could lie against a newspaper which cause the plaintiff loss, injury or damage by maliciously publishing material which made the plaintiff appear ridiculous or a fool, or which held him up to public hatred or attributed unpopular opinions to him.

142 The fourth set of circumstances, where statutory provisions or orders of court forbid the reporting of certain judicial proceedings, is described in Appendix I, paragraphs 46-50, and 74 and 75.

Protection by the Press Council

143 A person who is aggrieved by any action of the press may complain to the Press Council, the history and constitution of which we have referred to above (paragraphs 131 to 136). No fee is payable; the aggrieved person merely has to apply to the Secretary of the Council and set out the nature of his complaint. The Secretariat of the Council will give guidance on how this should be done. The complainant is required first to put his complaint to the editor of the newspaper complained about. This gives the editor the opportunity of making amends to the complainant or of otherwise satisfying him, so that the complaint can be dealt with in that way—as is often the case, we are told.

144 If the complainant remains dissatisfied with the action of the editor, the Press Council secretariat then investigates the complaint thoroughly and acquires all the relevant information it can. We were given instances of the thoroughness of this investigation. The Secretary then sends the editor concerned an account of the complaint and of the supporting evidence, inviting his comment and informing the editor and any journalists concerned of their right to appear in person. The Secretary decides, consulting the Chairman as necessary, in the light of the newspaper's reply whether further evidence, written or oral, is needed. Once he has all the material he considers relevant, he presents the file to the complaints committee of the Council. The Press Council in their evidence to us describe the subsequent procedure as follows:

"The Complaints Committee meets every month to consider the dossiers of complaints and any oral evidence thought necessary. It has executive authority to disallow complaints that are insufficiently substantial to warrant adjudication by the Council but otherwise the Committee proceeds by recommending an adjudication to the Council.

The Council meets every two months. Every member receives well in advance of the meeting the full dossier as presented to the Complaints Committee, plus an account of any oral evidence given before the Committee and the Committee's recommendation. The matter is then open for discussion before the Council which may adopt, vary or reverse the Committee's recommendation or may send it back for further consideration. The Council normally directs that its adjudication shall be issued to the Press for publication. Subsequently the Secretary of the Council issues a Press Release to the parties in the complaint and for publication generally."

145 The Press Council deals with a substantial number of complaints of all kinds each year. In 1970/71 for instance, 370 complaints were received. Of these, 267 were withdrawn or not pursued, usually because of explanations given to the complainant by the Secretariat; 34 were disallowed on first examination by the Secretariat and a further 31 were disallowed by the complaints committee of the Council. Only 38 resulted in adjudications, 13 being upheld and 25 rejected.[61]

146 The Press Council operates therefore on a fairly large scale and is experienced in dealing with complaints from the public. The number of these which concern privacy is, however, a tiny proportion of the whole. In the whole period from the Council's inception in 1953 up to 30 June 1970 a total of only 65 privacy cases were adjudicated upon, of which 37 were upheld and 28 rejected. The annual average number of cases adjudicated upon was thus three and a half, with two cases upheld and one and a half rejected. The three cases in the twelve months ending June 1970 concerned a complaint about the publication of the memoirs of Miss Christine Keeler, which was upheld, and two complaints about publication of the identities of those involved in heart transplants, both of which were rejected.

147 All press representatives spoke of the effectiveness of the Press Council in maintaining ethical standards in the profession; it is, we were assured, "respected, feared and obeyed". They maintained that its substantial press membership guarantees a high level of expertise in an understanding of the problems and constraints of practical journalism; while its small lay element

[61]Source: the Press Council; the figures for 1970/71 were substantially affected by the postal strike.

ensures that the viewpoint outside the profession is given due weight. They pointed out also that the independent chairman, an eminent former Lord of Appeal in Ordinary, brings to bear on their decisions the weight of judicial impartiality. The press maintained also that the Council commands not only the respect of Fleet Street but the confidence of the public, to whom its existence and function are well known. They thought that if a potential complainant were unaware of the Council's facilities, he would soon be made aware of them by any Member of Parliament, solicitor or citizens' advice bureau that he was likely to consult in pursuit of his complaint. Its spokesmen claimed that the cheap and simple procedure of the Council makes its use far less intimidating than recourse to a court of law.

148 To the point that the Press Council, unlike a court of law, operates on no established principles, the Council's representatives replied that, although the Council has prepared no statement of principles or code of conduct for the profession, its adjudications have been widely promulgated so that editors and journalists have ample precedent to guide them.

149 To the suggestion that the Council's secretariat and complaints committee have summary jurisdiction over complaints, with no provision for appeal to the Council itself, the Council's representatives assured us that this is not so: it is only when a complaint has nothing whatever to do with press ethics that the secretariat is authorised to tell a complainant that the Council would not be able to help him. Where press ethics are involved, but on a point without apparent substance, the secretariat may advise the complainant that the matter is not worth pursuing, but it would be made clear to him that it was for him alone to make the decision on whether or not to proceed with his complaint. The Press Council added that the secretariat do much useful work in handling complaints where some other course of action is more appropriate or other solution can be found. The summary jurisdiction exercised by the complaints committee is expressly limited by resolution of the Council to complaints which "are not sufficiently substantial to warrant adjudication by the Council" and to complaints which have been subject to unreasonable delay by the complainant. There was, however, a small measure of support among some press witnesses for the suggestion that there should be some appeal procedure to which dissatisfied complainants could resort; but most maintained that the present arrangements are the best that could be devised.

150 The same view was taken on the composition of the Council, though a lone voice among the representatives of journalists' organisations whom we saw thought that a bigger lay membership might be justified to help the Council in reaching properly balanced decisions when dealing with complaints of "investigative" journalism.

151 The representatives of all the press interests from which we received evidence held that the sanctions at the Council's disposal are adequate. From this evidence it was clear to us that the only sanction is the considerable moral pressure on an offending newspaper to publish a critical adjudication on its conduct. We were assured that this is highly effective, that editors find it a most obnoxious course to have to take and that some proprietors and editors take a successful complaint to the Press Council more seriously than a judgment against them in a court action. In practice, we were told, a paper is most unlikely to refuse to publish a critical adjudication, although there is ultimately no means to force it to do so. We were told that there have been only five instances where publication has not followed. Four involved local newspapers, in one of which the complainant himself requested the paper not

to publish the adjudication.[62] In the remaining instance, involving a national newspaper, it was not unequivocally clear that the Press Council expected its adjudication to be published. Nothing is laid down as to the manner in which the notice of a critical adjudication should be carried by the offending paper, and some occasionally consign it to an unobtrusive corner, while others publish it with a counter-attack alongside. In the former event, it would apparently be open to complainant or the Press Council itself to initiate a further complaint on that score. In the latter event, the newspaper, we were told, would risk losing its readers' sympathies. Some press representatives conceded that it might be a good move to enable the Press Council to direct that notice of critical adjudications should receive equal space and treatment to the publicity which was the source of the complaint.

152 The press representatives considered that it would be wrong for what is intended as an interpretative body to wield any sanction more severe than the promulgation by a newspaper to its readers of the condemnation of its conduct. So they were opposed to any power being given to the Press Council to order payment of compensation or to levy fines or stop publication.

Press Council: Waiver of Right to Legal Action

153 There is one particular feature of the workings of the Press Council that needs to be noted. In their evidence to us they said:

> "In order to avoid the Council being used tactically for the purposes of a law suit, the complainant is required in appropriate cases to surrender his right to sue the newspaper after an adjudication; in these cases the editor gives an undertaking to publish the adjudication."

Appropriate cases are those where the substance of the complaint could form grounds of an action in law, so this requirement would not be imposed in a complaint about, say, publication of true and non-confidential personal information. The Press Council defend the waiver requirement, which may at first sight seem obnoxious, on several grounds.

154 The first is that the right to go to law is jettisoned only if the complainant freely opts to take the alternative course of using the Press Council. Second there is no bar to a complainant bringing a complaint to the Press Council after he has tried, and either succeeded or failed, to obtain redress in the courts; there have been cases where this has been done, where, for instance, the substance of the complaint was insufficient to secure a judgment but may constitute a grave breach of taste or ethics. Complainants who seem inclined to pursue a legal remedy are warned that the Council will not handle their complaint until the legal processes are ended. The third reason for the waiver is that, without it, a plaintiff would be able to oblige the defendant newspaper to disclose its defence in advance in the Press Council without any of the protections afforded by a court of law: in such circumstances, we were told, newspapers would not be prepared to participate in the Press Council proceedings as they do now under the protection of the waiver. Fourth, a complainant who was in fact contemplating a law suit might use the free proceedings of the Press Council as a stalking horse; or, if the Council made an adjudication favourable to him, might pray it in aid when the case eventually went to court.

[62]The complainant did not make known to the Press Council itself his desire that the adjudication should not be published.

155 Although at first sight the waiver requirement may seem unacceptable because it blocks the possibility of subsequently obtaining damages, that is implicit in the complainant's decision, which is entirely a free one, to use the Press Council machinery first rather than the courts. The need to make the waiver may deter some potential complainants, but we accept that it is an unavoidable feature of the system by which the Council operates and we note that it is common to other binding arbitration procedures.

The problems

Publicity generally

156 The basic problem in our consideration of the mass media is that whenever unwanted publicity is given to personal matters there may be a conflict of interests between the need for the public to be informed and the need to respect the individual's privacy. Whatever practice is permitted may involve damage to one or other interest and the question to be decided is how far each interest should be upheld at the expense of the other. Knowledge of what other people are doing is essential to members of a society who are interdependent. The need extends beyond knowing just about those who live close by or with whom we work. It extends to a general knowledge of events in the wider society and in the world as a whole, which is the raw material out of which public opinion is formed, on which national and regional policies are made, and by which standards of public and private customs and morals are evolved. Much of the knowledge referred to is of a purely public character, relating to issues of international, national or local policy. These categories raise no issues of privacy. On the other hand it often extends into the personal activities of individuals and groups, where the borderline between the private and public domains is less distinct. Marriage customs, and upbringing of children, conventions and habits in education, entertainment and social life, are all examples of subjects which should be widely discussed in the public interest and yet involve examination of the way of life of individual citizens and their families, which most people regard as private. The question of where to draw the line between private and public becomes even more complex when the private activities of a public figure are in question. Where customs vary between different regions, age groups and social classes, the wide dissemination of knowledge about how others live is a necessary way of preventing the undue fragmentation of society. The mass media as well as writers and speakers of other kinds see this as one of their important functions and would deplore anything which seriously impaired their ability to discharge it.

157 The importance of a piece of news is not the only factor which prompts its publication. Much news is published to satisfy curiosity or a desire to be entertained. Such news we would say was "of" public interest, as distinct from the type of news described in the preceding paragraph, which was "in" the public interest. The distinction is of great importance in attempting to set the bounds at which the right to be informed should give way to the right to privacy. Even a determined and substantial invasion of privacy will often be justifiable where it can be shown that the object is to give news *in* the public interest, but much less often, if the object is to give news merely *of* public interest. However, the importance of privacy is not a constant value, any more than is the importance of publishing news in the public interest; and it may be that at the lower end of the scale an invasion of privacy could be justified merely to publish news for entertainment or to satisfy curiosity. This would

depend on how widely one was prepared to draw the limits of privacy. This does not bring us nearer to discerning a principle on which to decide when publication of the news is in the public interest. All we can say is that the invasion of privacy is justified only at the point where the importance of the news exceeds the importance of the privacy, but where does that point lie?

158 We are unable, for instance, to devise any general rule which could help a newspaperman to decide at how late an hour he would be justified in disturbing a private citizen, or for that matter a public figure, or how far he should pursue him to a holiday retreat in order to get information or comment on a piece of news; or how far the importance or urgency of the news should affect his decision.

159 Nor could we lay it down as an inflexible rule that, when newspapers judge it necessary in the public interest to comment on the methods of administration and discipline in a school, they should never approach the pupils or parents but always do so through the head or others in authority over the school.

Conclusion

651 We are agreed, as we explained in Chapter 6, that the concept of privacy embodies values which are essential to the work of a free society. We do not regard respect for privacy as merely a question of taste which can be left to the interplay of free discussion and the restraints of social convention. We recognise also that under modern conditions the growing interdependence and organisation of individuals, together with technological developments, has subjected privacy to dangerous pressures. In the light of these pressures we are further agreed that privacy requires additional protection. The fundamental decision which we have had to make concerns the method by which protection is given. Should the law provide a remedy against invasions of privacy as such? Or is it sufficient to rely on the protection of privacy in each social situation where it is likely to come in issue—whether that protection takes the form of direct remedies, civil or criminal, or of other social forces operating under the pressure of public opinion—reinforced, we hope, by the publication of this Report?

652 Any general civil remedy would require hardly less general qualification in order to enable the courts (the judge or judge and jury) to achieve an acceptable balance between values implicit in respect for privacy and other values of at least equal importance to the well-being of society. We have particularly in mind the importance in a free society of the unimpeded circulation of true information and the occasions which would inevitably arise, if there were a general civil remedy for the protection of privacy, in which the courts would be called upon to balance, by reference to the "public interest", society's interest in the circulation of truth against the individual's claim for privacy.

653 We appreciate that there are countries (of which we give examples in Appendix J) in which it is precisely this balancing function which is left to the courts; and we point out in Appendix I that in English law the protection which is given to privacy by the action for breach of confidence may involve the courts in deciding whether the remedy should be refused on the grounds that the disclosure in question (as, for example, when it relates to the commission of a crime) was in the public interest. The vital difference, however, between decisions on what is in the public interest, taken by the courts in

countries where a general remedy for invasions of privacy exists, and the decisions on the public interest taken by English courts in cases under existing laws which are relevant to the protection of specific aspects of privacy, is that the judicial function in the latter is much more circumscribed. Thus, in an action for breach of confidence the court is faced initially with a disclosure of information which has been given in confidence; similarly, in an action for defamation no question of the public interest arises until there is before the court a defamatory statement which is untrue. It is clear that the function of the courts in such circumstances is a less difficult one and one which is likely to give rise to less controversy than that which would face a court which was called upon to apply a much more general law to cases in which no relationship of confidence existed and no false statement had been made. In such cases a court would in effect have to make an unguided choice, in the light of the public interest, between values which, in the abstract, might appear to have equal weight. We recognise that the courts could be given the task of considering, in the factual context of each case, whether a general right to privacy should be upheld against the claims of other values, in particular the value of the free circulation of true information. But we think that such a task might first make the law uncertain, at least for some time until the necessary range of precedents covering a wide range of situations had been established; and it might secondly extend the judicial role, as it is generally understood in our society, too far into the determination of controversial questions of a social and political character.

654 If privacy can be protected in no other way these disadvantages may have to be accepted, but we have thought it right rather to conduct our examination of privacy in the first instance with reference to the differing social contexts in which a claim for protection of privacy is, or could be, asserted.

655 We have now examined in chapters 7 to 20 each of the specific areas in which substantial concern about intrusions into privacy has been brought to our attention. In some cases we have recommended that there should be legislation to create either a new offence in order to deal with new threats to privacy, for instance new technical surveillance devices; or a right of access by an individual to information held about him by a credit rating agency. In other cases we have thought it more effective to recommend that administrative controls should be established over a particular kind of activity, such as credit rating agencies and private detectives. In yet other cases where legal action has seemed too heavy an instrument and administrative control undesirable or unnecessary, we have preferred to rely on a measure of self-discipline being exercised by bodies whose activities involve a possible threat to privacy. Examples are the mass media, the universities, the medical profession and industrial employers.

656 Of these the mass media are by far the most important. On the one hand are the broadcasting authorities, which by virtue of Charter or Statute are already under extensive obligations to have regard to the interests of the public; on the other are the varied organs of the press, which are under no special legal restriction beyond the general law of the land, but have developed regulatory machinery of their own through the Press Council to handle complaints. As regards the broadcasting authorities and the press we have reached the conclusion that, in respect generally of their dissemination of information, it is best to rely for the protection of privacy upon improvements in the existing systems rather than upon new legislation. On the other hand we think that they should, along with ordinary citizens, be subject in

their information gathering activities to the restrictions on the use of technical surveillance devices which we have recommended. They are already bound by the law relating to the disclosure of information obtained in breach of confidence and would be subject to any restrictions in that branch of the law which might emerge as a result of the clarification recommended in Chapter 21.

657 Looking at the field as a whole, we have expressed the view that the existing law provides more effective relief from some kinds of intrusion into privacy than is generally appreciated. In particular it is our opinion that the law on breach of confidence, if some of its present ambiguities were to be authoritatively clarified (if necessary by legislation), would turn out to be a practical instrument for dealing with many complaints in the privacy field.

658 We have already referred to the need to balance the right of privacy against other countervailing rights, in particular freedom of information and the right to tell the truth freely unless compelling reasons for a legal limitation of this right can be adduced. We have often found this balance difficult to strike. At every stage we have been conscious of differing judgments about the precise area of privacy which should be protected under each heading and about the considerations of "public interest" which might be held in each case to justify intrusion and so to override the right of privacy. These uncertainties are, no doubt, largely the consequence of the acknowledged lack of any clear and generally agreed definition of what privacy itself is; and of the only slightly less intractable problem of deciding precisely what is "in the public interest" or, in a wider formulation, "of public interest".

659 Despite these difficulties we have reached broad agreement among ourselves about the practical approach which we wish to recommend under each of the headings dealt with in Chapters 7 to 21. We recognise that this piecemeal approach leaves some gaps. In the private sector (with which alone we are concerned) it is not difficult to think of some kinds of intrusion, most obviously by journalistic investigators or by prying neighbours, for which our recommendations provide no new legal remedy. In the second place, some of our proposals frankly rely, to an extent which some may find over-optimistic, upon the readiness of potentially intrusive agencies, such as the press, to respond not to legal sanctions but to the pressures of public and professional criticism and to the climate of society. Yet other proposals rely upon codes of conduct or on negotiated conditions of employment as means of maintaining ethical standards.

660 Questions therefore arise whether the area which our recommendations would still leave legally unprotected is so important that it must somehow be covered; whether it is realistic to count upon the sense of responsibility of interested parties, or whether there is not a way of providing the additional support of legal sanctions, without at the same time requiring the courts to apply unduly vague criteria and to hammer out, without clear guidance from the statute book, the very definitions of privacy and of the public interest which have defied the best efforts of scholars and of successive draftsmen of parliamentary bills.

661 With these conflicting considerations in mind, we therefore turn to discuss the question whether a general right of privacy should be recognised by the law, on the lines proposed in Mr. Walden's Right of Privacy Bill. In doing this we would emphasise our unanimous view that our various recommendations made in previous chapters should remain unaffected whatever the outcome of this argument. In particular the question whether the criminal law

should be invoked in some cases has, in our view, been sufficiently dealt with under our specific headings and need not be considered in relation to a general right. Any civil remedy provided for infringement of a general right of privacy must, we feel sure, be considered as an addition to measures proposed under specific headings and not as an alternative to them.

662 The case for including a general right of privacy in the domestic law of the United Kingdom may reasonably start from the fact, to which attention was called in Chapter 2, that the Government of the United Kingdom is a party to the Universal Declaration of Human Rights, the United Nations Covenant on Civil and Political Rights and the European Convention for the Protection of Human Rights and Fundamental Freedoms, all of which in one form or another recognise the right of privacy in somewhat general terms. The principle therefore, is not in dispute, only the nature of the domestic legislation which is needed to implement it.

663 A number of other countries in Europe, America and the Commonwealth, have adopted legislation in wide and general terms. While the effectiveness of these laws varies from country to country, there is evidence that some practical use is made of them and no evidence that the information media have complained that these laws unduly restrict their legitimate activities. It seems a natural deduction from this that similar action could usefully be undertaken in the United Kingdom without risk. We have naturally paid close attention to the experience of other countries, but we have noted that the methods of adjusting domestic legislation to the requirements of international agreements differ widely from one signatory state to another, and that this has been markedly true in the field of human rights. This is firstly because some legal systems are readier than others to declare a general right and then to leave to the courts the development of effective sanctions against violations of the right. The second relevant consideration is the difference in the extent to which existing laws in particular countries are already believed to provide sufficiently for the protection of the new right. With regard to the first point we think that the best way to ensure regard for privacy is to provide specific and effective sanctions against clearly defined activities which unreasonably frustrate the individual in his search of privacy. As far as the second point is concerned, we have already described in detail the considerable extent to which privacy is already protected by existing English law. We have noted that in some countries, where the law of defamation is less developed than in England, new laws for the protection of privacy are being used in cases which in England would fall squarely under the heading of defamation. In Germany, we were told, the dividing line between privacy and defamation is already blurred. We do not ourselves favour a similar development here, believing that the law should continue to distinguish clearly in the sanctions which it provides between statements which are both defamatory and untrue and statements which, even if they may be offensive on other grounds, are neither of these things.

664 This raises the question whether the method which we have adopted is nevertheless inadequate because it leaves the citizen without a legal remedy for important kinds of intrusion upon his privacy; and whether a general right of privacy, which would fill in these gaps, would in practice carry with it serious dangers to the legitimate circulation of information, which is an important value in any democratic society. We have concluded that, so far as the principal areas of complaint are concerned, and especially those which arise from new technological developments, our specific recommendations are likely to

be much more effective than any general declaration. Having covered these areas, we do not think that what remains uncovered is extensive; and our evidence does not suggest that the position in the uncovered area is deteriorating. We think moreover that to cover it by a blanket declaration of a right of privacy would introduce uncertainties into the law, the repercussions of which upon free circulation of information are difficult to foresee in detail but could be substantial.

665 We have found privacy to be a concept which means widely different things to different people and changes significantly over relatively short periods. In considering how the courts could handle so ill-defined and unstable a concept, we conclude that privacy is ill-suited to be the subject of a long process of definition through the building up of precedents over the years, since the judgments of the past would be an unreliable guide to any current evaluation of privacy. If, on the other hand, no body of judge-made precedent were built up, the law would remain, as it would certainly have to begin, highly uncertain and subject to the unguided judgments of juries from time to time. It is difficult to find any firm evidential base on which to assess the danger to the free circulation of information which might result from a legal situation of this kind. The press and broadcasting authorities have naturally expressed to us their concern about any extension into the field of truthful publication of the sort of restraints at present imposed on them by the law of defamation, especially if the practical limits of the extension are bound to remain somewhat indeterminable for a period of years. We do not think these fears can be discounted and we do not forget that others besides the mass media, for instance biographers, novelists or playwrights, might also be affected. We already have some experience of the uncertainties which result, for instance in obscenity cases, when courts of law are asked to make judgments on controversial matters, where statutory definitions are unsatisfactory, and social and moral opinion fluctuates rapidly.

666 It would, in our view, be unwise to extend this kind of uncertainty into a new branch of the law, unless there were compelling evidence of a substantial wrong, which must be righted even at some risk to other important values. Within the area covered by our terms of reference, evidence of this kind has been conspicuously lacking and we therefore see no reason to recommend that this risk should be taken.

667 Finally, we repeat what we said at the outset of this chapter. Privacy, however defined, embodies values which are essential to a free society. It requires the support of society as a whole. But the law is only one of the factors determining the climate of a democratic society and it is often only a minor factor. Education, professional standards and the free interplay of ideas and discussion through the mass media and the organs of political democracy can do at least as much as the law to establish and maintain standards of behaviour. We have explained in this report that we see risks in placing excessive reliance on the law in order to protect privacy. We believe that in our recommendations we have given to the law its due place in the protection of privacy and we see no need to extend it further.

Note: Two members of the Committee who were in favour of a general tort protecting against invasions of privacy, dissented.

Question

1. The Younger Committee posed the question: 'Should the law provide a remedy against invasions of privacy as such? Or is it sufficient to rely on the protection of privacy in each social situation where it is likely to come in issue—whether that protection takes the form of direct remedies, civil or criminal, or other social forces operating under the pressure of public opinion—reinforced, we hope, by the publication of this Report.' What do you think?

PRESS COUNCIL DECLARATION ON PRIVACY

Note: In April 1976 the Press Council issued the following declaration:

The Press Council exists primarily to protect the freedom of the Press, the maintenance of which in our democratic society has never been more important than now. It has however for some time had under study complaints which have been made about Press activities in relation to personal privacy and believes it opportune to declare its determination to uphold the right of individuals to be protected against unwarranted intrusion into their private lives or affairs.

The Council is convinced that the right of privacy is incapable of satisfactory definition by statute law and that any attempt to legislate on privacy would be contrary to the public interest.

No statutory enactment on privacy could itself secure that degree of protection which would satisfy those who consider it to be of paramount importance without at the same time curtailing the right of the public at large to be informed about and know of matters of public concern. Any such enactment would make it more difficult for the Press to carry out those duties of vigilance, inquiry and disclosure which are appropriate to a healthy democracy.

The following statement represents the policy which the Press Council has and will continue to support and which accords with the practice of responsible journalists:

    (i) The publication of information about the private lives or concerns of individuals without their consent is only acceptable if there is a legitimate public interest overriding the right of privacy.

   (ii) It is the responsibility of editors to ensure that inquiries into matters affecting the private life or concerns of individuals are only undertaken where in the Editor's opinion at the time a legitimate public interest in such matters may arise. The right to privacy is however not involved if the individuals concerned have freely and clearly consented to the pursuit of enquiries and publication.

  (iii) The public interest relied on as the justification for publication or inquiries which conflict with a claim to privacy must be a legitimate and proper public interest and not only a prurient or morbid curiosity. "Of interest to the public" is not synonymous with "in the public interest." It should be recognised that entry into public life does not disqualify an individual from his right to privacy about his private affairs, save when the circumstances relating to the private life of an individual occupying a public position may be likely to affect the performance of his duties or public confidence in him or his office.

(iv) Invasion of privacy by deception, eavesdropping or technological methods which are not in themselves unlawful can however only be justified when it is in pursuit of information which ought to be published in the public interest and there is no other reasonably practicable method of obtaining or confirming it.

(v) The Council expects the obtaining of news or pictures to be carried out with sympathy and discretion. Reporters and photographers should do nothing to cause pain or humiliation to bereaved or distressed people unless it is clear that the publication of the news or pictures will serve a legitimate public interest and there is no other reasonably practicable means of obtaining the material.

(vi) Editors are responsible for the actions of those employed by their newspapers and have a duty to ensure that all concerned are aware of the importance of respecting all legitimate claims to personal privacy.

This Declaration of Principle, which takes account of existing rulings of the Council and editorial directives on standards of journalists, should ensure the maintenance of a climate of opinion and behaviour amongst all concerned, protecting the right of privacy.

The Council has been and will seek to continue to be effective in establishing and maintaining ethical standards in the Press and by vigorous public condemnation discouraging undesirable practices. In the course of its consultations with editors the Council has welcomed widespread support for the acceptance by the Press of the responsibility for ensuring a proper balance between the right of the individual to privacy and the right of the public to know.

[*The Press and the People, Twenty-fourth Annual Report of the Press Council,* 1977 (London, 1979), pp. 109-11.]
Note: See also p. 302.

Case of Klass and others (1978)

European Courts of Human Rights

Five German lawyers sought to challenge the compatibility with the Convention of Article 10 (2) of the German Constitution and of an Act of August 13, on Restrictions on the secrecy of the mail, post and telecommunications (an Act referred to as "G 10") which provided authority for the German intelligence services to intercept communications. The Court (to which the matter had been referred by the Commission) decided first of all that although the complainants could not show that they had personally been affected by surveillance, measures taken by the intelligence services were nonetheless "victims" for the purpose of making a complaint under Article 25 (1) of the Convention. Turning to the alleged violation of Article 8 of the Convention the Court then said:

39. The applicants claim that the contested legislation, notably because the person concerned is not informed of the surveillance measures and cannot have recourse to the courts when such measures are terminated, violates Article 8 of the Convention which provides as follows:

[The Court here set out the text of Article 8 as found on p. 33.]

40. According to Article 10 § 2 of the Basic Law, restrictions upon the secrecy of the mail, post and telecommunications may be ordered but only pursuant to a statute. Article 1 § 1 of the G 10 allows certain authorities to open and inspect mail and post, to read telegraphic messages and to monitor and record telephone conversations (see paragraph 17 above). The Court's examination under Article 8 is thus limited to the authorisation of such measures alone and does not extend, for instance, to the secret surveillance effected in pursuance of the Code of Criminal Procedure (see paragraph 25 above).

41. The first matter to be decided is whether and, if so, in what respect the contested legislation, in permitting the above-mentioned measures of surveillance, constitutes an interference with the exercise of the right guaranteed to the applicants under Article 8 § 1.

Although telephone conversations are not expressly mentioned in paragraph 1 of Article 8, the Court considers, as did the Commission, that such conversations are covered by the notions of "private life" and "correspondence" referred to by this provision.

In its report, the Commission expressed the opinion that the secret surveillance provided for under the German legislation amounted to an interference with the exercise of the right set forth in Article 8 § 1. Neither before the Commission nor before the Court did the Government contest this issue. Clearly, any of the permitted surveillance measures, once applied to a given individual, would result in an interference by a public authority with the exercise of that individual's right to respect for his private and family life and his correspondence. Furthermore, in the mere existence of the legislation itself there is involved, for all those to whom the legislation could be applied, a menace of surveillance; this menace necessarily strikes at freedom of communication between users of the postal and telecommunication services and thereby constitutes an "interference by a public authority" with the exercise of the applicants' right to respect for private and family life and for correspondence.

The Court does not exclude that the contested legislation, and therefore the measures permitted thereunder, could also involve an interference with the exercise of a person's right to respect for his home. However, the Court does not deem it necessary in the present proceedings to decide this point.

42 The cardinal issue arising under Article 8 in the present case is whether the interference so found is justified by the terms of paragraph 2 of the Article. This paragraph, since it provides for an exception to a right guaranteed by the Convention, is to be narrowly interpreted. Powers of secret surveillance of citizens, characterising as they do the police state, are tolerable under the Convention only insofar as strictly necessary for safeguarding the democratic institutions.

43. In order for the "interference" established above not to infringe Article 8, it must, according to paragraph 2, first of all have been "in accordance with the law". This requirement is fulfilled in the present case since the "interference" results from Acts passed by Parliament, including one Act which was modified by the Federal Constitutional Court, in the exercise of its jurisdiction, by its judgment of 15 December 1970 (see paragraph 11 above). In addition, the Court observes that, as both the Government and the Commission

pointed out, any individual measure of surveillance has to comply with the strict conditions and procedures laid down in the legislation itself.

44. It remains to be determined whether the other requisites laid down in paragraph 2 of Article 8 were also satisfied. According to the Government and the Commission, the interference permitted by the contested legislation was "necessary in a democratic society in the interests of national security" and/or "for the prevention of disorder or crime". Before the Court, the Government submitted that the interference was additionally justified "in the interests of . . . public safety" and "for the protection of the rights and freedoms of others".

45. The G 10 defines precisely, and thereby limits, the purposes for which the restrictive measures may be imposed. It provides that, in order to protect against "imminent dangers" threatening "the free democratic constitutional order", "the existence or security of the Federation or of a *Land*", "the security of the [allied] armed forces" stationed on the territory of the Republic or the security of "the troops of one of the Three Powers stationed in the *Land* of Berlin", the responsible authorities may authorise the restrictions referred to above (see paragraph 17).

46. The Court, sharing the view of the Government and the Commission, finds that the aim of the G 10 is indeed to safeguard national security and/or to prevent disorder or crime in pursuance of Article 8 § 2. In these circumstances, the Court does not deem it necessary to decide whether the further purposes cited by the Government are also relevant.

On the other hand, it has to be ascertained whether the means provided under the impugned legislation for the achievement of the above-mentioned aim remain in all respects within the bounds of what is necessary in a democratic society.

47. The applicants do not object to the German legislation in that it provides for wide-ranging powers of surveillance; they accept such powers, and the resultant encroachment upon the right guaranteed by Article 8 § 1, as being a necessary means of defence for the protection of the democratic State. The applicants consider, however, that paragraph 2 of Article 8 lays down for such powers certain limits which have to be respected in a democratic society in order to ensure that the society does not slide imperceptibly towards totalitarianism. In their view, the contested legislation lacks adequate safeguards against possible abuse.

48. As the Delegates observed, the Court, in its appreciation of the scope of the protection offered by Article 8, cannot but take judicial notice of two important facts. The first consists of the technical advances made in the means of espionage and, correspondingly, of surveillance; the second is the development of terrorism in Europe in recent years. Democratic societies nowadays find themselves threatened by highly sophisticated forms of espionage and by terrorism, with the result that the State must be able, in order effectively to counter such threats, to undertake the secret surveillance of subversive elements operating within its jurisdiction. The Court has therefore to accept that the existence of some legislation granting powers of secret surveillance over the mail, post and telecommunications is, under exceptional conditions, necessary in a democratic society in the interests of national security and/or for the prevention of disorder or crime.

49. As concerns the fixing of the conditions under which the system of surveillance is to be operated, the Court points out that the domestic legislature enjoys a certain discretion. It is certainly not for the Court to substitute for the

assessment of the national authorities any other assessment of what might be the best policy in this field (cf., *mutatis mutandis*, the De Wilde, Ooms and Versyp judgment of 18 June 1971, Series A no. 12, pp. 45-46, § 93, and the Golder judgment of 21 February 1975, Series A no. 18, pp. 21-22, § 45; cf., for Article 10 § 2, the Engle and others judgment of 8 June 1976, Series A no. 22, pp. 41-42, § 100, and the Handyside judgment of 7 December 1976, Series A no. 24, p. 22, § 48).

Nevertheless, the Court stresses that this does not mean that the Contracting States enjoy an unlimited discretion to subject persons within their jurisdiction to secret surveillance. The Court, being aware of the danger such a law poses of undermining or even destroying democracy on the ground of defending it, affirms that the Contracting States may not, in the name of the struggle against espionage and terrorism, adopt whatever measures they deem appropriate.

50. The Court must be satisfied that, whatever system of surveillance is adopted, there exist adequate and effective guarantees against abuse. This assessment has only a relative character: it depends on all the circumstances of the case, such as the nature, scope and duration of the possible measures, the grounds required for ordering such measures, the authorities competent to permit, carry out and supervise such measures, and the kind of remedy provided by the national law.

The functioning of the system of secret surveillance established by the contested legislation, as modified by the Federal Constitutional Court's judgment of 15 December 1970, must therefore be examined in the light of the Convention.

51. According to the G 10, a series of limitative conditions have to be satisfied before a surveillance measure can be imposed. Thus, the permissible restrictive measures are confined to cases in which there are factual indications for suspecting a person of planning, committing or having committed certain serious criminal acts; measures may only be ordered if the establishment of the facts by another method is without prospects of success or considerably more difficult; even then, the surveillance may cover only the specific suspect or his presumed "contact-persons" (see paragraph 17 above). Consequently, so-called exploratory or general surveillance is not permitted by the contested legislation.

Surveillance may be ordered only on written application giving reasons, and such an application may be made only by the head, or his substitute, of certain services; the decision thereon must be taken by a Federal Minister empowered for the purpose by the Chancellor or, where appropriate, by the supreme *Land* authority (see paragraph 18 above). Accordingly, under the law there exists an administrative procedure designed to ensure that measures are not ordered haphazardly, irregularly or without due and proper consideration. In addition, although not required by the Act, the competent Minister in practice and except in urgent cases seeks the prior consent of the G 10 Commission (see paragraph 21 above).

52. The G 10 also lays down strict conditions with regard to the implementation of the surveillance measures and to the processing of the information thereby obtained. The measures in question remain in force for a maximum of three months and may be renewed only on fresh application; the measures must immediately be discontinued once the required conditions have ceased to exist or the measures themselves are no longer necessary; knowledge and documents thereby obtained may not be used for other ends, and documents

must be destroyed as soon as they are no longer needed to achieve the required purpose (see paragraphs 18 and 20 above).

As regards the implementation of the measures, an initial control is carried out by an official qualified for judicial office. This official examines the information obtained before transmitting to the competent services such information as may be used in accordance with the Act and is relevant to the purpose of the measure; he destroys any other intelligence that may have been gathered (see paragraph 20 above).

53. Under the G 10, while recourse to the courts in respect of the ordering and implementation of measures of surveillance is excluded, subsequent control or review is provided instead, in accordance with Article 10 § 2 of the Basic Law, by two bodies appointed by the people's elected representatives, namely the Parliamentary Board and the G 10 Commission.

The competent Minister must, at least once every six months, report on the application of the G 10 to the Parliamentary Board consisting of five Members of Parliament; the Members of Parliament are appointed by the *Bundestag* in proportion to the parliamentary groupings, the opposition being represented on the Board. In addition, the Minister is bound every month to provide the G 10 Commission with an account of the measures he has ordered. In practice, he seeks the prior consent of this Commission. The latter decides, *ex officio* or on application by a person believing himself to be under surveillance, on both the legality of and the necessity for the measures in question; if it declares any measures to be illegal or unnecessary, the Minister must terminate them immediately. The Commission members are appointed for the current term of the *Bundestag* by the Parliamentary Board after consultation with the Government; they are completely independent in the exercise of their functions and cannot be subject to instructions (see paragraph 21 above).

54. The Government maintain that Artile 8 § 2 does not require judicial control of secret surveillance and that the system of review established under the G 10 does effectively protect the rights of the individual. The applicants, on the other hand, qualify this system as a "form of political control", inadequate in comparison with the principle of judicial control which ought to prevail.

It therefore has to be determined whether the procedures for supervising the ordering and implementation of the restrictive measures are such as to keep the "interference" resulting from the contested legislation to what is "necessary in a democratic society".

55. Review of surveillance may intervene at three stages: when the surveillance is first ordered, while it is being carried out, or after it has been terminated. As regards the first two stages, the very nature and logic of secret surveillance dictate that not only the surveillance itself but also the accompanying review should be effected without the individual's knowledge. Consequently, since the individual will necessarily be prevented from seeking an effective remedy of his own accord or from taking a direct part in any review proceedings, it is essential that the procedures established should themselves provide adequate and equivalent guarantees safeguarding the individual's rights. In addition, the values of a democratic society must be followed as faithfully as possible in the supervisory procedures if the bounds of necessity, within the meaning of Article 8 § 2, are not to be exceeded. One of the fundamental principles of a democratic society is the rule of law, which is expressly referred to in the Preamble to the Convention (see the Golder judgment of 21 February 1975, Series A no. 18, pp. 16–17, § 34). The rule of

law implies, *inter alia*, that an interference by the executive authorities with an individual's rights should be subject to an effective control which should normally be assured by the judiciary, at least in the last resort, judicial control offering the best guarantees of independence, impartiality and a proper procedure.

56. Within the system of surveillance established by the G 10, judicial control was excluded, being replaced by an initial control effected by an official qualified for judicial office and by the control provided by the Parliamentary Board and the G 10 Commission.

The Court considers that, in a field where abuse is potentially so easy in individual cases and could have such harmful consequences for democratic society as a whole, it is in principle desirable to entrust supervisory control to a judge.

Nevertheless, having regard to the nature of the supervisory and other safeguards provided for by the G 10, the Court concludes that the exclusion of judicial control does not exceed the limits of what may be deemed necessary in a democratic society. The Parliamentary Board and the G 10 Commission are independent of the authorities carrying out the surveillance, and are vested with sufficient powers and competence to exercise an effective and continuous control. Furthermore, the democratic character is reflected in the balanced membership of the Parliamentary Board. The opposition is represented on this body and is therefore able to participate in the control of the measures ordered by the competent Minister who is responsible to the *Bundestag*. The two supervisory bodies may, in the circumstances of the case, be regarded as enjoying sufficient independence to give an objective ruling.

The Court notes in addition that an individual believing himself to be under surveillance has the opportunity of complaining to the G 10 Commission and of having recourse to the Constitutional Court (see paragraph 23 above). However, as the Government conceded, these are remedies which can come into play only in exceptional circumstances.

57. As regards review *a posteriori*, it is necessary to determine whether judicial control, in particular with the individual's participation, should continue to be excluded even after surveillance has ceased. Inextricably linked to this issue is the question of subsequent notification, since there is in principle little scope for recourse to the courts by the individual concerned unless he is advised of the measures taken without his knowledge and thus able retrospectively to challenge their legality.

The applicants' main complaint under Article 8 is in fact that the person concerned is not *always* subsequently informed after the suspension of surveillance and is not therefore in a position to seek an effective remedy before the courts. Their preoccupation is the danger of measures being improperly implemented without the individual knowing or being able to verify the extent to which his rights have been interfered with. In their view, effective control by the courts after the suspension of surveillance measures is necessary in a democratic society to ensure against abuses; otherwise adequate control of secret surveillance is lacking and the right conferred on individuals under Article 8 is simply eliminated.

In the Government's view, the subsequent notification which must be given since the Federal Constitutional Court's judgment (see paragraphs 11 and 19 above) corresponds to the requirements of Article 8 § 2. In their submission, the whole efficacy of secret surveillance requires that, both before and after the event, information cannot be divulged if thereby the purpose of the investigation is, or would be retrospectively thwarted. They stressed that recourse to the courts is no longer excluded after notification has been given, various legal remedies then becoming available to allow the individual, *inter alia*, to seek redress for any injury suffered (see paragraph 24 above).

58. In the opinion of the Court, it has to be ascertained whether it is even feasible in practice to require subsequent notification in all cases.

The activity or danger against which a particular series of surveillance measures is directed may continue for years, even decades, after the suspension of those measures. Subsequent notification to each individual affected by a suspended measure might well jeopardise the long-term purpose that originally prompted the surveillance. Furthermore, as the Federal Constitutional Court rightly observed, such notification might serve to reveal the working methods and fields of operation of the intelligence services and even possibly to identify their agents. In the Court's view, insofar as the "interference" resulting from the contested legislation is in principle justified under Article 8 § 2 (see paragraph 48 above), the fact of not informing the individual once surveillance has ceased cannot itself be incompatible with this provision since it is this very fact which ensures the efficacy of the "interference". Moreover, it is to be recalled that, in pursuance of the Federal Constitutional Court's judgment of 15 December 1970, the person concerned must be informed after the termination of the surveillance measures as soon as notification can be made without jeopardising the purpose of the restriction (see paragraphs 11 and 19 above).

59. Both in general and in relation to the question of subsequent notification, the applicants have constantly invoked the danger of abuse as a ground for their contention that the legislation they challenge does not fulfil the requirements of Article 8 § 2 of the Convention. While the possibility of improper action by a dishonest, negligent or over-zealous official can never be completely ruled out whatever the system, the considerations that matter for the purposes of the Court's present review are the likelihood of such action and the safeguards provided to protect against it.

The Court has examined above (at paragraphs 51 to 58) the contested legislation in the light, *inter alia*, of these considerations. The Court notes in particular that the G 10 contains various provisions designed to reduce the effect of surveillance measures to an unavoidable minimum and to ensure that the surveillance is carried out in strict accordance with the law. In the absence of any evidence or indication that the actual practice followed is otherwise, the Court must assume that in the democratic society of the Federal Republic of Germany the relevant authorities are properly applying the legislation in issue.

The Court agrees with the Commission that some compromise between the requirements for defending democratic society and individual rights is inherent in the system of the Convention (see, *mutatis mutandis*, the judgment of 23 July 1968 in the "Belgian Linguistic" case, Series A no. 6, p. 32, § 5). As the Preamble to the Convention states, "Fundamental Freedoms . . . are best maintained on the one hand by an effective political democracy and on the other by a common understanding and observance of the Human Rights upon which [the Contracting States] depend". In the context of Article 8, this means that a balance must be sought between the exercise by the individual of the right guaranteed to him under paragraph 1 and the necessity under paragraph 2 to impose secret surveillance for the protection of the democratic society as a whole.

60. In the light of these considerations and of the detailed examination of the contested legislation, the Court concludes that the German legislature was justified to consider the interference resulting from that legislation with the exercise of the right guaranteed by Article 8 § 1 as being necessary in a democratic society in the interests of national security and for the prevention of disorder or crime (Article 8 § 2). Accordingly, the Court finds no breach of Article 8 of the Convention.

The Court then considered possible violations of Article 13 and 6 (1) of the Convention, and held unanimously that there had been no violation of these Articles or of Article 8.

INTERCEPTION OF COMMUNICATIONS

Further Reading

De Smith, pp. 456–458; O'Higgins, pp. 51–56; Street, pp. 42–48; Wade & Phillips, pp. 527–429.

P. J. Duffy, "The case of Klass and others: Secret Surveillance of Communications and the European Convention on Human Rights," (1979) 4 *Human Rights Review* pp. 20–40.

REPORT OF PRIVY COUNCILLORS

In 1956 the Home Secretary authorised the police to hand-over to the Benchers of Lincoln's Inn transcripts of telephone conversations to which a barrister, subject to disciplinary proceedings before the Benchers, had been a party. A public outcry led to a committee of Privy Councillors (Lord Birkett, Lord Monckton and Mr. Patrick Gordon Walker) being set up to "consider and report upon the exercise by the Secretary of State of the executive power to intercept communications," including the extent of the use of such power and to make recommendations as to its future exercise. Considering the legality of the exercise of this power the Committee had this to say:

Part I

THE AUTHORITY OF THE SECRETARY OF STATE TO INTERCEPT COMMUNICATIONS

9. The origin of the authority of the Executive to intercept communications is obscure, and it is not surprising that conflicting views about the source of the power have been placed before us. The first public reference to the warrant of the Secretary of State authorising the opening of letters is in the Proclamation of May 25th, 1663, which forbade the opening of any letters or packets by anybody, except by the immediate warrant of the Principal Secretary of State. But long before this date the practice of opening letters had been followed.

10. It is a singular circumstance that the source of the power has never been the subject of judicial pronouncement, and the text-book writers have not discussed it in any fullness. In the fourth edition of Anson's Law and Custom of the Constitution, Vol. II, Part II, for example, the subject is thus dealt with:—

> "The right and the duty, if occasion requires, of detaining and opening letters in the Post Office rests in Great Britain upon the Home Secretary, in Northern Ireland upon the Governor. This power, which extends to telegraphic communications, is occasionally, though not frequently, used . . . and is extended to telegrams . . ."

11. The existence of the power from early times has frequently been acknowledged; its exercise has been publicly known; and the manner of its exercise has been the subject of public agitation from time to time, and has been made the subject of debate in the House of Commons and the House of Lords. In the year 1844, a great agitation arose in the country, because the Secretary of State, Sir James Graham, had issued a warrant to open the letters of Joseph Mazzini; and after debates in both Houses of Parliament, two Secret Committees were set up, one of the House of Commons and one of the House of Lords. Both Committees were asked to inquire into the state of the law in respect of the detaining and opening of letters at the General Post Office. It is significant that both Committees avoided any discussion of the source of the authority upon which the Secretary of State exercised his power, and were content to recognise the existence of the power to intercept communications, and to rely upon the various statutes which refer to the existence of the power. This is significant, because in the debates which preceded the setting up of the Committees, the origin of the power had been discussed. In the House of Lords, Lord Campbell, who was at that time a member of the Judicial Committee of the Privy Council, and afterwards was to be Lord Chief Justice and Lord Chancellor, discussed the question, and in his Autobiography he says:—

> "In the debates which arose this session upon the practice of opening letters at the Post Office under a warrant from the Secretary of State, I contended that it was neither authorised by common law nor statute, although the Secretary of State, like any other magistrate, or indeed any private individual, may seize and detain documents which constitute evidence of the commission of a crime."

12. On the question of law, the Committee of the House of Commons reported:—

> "The inquiry, therefore, what the state of the law now is respecting such detention and opening, is reduced to the inquiry what the state of the law was, respecting the same matter, immediately upon the passing of the Statute of Anne . . . the law on the matter in question was the same in 1711 that it is in 1844."

13. They also said on the point of law:—

> "In preference to discussing the purely legal question, how far the Statute of Anne, in recognising the practice, on the part of the Secretaries of State, of issuing Warrants to open Letters, rendered it lawful for the Secretaries of State to issue such Warrants, Your Committee propose, so far as they have materials for that purpose, to give the history of this

practice, prior and subsequent to the passing of that Statute: these materials being such as ought not to be overlooked in investigating the grounds on which the exercise of this authority rests."

14. Two further extracts from the history the Committee set out may be given:—

(a) "It does not appear at what precise period the Crown undertook to be the regular carrier of Letters for its subjects. The Crown, doubtless, found it necessary, at a very early period, to the exercise of the functions of Sovereignty, to be able to convey with speed and security its own despatches from one part of the realm to another, and from and to parts beyond the seas; and for that purpose it appointed certain messengers or runners, called the Posts. These Posts were also employed for the personal convenience of the Sovereign, and the individuals composing the Royal Court. In course of time, a Master of the Posts was appointed, and the first of these on record was Brian Tuke, Esq., . . . who held that office in 1516 . . ."

(b) "The practice probably began at an early period, and afterwards grew into a regular custom, of allowing private persons to avail themselves of the King's Posts for transmitting their correspondence. This probably became a perquisite to the Postmasters, while, at the same time, it gave to the Ministers of State the power of narrowly inspecting the whole of the written communications of the country."

15. The Committee of the House of Lords had two former Lord Chancellors as members, Lord Brougham and Lord Cottenham, and in their Report the Committee said:—

"The Committee have not thought it necessary to attempt to define the Grounds upon which the Government has exercised the Power afforded by public Conveyance of Letters of obtaining such Information, as might be though beneficial for the public Service; it seems sufficient for the present Purpose to state, that the Exercise of this Power can be traced from the earliest Institutions in this Country for the Conveyance of Letters, from Orders in Council of the 22nd of November, 1626, and 24th of February, 1627 . . . In 1657, upon the first Establishment of a regular Post Office, it was stated in the Ordinance to be the best Means to discover and prevent any dangerous and wicked Designs against the Commonwealth . . . The Power, therefore, appears to have been exercised from the earliest Period, and to have been recognised by several Acts of Parliament. This appears to the Committee to be the State of the Law in respect to the detaining and opening of Letters at the Post Office, and they do not find any other Authority for such detaining or opening."

16. The situation with regard to the opening and detaining of letters and postal packets is substantially the same in 1957 as it was in 1844, for section 58 (I) of the Post Office Act of 1953, which is the Act now governing the opening and detaining of letters, is substantially in the same terms as the earlier statutes of 1908, 1837 and 1710.

17. We have made these quotations from the two important Reports of 1844, because it is clear that not only were questions of law debated in both Houses of Parliament, but both Committees considered the questions of law with great care. Both Committees recognised that the Executive had exercised the power of opening letters over a very long period of time, and neither

Committee ever suggested or concluded that the exercise of the power was in any way unlawful. Nor did they suggest in terms that the exercise of the power was the exercise of a prerogative right of the Crown. They leaned heavily upon the Post Office statutes, although none of the statutes contain clauses conferring the power to intercept communications, but recognise the power as an existing power which it is lawful to exercise.

18. In view of the conflicting opinions that have been put before us on the source of the Secretary of State's power to intercept communications, we think it best to set out briefly the arguments as they were presented to us.

19. The first submission made was that the power of the Secretary of State to issue his warrant for the interception and opening of letters was in exercise of a prerogative right of the Crown. The Royal Prerogative has been defined as comprehending all the special liberties, privileges and powers and royalties allowed by common law. It is created and limited by the common law. Blackstone defined the Royal Prerogative in these words—

> "Prerogative can only be applied to those rights and capacities which the King enjoys alone in contradistinction to others and not to those which he enjoys in common with any of his subjects."

20. It was contended before us that the procedure of opening letters so far as it was known, and set out in the Secret Committees' Reports of 1844, was such that in all respects it was proper to describe it as a prerogative right. The nature of that right was said to be a right to intercept communications. It is true that for some centuries, communications in fact were confined to letters and postal packets, but as science invented new modes of communication, such as the telegraph and the telephone, and they came into general use, it was submitted that the prerogative power to intercept communications was wide enough to include not only letters and postal packets, but every subsequent means of communication that became known and was used. The prerogative right, therefore, to intercept communications applied now to letters and telegrams and telephonic communications alike.

21. It would appear that the view entertained by the Home Office has always been that the power exercised by the Secretary of State is not expressly conferred by statute, but that the statutes relating to the Post Office recognise the existence of the power as a lawful power for the purpose of making it clear that no offence is committed by a person who acts in obedience to a warrant of the Secretary of State issued by him in the exercise of that power. On this view the power exercised from the very earliest times is a prerogative power to intercept, examine, and disclose for certain purposes connected with the safety of the State or the preservation of public order, any messages carried by the Crown; and this Prerogative attached to the new methods of carrying messages that were undertaken by the Crown in the nineteenth century by means of the telegraph and the telephone. It was conceded that no new Prerogatives can be created, and the prerogative power to intercept a telephone message must therefore be the same prerogative power which authorises the interception of letters.

22. In connection with this argument the principle must be borne in mind that, where the legislature has intervened and covered by statute the ground covered by the Prerogative, the statute thereafter rules. But this doctrine does not seem applicable here, since there has been no intervention of this character by the legislature.

23. The opponents of the view that the power to intercept is a prerogative power emphasise the fact that no constitutional writer when dealing with the Royal Prerogative, mentions this particular power as being a prerogative power. In Chitty's Prerogatives of the Crown published in 1820, the learned author states that he has attempted "to present a comprehensive and connected, yet compressed and logical, view of every prerogative and corresponding right of the subject"; but nowhere is any reference made to a prerogative power of detaining and opening communications. Reliance is also placed on the doctrine laid down by Lord Camden in Entick v. Carrington, 19 State Trials 1030. In the year 1762, the Secretary of State issued a warrant directing certain persons to search for John Entick, the author of certain numbers of "The Monitor or British Freeholder," and to seize him, "together with his books and papers," and to bring them to the Secretary of State. Certain messengers, empowered by the warrant, seized Mr. Entick in his house, and seized his papers. Entick brought an action in trespass against the messengers for seizure of his papers. The case was tried before the Lord Chief Justice and a jury, and the jury returned a special verdict, which is very lengthy, and is set out in the report of the case. If the Defendants were liable, the jury assessed the damages at £300. This special verdict was twice argued in the Court of Common Pleas at great length, and with much learning; and finally in 1765 Lord Camden delivered the elaborate judgment which was the judgment of the Court. Many questions were argued and decided, but the main question was the legality of the general warrant. Lord Camden declared that the practice of issuing general warrants was illegal and unconstitutional. The jury found by their special verdict that the practice of issuing general warrants had been in existence for many years, but Lord Camden nevertheless denied their legality.

24. It was suggested that the arguments used to support the legality of general warrants before Lord Camden and his fellow judges were the same arguments used to support the prerogative power exercised by the Secretary of State to intercept communications, namely that no court of justice had ever declared the powers to be illegal, that the powers were essential to government, and the only means of quieting clamours and seditions. Lord Camden said—

> "With respect to the practice itself, if it goes no higher, every lawyer will tell you it is much too modern to be evidence of the common law; and if it be added that these warrants ought to acquire some strength by the silence of those courts which have heard them read so often upon returns without censure or animadversion, I am able to borrow my answer to that pretence from the Court of King's Bench, which lately declared with great unanimity in the case of General Warrants that as no objection was taken to them on the returns and the matter passed *sub silentio,* the precedents were of no weight. I most heartily concur in that opinion . . ."
>
> "To search, seize, and carry away all the papers of the subject on the first warrant: that such a right should have existed from the time whereof the memory of man runneth not to the contrary, and never yet have found a place in any book of law; is incredible. But if so strange a thing could be supposed, I do not see how we could declare the law upon such evidence."
>
> ". . . If it is law it will be found in our books. If it is not to be found there it is not law."

25. It was submitted in reply that there is a distinction to be drawn between the general warrants condemned by Lord Camden, and the limited, strictly governed use of the Secretary of State's warrant into the exercise of which we have been enquiring; and in this connexion we emphasise once more the exact nature of the procedure we set out in Part II of this Report.

26. It was further pointed out that the provisions of section 9 (I) of the Crown Proceedings Act of 1947 giving certain immunities to the Crown are inconsistent with the existence of a prerogative power for the section provides that ". . . no proceedings in tort shall lie against the Crown for anything done or omitted to be done in relation to a postal packet by any person while employed as a servant or agent of the Crown, or for anything done or omitted to be done in relation to a telephonic communication by any person whilst so employed; nor shall any officer of the Crown be subject, save at the suit of the Crown, to any civil liability for any of the matters aforesaid." It may very well be that in 1947 the question of intercepting a telephone message was not in contemplation, and therefore no reference was made to a prerogative power, but the words of the section are very wide in their terms.

27. An alternative view was put before us which differed in some respects from the assertion of the prerogative right, but scarcely differed in substance. It was submitted that the origin of the power of the Secretary of State to intercept communications lay in a common law right which was not a part of the Prerogative, but which derived from an inherent power in the Crown to protect the realm against the misuse of postal facilities by ill-disposed persons. This common law right, it was said, continues to exist and is recognised in the Post Office statutes. No statute has enacted the power in express terms, but in addition to recognising and acknowledging the power, the statutes have indicated certain ways in which the power should be exercised, as for example, by the issue of a warrant by the Secretary of State authorising the interception to be made.

28. No support for this view is to be found in any judicial pronouncement, or in any legal text book. Indeed in Chitty's Royal Prerogative in England published in 1830, the learned author says at page 166—

> "In modern times the prerogative of the Crown has been so strictly defined by law . . . . that though the old doctrines of absolute sovereignty and transcedent domination still disfigure our law books, they are little heard of elsewhere. Occasionally however it happens that in Parliamentary discussions, assertions are hazarded of latent prerogatives in the Crown which are supposed to be inherent in the very nature of sovereignty. That such pretensions are unfounded it is not difficult to make out."

29. It was said before us that this common law power which was clearly an ancient power and derived from the actions of the monarchy when seeking to safeguard the realm, was a power wide enough to cover every form of communication which might come into being at any time. This second view is difficult to distinguish from the first view save that the use of the word "Prerogative" is avoided.

30. A third argument was put before us, which we summarise in paragraphs 31-37, that from the earliest times the power to intercept and open letters had been in existence. Throughout many centuries the practice had continued. How it arose can only be conjectured because historical records

are wanting, but that the power existed and was used permits of no doubt whatever.

31. The Ordinance of 1657 recited in the Preamble that one of the advantages of erecting and settling one General Post Office was that it "was the best means to discover and prevent many dangerous and wicked designs which have been and are daily contrived against the peace and welfare of the Commonwealth, the intelligence whereof cannot well be communicated but by letter of escript." One of the principal objects of that Ordinance, it was suggested, was to prohibit persons other than the Postmaster-General from conveying letters, and the public reference to "discovering many dangerous and wicked designs" would seem to throw some light on the probable origin of the power. The Act of Parliament of 1660 followed the Ordinance of 1657 and agreed *mutatis mutandis* with its content. The Proclamation of 1663 prohibiting the opening of letters save by the warrant of the Secretary of State would seem to imply that it was not unlawful to open a letter before that Proclamation, otherwise the prohibition would have been superfluous. The object of the legislation of 1657 and 1660 was to create a monopoly for the Crown and to ensure that the letters would be carried by persons appointed or licensed by the Crown, with the object of enabling the Crown to inspect the contents of the letters carried. It was also pointed out that in none of these public declarations was there any assertion of the Royal Prerogative. The origin of the power to intercept letters, on this view, was the result of the creation of a monopoly, created and developed for this among other purposes; and the opening and detaining of letters by the Crown took place not because of any prerogative right, but upon the footing that those who entrusted their letters to the Posts would render them open to inspection at the wish of the Crown. It is of course understandable how this power should be referred to as a Prerogative, because the Crown alone could exercise the power; but, however the power is described, it was said that from the 17th century at least it cannot be doubted that the power to open letters has been lawfully exercised by the Crown.

32. In 1710, an Act was passed "for establishing a General Post Office for all Her Majesty's Dominions, etc." and again it was enacted by section 40 "that no person . . . . shall presume to open, detain, or delay . . . . any . . . . Letter after same is or shall be delivered into the General or other Post Office . . . . except by an express Warrant in Writing under the Hand of one of the Principal Secretaries of State for every such opening, detaining, or delaying . . . ."

33. Section 58 (I) of the Post Office Act, 1953 provides—

"If any officer of the Post Office, contrary to his duty, opens . . . . any postal packet in course of transmission by post, or wilfully detains or delays . . . . any such postal packet, he shall be guilty of a misdemeanour . . . .

Provided that nothing in this section shall extend to the opening, detaining or delaying of a postal packet returned for want of a true direction, or returned by reason that the person to whom it is directed has refused it, or has refused or neglected to pay the postage thereof, or that the packet cannot for any other reason be delivered, or to the opening, detaining or delaying of a postal packet under the authority of this Act or in obedience to an express warrant in writing under the hand of a Secretary of State."

34. Postal packet is defined in section 87 (I) as meaning—

"A letter, postcard, reply postcard, newspaper, printed packet, sample packet, or parcel, and every packet or article transmissible by post, and includes a telegram."

35. Section 58 of the Act of 1953 reproduces section 56 of the Post Office Act, 1908 which reproduces section 25 of the Post Office (Offences) Act, 1837 which in return re-enacted without material amendment section 40 of the Post Office (Revenue) Act of 1710.

36. The legal position since 1710 and now is that an officer of the Post Office who opens, delays or detains a postal packet commits an offence unless it is his duty to do so, or one of the conditions mentioned in the section as justifying his conduct is satisfied. It is a defence to show that the letter was opened, delayed or detained on the authority of the Secretary of State's warrant.

37. As telegrams are postal packets for the purposes of the Post Office Act of 1953, and are telegraphic messages for the purposes of the Telegraph Act of 1869 by virtue of section 3, it is an offence for an officer of the Post Office to "open, delay or detain" a telegram in course of transmission by post unless it is his duty so to do, or the opening, &c., is authorised by the warrant of the Secretary of State, or it is justified on one or other of the grounds mentioned in section 58 (I) of the Post Office Act, 1953.

38. We have thought it right to set out at some length the different views which were expressed to us by high legal authorities. We recognise that we have no authority ourselves to decide between these conflicting views and to declare the law. We have been impressed by the fact that many Secretaries of State in many Administrations for many years past have acted upon the view that the power to intercept communications was in the nature of a prerogative power. It had never been thought necessary for any statute to confer the right, but all the statutes had recognised the right as an existing right at the time of their enactment. It was beyond doubt that the power had existed independently of the statutes, its precise origin alone remaining in doubt.

39. If the problem confronting us had merely been concerned with letters, we should have been inclined to follow the example of the two Secret Committees in 1844, and to say that there can be no doubt whatever of these things—

(a) The power to intercept letters and postal packets and to disclose their contents and otherwise to make use of them had been used and frequently used through many centuries.

(b) Such a power existed and was exercised widely and publicly known as the debates in the House of Commons and the House of Lords plainly showed.

(c) At no time had it been suggested with any authority that the exercise of the power was unlawful.

But we recognise that the chief controversy which resulted in the setting up of the present committee was concerned with the interception of telephone messages, and therefore we do not feel able to leave the matters in question quite as the two Secret Committees were able to do.

40. The power to intercept telephone messages has been exercised in this country from time to time since the introduction of the telephone; and until the year 1937, the Post Office acted upon the view that the power, which the Crown exercised in intercepting telephone messages, was a power possessed

by any other operator of telephones and was not contrary to law. No warrants by the Secretary of State were therefore issued, and any arrangements for the interception of telephone conversations were made directly between the Security Service or the Police Authorities and the Director-General of the Post Office.

41. In 1937 the position was reviewed by the Home Secretary and the Postmaster-General and it was then decided, as a matter of policy, that it was undesirable that records of telephone conversations should be made by Post Office servants and disclosed to the Police or to the Security Service without the authority of the Secretary of State. Apart from thinking that the former practice was undesirable, the Home Office was of opinion that the power on which they had acted to intercept letters and telegrams on the authority of a warrant issued by the Secretary of State, was wide enough in its nature to include the interception of telephone messages also. It was accordingly decided to act on this view of the law, and it has since been the practice of the Post Office to intercept telephone conversations only on the express warrant of the Secretary of State, that is, upon the authority which had already been recognised in the statutes to which we have referred dealing with letters and telegrams.

42. If it be said that a prerogative right could not extend to the interception of telephone conversations, because telephones were undreamt of when the prerogative power was first taken and exercised, reference should be made to the case of In re a Petition of Right [1915] 3 K.B. 659 in the Court of Appeal (Cozens-Hardy, M.R., Pickford and Warrington L.JJ), when Lord Cozens-Hardy said in affirming the judgment of Avory J.—

> "If it be said that the prerogative right cannot extend to an aerodrome because aeroplanes were unknown in the reign of Richard I., I think that the answer is to be found in the somewhat analogous case of *Mercer* v. *Denne* (1905) 2 Ch. 538, 585, where this Court held that a customary right to 'cutch' fishing nets was not limited to materials known in the reign of Richard I., but extended to drying nets with suitable materials. So the prerogative applies to what is reasonably necessary for preventing and repelling invasion at the present time, regard being had to the invention of gunpowder and the use of aeroplanes in warfare."

WARRINGTON L.J. said—

> "The circumstances under which the power may be exercised and the particular acts which may be done in the exercise thereof must of necessity vary with the times and the advance of military science . . . ."

43. The prerogative power in question in that case was the power to take lands without compensation for the purposes of the Defence of the Realm, but if in the question we have to consider, the existence of a prerogative power to intercept all communications was established, the objection that the telephone was a modern invention would not defeat the application of the power.

44. But if the view accepted and followed by the Home Office for many years is rejected, then it was submitted that the power to intercept telephone messages was governed by special considerations which were somewhat different from those that govern the question of letters and telegrams. If there be no prerogative power governing all communications, and thus including telephonic communications, and if there be no power at common law to the

like effect, then the only relevant statutory reference to be considered, would be section 20 of the Telegraph Act of 1868.

45. The material words of the section are—

"Any person having official duties connected with the Post Office or acting on behalf of the Postmaster-General, who shall, contrary to his duty, disclose or in any way make known or intercept the contents or any part of the contents of any telegraphic messages or any message intrusted to the Postmaster-General for the purpose of transmission, shall in England and in Ireland be guilty of a misdemeanor, . . . and the Postmaster-General shall make regulations to carry out the intentions of this section, and to prevent the improper use of any person in his employment or acting on his behalf of any knowledge he may acquire of the contents of any telegraphic message."

46. No regulations have in fact been made under this section. It is a little difficult to think that the word "intercept" in section 20 of the Act of 1868 contemplated the listening in to telephone conversations for the telephone exchange was only instituted in England in 1879 and then there were only seven or eight subscribers.

47. In the case of the Attorney-General v. Edison Telephone Company, (1880) 6 Q.B.D. p. 244, it was held that a telephone conversation is a "telegraphic communication" for the purposes of the Telegraph Acts, though at the time of the decision the question of listening into or intercepting a telephone message was not being considered.

48. In view of the decision, however, it was argued that by reason of section 20 of the Telegraph Act of 1868 it was open to the Postmaster-General to instruct post office officials and those acting on his behalf to listen in, to record and disclose telephone conversations, just as he had the power to intercept, disclose and make known the contents of a telegram. It was also argued that the fact that it is not now the practice for the Postmaster-General to give any such instructions except on the authority of the Secretary of State's warrant had no legal significance.

49. If this argument is rejected, then it was submitted that, so far as the interception of telephone messages is concerned, reliance could be placed on the doctrine followed until 1937 that the Post Office was entitled to intercept and that it was not unlawful to do so, and that in any event the provisions of the Crown Proceedings Act made the Post Office immune from any legal action for any acts relating to the telephone.

50. We should not be happy to feel that so important a power as the power to intercept telephone messages rested on either of the grounds set out in paragraphs 44-49. We favour the view that it rests upon the power plainly recognised by the Post Office statutes as existing before the enactment of the statutes, by whatever name the power is described.

51. We are therefore of the opinion that the state of the law might fairly be expressed in this way.
(a) The power to intercept letters has been exercised from the earliest times, and has been recognised in successive Acts of Parliament.
(b) This power extends to telegrams.
(c) It is difficult to resist the view that if there is a lawful power to intercept communications in the form of letters and telegrams, then it is wide enough to cover telephone communications as well.

52. If, however, it should be thought that the power to intercept telephone messages was left in an uncertain state that was undesirable, it would be for Parliament to consider what steps ought to be taken to remove all uncertainty if the practice is to continue. So far as letters and telegrams are concerned, the provisions of the Post Office Act of 1953 appear to have worked in practice without any difficulty. If it were thought necessary, a suitable amendment to that section of the Act of 1953 would remove doubts whether telephonic communications were in the same position as letters and telegrams.

[*Report of the Committee of Privy Councillors appointed to inquire into the interception of communications (Cmnd. 283, 1957).*]

Note: The Committee took the view that making available transcripts to the Benchers of Lincoln's Inn was "a mistaken decision." They recommended that the practice of intercepting messages should continue subject to administrative safeguards. They published statistics of the use of the power of interception which showed that limited use of the power was used. These statistics are suspect, if only because it was subsequently revealed that every telegram coming into or going out of the country was intercepted by the security services, and no account was taken of this fact in the compilation of statistics.

Malone v. Metropolitan Police Commissioner [1979] 2 W.L.R. 700.

Chancery Division

In Crown Court proceedings against the plaintiff, charged with others with handling stolen property, it was admitted by the prosecution that there had been interception of the plaintiff's telephone conversations on the authority of a Secretary of State's warrant. A series of declarations were sought by the plaintiff impugning the legality of this interception. After having ruled that the Court did not have authority to issue a declaration that Article 8 of the European Convention on Human Rights had been violated ("In my judgment, the power to make declarations is confined to making declarations on matters which are justiciable in the courts") and having declined to grant a declaration "that the plaintiff has no remedy in this country for the tapping of his telephone lines" because it would not confer any benefit on the plaintiff beyond that conferred by a reasoned judgment of the court on the issue, **SIR ROBERT MEGARRY,** V.–C. said:
  . . . the question may be expressed in the simple form "Is telephone tapping in aid of the police in their functions relating to crime illegal?" However, I think that I should make it clear that the only form of telephone tapping that has been debated is tapping which consists of the making of recordings by Post Office officials in some part of the existing telephone system, and the making of those recordings available to police officers for the purposes of transcription and use. I am not concerned with any form of tapping that involved electronic devices which make wireless transmissions, nor with any process whereby anyone trespasses on to the premises of the subscriber or anyone else to affix tapping devices or the like. All that I am concerned with is

the legality of tapping effected by means of recording telephone conversations from wires which, though connected to the premises of the subscriber, are not on them.

Mr. Ross-Munro advanced a number of broad propositions. I do not propose to set them out verbatim, especially as they were to some extent modified during argument. Further, although the royal prerogative was mentioned from time to time, no claim was made that there was any prerogative power to tap telephones, and so I need say nothing of that. As they finally emerged, I think Mr. Ross-Munro's three main submissions may be summarised as follows. First, he said that it was unlawful for anyone to intercept or monitor the telephone conversations of another without the consent of that other. He rested this contention on the right of property, on the right of privacy, and on the right of confidentiality. Second, he relied on article 8 of the Convention, as construed by the European Court of Human Rights, especially in *Klass and Others,* July 4, 1978. He relied on this in two respects. First, he said that it conferred a direct right on all citizens of the United Kingdom. Second, he said that it aided the courts of this country. It guided those courts in interpreting and applying English law so as to make it accord as far as possible with the Convention; and it provided a guide in cases of ambiguity or a lack of clarity in English law. Mr. Ross-Munro's third main contention was based on the absence of any grant of powers to the executive to tap telephones, either by statute or by the common law. . . .

Before I examine Mr. Ross-Munro's contentions, I should indicate the basic thesis of the contentions of Mr. Rattee and the Solicitor-General to the contrary. This was that apart from certain limited statutory provisions, there was nothing to make governmental telephone tapping illegal; and the statutory provisions of themselves assume that such tapping is not in other respects illegal. That being so, there is no general right to immunity from such tapping. England, it may be said, is not a country where everything is forbidden except what is expressly permitted: it is a country where everything is permitted except what is expressly forbidden.

As the plaintiff's contentions overlap to some extent, I shall set them all out first, and in most cases postpone my consideration of their force and effect until after I have deployed them all. Mr. Ross-Munro's first proposition rested in the first place on a right of property. To tap a person's telephone conversation without his consent, he said, was unlawful because that person had rights of property in his words as transmitted by the electrical impulses of the telephone system, and so the tapping constituted an interference with his property rights. An analogy that he suggested was that the important part of a letter was the words that it contained rather than the paper that it was written on. I regret to say that Mr. Ross-Munro found it difficult to persuade me that there was any reality in this contention, and he did not struggle long. I do not see how words being transmitted by electrical impulses could themselves (as distinct from any copyright in them) fairly be said to be the subject matter of property. At all events, no argument which even began to support such a proposition was put before me.

The second ground on which Mr. Ross-Munro sought to support his first proposition was that of the right of privacy. He accepted that the books assert that in English law there is no general right to privacy, and he referred me to a passage in *Halsbury's Laws of England,* 4th ed., vol. 8 (1974), p. 557 to this effect. But he contended that there was a particular right of privacy which the books did not mention, namely, the right to hold a telephone conversation in the privacy of one's home without molestation. In support of his contention, Mr. Ross-Munro relied to a large extent on the common law offence of eavesdropping, the celebrated article on "The Right of Privacy" by Samuel D. Warren and the future Brandeis J. in (1890) 4 *Harvard Law Review* 193, the Fourth Amendment to the Constitution of the United States of America, *Katz* v. *United States* (1967) 389 U.S. 347 and *Rhodes* v. *Graham* (1931) 37 S.W. (2d) 46. I shall mention these in turn.

The offence of eavesdropping is described in *Blackstone's Commentaries* (1809), 15th ed., vol. 4, p. 168 as being committed by those who listen under walls or windows or the eaves of a house, and frame slanderous and mischievous tales. The offence constituted a common nuisance, punishable by fine and finding sureties for good behaviour. This offence fell under the same broad head, dealt with on the same page of *Blackstone,* as being a common scold, which was punishable by immersion in the trebucket or ducking stool. Section 13 of the Criminal Law Act 1967 abolished these and a number of other offences, so that eavesdropping can now speak in support of Mr. Ross-Munro with only a muted voice.

The article in the *Harvard Law Review* is, as Mr. Ross-Munro emphasised, to a large extent founded on English authorities. No summary can do it justice; but some indication of its general effect may be given by saying that decisions based on property, on implied terms in a contract or on trust or confidence, are said to be instances of a broad principle giving individuals a right to privacy. A number of limitations of this right are suggested. These include a provision that the right to privacy does not prohibit the publication of any matter which is of public or general interest. The detection of crime is not mentioned in this context. The article could be urged in support of the general right of privacy which Mr. Ross-Munro accepts does not exist in English law, but provides little or no support for the particular right of privacy for telephone conversations in the home for which he contends. . . .

I now turn to the third ground on which Mr. Ross-Munro supports his first proposition, the right of confidentiality. This is an equitable right which is still in course of development, and is usually protected by the grant of an injunction to prevent disclosure of the confidence. Under Lord Cairns' Act 1858 damages may be granted in substitution for an injunction; yet if there is no case for the grant of an injunction, as when the disclosure has already been made, the unsatisfactory result seems to be that no damages can be awarded under this head: see *Proctor* v. *Bayley* (1889) 42 Ch.D. 390. In such a case, where there is no breach of contract or other orthodox foundation for damages at common law, it seems doubtful whether there is any right to damages, as distinct from an account of profits. It may be, however, that a new tort is emerging (see *Goff and Jones, The Law of Restitution,* 2nd ed. (1978), pp. 518, 519, and Gareth Jones (1970) 86 L.Q.R. 463, 491), though this has been doubted: see *Street, The Law of Torts,* 6th ed. (1976), p. 377. Certainly the subject raises many questions that are so far unresolved, some of which are discussed in the Younger Report at pp. 296—299.

The application of the doctrine of confidentiality to the tapping of private telephone lines is that in using a telephone a person is likely to do it in the belief that it is probable (though by no means certain) that his words will be heard only by the person he is speaking to. I do not think that it can be put higher than that. As the Younger Report points out at p. 168, those who use the telephone are "aware that there are several well understood possibilites of being overheard. A realistic person would not therefore rely on the telephone system to protect the confidence of what he says because, by using the telephone, he would have discarded a large measure of security for his private speech." . . .

It is against that background that I must consider Mr. Ross-Munro's submissions. He contended that the categories of confidentiality were not closed, and that they should be extended. The leading case in this branch of the law is *Prince Albert* v. *Strange* (1849) 1 Mac. & G. 25 (affirming (1848) 2 De G. & Sm. 652), as applied in *Duchess of Argyll* v. *Duke of Argyll* [1967] Ch. 302; and without citing the former, Mr. Ross-Munro read me passages from the latter. If A makes a confidential communication to B, then A may not only restrain B from divulging or using the confidence, but also may restrain C from divulging or using it if C has acquired it from B, even if he acquired it without notice of any impropriety: see the authorities cited in *Snell's Principles of Equity,* 27th ed. (1973), p. 651, one of which, *Printers & Finishers Ltd.* v. *Holloway* [1965] 1 W.L.R. 1, 7, was put before me. In such cases it seems plain that however innocent the acquisition of the knowledge, what will be restrained is the use or disclosure of it after notice of the impropriety. In the case of a telephone conversation, said Mr. Ross-Munro, any conversation that was "reasonably intended to be private" (in the words of Harlan J. in *Katz* v. *United States,* 389 U.S. 347, 362), should be treated as a confidential communication. Even if the using of the telephone must be taken as implying some sort of consent to some risk of being overheard, that could not be taken to be any kind of consent to any publication to any third party.

Mr. Ross-Munro agreed that there were limits to the doctrine of confidentiality. He accepted the dictum of Page Wood V.-C. in *Gartside* v. *Outram* (1856) 26 L.J.Ch. 113, 114, that "there is no confidence as to the disclosure of iniquity." This view was applied in *Initial Services Ltd.* v. *Putterill* [1968] 1 Q.B. 396, 405, where Lord Denning M.R. held that it extended "to any misconduct of such a nature that it ought in the public interest to be disclosed to others," and was not confined to cases of crime or fraud. Mr. Ross-Munro agreed that if through what are often called "crossed lines" a person overhears what is plainly a confidential conversation, and this discloses plans to commit a crime, that person should inform the police, and he could not be said to have committed any breach of the obligation of confidentiality. But that, he contended, was very different from tapping a telephone in the hope of obtaining information about some crime, whether already committed or being planned. . . .

With that, I turn to Mr. Ross-Munro's second main contention, based on the Convention. As I have mentioned, there were two limbs; first, that the Convention conferred direct rights on citizens of the United Kingdom, and, second, that the Convention should be applied as a guide in interpreting and applying English law in so far as it is ambiguous or lacking in clarity. I have already read articles 8 and 13 of the Convention, but although I have mentioned the *Klass* case, I have not discussed it. It was a case referred to the European Court of Human Rights by the Commission of Human Rights in respect of an application by five German citizens against the Federal Republic of Germany under the Convention. The decision was by the court in plenary session. Fifteen judges joined in the main judgment, and one judge delivered a separate judgment, concurring in the result but giving different reasons. The complaint was that a statute of the Republic, which was called "the G.10," was contrary to the Convention in that, in permitting governmental surveillance of the post and telecommunications, (a) it did so without obliging the authorities in every case to notify those concerned after the event, and (b) it excluded any remedy in the courts against ordering and executing the surveillance. There was no challenge to the right of the state to carry out the surveillance; the challenge was as to the absence of these safeguards. . . .

. . . For the present, all that I say is that I take note of the Convention, as construed in the *Klass* case, and I shall give it due consideration in discussing English law on the point. As for the direct right which the Convention confers, it seems to me to be plain that this is a right in relation to the European Commission of Human Rights and the European Court of Human Rights, the bodies established by the Convention, but not in relation to the courts of this country. The Convention is plainly not of itself law in this country, however much it may fall to be considered as indicating what the law of this country should be, or should be construed as being.

Finally, there is the contention that as no power to tap telephones has been given by either statute or common law, the tapping is necessarily unlawful. The underlying assumption of this contention, of course, is that nothing is lawful that is not positively authorised by law. As I indicated, England is not a country where everything is forbidden except what is expressly permitted. One possible illustration is smoking. I inquired what positive authority was given by the law to permit people to smoke. Mr. Ross-Munro accepted that there was none; but tapping, he said, was different. It was in general disfavour, and if offended against usual and proper standards of behaviour, in that it was an invasion of privacy and an interference with the liberty of the individual and his right to be let alone when lawfully engaged on his own affairs.

I did not find this argument convincing. A stalwart non-smoker, whether life-long or redeemed, might consider that most or all of what Mr. Ross-Munro said applied with equal force to the not inconsiderable numbers of non-smokers. In leading an ordinary life they often find themselves unable to avoid inhaling in an enclosed space the products of a combustion deliberately caused by a smoker who knows that the fumes that he is creating will spread, and will affect other people. But in any case the answer destroys the underlying assumption and mutilates the proposition. The notion that some express authorisation of law is required for acts which meet with "general disfavour," and "offend against proper standards of behaviour," and so on, would make the state of the law dependent on subjective views on indefinite concepts, and would be likely to produce some remarkable and contentious results. Neither in principle not in authority can I see any justification for this view, and I reject it. If the tapping of telephones by the Post Office at the request of the police can be carried out without any breach of the law, it does not require any statutory or common law power to justify it: it can lawfully be done simply because there is nothing to make it unlawful. The question, of course, is whether tapping can be carried out without infringing the law. . . .

Now that I have dealt with these matters, I can consider the contentions of Mr. Ross-Munro that I have attempted to summarise. I propose to take his three main contentions by stages. His first main contention was that by reason of the right of privacy and the right of confidentiality it was unlawful to tap a telephone, even under the authority of a warrant of the Home Secretary. I need not mention the argument based on property as I have already rejected it.

First, I do not think that any assistance is obtained from the general warrant cases, or other authorities dealing with warrants. At common law, the only power to search premises under a search warrant issued by a justice of the peace is to search for stolen goods: see *Entick* v. *Carrington,* 19 St.Tr. 1029, 1067. However, many statutes authorise searches under search warrants for many different purposes; and there is admittedly no statute which in terms authorises the tapping of telephones, with or without a warrant. Nevertheless, any conclusion that the tapping of telephones is therefore illegal would plainly be superficial in the extreme. The reason why a search of premises which is not authorised by law is illegal is that it involves the tort of trespass to those premises: and any trespass, whether to land or goods or the person, that is made without legal authority is prima facie illegal. Telephone tapping by the Post Office, on the other hand, involves no act of trespass. The subscriber speaks into his telephone, and the process of tapping appears to be carried out by Post Office officials making recordings, with Post Office apparatus on Post Office premises, of the electrical impulses on Post Office wires provided by Post Office electricity. There is no question of there being any trespass on the plaintiff's premises for the purpose of attaching anything either to the premises themselves or to anything on them: all that is done is done within the Post Office's own domain. As Lord Camden C.J. said in *Entick* v. *Carrington,* 19 St.Tr. 1029, 1066, "the eye cannot by the laws of England be guilty of a trespass"; and, I would add, nor can the ear.

Second, I turn to the warrant of the Home Secretary. This contrasts with search warrants in that it is issued by one the great officers of state as such, and not by a justice of the peace acting as such. Furthermore, it does not purport to be issued under the authority of any statute or of the common law. From the Birkett Report (see paragraph 40 et seq.) it appears that the power to tap telephones has been exercised "from time to time since the introduction of the telephone," but that not until 1937 were any warrants issued. Until then, the Post Office took the view that any operator of telephones had a power to tap conversations without infringing any rule of law. The police authorities accordingly made arrangements directly with the Director-General of the Post Office for any tapping of telephones that might be required. In 1937, however, the Home Secretary and Postmaster General decided, as a matter of policy, that thenceforward records of telephone conversations should be made by the Post Office and disclosed to the police only on the authority of the Home Secretary. The view was taken that certain statutes which permitted the interception of letters and telegrams on the authority of a Secretary of State were wide enough to cover telephone tapping. The decision seems to have been based partly on what was desirable as a matter of policy, and partly on an application of the statutory power of interception, or some analogy to it. At all events, the decision seems plainly to have been an administrative decision not dictated or required by statute.

At that stage, the Home Secretary and the Postmaster General were both officers of state under the Crown, and the Post Office was a department of state. The Post Office Act 1969, which came into force on October 1, 1969, changed that. The office of Postmaster General was abolished, a new corporate public authority was established under the name of the Post Office, governed by a chairman and a number of members, and the office of Minister of Posts and Telecommunications was created, with certain supervisory functions in relation to the Post Office. In 1974 all these functions were transferred to the Home Secretary, and the Ministry of Posts and Telecommunications was dissolved: Ministry of Posts and Telecommunications (Dissolution) Order 1974 (S.I. 1974 No. 691).

One result of the change in the status of the Post Office in 1969 was that as it was no longer under the direct control of a Minister of the Crown, but had become a corporation with a large measure of independence from the Crown, no assumption could any longer be made that the Post Office would act upon a warrant of the Home Secretary to tap telephones. If previously the Postmaster General had wished not to obey such a warrant, there would have been a disagreement between two Ministers of the Crown which, in default of some other means of resolution, would presumably have been determined by the Cabinet. That, however, ceased to be the position in 1969; and one aspect of the change was dealt with by section 80 of the Act. This provision, on which the Solicitor-General placed great weight, runs as follows:

"A requirement to do what is necessary to inform designated persons holding office under the Crown concerning matters and things transmitted or in course of transmission by means of postal or telecommunication services provided by the Post Office may be laid on the Post Office for the like purposes and in the like manner as, at the passing of this Act, a requirement may be laid on the Postmaster General to do what is necessary to inform such persons concerning matters and things transmitted or in course of transmission by means of such services provided by him."

This, said the Solicitor-General, plainly showed that Parliament intended to provide lawful authority in the changed circumstances for what had previously been done in the old circumstances. The Home Secretary's warrant, which had previously been given under administrative arrangements, now had a statutory function as being a "requirement" under section 80, and, what is more, as a requirement that statute authorised to be "laid" on the Post Office. Although the previous arrangements had been merely administrative, they had been set out in the Birkett Report a dozen years earlier, and the section plainly referred to these arrangements; if not, it was difficult to see what the section had in view, and certainly nothing intelligible has been suggested. A warrant was not needed to make the tapping lawful: it was lawful without any warrant. But where the tapping was done under warrant (and that is the only matter before me) the section afforded statutory recognition of the lawfulness of the tapping. In their essentials, these contentions seem to me to be sound.

Section 80 of the Post Office Act 1969 does not stand alone, however; there is also paragraph 1 (1) of Schedule 5 to that Act. To explain the purport of this it is necessary to refer to three statutes which on the face of them appear to refer to telegrams rather than telephone conversations. Section 45 of the Telegraph Act 1863 made it an offence if any person employed by a telegraph company "improperly divulges to any person the purport of any message." Section 20 of the Telegraph Act 1868 made it an offence if any Post Office official:

"shall, contrary to his duty, disclose or in any way make known or intercept the contents or any part of the contents of any telegraphic messages or any message intrusted to the Postmaster General for the purpose of transmission . . ."

These provisions were both enacted before section 4 of the Telegraph Act 1869 had given the Postmaster General his monopoly of transmitting telegrams, and of course long before the telephone service came into being in 1879. Finally, there is section 11 of the Post Office (Protection) Act 1884. This made it an offence if any employee of a telegraph company (as defined) "improperly divulges to any person the purport of any telegram." These provisions all thus give rise to possible questions of the meaning of "improperly" divulging, or disclosing "contrary to his duty": if an instruction to divulge or disclose were to be given by an official superior who appeared to be acting within the scope of his duty, would an employee who obeyed the instruction be guilty of offence? At the same time, there is the question whether this had anything to do with telephone conversations as opposed to telegrams.

Now this latter point is subject to some authority. In *Attorney-General* v. *Edison Telephone Co. of London Ltd.* (1880) 6 Q.B.D. 244, a case in which the Crown had the opulent representation of both law officers and four other counsel, the question was whether the monopoly rights which section 4 of the Act of 1869 had given the Postmaster General for telegraphs was infringed by the operations of a telephone company. A Divisional Court of the Exchequer Division held that it was, and granted declarations, an injunction and an account against the company. As the patents for the telephone had not been granted until 1877 and 1878, and the system did not exist in this country until 1879, this construction of the Act of 1869 was striking. A "telephone" was held to be a "telegraph" within the meaning of the Acts of 1863 and 1869, and a telephone conversation was held to be a "message," or at all events "a communication transmitted by a telegraph" within the meaning of those Acts.

With that in mind I return to the Offences created by the Acts of 1863, 1868 and 1884. These are the subject of paragraph 1 (1) of Schedule 5 to the Post Office Act 1969, a Schedule which bears the title "Repair of minor Deficiencies in certain Acts." This sub-paragraph provides that in proceedings against any person for an offence under these provisions, "it shall be a defence for him to prove that the act constituting the offence was done in obedience to a warrant under the hand of a Secretary of State." If no more, this at least appears to recognise that the changed position of the Post Office and its employees made desirable some statutory provision giving some effect to a warrant of the Home Secretary in relation to the statutory offences in question. Whatever may be the position of an employee who makes a disclosure on the orders of a superior who appears to be acting within the scope of his duty (and it is difficult to see how such a disclosure could be said to be an "improper" act by the employee, or "contrary to his duty"), such an employee has the protection of statute if he acts under a warrant of the Home Secretary. It is true, as Mr. Ross-Munro pointed out, that Schedule 5 does not in terms empower the Home Secretary to issue a warrant in the way that is done by section 4 (1) of the Official Secrets Act 1920, which is expressed in very wide terms; and see the power given to the Governor by section 33 of the Hong Kong Telecommunication Ordinance 1963. That, however, does not alter the fact that by the Post Office Act 1969 Parliamentary recognition to such warrants was given. Accordingly, I leave this part of the case on the footing that by that Act Parliament has provided a clear recognition of the warrant of the Home Secretary as having an effective function in law, both as providing a defence to certain criminal charges, and also as amounting to an effective requirement for the Post Office to do certain acts.

I may add one comment. I do not think that the Telephone Regulations 1951 (S.I. 1951 No. 2075), regulation 55 (2), effects this case. That regulation gives the Post Office power to interrupt and terminate telephone conversations that are indecent or offensive, and so on; but I do not see how the fact that this power is given for limited purposes can negate any general power to tap telephones for police purposes in relation to crime.

Third, there is the right of privacy. Here the contention is that although at present no general right of privacy has been recognised by English law, there is a particular right of privacy, namely, the right to hold a telephone conversation in the privacy of one's home without molestation. This, it was said, ought to be recognised and declared to be part of English law, despite the absence of any English authority to this effect. As I have indicated, I am not unduly troubled by the absence of English authority: there has to be a first time for everything, and if the principles of English law, and not least analogies from the existing rules, together with the requirements of justice and common sense, pointed firmly to such a right existing, then I think the court should not be deterred from recognising the right.

On the other hand, it is no function of the courts to legislate in a new field. The extension of the existing laws and principles is one thing, the creation of an altogether new right is another. At times judges must, and do, legislate; but as Holmes J. once said, they do so only interstitially, and with molecular rather than molar motions: see *Southern Pacific Co.* v. *Jensen* (1917) 244 U.S. 205, 221, in a dissenting judgment. Anything beyond that must be left for legislation. No new right in the law, fully-fledged with all the appropriate safeguards, can spring from the head of a judge deciding a particular case: only Parliament can create such a right. . . .

Fourth, there is the right of confidentiality. Let me at the outset dispose of one point. If telephone services were provided under a contract between the telephone subscriber and the Post Office, then it might be contended that there was some implied term in that contract that telephone conversations should remain confidential and be free from tapping. To meet such a possible contention, the Solicitor-General took me through a series of statutes and cases on the point, ending with certain sections of the Post Office Act 1969. The combined effect of sections 9 and 28 is that the Post Office is under a duty to provide certain services, including telephone services (though this duty is not enforceable by proceedings in court), and that the Post Office has power to make a scheme of charges and other terms and conditions for those services, the charges being recoverable "as if" they were simple contract debts. Under section 28, the Post Office Telecommunication Scheme 1976 was duly made, bearing the name Scheme T1/1976: this was published as a supplement to the "London Gazette" of May 25, 1976. By paragraph 6 of the scheme, neither the scheme, nor anything done under it, nor any request for any service for which the scheme fixes or determines any charges, terms or conditions, is to "constitute or lead to the formation of a contract between the Post Office and any other person; . . ." At the end of the Solicitor-General's submissions on the point Mr. Ross-Munro conceded that there was no contract as such between the plaintiff and the Post Office; and that, I think, is the end of any contention based on implied terms.

The right of confidentiality accordingly falls to be considered apart from any contractual right. In such a case, it has been said that three elements are normally required if a case of breach of confidence is to succeed. First, the information itself, in the words of Lord Greene M.R. in *Saltman Engineering Co.*

Ltd. v. *Campbell Engineering Co. Ltd.* (1948) 65 R.P.C. 203, 215, "must 'have the necessary quality of confidence about it.' Secondly, that information must have been imparted in circumstances importing an obligation of confidence. Thirdly, there must be an unauthorised use of that information to the detriment of the party communicating it": see *Coco* v. *A. N. Clark (Engineers) Ltd.* [1969] R.P.C. 41, 47, cited by Lord Widgery C.J. in *Attorney-General* v. *Jonathan Cape Ltd.* [1976] Q.B. 752, 769. Of the second requirement, it was said in the *Coco* case, at pp. 47-48:

> "However secret and confidential the information, there can be no binding obligation of confidence if that information is blurted out in public or is communicated in other circumstances which negative any duty of holding it confidential."

What was in issue in the *Coco* case was a communication by an inventor or designer to a manufacturer, and the alleged misuse of that information by the manufacturer. In the present case, the alleged misuse is not by the person to whom the information was intended to be communicated, but by someone to whom the plaintiff had no intention of communicating anything: and that, of course, introduces a somewhat different element, that of the unknown overhearer.

It seems to me that a person who utters confidential information must accept the risk of any unknown overhearing that is inherent in the circumstances of communication. Those who exchange confidences on a bus or a train run the risk of a nearby passenger with acute hearing or a more distant passenger who is adept at lip-reading. Those who speak over garden walls run the risk of the unseen neighbour in a toolshed nearby. Office cleaners who discuss secrets in the office when they think everyone else has gone run the risk of speaking within earshot of an unseen member of the staff who is working late. Those who give confidential information over an office intercommunication system run the risk of some third party being connected to the conversation. I do not see why someone who had overheard some secret in such a way should be exposed to legal proceedings if he uses or divulges what he had heard. No doubt an honourable man would give some warning when he realises that what he is hearing is not intended for his ears; but I have to concern myself with the law, and not with moral standards. There are, of course, many moral precepts which are not legally enforceable.

When this is applied to telephone conversations, it appears to me that the speaker is taking such risks of being overheard as are inherent in the system. As I have mentioned, the Younger Report referred to users of the telephone being aware that there were several well-understood possibilities of being overheard, and stated that a realistic person would not rely on the telephone system to protect the confidence of what he says. That comment seems unanswerable. . . .

I think that one has to approach these matters with some measure of balance and common sense. The rights and liberties of a telephone subscriber are indeed important: but so also are the desires of the great bulk of the population not to be the victims of assault, theft or other crimes. The detection and prosecution of criminals, and the discovery of projected crimes, are important weapons in protecting the public. In the nature of things it will be virtually impossible to know beforehand whether any particular telephone conversation will be criminal in nature. The question is not whether there is a certainty that the conversation tapped will be iniquitous, but whether there is just cause or excuse for the tapping and for the use made of the material obtained by the tapping.

If certain requirements are satisfied, then I think that there will plainly be just cause or excuse for what is done by or on behalf of the police. These requirements are, first, that there should be grounds for suspecting that the tapping of the particular telephone will be of material assistance in detecting or preventing crime, or discovering the criminals, or otherwise assisting in the discharge of the functions of the police in relation to crime. Second, no use should be made of any material obtained except for these purposes. Third, any knowledge of information which is not relevant to those purposes should be confined to the minimum number of persons reasonably required to carry out the process of tapping. If those requirements are satisfied, then it seems to me that there will be just cause or excuse for carrying out the tapping, and using information obtained for those limited purposes. I am not, of course, saying that nothing else can constitute a just cause or excuse: what I am saying is that if these requirements are satisfied, then in my judgment there will be a just cause or excuse. I am not, for instance, saying anything about matters of national security: I speak only of what is before me in the present case, concerning tapping for police purposes in relation to crime.

So far as the evidence goes, it seems to me that the process of tapping, as carried out on behalf of the police in relation to crime, fully conforms with these requirements: indeed, there are restrictions on tapping, and safeguards, which go beyond these requirements. The only possible difficulty is in relation to the "strict conditions" laid down by the Home Office which have to be satisfied before the warrant of the Home Office is sought; for I do not know what these conditions are. However, Mr. Kelland's affidavit states in relation to the plaintiff that if a warrant had been sought by the Metropolitan Police (and he says nothing as to whether in fact it was) "the sole purpose in seeking such a warrant would have been to obtain information of value in the detection and prevention of serious crime." This, coupled with the other evidence, makes it clear enough, I think, that the first of the three requirements that I have stated would be satisfied. Accordingly, in my judgment, if, contrary to my opinion, telephone tapping on behalf of the police is a breach of any duty of confidentiality, there is just cause or excuse for that tapping in the circumstances of this case.

I would add one comment. I have already mentioned section 5 (b) of the Wireless Telegraphy Act 1949. Under this, there is no offence if the information is obtained by a Crown servant in the course of his duty or under the authority of the Postmaster General (now the Home Secretary). This, said Mr. Rattee, made it improbable that there was any general law against telephone tapping; for Parliament would hardly empower the Postmaster General to authorise such tapping as regards the criminal law if all the time it was tortious. This contention seems to me to have some force.

Fifth, there is Mr. Ross-Munro's second main head, based on the European Convention for the Protection of Human Rights and Fundamental Freedoms and the *Klass* case. The first limb of this relates to the direct rights conferred by the Convention. Any such right is, as I have said, a direct right in relation to the European Commission of Human Rights and the European Court of Human Rights, and not in relation to the courts of this country; for the Convention is not law here. Article 1 of the Convention provides that the High Contracting Parties "shall secure to everyone within their jurisdiction the rights and freedoms defined in Section I of this Convention"; and those rights and freedoms are those which are set out in articles 1 to 18 inclusive. The United Kingdom, as a High Contracting Party which ratified the Convention on March 8, 1951, has thus long been under an obligation to secure these rights and freedoms to everyone. That obligation, however, is an obligation under a treaty which is not justiciable in the courts of this country. Whether that obligation has been carried out is not for me to say. It is, I suppose, possible to contend that the de facto practice in this country sufficiently secures these rights and freedoms, without legislation for the purpose being needed. It is also plainly possible to contend that, among other things, the existing safeguards against unbridled telephone tapping, being merely administrative in nature and not imposed by law, fall far short of making any rights and freedoms "secure" to anyone. However, as I have said, that is not for me to decide. All that I do is to hold that the Convention does not, as a matter of English law, confer any direct rights on the plaintiff that he can enforce in the English courts.

Sixth, there is the second limb of Mr. Ross-Munro's contentions, based on the Convention and the *Klass* case as assisting the court to determine what English law is on a point on which authority is lacking or uncertain. Can it be said that in this case two courses are reasonably open to the court, one of which is inconsistent with the Convention and the other consonant with it? . . . I readily accept that if the question before me were one of construing a statute enacted with the purpose of giving effect to obligations imposed by the Convention, the court would readily seek to construe the legislation in a way that would effectuate the Convention rather than frustrate it. However, no relevant legislation of that sort is in existence. It seems to me that where Parliament has abstained from legislating on a point that is plainly suitable for legislation, it is indeed difficult for the court to lay down new rules of common law or equity that will carry out the Crown's treaty obligations, or to discover for the first time that such rules have always existed.

Now the West German system that came under scrutiny in the *Klass* case was laid down by statute, and it contained a number of statutory safeguards. There must be imminent danger: other methods of surveillance must be at least considerably more difficult; both the person making the request for surveillance and the method of making it are limited; the period of surveillance is limited in time, and in any case must cease when the need has passed; the person subjected to surveillance must be notified as soon as this will not jeopardise the purpose of surveillance; no information is made available to the police unless an official qualified for judicial office is satisfied that it is within the safeguards; all other information obtained must be destroyed; the process is supervised by a Parliamentary board on which the opposition is represented; and there is also a supervising commission which may order that surveillance is to cease, or that notification of it is to be given to the person who has been subjected to it. Not a single one of these safeguards is to be found as a matter of established law in England, and only a few corresponding provisions exist as a matter of administrative procedure.

It does not, of course, follow that a system with fewer or different safeguards will fail to satisfy article 8 in the eyes of the European Court of Human Rights. At the same time, it is impossible to read the judgment in the *Klass* case without its becoming abundantly clear that a system which has no legal safeguards whatever has small chance of satisfying the requirements of that court, whatever administrative provisions there may be. Broadly, the court was concerned to see whether the German legislation provided "adequate and effective safeguards against abuse." Though in principle it was desirable that there should be judicial control of tapping, the court was satisfied that the German system provided an adequate substitute in the independence of the board and Commission from the authorities carrying out the surveillance. Further, the provisions for the subsequent notification of the surveillance when this would not frustrate its purpose were also considered to be adequate. In England, on the other hand, the system in operation provides no such independence, and contains no provision whatever for subsequent notification. Even if the system were to be considered adequate in its conditions, it is laid down merely as a matter of administrative procedure, so that it is unenforceable in law, and as a matter of law could at any time be altered without warning or subsequent notification. Certainly in law any "adequate and effective safeguards against abuse" are wanting. In this respect English law compares most unfavourably with West German law: this is not a subject on which it is possible to feel any pride in English law.

I therefore find it impossible to see how English law could be said to satisfy the requirements of the Convention, as interpreted in the *Klass* case, unless that law not only prohibited all telephone tapping save in suitably limited classes of case, but also laid down detailed restrictions on the exercise of the power in those limited classes. It may perhaps be that the common law is sufficiently fertile to achieve what is required by the first limb of this; possible ways of expressing such a rule may be seen in what I have already said. But I see the greatest difficulty in the common law framing the safeguards required by the second limb. Various institutions or offices would have to be brought into being to exercise various defined functions. The more complex and indefinite the subject matter, the greater the difficulty in the court doing what it is really appropriate, and only appropriate, for the legislature to do. Furthermore, I find it hard to see what there is in the present case to require the English courts to struggle with such a problem. Give full rein to the Convenion, and it is clear that when the object of the surveillance is the detection of crime, the question is not whether there ought to be a general prohibition of all surveillance, but in what circumstances, and subject to what conditions and restrictions, it ought to be permitted. It is those circumstances, conditions and restrictions which are at the centre of this case; and yet it is they which are the least suitable for determination by judicial decision.

It appears to me that to decide this case in the way that Mr. Ross-Munro seeks would carry me far beyond any possible function of the Convention as influencing English law that has ever been suggested; and it would be most undesirable. Any regulation of so complex a matter as telephone tapping is essentially a matter for Parliament, not the courts; and neither the Convention nor the *Klass* case can, I think, play any proper part in deciding the issue before me. Accordingly, the second limb of Mr. Ross-Munro's second main contention also fails.

I would only add that, even if it was not clear before, this case seems to me to make it plain that telephone tapping is a subject which cries out for legislation. Privacy and confidentiality are, of course, subjects of considerable complexity. Yet however desirable it may be that they should at least to some extent be defined and regulated by statute, rather than being left for slow and expensive evolution in individual cases brought at the expense of litigants and the legal aid fund, the difficulty of the subject matter is liable to discourage legislative zeal. Telephone tapping lies in a much narrower compass; the difficulties in legislating on the subject ought not to prove insuperable; and the requirements of the Convention should provide a spur to action, even if belated. This, however, is not for me to decide. I can do no more than express a hope, and offer a proleptic welcome to any statute on the subject. However much the protection of the public against crime demands that in proper cases the police should have the assistance of telephone tapping, I would have thought that in any civilised system of law the claims of liberty and justice would require that telephone users should have effective and independent safeguards against possible abuses. The fact that a telephone user is suspected of crime increases rather than diminishes this requirement: suspicions, however reasonably held, may sometimes prove to be wholly unfounded. If there were effective and independent safeguards, these would not only exclude some cases of excessive zeal but also, by their mere existence, provide some degree of reassurance for those who are resentful of the police or believe themselves to be persecuted. I may perhaps add that it would be wrong to allow any decision in this case to be influenced by the consideration that if the courts were to hold that all telephone tapping was illegal, this might well offer a strong and prompt inducement to the government to persuade Parliament to legislate on the subject.

Seventh, there is Mr. Ross-Munro's third main contention, based on the absence of any grant of powers to the executive to tap telephones. I have already held that if such tapping can be carried out without committing any breach of the law, it requires no authorisation by statute or common law; it can lawfully be done simply because there is nothing to make it unlawful. Now that I have held that such tapping can indeed be carried out without committing any breach of the law, the contention necessarily fails. I may also say that the statutory recognition given to the Home Secretary's warrant seems to me to point clearly to the same conclusion.

CHAPTER 13

SPECIAL GROUPS

In the absence of any constitutional provision outlawing discrimination against minorities little attention has been paid in this country to legal and administrative discrimination against certain groups. There are signs of change especially where the groups concerned are sufficiently powerful, vociferous or socially or economically significant to lead to legislative action outlawing discrimination against them. This has happened in a number of cases, including of course, legislation dealing with discrimination against women, the Equal Pay Act 1970 and the Sex Discrimination Act 1975, and against racial minorities, the Race Relations Act 1976. There are many other groups where equality of treatment is denied in particular respects, and this Chapter deals with four of them.

Further Reading

The best book on discrimination generally is Folke Schmidt (ed.), *Discrimination in Employment* (Stockholm, 1978). Despite its title the book discusses the social and legal problems raised by discrimination generally, although the emphasis of the book is on the operation of discrimination in the area of employment. Also useful are B. Sundberg-Weitman, *Discrimination on Grounds of Nationality: Free Movement of Workers & Freedom of Establishment under the EEC Treaty* (North Holland Publishing Co., 1977) and Bob Hepple, *Race, Jobs and the Law* (Penguin, 2nd ed., 1970).

See also pp. 106, 112, 115, 116 and 118.

1. *ALIENS*

De Smith, pp. 405–426; Street, pp. 276–286; Wade & Phillips, pp. 409–433.

J. M. Evans, *Immigration Law* (Sweet & Maxwell, 1976); F. Lafitte, *The Internment of Aliens* (Penguin, 1940) [This is a classic study of the treatment of German and Austrian anti-fascist refugees in Britain, September 1939–August 1940]; H. Norden, "Agee and Hosenball: A Nasty, Sordid Business," (1977) 6(2) *Index on Censorship* pp. 34–40; C. Thornberry, "Dr. Soblen and the Alien Law of the United Kingdom," (1963) 12 *International & Comparative Law Quarterly* pp. 414–000; *ibid, Stranger at the Gate* (1964) Fabian Research Series No. 264.

See also pp. 134 and 137.

ALIENS RESTRICTIONS ACT 1914

1. Powers with respect to aliens in case of national emergency

(1) His Majesty may at any time when a state of war exists between His Majesty and any foreign power, or when it appears that an occasion of imminent national danger or great emergency has arisen, by Order in Council impose restrictions on aliens, and provision may be made by the Order—

(a) for prohibiting aliens from landing in the United Kingdom, either generally or at certain places, and for imposing restrictions or conditions on aliens landing or arriving at any port in the United Kingdom; and

(b) for prohibiting aliens for embarking in the United Kingdom, either generally or at certain places, and for imposing restrictions and conditions on aliens embarking or about to embark in the United Kingdom; and

(c) for the deportation of aliens from the United Kingdom; and

(d) for requiring aliens to reside and remain within certain places or districts; and

(e) for prohibiting aliens from residing or remaining in any areas specified in the Order; and

(f) for requiring aliens residing in the United Kingdom to comply with such provisions as to registration, change of abode, travelling, or otherwise as may be made by the Order; and

(g) for the appointment of officers to carry the Order into effect, and for conferring on such officers and on the Secretary of State such powers as may be necessary or expedient for the purposes of the Order; and

(h) for imposing penalties on persons who aid or abet any contravention of the Order, and for imposing such obligations and restrictions on masters of ships or any other persons specified in the Order as appear necessary or expedient for giving full effect to the Order; and

(i) for conferring upon such persons as may be specified in the Order such powers with respect to arrest, detention, search of premises or persons, and otherwise, as may be specified in the Order, and for any other ancillary matters for which it appears expedient to provide with a view to giving full effect to the Order; and

(k) for any other matters which appear necessary or expedient with a view to the safety of the realm;

(l) for determining what nationality is to be ascribed to aliens in doubtful circumstances, and for disregarding, in the case of any person against whom a deportation or expulsion order has been made, any subsequent change of nationality.

(2) If any person acts in contravention of, or fails to comply with, any provisions of any such Order, he shall be liable on conviction under the Summary Jurisdiction Acts to a fine not exceeding one hundred pounds or to imprisonment with or without hard labour for a term not exceeding six months, and the court before which he is convicted may, either in addition to, or in lieu of, any such punishment, require that person to enter into recognizances with or without sureties to comply with the provisions of the Order in Council or such provisions thereof as the court may direct.

If any person fails to comply with an order of the court requiring him to enter into recognizances the court, or any court of summary jurisdiction sitting for the same place, may order him to be imprisoned with or without hard labour for any term not exceeding six months.

(3) Any provision of any Order in Council made under this section with respect to aliens may relate either to aliens in general or to any class or description of aliens.

(4) If any question arises on any proceedings under any such Order, or with reference to anything done or proposed to be done under any such Order, whether any person is an alien or not, or is an alien of a particular class or not, the onus of proving that that person is not an alien, or, as the case may be, is not an alien of that class, shall lie upon that person.

(5) His Majesty may by Order in Council revoke, alter, or add to any Order in Council made under this section as occasion requires.

(6) Any powers given under this section, or under any Order in Council made under this section, shall be in addition to, and not in derogation of, any other powers with respect to the expulsion of aliens, or the prohibition of aliens from entering the United Kingdom or any other powers of His Majesty.

The Aliens Restriction (Amendment) Act 1919

Continuance and Extension of Emergency Powers

1. Continuance of emergency powers

(1) The powers which under subsection (1) of section one of the Aliens Restriction Act, 1914 (which Act, as amended by this Act, is herein-after in this Act referred to as the principal Act), are exerciseable with respect to aliens at any time when a state of war exists between His Majesty and any foreign power, or when it appears that an occasion of imminent national danger or great emergency has arisen, shall, for a period of one year after the passing of this Act, be exerciseable, not only in those circumstances, but at any time; and accordingly that subsection shall, for such period as aforesaid, have effect as though the words "at any time when a state of war exists between "His Majesty and any foreign power, or when it appears that an occasion "of imminent national danger or great emergency has arisen" were omitted.

(2) Any order made under the principal Act during the currency of this section shall be laid before each House of Parliament forthwith, and, if an address is presented to His Majesty by either House of Parliament within the next subsequent twenty-one days on which that House has sat after any such order is laid before it praying that the order may be annulled, His Majesty in Council may annul the order, and it shall thenceforth be void, but without prejudice to the validity of anything previously done thereunder:

Provided that this provision shall not apply in the case of an order the operation of which is limited to a time when a state of war exists between His Majesty and any foreign power, or when it appears that an occasion of imminent national danger or great emergency has arisen.

2. Extension of powers

(2) For the purpose of enforcing the provisions of any Treaty of Peace concluded or to be concluded between His Majesty and any Power with which His

Majesty was at war in the year nineteen hundred and eighteen His Majesty may by Order in Council under the principal Act make regulations requiring information to be given as to the property, liabilities, and interests of former enemy aliens, and for preventing (without notice or authority) the transfer of or other dealings with the property of such aliens.

Further Restrictions of Aliens

3. Incitement to sedition, etc.

(1) If any alien attempts or does any act calculated or likely to cause sedition or disaffection amongst any of His Majesty's Forces or the forces of His Majesty's allies, or amongst the civilian population, he shall be liable on conviction on indictment to penal servitude for a term not exceeding ten years, or on summary conviction to imprisonment for a term not exceeding three months.

(2) If any alien promotes or attempts to promote industrial unrest in any industry in which he has not been bona fide engaged for at least two years immediately preceding in the United Kingdom, he shall be liable on summary conviction to imprisonment for a term not exceeding three months.

4. Pilotage certificates

No alien shall hold a pilotage certificate for any pilotage district in the United Kingdom; except that the provisions of section twenty-four of the Pilotage Act, 1913, shall continue to apply to the renewal and issue of certificates entitling a master or mate of French nationality to navigate his ship into the ports of Newhaven or Grimsby.

5. Employment of aliens in ships of the mercantile marine

(1) No alien shall act as master, chief officer, or chief engineer of a British merchant ship registered in the United Kingdom, or as skipper or second hand of a fishing boat registered in the United Kingdom, except in the case of a ship or boat employed habitually in voyages between ports outside the United Kingdom:

Provided that this prohibition shall not apply to any alien who has acted as a master, chief officer, or chief engineer of a British ship, or as skipper or second hand of a British fishing boat, at any time during the war, and is certified by the Admiralty to have performed good and faithful service in that capacity.

(2) No alien shall be employed in any capacity on board a British ship registered in the United Kingdom at a rate of pay less than the standard rate of pay for the time being current on British ships for his rating:

Provided that, where the Board of Trade are satisfied that aliens of any particular race . . . are habitually employed afloat in any capacity, or in any climate, for which they are specially fitted, nothing in this section shall prejudice the right of aliens of such race to be employed upon British ships at rates of pay which are not below those for the time being fixed as standard rates for British subjects of that race.

(3) No alien shall be employed in any capacity on board a British ship registered in the United Kingdom unless he has produced to the officer before whom he is engaged satisfactory proof of his nationality.

(4) Any person who engages an alien for employment on a British ship in contravention of the provisions of this section shall be guilty of an offence under this Act.

6. Appointment of aliens to the Civil Service

After the passing of this Act no alien shall be appointed to any office or place in the Civil Service of the State.

7. Restriction of change of name by aliens

(1) An alien shall not for any purpose assume or use or purport to assume or use or continue after the commencement of this Act the assumption or use of any name other than that by which he was ordinarily known on the fourth day of August, nineteen hundred and fourteen.

(2) Where any alien carries on or purports or continues to carry on, or is a member of a partnership or firm which carries on, or which purports or continues to carry on any trade or business in any name other than that under which the trade or business was carried on on the fourth of August, nineteen hundred and fourteen, he shall, for the purpose of this section, be deemed to be using or purporting or continuing to use a name other than that by which he was ordinarily known on the said date.

(3) A Secretary of State may, if it appears desirable on special grounds in any particular case, grant an exemption from the provisions of this section, but shall not do so unless he is satisfied that the name proposed to be assumed, used, or continued is in the circumstances of the case a suitable name.

(4) Nothing in this section shall—

(a) affect the assumption or use or continued assumption or use of any name in pursuance of a royal licence; or

(b) affect the continuance of the use by any person of a name which he has assumed before the commencement of this Act if he has been granted an exemption under the Defence of the Realm Regulations or the Aliens Restriction Order in force on the first day of January nineteen hundred and nineteen.

(c) prevent the assumption or use by a married woman of her husband's name.

(5) A fee of ten guineas shall be paid by any alien on obtaining an exemption under this section; but the Secretary of State may remit the whole or any part of such fee in special cases.

(6) A list of the persons to whom the Secretary of State has granted an exemption under this section shall be published in the Gazette as soon as may be after the granting of the exemption.

(7) Any person to whom any such exemption is granted shall, unless the Secretary of State shall expressly dispense with such publication, within one calendar month thereafter publish at his own expense, in some paper circulating in the district in which he resides, an advertisement stating the fact that the exemption has been granted.

8. Provisions as to aliens on juries

No alien shall sit upon a jury in any judicial or other proceedings if challenged by any party to such proceedings.

General

13. Offences and penalties

(1) If any person acts in contravention of or fails to comply with the provisions of this Act or any order or rules made or conditions imposed thereunder, he shall be guilty of an offence against this Act.

(2) If any person aids or abets any person in any contravention of this Act or knowingly harbours any person whom he knows or has reasonable ground for believing to have acted in contravention of this Act, he shall be guilty of an offence against this Act.

(3) Where a person lands in the United Kingdom in contravention of this Act, the master of the ship or the pilot or commander of the aircraft from which he lands shall, unless he proves to the contrary, be deemed to have aided and abetted the offence.

(4) A person who is guilty of an offence against this Act shall be liable on summary conviction to a fine not exceeding one hundred pounds or to imprisonment, with or without hard labour, for a term not exceeding six months, or, on a second or subsequent conviction, twelve months, or, in either case, to both such fine and imprisonment.

ALIENS' EMPLOYMENT ACT 1955

1. Provision for civil employment of aliens

(1) Notwithstanding anything in section three of the Act of Settlement, or in section six of the Aliens Restriction (Amendment) Act, 1919, an alien may be employed in any civil capacity under the Crown—

(a) if he is appointed in any country or territory outside the United Kingdom, the Channel Islands and the Isle of Man and employed in any such country or territory in service of a class or description which appears to the responsible Minister to be appropriate for the employment of aliens; or

(b) if a certificate in respect of his employment, issued by the responsible Minister with the consent of the Treasury, is for the time being in force under this section;

and so much of the said section three imposes disability for employment in any such capacity shall cease to have effect in relation to British protected persons.

(2) A certificate may be issued under this section either in respect of the employment of a specified alien in specified service, or in respect of the employment of aliens generally in specified service or in service of any specified class or description; but no such certificate shall be issued unless it appears to the responsible Minister, at the time of the issue of the certificate,—

(a) in the case of a certificate in respect of the employment of a specified alien in specified service, either that no suitably qualified person being a British subject is available for employment in that service or that the alien possesses exceptional qualifications or experience fitting him for such employment;

(b) in the case of any other certificate, that suitably qualified persons being British subjects are not readily available, or available in sufficient numbers, for employment in the service, or class or description of service, specified in the certificate.

(3) A certificate under this section shall cease to have effect, unless previously revoked, at the expiration of a period of five years from the date on which it is issued, but without prejudice to the power of the responsible Minister to issue a fresh certificate.

(4) The Treasury shall lay before each House of Parliament in every financial year a list containing particulars of all certificates in force under this section during the previous financial year, including the number of aliens employed during that year in pursuance of such certificates.

2. Supplementary provisions

(1) In this Act "alien" and "British protected person" have the same meaning as in the British Nationality Act, 1948; "Minister" includes the Treasury, the Admiralty and the Board of Trade; and "responsible Minister", in relation to any service, means the Minister concerned with the administration of that service.

(2) Any question arising under this section what Minister is the responsible Minister in relation to any service shall be referred to and determined by the Treasury. . . .

2. CONVICTED PERSONS AND PRISONERS

Further Reading

S. Cohen & Laurie Taylor, *Prison Secrets* (Cobden Trust, 1973); P. English, "Prisoners' Rights, Quis Custodiet Ipso Custodes," in *Fundamental Rights* (J. W. Bridge *et al* ed.) (1973) at pp. 201–218; M. FitzGerald, *Prisoners in Revolt* (Penguin, 1977); L. Grant, *et al., Civil Liberty: The NCCL Guide to Your Rights* (Penguin, 1978), Chap. 3; Howard League, *Losing Touch: restrictions on prisoners' contacts* (London, 1979); T. Piney, "Prison Censorship in Britain," (1977) 6(1) *Index on Censorship* pp. 39–43; G. Zellick, "Prisoners' Rights in England," (1974) 24 *University of Toronto Law Journal* pp. 331–346; *ibid,* "The Rules in Prison," February 20, 1975 *New Society; ibid,* "The Forcible Feeding of Prisoners: An Examination of the Legality of Enforced Therapy," (1967) *Public Law* pp. 153–187.

THE PRISON RULES 1964

Part 1

Prisoners

General

Purpose of prison training and treatment

1.—The purpose of the training and treatment of convicted prisoners shall be to encourage and assist them to lead a good and useful life.

Maintenance of order and discipline

2.—(1) Order and discipline shall be maintained with firmness, but with no more restriction than is required for safe custody and well ordered community life.

(2) In the control of prisoners, officers shall seek to influence them through their own example and leadership, and to enlist their willing co-operation.

(3) At all times the treatment of prisoners shall be such as to encourage their self-respect and a sense of personal responsibility, but a prisoner shall not be employed in any disciplinary capacity.

Classification of prisoners

3.—(1) Prisoners shall be classified, in accordance with any directions of the Secretary of State, having regard to their age, temperament and record and with a view to maintaining good order and facilitating training and, in the case of convicted prisoners, of furthering the purpose of their training and treatment as provided by Rule 1 of these Rules.

(2) Unconvicted prisoners shall be kept out of contact with convicted prisoners as far as this can reasonably be done.

(3) Nothing in this Rule shall require a prisoner to be deprived unduly of the society of other persons.

Privileges

4.—There shall be established at every prison systems of privileges approved by the Secretary of State and appropriate to the classes of prisoners there, which shall include arrangements under which money earned by prisoners in prison may be spent by them within the prison.

Information to prisoners

7.—(1) Every prisoner shall be provided, in his cell or room, with information in writing about those provisions of these Rules and other matters which it is necessary that he should know, including earnings and privileges, and the proper method of making complaints and of petitioning the Secretary of State.

(2) The governor, or an officer deputed by him, shall ensure that every prisoner has as soon as possible after his reception into prison, and in any case within 24 hours, read the information so provided or, in the case of a prisoner who cannot read or has difficulty in understanding, had it so explained to him that he can understand his rights and duties.

Women prisoners

9.—(1) Women prisoners shall be kept entirely separate from male prisoners.

(3) The Secretary of State may, subject to any conditions he thinks fit, permit a woman prisoner to have her baby with her in prison, and everything necessary for the baby's maintenance and care may be provided there.

Religious denomination

10.—A prisoner shall be treated as being of the religious denomination stated in the record made in pursuance of section 10(5) of the Prison Act 1952 but the governor may, in a proper case and after due enquiry, direct that record to be amended.

Sunday work

15.—Arrangements shall be made so as not to require prisoners of the Christian religion to do any unnecessary work on Sunday, Christmas Day or Good Friday, or prisoners of other religions on their recognised days of religious observance.

Religious books

16.—There shall, so far as reasonably practicable, be available for the personal use of every prisoner such religious books recognised by his denomination as are approved by the Secretary of State for use in prisons.

Work

28.—(1) A convicted prisoner shall be required to do useful work for not more than ten hours a day, and arrangements shall be made to allow prisoners to work, where possible, outside the cells and in association with one another.

(2) The medical officer may excuse a prisoner from work on medical grounds, and no prisoner shall be set to do work which is not of a class for which he has been passed by the medical officer as being fit.

(3) No prisoner shall be set to do work of a kind not authorised by the Secretary of State.

(4) No prisoner shall work in the service of another prisoner or an officer, or for the private benefit of any person, without the authority of the Secretary of State.

(5) An unconvicted prisoner shall be permitted, if he wishes, to work as if he were a convicted prisoner.

(6) Prisoners may be paid for their work at rates approved by the Secretary of State, either generally or in relation to particular cases.

Letters and visits

Letters and visits generally

33.—(1) The Secretary of State may, with a view to securing discipline and good order or the prevention of crime or in the interests of any persons, impose restrictions, either generally or in a particular case, upon the communications to be permitted between a prisoner and other persons.

(2) Except as provided by statute or these Rules, a prison shall not be permitted to communicate with any outside person, or that person with him, without the leave of the Secretary of State.

(3) Except as provided by these Rules, every letter or communication to or from a prisoner may be read or examined by the governor or an officer deputed by him, and the governor may, at his discretion, stop any letter or communication on the ground that its contents are objectionable or that it is of inordinate length.

(4) Every visit to a prisoner shall take place within the sight of an officer, unless the Secretary of State otherwise directs.

(5) Except as provided by these Rules, every visit to a prisoner shall take place within the hearing of an officer, unless the Secretary of State otherwise directs.

(6) The Secretary of State may give directions, generally or in relation to any visit or class of visits, concerning the days and times when prisoners may be visited.

Personal letters and visits

34.—(1) An unconvicted prisoner may send and receive as many letters and may receive as many visits as he wishes within such limits and subject to such conditions as the Secretary of State may direct, either generally or in a particular case.

(2) A convicted prisoner shall be entitled—

(*a*) to send and to receive a letter on his reception into a prison and thereafter once a week; and

(*b*) to receive a visit once in four weeks if he is under the age of 21 years, and otherwise once in eight weeks.

(3) The governor may allow a prisoner an additional letter or visit where necessary for his welfare or that of his family.

(4) The governor may allow a prisoner entitled to a visit to send and to receive a letter instead.

(5) The governor may defer the right of a prisoner to a visit until the expiration of any period of cellular confinement.

(6) The visiting committee or board of visitors may allow a prisoner an additional letter or visit in special circumstances, and may direct that a visit may extend beyond the normal duration.

(7) The Secretary of State may allow additional letters and visits in relation to any prisoner or class of prisoners.

(8) A prisoner shall not be entitled under this Rule to communicate with any person in connection with any legal or other business, or with any person other than a relative or friend, except with the leave of the Secretary of State.

(9) Any letter or visit under the succeeding provisions of these Rules shall not be counted as a letter or visit for the purposes of this Rule.

Police interviews

35.—A police officer may, on production of an order issued by or on behalf of a chief officer of police, interview any prisoner willing to see him.

Securing release

36.—A person detained in prison in default of finding a surety, or of payment of a sum of money, may communicate with, and be visited at any reasonable time on a weekday by, any relative or friend to arrange for a surety or payment in order to secure his release from prison.

Legal advisers

37.—(1) The legal adviser of a prisoner in any legal proceedings, civil or criminal, to which the prisoner is a party shall be afforded reasonable facilities for interviewing him in connection with those proceedings, and may do so out of hearing but in the sight of an officer.

(2) A prisoner's legal adviser may, with the leave of the Secretary of State, interview the prisoner in connection with any other legal business in the sight and hearing of an officer.

Further facilities in connection with legal proceedings

37A.—(1) A prisoner who is a party to any legal proceedings may correspond with his legal adviser in connection with the proceedings and unless the Governor has reason to suppose that any such correspondence contains matter not relating to the proceedings it shall not be read or stopped under Rule 33(3) of these Rules.

(2) A prisoner shall on request be provided with any writing materials necessary for the purposes of paragraph (1) of this Rule.

(3) Subject to any directions given in the particular case by the Secretary of State, a registered medical practitioner selected by or on behalf of such a prisoner as aforesaid shall be afforded reasonable facilities for examining him in connection with the proceedings, and may do so out of hearing but in the sight of an officer.

(4) Subject to any directions of the Secretary of State, a prisoner may correspond with a solicitor for the purpose of obtaining legal advice concerning any cause of action in relation to which the prisoner may become a party to civil proceedings or for the purpose of instructing the solicitor to issue such proceedings.

Special control and restraint

Removal from association

43.—(1) Where it appears desirable, for the maintenance of good order or discipline or in his own interests, that a prisoner should not associate with other prisoners, either generally or for particular purposes, the governor may arrange for the prisoner's removal from association accordingly.

(2) A prisoner shall not be removed under this Rule for a period of more than 24 hours without the authority of a member of the visiting committee or board of visitors, or of the Secretary of State. An authority given under this paragraph shall be for a period not exceeding one month, but may be renewed from month to month.

(3) The governor may arrange at his discretion for such a prisoner as aforesaid to resume association with other prisoners, and shall do so if in any case the medical officer so advises on medical grounds.

Use of force

44.—(1) An officer in dealing with a prisoner shall not use force unnecessarily and, when the application of force to a prisoner is necessary, no more force than is necessary shall be used.

(2) No officer shall act deliberately in a manner calculated to provoke a prisoner.

Temporary confinement

45.—The governor may order a refractory or violent prisoner to be confined temporarily in a special cell, but a prisoner shall not be so confined as a punishment, or after he has ceased to be refractory or violent.

Offences against discipline

Offences against discipline

47.—A prisoner shall be guilty of an offence against discipline if he—
(1) mutinies or incites another prisoner to mutiny;
(2) does gross personal violence to an officer;
(3) does gross personal violence to any person not being an officer;
(4) commits any assault;
(5) escapes from prison or from legal custody;
(6) absents himself without permission from any place where he is required to be, whether within or outside prison;
(7) has in his cell or room or in his possession any unauthorised article, or attempts to obtain such an article;
(8) delivers to or receives from any person any unauthorised article;
(9) sells or delivers to any other person, without permission, anything he is allowed to have only for his own use;
(10) takes improperly or is in unauthorised possession of any article belonging to another person or to a prison;
(11) wilfully damages or disfigures any part of the prison or any property not his own;
(12) makes any false and malicious allegation against an officer;
(13) treats with disrespect an officer or any person visiting a prison;
(14) uses any abusive, insolent, threatening or other improper language;
(15) is indecent in language, act or gesture;
(16) repeatedly makes groundless complaints;
(17) is idle, careless or negligent at work or, being required to work, refuses to do so;
(18) disobeys any lawful order or refuses or neglects to conform to any rule or regulation of the prison;
(19) attempts to do any of the foregoing things;
(20) in any way offends against good order and discipline; or
(21) does not return to prison when he should have returned after being temporarily released from prison under Rule 6 of these Rules, or does not comply with any condition upon which he was so released.

Disciplinary charges

48.—(1) Where a prisoner is to be charged with an offence against discipline, the charge shall be laid as soon as possible.

(2) A prisoner who is to be charged with an offence against discipline may be kept apart from other prisoners pending adjudication.

(3) Every charge shall be inquired into, in the first instance, by the governor.

(4) Every charge shall be first inquired into not later, save in exceptional circumstances, than the next day, not being a Sunday or public holiday, after it is laid.

Rights of prisoners charged

49.—(1) Where a prisoner is charged with an offence against discipline, he shall be informed of the charge as soon as possible and, in any case, before the time when it is inquired into by the governor.

(2) At any inquiry into a charge against a prisoner he shall be given a full opportunity of hearing what is alleged against him and of presenting his own case.

Governor's awards

50.—Subject to Rules 51 and 52 of these Rules, the governor may make any one of more of the following awards for an offence against discipline:—

(a) caution;

(b) forfeiture for a period not exceeding 28 days of any of the privileges under Rule 4 of these Rules;

(c) exclusion from associated work for a period not exceeding 14 days;

(d) stoppage of earnings for a period not exceeding 28 days;

(e) cellular confinement for a period not exceeding 3 days;

(f) forfeiture of remission of a period not exceeding 28 days;

(g) forfeiture for any period, in the case of a prisoner otherwise entitled thereto, of any of the following:—

   (i) the right to be supplied with food and drink under Rule 21(1) of these Rules; and

   (ii) the right under Rule 41(1) of these Rules to have the articles there mentioned;

(h) forfeiture for any period, in the case of a prisoner otherwise entitled thereto who is guilty of escaping or attempting to escape, of the right to wear clothing of his own under Rule 20(1) of these Rules.

Graver offences

51.—(1) Where a prisoner is charged with any of the following offences against discipline:—

(a) escaping or attempting to escape from prison or from legal custody,

(b) assaulting an officer, or

(c) doing gross personal violence to any person not being an officer,

the governor shall, unless he dismisses the charge, forthwith inform the Secretary of State and shall, unless otherwise directed by him, refer the charge to the board of visitors.

(2) Where a prisoner is charged with any serious or repeated offence against discipline (not being an offence to which Rule 52 of these Rules applies) for which the awards the governor can make seem insufficient, the governor may, after investigation, refer the charge to the board of visitors.

(3) Where a charge is referred to the board of visitors under this Rule, the chairman thereof shall summon a special meeting at which not more than five nor fewer than two members shall be present.

(4) The Board so constituted shall inquire into the charge and, if they find the offence proved, shall make one or more of the following awards:—

(a) caution;

(b) forfeiture for any period of any of the privileges under Rule 4 of these Rules;

(c) exclusion from associated work for a period not exceeding 56 days;

(d) stoppage of earnings for a period not exceeding 56 days;

(e) cellular confinement for a period not exceeding 56 days;

(f) forfeiture of remission of a period not exceeding 180 days;

(g) forfeiture for any period, in the case of a prisoner otherwise entitled thereto, of any of the following:—

(i) the right to be supplied with food and drink under Rule 21(1) of these Rules; and

(ii) the right under Rule 41(1) of these Rules to have the articles there mentioned;

(*h*) forfeiture for any period, in the case of a prisoner otherwise entitled thereto who is guilty of escaping or attempting to escape, of the right to wear clothing of his own under Rule 20(1) of these Rules.

(5) The Secretary of State may require any charge to which this Rule applies to be referred to him, instead of to the board of visitors, and in that case an officer of the Secretary of State (not being an officer of a prison) shall inquire into the charge and, if he finds the offence proved, make one or more of the awards listed in paragraph (4) of this Rule.

Especially grave offences

52.—(1) Where a prisoner is charged with one of the following offences:—

(*a*) mutiny or incitement to mutiny; or

(*b*) doing gross personal violence to an officer,

the governor shall forthwith inform the Secretary of State and shall, unless otherwise directed by him, refer the charge to the board of visitors.

(2) Where a charge is referred to the board of visitors under this Rule, the chairman thereof shall summon a special meeting at which not more than five nor fewer than three members, at least two being justices of the peace, shall be present.

(3) The board constituted as aforesaid shall inquire into the charge and, if they find the offence proved, shall make one or more of the awards listed in Rule 51(4) of these Rules, so however that, if they make an award of forfeiture of remission, the period forfeited may exceed 180 days.

Provisions in relation to particular awards

53.—(1) An award of stoppage of earnings may, instead of forfeiting all a prisoner's earnings for a specified period not exceeding 28 or as the case may be 56 days, be expressed so as to forfeit a proportion (not being less than one half) of his earnings for a specified period not exceeding a correspondingly greater number of days.

(2) No award of cellular confinement shall be made unless the medical officer has certified that the prisoner is in a fit state of health to be so dealt with.

Prospective forfeiture of remission

54.—(1) In the case of an offence against discipline committed by a prisoner who has attained the age of 21 years and is detained only on remand or to await trial or sentence, an award for forfeiture of remission may be made notwithstanding that the prisoner has not (or had not at the time of the offence) been sentenced to imprisonment.

(2) An award under paragraph (1) above shall have effect only in the case of a sentence of imprisonment being imposed which is reduced, by section 67 of the Criminal Justice Act 1967 (a), by a period which includes the time when the offence against discipline was committed.

(a) 1967 c. 80.

Suspended awards

55.—(1) Subject to any directions of the Secretary of State, the power to make a disciplinary award (other than a caution) shall include power to direct that the award is not to take effect unless, during a period specified in the direction (not being more than 6 months from the date of the direction), the prisoner commits another offence against discipline and a direction is given under paragraph (2) below.

(2) Where a prisoner commits an offence against discipline during the period specified in a direction given under paragraph (1) above the person or board dealing with that offence may—

    (a) direct that the suspended award shall take effect; or

    (b) reduce the period or amount of the suspended award and direct that it shall take effect as so reduced; or

    (c) vary the original direction by substituting for the period specified therein a period expiring not later than 6 months from the date of variation; or

    (d) give no direction with respect to the suspended award.

Remission and mitigation of awards

56.—(1) The Secretary of State may remit a disciplinary award or mitigate it either by reducing it or by substituting another award which is, in his opinion, less severe.

(2) Subject to any directions of the Secretary of State, the governor may remit or mitigate any award made by a governor and the board of visitors may remit or mitigate any disciplinary award.

Prisoners committed for contempt, &c.

63.—(1) A prisoner committed or attached for contempt of court, or for failing to do or abstain from doing anything required to be done or left undone, shall have the same privileges as an unconvicted prisoner under Rules 20(1) and 34(1) of these Rules.

(2) Such prisoners shall be treated as a separate class for the purposes of Rule 3 of these Rules but, notwithstanding anything in that Rule, such prisoners may be permitted to associate with any other class of prisoners if they are willing to do so.

(3) A prisoner detained in a prison for a stated term of more than one month on committal or attachment for contempt of court shall, for the purposes of Rule 5 of these Rules, be treated as serving a sentence of imprisonment for a like term.

Prisoners convicted of sedition, &c.

64.—(1) A prisoner serving a sentence on conviction of sedition, seditious conspiracy or seditious libel shall have the same privileges as an unconvicted prisoner under Rules 17(4), 20(1), 21(1), 25, 28, 34(1) and 41(1) of these Rules.

(2) Such a prisoner shall not be required to associate with other prisoners.

(3) Such a prisoner shall be permitted to work at his ordinary employment or vocation as far as conditions in the prison and the needs of discipline and safe custody allow.

Part II

Officers of Prisons

Contact with former prisoners, &c.

81.—No officer shall, without the knowledge of the governor, communicate with any person whom he knows to be a former prisoner or a relative or friend of a prisoner or former prisoner.

Communications to the press, &c.

82.—(1) No officer shall make, directly or indirectly, any unauthorised communication to a representative of the press or any other person concerning matters which have become known to him in the course of his duty.

(2) No officer shall, without authority, publish any matter or make any public pronouncement relating to the administration of any institution to which the Prison Act 1952 applies or to any of its inmates.

Quarters

83.—An officer shall occupy any quarters which may be assigned to him.

Code of discipline

84.—The Secretary of State may approve a code of discipline to have effect in relation to officers, or such classes of officers as it may specify, setting out the offences against discipline, the awards which may be made in respect of them and the procedure for dealing with charges.

Note: These rules (S.I. 1964 No. 388) were made under the Prisons Act 1952 (as amended) and are reproduced here as amended by S.I. 1968 No. 440; S.I. 1971 No. 2019; S.I. 1972 No. 1860; S.I. 1974 No. 713 and S.I. 1976 No. 503. Rule 37A (1), (2) and (3) was added in 1972. Rule 37A (4) was added in 1976 (*Cf. Golder Case*, below). Rule 64 was deleted in 1972. In Rule 33 (3), line 2 the word "may" was inserted in place of "shall" in 1974. See also *R.* v. *Hull Prison Board of Visitors, ex parte St. Germain and others* [1979] 1 All E.R. 701.

Tyrer v. United Kingdom (1978)

European Court of Human Rights

When aged 15 Tyrer was sentenced by a Manx juvenile court to three strokes of the birch for an assault on a fellow school pupil. Under Manx law the birch was available as a punishment for male juveniles. "In strict law, the United Kingdom Parliament has full power to pass laws applicable to the Isle of Man, but, by constitutional convention, does not in the ordinary course legislate on the island's domestic affairs, such as penal policy, without its consent" (para. 13 of Court's judgment). Tyrer presented a complaint to the Commission, who referred the matter to the Court. The complaint had alleged that his treatment involved a violation of Article 3 of the European Convention on Human Rights and Fundamental, Freedoms (see p. 31 above). The Court said:

In its report, the Commission expressed the opinion that judicial corporal punishment, being degrading, constituted a breach of Article 3 and that, consequently, its infliction on the applicant was in violation of that provision.

29. The Court shares the Commission's view that Mr. Tyrer's punishment did not amount to "torture" within the meaning of Article 3. The Court does not consider that the facts of this particular case reveal that the applicant underwent suffering of the level inherent in this notion as it was interpreted and applied by the Court in its judgment of 18 January 1978 (Ireland v. the United Kingdom, Series A no. 25, pp. 66-67 and 68, §§ 167 and 174).

That judgment also contains various indications concerning the notions of "inhuman treatment" and "degrading treatment" but it deliberately left aside the notions of "inhuman punishment" and "degrading punishment" which alone are relevant in the present case (*ibid.*, p. 65, § 164). Those indications accordingly cannot, as such, serve here. Nevertheless, it remains true that the suffering occasioned must attain a particular level before a punishment can be classified as "inhuman" within the meaning of Article 3. Here again, the Court does not consider on the facts of the case that that level was attained and it therefore concurs with the Commission that the penalty imposed on Mr. Tyrer was not "inhuman punishment" within the meaning of Article 3. Accordingly, the only question for decision is whether he was subjected to a "degrading punishment" contrary to that Article.

30. The Court notes first of all that a person may be humiliated by the mere fact of being criminally convicted. However, what is relevant for the purposes of Article 3 is that he should be humiliated not simply by his conviction but by the execution of the punishment which is imposed on him. In fact, in most if not all cases this may be one of the effects of judicial punishment, involving as it does unwilling subjection to the demands of the penal system.

However, as the Court pointed out in its judgment of 18 January 1978 in the case of Ireland v. the United Kingdom (Series A no. 25, p. 65, § 163), the prohibition contained in Article 3 of the Convention is absolute: no provision is made for exceptions and, under Article 15 § 2, there can be no derogation from Article 3. It would be absurd to hold that judicial punishment generally, by reason of its usual and perhaps almost inevitable element of humiliation, is "degrading" within the meaning of Article 3. Some further criterion must be read into the text. Indeed, Article 3, by expressly prohibiting "inhuman" and "degrading" punishment, implies that there is a distinction between such punishment and punishment in general.

In the Court's view, in order for a punishment to be "degrading" and in breach of Article 3, the humiliation or debasement involved must attain a particular level and must in any event be other than that usual element of humiliation referred to in the preceding sub-paragraph. The assessment is, in the nature of things, relative: it depends on all the circumstances of the case and, in particular, on the nature and context of the punishment itself and the manner and method of its execution.

31. The Attorney-General for the Isle of Man argued that the judicial corporal punishment at issue in this case was not in breach of the Convention since it did not outrage public opinion in the Island. However, even assuming that local public opinion can have an incidence on the interpretation of the

concept of "degrading punishment" appearing in Article 3, the Court does not regard it as established that judicial corporal punishment is not considered degrading by those members of the Manx population who favour its retention: it might well be that one of the reasons why they view the penalty as an effective deterrent is precisely the element of degradation which it involves. As regards their belief that judicial corporal punishment deters criminals, it must be pointed out that a punishment does not lose its degrading character just because it is believed to be, or actually is, an effective deterrent or aid to crime control. Above all, as the Court must emphasise, it is never permissible to have recourse to punishments which are contrary to Article 3, whatever their deterrent effect may be.

The Court must also recall that the Convention is a living instrument which, as the Commission rightly stressed, must be interpreted in the light of present-day conditions. In the case now before it the Court cannot but be influenced by the developments and commonly accepted standards in the penal policy of the member States of the Council of Europe in this field. Indeed, the Attorney-General for the Isle of Man mentioned that, for many years, the provisions of Manx legislation concerning judicial corporal punishment had been under review.

32.   As regards the manner and method of execution of the birching inflicted on Mr. Tyrer, the Attorney-General for the Isle of Man drew particular attention to the fact that the punishment was carried out in private and without publication of the name of the offender.

Publicity may be a relevant factor in assessing whether a punishment is "degrading" within the meaning of Article 3, but the Court does not consider that absence of publicity will necessarily prevent a given punishment from falling into that category: it may well suffice that the victim is humiliated in his own eyes, even if not in the eyes of others.

The Court notes that the relevant Isle of Man legislation, as well as giving the offender a right of appeal against sentence, provides for certain safeguards. Thus, there is a prior medical examination; the number of strokes and dimensions of the birch are regulated in detail; a doctor is present and may order the punishment to be stopped; in the case of a child or young person, the parent may attend if he so desires; the birching is carried out by a police constable in the presence of a more senior colleague.

33.   Nevertheless, the Court must consider whether the other circumstances of the applicant's punishment were such as to make it "degrading" within the meaning of Article 3.

The very nature of judicial corporal punishment is that it involves one human being inflicting physical violence on another human being. Furthermore, it is institutionalised violence, that is in the present case violence permitted by the law, ordered by the judicial authorities of the State and carried out by the police authorities of the State (see paragraph 10 above). Thus, although the applicant did not suffer any severe or long-lasting physical effects, his punishment—whereby he was treated as an object in the power of the authorities—constituted an assault on precisely that which it is one of the main purposes of Article 3 to protect, namely a person's dignity and physical integrity. Neither can it be excluded that the punishment may have had adverse psychological effects.

The institutionalised character of this violence is further compounded by the whole aura of official procedure attending the punishment and by the fact that those inflicting it were total strangers to the offender.

Admittedly, the relevant legislation provides that in any event birching shall not take place later than six months after the passing of sentence. However, this does not alter the fact that there had been an interval of several weeks since the applicant's conviction by the juvenile court and considerable delay in the police station where the punishment was carried out. Accordingly, in addition to the physical pain he experienced, Mr. Tyrer was subjected to the mental anguish of anticipating the violence he was to have inflicted on him.

34.   In the present case, the Court does not consider it relevant that the sentence of judicial corporal punishment was imposed on the applicant for an offence of violence. Neither does it consider it relevant that, for Mr. Tyrer, birching was an alternative to a period of detention: the fact that one penalty may be preferable to, or have less adverse effects or be less serious than, another penalty does not of itself mean that the first penalty is not "degrading" within the meaning of Article 3.

35.   Accordingly, viewing these circumstances as a whole, the Court finds that the applicant was subjected to a punishment in which the element of humiliation attained the level inherent in the notion of "degrading punishment" as explained at paragraph 30 above. The indignity of having the punishment administered over the bare posterior aggravated to some extent the degrading character of the applicant's punishment but it was not the only or determining factor.

The Court therefore concludes that the judicial corporal punishment inflicted on the applicant amounted to degrading punishment within the meaning of Article 3 of the Convention.

The Court then considered whether Article 63 (3) of the Convention affected their conclusion and decided that it did not. They declined to consider whether confining birching to *male* juveniles involved a violation of Article 14. Their conclusion on Article 3 was by a majority of six votes to one.

Golder v. United Kingdom (1976)

European Court of Human Rights

Golder while serving a prison sentence was accused by a prison officer of having assaulted him in the course of disturbance. This caused Golder some inconvenience and in March 1970 he petitioned the Home Secretary requesting a transfer to some other prison and adding:

> "I understand that a statement wrongly accusing me of participating in the events of 24th October last, made by Officer Laird, is lodged in my prison record. I suspect that it is this wrong statement that has recently prevented my being recommended by the local parole board for parole.
>   "I would respectfully request permission to consult a solicitor with a view to taking civil action for libel in respect of this statement. . . ."

Acting under the Prisons Act 1952 and the Prison Rules 1964, rules 33 and 34, the Home Secretary declined the permission requested. Golder was released on parole in July 1972 and petitioned the European Commission of Human Rights alleging a violation of the European Convention. The Commission in 1974 decided unanimously that there had been a violation of Article 6 (1) and by seven votes to two that there had been a violation of

Article 8 (1). The issue was then referred to the Court as to whether there had been a violation of the Convention.

The Court concluded on the issue whether Article 6 (1) covered the situation of Golder:

36. . . . that Article 6 § 1 secures to everyone the right to have any claim relating to his civil rights and obligations brought before a court or tribunal. In this way the Article embodies the "right to a court", of which the right of access, that is the right to institute proceedings before courts in civil matters, constitutes one aspect only. To this are added the guarantees laid down by Article 6 § 1 as regards both the organisation and composition of the court, and the conduct of the proceedings. In sum, the whole makes up the right to a fair hearing. The Court has no need to ascertain in the present case whether and to what extent Article 6 § 1 further requires a decision on the very substance of the dispute (English "determination", French "*decidera*").

B. On The "Implied Limitations"

37. Since the impediment to access to the courts, mentioned in paragraph 26 above, affected a right guaranteed by Article 6 § 1, it remains to determine whether it was nonetheless justifiable by virtue of some legitimate limitation on the enjoyment or exercise of that right.

38. The Court considers, accepting the views of the Commission and the alternative submission of the Government, that the right of access to the courts is not absolute. As this is a right which the Convention sets forth (see Articles 13, 14, 17 and 25) without, in the narrower sense of the term, defining, there is room, apart from the bounds delimiting the very content of any right, for limitations permitted by implication.

The first sentence of Article 2 of the Protocol of 20 March 1952, which is limited to providing that "no person shall be denied the right to education", raises a comparable problem. In its judgment of 23 July 1968 on the merits of the case relating to certain aspects of the laws on the use of languages in education in Belgium, the Court ruled that:

> "The right to education . . . by its very nature calls for regulation by the State, regulation which may vary in time and place according to the needs and resources of the community and of individuals. It goes without saying that such regulation must never injure the substance of the right to education nor conflict with other rights enshrined in the Convention." (Series A no. 6, p. 32, § 5).

These considerations are all the more valid in regard to a right which, unlike the right to education, is not mentioned in express terms.

39. The Government and the Commission have cited examples of regulations, and especially of limitations, which are to be found in the national law of States in matters of access to the courts, for instance regulations relating to minors and persons of unsound mind. Although it is of less frequent occurrence and of a very different kind, the restriction complained of by Golder constitutes a further example of such a limitation.

It is not the function of the Court to elaborate a general theory of the limitations admissible in the case of convicted prisoners, nor even to rule *in abstracto* on the compatibility of Rules 33 § 2, 34 § 8 and 37 § 2 of the Prison Rules 1964 with the Convention. Seised of a case which has its origin in a petition presented by an individual, the Court is called upon to pronounce itself only on the point whether or not the application of those Rules in the present case violated the Convention to the prejudice of Golder (De Becker judgment of 27 March 1962, Series A no. 4, p. 26).

40.   In this connection, the Court confines itself to noting what follows.

In petitioning the Home Secretary for leave to consult a solicitor with a view to suing Laird for libel, Golder was seeking to exculpate himself of the charge made against him by that prison officer on 25 October 1969 and which had entailed for him unpleasant consequences, some of which still subsisted by 20 March 1970 (paragraphs 12, 15 and 16 above). Furthermore, the contemplated legal proceedings would have concerned an incident which was connected with prison life and had occurred while the applicant was imprisoned. Finally, those proceedings would have been directed against a member of the prison staff who had made the charge in the course of his duties and who was subject to the Home Secretary's authority.

In these circumstances, Golder could justifiably wish to consult a solicitor with a view to instituting legal proceedings. It was not for the Home Secretary himself to appraise the prospects of the action contemplated; it was for an independent and impartial court to rule on any claim that might be brought. In declining to accord the leave which had been requested, the Home Secretary failed to respect, in the person of Golder, the right to go before a court as guaranteed by Article 6 § 1.

II.   *On the alleged violation of article 8*

41.   In the opinion of the majority of the Commission (paragraph 123 of the report) "the same facts which constitute a violation of Article 6 § 1 constitute also a violation of Article 8". The Government disagree with this opinion.

42.   Article 8 of the Convention reads as follows:

> "1.   Everyone has the right to respect for his private and family life, his home and his correspondence.
>
> 2.   There shall be no interference by a public authority with the exercise of this right except such as is in accordance with the law and is necessary in a democratic society in the interests of national security, public safety or the economic well-being of the country, for the prevention of disorder or crime, for the protection of health or morals, or for the protection of the rights and freedoms of others."

43.   The Home Secretary's refusal of the petition of 20 March 1970 had the direct and immediate effect of preventing Golder from contacting a solicitor by any means whatever including that which in the ordinary way he would have used to begin with, correspondence. While there was certainly neither stopping nor censorship of any message, such as a letter, which Golder would have written to a solicitor—or vice-versa—and which would have been a piece of correspondence within the meaning of paragraph 1 of Article 8, it would be wrong to conclude therefrom, as do the Government, that this text is inapplicable. Impeding someone from even initiating correspondence constitutes the most far-reaching form of "interference" (paragraph 2 of Article 8) with the exercise of the "right to respect for correspondence"; it is inconceivable that that should fall outside the scope of Article 8 while mere supervision indisputably falls within it. In any event, if Golder had attempted to write to a solicitor notwithstanding the Home Secretary's decision or without requesting the required permission, that correspondence would have been stopped and he could have invoked Article 8; one would arrive at a paradoxical and hardly equitable result, if it were considered that in complying with

the requirements of the Prison Rules 1964 he lost the benefit of the protection of Article 8.

The Court accordingly finds itself called upon to ascertain whether or not the refusal of the applicant's petition violated Article 8.

44. In the submission of the Government, the right to respect for correspondence is subject, apart from interference covered by paragraph 2 of Article 8, to implied limitations resulting, *inter alia*, from the terms of Article 5 § 1 (a): a sentence of imprisonment passed after conviction by a competent court inevitably entails consequences affecting the operation of other Articles of the Convention, including Article 8.

As the Commission have emphasised, that submission is not in keeping with the manner in which the Court dealt with the issue raised under Article 8 in the "Vagrancy" cases (De Wilde, Ooms and Versyp judgment of 18 June 1971, Series A no. 12, pp. 45-46, § 93). In addition and more particularly, that submission conflicts with the explicit text of Article 8. The restrictive formulation used at paragraph 2 ("There shall be no interference . . . except such as . . .") leaves no room for the concept of implied limitations. In this regard, the legal status of the right to respect for correspondence, which is defined by Article 8 with some precision, provides a clear contrast to that of the right to a court (paragraph 38 above).

45. The Government have submitted in the alternative that the interference complained of satisfied the explicit conditions laid down in paragraph 2 of Article 8.

It is beyond doubt that the interference was "in accordance with the law", that is Rules 33 § 2 and 34 § 8 of the Prison Rules 1964 (paragraph 17 above).

The Court accepts, moreover, that the "necessity" for interference with the exercise of the right of a convicted prisoner to respect for his correspondence must be appreciated having regard to the ordinary and reasonable requirements of imprisonment. The "prevention of disorder or crime", for example, may justify wider measures of interference in the case of such a prisoner than in that of a person at liberty. To this extent, but to this extent only, lawful deprivation of liberty within the meaning of Article 5 does not fail to impinge on the application of Article 8.

In its judgment of 18 June 1971 cited above, the Court held that "even in cases of persons detained for vagrancy" (paragraph 1 (e) of Article 5)—and not imprisoned after conviction by a court—the competent national authorities may have "sufficient reason to believe that it (is) 'necessary' to impose restrictions for the purpose of the prevention of disorder or crime, the protection of health or morals, and the protection of the rights and freedoms of others". However, in those particular cases there was no question of preventing the applicants from even initiating correspondence; there was only supervision which in any event did not apply in a series of instances, including in particular correspondence between detained vagrants and the counsel of their choice (Series A no. 12, p. 26, § 39, and p. 45, § 93).

In order to show why the interference complained of by Golder was "necessary", the Government advanced the prevention of disorder or crime and, up to a certain point, the interests of public safety and the protection of the rights and freedoms of others. Even having regard to the power of appreciation left to the Contracting States, the Court cannot discern how these considerations, as they are understood "in a democratic society", could oblige the Home Secretary to prevent Golder from corresponding with a solicitor with a view to suing Laird for libel. The Court again lays stress on the fact that

Golder was seeking to exculpate himself of a charge made against him by that prison officer acting in the course of his duties and relating to an incident in prison. In these circumstances, Golder could justifiably wish to write to a solicitor. It was not for the Home Secretary himself to appraise—no more than it is for the Court today—the prospects of the action contemplated; it was for a solicitor to advise the applicant on his rights and then for a court to rule on any action that might be brought.

The Home Secretary's decision proves to be all the less "necessary in a democratic society" in that the applicant's correspondence with a solicitor would have been a preparatory step to the institution of civil legal proceedings and, therefore, to the exercise of a right embodied in another Article of the Convention, that is, Article 6.

The Court thus reaches the conclusion that there has been a violation of Article 8.

The Court held by nine votes to three that there had been a violation of Article 6 (1); held unanimously that there had been violation of Article 8, and held unanimously that these findings in themselves amounted to adequate just satisfaction under Article 50.

3. *GIPSIES*

Further Reading

L. Grant, *et al.* (ed.), *Civil Liberty: The NCCL Guide to your Rights* (Penguin, 1978), Chap. 18; F.-J. Bryan Long, "Gypsies in Britain" in *Human Rights: A Study Guide for the International Year for Human Rights, 1968* (Heinemann, 1967), pp. 147–151; Ministry of Housing and Local Government, *Gypsies and other travellers* (London, 1967); Grattan Puxon, *On the Road* (NCCL, 1968); Martin Smith, *Gypsies: where now?* (Young Fabian pamphlet no. 42, 1975); R. Zara, *Travelling People and the Law* (Walsall, 1974).

Mills v. Cooper [1967] 2 All E.R. 100

Queens Bench Division

Section 127 of the Highways Act 1959 provides *inter alia* "If, without lawful authority or excuse, . . . (c) a hawker or other itinerant trader or a gipsy pitches a booth, a stall or stand, or encamps, on a highway, he shall be guilty of an offence . . ." The respondent was charged that, he, being a gipsy, did without lawful excuse or authority encamp on the highway contrary to section 127. The magistrates dismissed the charge on the ground that they were not satisfied that the respondent was a gipsy. On appeal by the prosecutor the court had to consider the proper meaning to be given to the term "gipsy." **LORD PARKER**, C.J.:

That a man is of the Romany race is, as it seems to me, something which is really too vague of ascertainment, and impossible to prove; moreover, it is, I think difficult to think that Parliament intended to subject a man to a penalty in the context of causing litter and obstruction on the highway merely by reason of his race. I think that, in this context, "gipsy" means no more than a person leading a nomadic life with no, or no fixed, employment and with no fixed abode. In saying that, I am hoping that those words will not be considered as the words of a statute, but merely as conveying the general colloquial idea of a gipsy. Looked at in that way, a man might well not be a gipsy on one date and yet be one on a later date. I cannot think that the doctrine of issue estoppel, even if applicable at all in criminal cases, is applicable except in cases where the determination is as to something which has taken place on a particular day, or as to something like the date of a man's birth, which can never vary and has no application whatever to a state of affairs, as here, when a man may be described as a gipsy on one day, and may well not be so described on another day.

DIPLOCK, L.J.: I agree that the word "gipsy" as used in s. 127 (c) the Highways Act, 1959, cannot bear its dictionary meaning of a member of a wandering race (by themselves called Romany) of Hindu origin. If it did, it would mean that Parliament in 1959 had amended the corresponding section of the Highway Act, 1835, (1) which referred to "gipsy or other person" so as to discriminate against persons by reason of their racial origin alone. It would raise other difficulties too. How pure blooded a Romany must one be to fall into the definition? The section is a penal section and should, I suppose, be strictly construed as requiring pure Romany descent. As members of this race first appeared in England not later than the beginning of the sixteenth century, and have not in the intervening centuries been notorious for the abundance of their written records, it would be impossible to prove Romany origin even as far back as the sixteenth century, let alone through the earlier centuries of their peripatetic history from India to the shores of this island. The section, so far as it referred to "gipsy", would be incapable in practice of having any application at all. Confronted by these difficulties, counsel for the respondant only faintly argued that the word "gipsy" in the context of the section does not bear its popular meaning, which I would define as a person without fixed abode who leads nomadic life, dwelling in tents or other shelters, or in caravans or other vehicles. If this meaning is adopted, it follows that being a gipsy is not an unalterable status. It cannot be said "once a gipsy always a gipsy". By changing his way of life a modern Borrow may be a gipsy at one time and not a gipsy at another. . . .

Ashworth, J. agreed.

The Caravan Sites Act 1968

An Act to restrict the eviction from caravan sites of occupiers of caravans and make other provision for the benefit of such occupiers; to secure the establishment of such sites by local authorities for the use of gipsies and other persons of nomadic habit, and control in certain areas the unauthorised occupation of land by such persons; to amend the definition of "caravan" in Part I of the Caravan Sites and Control of Development Act 1960, and for purposes connected with the matters aforesaid.

Part II

Gipsy Encampments

Provision of sites by local authorities

6. Duty of local authorities to provide sites for gipsies

(1) Subject to the provisions of this and the next following section, it shall be the duty of every local authority being the council of a county, county

borough or London borough to exercise their powers under section 24 of the Caravan Sites and Control of Development Act 1960 (provision of caravan sites) so far as may be necessary to provide adequate accommodation for gipsies residing in or resorting to their area.

(2) The council of a county borough or London borough shall not in any case be required under subsection (1) of this section to provide accommodation for more than fifteen caravans at a time, and the Minister may give directions exempting from the duty imposed by that subsection—

(a) any county borough or London borough in the case of which he is satisfied, after such inquiries as appear to him to be appropriate, that suitable land within the borough is not available;

(b) any county borough in the case of which he is so satisfied that the number of gipsies resorting to the borough in the period of five years ending on 1st May 1968 was not such as to warrant the provision by the council of accommodation for them.

(3) Any local authority may defray or contribute towards expenditure incurred under this Part of this Act by any other authority.

(4) The powers of a local authority under the said section 24 shall include power to provide, in or in connection with sites for the accommodation of gipsies, working space and facilities for the carrying on of such activities as are normally carried on by them; but subsection (1) of this section shall not apply to the powers conferred by this subsection.

9. Powers of Minister

(1) Every local authority to which subsection (1) of section 6 of this Act applies shall, as soon as may be after the commencement of this Part of this Act, give notice to the Minister describing the number and location of sites proposed to be provided by them pursuant to that section and the numbers of caravans for which accommodation thereon is designed; and where any site has been so provided they shall give notice to that effect to the Minister.

(2) The Minister may, if at any time it appears to him to be necessary so to do, give directions to any such local authority requiring them to provide, pursuant to the said section 6, such sites or additional sites, for the accommodation of such numbers of caravans, as may be specified in the directions; and any such directions shall be enforceable, on the application of the Minister, by mandamus.

(3) If it appears to the Minister, upon representations made by the council of a county, that the council of any county district within the county have failed to carry out adequately their functions under this Part of this Act in relation to any site provided pursuant thereto, the Minister may by order—

(a) transfer to the council of the county the functions of the council of the district in relation to that site; and

(b) authorise the council of the county to make such other arrangements for the equipment and management of the site as appear to him to be appropriate.

(4) The Minister may cause a local inquiry to be held for the purposes of the exercise of any of his functions under this Part of this Act; and subsections (2) to (5) of section 290 of the Local Government Act 1933 (evidence at and costs of local inquiries) shall have effect with respect to any inquiry held by virtue of this section as if the Minister were a department for the purposes of that section.

Control of unauthorised encampments

10. Prohibition of unauthorised camping in designated areas

(1) In any area designated under the following provisions of this Act as an area to which this section applies it shall be an offence for any person being a gipsy to station a caravan for the purpose of residing for any period—

(a) on any land situated within the boundaries of a highway; or

(b) on any other unoccupied land; or

(c) on any occupied land without the consent of the occupier.

(2) In proceedings against any person for an offence under this section it shall be a defence to prove that the caravan was stationed on the land in consequence of illness, mechanical breakdown or other immediate emergency and that he removed it (or intended to remove it) as soon as reasonably practicable.

(3) A person guilty of an offence under this section shall be liable on summary conviction to a fine not exceeding £20; and if the offence of which he is convicted is continued after the conviction he shall be guilty of a further offence and shall be liable in respect thereof to a fine not exceeding £5 for every day on which the offence is so continued.

11. Removal of unlawful encampments

(1) In any area to which section 10 of this Act applies, a magistrates' court may, on the complaint of any local authority, by order authorise that authority to take such steps as may be specified in the order for the removal from land in that area of caravans proved to the satisfaction of the court to be stationed thereon in contravention of the said section 10, and of persons residing therein.

(2) Notice of any summons issued pursuant to a complaint under this section shall be given by the local authority to the owner and occupier (if any) of the land on which the caravans are alleged to be stationed unless, after reasonable inquiries, the authority are unable to ascertain his name and address; and the owner and occupier of any such land shall be entitled to appear and be heard in the proceedings.

(3) Any order under this section may authorise the local authority, by their officers and servants—

(a) to enter upon any land specified in the order for the purpose of carrying out the order;

(b) to take, in relation to any caravan to be removed pursuant to the order, such steps for securing entry and rendering it suitable for removal as may be so specified:

Provided that the local authority shall not so enter upon any occupied land unless they have given to the owner and occupier at least twenty-four hours' notice of their intention to do so, or unless after reasonable inquiries they are unable to ascertain their names and addresses.

(4) A person who wilfully obstructs any person in the execution of an order under this section shall be liable on summary conviction to a fine not exceeding £20 or, if he has previously been convicted of an offence under this subsection, not exceeding £50; and a constable may arrest without warrant any person found committing an offence under this subsection.

12. Designation of areas

(1) The Minister may by order made on the application of any local authority being the council of a county, a county borough or a London borough, designate the area of that authority as an area to which section 10 of this Act applies.

(2) The Minister shall not make such an order in respect of any area unless it appears to him either that adequate provision is made therein for the accommodation of gipsies residing in or resorting to the area, or that in all the circumstances it is not necessary or expedient to make any such provision.

(3) An order under this section may be revoked by an order made by the Minister, either on the application of the local authority or without such an application.

(5) Where an order under this section is made in respect of any area it shall be the duty of the local authority for that area to take such steps as are reasonably practicable to inform gipsies within the area of the making and effects of the order.

16. Interpretation

In this Act the following expressions have the following meanings that is to say— . . .

"gipsies" means persons of nomadic habit of life, whatever their race or origin, but does not include members of an organised group of travelling showmen, or of persons engaged in travelling circuses, travelling together as such; . . .

Note: See *Report of the Mobile Homes Review—A Study carried out within the Department of the Environment* (London, 1974).

4. THE POOR

Note: There curiously exists no study of the ways in which the law penalises the poor for the fact of their being poor. Some illustrations will have to suffice here.

THE VAGRANCY ACT 1824

An Act for the Punishment of idle and disorderly Persons, and Rogues and Vagabonds, in that Part of Great Britain called England.

3. Persons refusing to maintain themselves and families, or leaving place to which they were removed, and unlicensed pedlars, prostitutes, and beggars shall be deemed idle and disorderly persons, and may be imprisoned for one month with hard labour

. . . Every petty chapman or pedlar wandering abroad, and trading without being duly licensed, or otherwise authorized by law; every common prostitute wandering in the public streets or public highways, or in any place of public resort, and behaving in a riotous or indecent manner; and every person wandering abroad, or placing himself or herself in any public place, street, highway, court, or passage, to beg or gather alms, or causing or procuring or encouraging any child or children so to do; shall be deemed an idle and disorderly person within the true intent and meaning of this Act; and it shall be lawful for any justice of the peace to commit such offender (being thereof convicted before him by his own view, or by the confession of such offender, or by the evidence on oath of one or more credible witness or witnesses,) to the house of correction . . . for any time not exceeding one calendar month.

4. Persons committing certain offences shall be deemed rogues and vagabonds and may be imprisoned for three months with hard labour

. . . Every person committing any of the offences herein-before mentioned, after having been convicted as an idle and disorderly person; every person pretending or professing to tell fortunes, or using any subtle craft, means, or device, by palmistry or otherwise, to deceive and impose on any of his Majesty's subjects; every person wandering abroad and lodging in any barn or outhouse, or in any deserted or unoccupied building, or in the open air, or under a tent, or in any cart or wagon, . . . and not giving a good account of himself or herself; every person wilfully exposing to view, in any street, road, highway, or public place, any obscene print, picture, or other indecent exhibition; every person wilfully, openly, lewdly, and obscenely exposing his person . . ., with intent to insult any female; every person wandering abroad, and endeavouring by the exposure of wounds or deformities to obtain or gather alms; every person going about as a gatherer or collector of alms, or endeavouring ot procure charitable contributions of any nature or kind, under any false or fraudulent pretence; . . . every person . . . being armed with any gun, pistol, hanger, cutlass, bludgeon, or other offensive weapon, or having upon him or her any instrument, with intent to commit an arrestable offence; every person being found in or upon any dwelling house, warehouse, coach-house, stable, or outhouse, or in any inclosed yard, garden, or area, for any unlawful purpose; every suspected person or reputed thief, frequenting any river, canal, or navigable stream, dock, or basin, or any quay, wharf, or warehouse near or adjoining thereto, or any street, highway, or avenue leading thereto, or any place of public resort, or any avenue leading thereto, or any street or any highway or any place adjacent to a street or highway with intent to commit an arrestable offence; and every person apprehended as an idle and disorderly person, and violently resisting any constable, or other peace officer so apprehending him or her, and being subsequently convicted of the offence for which he or she shall have been so apprehended; shall be deemed a rogue and vagabond, within the true intent and meaning of this Act; and it shall be lawful for any justice of the peace to commit such offender (being thereof convicted before him by the confession of such offender, or by the evidence on oath of one or more credible witness or witnesses,) to the house of correction . . . for any time not exceeding three calendar months; . . . and every such gun, pistol, hanger, cutlass, bludgeon, or other offensive weapon, and every such instrument as aforesaid, shall, by the conviction of the offender, become forfeited to the King's Majesty.

5. Certain offenders shall be deemed incorrigible rogues and may be committed for trial at quarter sessions

Every person breaking or escaping out of any place of legal confinement before the expiration of the term for which he or she shall have been committed or ordered to be confined of this Act; every person committing any offence against this Act shall subject him or her to be dealt with as a rogue and vagabond, such person having been at some former time adjudged so to be, and duly convicted thereof; and every person apprehended as a rogue and vagabond, and violently resisting any constable or other peace officer so apprehending him or her, and being subsequently convicted of the offence for which he or she shall have been so apprehended; shall be deemed an incorrigible rogue within the true intent and meaning of this Act; and it shall be lawful for any justice of the peace to commit such offender (being thereof convicted before him by the confession of such offender, or by the evidence on oath of one or more credible witness or witnesses,) to quarter sessions, either in custody or on bail . . .

6. Any person may apprehend offenders—Constables, etc., refusing to apprehend, to be deemed guilty of neglect of duty

It shall be lawful for any person whatsoever to apprehend any person who shall be found offending against this Act, and forthwith to take and convey him or her before some justice of the peace, to be dealt with in such manner as is herein-before directed, or to deliver him or her to any constable or other peace officer of the place where he or she shall have been apprehended, to be so taken and conveyed as aforesaid . . .

8. Offenders may be searched and their trunks, bundles, etc., inspected —Money and effects found upon offenders may be applied towards the expenses of apprehending them, etc.

It shall be lawful for any constable, peace officer, or other person apprehending any person charged with being an idle and disorderly person, or a rogue and vagabond, or an incorrigible rogue, to take any horse, mule, ass, cart, car, caravan, or other vehicle or goods in the possession or use of such person, and to take and convey the same, as well as such person, before some justice of the peace, and for every justice of the peace by whom any person shall be adjudged to be an idle and disorderly person, or a rogue and vagabond, or an incorrigible rogue, to order that such offender shall be searched, and that his or her trunks, boxes, bundles, parcels, or packages shall be inspected in the presence of the said justice, and of him or her, and also that any cart, car, caravan, or other vehicle which may have been found in his or her possession or use shall be searched in his or her presence; and it shall be lawful for the said justice to order that any money which may be then found with or upon such offender shall be paid and applied for and towards the expense of apprehending, conveying to the house of correction, and maintaining such offender during the time for which he or she shall have been committed; and if upon such search money sufficient for the purposes aforesaid be not found, it shall be lawful for such justice to order that a part, or, if necessary, the whole of such other effects then found shall be sold, and that the produce of such sale shall be paid and applied as aforesaid, and also that the overplus of such money or effects, after deducting the charges of such sale, shall be returned to the said offender.

Vagrancy Act 1935

1. Amendment of 5 Geo. 4 c. 83, s. 4

(1) So much of section four of the Vagrancy Act, 1824, as enacts that a person wandering abroad and lodging in any barn or outhouse, or in any deserted or unoccupied building, or in the open air, or under a tent, or in any cart or waggon, not having any visible means of subsistence, and not giving a good account of himself, shall be deemed a rogue and vagabond within the meaning of that Act, shall have effect subject to the following provisions of this section.

(2) The words "not having any visible means of subsistence" in the said enactment are hereby repealed.

(3) A person wandering abroad and lodging as aforesaid shall not be deemed by virtue of the said enactment a rogue and vagabond within the meaning of the said Act unless it is proved either—

(a) that, in relation to the occasion on which he lodged as aforesaid, he had been directed to a reasonably accessible place of shelter and failed to apply for, or refused, accommodation there;

(b) that he is a person who persistently wanders abroad and, notwithstanding that a place of shelter is reasonably accessible, lodges or attempts to lodge as aforesaid; or

(c) that by, or in the course of, lodging as aforesaid he caused damage to property, infection with vermin, or other offensive consequence, or that he lodged as aforesaid in such circumstances as to appear to be likely so to do.

In this subsection the expression "a place of shelter" means a place where provision is regularly made for giving (free of charge) accommodation for the night to such persons as apply therefor.

(4) The reference in the said enactment to a person lodging under a tent or in a cart or waggon shall not be deemed to include a person lodging under a tent or in a cart or waggon with or in which he travels.

Note: These Acts do not apply in Scotland or Northern Ireland. For a discussion of the application of these Acts see Clare Demuth, *'Sus' a Report on the Vagrancy Act 1824* (Runnymede Trust, 1978); Home Office, *Working Party on Vagrancy and Street Offences Working Paper* (HMSO, 1974), and *Home Office, Report of the Working Party on Vagrancy and Street Offences* (1976). See also L. H. Leigh, "Powers of Arrest in relation to Vagrancy and Related Offences," (1974) Crim. L.R. pp. 157–165; *ibid* "Vagrancy, Morality and Decency," (1975) Crim. L.R. pp. 381–390; *ibid, Police Powers in England and Wales* (Butterworths, 1975), Chap. 5.

Mathers v. Penfold [1915] 1 K.B. 514

Divisional Court

The respondent, a member of the Shamrock Branch of the United Order of General Labourers was acquitted of begging contrary to the Vagrancy Act 1824, s. 3. He had been soliciting contributions, in exchange for which tickets were issued, of donations to help members of the branch who were out of work on strike. The respondent was himself one of those out of work.

A case was stated. The Divisional Court upheld the magistrate in dismissing the summons.

DARLING J.:

In this case the respondent, who belonged to an association of persons some of whom were out of work, solicited alms in the street, and was charged under s. 3 of the Vagrancy Act, 1824, with unlawfully wandering abroad in a public place there to beg, which under the terms of the section involves a charge of being an idle and disorderly person. The magistrate declined to convict. The question which we have to decide turns upon the language of s. 3 of the Act of 1824, because the charge against him is that he is an idle and disorderly person within the meaning of that section, which enacts that "every person wandering abroad, or placing himself or herself in any public place, street, highway, court or passage, to beg or gather alms . . . shall be deemed an idle and disorderly person within the true intent and meaning of this Act."

Now the respondent did undoubtedly place himself in a street, and he solicited contributions to a fund for the relief of persons who were out of work and were members of the society to which he himself belonged. He would or might benefit to some extent by any contributions that might be received. In my judgment the magistrate was right in refusing to convict him. I think that the Vagrancy Act, 1824, which enacts that a person infringing its provisions is to be deemed to be an idle and disorderly person, is aimed not at persons collecting for an object of a charitable nature in which possibly they themselves have an interest, but that it is directed at persons of a different type. It is not a statute which stands by itself. It is the result of a number of statues dealing with persons who were a danger to society, persons wandering about the country without work. I am not in the least saying that when they were first passed the persons at whom those statutes were aimed were without work by their own fault, but they were without work, and being without work and without means, no doubt they were dangerous people, and it was necessary to deal with them. How they came to be in such a state is a matter of history, and one need not go into it, but there they were; and there having been these masses of persons about the country for many years, the Vagrancy Act, 1824, was passed to deal with them, as other statutes had been. I think that the preamble to the Act is important. It says: "Whereas . . . . it is expedient to make further provision for the suppression of vagrancy, and for the punishment of idle and disorderly persons, rogues and vagabonds, and incorrigible rogues in England . . . ." Sect. 3 commences by enacting that "every person being able wholly or in part to maintain himself or herself, or his or her family, by work or other means, and wilfully refusing or neglecting so to do, by which refusal or neglect he or she, or any of his or her family whom he or she may be legally bound to maintain, shall have become chargeable to any parish, township or place . . . ." That shows the kind of person, amongst others, who is aimed at. The section then uses the words which I read at the commencement of my judgment.

In my opinion what the respondent was doing was not begging in the sense in which the statute uses the word "beg." The word is one which may be used in many senses, e.g., you may say "I beg your pardon." The word used in that sense has very little similarity to the kind of begging which is done by a person whom the statutes designate a sturdy beggar and vagrant. This last kind of begging would be thought by most people to be rather a humiliating thing to do. It is done by persons—sturdy and troublesome beggars—of quite a distinct turn of mind. Following the word "beg" the section uses the expression "or gather alms." I think the respondent can hardly say he was not gathering alms. I think he was gathering alms, but it is to be noticed that he did not do it for the same kind of purpose as those persons did who were denominated by the statute idle and disorderly persons. He somewhat resembled in his attitude the monk who waited on Mr. Sterne in "The Sentimental Journey." In my opinion, it would be a misuse of language to say that the respondent, simply because he stood in the street and asked for contributions to a fund from which he and others were to profit, they being temporarily out of work, had become an idle and disorderly person. The words of the statute are obviously aimed at persons in a different category altogether, namely, persons who are wandering abroad, who are placing themselves at the corners of streets and begging or soliciting alms, such persons as are described in the judgment of Cave J. in *Pointon* v. *Hill* (1), which was concurred in by A. I. Smith J., as having given up work and adopted begging as a habit or mode of life. Those persons are clearly, I think, within the statute. I do not differ from the judgment of Cave J. in *Pointon* v. *Hill* (1), but I do not think that his definition in that case is exhaustive, inasmuch as it places a magistrate in the difficulty of having to ascertain whether a person has begged as a habit or mode of life, and magistrates have felt a difficulty if they find a person begging for the first time in holding that he is a beggar by habit or by mode of life. I do not agree that the right test is whether it is the first time a person has begged. I think that it is possible to say whether or not it is a person's habit or mode of life even though he has only just adopted it. If it were proved that a person, although having been in work, had definitely come to the conclusion, for reasons satisfactory to himself, that he did not wish to work and that he meant to lead the life of a gipsy—to live on alms which he might gather—I should say that a magistrate, being convinced by the evidence that this was so, might convict him under the statute and hold that the fact that he was demanding alms made him an idle and disorderly person within the statute, although there was no proof that he had ever done it before; because the proof that he had done it before would be only one way of proving what was his habit and mode of life, as Cave J. expresses it. You might prove by evidence, although it did not show that he had done it before, that such was his habit and mode of life; becuase a man may have a habit or mode of life although he has only just taken to it. For example, a barrister who has been called to the Bar, and has not yet had a brief, could on the first day that he is called say that he has adopted the habit or mode of life of a barrister, that he intends to get his living in that way although nobody has ever yet given him a brief. I should say of a beggar that it might perfectly well be proved, if the evidence was satisfactory to the magistrate, that he was a beggar by mode of life although he had not yet received a contribution, and although it was the first time he asked for one, and on that occasion in fact he did not obtain it. It might be difficult to prove, but the view I have expressed gets rid of the kind of notion that a beggar is like a vicious dog which cannot be proved to be vicious till it has bitten somebody. That is commonly taken to be so, although I should myself hardly say an actual bite is necessary if it had tried to bite some one. But it is not necessary to go as far as that with a beggar. If the magistrate is satisfied that the person charged with begging has taken to this

(1) 12 Q.B.D. 306.

mode of collecting alms, as a habit and mode of life, for his own benefit, he could be convicted although it was the first occasion that he had done it. I think that all that kind of evidence is rebutted when you come to the proof that although he may have solicited alms a hundred times he was soliciting them for a charitable purpose—for the sake of those who, like himself, were in misfortune—and that there was nothing disorderly in his conduct, that it was a well-arranged charitable collection, just as much as are the collections for many recognized charities. In that case, I think it would be an absolute misuse of language to say that he must be deemed to be an idle and disorderly person when he is not idle, when he is not disorderly, but simply because he has done one of those things which other persons who really are idle and dis-orderly are in the habit of doing. . . .

LUSH J.:

It is, I think, impossible to read the preamble of this Act, or to observe the context in which this passage with regard to begging, which we have to con-sider, occurs, without seeing fairly clearly what the class of persons is against whom this legislation was directed. It seems to me to be clear that it was directed against that idle class of persons who, instead of endeavouring to earn their livelihood by work, prefer to loaf about or wander abroad, as the section says, or place themselves in a public street, and to beg or gather alms. That is the class of persons against whom this part of the section was directed, who are not improperly called "idle and disorderly persons."

It seems to me quite impossible to say that a person who, like the respon-dent, was engaged in collecting funds on behalf of the trade union to which he belonged is within the class of idle and disorderly persons against whom this part of the section is directed.

Atkin, Avery and Bankes, JJ. delivered judgments to the same effect.

Questions

1. "The Vagrancy Laws have a long and tangled history and have gradually gathered to themselves a miscellaneous collection of odd offences; but in essence they consist in blind, ill-tempered and vindictive hitting out at people who are guilty of the unpardonable offence of being poor"—"Barrister," *Justice in England* (1938). Discuss.

2. Article 3 (1) of the Italian Constitution provides: "All citizens are invested with equal social status and are equal before the law, without distinction as to sex, race, language, political opinion and personal or social condition." What would be the practical and legal implications of the enactment of such a provision as part of British law?

CHAPTER 14

EMERGENCY POWERS

Further Reading

De Smith, Chap. 23; Wade & Phillips, Chap. 29.

G. Wilson, *Cases and Materials on Constitutional and Administrative Law* (2nd ed., C.U.P., 1976), pp. 729–738.

See also Chapter 15.

EMERGENCY POWERS ACT 1920

1. Issue of proclamations of emergency

(1) If at any time it appears to His Majesty that there have occurred, or are about to occur, events of such a nature as to be calculated, by interfering with the supply and distribution of food, water, fuel, or light, or with the means of locomotion, to deprive the community, or any substantial portion of the community, of the essentials of life, His Majesty may, by proclamation (hereinafter referred to as a proclamation of emergency), declare that a state of emergency exists.

No such proclamation shall be in force for more than one month, without prejudice to the issue of another proclamation at or before the end of that period.

(2) Where a proclamation of emergency has been made the occasion thereof shall forthwith be communicated to Parliament, and, if Parliament is then separated by such adjournment or prorogation as will not expire within five days, a proclamation shall be issued for the meeting of Parliament within five days, and Parliament shall accordingly meet and sit upon the day appointed by that proclamation, and shall continue to sit and act in like manner as if it had stood adjourned or prorogued to the same day.

2. Emergency regulations

(1) Where a proclamation of emergency has been made, and so long as the proclamation is in force, it shall be lawful for His Majesty in Council, by Order, to make regulations for securing the essentials of life to the community, and those regulations may confer or impose on a Secretary of State or other Government department, or any other persons in His Majesty's service or acting on His Majesty's behalf, such powers and duties as His Majesty may deem necessary for the preservation of the peace, for securing and regulating the supply and distribution of food, water, fuel, light, and other necessities, for maintaining the means of transit or locomotion, and for any other purposes essential to the public safety and the life of the community, and may

make such provisions incidental to the powers aforesaid as may appear to His Majesty to be required for making the exercise of those powers effective:

Provided that nothing in this Act shall be construed to authorise the making of any regulations imposing any form of compulsory military service or industrial conscription:

Provided also that no such regulation shall make it an offence for any person or persons to take part in a strike, or peacefully to persuade any other person or persons to take part in a strike.

(2) Any regulations so made shall be laid before Parliament as soon as may be after they are made, and shall not continue in force after the expiration of seven days from the time when they are so laid unless a resolution is passed by both Houses providing for the continuance thereof.

(3) The regulations may provide for the trial, by courts of summary jurisdiction, of persons guilty of offences against the regulations; so, however, that the maximum penalty which may be inflicted for any offence against any such regulations shall be imprisonment with or without hard labour for a term of three months, or a fine of one hundred pounds, or both such imprisonment and fine, together with the forfeiture of any goods or money in respect of which the offence has been committed: Provided that no such regulations shall alter any existing procedure in criminal cases, or confer any right to punish by fine or imprisonment without trial.

(4) The regulations so made shall have effect as if enacted in this Act, but may be added to, altered, or revoked by resolution of both Houses of Parliament or by regulations made in like manner and subject to the like provisions as the original regulations . . .

(5) The expiry or revocation of any regulations so made shall not be deemed to have affected the previous operation thereof, or the validity of any action taken thereunder, or any penalty or punishment incurred in respect of any contravention or failure to comply therewith, or any proceeding or remedy in respect of any such punishment or penalty.

EMERGENCY POWERS ACT 1964

2. Defence (Armed Forces) Regulations 1939 made permanent

The Defence (Armed Forces) Regulations 1939 in the form set out in Part C of Schedule 2 to the Emergency Laws (Repeal) Act 1959 (which regulations enable the temporary employment in agricultural work or in other work, being urgent work of national importance, of members of the armed forces of the Crown to be authorised) shall become permanent.

PREVENTION OF TERRORISM (TEMPORARY PROVISIONS) ACT 1976

Part 1

PROSCRIBED ORGANISATIONS

1. Proscribed organisations

(1) Subject to subsection (6) below, if any person—
    (a) belongs or professes to belong to a proscribed organisation:
    (b) solicits or invites financial or other support for a proscribed organisation, or knowingly makes or receives any contribution in money or otherwise to the resources of a proscribed organisation; or

(c) arranges or assists in the arrangement or management of, or addresses, any meeting of three or more persons (whether or not it is a meeting to which the public are admitted) knowing that the meeting is to support or to further the activities of, a proscribed organisation, or is to be addressed by a person belonging or professing to belong to a proscribed organisation

he shall be liable—

(i) on summary conviction to imprisonment for a term not exceeding six months or to a fine not exceeding £400, or both, or

(ii) on conviction on indictment to imprisonment for a term not exceeding five years or to a fine, or both.

(2) Any organisation for the time being specified in Schedule I to this Act is a proscribed organisation for the purposes of this Act: and any organisation which passes under a name mentioned in that Schedule shall be treated as proscribed, whatever relationship (if any) it has to any other organisation of the same name.

(3) The Secretary of State may by order add to Schedule I to this Act any organisation that appears to him to be concerned in terrorism occurring in the United Kingdom and connected with Northern Irish affairs, or in promoting or encouraging it.

(4) The Secretary of State may also by order remove an organisation from Schedule I to this Act.

(5) In this section "organisation" includes an association or combination of persons.

(6) A person belonging to a proscribed organisation shall not be guilty of an offence under this section by reason of belonging to the organisation if he shows that he became a member when it was not a proscribed organisation and that he has not since he became a member taken part in any of its activities at any time while it was a proscribed organisation.

In this subsection the reference to a person becoming a member of an organisation shall be taken to be a reference to the only or last occasion on which he became a member.

(7) The court by or before which a person is convicted of an offence under this section may order the forfeiture of any money or other property which, at the time of the offence, he had in his possession or under his control for the use or benefit of the proscribed organisation.

2. Display of support in public for a proscribed organisation

(1) Any person who in a public place—

(a) wears any item of dress, or

(b) wears, carries or displays any article,

in such a way or in such circumstances as to arouse reasonable apprehension that he is a member or supporter of a proscribed organisation, shall be liable on summary conviction to imprisonment for a term not exceeding six months or to a fine not exceeding £400, or both.

(2) A constable may arrest without warrant a person whom he reasonably suspects to be a person guilty of an offence under this section.

(3) In this section "public place" includes any highway and any other premises or place at the material time the public have, or are permitted to have, access whether on payment or otherwise.

Part II

Exclusion Orders

3. Exclusion orders: general

(1) The Secretary of State may exercise the powers conferred on him by this Part of this Act in such way as appears to him expedient to prevent acts of terrorism (whether in the United Kingdom or elsewhere) designed to influence public opinion or Government policy with respect of affairs in Northern Ireland.

(2) An order under section 4, 5 or 6 of this Act is referred to in this Act as an "exclusion order".

An exclusion order may be revoked at any time by a further order made by the Secretary of State.

4. Orders excluding persons from Great Britain

(1) If the Secretary of State is satisfied that any person—
- (a) is or has been concerned (whether in Great Britain or elsewhere) in the commission, preparation or instigation of acts of terrorism, or
- (b) is attempting or may attempt to enter Great Britain with a view to being concerned in the commission, preparation or instigation of acts of terrorism,

the Secretary of State may make an order against that person prohibiting him from being in, or entering, Great Britain.

(2) In deciding whether to make an order under this section against a person who is ordinarily resident in Great Britain, the Secretary of State shall have regard to the question whether that person's connection with any territory outside Great Britain is such as to make it appropriate that such an order should be made.

(3) An order shall not be made under this section against a person who is a citizen of the United Kingdom and Colonies and who—
- (a) is at the time ordinarily resident in Great Britain, and has then been ordinarily resident in Great Britain throughout the last 20 years, or
- (b) was born in Great Britian and has, throughout his life, been ordinarily resident in Great Britain, or
- (c) is at the time subject to an order under section 5 of this Act.

Paragraph (a) shall be construed in accordance with Schedule 2 to this Act.

5. Orders excluding persons from Northern Ireland

(1) If the Secretary of State is satisfied that any person—
- (a) is or has been concerned (whether in Northern Ireland or elsewhere) in the commission, preparation or instigation of acts of terrorism, or
- (b) is attempting or may attempt to enter Northern Ireland with a view to being concerned in the commission, preparation or instigation of acts of terrorism,

the Secretary of State may make an order against that person prohibiting him from being in, or entering, Northern Ireland.

(2) In deciding whether to make an order under this section against a person who is ordinarily resident in Northern Ireland, the Secretary of State shall have regard to the question whether that person's connection with any

territory outside Northern Ireland is such as to make it appropriate that such an order should be made.

(3) An order shall not be made under this section against a person who is a citizen of the United Kingdom and Colonies and who—

(a) is at the time ordinarily resident in Northern Ireland, and has then been ordinarily resident in Northern Ireland throughout the last 20 years, or

(b) was born in Northern Ireland and has, throughout his life, been ordinarily resident in Northern Ireland, or

(c) is at the time subject to an order under section 4 of this Act.

Paragraph (a) shall be construed in accordance with Schedule 2 to this Act.

6. Orders excluding persons from the United Kingdom

(1) If the Secretary of State is satisfied that any person—

(a) is or has been concerned (whether in the United Kingdom or elsewhere) in the commission, preparation or instigation of acts of terrorism, or

(b) is attempting or may attempt to enter Great Britain or Northern Ireland with a view to being concerned in the commission, preparation or instigation of acts of terrorism,

the Secretary of State may make an order against that person prohibiting him from being in, or entering, the United Kingdom.

(2) In deciding whether to make an order under this section against a person who is ordinarily resident in the United Kingdom, the Secretary of State shall have regard to the question whether that person's connection with any territory outside the United Kingdom is such as to make it appropriate that such an order should be made.

(3) An order shall not be made under this section against a person who is a citizen of the United Kingdom and Colonies.

7. Right to make representations etc. to Secretary of State

(1) As soon as may be after the making of an exclusion order, notice of the making of the order shall be served on the person against whom it is made, and the notice shall—

(a) set out the rights afforded to him by this section, and

(b) specify the manner in which those rights are to be exercised.

(2) Subsection (1) above shall not impose an obligation to take any steps to serve a notice on a person at a time when he is outside the United Kingdom.

(3) If a person served with notice of the making of an exclusion order objects to the order, he may within 96 hours of service of the notice—

(a) make representations in writing to the Secretary of State setting out the grounds of his objection, and

(b) include in those representations a request for a personal interview with the person or persons nominated by the Secretary of State under subsection (4) below.

(4) Where representations are duly made under this section, the Secretary of State shall, unless he considers the grounds to be frivolous, refer the matter for the advice of one or more persons nominated by him.

(5) Where a matter is referred for the advice of one or more persons nominated by the Secretary of State and the person against whom the order was made—

(a) included in his representations a request under subsection (3) (b) above, and

(b) has not been removed, with his consent, from Great Britain, Northern Ireland or the United Kingdom, as the case may be, under section 8 of this Act,

that person shall be granted a personal interview with the person or persons so nominated.

(6) After receiving the representations and the report of the person or persons nominated by him under subsection (4) above, the Secretary of State shall, as soon as may be, reconsider the case.

(7) Where representations are duly made under this section the Secretary of State shall, if it is reasonably practicable, notify the person against whom the order was made of any decision he takes as to whether or not to revoke the order.

Part III

General and Miscellaneous

10. Contributions towards acts of terrorism

(1) If any person—

(a) solicits or invites any other person to give or lend, whether for consideration or not, any money or other property, or

(b) receives or accepts from any other person, whether for consideration or not, any money or other property,

intending that the money or other property shall be applied or used for or in connection with the commission, preparation or instigation of acts of terrorism to which this section applies, he shall be guilty of an offence.

(2) If any person gives, lends or otherwise makes available to any other person, whether for consideration or not, any money or other property, knowing or suspecting that the money or other property will or may be applied or used for or in connection with the commission, preparation or instigation of acts of terrorism to which this section applies, he shall be guilty of an offence.

(3) A person guilty of an offence under subsection (1) or subsection (2) above shall be liable—

(a) on summary conviction to imprisonment for a term not exceeding six months, or to a fine not exceeding £400, or both, or

(b) on conviction on indictment to imprisonment for a term not exceeding five years or to a fine, or both.

(4) A court by or before which a person is convicted of an offence under subsection (1) above may order the forfeiture of any money or other property—

(a) which, at the time of the offence, he had in his possession or under his control, and

(b) which, at that time, he intended should be applied or used for or in connection with the commission, preparation or instigation of acts of terrorism to which this section applies.

(5) This section and section 11 of this Act apply to acts of terrorism occurring in the United Kingdom and connected with Northern Irish affairs.

11. Information about acts of terrorism

(1) If a person who has information which he knows or believes might be of material assistance—

(a) in preventing an act of terrorism to which this section applies, or

(b) in securing the apprehension, prosecution or conviction of any person

for an offence involving the commission, preparation or instigation of
an act of terrorism to which this section applies,
fails without reasonable excuse to disclose that information as soon as
reasonably practicable—
(i) in England and Wales, to a constable,
he shall be guilty of an offence.

(2) A person guilty of an offence under subsection (1) above shall be
liable—
(a) on summary conviction to imprisonment for a term not exceeding six
months, or to a fine not exceeding £400, or both, or
(b) on conviction on indictment to imprisonment for a term not exceeding
five years, or to a fine, or both.

12. Powers of arrest and detention

(1) A constable may arrest without warrant a person whom he reasonably
suspects to be—
(a) a person guilty of an offence under section 1, 9, 10 or 11 of this Act;
(b) a person who is or has been concerned in the commission, preparation
or instigation of acts of terrorism;
(c) a person subject to an exclusion order.

(2) A person arrested under this section shall not be detained in right of the
arrest for more than 48 hours after this arrest; but the Secretary of State may,
in any particular case, extend the period of 43 hours by a further period not
exceeding 5 days.

(3) The following provisions (requirement to bring arrested person before
a court after his arrest) shall not apply to a person detained in right of the
arrest.
The said provisions are—
Section 38 of the Magistrates' Court Act 1952,
Section 29 of the Children and Young Persons Act 1969,
Section 321(3) of the Criminal Procedure (Scotland) Act 1975, Section
132 of the Magistrates' Courts Act (Northern Ireland) 1964, and Section
50(3) of the Children and Young Persons Act (Northern Ireland) 1968.

(4) In Scotland section 295(1) of the Criminal Procedure (Scotland) Act
1975 (chief constable may in certain cases accept bail) shall not apply to a
person detained in right of an arrest under this section.

(5) The provisions of this section are without prejudice to any power of
arrest conferred by law apart from this section.

13. Control of entry and procedure for removal

(1) The Secretary of State may by order provide for—
(a) the examination of persons arriving in, or leaving, Great Britain or
Northern Ireland, with a view to determining—
(i) whether any such person appears to be a person who is or has
been concerned in the commission, preparation or instigation of
acts of terrorism, or
(ii) whether any such person is subject to an exclusion order, or
(iii) whether there are grounds for suspecting that any such person has
committed an offence under section 9 or 11 of this Act,
(b) the arrest and detention of persons subject to exclusion orders, pending
their removal pursuant to section 8 of this Act, and

(c) arrangements for the removal of persons pursuant to section 8 of this Act.

(2) An order under this section may confer powers on examining officers (appointed in accordance with paragraph 1 (2) of Schedule 3 to this Act), including—

(a) the power of arresting and detaining any person pending—
  (i) his examination,
  (ii) the taking of a decision by the Secretary of State as to whether or not to make an exclusion order against him, or
  (iii) his removal pursuant to section 8 of this Act,

(b) the power of searching persons, of boarding ships or aircraft, of searching in ships or aircraft, or elsewhere and of detaining articles—
  (i) for use in connection with the taking of a decision by the Secretary of State as to whether or not to make an exclusion order. or
  (ii) for use as evidence in criminal proceedings.

14. Supplement provisions

(1) In this Act, unless the context otherwise requires—
"aircraft" includes hovercraft,
"captain" means master (of a ship) or commander (of an aircraft),
"exclusion order" has the meaning given by section 3 (2) of this Act,
"port" includes airport and hoverport,
"ship" includes every description of vessel used in navigation,
"terrorism" means the use of violence for political ends, and includes any use of violence for the purpose of putting the public or any section of the public in fear.

(2) The powers conferred by Part II and section 13 of this Act shall be exercisable notwithstanding the rights conferred by section I of the Immigration Act 1971 (general principles regulating entry into and staying in the United Kingdom).

(3) An reference in a provision of this Act to a person's having been concerned in the commission, preparation or instigation of acts of terrorism shall be taken to be a reference to his having been so concerned at any time, whether before or after the coming into force of that provision.

(4) When any question arises under this Act whether or not a person is exempted from the provisions of section 4, 5 or 6 of this Act, it shall lie on the person asserting it to prove that he is.

(9) No order under section 1 or 17 of this Act shall be made unless—
(a) a draft of the order has been approved by resolution of each House of Parliament, or
(b) it is declared in the order that it appears to the Secretary of State that by reason of urgency it is necessary to make the order without a draft having been so approved.

(10) Every order under section 1 or 17 of this Act (except such an order of which a draft has been so approved)—
(a) shall be laid before Parliament, and
(b) shall cease to have effect at the expiration of a period of 40 days beginning with the date on which it was made unless, before the expiration of that period, the order has been approved by resolution of each House of Parliament, but without prejudice to anything previously done or to the making of a new order.

17. Duration, expiry and revival of Act

(1) The provisions of—
> sections 1 to 13 of this Act,
> section 14 of this Act except in so far as it relates to orders under subsection (2) (*a*) or (*b*) below,
> subsection (2) (*c*) below, and
> Schedules 1 to 3 to this Act

shall remain in force until the expiry of the period of twelve months beginning with the passing of this Act and shall then expire unless continued in force by an order under subsection (2) (*a*) below.

(2) The Secretary of State may by order provide—

(*a*) that all or any of the said provisions which are for the time being in force (including any in force by virtue of an order under this paragraph or paragraph (*c*) below) shall continue in force for a period not exceeding twelve months from the coming into operation of the order;

(*b*) that all or any of the said provisions which are for the time being in force shall cease to be in force; or

(*c*) that all or any of the said provisions which are not for the time being in force shall come into force again and remain in force for a period not exceeding twelve months from the coming into operation of the order.

SCHEDULES

SCHEDULE 1

Proscribed Organisations

Irish Republican Army

SCHEDULE 3

Supplemental Provisions for Sections 1 to 13

PART II

Offences, Detention, etc.

Prosecution of offences

3. Proceedings shall not be instituted—

(*a*) in England and Wales for an offence under section 1, 2, 9, 10 or 11 of this Act, except by or with the consent of the Attorney General.

Search warrants

4.—(1) If a justice of the peace is satisfied that there is reasonable ground for suspecting that—

(*a*) evidence of the commission of an offence under section 1, 9, 10 or 11 of this Act, or

(*b*) evidence sufficient to justify the making of an order under section 1 of this Act or an exclusion order, is to be found at any premises or place, he may grant a search warrant authorising entry to the premises or place.

(2) An application for a warrant under sub-paragraph (1) above shall be made by a member of a police force of a rank not lower than the rank of an inspector, and he shall give his information to the justice on oath.

(3) The warrant shall authorise the applicant, and any other member of any police force, to enter the premises or place, if necessary by force, and to search the premises or place and every person found therein and to seize anything found on the premises or place, or on any such person, which any member of a police force acting under the warrant has reasonable grounds for suspecting to be evidence falling within sub-paragraph (1) above.

(4) If a member of a police force of a rank not lower than the rank of superintendent has reasonable grounds for believing that the case is one of great emergency and that in the interests of the State immediate action is necessary, he may by a written order signed by him give to any member of a police force the authority which may be given by a search warrant under this paragraph.

(5) Where any authority is so given, particulars of the case shall be notified as soon as may be to the Secretary of State.

Powers of search without Warrant

6.—(1) In any circumstances in which a constable has power under section 12 of this Act to arrest a person, he may also, for the purpose of ascertaining whether he has in his possession any document or other article which may constitute evidence that he is a person liable to arrest, stop that person, and search him.

(2) Where a constable has arrested a person under the said section, for any reason other than for the commission of a criminal offence he, or any other constable, may search him for the purpose of ascertaining whether he has in his possession any document or other article which may constitute evidence that he is a person liable to arrest.

(3) No woman shall in pursuance of this paragraph be searched except by a woman.

Note: See *Review of the Operation of the Prevention of Terrorism (Temporary Provisions) Acts 1974 and 1976 by the Rt. Hon. Lord Shackleton, KG, OBE,* Cmnd. 7324, 1978.

Question

1. "The taking of effective measures to deal with terrorism is not compatible with a free society." Discuss.

CHAPTER 15

NORTHERN IRELAND

Further Reading

De Smith, pp. 629–634; Wade & Phillips, pp. 36–38, 75–76, 84–85, 374–375, 517–519.

The literature on recent problems in Northern Ireland is enormous. Listed below is a selection of some of the more significant materials.

D. P. Barritt and A. Booth, *Orange and Green* (Northern Friends Peace Bd., 2nd ed., 1972); J. C. Beckett, *The Making of Modern Ireland 1603–1923* (Faber, 1966); A. Cocatre-Zilgien, "Les raisons due malaise Nord-Irlandais," (1972) 86 *Rev. du Dr. Public et de la Science Politique en France et a l'Etranger* 91–107; S. Dash, *Justice denied: A Challenge to Lord Widgery's Report on "Bloody Sunday"* (National Council for Civil Liberties, 1972); Martin Dillon and D. Lehane, *Political Murder in Northern Ireland* (Penguin, 1973); R. Evelegh, *Peace-Keeping in a Democratic State: The Lessons of Northern Ireland* (C. Hurst & Co., 1978); M. Farrell, *Northern Ireland: The Orange State* (Pluto Press Ltd., 1976); *Emergency Powers: A Fresh Start* (1972) Fabian tract no. 416; T. Hadden and P. Hillyard, *Justice in Northern Ireland* (Cobden Trust, 1973); Roger H. Hull, *The Irish Triangle: Conflict in Northern Ireland* (Princeton University Press, 1976); H. Jackson, *The Two Irelands* (Minority Rights Group, 1972); F. S. L. Lyons, *Ireland Since the Famine* (Fontana, 2nd ed., 1971); C. Mertens, "Report on Civil and Social Rights in Northern Ireland," (1969) 2 *Human Rights Journal* 507–43; E. T. McGovern, "Internment and Detention in the Light of the European Convention on Human Rights," in *Fundamental Rights* (Bridge, J. W. et. al. ed. 1973), pp. 219–31; J. McGuffin, *Guineapigs* (Penguin, 1970); *ibid, Internment* (Anvil Books, 1973); B. McMahon, *The Impaired Asset: A Legal Commentary on the Report on the Widgery Tribunal* (Cork, 1972); NCCL, *The Special Powers Acts of Northern Ireland: Report of a Commission of Inquiry appointed to examine the purpose and effect of the Civil Authorities (Special Powers) Acts (Northern Ireland) 1922 & 1923* (London, 1936); P. O'Higgins, "The Northern Ireland Act 1972," (1972) 35 MLR 295–9; Claire Palley, *Constitutional Law and Minorities* (Minority Rights Group, 1978); *ibid,* "The Evolution, Disintegration & Eventual Reconstruction of the Northern Ireland Constitution," (1972) 1 *Anglo-American Law Review* 368–476; R. Rose, *Northern Ireland: A Time of Crisis* (MacMillan, 1976); C. Scorer, *The Prevention of Terrorism Acts 1974 and 1976* (National Council for Civil Liberties, 1976); R. J. Spjut, "The Northern Ireland Constitutional Settlement of 1973 and the Loyalist Opposition," 12 *Irish Jurist* (1977) 243–60; P. Taylor, "Reporting Northern Ireland," 7 (6) *Index on Censorship* (1978) 3–11 K. Boyle, *et al., Law and State: The Case of Northern Ireland* (Martin Robertson, 1975).

There have been numerous official reports and inquiries relevant to civil liberties. The following are the most relevant:

Disturbances in Northern Ireland. Report of the Commission appointed by the Governor of Northern Ireland, Cmd. 532, (1969) (HMSO, Belfast); *A Commentary by the Government of Northern Ireland to accompany the Cameron Report,* Cmd. 534 (1969) (HMSO, Belfast); *Report of The Advisory Committee on Police in Northern Ireland,* Cmd. 535 (1969) (HMSO, Belfast); *Report of the enquiry into allegations against the security forces of physical brutality in Northern Ireland arising out of events on the 9th August, 1971. Chairman Sir Edmund Compton, G.C.B., K.B.E.,* Cmnd. 4823 (1971) (HMSO, London); *Report of the Committee of Privy Counsellors appointed to consider authorised procedures for the interrogation of persons suspected of terrorism. Chairman: Lord Parker of Waddington,* Cmnd. 4901 (1972) (HMSO, London); *Government of Northern Ireland. Violence and Civil Disturbances in Northern Ireland in 1969. Report of Tribunal of Inquiry,* Cmd. 566 (1972) (HMSO, Belfast); *Report of the Tribunal appointed to inquire into the events on Sunday, 30th January 1972, which led to loss of life in connection with the procession in Londonderry on that day by The Rt. Hon. Lord Widgery, O.B.E., T.D.,* (1972) H.L. 101 H.C. 220, 1972 (HMSO, London); *Report of the Commission to consider legal procedures to deal with terrorist activities in Northern Ireland. Chairman Lord Diplock,* Cmnd. 5185 (1972) (HMSO, London); *Report of a Committee to consider, in the context of civil liberties and human rights, measures to deal with terrorism in Northern Ireland. Chairman: Lord Gardiner,* Cmnd. 5847 (1975) (HMSO, London); *The Protection of human rights by law in Northern Ireland,* Cmnd. 7009 (1977) (HMSO, London); *Report of The Committee of Inquiry into Police Interrogation Procedures In Northern Ireland,* Cmnd. 7497 (1979) (HMSO, London).

Reference should also be made to the unofficial *Report of an Amnesty International Mission to Northern Ireland (November 28–December 6, 1977)* (London, 1978), as well as to the decision of the European Court of Human Rights in 1978 in the *Case of Ireland* v. *the United Kingdom* (Strasbourg, 1978).

THE CAMERON COMMISSION'S SUMMARY OF CONCLUSIONS ON CAUSES OF DISORDERS

229. Having carried out as full an investigation as lay within our competence we can summarise our conclusions upon the immediate and precipitating causes of the disorders which broke out in Londonderry on 5th October 1968 and continued thereafter both in Londonderry and elsewhere on subsequent dates. These are both general and particular.

(a) **General**

(1) A rising sense of continuing injustice and grievance among large sections of the Catholic population in Northern Ireland, in particular in Londonderry and Dungannon, in respect of (i) inadequacy of housing provision by certain local authorities (ii) unfair methods of allocation of houses built and let by such authorities, in particular, refusals and omissions to adopt a 'points' system in determining priorities and making allocations (iii) misuse in

certain cases of discretionary powers of allocation of houses in order to perpetuate Unionist control of the local authority (paragraphs 128–131 and 139).

(2) Complaints, now well documented in fact, of discrimination in the making of local government appointments, at all levels but especially in senior posts, to the prejudice of non-Unionists and especially Catholic members of the community, in some Unionist controlled authorities (paragraphs 128 and 138).

(3) Complaints, again well documented, in some cases of deliberate manipulation of local government electoral boundaries and in others a refusal to apply for their necessary extension, in order to achieve and maintain Unionist control of local authorities and so to deny to Catholics influence in local government proportionate to their numbers (paragraphs 133–137).

(4) A growing and powerful sense of resentment and frustration among the Catholic population at failure to achieve either acceptance on the part of the Government of any need to investigate these complaints or to provide and enforce a remedy for them (paragraphs 126–147).

(5) Resentment, particularly among Catholics, as to the existence of the Ulster Special Constabulary (the 'B' Specials) as a partisan and paramilitary force recruited exclusively from Protestants (paragraph 145).

(6) Widespread resentment among Catholics in particular at the continuance in force of regulations made under the Special Powers Act, and of the continued presence in the statute book of the Act itself (paragraph 144).

(7) Fears and apprehensions among Protestants of a threat to Unionist domination and control of Government by increase of Catholic population and powers, inflamed in particular by the activities of the Ulster Constitution Defence Committee and the Ulster Protestant Volunteers, provoked strong hostile reaction to civil rights claims as asserted by the Civil Rights Association and later by the People's Democracy which was readily translated into physical violence against Civil Rights demonstrators (paragraphs 148–150 and 216–226).

(b) Particular

(8) There was a strong reaction of popular resentment to the Minister's ban on the route of the proposed Civil Rights march in Londonderry on 5th October 1968 which swelled very considerably the number of persons who ultimately took part in the march. Without this ban the numbers taking part would in all probability have been small and the situation safely handled by available police forces (paragraphs 157–165).

(9) The leadership, organisation and control of the demonstrations in Londonderry on 5th October 1968, and in Newry on 11th January 1969, was ineffective and insufficient to prevent violent or disorderly conduct among certain elements present on these occasions (paragraphs 54 and 118).

(10) There was early infiltration of the Civil Rights Association both centrally and locally by subversive left wing and revolutionary elements which were prepared to use the Civil Rights movement to further their own purposes, and were ready to exploit grievances in order to provoke and foment, and did provoke and foment, disorder and violence in the guise of supporting a non-violent movement (paragraphs 187–189 and 193).

(11) This infiltration was assisted by the declared insistence of the Civil Rights Association that it was non-sectarian and non-political, and its consequent refusal to reject support from whatever quarter it came provided that

support was given and limited to the published aims of the Association (paragraph 187).

(12) What was originally a Belfast students' protest against police action in Londonderry on 5th October and support for the Civil Rights movement was transformed into the People's Democracy—itself an unnecessary adjunct to the already existing and operative Civil Rights Association. People's Democracy provided a means by which politically extreme and militant elements could and did invite and incite civil disorder, with the consequence of polarising and hardening opposition to Civil Rights claims (paragraphs 194–204).

(13) On the other side the deliberate and organised interventions by followers of Major Bunting and the Rev. Dr. Paisley, especially in Armagh, Burntollet and Londonderry, substantially increased the risk of violent disorder on occasions when Civil Rights demonstrations or marches were to take place, were a material contributory cause of the outbreaks of violence which occurred after 5th October, and seriously hampered the police in their task of maintaining law and order, and of protecting members of the public in the exercise of their undoubted legal rights and upon their lawful occasions (paragraphs 222–224).

(14) The police handling of the demonstration in Londonderry on 5th October 1968 was in certain material respects ill co-ordinated and inept. . . .

[*Disturbances in Northern Ireland. Report of the Commission Appointed by the Governor of Northern Ireland*, Cmd. 532, 1969 (Belfast).]

NORTHERN IRELAND CONSTITUTION ACT 1973

PART III

PREVENTION OF RELIGIOUS AND POLITICAL DISCRIMINATION

Discrimination in legislation

17.—(1) Any Measure, any Act of the Parliament of Northern Ireland and any relevant subordinate instrument shall, to the extent that it discriminates against any person or class of persons on the ground of religious belief or political opinion, be void.

(2) In this section "relevant subordinate instrument" means an instrument of a legislative character (including a byelaw) made (whether before or after the coming into force of this section) under any Act of the Parliament of the United Kingdom or the Parliament of Northern Ireland or under any Measure and extending only to Northern Ireland or a part of Northern Ireland.

Special procedure for determining validity of legislation

18.—(1) If it appears to the Secretary of State to be expedient in the public interest that steps should be taken for the speedy decision of any question whether a provision of a Measure, Act of the Parliament of Northern Ireland or relevant subordinate instrument within the meaning of section 17 above is void by virtue of that section, he may recommend to Her Majesty that the question be referred for decision to the Judicial Committee of the Privy Council. . . .

19. Discrimination by public authorities

(1) It shall be unlawful for a Minister of the Crown, a member of the Northern Ireland Executive or other person appointed under section 8 above, the Post Office and any authority or body listed in Schedule 2 to the Parliamentary Commissioner Act 1967, Schedule 1 to the Parliamentary Commissioner Act (Northern Ireland) 1969 or Schedule 1 to the Commissioner for Complaints Act (Northern Ireland) 1969 to discriminate, or aid, induce or incite another to discriminate, in the discharge of functions relating to Northern Ireland against any person or class of persons on the ground of religious belief or political opinion.

(2) The obligation to comply with subsection (1) above is a duty owed to any person who may be adversely affected by a contravention of that subsection, and any breach of that duty is actionable in Northern Ireland accordingly.

(3) Without prejudice to the right of any person apart from this subsection to claim an injunction restraining another from continuing or repeating any act which is unlawful by virtue of subsection (1) above, the plaintiff may in an action in respect of an act alleged to be unlawful as aforesaid claim any such injunction as is mentioned below on the grounds—

    (a) that the act was done by the defendant and was unlawful as aforesaid;

    (b) that the defendant had previously done such unlawful acts of the same kind as, or of a similar kind to, that act; and

    (c) that he is likely, unless restrained by order of the court, to do further acts of the same or of a similar kind;

and the court may, if satisfied as to those grounds and whether or not damages are awarded, grant such injunction as appears to the court to be proper in all the circumstances, being an injunction restraining the defendant from doing, or causing or permitting others to do, further acts of the same or a similar kind.

20. The Standing Advisory Commission on Human Rights

(1) There shall be constituted a Commission to be known as the Standing Advisory Commission on Human Rights (and hereafter in this section referred to as the Advisory Commission) for the purpose of—

    (a) advising the Secretary of State on the adequacy and effectiveness of the law for the time being in force in preventing discrimination on the ground of religious belief or political opinion and in providing redress for persons aggrieved by discrimination on either ground;

    (b) keeping the Secretary of State informed as to the extent to which the persons, authorities and bodies mentioned in section 19 (1) above have prevented discrimination on either ground by persons or bodies not prohibited from discriminating by that law.

(2) The Advisory Commission shall consist of—

    (a) a chairman appointed by the Secretary of State from among the members of the Advisory Commission;

    (b) the chairman of the Northern Ireland Community Relations Commission;

    (c) the Northern Ireland Commissioner for Complaints;

    (d) the Northern Ireland Parliamentary Commissioner for Administration; and

    (e) such other members as may be appointed by the Secretary of State;

and any member mentioned in paragraphs (b) to (d) above is hereafter in this section referred to as an ex-officio member.

(3) An ex-officio member of the Advisory Commission shall on ceasing to hold the office by virtue of which his is a member of the Commission cease to be a member of the Commission and, if he is the chairman, to be chairman.

(4) The members of the Advisory Commission, other than the ex-officio members, shall hold and vacate office in accordance with the terms of their respective appointments and shall, on ceasing to hold office, be eligible for reappointment, but any such member may at any time by notice addressed to the Secretary of State resign his office.

(5) The Secretary of State may out of moneys provided by Parliament pay the members of the Advisory Commission, other than the ex-officio members, such remuneration and such allowances as may be determined by the Secretary of State with the consent of the Minister for the Civil Service.

(6) The Secretary of State shall provide the Advisory Commission with such officers and such accommodation as may be appropriate.

(7) The Advisory Commission shall make annual reports to the Secretary of State with respect to the exercise of their functions and make copies of those reports available to the Assembly; and the Secretary of State shall lay any such report before each House of Parliament.

21. Unlawful oaths, undertakings and declarations

(1) Subject to subsections (2) and (3) below, it shall be unlawful for an authority or body to which this section applies to require any person to take an oath, make an undertaking in lieu of an oath or make a declaration, as a condition of his being appointed to or acting as a member of that authority or body, or of serving with or being employed under that authority or body.

(2) Subsection (1) above shall not prevent a person being required to take an oath or make an undertaking or a declaration which is specifically required or authorised to be taken or made—

(a) by the law in force immediately before the coming into force of that subsection; or

(b) by or under this Act or by a subsequent Measure for the time being in force;

but, except as aforesaid, has effect notwithstanding anything in any enactment, any Measure or any instrument made under an enactment or a Measure.

(3) Subsection (1) above shall not prevent a person being required to make a declaration of acceptance of office or a declaration that he is qualified to act, serve or be employed, or not disqualified from acting, serving or being employed, in any capacity.

(4) This section applies to the Assembly and to any authority or body listed in Schedule 1 to the Parliamentary Commissioner Act (Northern Ireland) 1969 or Schedule 1 to the Commissioner for complaints Act (Northern Ireland) 1969.

(5) Subsections (1) to (3) above shall apply with the necessary modifications to a member of the Northern Ireland Executive or other person appointed under section 8 above as they apply to any such authority or body.

(6) Subsections (2) and (3) of section 19 above shall apply in relation to subsection (1) above as they apply in relation to subsection (1) of that section.

Note: See also Fair Employment (Northern Ireland) Act 1976

NORTHERN IRELAND (EMERGENCY PROVISIONS) ACT 1978

Note: In force 1st June 1978

PART 1

SCHEDULED OFFENCES

Preliminary enquiries, bail and young persons in custody

1. Preliminary enquiry into scheduled offences

(1) Where in any proceedings before a magistrates' court for a scheduled offence (not being an extra-territorial offence as defined in section 1 (3) of the Criminal Jurisdiction Act 1975) the prosecutor requests the court to conduct a preliminary enquiry into the offence under the Criminal Procedure (Committal for Trial) Act (Northern Ireland) 1968, the court shall, notwithstanding anything in section 1 of that Act of 1968, conduct a preliminary enquiry into the offence unless the court is of opinion that in the interests of justice a preliminary investigation should be conducted into the offence under Part VI of the Magistrates' Courts Act (Northern Ireland) 1964.

(2) Where in any proceedings a person charged with a scheduled offence is also charged with another offence which is not a scheduled offence, that other offence shall be treated as a scheduled offence for the purposes of subsection (1) above.

2. Limitation of power to grant bail in case of scheduled offences

(1) Subject to the provisions of this section, a person to whom this section applies shall not be admitted to bail except—
  (*a*) by a judge of the Supreme Court; or
  (*b*) by the judge of the court of trial, on adjourning the trial of a person so charged.

(2) A judge shall not admit any such person to bail unless he is satisfied that the applicant—
  (*a*) will comply with the conditions on which he is admitted to bail; and
  (*b*) will not interfere with any witness; and
  (*c*) will not commit any offence while he is on bail.

(3) Without prejudice to any other power to impose conditions on admission to bail, a judge may impose such conditions on admitting a person to bail under this section as appear to him to be likely to result in that person's appearance at the time and place required or to be necessary in the interests of justice or for the prevention of crime.

(4) Nothing in this section shall prejudice any right of appeal against the refusal of a judge to grant bail.

(5) This section applies, subject to subsection (6) below, to any person—
  (*a*) who is charged with a scheduled offence; and
  (*b*) who has attained the age of 14; and
  (*c*) who is not a serving member of any of Her Majesty's regular naval, military or air forces.

(6) This section does not apply to a person charged with a scheduled offence—

    (a) which is being tried summarily; or

    (b) which the Director of Public Prosecutions for Northern Ireland certifies is in his opinion suitable to be tried summarily.

3. Legal aid to applicants for bail in case of scheduled offences

(1) Where it appears to a judge of the Supreme Court—

    (a) that a person charged with a scheduled offence intends to apply to be admitted to bail; and

    (b) that it is desirable in the interests of justice that that person should have legal aid but that he has not sufficient means to enable him to obtain that aid,

the judge may assign to him a solicitor and counsel, or counsel only, in the application for bail.

(2) If, on a question of granting a person free legal aid under this section, there is a doubt whether his means are sufficient to enable him to obtain legal aid or whether it is desirable in the interests of justice that he should have free legal aid, the doubt shall be resolved in favour of granting him free legal aid.

4. Holding in custody of young persons charged with scheduled offences

(1) Where a person to whom this section applies has been remanded or committed for trial as respects a scheduled offence and is not released on bail, he may—

    (a) notwithstanding the provisions of any enactment, and

    (b) whether or not he was remanded or committed for trial at a time when this section was not in force,

be held in custody in such prison or other place as may be specified in a direction given by the Secretary of State under this section (in this section and section 5 below referred to as "a direction").

(2) The Secretary of State may give a direction in respect of a person to whom this section applies if he considers that it is necessary, in order to prevent his escape or to ensure his safety or the safety of others, to make special arrangements as to the place at which that person is to be held in custody while on remand or while committed for trial.

(3) A direction may be given by the Secretary of State at any time after the young person to whom it relates has been charged with a scheduled offence, and may be varied or revoked by a further direction.

(4) This section applies to any young person charged with a scheduled offence.

(5) In this section "young person" means a person who has attained the age of 14 and is under the age of 17.

5. Directions under s. 4

(1) A direction shall, if it has not previously ceased to have effect, cease to have effect at the expiration of such period as may be specified in the direction (being a period not exceeding two months beginning with the date of the direction), unless continued in force by a further direction.

(2) Where, by virtue of a direction, a young person is held in custody in a prison or other place and the direction ceases to have effect (whether or not by

reason of the expiry or cesser of section 4 above) it shall be lawful for him to continue to be held in custody in that prison or place until arrangements can be made for him to be held in custody in accordance with the law then applicable to his case.

(3) Nothing in subsection (2) above shall be taken to make lawful the holding in custody of any person who would, disregarding that subsection, be entitled to be released from custody.

Court and mode of trial

6. Court of trial on indictment of scheduled offences

(1) A trial on indictment of a scheduled offence shall be held only at the Belfast City Commission.

(2) A magistrates' court which commits a person for trial on indictment for a scheduled offence or two or more offences which are or include scheduled offences shall commit him for trial to the Belfast City Commission and section 47 of the Magistrates' Courts Act (Northern Ireland) 1964 (committal to assize or county court) shall have effect accordingly.

(3) A county court judge may at any time, at the request of the Lord Chief Justice of Northern Ireland, sit and act as a judge at the Belfast City Commission for the trial on indictment of a scheduled offence, or for two or more such trials, and while so sitting and acting shall have all the jurisdiction, powers and privileges of a High Court judge included in the Commission, so far as concerns any such trial.

(4) A county court judge requested to sit and act as aforesaid for a period of time may, notwithstanding the expiry of that period, attend at the Belfast City Commission for the purpose of continuing to deal with, giving judgment in or dealing with any ancillary matter relating to, any case which may have begun before him when sitting as a judge at the Commission and shall have the same jurisdiction, powers and privileges as under subsection (3) above.

7. Mode of trial on indictment of scheduled offences

(1) A trial on indictment of a scheduled offence shall be conducted by the court without a jury.

(2) The court trying a scheduled offence on indictment under this section shall have all the powers, authorities and jurisdiction which the court would have had if it had been sitting with a jury, including power to determine any question and to make any finding which would, apart from this section, be required to be determined or made by a jury, and references in any enactment to a jury or the verdict or finding of a jury shall be construed accordingly in relation to a trial under this section.

(3) Where separate counts of an indictment allege a scheduled offence and an offence which is not a scheduled offence, the trial on indictment shall, without prejudice to section 5 of the Indictments Act (Northern Ireland) 1945 (orders for amendment of indictment, separate trial and postponement of trial), be conducted as if all the offences alleged in the indictment were scheduled offences.

(4) Without prejudice to subsection (2) above, where the court trying a scheduled offence on indictment—

(a) is not satisfiied that the accused is guilty of that offence but

(b) is satisfied that he is guilty of some other offence which is not a

scheduled offence, but of which a jury could have found him guilty on a trial for the scheduled offence,
the court may convict him of that other offence.

(5) Where the court trying a scheduled offence convicts the accused of that or some other offence, then, without prejudice to its power apart from this subsection to give a judgment, it shall, at the time of conviction or as soon as practicable thereafter, give a judgment stating the reasons for the conviction.

(6) A person convicted of any offence on a trial under this section without a jury may, notwithstanding anything in section 8 of the Criminal Appeal (Northern Ireland) Act 1968, appeal to the Court of Criminal Appeal under that section—

(a) against his conviction, on any ground, without the leave of the Court of Criminal Appeal or a certificate of the judge of the court of trial; and

(b) against sentence passed on conviction, without that leave, unless the sentence is one fixed by law.

(7) Where a person is so convicted, the time for giving notice of appeal under subsection (1) of section 20 of that Act of 1968 shall run from the date of judgment, if later than the date from which it would run under that subsection.

Evidence, onus of proof and treatment of convicted young persons

8. Admissions by persons charged with scheduled offences

(1) In any criminal proceedings for a scheduled offence, or two or more offences which are or include scheduled offences, a statement made by the accused may be given in evidence by the prosecution in so far as—

(a) it is relevant to any matter in issue in the proceedings; and

(b) it is not excluded by the court in pursuance of subsection (2) below.

(2) If, in any such proceedings where the prosecution proposes to give in evidence a statement made by the accused, prima facie evidence is adduced that the accused was subjected to torture or to inhuman or degrading treatment in order to induce him to make the statement, the court shall, unless the prosecution satisfies it that the statement was not so obtained—

(a) exclude the statement, or

(b) if the statement has been received in evidence, either—

(i) continue the trial disregarding the statement; or

(ii) direct that the trial shall be restarted before a differently constituted court (before which the statement in question shall be inadmissible).

(3) This section does not apply to a summary trial.

9. Onus of proof in relation to offences of possession

(1) Where a person is charged with possessing a proscribed article in such circumstances as to constitute an offence to which this section applies and it is proved that at the time of the alleged offence—

(a) he and that article were both present in any premises; or

(b) the article was in premises of which he was the occupier or which he habitually used otherwise than as a member of the public,

the court may accept the fact proved as sufficient evidence of his possessing (and, if relevant, knowingly possessing) that article at that time unless it is further proved that he did not at that time know of its presence in the premises in question, or, if he did know, that he had no control over it.

(2) This section applies to vessels, aircraft and vehicles as it applies to premises.

(3) In this section "proscribed article" means an explosive, firearm, ammunition, substance or other thing (being a thing possession of which is an offence under one of the enactments mentioned in subsection (4) below).

(4) This section applies to scheduled offences under the following enactments, that is to say—

The Explosive Substances Act 1883

Section 3, so far as relating to subsection (1) (b) thereof (possessing explosive with intent to endanger life or cause serious damage to property).

Section 4 (possessing explosive in suspicious circumstances).

The Firearms Act (Northern Ireland) 1969

Section 1 (possessing firearm or ammunition without, or otherwise than as authorised by, a firearm certificate).

Section 4 (possessing machine gun, or weapon discharging, or ammunition containing, noxious substance).

Section 14 (possessing firearm or ammunition with intent to endanger life or cause serious damage to property).

Section 15 (2) (possessing firearm or imitation firearm at time of committing, or being arrested for, a specified offence).

Section 19 (1) to (3) (possession of a firearm or ammunition by a person who has been sentenced to imprisonment, etc.).

Section 19A (possessing firearm or ammunition in suspicious circumstances).

The Protection of the Person and Property Act (Northern Ireland) 1969

Section 2 (possessing petrol bomb, etc., in suspicious circumstances).

(5) This section does not apply to a summary trial.

10. Treatment of young persons convicted of scheduled offences

(1) Section 73 (2) of the Children and Young Persons Act (Northern Ireland) 1968 (under which a court may sentence a child or young person convicted on indictment of an offence punishable in the case of an adult with imprisonment for fourteen years or more to detention for a period specified in the sentence) shall have effect in relation to a young person convicted of a scheduled offence committed while this subsection is in force with the substitution of the word "five" for the word "fourteen".

(2) Subsection (3) of section 74 of that Act (under which the maximum length of the term or the aggregate of the terms for which a person may be committed in custody to a remand home under section 74 (1) (e) is one month) shall have effect in relation to a young person found guilty of a scheduled offence committed while this subsection is in force with the substitution of the words "six months" for the words "one month".

PART II

POWERS OF ARREST, DETENTION, SEARCH AND SEIZURE, ETC.

11. Arrest of terrorists

(1) Any constable may arrest without warrant any person whom he suspects of being a terrorist.

(2) For the purpose of arresting a person under this section a constable may enter and search any premises or other place where that person is or where the constable suspects him of being.

(3) A person arrested under this section shall not be detained in right of the arrest for more than seventy-two hours after the arrest, and section 132 of the Magistrates' Courts Act (Northern Ireland) 1964 and section 50 (3) of the Children and Young Persons Act (Northern Ireland) 1968 (requirement to bring arrested person before a magistrates' court not later than forty-eight hours after his arrest) shall not apply to any such person.

(4) Where a person is arrested under this section, an officer of the Royal Ulster Constabulary not below the rank of chief inspector may order him to be photographed and to have his finger prints and palm prints taken by a constable, and a constable may use such reasonable force as may be necessary for that purpose.

15. Power to search for munitions and radio transmitters

(1) Any member of Her Majesty's forces on duty or any constable may enter any premises or other place other than a dwelling-house for the purpose of ascertaining—

(a) whether there are any munitions unlawfully at that place; or

(b) whether there is a transmitter at that place;

and may search the place for any munitions or transmitter with a view to exercising the powers conferred by subsection (4) below.

(2) Any member of Her Majesty's forces on duty authorised by a commissioned officer of those forces or any constable authorised by an officer of the Royal Ulster Constabulary not below the rank of chief inspector may enter any dwelling-house in which it is suspected that there are unlawfully any munitions or that there is a transmitter and may search it for any munitions or transmitter with a view to exercising the said powers.

(3) Any member of Her Majesty's forces on duty or any constable may—

(a) stop any person in any public place and, with a view to exercising the said powers, search him for the purpose of ascertaining whether he has any munitions unlawfully with him or any transmitter with him; and

(b) with a view to exercising the said powers, search any person not in a public place whom he suspects of having any munitions unlawfully with him or any transmitter with him.

(4) A member of Her Majesty's forces or a constable—

(a) authorised to search any premises or other place or any person under this Act, may seize any munitions found in the course of the search unless it appears to the person so authorised that the munitions are being, have been and will be used only for a lawful purpose and may retain and, if necessary, destroy them;

(b) authorised to search any premises or other place or any person, may seize any transmitter found in the course of the search unless it appears to the person so authorised that the transmitter has been, is being and is likely to be used only lawfully and may retain it.

(5) In this section—

"munitions" means—

(a) explosives, explosive substances, firearms and ammunition; and

(b) anything used or capable of being used in the manufacture of any explosive, explosive substance, firearm or ammunition;

"transmitter" means any apparatus for wireless telegraphy designed or adapted for emission, as opposed to reception, and includes part of any such apparatus;

"wireless telegraphy" has the same meaning as in section 19 (1) of the Wireless Telegraphy Act 1949.

16. Powers of explosives inspectors

(1) An inspector appointed under section 53 of the Explosives Act 1875 may, for the purpose of ascertaining whether there is unlawfully in any premises or other place other than a dwelling-house any explosive or explosive substance, enter that place and search it with a view to exercising the powers conferred by subsection (3) below.

(2) Any such inspector may stop any person in a public place and search him for the purpose of ascertaining whether he has any explosive or explosive substance unlawfully with him with a view to exercising the said powers.

(3) Any such inspector may seize any explosive or explosive substance found in the course of a search under this section unless it appears to him that it is being, has been and will be used only for a lawful purpose and may retain and, if necessary, destroy it.

17. Entry to search for persons unlawfully detained

(1) Where any person is believed to be unlawfully detained in such circumstances that his life is in danger, any member of Her Majesty's forces on duty or any constable may, subject to subsection (2) below, enter any premises or other place for the purpose of ascertaining whether that person is so detained there.

(2) A dwelling-house may be entered in pursuance of subsection (1) above—

(a) by a member of Her Majesty's forces, only when authorised to do so by a commissioned officer of those forces; and

(b) by a constable, only when authorised to do so by an officer of the Royal Ulster Constabulary not below the rank of chief inspector.

18. Power to stop and question

(1) Any member of Her Majesty's forces on duty or any constable may stop and question any person for the purpose of ascertaining—

(a) that person's identity and movements;

(b) what he knows concerning any recent explosion or any other incident endangering life or concerning any person killed or injured in any such explosion or incident; or

(c) any one or more of the matters referred to in paragraphs (a) and (b) above.

(2) Any person who—
  (a) fails to stop when required to do so under this section, or
  (b) refuses to answer, or fails to answer to the best of his knowledge and
      ability, any question addressed to him under this section,
shall be liable on summary conviction to imprisonment for a term not exceeding six months or to a fine not exceeding £400, or both.

19. General powers of entry and interference with rights of property and with highways

(1) Any member of Her Majesty's forces on duty or any constable may enter any premises or other place—
  (a) if he considers it necessary to do so in the course of operations for the
      preservation of the peace or the maintenance of order; or
  (b) if authorised to do so by or on behalf of the Secretary of State.

(2) Any member of Her Majesty's forces on duty, any constable or any person specifically authorised to do so by or on behalf of the Secretary of State may, if authorised to do so by or on behalf of the Secretary of State—
  (a) take possession of any land or other property;
  (b) take steps to place buildings or other structures in a state of defence;
  (c) detain any property or cause it to be destroyed or moved;
  (d) do any other act interfering with any public right or with any private
      rights of property, including carrying out any works on any land of
      which possession has been taken under this subsection.

(3) Any member of Her Majesty's forces on duty, any constable or any person specifically authorised to do so by or on behalf of the Secretary of State may, so far as he considers it immediately necessary for the preservation of the peace or the maintenace of order—
  (a) wholly or partly close a highway or divert or otherwise interfere with a
      highway or the use of a highway; or
  (b) prohibit or restrict the exercise of any right of way or the use of any
      waterway.

(4) Any person who, without lawful authority or reasonable excuse (the proof of which lies on him), interferes with works executed, or any apparatus, equipment or any other thing used, in or in connection with the exercise of powers conferred by this section, shall be liable on summary conviction to imprisonment for a term not exceeding six months or to a fine not exceeding £400, or both.

(5) Any authorisation to exercise any powers under any provision of this section may authorise the exercise of all those powers, or powers of any class or a particular power specified, either by all persons by whom they are capable of being exercised or by persons of any class or a particular person specified.

20. Supplementary provisions

(1) Any power conferred by this Part of this Act—
  (a) to enter any premises or other place includes power to enter any vessel,
      aircraft or vehicle;
  (b) to search any premises or other place includes power to stop and search
      any vehicle or vessel or any aircraft which is not airborne and search
      any container;
and in this Part of this Act references to any premises or place shall be construed accordingly.

(2) In this Part of this Act references to a dwelling-house includes references to a vessel or vehicle which is habitually stationary and used as a dwelling.

(3) Any power conferred by this Part of this Act to enter any place, vessel, aircraft or vehicle shall be exercisable, if need be, by force.

(4) Any power conferred by virtue of this section to search a vehicle or vessel shall, in the case of a vehicle or vessel which cannot be conveniently or thoroughly searched at the place where it is, include power to take it or cause it to be taken to any place for the purpose of carrying out the search.

(5) Any power conferred by virtue of this section to search any vessel, air-craft vehicle or container includes power to examine it.

(6) Any power conferred by this Part of this Act to stop any person includes power to stop a vessel or vehicle or an aircraft which is not airborne.

(7) Any person who, when required by virtue of this section to stop a vessel or vehicle or any aircraft which is not airborne, fails to do so shall be liable on summary conviction to imprisonment to a term not exceeding six months or to a fine not exceeding £400, or both.

(8) A member of Her Majesty's forces exercising any power conferred by this Part of this Act when he is not in uniform shall, if so requested by any person at or about the time of exercising that power, produce to that person documentary evidence that he is such a member.

(9) The Documentary Evidence Act 1868 shall apply to any authorisation given in writing under this Part of this Act by or on behalf of the Secretary of State as it applies to any order made by him.

PART III

OFFENCES AGAINST PUBLIC SECURITY AND PUBLIC ORDER

21. Proscribed organisations

(1) Subject to subsection (7) below, any person who—
   (a) belongs or professes to belong to a proscribed organisation; or
   (b) solicits or invites financial or other support for a proscribed organisa-tion, or knowingly makes or receives any contribution in money or otherwise to the resources of a proscribed organisation; or
   (c) solicits or invites any person to become a member of a proscribed organisation or to carry out on behalf of a proscribed organisation orders or directions given, or requests made, by a member of that organisation,
shall be liable on summary conviction to imprisonment for a term not exceed-ing six months or to a fine not exceeding £400, or both, and on conviction on indictment to imprisonment for a term not exceeding ten years or to a fine, or both.

(2) The court by or before which a person is convicted of an offence under this section may order the forfeiture of any money or other property which at the time of the offence he had in his possession or under his control for the use or benefit of the proscribed organisation.

(3) The organisations specified in Schedule 2 to this Act are proscribed organisations for the purposes of this section; and any organisation which passes under a name mentioned in that Schedule shall be treated as pro-scribed, whatever relationship (if any) it has to any other organisation of the same name.

(4) The Secretary of State may by order add to Schedule 2 to this Act any organisation that appears to him to be concerned in terrorism or in promoting or encouraging it.

(5) The Secretary of State may also by order remove an organisation from Schedule 2 to this Act.

(6) The possession by a person of a document—

    (a) addressed to him as a member of a proscribed organisation; or

    (b) relating or purporting to relate to the affairs of a proscribed organisation; or

    (c) emanating or purporting to emanate from a proscribed organisation or officer of a proscribed organisation,

shall be evidence of that person belonging to the organisation at the time when he had the document in his possession.

(7) A person belonging to a proscribed organisation shall—

    (a) if the organisation is a proscribed organisation by virtue of an order under subsection (4) above; or

    (b) if this section has ceased to be in force but has been subsequently brought into force by an order under section 33 (3) below,

not be guilty of an offence under this section by reason of belonging to the organisation if he has not after the coming into force of the order under subsection (4) above or the coming into force again of this section, as the case may be, taken part in any activities of the organisation.

(8) Subsection (7) above shall apply in relation to a person belonging to the Red Hand Commando, the Ulster Freedom Fighters or the Ulster Volunteer Force as if the organisation were proscribed by virtue of an order under subsection (4) above with the substitution, in subsection (7), for the reference to the coming into force of such an order of a reference—

    (a) as respects a person belonging to the Red Hand Commando or the Ulster Freedom Fighters, to 12th November 1973;

    (b) as respects a person belonging to the Ulster Volunteer Force, to 4th October 1975.

22. Unlawful collection, etc. of information

(1) No person shall, without lawful authority or reasonable excuse (the proof of which lies on him)—

    (a) collect, record, publish, communicate or attempt to elicit any information with respect to any person to whom this paragraph applies which is of such a nature as is likely to be useful to terrorists;

    (b) collect or record any information which is of such a nature as is likely to be useful to terrorists in planning or carrying out any act of violence; or

    (c) have in his possession any record of or document containing any such information as is mentioned in paragraph (a) or (b) above.

(2) Subsection (1) (a) above applies to any of the following persons, that is to say—

    (a) any constable or member of Her Majesty's forces;

    (b) any person holding judicial office;

    (c) any officer of any court; and

    (d) any person employed for the whole of his time in the prison service in Northern Ireland.

(3) In subsection (1) above any reference to recording information includes a reference to recording it by means of photography or by any other means.

(4) If any person contravenes this section, he shall be liable—

(a) on summary conviction, to imprisonment for a term not exceeding six months or to a fine not exceeding £400, or both;

(b) on conviction on indictment, to imprisonment for a term not exceeding ten years or a fine, or both.

(5) The court by or before which a person is convicted of an offence under this section may order the forfeiture of any record or document mentioned in subsection (1) above which is found in his possession.

(6) Without prejudice to section 33 of the Interpretation Act 1889 (offences under two or more laws), nothing in this section shall derogate from the operation of the Official Secrets Act 1911 and 1920.

23. Training in making or use of firearms, explosives or explosive substances

(1) Subject to subsection (2) below, any person who instructs or trains another or receives instruction or training in the making or use of firearms, explosives or explosive substances shall be liable—

(a) on summary conviction, to imprisonment for a term not exceeding six months or to a fine not exceeding £400, or both;

(b) on conviction on indictment, to imprisonment for a term not exceeding ten years or to a fine, or both.

(2) In any prosecution for an offence under this section it shall be a defence for the person charged to prove that the instruction or training was given or received with lawful authority or for industrial, agricultural or sporting purposes only or otherwise with good reason.

(3) The court by or before which a person is convicted of an offence under this section may order the forfeiture of any thing which appears to the court to have been in his possession for purposes connected with the offence.

(4) Without prejudice to section 33 of the Interpretation Act 1889 (offences under two or more laws), nothing in this section shall derogate from the operation of the Unlawful Drilling Act 1819.

24. Failure to disperse when required to do so

(1) Where any commissioned officer of Her Majesty's forces or any officer of the Royal Ulster Constabulary not below the rank of chief inspector is of opinion that any assembly of three or more persons—

(a) may lead to a breach of the peace or public disorder; or

(b) may make undue demands on the police or Her Majesty's forces,

he, or any member of those forces on duty or any constable, may order the person constituting the aseembly to disperse forthwith.

(2) Where an order is given under this section with respect to an assembly, any person who thereafter joins or remains in the assembly or otherwise fails to comply with the order shall be liable on summary conviction to imprisonment for a term not exceeding six months or to a fine not exceeding £400, or both.

25. Dressing or behaving in a public place like a member of a proscribed organisation

Any person who in a public place dresses or behaves in such a way as to arouse reasonable apprehension that he is a member of a proscribed organisation shall be liable on summary conviction to imprisonment for a term not exceeding six months or to a fine not exceeding £400, or both.

26. Wearing of hoods, etc. in public places

Any person who, without lawful authority or reasonable excuse (the proof of which lies on him), wears in a public place or in the curtilage of a dwelling-house (other than one in which he is residing) any hood, mask or other article whatsoever made, adapted or used for concealing the identity or features shall be liable on summary conviction to imprisonment for a term not exceeding six months or to a fine not exceeding £400, or both.

PART VI

MISCELLANEOUS AND GENERAL

27. Supplementary regulations for preserving the peace, etc.

(1) The Secretary of State may by regulations make provision additional to the foregoing provisions of this Act for promoting the preservation of the peace and the maintenance of order.

(2) Any person contravening or failing to comply with the provisions of any regulations under this section or any instrument or directions under any such regulations shall be liable on summary conviction to imprisonment for a term not exceeding six months or to a fine not exceeding £400, or both.

(3) The regulations contained in Schedule 3 to this Act shall be deemed to have been made under this section and to have been approved in draft by each House of Parliament, and may be varied or revoked accordingly.

28. Compensation

(1) Where under this Act any real or personal property is taken, occupied, destroyed or damaged, or any other act is done interfering with private rights of property, compensation shall, subject to the provisions of this section, be payable by the Secretary of State.

(2) Any question as to compensation under this section shall, in default of agreement, be referred for determination to the county court or an arbitrator to be appointed by that court.

(3) The procedure for determining any question referred under subsection (2) above shall be that prescribed by rules made by the Lord Chief Justice of Northern Ireland after consultation with the Secretary of State.

(4) Nothing in this section shall be construed as giving to any person by whom an offence has been committed any right to compensation in respect of property taken, occupied, destroyed or damaged or in respect of any other act done in connection with the offence.

29. Restriction of prosecutions

(1) A prosecution shall not be instituted in respect of any offence under this Act except by or with the consent of the Director of Public Prosecutions for Northern Ireland.

(2) Article 7 of the Prosecution of Offences (Northern Ireland) Order 1972 shall apply in relation to any offence under this Act as if subsection (1) above were a consent provision within the meaning of that Article.

30. The scheduled offences

(1) In this Act "scheduled offence" means an offence specified in Part 1 or Part III of Schedule 4 to this Act, subject, however, to any relevant note contained in the said Part 1.

(2) Part II of that Schedule shall have effect with respect to offences related to those specified in Part 1 of that Schedule.

(3) The Secretary of State may by order amend Parts I and II of that Schedule (whether by adding an offence to, or removing an offence from, either of those Parts, or otherwise).

31. Interpretation

(1) In this Act, except so far as the context otherwise requires—

"constable" includes any member of the Royal Naval, Military or Air Force Police;

"dwelling-house" means any building or part of a building used as a dwelling;

"enactment" includes an enactment of the Parliament of Northern Ireland and a Measure of the Northern Ireland Assembly;

"explosive" means any article or substance manufactured for the purpose of producing a practical effect by explosion;

"explosive substance" means any substance for the time bring specified in regulations made under section 3 of the Explosives Act (Northern Ireland) 1970;

"firearm" includes an air gun or air pistol;

"proscribed organisation" means an organisation for the time being specified in Schedule 2 to this Act, including an organisation which is to be treated as a proscribed organisation by virtue of section 21 (3) above;

"public place" means a place to which for the time being members of the public have or are permitted to have access, whether on payment or otherwise;

"scheduled offence" has the meaning ascribed to it by section 30 above;

"terrorism" means the use of violence for political ends and includes any use of violence for the purpose of putting the public or any section of the public in fear;

"terrorist" means a person who is or has been concerned in the commission or attempted commission of any act of terrorism or in directing, organising or training persons for the purpose of terrorism;

"vehicle" includes a hovercraft.

(2) Any reference in this Act, except so far as the context otherwise requires, to an enactment shall be construed as a reference to that enactment as amended, applied or extended by or under any other enactment, including this Act.

(3) It is hereby declared that in applying section 38 (1) of the Interpretation Act 1889 (effect of repeal and re-enactment) for the construction of references in this Act to other Acts or enactments, account is to be taken of repeal and re-enactment by a Measure of the Northern Ireland Assembly or an Order in Council.

SCHEDULE 1

DETENTION OF TERRORISTS

Advisers

1. The Secretary of State shall for the purposes of this Act appoint such number of Advisers as he may determine to advise him on matters concerning the detention and release of terrorists.

2. An Adviser shall be a person who holds or has held judicial office in any part of the United Kingdom or is a barrister, advocate or solicitor, in each case of not less than ten years' standing in any part of the United Kingdom.

3.—(1) An Adviser shall hold and vacate his office in accordance with the terms of his appointment and shall, on ceasing to hold office, be eligible for reappointment.

(2) An Adviser may at any time by notice in writing to the Secretary of State resign his office.

(3) The Secretary of State may pay to the Advisers such remuneration and allowances as he may determine.

Interim Custody Orders

4.—(1) Where it appears to the Secretary of State that there are grounds for suspecting that a person has been concerned—

(*a*) in the commission or attempted commission of any act of terrorism; or

(*b*) in directing, organising or training persons for the purpose of terrorism,

the Secretary of State may make an interim custody order for the temporary detention of that person.

(2) An interim custody order shall be signed by the Secretary of State or a Minister of State or Under Secretary of State.

5.—(1) The Secretary of State may, at any time before the expiration of the period of fourteen days following the date of an interim custody order, refer the case to an Adviser and, unless the case is so referred, the order shall cease to have effect at the expiration of that period.

(2) A reference to an Adviser under this paragraph shall be by notice in writing signed on behalf of the Secretary of State and a copy of the notice shall be sent to the person detained.

Reference to an Adviser

6.—(1) As soon as possible after a case is referred to an Adviser under paragraph 5 above, the person detained shall be served with a statement in writing as to the nature of the terrorist activities of which he is suspected.

(2) A person detained may, within seven days following the date on which he receives any such statement as is mentioned in sub-paragraph (1) above, send to the Secretary of State—

(*a*) written representations concerning his case; and

(*b*) a written request that he be seen personally by an Adviser;

and the Secretary of State shall send a copy of such representations or request to the Adviser concerned.

(3) The Secretary of State may pay any reasonable costs or expenses incurred by a person detained in obtaining legal advice or legal assistance in

connection with the preparation of any representations he may make concerning his case.

7.—(1) Where the case of a person detained under an interim custody order is referred to an Adviser, he shall consider it and report the Secretary of State whether or not in his opinion—

(a) the person detained has been concerned in terrorist activities; and

(b) the detention of that person is necessary for the protection of the public.

(2) In considering any case referred to him an Adviser shall have regard to any information (whether oral or in writing) which is made available to, or obtained by, him and to any representations (whether oral or in writing) made by the person detained.

(3) No person shall be present during the consideration by an Adviser of the case of any person referred to him, except—

(a) any person who for the time being is being seen by the Adviser;

(b) any assistant to the Adviser; and

(c) any person who is present in the interests of security.

(4) The Secretary of State may, at the request of an Adviser, pay any reasonable expenses incurred by any person in connection with a reference to the Adviser.

Detention Orders

8.—(1) After receiving a report made by an Adviser under paragraph 7 (1) above, the Secretary of State shall consider the case of the person to whom it relates and, if he is satisfied—

(a) that that person has been concerned in the commission or attempted commission of any act of terrorism, or in directing, organising or training persons for the purpose of terrorism; and

(b) that the detention of that person is necessary for the protection of the public,

the Secretary of State may make a detention order for the detention of that person.

(2) If, on considering any case under sub-paragraph (1) above, the Secretary of State is not satisfied as mentioned in that sub-paragraph, he shall direct the release of the person concerned.

(3) Subject to sub-paragraphs (4) and (5) below, where—

(a) a person is detained under an interim custody order; and

(b) a detention order is not made in respect of that person within the period of seven weeks following the date of the interim custody order,

the interim custody order shall cease to have effect.

(4) The Secretary of State may, where a person is required to be detained under an interim custody order, give a direction in writing extending the period of seven weeks mentioned in sub-paragraph (3) above (or that period as extended under this sub-paragraph) for a further period of one week if it is stated in the direction that the report of the Adviser in relation to that person's case has not been received before the sixth day immediately preceding the day on which the interim custody order would, but for the direction, cease to have effect.

(5) Not more than three directions under sub-paragraph (4) above shall be given in respect of any one interim custody order.

(6) A detention order shall be signed by the Secretary of State, and a direction under sub-paragraph (4) above shall be signed by the Secretary of State or a Minister of State or Under Secretary of State.

Supplemental

9.—(1) The Secretary of State may at any time refer the case of a person detained under a detention order to an Adviser and, if so requested in writing in accordance with sub-paragraph (2) below by a person so detained, shall do so within fourteen days beginning with the receipt of the request.

(2) A person detained under a detention order shall not be entitled to make a request for the purpose of sub-paragraph (1) above—

(a) before the expiration of the period of one year beginning with the date of the detention order; or

(b) within a period of six months from the date of the last notification under sub-paragraph (5) below.

(3) On any reference under this paragraph, an Adviser shall consider the case and report to the Secretary of State whether or not the person's continued detention is necessary for the protection of the public.

(4) Paragraphs 6 (3) and 7 (2) to (4) above shall apply for the purposes of a reference under this paragraph as they apply for the purposes of a reference under paragraph 5 above.

(5) Where a case is referred to an Adviser in consequence of a request made in accordance with this paragraph, the Secretary of State shall, after receiving the report of the Adviser, reconsider the case of the person to whom it relates and, if he decides not to release that person, shall notify him of his decision.

(6) A notification under sub-paragraph (5) above shall be by notice in writing and signed by the Secretary of State.

10.—(1) The Secretary of State may, as respects a person detained under an interim custody order—

(a) direct his discharge unconditionally; or

(b) direct his release (whether or not subject to conditions) for a specified period.

(2) The Secretary of State may, as respects a person detained under a detention order,—

(a) direct his discharge unconditionally; or

(b) direct his release subject to conditions or for a specified period, or both.

(3) The Secretary of State may recall to detention a person released under sub-paragraph (1) (b) or (2) (b) above and a person so recalled may be detained under the original interim custody or detention order, as the case may be.

(4) Where a person is released under sub-paragraph (1) (b) above, any period during which he is not in detention shall be left out of account for the purposes of paragraphs 5 (1), 6 (2) and 8 (3) above.

11.—(1) A person required to be detained under an interim custody order or a detention order may be detained in a prison or in some other place approved for the purposes of this paragraph by the Secretary of State.

(2) A person for the time being having custody of a person required to be detained as aforesaid shall have all the powers, authorities, protection and privileges of a constable.

(3) Subject to any directions of the Secretary of State, a person required to be detained as aforesaid shall be treated as nearly as may be as if he were a prisoner detained in a prison on remand and any power of temporary removal for judicial, medical or other purposes shall apply accordingly.

(4) A person required to be detained as aforesaid who is unlawfully at large may be arrested without warrant by any constable or any member of Her Majesty's forces on duty.

12. Where a person required to be detained under an interim custody order is unlawfully at large, the interim custody order shall not cease to have effect under paragraph 5 or 8 above while he remains at large; and, upon his being taken again into custody, those paragraphs shall have effect as if the date of the interim custody order were that of his being taken again into custody.

13. Any person who—

(a) being detained under an interim custody order or detention order, escapes;

(b) rescues any person detained as aforesaid, or assists a person so detained in escaping or attempting to escape;

(c) fails to return to detention at the expiration of a period for which he was released under paragraph 10 (1) (b) or (2) (b) above; or

(d) knowingly harbours any person required to be detained under an interim custody order or detention order, or gives him any assistance with intent to prevent, hinder or interfere with his being taken into custody,

shall be liable on conviction on indictment to imprisonment for a term not exceeding five years or to a fine, or to both.

14.—(1) Any document purporting to be an order, notice or direction made or given by the Secretary of State for the purposes of this Schedule and to be signed in accordance with this Schedule shall be received in evidence and shall, until the contrary is proved, be deemed to be duly made or given and signed.

(2) Prima facie evidence of any such order, notice or direction may in any legal proceedings, be given by the production of a document bearing a certificate purporting to be signed by or on behalf of the Secretary of State and stating that the document is a true copy of the order, notice or direction; and the certificate shall be received in evidence, and shall, until the contrary is proved, be deemed to be duly made and signed.

15. The Secretary of State may make such payments to persons released or about to be released from detention under this Schedule as he may, with the consent of the Treasury, determine.

SCHEDULE 2

PROSCRIBED ORGANISATIONS

The Irish Republican Army.
Cumann na mBan.
Fianna na hEireann.
The Red Hand Commando.
Saor Eire.
The Ulster Freedom Fighters.
The Ulster Volunteer Force.

SCHEDULE 3

Section 27

THE NORTHERN IRELAND (EMERGENCY PROVISIONS) REGULATIONS 1978

Title

1. These regulations may be cited as the Northern Ireland (Emergency Provisions) Regulations 1978.

Road Traffic

2. The Secretary of State may by order prohibit, restrict or regulate in any area the use of vehicles or any class of vehicles on highways or the use by vehicles or any class of vehicles of roads or classes of roads specified in the order, either generally or in such circumstances as may be so specified.

Railways

3. The Secretary of State, or any officer of the Royal Ulster Constabulary not below the rank of assistant chief constable, may direct any person having the management of a railway to secure that any train specified in the direction or trains of any class so specified shall stop, or shall not stop, at a station or other place so specified.

4. Where it appears to an officer of the Royal Ulster Constabulary not below the rank of chief inspector that a funeral may—

    (a) occasion a breach of the peace or serious public disorder, or

    (b) cause undue demands to be made on Her Majesty's forces or the police,

he may give directions imposing on the persons organising or taking part in the funeral such conditions as appear to him to be necessary for the preservation of public order including (without prejudice to the generality of the foregoing) conditions—

    (i) prescribing the route to be taken by the funeral;

    (ii) prohibiting the funeral from entering any place specified in the directions;

    (iii) requiring persons taking part in the funeral to travel in vehicles.

Closing of licensed premises, clubs, etc.

5. The Secretary of State may by order require that premises licensed under the Licensing Act (Northern Ireland) 1971, premises registered under the Registration of Clubs Act (Northern Ireland) 1967 or any place of entertainment or public resort—

    (a) shall be closed and remain closed, either for an indefinite period or for a period, or until an event, specified in the order, or

    (b) shall be closed at a particular time either on all days or on any day so specified.

SCHEDULE 4

THE SCHEDULED OFFENCES

PART 1

SUBSTANTIVE OFFENCES

Common law offences

1. Murder, subject to note 1 below.
2. Manslaughter, subject to note 1 below.
3. The common law offence of riot.
4. Kidnapping.
5. False imprisonment.
6. Assault occasioning actual bodily harm, subject to note 1 below.

Malicious Damage Act 1861

7. Offences under section 35 of the Malicious Damage Act 1861 (interference with railway).

Offences against the Person Act 1861

8. Offences under the following provisions of the Offences against the Person Act 1861, subject as mentioned below,—
   (a) Section 4 (conspiracy, etc. to murder) subject to note 2 below;
   (b) section 16 (threats to kill) subject to note 2 below;
   (c) section 18 (wounding with intent to cause grievous bodily harm) subject to note 2 below;
   (d) section 20 (causing grievous bodily harm) subject to note 2 below;
   (e) section 28 (causing grievous bodily harm by explosives);
   (f) section 29 (causing explosion or sending explosive substance or throwing corrosive liquid with intent to cause grievous bodily harm);
   (g) section 30 (placing explosive near building or ship with intent to do bodily injury).

Explosive Substances Act 1883

9. Offences under the following provisions of the Explosive Substances Act 1883—
   (a) section 2 (causing explosion likely to endanger life or damage property);
   (b) section 3 (attempting to cause any such explosion, and making or possessing explosive with intent to endanger life or cause serious damage to property);
   (c) section 4 (making or possessing explosives in suspicious circumstances).

Prison Act (Northern Ireland) 1953

10. Offences under the following provisions of the Prison Act (Northern Ireland) 1953, subject to note 2 below,—
    (a) section 25 (being unlawfully at large while under sentence);

(*b*) section 26 (escaping from lawful custody and failing to surrender to bail);

(*c*) section 27 (attempting to break prison);

(*d*) section 28 (breaking prison by force or violence);

(*e*) section 29 (rescuing or assisting or permitting to escape from lawful custody persons under sentence of death or life imprisonment);

(*f*) section 30 (rescuing or assisting or permitting to escape from lawful custody persons other than persons under sentence of death or life imprisonment);

(*g*) section 32 (causing discharge of prisoner under pretended authority);

(*h*) section 33 (assisting prisoners to escape by conveying things into prisons).

Firearms Act (Northern Ireland) 1969

11. Offences under the following provisions of the Firearms Act (Northern Ireland) 1969—

(*a*) section 1 (1) (possessing, purchasing or acquiring firearm or ammunition without certificate);

(*b*) section 2 (1), (2), (3) or (4) (manufacturing, dealing in, repairing, etc. firearm or ammunition without being registered);

(*c*) section 3 (shortening barrel of shotgun or converting imitation firearm into firearm);

(*d*) section 4 (1) (manufacturing, dealing in or possessing machine gun, or weapon discharging, or ammunition containing, noxious substance);

(*e*) section 14 (possessing firearm or ammunition with intent to endanger life or cause serious damage to property);

(*f*) section 15 (use or attempted use of firearm or imitation firearm to prevent arrest of self or another, etc.);

(*g*) section 16 (carrying firearm or imitation firearm with intent to commit indictable offence or prevent arrest of self or another);

(*h*) section 17 (carrying firearm, etc., in public place) subject to note 3 below;

(*i*) section 19 (possession of firearm or ammunition by person who has been sentenced to imprisonment, etc., and sale of firearm or ammunition to such a person);

(*j*) section 19A (possessing firearm or ammunition in suspicious circumstances).

Theft Act (Northern Ireland) 1969

12. Offences under the following provisions of the Theft Act (Northern Ireland) 1969, subject to note 4 below,—

(*a*) section 8 (robbery);

(*b*) section 10 (aggravated burglary).

Protection of the Person and Property Act (Northern Ireland) 1969

13. Offences under the following provisions of the Protection of the Person and Property Act (Northern Ireland) 1969—

(*a*) section 1 (intimidation);

(*b*) section 2 (making or possessing a petrol bomb, etc. in suspicious circumstances);

(*c*) section 3 (throwing or using petrol bomb, etc.).

Hijacking

14. Offences under section 1 of the Hijacking Act 1971 (aircraft).

15. Offences in Northern Ireland under section 2 of the Criminal Jurisdiction Act 1975 (vehicles and ships).

Prevention of Terrorism (Temporary Provisions) Act 1976

16. Offences under the following provisions of the Prevention of Terrorism (Temporary Provisions) Act 1976—
   (*a*) section 9 (breach of exclusion orders);
   (*b*) section 10 (contributions towards acts of terrorism);
   (*c*) section 11 (information about acts of terrorism).

Criminal Damage (Northern Ireland) Order 1977

17. Offences under the following provisions of the Criminal Damage (Northern Ireland) Order 1977, subject to note 2 below—
   (*a*) Article 3 (1) and (3) or Article 3 (2) and (3) (arson);
   (*b*) Article 3 (2) (destroying or damaging property with intent to endanger life);
   (*c*) Article 4 (threats to destroy or damage property);
   (*d*) Article 5 (possessing anything with intent to destroy or damage property).

Criminal Law (Amendment) (Northern Ireland) Order 1977

18. Offences under Article 3 of the Criminal Law (Amendment) (Northern Ireland) Order 1977 (bomb hoaxes), subject to note 2 below.

This Act

19. Offences under the following provisions of this Act—
   (*a*) section 21;
   (*b*) section 22;
   (*c*) section 23;
   (*d*) paragraph 13 of Schedule 1.

NOTES

1. Murder, manslaughter or an assault occasioning actual bodily harm is not a schedule offence in any particular case in which the Attorney General for Northern Ireland certifies that it is not to be treated as a scheduled offence.

2. An offence under—
   (*a*) section 4, 16, 18 or 20 of the Offences Against the Person Act 1861; or
   (*b*) section 25, 26, 27, 28, 29, 30, 32 or 33 of the Prison Act (Northern Ireland) 1953; or
   (*c*) Article 3, 4, or 5 of the Criminal Damage (Northern Ireland) Order 1977; or
   (*d*) Article 3 of the Criminal Law (Amendment) (Northern Ireland) Order 1977,

is not a scheduled offence in any particular case in which the Attorney General for Northern Ireland certifies that it is not to be treated as a scheduled offence.

3. An offence under section 17 of the Firearms Act (Northern Ireland) 1969 is a scheduled offence only where it is charged that the offence relates to a weapon other than an air weapon.

4. Robbery and aggravated burglary are scheduled offences only where it is charged that an explosive, firearm, imitation firearm or weapon of offence was used to commit the offence; and expressions defined in section 10 of the Theft Act (Northern Ireland) 1969 have the same meaning when used in this note.

PART II

INCHOATE AND RELATED OFFENCES

20. Each of the following offences, that is to say—
  (a) aiding, abetting, counselling, procuring or inciting the commission of an offence specified in Part I of this Schedule (hereafter in this paragraph referred to as a "substantive offence");
  (b) attempting or conspiring to commit a substantive offence;
  (c) an offence under section 4 of the Criminal Law Act (Northern Ireland) 1967 of doing any act with intent to impede the arrest or prosecution of a person who has committed a substantive offence;
  (d) an offence under section 5 (1) of the Criminal Law Act (Northern Ireland) 1967 of failing to give information to a constable which is likely to secure, or to be of material assistance in securing the apprehension, prosecution or conviction of a person for a substantive offence,

shall be treated for the purposes of this Act as if it were the substantive offence.

PART III

EXTRA-TERRITORIAL OFFENCES

21. Any extra-territorial offence as defined in section 1 of the Criminal Jurisdiction Act 1975.

Question
"Anyone seeking a demonstration of the deficiencies in the British approach either to the protection of basic civil liberties or to the maintenance of law and order in an emergency situation will find it in the experience of Northern Ireland." Discuss.

CHAPTER 16

THE FUTURE?

Further Reading

Robert Jungk, *The Nuclear State* (J. Calder, 1979); Report by Justice, *Plutonium and Liberty: Some Possible consequences of nuclear reprocessing for an open society* (London, 1978).

322. The hazards of plutonium arise from its extreme radiotoxicity and from its explosive properties. The dispersion of a small amount of plutonium into the atmosphere with conventional explosives would pose a very serious radiological hazard since an individual dose of only a few milligrams is sufficient, if inhaled, to cause massive fibrosis of the lungs and death within a few years. Much smaller quantities can cause lung cancer after a latent period of perhaps 20 years. In fact it appears highly probable that only a small proportion of the plutonium would be disseminated in the particle size range that is respirable, but apart from the actual threat the psychological effect of a dispersion device would be very great. If such a device were to be detonated in a populous area, very expensive decontamination operations would certainly be needed.

323. The construction of a nuclear bomb by a terrorist group would certainly present considerable difficulties and dangers to those attempting it. The equipment required would not be significantly more elaborate than that already used by criminal groups engaged in the illicit manufacture of heroin, but great care would need to be taken in the handling of dangerous materials and in avoiding accidental criticality. A substantial knowledge would be needed of the physical and chemical processes involved, of the properties of high explosives and of the principles of bomb construction. We have been impressed and disturbed by the extent to which information on all these topics is now available in open technical literature.

324. There seems no reason to doubt that a sufficiently determined group with the necessary expertise could construct a very crude bomb which might explode with the force of a few tonnes of TNT. The amount of plutonium required could easily be carried by hand. Though extremely inefficient in nuclear terms such a device would still cause much damage and would create immediate radiation which would be lethal over a range of several hundred metres as well as dispersing radioactive material over a wide area. More doubt attaches to whether an illicit group could construct a weapon with a much greater yield, say 100 tonnes of TNT or more. There is some dispute about this possibility. From the discussions we have had we have formed the impression that the British authorities are less persuaded than those in the USA about the credibility of the construction of such a weapon. We felt it necessary to settle the matter in our own minds and we therefore consulted eminent

physicists both in the UK and the USA who are expert in the subject. Their judgment was that the construction of a bomb that would give such a yield was indeed possible, though the actual yield would be very uncertain, for it would be as much a matter of luck as of good judgment.

325. We have concluded therefore that it is entirely credible that plutonium in the requisite amounts could be made into a crude but very effective weapon that would be transportable in a small vehicle. The threat to explode such a weapon unless certain conditions were met would constitute nuclear blackmail, and would present any government with an appalling dilemma. We are by no means convinced that the British government has reaslised the full implications of this issue.

International safeguards

326. We conclude our discussion of the plutonium diversion problem with a brief description of the system of international safeguards. Security arrangements are no stronger than their weakest component, for plutonium stolen in one country could be put to illicit use in another. A number of observers have suggested that large parts of the world are inherently unsafe for nuclear power from this and other viewpoints; we were interested to learn that the CEGB agreed with this view. A system of international safeguards to prevent the diversion of fissile materials has been set up under the International Atomic Energy Agency (IAEA) in Vienna. These safeguards are mandatory on all non-nuclear weapons nations party to the Nuclear Non-Proliferation Treaty (NPT); we referred to general aspects of the proliferation problem in paragraphs 165-7 (Chapter IV). The safeguards have also been accepted on a bilateral basis by a number of other nations which do not subscribe to the treaty but wish to benefit from peaceful uses of nuclear power promoted by the IAEA.†

327. Under these safeguards, a national system of accounting for fissile material has to be devised and implemented, and duplicate copies of the inventories of each Materials Balance Area* (MBA) and of additons to and subtractions from them, have to be submitted regularly to the IAEA. The Agency employ inspectors who check the system at intervals, and ensure that all is in order. Penalties for infractions could include the return of fissile material and the loss of technical assistance by the Agency, but it is likely that international pressures would be applied if it were suspected that there was a significant amount of Material Unaccounted For (MUF) that had been diverted at the orders of the national Government.

328. The IAEA safeguards are carefully designed to provide essential checks without infringing national susceptibilities but it seems probable that there will be difficulty in preserving the effectiveness of the system given the tremendous expansion of nuclear power that is projected for the future, which would imply a great increase in the work of the inspectorate. The extent of this increase may be gauged from the fact that under the formula relating the maximum number of inspections to the throughput of plutonium at a plant,

---

†Safeguards under the NPT differ somewhat from non-NPT ones and are generally more rigorous. Attention is focussed on the accountancy of fissile material rather than on the security of the plant.

*This is an area of operation which can be treated as independent for accounting purposes. There are about six MBAs in the Windscale works.

Windscale could receive the attentions full-time of nearly six inspectors at present, and twenty five inspectors by the end of the century. There are at present only seventy four inspectors to cover the whole world.

329. In practice Windscale, being in a nuclear-weapons state, does not receive full inspections, and even after the voluntary offer by the British Government (in parallel with one by the USA Government) to place all our civil nuclear power activities under IAEA/NPT Safeguards has been implemented (probably late in 1977), it is likely that the IAEA will still concentrate their attention on nuclear facilities in non-nuclear weapons states. In fact Windscale has been subject to international safeguards inspection since 1973, when the UK joined the European Communities and consequently EURATOM. EURATOM operates a system of safeguards similar to but not identical with those of the IAEA; this is regarded by the IAEA as a "national" system, requiring some further independent checking by IAEA inspectors. The EURATOM inspectors visit the Windscale site about once a month, and details of the movements of fissile materials are forwarded to EURATOM headquarters at this frequency.

Effects on civil liberties

330. The presence of international inspectors and a system whereby the movements of fissile material are carefully monitored are both developments that we welcome. In fact the nominal loss of national sovereignty involved in having our civil nuclear power activities checked by foreign inspectors is the inevitable price of reciprocal arrangements being agreed in other countries where we might have more cause for concern about the chances of diversion of fissile material. But fears have been expressed that a safeguards system, to be really effective in deterring theft, in recovering stolen plutonium and in dealing with threats of terrorism or blackmail, may have to take on a more active role in the population at large. We referred to these concerned in Chapter IV: they have been most apparent in the United States where there is a Bill of Rights guaranteeing individuals against the excessive power of the state.

331. There are three main grounds for concern. The first is with the rights of employees who work in a plutonium factory. They will require to be screened before being employed, as they already are, and they may be subject to unusual surveillance during the course of their employment. Security screening is of course usual in some other areas of employment; though the need for it may be accepted by prospective employees, its more disagreeable aspects, especially the approaches made to friends, are resented by many. Security requirements are relevant to the question whether private, non-state, organisations and employees should be involved with the handling of plutonium and other fissile materials in the nuclear fuel cycle. This happens in the USA, where there have been quite a large number of prosecutions (and fines) for breaches of security. In the UK, there exists at present a monopoly exercised by BNFL, which, although nominally a private limited company, is in fact owned by the state, and required to observe the same security standards as the AEA, which is additionally charged with ensuring compliance. (The two organisations use the same security arm, the AEA constabulary). The Secretary of State for Energy retains the residual power to permit other organisations to hold or make fissile material, and we do not think that such permission should be granted to non-State organisations.

332. The second issue is over the secret surveillance of members of the public and possibly of employees who may make "undesirable" contacts. The activities might include the use of informers, infiltrators, wiretapping, checking on bank accounts and the opening of mail, and they would be practised on members or suspected members of extremist or terrorist groups or agents of foreign powers who it was thought might plan an attack on, or theft from, a plutonium plant. We regard such activities as highly likely, and indeed inevitable. No doubt these methods are already applied to certain small groups that are regarded as dangerous, so that their use in relation to the plutonium threat would constitute nothing new in principle. It is a matter of degree, and the real question is the extent of the surveillance that might become necessary in the future if there were to be great reliance on plutonium. If there were a significant number of factions or individuals who might be prepared to use plutonium in threats against society, then widespread surveillance could scarely be avoided. We find it hard to believe that such an intolerable situation could arise in this country, though it might do so in countries with repressive régimes. It must be remembered, however, that in considering the hazards of the plutonium economy we are concerned with conditions as they might be fifty or more years ahead. What is most to be feared is an insidious growth in surveillance in response to a growing threat as the amount of plutonium in existence, and familiarity with its properties, increases; and the possibility that a single serious incident in the future might bring a realisation of the need to increase security measures and surveillance to a degree that would be regarded as wholly unacceptable, but which could not then be avoided because of the extent of our dependence on plutonium for energy supplies. The unquantifiable effects of the security measures that might become necessary in the plutonium economy of the future should be a major consideration in any decision concerning a substantial increase in the nuclear power programme.

333. The third area of concern is over the action that would need to be taken to recover plutonium that was known to have been stolen, or in the circumstances in which a nuclear threat had been made. There would be a wide-scale and determined search for the missing plutonium, and general search warrants (which are at present illegal) might be required. The degree of disturbance to people in the course of a nation-wide search, or in the evacuation of a threatened area, could be considerable. There might well also need to be restrictions on the rights of movement and assembly and the suspension of *habeas corpus* if the threat of the plutonium being exploded were serious. Such powers already exist in theory under the Emergency Powers Act, 1920, but there might be doubts whether the occasion justified their use. It should be noted that the problems of enforced evacuation would also arise if there were a serious release of radioactivity as a result of a reactor accident.

Security arrangements in the UK

334. As we stated at the start of this chapter, we have not attempted to assess the present security arrangements but rather to obtain an understanding of how the security problems that might arise through developments in nuclear power are viewed by the authorities concerned. We note here, however, that the visits we made to nuclear installations left us with the impression that insufficient attention had been given to some aspects of security. We were accordingly glad to learn from the discussions we have since had on security matters that the arrangements have been thoroughly reviewed and

that improvements have been, and are being, introduced. One of these is that the UKAEA constabulary now have access to firearms and permanent statutory authorisation for this has been provided through the Atomic Energy Authority (Special Constables) Act recently passed by Parliament. We accept the necessity for this measure though we share the disquiet that was expressed by some Members of Parliament during the debate on the Bill about the potential implications of this step.

335. We are confident that the security hazards associated with the present level of nuclear development in the UK are now fully appreciated by the Government and the authorities concerned, and that the security measures now in force or planned are adequate for present circumstances. We have no doubt that these measures will be periodically reviewed, and if necessary strengthened, in the light of nuclear and other developments that would affect assessment of the risks. However, a flexible response to security risks in the light of events is one thing; it is quite another to question whether the hazards of nuclear development in the future could become so great that adequate security could not be ensured, or alternatively whether the implications of the security measures needed could become unacceptable to society. We cannot see that the present system by which decisions are reached on nuclear development allows us to address ourselves to such questions.

336. The issues we have discussed in this Chapter—the risk of sabotage against nuclear installations, the risk of plutonium diversion and its use in terrorist action or threats against society, and the extent of the security measures that might become necessary to provide adequate safeguards—are by their nature very difficult to assess. The significance that they might assume in the future can be only a matter of opinion, depending on speculative judgments about likely developments in society, and to some degree in the world at large, which no one can make with certainty. Nevertheless, these issues are real and important and of a kind which, in our view, require wide appreciation and discussion. Public debate will not resolve them but it may form a climate of opinion which would assist Government in assessing the weight that should be given to these matters in decisions on nuclear development. Though serious risks from such development probably lie well into the future, judgment about their possible severity and acceptability could react on decisions that need to be taken now.

[Royal Commission on Environmental Pollution (Chairman: Sir Brian Flowers), *Sixth Report: Nuclear Power and the Environment* (Cmnd. 6618, 1976), pp. 126-30.]

THE GOVERNMENT'S RESPONSE

34. In relation to terrorist groups, the Commission concluded that, given the adequacy of existing or planned security measures, the risks at the present level of nuclear development are small. They accepted that security measures will be periodically reviewed and if necessary strengthened. They expressed considerable concern however about the security situation that would exist in what they term a "plutonium economy": in other words a society, which could conceivably exist in the early part of the next century, in which there were much larger stocks, and much more frequent movements, of

plutonium than at present. Their anxiety was that under these circumstances the risks might be such that either adequate security could no longer be assured or the security measures introduced would do serious damage to civil liberties.

35.   So far as the present situation is concerned, the Commission were not convinced that the Government had fully appreciated the implications of the possible illicit construction of a crude nuclear weapon. In fact, security measures in connection with the transport and storage of plutonium have been greatly strengthened over the last two years, and will be reviewed at regular intervals.

36.   The Commission are right to draw attention to the need to consider carefully, in making future decisions about large-scale nuclear development, the effect of possible security measures. In the context of trying find an appropriate balance between any possible effects of nuclear power on civil liberties and its possible benefits for economic growth, the Government advance the following considerations which seem to be of significance.

37.   However the hazards of plutonium are rated in relation to those posed by other dangerous substances, it is certainly a possible target for terrorists. But by giving careful attention to security considerations at the design stage of nuclear installations, we could ensure that its availability in an accessible form remained severely restricted, even in a society which made extensive use of plutonium-fuelled power stations. Designing security into nuclear systems in this way would not only reduce the risk of successful terrorist action but should also reduce the need for the types of measures (such as any large-scale increase in checks on personnel) which could be regarded as a threat to civil liberties. The Government will ensure that full attention is given to this aspect at the planning and design stages of nuclear systems. Cost comparisons between nuclear and other systems will have to take into account the additional cost imposed by security measures.

38.   The degree of surveillance needed to detect and watch terrorists at any given time depends more on the prevalence of terrorism than on the availability of plutonium. Moreover, terrorism is in large measure an international phenomenon. On the one hand, this means that the United Kingdom could not necessarily avoid the potential problems of nuclear terrorism by a unilateral decision not to use plutonium. On the other hand, this fact clearly makes it important for the governments concerned to co-operate fully in adequate security arrangements in all countries in which stocks of plutonium exist now or may exist in the future. This aspect is therefore being taken fully into account in current international discussions. In the nuclear field as in other fields, the Government will continue to preserve civil liberties and to relate any security measures strictly to the nature and scope of the specific threat at any given time.

[*Nuclear Power and the Environment: The Government's Response to the Sixth Report of the Royal Commission on Environmental Pollution* (Cmnd. 6618). Cmnd. 6820, 1977.]

APPENDIX

Some foreign constitutional provisions concerning civil liberties

1. *FRANCE*

1. DECLARATION OF THE RIGHTS OF MAN AND OF THE CITIZEN, 1789

The representatives of the French people, organized in National Assembly, believing that ignorance, forgetfulness, or contempt of the rights of man are the sole causes of the public miseries and of the corruption of governments, have resolved to set forth in a solemn declaration the natural, inalienable, and sacred rights of man, in order that this declaration, being ever present to all the members of the social body, may unceasingly remind them of their rights and their duties; in order that the acts of the legislative power and those of the executive power may be each moment compared with the aim of every political institution and thereby may be more respected; and in order that the demands of the citizens, grounded henceforth upon simple and incontestable principles, may always take the direction of maintaining the constitution and the welfare of all.

In consequence, the National Assembly recognizes and declares, in the presence and under the auspices of the Supreme Being, the following rights of man and citizen.

1. Men are born and remain free and equal in rights. Social distinctions can be based only upon public utility.

2. The aim of every political association is the preservation of the natural and imprescriptible rights of man. These rights are liberty, property, security, and resistance to oppression.

3. The source of all sovereignty is essentially in the nation; no body, no individual can exercise authority that does not proceed from it in plain terms.

4. Liberty consists in the power to do anything that does not injure others; accordingly, the exercise of the natural rights of each man has no limits except those that secure to the other members of society the enjoyment of these same rights. These limits can be determined only by law.

5. The law has the right to forbid only such actions as are injurious to society. Nothing can be forbidden that is not interdicted by the law, and no one can be constrained to do that which it does not order.

6. Law is the expression of the general will. All citizens have the right to take part personally, or by their representatives, in its formation. It must be the same for all, whether it protects or punishes. All citizens, being equal in its eyes, are equally eligible to all public dignities, places and employments, according to their capacities, and without other distinction than that of their virtues and their talents.

7. No man can be accused, arrested, or detained, except in the cases deter-mined by the law and according to the forms that it has prescribed. Those who procure, expedite, execute, or cause to be executed arbitrary orders ought to be punished: but every citizen summoned or seized by virtue of the law ought to render instant obedience; he makes himself guilty by resistance.

8. The law ought to establish only penalties that are strictly and obviously necessary, and no one can be punished except by virtue of a law established and promulgated prior to the offence and legally applied.

9. Every man being presumed innocent until he has been pronounced guilty, if it is thought indispensable to arrest him, all severity that may not be necessary to secure his person ought to be strictly suppressed by law.

10. No one should be disturbed on account of his opinions, even religious, provided their manifestation does not disturb the public order established by law.

11. The free communication of ideas and opinions is one of the most precious of the rights of man; every citizen then can freely speak, write, and print, subject to responsibility for the abuse of this freedom in cases deter-mined by law.

12. The guarantee of the rights of man and citizen requires a public force; this force is instituted for the advantage of all and not for the personal benefit of those to whom it is entrusted.

13. For the maintenance of the public force and for the expenses of admin-istration a general tax is indispensable; it ought to be equally apportioned among all the citizens according to their names.

14. All the citizens have the right to ascertain, by themselves or by their representatives, the necessity of the public tax, to consent to it freely, to follow the employment of it, and to determine the quota, the assessment, the collec-tion, and the duration of it.

15. Society has the right to call for an account of his administration from every public agent.

16. Any society in which the guarantee of the rights is not secured, or the separation of powers not determined, has no constitution at all.

17. Property being a sacred and inviolable right, no one can be deprived of it, unless a legally established public necessity obviously requires it, under the condition of a just and prior indemnity.

2. PREAMBLE TO THE CONSTITUTION OF THE FOURTH FRENCH REPUBLIC, 1946

On the morrow of the victory of the free peoples over the regimes that attempted to enslave and degrade the human person, the French people proclaims once more that every human being, without distinction of race, religion or belief, possesses inalienable and sacred rights. It solemnly reaffirms the rights and freedoms of man and of the citizen consecrated by the Declaration of Rights of 1789 and the fundamental principles recognized by the laws of the Republic.

It further proclaims as most vital in our time the following political, economic and social principles:

The law guarantees to women equal rights with men in all domains.

Anyone persecuted because of his activities in the cause of freedom has the right of asylum within the territories of the Republic.

Everyone has the duty to work and the right to obtain employment. No one may suffer in his work or his employment because of his origin, his opinions or his beliefs.

Everyone may defend his rights and interests by trade-union action and may join the union of his choice.

The right to strike may be exercised within the framework of the laws that govern it.

Every worker through his delegates may participate in collective bargaining to determine working conditions, as well as in the management of business.

All property and all enterprises that now have or subsequently shall have the character of a national public service or a monopoly in fact must become the property of the community.

The nation ensures to the individual and the family the conditions necessary to their development.

It guarantees to all, and notably to the child, the mother and the aged worker, protection of health, material security, rest and leisure. Every human being who because of his age, his physical or mental condition, or because of the economic situation, finds himself unable to work, has the right to obtain from the community the means to lead a decent existence.

The nation proclaims the solidarity and equality of all Frenchmen with regard to the burdens resulting from national disasters.

The nation guarantees equal access of children and adults to education, professional training and culture. The establishment of free, secular, public education on all levels is a duty of the State.

The French Republic, faithful to its traditions, abides by the rules of international public law. It will not undertake wars of conquest and will never use its arms against the freedom of any people.

On condition of reciprocity, France accepts the limitations of sovereignty necessary to the organization and defense of peace.

France forms with the people of its overseas territories a Union based upon equality of rights and duties without distinction of race or religion.

The French Union is composed of nations and peoples who wish to place in common or coordinate their resources and their efforts in order to develop their civilization, increase their well-being and ensure their security.

Faithful to her traditional mission, France proposes to guide the peoples for whom she has assumed responsibility toward freedom to govern themselves and democratically to manage their own affairs; putting aside any system of colonization based upon arbitrary power, she guarantees to all equal access to public office and the individual or collective exercise of the rights and liberties proclaimed or confined above.

3. CONSTITUTION OF FRANCE, 1958

(amended 1960, 1962 and 1963)

PREAMBLE

The French people hereby solemnly proclaims its attachment to the Rights of Man and the principles of national sovereignty as defined by the Declaration of 1789, reaffirmed and complemented by the Preamble of the Constitution of 1946.

By virtue of these principles and that of the free determination of peoples, the Republic hereby offers to the Overseas Territories which express the desire to adhere to them, new institutions based on the common ideal of liberty, equality and fraternity and conceived with a view to their democratic evolution.

Art. 1. The Republic and the peoples of the Overseas Territories who, by an act of free determination, adopt the present Constitution thereby institute a Community.

The Community shall be based on the equality and the solidarity of the peoples composing it.

TITLE I

ON SOVEREIGNTY

Art. 2. France is a Republic, indivisible, secular, democratic and social. It shall ensure the equality of all citizens before the law, without distinction of origin, race or religion. It shall respect all beliefs.

The national emblem is the tricolor flag, blue, white and red.

The national anthem is the *Marseillaise*.

The motto of the Republic is "Liberty, Equality, Fraternity."

Its principle is government of the people, by the people and for the people.

Art. 3. National sovereignty belongs to the people, which shall exercise this sovereignty through its representatives and by means of referendums.

No section of the people, nor any individual, may attribute to themselves or himself the exercise thereof.

Suffrage may be direct or indirect under the conditions stipulated by the Constitution. It shall always be universal, equal and secret.

All French citizens of both sexes who have reached their majority and who enjoy civil and political rights may vote under the conditions determined by law.

Art. 4. Political parties and groups shall be instrumental in the expression of the suffrage. They shall be formed freely and shall carry on their activities freely. They must respect the principles of national sovereignty and democracy.

TITLE V

RELATIONS BETWEEN PARLIAMENT AND THE GOVERNMENT

Art. 34. Legislation shall be passed by Parliament.

Laws shall establish the regulations concerning:

— civil rights and the fundamental guarantees granted to the citizens for the exercise of their public liberties; the obligations imposed by national defence upon the persons and property of citizens;

— nationality, status and legal capacity of persons, marriage contracts, inheritance and gifts;

— determination of crimes and misdemeanors as well as the penalties imposed therefor; criminal procedure; amnesty; the creation of new juridical systems and the status of magistrates;

— the basis, the rate and the methods of collecting taxes of all types; the issuance of currency.

Laws shall likewise determine the regulations concerning:

— the electoral system of the Parliamentary assemblies and the local assemblies;

— the establishment of categories of public institutions;

— the fundamental guarantees granted to civil and military personnel employed by the States;

— the nationalization of enterprises and the transfer of the property of enterprises from the public to the private sector.

Laws shall determine the fundamental principles of:

— the general organization of national defence;

— the free administration of local communities, the extent of their jurisdiction and their resources;

— education;

— property rights, civil and commercial obligations;

— legislation pertaining to employment, unions and social security.

Financial laws shall determine the financial resources and obligations of the State under the conditions and with the reservations to be provided for by an organic law.

Laws pertaining to national planning shall determine the objectives of the economic and social action of the State.

The provisions of the present article may be developed in detail and amplified by an organic law.

Art. 35. Parliament shall authorize the declaration of war.

Art. 36. Martial law shall be decreed in a meeting of the Council of Ministers.

Its prorogation beyond twelve days may be authorized only by Parliament.

TITLE VIII

JUDICIAL AUTHORITY

Art. 64. The President of the Republic shall be the guarantor of the independence of the judicial authority.

He shall be assisted by the High Council of the Judiciary.

An organic law shall determine the status of the judiciary.

Judges may not be removed from office.

Art. 66. No one may be arbitrarily detained.

The judiciary, guardian of individual liberty, shall ensure respect for this principle under the conditions stipulated by law.

2. *REPUBLIC OF IRELAND*

THE CONSTITUTION OF 1936

FUNDAMENTAL RIGHTS

Personal rights

Article 40

1. All citizens shall, as human persons, be held equal before the law.

This shall not be held to mean that the State shall not in its enactments have due regard to differences of capacity, physical and moral, and of social function.

2. (1) Titles of nobility shall not be conferred by the State.

(2) No title of nobility or of honour may be accepted by any citizen except with the prior approval of the Government.

3. (1) The State guarantees in its laws to respect, and, as far as practicable, by its laws to defend and vindicate the personal rights of the citizen.

(2) The State shall, in particular, by its laws protect as best it may from unjust attack and, in the case of injustice done, vindicate the life, person, good name, and property rights of every citizen.

4. (1) No citizen shall be deprived of his personal liberty save in accordance with law.

(2) Upon complaint being made by or on behalf of any person to the High Court or any judge thereof alleging that such person is being unlawfully detained, the High Court and any and every judge thereof to whom such complaint is made shall forthwith enquire into the said complaint and may order the person in whose custody such person is detained to produce the body of such person before the High Court on a named day and to certify in writing the grounds of his detention, and the High Court shall, upon the body of such person being produced before that Court and after giving the person in whose custody he is detained an opportunity of justifying the detention, order the release of such person from such detention unless satisfied that he is being detained in accordance with the law.

(3) Where the body of a person alleged to be unlawfully detained is produced before the High Court in pursuance of an order in that behalf made under this section and that Court is satisfied that such person is being detained in accordance with a law but that such law is invalid having regard to the provision of this Constitution, the High Court shall refer the question of the validity of such law to the Supreme Court by way of case stated and may, at the time of such reference or at any time thereafter, allow the said person to be at liberty on such bail and subject to such conditions as the High Court shall fix until the Supreme Court has determined the question referred to it.

(4) The High Court before which the body of a person alleged to be unlawfully detained is to be produced in pursuance of an order in that behalf made under this section shall, if the President of the High Court or, if he is not available, the senior judge of that Court who is available so directs in respect of any particular case, consist of three judges and shall, in every other case, consist of one judge only.

(5) Where an order is made under this section by the High Court or a judge thereof for the production of the body of a person who is under sentence of death, the High Court or such judge thereof shall further order that the execution of the said sentence of death shall be deferred until after the body of such person has been produced before the High Court and the lawfulness of his detention has been determined and if, after such deferment, the detention of such person is determined to be lawful, the High Court shall appoint a day for the execution of the said sentence of death and that sentence shall have effect with the substitution of the day so appointed for the day originally fixed for the execution thereof.

(6) Nothing in this section, however, shall be invoked to prohibit, control, or interfere with any act of the Defence Forces during the existence of a state of war or armed rebellion.

5. The dwelling of every citizen is inviolable and shall not be forcibly entered save in accordance with law.

6. (1) The State guarantees liberty for the exercise of the following rights, subject to public order and morality:—

(i) The right of the citizens to express freely their convictions and opinions.

The education of public opinion being, however, a matter of such grave import to the common good, the State shall endeavour to ensure that organs of public opinion, such as the radio, the press, the cinema, while preserving their rightful liberty of expression, including criticism of Government policy, shall not be used to undermine public order or morality or the authority of the State.

The publication or utterance of blasphemous, seditious, or indecent matter is an offence which shall be punishable in accordance with law.

(ii) The right of the citizens to assemble peaceably and without arms.

Provision may be made by law to prevent or control meetings which are determined in accordance with law to be calculated to cause a breach of the peace or to be a danger or nuisance to the general public and to prevent or control meetings in the vicinity of either House of the Oireachtas.

(iii) The right of the citizens to form associations and unions.

Laws, however, may be enacted for the regulation and control in the public interest of the exercise of the foregoing right.

(2) Laws regulating the manner in which the right of forming associations and unions and the right of free assembly may be exercised shall contain no political, religious or class discrimination.

The Family

Article 41

1. (1) The state recognises the Family as the natural primary and fundamental unit group of Society, and as a moral institution possessing inalienable and imprescriptible rights, antecedent and superior to all positive law.

(2) The State, therefore, guarantees to protect the Family in its constitution and authority, as a necessary basis of social order and as indispensable to the welfare of the Nation and the State.

2. (1) In particular, the State recognises that by her life within the home, woman gives to the State a support without which the common good cannot be achieved.

(2) The State shall, therefore, endeavour to ensure that mothers shall not be obliged by economic necessity to engage in labour to the neglect of their duties in the home.

3. (1) The State pledges itself to guard with special care the institution of Marriage, on which the Family is founded, and to protect it against attack.

(2) No law shall be enacted providing for the grant of a dissolution of marriage.

(3) No person whose marriage has been dissolved under the civil law of any other State but is a subsisting valid marriage under the law for the time being in force within the jurisdiction of the Government and Parliament established by this Constitution shall be capable of contracting a valid marriage within that jurisdiction during the lifetime of the other party to the marriage so dissolved.

Education

Article 42

1. The State acknowledges that the primary and natural educator of the child is the Family and guarantees to respect the inalienable right and duty of parents to provide, according to their means, for the religious and moral, intellectual, physical and social education of their children.

2. Parents shall be free to provide this education in their homes or in private schools or in schools recognised or established by the State.

3. (1) The State shall not oblige parents in violation of their conscience and lawful preference to send their children to schools established by the State, or to any particular type of school designated by the State.

(2) The State shall, however, as guardian of the common good, require in view of actual conditions that the children receive a certain minimum education, moral, intellectual and social.

4. The State shall provide for free primary education and shall endeavour to supplement and give reasonable aid to private and corporate educational initiative, and, when the public good requires it, provide other educational facilities or institutions with due regard, however, for the rights of parents, especially in the matter of religious and moral formation.

5. In exceptional cases, where the parents for physical and moral reasons fail in their duty towards their children, the State as guardian of the common good, by appropriate means shall endeavour to supply the place of the parents, but always with due regard for the natural and imprescriptible rights of the child.

Private Property

Article 43

1. (1) The State acknowledges that man, in virtue of his rational being, has the natural right, antecedent to positive law, to the private ownership of external goods.

(2) The State accordingly guarantees to pass no law attempting to abolish the right of private ownership or the general right to transfer, bequeath, and inherit property.

2. (1) The State recognises, however, that the exercise of the rights mentioned in the foregoing provisions of this Article ought, in civil society, to be regulated by the principles of social justice.

(2) The State, accordingly, may as occasion requires delimit by law the exercise of the said rights with a view to reconciling their exer-cise with the exigencies of the common good.

Religion

Article 44

1. The State acknowledges that the homage of public worship is due to Almighty God. It shall hold His Name in reverence, and shall respect and honour religion.

2. (1) Freedom of conscience and the free profession and practice of religion are, subject to public order and morality, guaranteed to every citizen.

(2) The State guarantees not to endow any religion.

(3) The State shall not impose any disabilities or make any discrimination on the ground of religious profession, belief or status.

(4) Legislation providing State aid for schools shall not discriminate between schools under the management of different religious denominations, nor be such as to affect prejudicially the right of any child to attend a school receiving public money without attending religious instruction at that school.

(5) Every religious denomination shall have the right to manage its own affairs, own, acquire and administer property, movable and immovable, and maintain institutions for religious or charitable purposes.

(6) The property of any religious denomination or any educational institution shall not be diverted save for necessary works of public utility and on payment of compensation.

3. *UNITED STATES OF AMERICA*

Articles in addition to, and amendment of, the constitution of the United States of America, proposed by Congress, and ratified by the several States, pursuant to the fifth article of the original constitution

Article I

Congress shall make no law respecting an establishment of religion, or prohibiting the free exercise thereof; or abridging the freedom of speech, or of the press; or the right of the people peaceably to assemble, and to petition the Government for a redress of grievances.

Article II

A well regulated Militia, being necessary to the security of a free State, the right of the people to keep and bear Arms, shall not be infringed.

Article III

No Soldier shall, in time of peace be quartered in any house, without the consent of the Owner, nor in time of war, but in a manner to be prescribed by law.

Article IV

The right of the people to be secure in their persons, houses, papers, and effects, against unreasonable searches and seizures, shall not be violated, and no Warrants shall issue, but upon probable cause, supported by Oath or affirmation, and particularly describing the place to be searched, and the persons or things to be seized.

Article V

No person shall be held to answer for a capital, or otherwise infamous crime, unless on a presentment or indictment of a Grand Jury, except in cases arising in the land or naval forces, or in the Militia, when in actual service in time of War or public danger; nor shall any person be subject for the same offence to be twice put in jeopardy of life or limb; nor shall be compelled in any criminal case to be a witness against himself, nor be deprived of life, liberty, or property, without due process of law; nor shall private property be taken for public use, without just compensation.

Article VI

In all criminal prosecutions, the accused shall enjoy the right to a speedy and public trial, by an impartial jury of the State and district wherein the crime shall have been committed, which district shall have been previously ascertained by law, and to be informed of the nature and cause of the accusation; to be confronted with the witnesses against him; to have compulsory process for obtaining witnesses in his favor, and to have the Assistance of Counsel for his defence.

Article VII

In Suits at common law, where the value in controversy shall exceed twenty dollars, the right of trial by jury shall be preserved, and no fact tried by a jury, shall be otherwise re-examined in any Court of the United States, than according to the rules of the common law.

Article VIII

Excessive bail shall not be required, nor excessive fines imposed, nor cruel and unusual punishments inflicted.

Article IX

The enumeration in the Constitution, of certain rights, shall not be construed to deny or disparage others retained by the people.

Article X

The powers not delegated to the United States by the Constitution, nor prohibited by it to the States, are reserved to the States respectively, or to the people.

Article XI

The Judicial power of the United States shall not be construed to extend to any suit in law or equity, commenced or prosecuted against one of the United States by Citizens of another State, or by Citizens or Subjects of any Foreign State.

Article XIII

Section 1. Neither slavery nor involuntary servitude, except as a punishment for crime whereof the party shall have been duly convicted, shall exist within the United States, or any place subject to their jurisdiction.

Section 2. Congress shall have power to enforce this article by appropriate legislation.

Article XIV

Section 1. All persons born or naturalized in the United States, and subject to the jurisdiction thereof, are citizens of the United States and of the State wherein they reside. No State shall make or enforce any law which shall abridge the privileges or immunities of citizens of the United States; nor shall any State deprive any person of life, liberty, or property, without due process of law; nor deny to any person within its jurisdiction the equal protection of the laws.

Article XV

Section 1. The right of citizens of the United States to vote shall not be denied or abridged by the United States or by any State on account of race, color, or previous condition of servitude.
Section 2. The Congress shall have power to enforce this article by appropriate legislation.

Article XIX

The right of citizens of the United States to vote shall not be denied or abridged by the United States or by any State on account of sex.

Congress shall have power to enforce this article by appropriate legislation.

INDEX